PostgreSQL 12 High Availability Cookbook
Third Edition

Over 100 recipes to design a highly available server with the advanced features of PostgreSQL 12

Shaun Thomas

BIRMINGHAM - MUMBAI

PostgreSQL 12 High Availability Cookbook
Third Edition

Copyright © 2020 Packt Publishing

Commissioning Editor: Amey Varangaonkar
Acquisition Editor: Devika Battike
Content Development Editor: Roshan Kumar
Senior Editor: Jack Cummings
Technical Editor: Manikandan Kurup
Copy Editor: Safis Editing
Project Coordinator: Aishwarya Mohan
Proofreader: Safis Editing
Indexer: Priyanka Dhadke
Production Designer: Deepika Naik

First published: July 2014
Second edition: February 2017
Third edition: February 2020

Production reference: 1250220

Published by Packt Publishing Ltd.
Livery Place
35 Livery Street
Birmingham
B3 2PB, UK.

ISBN 978-1-83898-485-4

www.packt.com

Packt.com

Subscribe to our online digital library for full access to over 7,000 books and videos, as well as industry leading tools to help you plan your personal development and advance your career. For more information, please visit our website.

Why subscribe?

- Spend less time learning and more time coding with practical eBooks and Videos from over 4,000 industry professionals

- Improve your learning with Skill Plans built especially for you

- Get a free eBook or video every month

- Fully searchable for easy access to vital information

- Copy and paste, print, and bookmark content

Did you know that Packt offers eBook versions of every book published, with PDF and ePub files available? You can upgrade to the eBook version at www.packt.com and as a print book customer, you are entitled to a discount on the eBook copy. Get in touch with us at customercare@packtpub.com for more details.

At www.packt.com, you can also read a collection of free technical articles, sign up for a range of free newsletters, and receive exclusive discounts and offers on Packt books and eBooks.

Contributors

About the author

Shaun Thomas has been experimenting with PostgreSQL since late 2000 and serves as a database consultant, teacher, blogger, and support engineer with 2ndQuadrant. He has presented at conferences such as Postgres Open, 2Q PGCONF, and PgConf on topics such as handling extreme throughput, high availability, failover techniques, monitoring tools, database architecture, multi-master conflict avoidance, and high availability upgrade concepts. He believes in a multi-disciplinary approach when it comes to high availability.

He believes that PostgreSQL has a stupendous future ahead, and he can't wait to see the advancements subsequent versions will bring.

About the reviewers

Ilja Everilä is a software developer and consultant with over a decade of experience in various projects, currently employed at Siili Solutions Oyj. He has done both frontend and backend work and database administration in PostgreSQL. All in all, he is very much into database work and found this book an interesting read on an important subject.

Richard Yen received a bachelor of science in electrical engineering and computer science from the University of California, Berkeley. He started his career as a developer and DBA for Turnitin, an ed-tech start-up, and went on to work as a support engineer for EnterpriseDB, a professional services and software company focusing on PostgreSQL. His wealth of experience interacting with many clients, ranging from small start-ups to large financial and governmental institutions, has exposed him to many technologies, several of which are covered in this book.

Packt is searching for authors like you

If you're interested in becoming an author for Packt, please visit `authors.packtpub.com` and apply today. We have worked with thousands of developers and tech professionals, just like you, to help them share their insight with the global tech community. You can make a general application, apply for a specific hot topic that we are recruiting an author for, or submit your own idea.

Table of Contents

Preface

Database outages are costly and largely avoidable. This book will help you design and build an indestructible PostgreSQL 12 cluster that can remain online even in the most dire circumstances.

From cluster layout and hardware selection to software stacks and horizontal scalability, this book will help you build a versatile PostgreSQL cluster that will survive crashes, resist data corruption, and grow smoothly with customer demand. Configuration, troubleshooting, monitoring and alerting, backups, replication, decoupling through proxies, failover automation, horizontal scaling, upgrades, and several other considerations are all part of a healthy PostgreSQL cluster. By the end of this book, you will have learned all the new features of PostgreSQL 12 to help you build a more efficient and adaptive database.

Who this book is for

PostgreSQL administrators and developers who wish to build and maintain a highly reliable PostgreSQL cluster will find this book to be an extremely useful resource.

What this book covers

Chapter 1, *Architectural Considerations*, explains how the layout of the nodes in our PostgreSQL cluster can drastically influence its availability.

Chapter 2, *Hardware Planning*, explains the selection and provisioning of hardware required to build a highly available PostgreSQL database.

Chapter 3, *Minimizing Downtime*, explains how we should react when outages inevitably occur and how to prepare ourselves for them.

Chapter 4, *Proxy and Pooling Resources*, explains how to combine and abstract connectivity to isolate and protect the database.

Chapter 5, *Troubleshooting*, covers several techniques to track sources of poor performance or stop potential outages before they occur.

Chapter 6, *Monitoring*, focuses on what we should monitor, how often we should check system status, and how to present the data for easy consumption. We will learn how to effectively monitor PostgreSQL's server status and database performance.

Chapter 7, *PostgreSQL Replication*, shows how to utilize PostgreSQL replication as well as third-party table synchronization tools. We will learn several methods to copy entire databases or individual tables.

Chapter 8, *Backup Management*, shows where to turn when backing up large PostgreSQL clusters becomes a concern. This chapter will help ensure backups not only fulfill their stated role but are also reliable, fast, and efficient.

Chapter 9, *High Availability with repmgr*, discusses all the capabilities so that we can construct a fully automated high-availability stack. This chapter is dedicated to building a fully automated high-availability stack using the repmgr replica and cluster management tools by 2ndQuadrant.

Chapter 10, *High Availability with Patroni*, explains how to build a quick, yet adaptable, high-availability stack to keep our PostgreSQL servers online.

Chapter 11, *Low-Level Server Mirroring*, shows how to build and manipulate a fault-tolerant, high-performance foundation for our PostgreSQL clusters.

Chapter 12, *High Availability via Pacemaker*, shows how to automate cluster management and ensure high availability. This chapter covers Corosync and Pacemaker and the steps to manage dual-node servers with this software.

Chapter 13, *High Availability with Multi-Master Replication*, explains how multiple writable PostgreSQL nodes affect the concept of high availability. This chapter explores the inherent limitations of multi-master database technology as applied to PostgreSQL, as well as how to best utilize it to maximize application availability.

Chapter 14, *Data Distribution*, shows how clever data management can increase uptime even further.

Chapter 15, *Zero Downtime Upgrades*, explains how to upgrade a cluster while remaining fully online.

To get the most out of this book

This book concentrates on Unix systems with a focus on Linux in particular. Such servers have become increasingly popular for hosting databases for large and small companies. As such, we highly recommend that you use a virtual machine or development system running a recent copy of Debian, Ubuntu, Red Hat Enterprise Linux, or a variant such as CentOS or Scientific Linux.

You will also need a copy of PostgreSQL. If your chosen Linux distribution isn't keeping the included PostgreSQL packages sufficiently up to date, the PostgreSQL website maintains binaries for most popular distributions. You can find them at https://www.postgresql.org/download/.

Users of Red Hat Enterprise Linux and its variants should refer to the following URL to add the official PostgreSQL YUM repository to important database systems: https://yum.postgresql.org/repopackages.php.

Users of Debian, Ubuntu, Mint, and other related Linux systems should refer to the PostgreSQL APT wiki page at this URL instead: https://wiki.postgresql.org/wiki/Apt.

Be sure to include any `contrib` packages in your installation. They include helpful utilities and database extensions that we will use in some recipes.

Users of BSD should still be able to follow along with these recipes. Some commands may require slight alterations to run properly on BSD. Otherwise, all commands have been confirmed to work on Bash and recent GNU tools.

Download the color images

We also provide a PDF file that has color images of the screenshots/diagrams used in this book. You can download it here: https://static.packt-cdn.com/downloads/9781838984854_ColorImages.pdf.

Conventions used

There are a number of text conventions used throughout this book.

`CodeInText`: Indicates code words in text, database table names, folder names, filenames, file extensions, pathnames, dummy URLs, user input, and Twitter handles. Here is an example: "The `Environment` column has another goal related to physical separation."

A block of code is set as follows:

```
[global]
repo1-host=pg-primary
repo1-host-user=postgres
repo1-path=/var/lib/pgbackrest
repo1-retention-full=1
start-fast=y
```

Any command-line input or output is written as follows:

```
sudo yum install pgbackrest
```

Bold: Indicates a new term, an important word, or words that you see onscreen. For example, words in menus or dialog boxes appear in the text like this. Here is an example: "Select **System info** from the **Administration** panel."

 Warnings or important notes appear like this.

 Tips and tricks appear like this.

Sections

In this book, you will find several headings that appear frequently (*Getting ready, How to do it..., How it works..., There's more...,* and *See also*).

To give clear instructions on how to complete a recipe, use these sections as follows:

Getting ready

This section tells you what to expect in the recipe and describes how to set up any software or any preliminary settings required for the recipe.

How to do it...

This section contains the steps required to follow the recipe.

How it works...

This section usually consists of a detailed explanation of what happened in the previous section.

There's more...

This section consists of additional information about the recipe in order to make you more knowledgeable about the recipe.

See also

This section provides helpful links to other useful information for the recipe.

Get in touch

Feedback from our readers is always welcome.

General feedback: If you have questions about any aspect of this book, mention the book title in the subject of your message and email us at `customercare@packtpub.com`.

Errata: Although we have taken every care to ensure the accuracy of our content, mistakes do happen. If you have found a mistake in this book, we would be grateful if you would report this to us. Please visit `www.packtpub.com/support/errata`, selecting your book, clicking on the Errata Submission Form link, and entering the details.

Piracy: If you come across any illegal copies of our works in any form on the Internet, we would be grateful if you would provide us with the location address or website name. Please contact us at `copyright@packt.com` with a link to the material.

If you are interested in becoming an author: If there is a topic that you have expertise in and you are interested in either writing or contributing to a book, please visit `authors.packtpub.com`.

Reviews

Please leave a review. Once you have read and used this book, why not leave a review on the site that you purchased it from? Potential readers can then see and use your unbiased opinion to make purchase decisions, we at Packt can understand what you think about our products, and our authors can see your feedback on their book. Thank you!

For more information about Packt, please visit `packt.com`.

Architectural Considerations

In many ways, database server architecture is treated as a mere afterthought. It's often much easier to simply create a single node, install some software, and consider the whole affair resolved. If a company is particularly paranoid, they may even spare some thought for a replica server, or perhaps some kind of backup.

The true importance of database cluster architecture is easily overlooked as a result. But what is server architecture? Why does it matter?

Look down the street. Any street is fine. What do you see? Homes, offices, and buildings of various descriptions. With very rare exceptions, each one of these was meticulously planned, from the foundation to the walls to the electrical wires, pipes, up to the roof and drainage systems. A failure in any of these components could lead to the ultimate demise of the entire structure, given enough time.

The same also applies to a PostgreSQL cluster! Database architecture defines *what* goes into a database server cluster, and the reason for each element. How does it communicate? How many nodes are required? Where do we put those nodes, and why? What common problems are inherent in those decisions? How will our decisions influence the underlying cost? What trade-offs can we make, given some important constraints? How does all of this affect data availability? We *need* those answers before we even consider hardware or virtualization. There are many important considerations we must entertain when designing a highly available PostgreSQL cluster.

Why then is it so common for critical application and user data that drives the entire application stack behind the company itself to be treated so callously? We direct so much attention and focus on the application, with its various layers of indirection, queues, caches, container automation, and microarchitecture, that the data layer is overlooked or considered a nuisance.

This is actually highly understandable. In most cases, a PostgreSQL database layer demands an entirely different approach that development, system administration, and other information technology fields may not be entirely familiar with managing. Even experienced database administrators may not comprehend the scale and necessary theoretical concepts that drive the high availability of databases.

While we can't reduce the subtle art of database server architecture to a few memorable quips sure to entertain at parties, we can make the subject far more *approachable*. It shouldn't be necessary to have a Ph.D. in abstract theoretical frameworks to prevent a costly database outage.

In this chapter, we will learn how the layout of the nodes in our PostgreSQL cluster can drastically influence its availability. We will cover the following recipes:

- Setting expectations with RPO
- Defining timetables through RTO
- Picking redundant copies
- Selecting locations
- Having enough backups
- Considering quorum
- Introducing indirection
- Preventing split brain
- Incorporating multi-master
- Leveraging multi-master

Setting expectations with RPO

RPO is a common term in **business continuity** known as **Recovery Point Objective**. In the context of a database system, it describes the amount of data that may be lost following an unexpected outage before it is once again operational. It's important to understand this at an early stage because it will drive decisions such as node count, data synchronization methods, and backup technologies.

In this recipe, we will examine the ingredients for concocting a comprehensive RPO that will influence the PostgreSQL cluster composition itself.

Getting ready

The first thing we need to do is set expectations. These are most often defined by upper management or some other decision-making entity. Data loss is never desirable but is unavoidable in catastrophic scenarios. How much data loss can the business tolerate under these circumstances? Seconds, minutes, or hours' worth?

This recipe will mainly focus on information gathering from key individuals, so make sure it's possible to at least email anyone involved with the application stack. Hardware purchases depend on budget proposals, so it may even be necessary to interact with VP and C-level executives as well. Even if we don't do this right away, try to determine the extent of influence available to you.

How to do it...

Since we're dealing with many vectors, we should iterate them if possible. Try to follow a process like this:

1. Seek the input of major decision makers:

   - VP and C-level executives involved with technology
   - Product manager
   - Application designers and architects
   - Infrastructure team lead

2. Find an amount of time that will satisfy most or all of the above.
3. Follow the rest of the advice in this chapter to find a suitable architecture.
4. Try to determine a rough cost for this and the closest alternative.
5. Present one or more designs and cost estimates to decision makers.
6. Document the final RPO decision and architecture as reference material.

How it works...

Decision makers such as the technology VP, CEO, CTO, and such are the final word in most cases. Their input is vital and should be considered a requirement before ever taking a step further. Keep in mind that these people are likely not familiar with the technical feasibility of their demands at this extreme implementation level. When asked a question such as *How much data can we lose in a major outage?* they're probably going to say *None!* Regardless, this is a vital first step for reasons that will shortly become apparent.

Then, we simply traverse the stack of people who helped define the features the application stack fulfills, those who designed and implemented it, and whoever may be in charge of the requisite hardware and network where everything runs. Perhaps the design has a built-in tolerance for certain amounts of loss. Perhaps inherent queues or caches act as a sort of buffer for data backend difficulties. Maybe the design assumes there are multiple data systems all ingesting the same stream for redundancy. The architecture and those who built it are the best sources of this information.

Once we know the maximum amount of data the backend can lose before being restored, we must apply what we learn from the rest of this chapter and choose one or two best-case designs that can deliver that promise. The point here is that we will be executing this recipe several times until everyone agrees to all inherent design costs and limitations before continuing.

The best way to estimate cost is to take the chosen database server architectures and iterate a gross cost for each element. The next chapter on *Hardware Planning* describes in detail how to do this. We don't have to be exact here; the goal is to have some numbers we can present to decision makers. Do they still want zero RPO if it costs 10x as much as ten seconds of data loss? Are they willing to compromise on a hybrid design?

Once we have chosen a final structure, possibly the most important step is to produce a document describing that architecture, why it was chosen, the known limitations, and the RPO it delivers. Present this document to decision makers and encourage them to sign it if possible. Save it in any corporate documentation management system available, and make sure it's one of the first things people see regarding the database cluster layer. This document will single-handedly answer multiple questions about the capabilities of the database cluster, all while acting as a reference specification.

There's more...

RPO is considered a vital part of **business continuity planning**. Entire books have been written on this subject, and what we've presented here is essentially a functional summary. The subject is deep and varied, rich with its own inherent techniques beyond simply architecture and design. It is the language of business and resource management, so it can be a key component when interacting with decision makers.

Learning these concepts in depth can help influence the overall application stack to a more sustainable long-term structure. We'll cover more of these techniques in this chapter, but don't be afraid to proactively incorporate these techniques into your repertoire.

Defining timetables through RTO

Like RPO, **RTO** refers to a common business continuity term known as **Recovery Time Objective**. In practice, this is the amount of time an outage of the database layer may last. Often, it is incorporated into a **Service Level Agreement** (**SLA**) contract presented to clients or assumed as a metric within the application stack. Like RPO, this is a contractual-level element that can determine the number of required nodes at steadily increasing expense as the amount of tolerable downtime decreases.

In this recipe, we will examine the necessary steps to defining a realistic RTO, and what that could mean given known industry standards.

Getting ready

As with RPO, our goal in determining a functional RTO is to set expectations regarding inherent architecture limitations. The primary difference here is that RTO is more easily quantifiable. Fire up your favorite spreadsheet program, such as OpenOffice, Microsoft Excel, or Google Sheets; we'll be using it to keep track of how much time each layer of the application, including the database layer contributes to a potential outage scenario.

How to do it...

We simply need to produce a spreadsheet to track all of the elements of known RTO that depend on the database. We can do this with the following steps:

1. Locate an already-defined RTO SLA for each portion of the application dependent on PostgreSQL if possible.
2. If this does not exist, seek the input of major decision makers:

    - VP and C-level executives involved with technology
    - Product manager
    - Application designers and architects
    - Infrastructure team lead

3. Find an amount of time that will satisfy most or all of the above.
4. Create a new spreadsheet for RTO.
5. Create a heading row with the following columns:

    - `Activity`
    - `Time (seconds)`
    - `Count`
    - `Total (seconds)`

6. In the `Total` column, create the following formula:

    `=B2*C2`

7. Create one row for each type of the following `Activity` categories:

    - `Minor Upgrade`
    - `Major Upgrade`
    - `Reboot`
    - `Switchover`
    - `Failover`
    - `OS Upgrade`
    - `Etc.`

8. Copy and paste the formula into the `Total` column for all the rows we created.

9. At the bottom of the `Total` column, after all relevant rows (row 21, for example), create the following formula:

```
=SUM(D2:D20)
```

10. Ensure that the end result looks something like the following screenshot:

	A	B	C	D
1	Activity	Time (s)	Count	Total (s)
2	Minor Upgrade	30	4	120
3	Major Upgrade	120	1	120
4	Reboot	300	1	300
5	Switchover	60	2	120
6				
7				660

11. Follow the rest of the advice in this chapter to find a suitable architecture.
12. Try to determine a rough cost for this and the closest alternative(s).
13. Present the design and cost estimates to decision makers.
14. Document this final RTO decision and architecture as reference material.

How it works...

In order to see where our PostgreSQL cluster fits company expectations, we need to know whether the company and each individual part of the existing application stack has an overall target RTO. If it doesn't, it's our job to approximate one. This means contacting any decision-makers, product owners, architects, and so on, to know what RTO target we're trying to attain and how other resources may contribute. These will act as a type of maximum value we can't exceed.

Keep in mind that RTO values tend to be amplified between layers. If our RTO is higher than some portion of the application stack, that will necessarily raise the RTO of that layer as well, which may increase the RTO of each subsequent layer. This is the exact scenario we're trying to avoid.

Once we have an RTO expectation, we need to examine how possible it is to fall under that target. The easiest way to accomplish this is to build a spreadsheet that essentially consists of a list of dependencies, maintenance tasks, or other occurrences related to PostgreSQL.

The rows we used for `Activity` are mainly suggestions, and producing an exhaustive list is generally dependent on the architecture to a certain extent. However, all software requires upgrades, machines need to be rebooted, switchover tests to prove high availability functionality may be required, past experience with the full application stack and hardware may imply two unexpected outages per year, and so on. Each of these will contribute to the cumulative RTO for PostgreSQL which we can use as a reference value.

The number we use for the `Count` column should be the number of times the `Activity` happens on a yearly basis. As an example, PostgreSQL has a quarterly release schedule for non-critical bug and security enhancements. If you want to follow along with these, it could make sense to set the `Count` column of `Minor Upgrade` to 4.

> A number of architectural examples that we'll discuss later in this chapter will make it possible to set the `Time` column to 0 for some actions, or at least to a much lower value. We'll discuss these where relevant. This is also one of the reasons we'll need to execute this recipe multiple times when deciding on an appropriate architecture.

Once we have accounted for as many foreseeable `Action` components that may be necessary over the course of a year, we'll have a cumulative total that may represent the RTO that PostgreSQL can achieve for a given architecture. As a sanity check, we should compare that value to the lowest RTO for any parts of the application stack that depend on PostgreSQL. It's important we don't exceed this target.

Then, as with RPO, we need to present the possible RTO to decision-makers so that it can be integrated into the overall company RTO. To do that, we must continue with the rest of the chapter to find one or two architectures with either higher or lower expected RTO, estimate the cost of each, and work on a suitable compromise.

Deriving an appropriate RTO may require multiple iterations of this recipe, from estimation, architecture selection, presenting it to appropriate parties, and so on. This isn't a fast or simple process, and it pays to get it right early. We need to know how many PostgreSQL nodes to purchase, where each will reside, how we switch to alternatives, how much time each step may take, and so on.

There's more...

Besides what we discussed in the main recipe, there are other RTO concepts we would like to explore.

This may seem familiar

Believe it or not, it's very likely you've encountered this concept without even realizing it. Internet service providers or application hosts often advertise how many *9s* of availability their platform can maintain. It's often presented as a chart like this:

Uptime (%)	Daily	Weekly	Monthly	Yearly
99	14m 24s	1h 40m 48s	7h 18m 18s	3d 15h 39m 30s
99.9	1m 26s	10m 5s	43m 50s	8h 45m 57s
99.99	8.6s	1m 1s	4m 23s	52m 36s
99.999	0.9s	6s	26.3s	5m 16s

As you can imagine, it's generally more desirable to stay toward the higher end of 9s to minimize downtime. On the other hand, this is highly restrictive, as *Five 9s* only allows just over five minutes of downtime over the course of an entire year. This doesn't leave much room for database maintenance tasks or unexpected outages at any other layer of the stack.

Node counts

Generally, the more nodes we have, the lower our RTO will be. It may make sense to start with an initial estimate spreadsheet, and then create another for each architecture or variant that seems applicable. This will make it easier to rank the monetary cost and associated RTO for each. This may influence the final decision, and hence make it easier to track what options we may have.

Picking redundant copies

How many database servers should any architecture have as part of the inherent design? There are several factors that contribute to this answer, including the design of the final architecture itself. The number of redundant data copies ultimately determines how many nodes must exist, irrespective of whether we require more data centers, irrespective of whether we should account for latency, and so on.

The goal in this recipe is to consult our needs to derive a node count that won't break the bank, but still deliver the level of availability we want. In other words, aside from our primary data node, we will explain how to figure out the number of redundant data nodes necessary to adequately represent the entire cluster safely and ensure high availability.

Getting ready

Luckily, this recipe is a simple counting exercise. The only necessary elements are a healthy imagination and perhaps some idea of the budgetary constraints before we begin. Just consider that, for any of our reference designs, we will always require more than one server node as a minimum.

How to do it...

Observe the following steps when considering node counts driven by high availability architectures:

1. Always add one separate server for backups.
2. Always allocate one server for a logical or physical replica.
3. For automated failover, allocate the following:

   - An additional small VM / node to act as a voter
   - OR a fully qualified replica

4. For every active data center beyond the first two, allocate one replica.
5. If non-local data access latency is a concern, allocate the following:

   - An additional replica in the primary location
   - An additional replica in each location for symmetric clusters

How it works...

Why do we demand at least one backup server? The full answer to this question actually has its own recipe in this chapter. However, catastrophic failure is a fact of life and we must be ready for such an event. Even if the separate server is not a fully operational PostgreSQL node, it must exist and should be part of the reference design.

Likewise, we must have at least one PostgreSQL replica. Some of our designs work with either physical or logical replicas, so we won't differentiate between them here. Simply assume that every highly active PostgreSQL cluster must have at least two nodes that can fulfill the role of a primary database. Backups take time to restore, whereas replicas are generally writable in a minute or less.

One replica only really covers the case where switching from one PostgreSQL node to the alternate is a manual procedure. Fully automated failure detection mechanisms require an odd number of nodes for voting purposes. This third node can either be a mere voting entity, or a full PostgreSQL replica. We cover this in greater depth in the *Considering quorum* recipe.

Once we start accounting for multiple geographic locations at different data centers, things don't change exceptionally. By now, we have at least one PostgreSQL replica that is probably at the first alternate location. If we have three or more active data centers where the application is using PostgreSQL, we'll want a local replica for each.

Then, consider the implications of limiting ourselves to merely one PostgreSQL node per location. This means any minor upgrade or other maintenance task will mean switching to an alternate data center while the maintenance is active. This can introduce unwanted latency that will affect the application. To reduce this, add one replica to the primary location to account for this effect. For symmetrical data centers that have no primary location, add a PostgreSQL replica to each location for the same reasons.

As a quick example, consider two scenarios. Our first company (Company A) only uses two data centers, and doesn't need automated database failover, nor is it necessary to worry about downtime caused by minor upgrades. In this case, they decided to use two PostgreSQL servers and a backup system. This is a minimum of three nodes related to PostgreSQL, and their cluster looks like this:

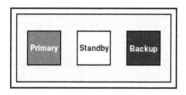

Company A

In the second case (Company B), we have a much more demanding financial institution that requires all three of their data centers to be active at all times. They chose to have one **Primary** PostgreSQL server, two **Replicas** per data center, a **Witness** node, and a **Backup** server. In that extreme case, they used a total of eight nodes dedicated to PostgreSQL.

Their cluster would look like this:

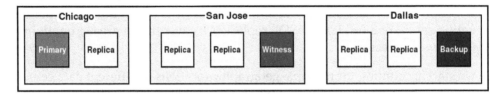

Company B

 Nodes denoted here are specifically meant to be running PostgreSQL. Architectures discussed in this chapter will include various abstraction layers and, as a result, will likely require even more nodes in the cluster. PostgreSQL nodes tend to be much larger and do far more work, so are the focus of this recipe.

There's more...

Chosen node counts will naturally suggest certain architectures over others. The reason we're performing this recipe so early is to get an idea of compatible architectures. It may be necessary to revise these counts once we learn information from other recipes in this chapter.

Selecting locations

Once we've decided how many PostgreSQL nodes to allocate in our cluster, where should we put them? Generally, this is easy to answer, but there are some subtleties we need to consider as well. A truly **high availability cluster** can resist many different types of failure, including where the servers themselves reside.

In this recipe, we will learn all about the ways separate geographical locations can affect our chosen design.

Getting ready

It's time to start drawing diagrams. Find your favorite drawing program, such as Visio, Dia, or Draw.io, or a convenient sheet of paper or whiteboard.

Keep in mind that the *ideal* design may require more data centers than the company currently utilizes. In these cases, it may be possible to supply sufficient justification to contract at least one more location if it benefits the RPO or RTO. Hence, we recommend following the *Setting expectations with RPO* recipe and *Defining timetables through RTO* recipe before continuing here.

How to do it...

Consider these basic guidelines while thinking about how many data centers are necessary, and which nodes should be placed in each:

1. If data must be available in case of a site outage, use one additional location.
2. Always place the backup in a separate location if possible.
3. If two locations are in the same general geographical area, use one additional location at least 100 miles (160 km) away.
4. If automated failover is desirable, consider at least three data centers.
5. Place one PostgreSQL server (or witness) in each location.
6. Continue placing PostgreSQL servers evenly until the count is exhausted.
7. Try to place witness servers in a location that is unlikely to lose contact with more than one location simultaneously.

How it works...

Let's consider an extreme example to explain how this works: a financial institution wants to place six PostgreSQL nodes, one witness server, and a backup system. This would clearly be a silly design, as shown in the following diagram:

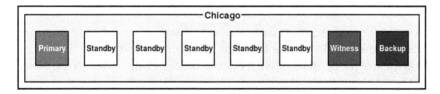

This places every node in a single location that could lose its connection to the internet, lose power, or suffer some other catastrophe that would render the entire database stack unusable or even destroyed.

Now, let's apply the guidelines. First of all, we want to protect the backup; let's place that elsewhere, as seen in this following diagram:

Now, one PostgreSQL server and the backup are safe in case something happens to the first data center. Now of course, we have a new problem: what happens if Chicago itself is somehow isolated from the rest of the internet. Though incredibly rare, major internet backbone outages like this are possible.

So, let's add a third data center in Dallas. This allows us to actually follow three separate rules. We can move the backup to that remote location so it's even safer. We can relocate at least one more PostgreSQL server to that data center as well, so it acts as an alternate in case Chicago becomes unavailable. And finally, we have three data centers, so it's possible to safely use automated failover.

Recipes later in this chapter will explain why we keep insisting that safety comes in odd numbers. For now, just keep it in mind when considering the design.

With these revisions, our cluster looks more like the following diagram:

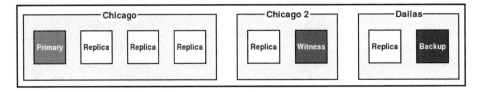

The only remaining rules suggest that our node distributions should be more even, and that the witness should be less likely to lose contact with more than one location at once. This means we need to move a couple more of our nodes to the other data centers. But what about the witness node? It's actually best to leave it in the second Chicago location. If Chicago is separated from Dallas, the witness is still at least in another data center, and is less likely to lose contact with Chicago, thereby preserving its voting abilities.

Given we're discussing a large financial institution that likely has access to multiple data centers, perhaps there's an even better solution. Following one final node reorganization, the cluster probably looks more like this diagram:

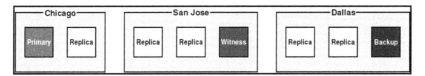

Now, we can utilize three data centers that are relatively diverse in their geographic isolation. This may appear to be an extreme case, but is merely illustrative of the process we recommend to ensure that the overall state of the cluster is as safe as possible.

There's more...

As database sizes increase, sometimes having only a single offsite backup as the only recovery source can be somewhat inconvenient. Not only do we have to wait to copy data from the backup location, but potentially any related time to restore the database instance to working order, and any further recovery steps.

In these cases, it's reasonable and even suggested to maintain a backup server at each major data center. This can be done by backing up a local replica, or by using some other kind of filesystem copy or distribution mechanism synchronizing between the locations.

See also

Please refer to this short list of companies that offer virtual hosting to use as quick supplementary data center locations:

- **Amazon AWS**: https://aws.amazon.com/
- **Rackspace**: https://www.rackspace.com/
- **Microsoft Azure**: https://azure.microsoft.com/en-us/
- **Google Cloud**: https://cloud.google.com/
- **Linode**: https://www.linode.com/

Additionally, diagram software is various and widely available. Here are some of our favorites:

- **Draw.io**: https://www.draw.io/
- **Visio**: https://office.live.com/start/Visio.aspx?auth=2&nf=1
- **Dia**: http://dia-installer.de/

Having enough backups

Database backups are a crucial component to any architecture, and should be considered a required part of the central design. The only real question in most cases is: how many backups? All highly available clusters account for relevant backup copies, lest the cluster itself is lost.

In this recipe, we'll cover one simple set of rules to provide an answer.

Getting ready

This is very important, so write it down if necessary. Put it in company documentation if possible.

How to do it...

When considering how many backups to allocate, follow the 3-2-1 backup rule, which consists of these elements:

1. Keep at least **three** copies of your data.
2. Store **two** copies on different devices.
3. Keep at least **one** copy offsite.

Take note that many things may qualify as a copy, including PostgreSQL replicas, and the original data itself.

How it works...

Notice how we don't really recommend a specific backup method, how it should be stored, or how filesystem-based features might contribute. All of those things are implementation details and don't matter as much as the rules themselves.

Consider the first rule: **keep at least three copies of your data**. Since our PostgreSQL instance is the first copy, we need two more. What might these two be? Could we use one replica and a backup? Maybe we could use two replicas? Perhaps, but let's examine the remaining rules first.

Imagine we've produced a PostgreSQL backup, and it's stored on our primary server and the same filesystem as the database instance. What happens if that storage device is damaged or destroyed? Now, we've lost the database *and* the backup.

That naturally leads to the second rule: **store two copies on different devices**. It's fine to retain a copy on the local PostgreSQL server and even the same physical storage device, provided we store a copy of the backup on a device that won't be lost simultaneously. Store another copy of the backup on a second physical device. This can be a separate set of storage drives, a SAN, a shared NFS filesystem, or anything else, so long as it's separate from the database itself.

Be wary of relying on shared infrastructure for following the second rule. If we have two separate LUNs from the same SAN mounted on our database server for PostgreSQL and the backup, this means nothing if the SAN itself is lost. If possible, try to ensure that the backup is actually on a physically distinct device.

So, to fulfill the second rule, we merely need to ensure that the second copy of our PostgreSQL instance is on another device. This is most easily done by creating a replica on another server, or a VM hosted on a different hypervisor. That's two copies of the data.

Finally there's rule three: **keep at least one copy offsite**. This is the third copy of our data, and it's best to place it somewhere that's immune from a catastrophic failure of the data center itself. In limited circumstances, it may be safe enough to place the backup on a server in another rack of the same data center, but why take the risk?

There are ample cloud providers, vault systems, and cheap storage services that can fill the role of hosting the third and final copy of our data. If we have our own second data center, that's an easy choice of venue. If not, it's important to select, allocate, and designate some tertiary location that won't be lost if the worst happens. This third data copy is an insurance policy, and it doesn't even have to be easily available. As long as we can obtain the backup upon request, that fits the minimum requirement.

There's more...

There's one important corollary here. PostgreSQL replicas tend to immediately reflect every change made to the primary node. What happens if someone accidentally drops a table? In this case, the 3-2-1 rule by itself is not sufficient. Relying on replicas alone means we've permanently lost this data.

Thus, we strongly recommend the following additional rule: **At least one copy must be a true backup**.

Databases such as PostgreSQL are equipped with **Point-In-Time-Recovery** (**PITR**), which allows the user to start with any past backup and apply changes until it reaches a specific point where recovery is stopped. This lets us recover a backup to the point before a table was damaged or removed, capture the desired contents, and reintroduce them into the original database. This can only be done with a real binary-level backup, and there are multiple tools dedicated to performing this task. This book even contains a chapter dedicated to *Backup Management*.

See also

To make the 3-2-1 rule easier to follow, consider the following long-term storage solutions:

- **Amazon Glacier**: https://aws.amazon.com/glacier/
- **Backblaze**: https://www.backblaze.com/
- **Azure Backup**: https://azure.microsoft.com/en-us/services/backup/
- **Google Cloud Storage**: https://cloud.google.com/storage/

Considering quorum

Quorum can best be explained by imagining any voting system. It's a result of trusted consensus and relies on multiple implementations backed by dissertation and quantitative study. The most common way to guarantee a quorum for a PostgreSQL cluster is by utilizing a **witness** node. This exists only to vote and observe the state of the cluster. This helps us reach maximum availability by guaranteeing there's always an active primary node.

In this recipe, we'll examine why it's important to apply the concept of quorum to our PostgreSQL cluster, and how we may do so.

Getting ready

The primary criteria for establishing a quorum is that we must satisfy the capability for avoiding tie votes, also known as establishing consensus. Basically, this means we must have an odd number of PostgreSQL nodes within our cluster such that there's always a majority. We should already have a preliminary node count by working through previous recipes in this chapter, in particular, the *Picking redundant copies* recipe and the *Selecting locations* recipe.

That being said, the concept of quorum is only necessary in clusters that intend to provide automated failover capabilities. If this is not going to be a feature of the end architecture, this recipe may be skipped.

How to do it...

Once we have an initial node count, we should apply these guidelines to adjust the total count and node distribution:

1. If the initial PostgreSQL node count is even, add one witness node.
2. If the initial PostgreSQL node count is odd, convert one replica into a witness node.
3. In the presence of two locations, the witness node should reside in the same data center as the primary node.
4. If possible, allocate witness nodes in an independent tertiary location.

How it works...

While deceptively simple, there's actually a lot of thought involved in correctly placing an odd node, and why we use witness nodes rather than yet another PostgreSQL replica:

1. Our first guideline is the most straightforward of these, such that we ensure there are an odd number of nodes in the cluster. Once we have that, any event in the cluster is submitted to the entire quorum for a decision, and only agreement guarantees subsequent action. Further, since the witness cannot vote for itself, only one eligible node will ever win the election. Consider this sample cluster diagram:

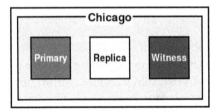

We have three nodes in this cluster and, in the event of a failure of the **Primary** node, the **Witness** must vote for the only remaining **Replica**. If the **Witness** had been a standard replica node, it could have voted for itself and potentially led to a tied vote. In an automated scenario, this would prevent the cluster from promoting a replacement **Primary** node.

2. The second guideline is a variant of this concept. If we already had an odd number of nodes, one of these should be a **Witness** rather than a standard replica. Consider this diagram:

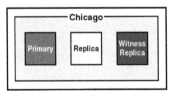

We can see here that the third node is still a replica, but it also acts as a **Witness**. Essentially, we don't allow this node to vote for itself to become the new **Primary**. This kind of role works well for read-only replicas that exist only for application use and is a good way to reuse existing resources.

3. The third guideline, of placing the **Witness** in the same location as the **Primary** node, safeguards node visibility. More important than automation is safety. By placing the **Witness** in the same location as the **Primary** when there are only two data centers, we can ensure that a **network partition**—a situation where we lose network connectivity between the data centers—won't result in the alternate location incorrectly promoting one of its replicas. Consider this diagram:

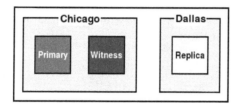

If the connection between **Chicago** and **Dallas** is lost, Chicago still has the majority of voting nodes, and Dallas does not. As a result, the cluster will continue operating normally until the network is repaired, and we didn't experience an accidental activation of a node in Dallas.

 Some failover automation systems also take physical location into account by verifying that all nodes in one location agree that all nodes in the other location are not responding. In these cases, the only time where automation will not work normally is when a network partition has occurred. This approach is only viable when more than one node exists in each location. Such can be accomplished by allocating further replicas, or even witness nodes.

Unfortunately, our cluster is no longer symmetrical. If we activate the node in Dallas, there are no witnesses in that location, so we must eventually move the Primary back to Chicago. This means every failover will be followed by a manual switch to the other location, thus doubling our downtime.

The easiest way to permanently address these concerns is to add a third location and assign a node there. In most cases, this will be the **Witness** node itself. Consider this example:

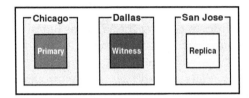

In this case, we may desire that only Chicago or San Jose host the active PostgreSQL node. In the event of a failure of our Primary node, San Jose should take over instead. The Witness can see both data centers and decide voting based on this. Furthermore, it doesn't matter if the Primary is active in Chicago or San Jose, because the Witness is not tied directly to either location.

There's more...

What happens in the case of a tie? Even if the original cluster contained an odd number of nodes, when the Primary node goes offline, this is no longer true. In simple quorum systems, each node votes for itself. However, a Witness, by its definition, must vote for some other node. This means some replica in the cluster will have more than one vote, and thus win the election.

In case there are somehow multiple witnesses, and votes are split anyway, PostgreSQL quorum systems usually account for the **Log Sequence Number** (**LSN**) from the Primary node. Even if it's only a single transaction, one of the nodes with the most votes will have replicated more data than the other, and this will break the tie.

Introducing indirection

What happens to connections to a PostgreSQL system when the service must be shut down for maintenance, or the node itself experiences a hardware problem? Previous recipes have already recommended we integrate at least one data replica into our design, but how should we handle switching between these resources? A great way to achieve high availability is to make server maintenance or replacement as simple as possible.

The concept we'll be exploring in this recipe will be one of anticipating system outages, and even welcoming them, by incorporating **proxy** techniques into the design.

Getting ready

There are actually several methods for switching from one PostgreSQL node to another. However, when considering the node architecture as a whole, we need to know the four major techniques to handle node indirection:

1. Domain name reassignment
2. Virtual IP address
3. Session multiplexing software
4. Software or hardware load balancer

In real terms, these are all basically the same thing: a proxy for our PostgreSQL primary node. Keep this in mind as we consider how they may affect our architecture. It would also be a good idea to have some diagram software ready to describe how communication flows through the cluster.

How to do it...

Integrating a proxy into a PostgreSQL cluster is generally simple if we consider these steps in the design phase:

1. Assign a proxy to the primary node.
2. Redirect all communication to the primary node through the proxy.
3. If the proxy requires dedicated hardware or software, designate two to account for failures.

How it works...

These rules are simple, but that's one of the reasons they're often overlooked. Always communicate with the Primary node through at least one proxy.

Even if this is merely an abstract network name, or an ephemeral IP address, doing so prevents problems that could occur, as seen in the following diagram:

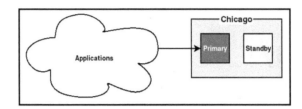

What happens when the **Primary** PostgreSQL node is offline and the cluster is now being managed by the **Standby**? We have to reconfigure—and possibly restart—any and all applications that connect directly to it. With one simple change, we can avoid that concern, as seen here:

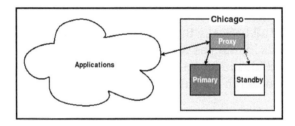

By following the second guideline, all traffic is directed through the **Proxy**, thus ensuring that either the **Primary** or **Standby** will stay online and remain accessible without further invasive changes. Now, we can switch the active primary node, perform maintenance, or even replace nodes entirely, and the application stack will only see the proxy.

We've encountered clusters that do not follow these two guidelines. Sometimes, applications will actually communicate directly with the primary node as assigned by the inventory reference number. This means any time the infrastructure team or vendor needs to reassign or rename nodes, the application becomes unusable for a short period of time.

Sometimes, hardware load balancers are utilized to redirect application traffic to PostgreSQL. On other occasions, this is done with connection multiplexing software such as PgBouncer or HAProxy. In these cases the proxy is not simply a permanent network name or IP address that is associated with the PostgreSQL cluster, but a piece of hardware. This means that a software or hardware failure could also affect the proxy itself.

In this case, we recommend using two proxies, as seen here:

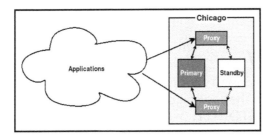

This is especially useful in microarchitectures, which may consist of dozens or even hundreds of different application servers. Each may target a different proxy such that a failure of either only affects the application servers assigned to it.

There's more...

Given that applications must always access PostgreSQL exclusively through the Proxy, we always recommend assigning a reference hostname that is as permanent as possible. This may fit with the company naming scheme, and should always be documented. PostgreSQL nodes may come and go and, in extreme cases, the cluster itself can be swapped for a replacement, but the Proxy is (or should be) forever.

Physical proxy nodes themselves are not immune to maintenance or failure. Thus, it may be necessary to contact the network team to assign a CNAME or other fixture that can remain static even as the proxy hardware fluctuates.

See also

If you want to learn more about how proxies work, check out this resource: https://whatis.techtarget.com/definition/proxy-server

Preventing split brain

Split brain is the scenario that occurs when more than one primary node is active in a PostgreSQL cluster simultaneously. In these circumstances, if any data was written to both nodes from the application, it becomes extremely difficult to rectify. Certainly, no cluster with such data corruption can be considered highly available!

In this recipe, we will further explore the concept, and how we might mitigate this problem.

Getting ready

An important concept necessary for preventing split brain scenarios is **fencing**, or isolation of a node from the application and database stack. Often, this is accomplished through **STONITH** (which stands for **Shoot The Other Node In The Head**). After accounting for situations where this is not possible, the old primary must invoke **SMITH** instead, or **Shoot Myself In The Head**. While it may sound extreme, for servers, this is really a temporary solution to prevent a more worrying complication.

Keep these terms in mind while we explore how they may affect our architecture.

How to do it...

Apply these steps when designing a cluster to help minimize or eliminate the risk of split brain:

1. If available, allocate STONITH hardware for nodes that may take the role of the Primary.
2. Consider situations where SMITH must be used instead, during network interruptions.
3. Ensure PostgreSQL does not start automatically following a system reboot.

How it works...

Modern servers are often equipped with hardware that enables remote administration. These components often allow network access to the boot process itself. In the case where PostgreSQL is installed on virtual servers, the hypervisor serves this role. Many companies commonly install **Power Distribution Units** (PDU) that can be remotely instructed to cut power to a server.

Whatever the approach, working with infrastructure or systems operations teams is likely necessary to gain access to interact with these devices. As an example, imagine we have a 2-node cluster consisting of a **Primary** and **Standby**, and a **PDU** is available for each. We could do something like this:

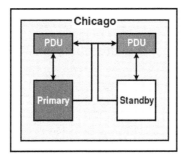

In this case, in the case of a failover and subsequent promotion, the **Standby** could instruct the **PDU** to cut power to the **Primary** to ensure that it wasn't possible for applications to be connected. But what about a scenario where it's far more common for network interruptions, such as between two data centers, as seen here:

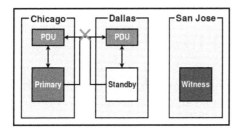

In this scenario, the **Standby** would be unable to shut down the **Primary** node in the case of a failover. This is why it's important to consider SMITH approaches as well. In this case, the **Primary** should monitor the state of the **Standby** and **Witness**, and if both disconnect for a sufficient period, it should assume the **Standby** will be promoted. In this case, it would power itself down to prevent applications from interacting with it.

Finally, always disable the PostgreSQL start up mechanism on clusters equipped with high availability management software. That software should manage starting and stopping the service, and this will also prevent unintended events such as accidentally having two primary nodes active simply because a reboot started a previously failed PostgreSQL node.

Advanced recipes later in this book will adhere to the rule of disabling PostgreSQL on startup and provide exact instructions for doing so.

There's more...

The reason preventing split brain is so difficult is that it's not an easy problem to solve. This is why dedicated software for managing high availability exists. While these are not immune to the issue, they greatly reduce the potential of occurrence.

Pacemaker has components specifically for interacting with STONITH hardware. repmgr implements the concept of hook scripts for event notifications, and accounts for scenarios where the Primary is isolated from the remainder of the cluster as seen in the previous diagram. Patroni uses a sophisticated locking mechanism that only allows one primary node to be registered at once.

Don't try to invent a solution for an already solved problem when most of the work has already been done by companies dedicated to the cause.

Incorporating multi-master

Some PostgreSQL vendors provide proprietary extended functionality that makes it possible for a cluster to contain multiple writable Primary nodes simultaneously. Users of this kind of software can expect certain enhanced capabilities, though concessions are often necessary. This recipe will explore how PostgreSQL multi-master can influence cluster topology.

Getting ready

This recipe will require some knowledge of where the nodes are likely to reside on a global scale. Will some PostgreSQL nodes be in Dubai, while others are in Cairo or Toronto? We will also need to have a very basic understanding of how the application operates. This may mean interacting with application developers or designers to derive a rough approximation of queries required for basic operation.

How to do it...

When considering deploying multiple writable PostgreSQL nodes, utilize these guiding questions:

1. Is there significant geographical distance between nodes?
2. Does the application use multiple transactions or queries per operation?
3. Are accounts or users likely to operate primarily in a certain region?

How it works...

Probably the most obvious benefit arising from using multiple writable PostgreSQL nodes is one of reduced write latency. Consider an initial cluster that may resemble this diagram:

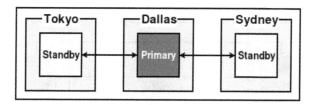

Each write to Tokyo or Sydney must first cross thousands of miles before being committed. And due to how replication works, the local replicas in those regions will have to wait for the transaction to be replayed before it will be visible there. These times can be considerable. Consider this table of round-trip-times for network traffic for the locations we've chosen:

	Dallas	Sydney	Tokyo
Dallas	X	205 ms	145 ms
Sydney	200 ms	X	195 ms
Tokyo	145 ms	195 ms	X

Each write may require over 200 ms simply to reach the primary node. Then, the same data must be transmitted from the **Primary** to each **Standby**, doubling the time necessary before the transaction may be visible in the continent where it originated. Since many application actions can invoke multiple transactions, this can cause a time amplification effect that could last for several minutes in extreme cases.

This is why we ask whether or not an application performs multiple actions per task. Displaying a web page may require a dozen queries. Submitting a credit application can mean several writes and polling for results. With competition around every corner, every second of waiting increases the chances a user may simply use another application without such latency issues. If each of those nodes were a **Primary**, the transaction write overhead would be effectively zero.

The last question we should answer is one of expandability. As the usage volume of the cluster increases, we will inevitably require further nodes. A popular method of addressing this is to regionalize the primary nodes, but otherwise follow standard replication concepts. As an example, imagine we needed a further two nodes in each region to fulfill read traffic. It could look something like this:

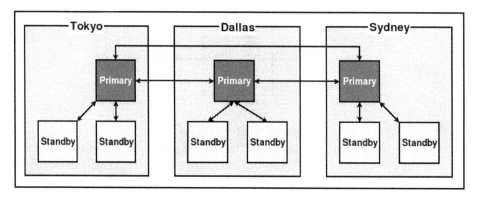

This **Hub + Spoke** model helps ensure each region can keep up with demand, without adding latency by including nodes outside of a particular region. Note also that, when using these multi-master clusters, all nodes often require direct connections to each other.

There's more...

These types of multi-master PostgreSQL clusters often require two direct connections between all participating nodes, one for each direction of communication. This is called a **Mesh** topology, and is considered by some to be a source of excessive communication overhead. If we think about it, that's a valid criticism given that every transaction in the cluster must eventually be acknowledged by every other primary node. In very active systems, the impact could be significant.

A scenario along the lines of the following diagram, for example, may present complications:

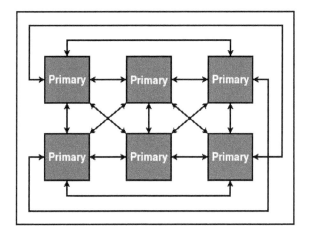

By merely adding three more primary nodes, we've increased the number of communication channels to 30. In fact, the general formula for this can be expressed for PostgreSQL multi-master as follows:

```
C = N * (N - 1)
```

So, if we have 3 nodes, we can expect 6 channels, but if we have 10 nodes, there are 90 instead. This is one major reason for the Hub + Spoke model, since the local Replica nodes do not need to be primary nodes and contribute to the topology communication overhead.

Consider the potential impact of this before simply embracing the benefits of operating in multiple locations simultaneously.

See also

If interested, feel free to explore some of these concepts in greater depth using the resources listed here: https://wondernetwork.com/pings/

Leveraging multi-master

One significant benefit to using software that enables multiple primary nodes in a PostgreSQL cluster is the associated increase in availability. This functionality can eliminate node promotion time and allow a fully active application stack on all data backends if properly configured.

In this recipe, we'll explore advanced usage of a **multi-master** cluster, and how it can help us reach the pinnacle of high availability.

Getting ready

It's crucially important to become familiar with the benefits and drawbacks of how multi-master operation can affect the cluster. The previous *Incorporating multi-master* recipe is a good place to start. Additionally, information we cover here can be directly relevant to the *Defining timetables through RTO* recipe and the *Picking redundant copies* recipe.

In a way, this recipe will bring together a lot of concepts we've covered through the chapter, so we recommend covering it last if possible.

How to do it...

To really make the most of multi-master architecture, follow these guidelines:

1. Always allocate a proxy layer.
2. If cross-data center latency is relevant, allocate at least two nodes per location.
3. It's no longer necessary to worry about adding nodes specifically to maintain quorum.
4. Geographically partition data if possible.

How it works...

We actually recommend applying the first rule to all clusters, as suggested in the *Introducing indirection* recipe. It's especially important here as the focus is specifically centered on maximizing availability.

Unlike a standard PostgreSQL node, a cluster containing multiple primary nodes does not require the promotion of alternate systems to writable status. This means we can switch to them in a nearly instantaneous manner. A properly configured proxy layer means this is possible without directly alerting the application layer. Such a cluster could resemble this diagram:

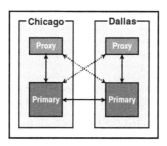

Given this configuration, it's possible to switch from one **Primary** to the other with a pause of mere milliseconds in between. This effectively means zero RTO contribution for that action. This allows us to perform maintenance on any node, essentially without disturbing the application layer at all.

In the preceding configuration, however, we only have one node per location. In the event that the **Primary** in Chicago fails or is undergoing maintenance, applications in that location will be interacting with the Dallas node. A better design would be something like this:

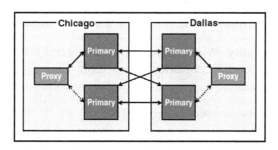

With two nodes per data center, we're free to swap between them as necessary. If the proxy uses a connection check mechanism, it can even autodetect online status and ensure traffic always goes to the online node in the same location.

The extra Primary per data center need not remain idle when not in use. Some proxy systems can allocate application sessions by user, account, or some other identifying characteristic. This allows safe load balancing that avoids risks associated with multi-master systems, such as conflict resolution.

Pay attention to the preceding diagrams and try to find one common attribute they both share.

Find it yet?

Each cluster has an even number of nodes. Also note that we didn't compensate for this by adding any kind of witness node to help arbitrate the quorum state. This is because each node is a Primary with no failover process to manage. As a consequence, we no longer have the usual cause of split brain, nor must we worry too much about network partition events.

Finally, try, if possible, to arrange the cluster such that data is as closely associated with its users as possible. If users are bank clients interacting with their own account and can be regionalized by country, this is an easy choice. If it's a shared service microarchitecture with applications indiscriminately modifying data from arbitrary accounts, that's not so simple.

For those more advanced circumstances, it's possible to approach the problem from a smaller scale. Perhaps servers in the same rack only communicate with the database nearest to them physically. Perhaps the proxy layer can use sticky sessions and route connections to specific primary nodes based on a stable metric.

The goal here is data locality. While multi-master PostgreSQL allows multiple nodes to ingest writes simultaneously, consider transmission latency. We can observe this in a simple two-node interaction:

1. Node A accepts a write for Account X.
2. Node A sends the result to Node B.
3. The application is stateless and connects to Node B.
4. The application notices data is missing in node B and submits a change again.
5. Node B replays data from Node A.
6. Account X has now been modified twice.

If the application session was tightly coupled to one primary node, this scenario would not be possible. There are numerous ways to accomplish this coupling, and it helps ensure fastest turnaround for associated data that was previously modified in any case.

There's more...

PostgreSQL multi-master solutions use logical replication to transfer data between nodes by necessity. As a result, software versions need not match. This means that PostgreSQL 11 and PostgreSQL 12 nodes may coexist in the same cluster. Combined with a proxy layer as recommended, this allows fully online, major-version upgrades. From an RTO perspective, this means the following elements may all be assumed to contribute zero or a small number of milliseconds:

- Node failover and switchover
- Minor upgrades (v12.1 to v12.2)
- Node maintenance
- Major upgrades (v11 to v12)

Due to its proprietary nature, PostgreSQL multi-master is generally not available without additional cost. Consider any associated pricing when tabulating RTO architecture variant cost sheets. This should enable management to make an informed decision based on expenses associated with pursuing extremely low RTO features such as these.

See also

Further reading to consider regarding the concepts introduced in this recipe include the following:
```
https://www.postgresql.org/docs/current/logical-replication.html
```

Hardware Planning

What does high availability mean? In the context of what we're trying to build, it means we want our database to start and remain online for as long as possible. A critical component of this is the hardware that hosts the database itself. No matter how perfect a machine and its parts may be, the failure, of or unexpected behavior from, any element can result in an outage.

So how do we avoid these unwanted outages? We expect them. We must start by assuming hardware can and will fail, and at the worst possible moment. If we start with that in mind, it becomes much easier to make decisions regarding the composition of each server we are building.

Make no mistake! Much of this planning will rely on worksheets, caveats, and compromise. Some of our choices will have several expensive options, and we will have to weigh the benefits offered against our total cost outlay. We want to build something stable, which is not always easy. Depending on the size of our company, our purchasing power, and available hosting choices, we may be in for a rather complicated path to that goal.

This chapter will attempt to paint a complete picture of a highly available environment in such a way that you can pick and choose the best solution without making too many detrimental compromises. Of course, we'll offer advice on what we believe is the best overall solution, but you don't always have to take our word for it.

In this chapter, we will learn about the selection and provisioning of hardware necessary to build a highly available PostgreSQL database. We will cover the following recipes in this chapter:

- Planning for redundancy
- Having enough IOPS
- Sizing storage

- Investing in a RAID
- Picking a processor
- Allocating enough memory
- Exploring nimble networking
- Managing motherboards
- Selecting a chassis
- Saddling up to a SAN
- Tallying up
- Protecting your eggs

 For the purposes of this chapter, we will not cover cloud computing or other elastic allocation options. Many of the concepts we introduce can be adapted to those solutions, yet many are implementation-specific. If you want to use a cloud vendor such as Amazon or Rackspace, you will need to obtain manuals and appropriate materials for applying what you learn here.

Planning for redundancy

Redundancy means having a spare, but a spare for what? Everything. Every single part, from the motherboard to the chassis, power supply to network cable, disk space to throughput, should have at least one piece of excess equipment or capacity available for immediate use.

The intent of this recipe is to consider as many of these elements as we can imagine before committing to a final inventory purchase.

Getting ready

Fire up your favorite spreadsheet program; we'll be using it to keep track of all the parts that go into the server, and any capacity concerns. If you don't have one, OpenOffice and LibreOffice are good free alternatives for building these spreadsheets, as is Google Sheets. The subsequent sections will help determine most of the row contents.

How to do it...

We simply need to produce a hardware spreadsheet to track our purchase needs. We can do that with the following steps:

1. Create a new spreadsheet for parts and details.
2. Create a heading row with the following columns:

   - Type
   - Capacity
   - Supplier
   - Price
   - Count
   - Total cost

3. Create a new row for each type of the following components:

   - Chassis
   - CPU
   - Hard Drive (3.5")
   - Hard Drive (2.5")
   - Hard Drive (SSD)
   - Motherboard
   - XPower Supply
   - RAID Controller
   - RAM
   - SAN

4. In the Chassis row, under the Total Cost column, enter the formula: =D2*E2.
5. Copy and paste the formula into the Total Cost column for all the rows we created. The end result should look something like the following screenshot:

	A	B	C	D	E	F
1	Type	Capacity	Supplier	Price	Count	Total Cost
2	Chassis					0
3	CPU					0

How it works...

What we've done is prepare a spreadsheet that we can fill in with information collected throughout the remainder of this chapter. We will have very long discussions regarding each part of the server we want to build, so we need a place to collect each decision we make along the way.

The heading column can include any other details you wish to retain about each part, but for the sake of simplicity, we have stuck to the bare minimum. This also goes for the parts we chose for each column. Depending on the vendor you select to supply your server, many of these decisions will already be made. It's still a good idea to include each component in case you need an emergency replacement.

The Total Cost column exists for one purpose: to itemize the cost of each part, multiplied by how many we will need to complete the server.

To make sure we account for the redundancy element of the spreadsheet, we strongly suggest inflating the number you use for the Count column, which will also increase the price automatically. This ensures that we automatically include extra capacity in case something fails. If you would rather track this separately, add a Spare Count column to the spreadsheet instead.

We'll have discussions later as to the failure rates of different types of hardware, which will influence how many excess components to allocate. Don't worry about that for now.

There's more...

We also recommend including a summary for all Total Cost columns so we get an aggregate cost estimate for the whole server. To do that with our spreadsheet example, keep in mind that the Total Cost column is listed as column **F**.

To add a Sum Total column to your spreadsheet in row **15**, column **F**, enter the formula =SUM(F2:F12). If you've added more columns, substitute for column **F** whichever column now holds Total Cost. Likewise, if you have more than 13 rows of different parts, use a different row to represent your summary price than row **15**.

See also

There are a lot of spreadsheet options available. Many corporations supply a copy of Microsoft Excel. However, if this is not the case, there are many alternatives, including the following:

- Google Sheets: `https://docs.google.com/spreadsheets/`
- Open Office: `https://www.openoffice.org/`
- Libre Office: `https://www.libreoffice.org/`

All of these options are free to use and popular enough that support and documentation are readily available.

Having enough IOPS

IOPS (stands for **Input/Output Operations Per Second**) describes how many operations a device can perform per second before it should be considered saturated. If a device is saturated, further requests must wait until the device has spare bandwidth. A server overwhelmed with requests can amount to seconds, minutes, or even hours of delayed results.

Depending on application timeout settings and user patience, a device with low IOPS appears as a bottleneck that reduces both system responsiveness and the perception of quality. A database with insufficient IOPS to service queries in a timely manner is unavailable for all intents and purposes. It doesn't matter if PostgreSQL is still online and serving requests in this scenario, as its availability has already suffered.

In this recipe, we will attempt to account for future storage and throughput needs based on monthly increases in storage utilization.

Getting ready

This process is more of a thought experiment. We will present some very rough estimates of I/O performance for many different disk types. We should increment the entries in our hardware spreadsheet based on the perceived need for each.

The main things we will need for this process are numbers. During development, applications commonly have a goal, expected client count, table count, estimated growth rates, and so on. Even if we must guess many of these, each will contribute to our IOPS requirements. Have these numbers ready, even if they're simply guesses.

 If the application already exists on a development or stage environment, try to get the development or QA team to run operational tests. This is a great opportunity to gather statistics before choosing potential production hardware.

How to do it...

We need to figure out how many operations per second we can expect. We can estimate this by using the following steps:

1. Collect the number of simultaneous database connections. Start with the expected user count, and divide by 50.
2. Obtain the average number of queries per page. If this is unavailable, use 10.
3. Count the number of tables used in those queries. If this is unavailable, use 3.
4. Multiply these numbers together, and double the result.
5. Multiply the previous total by 8.
6. Increment the Count column in our hardware spreadsheet for one or more of the following, and round up:

    - For 3.5" hard drives, divide by 200.
    - For 2.5" hard drives, divide by 150.
    - For SSD hard drives, divide by 50,000, and then add two.

7. Add 10% to any count greater than 0 and then round up.

How it works...

Wow, that's a lot of work! There's a reason for everything, of course.

In the initial three steps, we're trying to determine how many operations might touch an object on disk. For every user that's actively loading a page, for every query in that page, and for every table in that query, that's a potential disk read or write.

We double that number to account for the fact we're estimating these values. It's a common engineering trick to double or triple calculations to absorb unexpected capacity, variance in materials, and so on. We can use that same technique here.

 Why did we suggest dividing the user count by 50 to get the connection total? Since we do not know the average query runtime, we assume 20 ms for each query. For every query that's executing, a connection is in use. Assuming full utilization, up to 50 queries can be active per second. If you have a production system that can provide a better query runtime average, we suggest using that value instead.

But why do we then multiply by eight? In a worst- (or best-) case scenario, it's not uncommon for an application to double the number of users or requests on a yearly basis. Doubled usage means doubled hardware needs. If requirements double in one year, we would need a server three times more powerful (1 + 2) than the original estimates to account for the second year. Another doubling would mean a server seven times better (1 + 2 + 4). CPUs, RAM, and storage are generally available as powers of two. Since it's fairly difficult to obtain storage seven times faster than what we already have, we multiply the total by eight.

That gives a total IOPS value roughly necessary for our database to immediately serve every request for the next 3 years, straight from the disk device. Several companies buy servers every three or four years as a balance between cost and capacity, so these estimates are based on that assumption.

In the next step, we get a rough estimate of the number of disks necessary to serve the required IOPS. Our numbers in these steps are based on hard drive performance. A 15,000 RPM SAS hard drive can serve, under ideal conditions, roughly 200 operations per second. Likewise, a 10,000 RPM drive can provide about 150 operations per second.

Current SSDs as of the time of writing commonly reach 200,000-300,000 IOPS, and some even regularly eclipse a cool million. However, their extreme speed suggests fewer of them are necessary to reach IOPS goals, and thus failure risk is not as evenly distributed. We artificially increase the number of these drives because, again, we are erring toward availability.

Finally, we add a few extra devices for spares that will reside in long-term storage, just in case one or more drives fail. This also insulates us from the rare event that hardware is discontinued or otherwise becomes difficult to obtain.

There's more...

Figuring out the number of IOPS we need and the devices involved is only part of the story. Let's take a look at an example using values we might encounter in a real application. After that, we'll discuss other things we may need to consider when adjusting these numbers.

A working example

Sometimes, these large lists of calculations make more sense if we see them in practice. So let's make the assumption that 2,000 users will use our application each second. This is how this would look:

- $2000 / 50 = 40$
- Default queries per page = 10
- Default tables per query = 3
- $40 * 10 * 3 * 2 = 2,400$
- $2,400 * 8 = 19,200$
- 19,200 IOPS in drives:
    - 5" drives: $19,200 / 200 = 96$
    - 5" drives: $19,200 / 150 = 128$
    - SSDs: $2 + (19,200 / 50,000) = 2.38 \sim 3$
- Add 10%:
    - 5" drives: $96 + 9.6 = 105.6 \sim 106$
    - 5" drives: $128 + 12.8 = 140.8 \sim 141$
    - SSDs: $3 + 0.3 = 3.3 \sim 4$

We are not taking storage capacity into account, which would likely increase our SSD total. We will be discussing capacity soon.

Making concessions

Our calculations always assume worst-case scenarios. This is both expensive and, in most cases, monumentally overzealous. We ignore RAM caching of disk blocks, we don't account for application frontend caches, and the PostgreSQL shared buffers are also not included.

Why? Crashes are always a concern. If a database crashes, buffers are forfeit. If the application frontend cache gets emptied or has problems, reads will be served directly from the database. Until caches are rebuilt, query results can be multiple orders of magnitude slower than normal for minutes or even hours. We will discuss methods of circumventing these effects, but these IOPS numbers give us a baseline.

The number of necessary IOPS, and hence disk requirements, are subject to risk evaluation and cost-benefit analysis. Deciding between 100% coverage and an acceptable fraction is a careful balancing act.

Feel free to reduce these numbers; just consider the cost of an outage as part of the total. If a delay is considered as part of standard operating procedures, fractions up to 50% are relatively low risk. If possible, try to run tests for an ultimate decision before purchase.

Sizing storage

Capacity planning for a database server involves a lot of variables. We must account for table count, user activity, compliance storage requirements, indexes, object bloat, maintenance, archival, and more. We may even need to consider application features that do not yet exist. New functionality often brings additional tables, extra storage standards, and increased archival needs. Planning done now may have little relevance to future usage.

So how do we produce functional estimates for disk space with so many uncertain or fluctuating elements? We primarily want to avoid a scenario where we lack sufficient capacity to continue operating. Exhausting disk space results in ignored queries at best, and a completely frozen and difficult to repair database at worst. Neither are the ingredients of a highly available environment.

In this recipe, we will explore a possible approach to determine minimum storage for long-term operations. Our goal is to provision enough to avoid outright catastrophe, though it's in our best interest to allocate more than the bare minimum.

Getting ready

Since there are numerous variables that contribute to the volume of storage we want, we need information about each of them. Gather as many data points as possible regarding things such as the largest expected tables and indexes, row counts per day, indexes per table, desired excess, and anything else imaginable. We'll use all of it.

This is much easier if we already have a database, and are now trying to ensure it is highly available. Even if the database is only in development or staging environments at this moment, a few activity simulations at expected user counts should provide a basis for many of our numbers. No matter the case, revisit estimates as concrete details become available.

How to do it...

We can collect some of the information we want from PostgreSQL if we have a running instance already. If not, we can use baseline numbers. Follow these steps if you already have a PostgreSQL database available:

1. Submit this query to get the amount of space used by all databases:

```
SELECT pg_size_pretty(sum(pg_database_size(oid))::BIGINT)
   FROM pg_database;
```

2. Wait for one week.
3. Perform the preceding query again.
4. Subtract the first reading from the second.

Downloading the example code:
You can download the example code files for all Packt books you have purchased from your account at http://www.packtpub.com. If you purchased this book elsewhere, you can visit http://www.packtpub.com/support and register to have the files emailed directly to you.

If we don't have an existing installation and are working with a project that has yet to start development, we can substitute a few guesses instead. Without a running PostgreSQL instance, consider using these sample values obtained from a real-world system:

- Our databases have a total size of 100 GB.
- After 1 week, our install grew by 1.5 GB.

 Of course, you don't have to start with these rather arbitrary numbers for your own use case. Without a source database, we simply recommend starting with medium-size growth values to avoid underestimating. If our estimates are too low, the database could exceed our plans and require emergency resource allocation. That's not something we want in a highly available cluster!

Next, we can calculate our growth needs for the next 3 years. Perform the following steps:

1. Multiply the data size delta by four.
2. Apply the following formula, where x is the most recent size of the databases, and y is the value from the previous step: $x * (1 + y/x)^{36}$.
3. Multiply the previous result by two.

How it works...

The process we illustrate here is the magic of compounding interest. If we have an existing database directory, it can tell us not only how much space it currently consumes, but also how quickly it's currently growing. If not, we can start with a medium-size configuration and substitute a growth assumption that will cause the cumulative total to double in size every year. Remember, we begin by working with worst-case scenarios, and modify the numbers afterward.

 What if we don't need compounding interest because our expected growth is linear? It's always easier to start with too much space than to add more later. If you know your table count will rarely change, users will not increase in number, or data streams are relatively consistent, feel free to drop the compounded interest formula. Otherwise, we suggest using it anyway.

The PostgreSQL query we provide takes advantage of the system catalog and known statistics regarding the database contents. The `pg_database_size` function always returns the number of bytes a database uses, so we must use the `pg_size_pretty` function to make it more human-readable.

Once we know the size of the database instance and its growth rate, we can apply a simple compounding interest function to estimate the volume at any point in the future. This not only accounts for the current growth rate, but also incorporates additional accumulation caused by increases in clients, table counts, and other unspecified sources. It's extremely aggressive, since we take the weekly growth rate, translate that to a monthly rate, and apply the compounding monthly instead of yearly.

And then we use a standard engineering tactic and double the estimate, just in case. Using the provided values—that of a 100 GB database that grows at 1.5 GB per week—we would have an 815 GB database install in 3 years. With a system that large, we should allocate at least 1,630 GB.

Alternatively, if our growth rate were more linear, we could simply add the 1.5 GB weekly growth rate for 3 years. In that case, the final tally after 3 years of accumulation would only be 334 GB, and we could be safe with a total capacity of 668 GB.

There's more...

Don't let our formulas define your only path. Let's explore how they apply in a real-world situation, and how we can modify them to better fit our systems.

Real-world example

There are quite a few very large databases using PostgreSQL. Whether or not they have thousands of tables and indexes, billions of rows, or handle billions of queries per day, statistics help us plan for the future. Let's apply the previous steps to an example database that actually exists:

- The database is currently 875 GB.
- The database was 865 GB last week.
- The database grows by 10 GB per week.
- Thus, the database grows by 40 GB every 4 weeks.

- Using the formula we discussed in *step two* of this recipe, our size estimate after 3 years is: *875 * (1 + 40/875)^36 = 4,374 GB*.
- Doubled, this is 8,748 GB.

Keep in mind that this estimation technique may grossly exaggerate the necessary space. If we take the existing 40 GB monthly growth rate, the database would only be 2,315 GB in 3 years. Of course, 2.3 TB is still a very large database; it's just half as large as our estimate.

Adjusting the numbers

We already mentioned that the growth curve used here is extremely aggressive. We can't risk ever running out of space in a production database and still consider ourselves highly available. However, there is probably a safe position between the current growth rate of the database, and the compounded estimate, especially since we are doubling the allocation anyway.

In the preceding real-world example, the database is likely to have a size between 2,315 GB and 4,374 GB. If we split the difference, that's 3,345 GB. Furthermore, we don't necessarily have to double that number if we're comfortable having a disk device that's 70% full 3 years from now, instead of 50%. With that in mind, we would probably be safe with 5 TB of space instead of 9 TB. That's a vast saving if we're willing to make those compromises.

Incorporating the spreadsheet

At the beginning of this chapter, in the *Planning for redundancy* recipe, we created a hardware cost spreadsheet to estimate the total cost of a highly available server. If we were following the chapter, our spreadsheet already accounts for the minimum number of devices necessary to provide the IOPS we want.

Suppose we needed 5,000 IOPS, and decided to use 2.5-inch drives. That would require about 33 devices. Even at only 300 GB each, that's 9 TB of total available space. Yet the case for SSDs is the opposite. For our previous example, we would need at least five 1 GB SSD drives, or one very large PCIe SSD to provide 5 TB of space for the adjusted sample.

Whichever solution we finally choose, we can take the advice from every section so far. At this point, the spreadsheet should have a device count that should satisfy most, if not all, of our space and IOPS requirements.

Investing in a RAID

A **Redundant Array of Independent (or Inexpensive) Disks** (**RAID**) often requires a separate controller card for management. The primary purpose of a RAID is to combine several physical devices into a single logical unit for the sake of redundancy and performance.

This is especially relevant to our interests. Carnegie Mellon University published a study in 2007 on hard drive failure rates. They found that hard drives fail at a rate of about 3% per year. Furthermore, they found that drive type and interface contributed little to disk longevity, and that hard drives do not reflect a tendency to fail early as was commonly accepted. These findings were largely corroborated by a parallel study released the same year by Google.

What does this mean? For our purposes in building a highly available server, it means hard drives should be looked at with great disdain. Larger databases will depend on tens or hundreds of hard drives in order to represent several terabytes of data. With a 3% failure rate per year, a 100-drive array would lose roughly nine devices after 3 years.

This is the primary reason that all of our calculations regarding disk devices automatically assume a 10% excess inventory allotment. If a drive fails, we need an immediate replacement. Vendors are not always capable of delivering a new drive quickly enough. Having a spare on hand, ideally at the hosting facility or in the server itself, helps ensure continuous uptime.

So how does RAID figure into this scenario? If we hosted our database on several bare hard drives knowing that around 10% of these drives will fail in 3 years, outages would be inevitable. What we want is an abstraction layer that can present any number of hard drives as a single whole, keeping reserves for drive errors, handling checksums for integrity, and mirroring for redundancy.

RAID provides all of that in several convenient configurations. Good controller cards often include copious amounts of cache and other management capabilities. Instead of manually assigning dozens of drives, it's fairly common to split them into several usable array allocations that reflect much lower operational risk.

Knowing all of this, databases have special needs when it comes to RAID and the performance characteristics associated with each RAID type. This recipe will explore the selection criteria for our database, and how to simplify the process.

Getting ready

That was a long introduction, wasn't it? Well, we also strongly suggest taking a look at the *Having enough IOPS* and *Sizing storage* recipes before continuing. Make sure the hardware spreadsheet has a drive count for the type of drives going into the server we're designing. If we're using PCIe instead of standard SSD drives, this section can be skipped.

How to do it...

Only a few RAID levels matter in a database context. Perform these steps to decide which one is right for this server:

- If this is an **Online Transaction Processing** (**OLTP**) database primarily for handling very high-speed queries, use RAID level 1+0.
- If this is a non-critical development or staging system, use RAID level 5.
- If this is a non-critical **Online Analytic Processing** (**OLAP**) reporting system, use RAID level 5.
- If this is a critical OLAP reporting system, use RAID level 6.
- If this is a long-term storage OLAP warehouse, use RAID level 6.

How it works...

We have made a lot of snap decisions here. There are quite a few RAID levels we simply ignored, so there should be some discussion regarding the reasoning we used.

Let's begin with RAID level 0. Level 0 stripes data across all disks at once. It's certainly convenient, but a single drive failure will lose all stored information in the array. What about RAID level 1? Level 1 acts as a full mirror of all data stored. For every set of drives, a second set of drives holds an exact copy. If a drive fails in one set, the second set is still available. However, if that set also experiences any failure, all data is lost.

When we talk about RAID 1+0, we actually combine the mirroring capability of RAID 1 with the striping of RAID 0. How? Take a look at the following diagram:

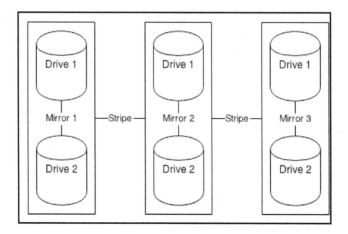

In this RAID 1+0, we have three sets, each consisting of two disks. Each of the two disks mirrors the other, and the data is striped across all three sets. We could lose a disk from each set and still retain all of our data. We only have a problem if we lose two disks from the same set since they mirror each other. Overall, this is the most robust RAID level available, and the most commonly used for OLTP systems.

RAID level 5 and 6 take a different approach. Again, let's look at six drives and see a very simplified view of how RAID 5 would operate in that situation:

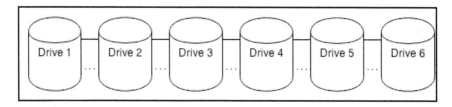

The solid line shows that the data is spread across all six drives. The dotted line is the parity information. If a drive fails and the block can't be read directly from the necessary location, a RAID 5 array will use the remaining parity information from all drives to reconstruct the missing data. The only real difference between a RAID 5 and a RAID 6 array is that a RAID 6 array contains a second parity line, so up to two drives can fail before the array begins operating in a degraded manner.

Using RAID 5 or 6 offers more protection than RAID 0, with fewer costs than RAID 1+0, which requires double the amount of required devices. We selected these for non-critical OLAP systems because they usually prioritize storage over performance and are not as sensitive to immediate availability pressures as an OLTP system.

There's more...

We mentioned controller cards earlier and noted that they also offer onboard cache. RAID has been around for a long time, and though disks are getting much larger, they haven't experienced an equivalent increase in speed. In scenarios that use RAID 5 or 6, writes can also be slowed since each write must be committed to several devices simultaneously in the form of parity.

To combat this, RAID controllers allow configuration of the cache to buffer writes in favor of reads, or vice versa. Don't be afraid to adjust this and run tests to determine the best cache mix. If everything else fails, start with 100% for writes, as they are the most in need of caching. Keep a close eye on write performance and give it priority if possible. Generally, the OS cache does a better job of caching reads, and has much more memory available to do so.

See also

For more details, refer to the following link:

- **Disk failures in the real world**: http://www.cs.cmu.edu/~bianca/fast07.pdf
- **Failure Trends in a Large Disk Drive Population**: http://research.google.com/pubs/pub32774.html

Picking a processor

In selecting a CPU for our server, we have much to consider. At the time of writing, the current trend among processors in every space—including mobile—is toward multiple cores per chip. CPU manufacturers have found that providing a large number of smaller processing units spreads workload horizontally for better overall scalability.

As users of PostgreSQL, this benefits us tremendously. PostgreSQL is based on processes instead of threads. This means each connected client is assigned to a process that can use a CPU core when available. The host operating system can perform such allocations without any input from the database software. Motherboards have limited space, so we need more cores on the same limited real estate, which means more simultaneously active database clients.

Once again, our discussion veers toward capacity planning for a three- or four-year cycle. Limited processing capability leads to slow or delayed queries, or a database that is incapable of adequately handling increasing numbers of simultaneous users. Yet simply choosing the fastest CPU with the most cores and filling the motherboard can be a staggering waste of resources. So how, then, do we know what to buy?

This recipe will attempt to answer that question.

Getting ready

Luckily, there are only really two manufacturers that produce commodity server-class CPUs. Furthermore, each vendor has a line of CPUs designed specifically for server use. AMD and Intel both provide similar price-to-performance curves, but that's where the comparison ends.

This is an exciting time to purchase a CPU. At the time of writing, AMD Threadripper chips compare quite favorably to Intel Xeon processors, and often provide higher core counts. Unlike previous CPU architecture iterations, choosing a CPU isn't as simple as it once was.

Before going through this recipe, it would be a good idea to visit AnandTech, Tom's Hardware, Intel, and AMD, just to get a basic idea of the landscape. There are a lot of benchmarks that compare various models of CPUs, so don't take our word for it.

Generally, however, we can count on one thing for now: AMD CPUs tend toward higher core counts, while Intel chips prioritize per-core clock speed. This may affect which we choose for each environment, so we recommend cultivating a passing familiarity with these processor architectures if possible.

How to do it...

We can collect some of the information we want from the database if we have one already. If we already have a PostgreSQL database available, we can execute a query to start our calculations. This works best if used at the most active time of day.

If you have PostgreSQL 9.2 or higher, execute this query as a superuser to get the count of simultaneous active users:

```
SELECT count(*)
  FROM pg_stat_activity
 WHERE state = 'active';
```

Use this query if you have an older version:

```
SELECT count(*)
  FROM pg_stat_activity
 WHERE current_query NOT LIKE '<IDLE>%';
```

If we don't have a PostgreSQL server, we need to make an educated guess. Use these steps to approximate:

1. Work with the application developers to obtain a count of expected active clients per second.
2. Divide the previous number by 50 to remain consistent with our 20 ms query assumption.

Once we have some idea of how many queries will be active simultaneously, we need to estimate the processor count. Follow these steps:

1. If we already know how many disks will store our data, use this number. In the case of an SSD base, use 0.
2. Subtract the previous number from our count of active users.

3. Divide the previous result by 2.
4. Apply the following formula, where x is the value from the previous step:

```
x * (1.4)^3
```

How it works...

Before we can even begin to decide on a processor count, we need a baseline. With a working PostgreSQL server to base our numbers on, we can just use the number of existing users during a busy period. Without that, we need to guess. This guess can actually be fairly accurate depending on how the application functions. For example, if the intent is to service 1,000 users per second, we can start with the same assumption.

After that, we apply a commonly accepted formula used by PostgreSQL administrators for a very long time. The ideal number of active connections is equal to twice the amount of available processor cores, plus the amount of disk spindles. Amusingly, the disk spindles increase the ideal number of connections because they contribute seek time, which forces the processor to wait for information. While a processor is waiting for input intended for one connection, the operating system may decide to lend the processor to another until the data is retrieved.

Thus, we apply that accepted formula in reverse. First, we subtract the number of spindles, and then divide by two to obtain how many CPUs we should have for our expected workload.

Afterward, we assume a 40% increase in active clients on a yearly basis, and increase the CPU core count accordingly for 3 years.

Note that this is a very aggressive growth rate. If we have historical growth data available, or the company is expecting a different value, we should use that instead. This is one problem inherent in estimating expected usage rather than projecting based on existing patterns.

When purchasing CPUs, no matter how cores are distributed, the final total should be equal to or greater than the number we calculated. If it isn't, the application may require more aggressive caching than expected, or we may need to horizontally scale the database. We're not ready to introduce that yet, but keep it in mind for later.

There's more...

The processor count is only part of the story. Modern CPUs have a few additional elements we need to consider.

Simultaneous multithreading

Essentially, all modern server-class processors provide a feature that essentially splits each physical processor core into two virtual cores. Intel calls this **hyper-threading**, while AMD uses the standard **Simultaneous Multithreading (SMT)** terminology. Historically, this was not well received as benchmarks often illustrated performance degradation when the feature was enabled.

> Recently, several security vulnerabilities have been discovered in SMT-enabled CPUs. Be sure to check for security advisories before enabling this feature in earnest.

Since the introduction of Intel's Nehalem-based architecture in 2008 and AMD's Ryzen architecture in 2017, this is no longer the case. While doubling the processor count does not result in a doubling of throughput, we've run several tests that show up to a 40% improvement over using physical cores alone. This may not be universal, but it does apply to PostgreSQL performance tests. What this means is that the commonly accepted formula for determining the ideal connection count requires modification.

The current advice is to only multiply the physical core count by two. Assuming a 40% increase by enabling SMT, the new formula becomes *2 * 1.4 * CPUs + spindles*. With that in mind, if we wanted to serve 1,000 connections per second and used SSDs to host our data, our minimum CPU count would be *1000 / 50 / 1.4*, or 14. Half of that is seven, but no CPU has seven physical cores, so we would need at least eight. If we used the physical cores alone for our calculation, we would need 10.

Clock boosting

Recent processors also tend to provide adaptive CPU clock boosting based on perceived workload. Some vendor motherboards disable this by default.

> Make sure to go through the BIOS settings before performing acceptability tests, as this functionality can provide up to 25% better performance in isolated cases.

This is possible because the maximum speed of the core itself is increased when resources are available or demand is high. A 4.2 GHz core might operate temporarily at 4.5 GHz. For queries that are dependent on nested loops or other CPU-intensive operations, this can drastically reduce query execution times.

Power usage

Intel family chips often have low voltage versions of their high-performance offerings. While these processors require up to 30% less electricity, they also run up to 25% slower. Low-power name designations are not always consistent, so when choosing an Intel processor, make sure to compare specifications of all similarly named chips.

Beware of accidentally choosing a low-power chip meant for a high-performance database. However, these chips may be ideal for warehouse or reporting database use, since those systems are not meant for high throughput or vast amounts of simultaneous users. They often cost less than their high-performance counterparts, making them perfect for systems expecting low utilization.

See also

For more details, refer to the following links:

- AnandTech: https://www.anandtech.com/
- Tom's Hardware: https://www.tomshardware.com/

Allocating enough memory

The primary focus when selecting memory for a highly available system is stability. It's no accident that most, if not all, server-class RAM is of the error-correcting variety. There are a few other things to consider that may not appear obvious at first glance.

Due to the multi-core nature of our CPUs, the amount of addressable memory may depend on the core count. In addition, speed, latency, and parity are all considerations. We also must include the number of channels reported by each CPU; failing to match this with an equal count of memory sticks can drastically degrade performance.

This recipe will help ensure our server remains fast and stable by considering memory options.

Getting ready

Some of the decisions we will make depend on the capabilities of the CPU. Make sure to read through the *Picking a processor* recipe before continuing. If we have a PostgreSQL database available, there's also a query that can prepare us for selecting the most advantageous count of memory modules. It's also a very good idea to complete the *Sizing storage* recipe to get a better idea for choosing an amount of memory.

How to do it...

We can collect some of the information we want from PostgreSQL if we have an install already. Follow these steps if there's an existing database instance that we can use:

1. Execute the following query to obtain the size of all databases in the instance:

```
SELECT pg_size_pretty(sum(pg_database_size(oid))::BIGINT)
  FROM pg_database;
```

2. Multiply the result by eight.

If we don't have an existing database, we should use a size estimate of the database install after 3 years. Refer to the *Sizing storage* recipe to obtain this estimate. Then, perform the following steps:

1. Divide the current or estimated database storage size by ten to obtain the minimum amount of memory.
2. Multiply our ideal CPU chip count by four to get the memory module count.
3. Divide the minimum memory amount by the module count to get the minimum module size.
4. Round up to the nearest available memory module size.

How it works...

The important part of this recipe is starting with a viable estimate of the database size. Since a lack of RAM usually won't cause the database to crash or operate improperly, we can use looser guidelines to obtain this number. Hence, 3 years down the road, an existing database install could be eight times larger than its current size. We use eight based on previous assumptions that the database roughly doubles in size every year.

Why do we then divide that number by ten? Our goal here is to maximize the benefit of the OS-level cache, which will consume a majority of our RAM. This estimate gives us a value that is ten times smaller than the space our database consumes. At this scale, data that is frequently fetched from disk is likely to be served from memory instead. The alternative is read latency due to insufficient memory for disk caching.

Most current CPUs are quad-channel, and thus operate best when the number of modules per processor is a multiple of four. Assuming we previously determined how many processor cores would be ideal for our system in the *Picking a processor* recipe, we automatically know the most efficient memory module count. Why do we multiply by four, regardless of how many memory channels the CPU has? Adding more memory modules is not wasted on chips with fewer channels, and provides a possible upgrade path.

Dividing the memory amount by the module count gives our minimum module size. RAM comes in many dimensions, and our calculation is not likely to match any of the available dimensions for purchase, so we need to round up. Why not round down? The operating system will utilize all available RAM to cache and buffer important data. Unless the greater amount is extremely expensive in comparison, any *excess* memory will not be wasted.

Imagine we have a 200 GB PostgreSQL installation, and chose to buy a single CPU chip. If we follow the preceding procedure, we would want at least 20 GB of RAM distributed over four RAM chips. Since 20/4 = 5, we would likely want four 8 GB RAM chips, or a total of 32 GB. This is actually a fairly good starting value in general, and allows our database to grow before 10% of its current size is greater than 32 GB.

There's more...

We didn't focus on memory speed, timings, or latency here. Timing and latency can affect performance, but our primary focus is stability. We're always free to order faster or better memory as our budget allows.

Memory speed, on the other hand, is a more visible factor. Memory speed works with a multiplier to match the highest compatible motherboard bus speed. This directly controls how quickly the CPU can utilize available RAM. Before buying memory, research the stated clock speed and try to match it with one of the faster settings compatible with both the CPU and motherboard.

For example, DDR4-3200 is twice as fast as DDR4-1600 since it operates at 400 MHz, as opposed to 200 MHz. Database benchmarks would be vastly different between these two memory speeds, even with the same CPU. Fast memory means that PostgreSQL can make more immediate use of cached data and produce results more quickly.

Exploring nimble networking

The network card enables the database server to exchange data with the outside world. This includes far more than web servers, spreadsheets, loading jobs, application servers, and other data consumers. The database server is part of a large continuum of activity, much of which will center around maintenance, management, and even filesystem availability.

Little of this other traffic involves PostgreSQL directly. Much happens in the background regardless of the database and its current workload. Yet even one mishandled network packet across an otherwise normal driver can render the entire server invisible to the outside world or, in extreme cases, even lead to a system panic and subsequent shutdown. On a busy database server, network cards can handle several terabytes of traffic on a daily basis; the margin of error for such a critical piece of hardware is exceptionally slim.

What's more, network bandwidth can easily be saturated by an aggressive backup strategy, which is something critical to a highly available database. For PostgreSQL systems utilizing streaming replication or WAL archival, that traffic contributes quite a bit of bandwidth to the overall picture. If our backups are delayed, or replicas sit idly waiting for network packets, our exposure to risk is high indeed.

That's not to say everything is doom and gloom! With the right network setup and accompanying hardware, there should be more than enough room for any and all traffic our database server needs. This recipe will explore all the copious options for connecting our database to the outside world, and making sure it stays there.

Getting ready

This is one of those times when it pays to do research. At the time of writing, the current high-speed network standards include 1 Gb/s (gigabits per second), 10 Gb/s, 40 Gb/s, and even 100 Gb/s Ethernet. However, 40 Gb/s network cards are still extremely rare, and 100 Gb/s is generally reserved for fiber-based switches and data center use.

This means we will be covering 1 Gb/s and 10 Gb/s interfaces. While we will do our best to outline all of the important aspects of these technologies to simplify the process, we strongly encourage using the internet to validate current availability and performance characteristics.

How to do it...

Let's begin with a few basic calculations. Look at these following numbers that represent an estimate of interface speed after accounting for network overhead:

- *1,000 Mb/s * B/10 b = 100 MB/s (Megabytes per second)*
- *10,000 Mb/s * B/10 b = 1,000 MB/s*

Next, consider how many ways this will be distributed. If we have an existing PostgreSQL setup, follow these steps:

1. Execute the following query to determine the number of existing replicas:

```
SELECT count(*)+1 AS streams
  FROM pg_stat_replication;
```

2. Multiply streams by 160 to find the maximum MB/s needed by replication streams.
3. Execute the following queries together in a psql connection during a busy time of day on a production database:

```
SELECT SUM(pg_stat_get_db_tuples_fetched(oid)) AS count1
  FROM pg_database;
SELECT pg_sleep(1);
SELECT SUM(pg_stat_get_db_tuples_fetched(oid)) AS count2
  FROM pg_database;
```

4. Subtract the results of `count1` from `count2` for the number of rows fetched from the database per second.

5. Divide the number of rows per second by 10,000 to get the MB/s used by PostgreSQL connections.

6. Add the calculated value of MB/s for streams to the value of MB/s for connections.

Without an existing database, follow these steps for some basic bandwidth numbers:

1. Multiply the desired number of PostgreSQL replicas by 160 to get the maximum MB/s needed by replication streams.

2. Assume one WAL stream for an off-site disaster recovery database copy.

3. Start with at least one live hot-streaming standby copy.

4. Include any additional database mirrors.

5. Estimate the active client count, as discussed in *Picking a Processor*.

6. Multiply the active client count estimate by five for MB/s used by PostgreSQL connections.

7. Add the value of MB/s for streams to the value of MB/s for connections.

No matter which checklist we follow, we should double the final tally.

How it works...

If we have an existing database, there is a wealth of statistical information at our fingertips. The first query we ran gave us a slightly inflated count of PostgreSQL replicas. For each replica, data must be transferred from the database to another server. This data is based on PostgreSQL WAL output, and these files are 16 MB each. A busy server can produce more than ten of these per second, so we multiply the count of streams by 160 to produce an aggressive amount of network overhead used by database replicas. As usual, this may be overzealous; it's always best to observe an actual system to measure maximum WAL segments generated during heavy write loads.

In PostgreSQL 9.2 and higher, database replicas can stream from other database replicas. This means network traffic can be distributed better among streaming clients, reducing network bandwidth pressure on production systems. PostgreSQL 9.2 and greater also allow direct backup of streaming replicas. This means one or two replicas may be the most the production database ever needs to supply with WAL traffic.

For the next set of numbers, we need to know how much data the database connections commonly retrieve. PostgreSQL tracks the number of table rows fetched, but it's a cumulative total. By waiting until a busy time of day and asking the database how many rows have been fetched before and after a one-second wait, we know how many rows are fetched per second.

However, we still don't know how many bytes these rows consume. A good estimate of this is 100 bytes per row. Then, we only have to multiply the number of rows by 100 to find the amount of bandwidth we would need. So why do we divide by 10,000? What's 10,000 multiplied by 100? One million. On dividing by 10,000, we produce the number of megabytes per second those tuple fetches probably used.

If an average of 100 bytes per row isn't good enough, we can connect to one of our primary databases and calculate the average tuple size. Use the query in the following code snippet:

```
SELECT sum(pg_relation_size(oid)) / sum(reltuples)
    FROM pg_class;
```

By adding the amount of streaming traffic to the amount of connection traffic, we have a good, if slightly inflated, idea of how much bandwidth the server needs.

Without a working database to go by, we need to use a few guesses instead. Luckily, the number of streams for a reliable database infrastructure starts at two: one for a live standby, and one for an off-site archive. Each additional desired mirror should increase this total. Again, we multiply the number of streams by 160 to obtain the maximum MB/s that all these replicas are likely to require.

The amount of bandwidth client connections use is slightly harder to estimate. However, if we worked through previous chapter sections, we have a CPU estimate, which also tells us the maximum number of database clients the server can reliably support. If we take that value and multiply by five, that provides a rough value in MB/s as well.

Again, we just add those two totals together, and we know the minimum speed of our network.

Finally, we multiply the final tally by two to account for any unknown maintenance, backup, and filesystem synchronization overhead.

There's more...

Besides producing an estimate through some simple calculations, we also want to make note of a few other networking details.

A networking example

This may be easier to visualize with a real example. Let's start with a very active database that has one streaming replica, and one off-site archive. Furthermore, connected clients regularly fetch five million rows per second. Let's work through our steps:

1. *2 * 160 = 320 MB/s*
2. *5,000,000 / 10,000 = 50 MB/s*
3. *320 + 50 = 370 MB/s*
4. *370 * 2 = 740 MB/s*

That's a very high value! A 1 Gb/s interface can only supply 100 MB/s at most, so we would need eight of those to produce the necessary bandwidth. Yet a 10 Gb/s interface can supply 1,000 MB/s, so it can easily handle 740 MB/s and have room to spare. Would we rather have eight network cables coming out of our server, or one?

Remember redundancy

One of the first things this chapter suggested was to consider extra inventory. Yet we haven't really covered online backups. Most server-class motherboards include not just one, but two onboard network modules. Each module commonly provides four Ethernet interfaces.

Usually, each interface is considered separate, and two interfaces from each module are connected to two switches in the data center. This allows server administrators to seamlessly perform maintenance on either switch without disrupting our network traffic. Furthermore, if a switch or network module fails, there's always a backup available.

In our working example, we would need eight 1 Gb/s interfaces to avoid experiencing network congestion. However, we've already used four of our eight available interfaces simply to satisfy basic server hosting requirements. That doesn't leave enough available capacity, and as a consequence, this server would experience a network bottleneck.

This would not be the case with a 10 Gb/s interface. Each of the interfaces connected to redundant switches can carry the entire network requirements of the server.

Saving the research

We suggested doing research on 1 Gb/s and 10 Gb/s network cards. Well, don't do too much. It's very likely the infrastructure department already has a standard server profile for high-bandwidth systems. This is primarily due to the fact 10 Gb/s is a very complicated standard compared to 1 Gb/s or lower. There are several different cable types available along with complimentary network modules, one or more of which are probably already deployed in the data center.

Just make sure that the infrastructure knows to allocate high-bandwidth resources if our calculations call for it.

Managing motherboards

We have been working up to this for quite some time. None of our storage, memory, CPU, or network matters if we have nothing to plug all of it into.

This could have been a long section dedicated to properly weighing the pros and cons of selecting a motherboard manufacturer for maximum stability. It turns out that most server vendors have already done all the hard work in that regard. In fact, a few vendors even disclose many details about the motherboard in their servers outside the model documentation. We can't really read hundreds of pages of documentation about every potential server we would like to consider, so what is the alternative?

No matter where we decide to purchase our server, vendors will not sell—or even present—incompatible choices. If we approached this chapter as intended, we already have a long list of parts, counts, and necessary details to exclude potential offerings very quickly. These choices will often come in the form of drop-down lists for every component the motherboard and chassis will accept.

The chassis will come later. For now, this recipe will focus on CPU, RAM, RAID, and network compatibility.

Keep in mind that motherboards and the requisite case are almost exclusively a package deal. This means we can't keep an extra motherboard available in case of failure, unlike other swappable elements. This breaks our redundancy rule, but there are ways of circumventing that problem.

Getting ready

This is one of the times when the hardware spreadsheet will show its true usefulness. As long as we have been keeping track of our counts through each section, this segment of server selection will be much simpler. By this point, our spreadsheet should look something like the following screenshot:

	A	B	C	D	E
1	Type	Capacity	Supplier	Price	Count
2	CPU	10-core			3
3	Network Card	10GbE			3
4	RAID Controller	1GB, RAID 10			3
5	RAM	16GB			10

We don't care about the total cost for each part yet. It might be a good idea to create a separate tab or copy of the spreadsheet for each vendor we want to consider. This way, we can do some comparison shopping. Also, remember that the counts are inflated by at least one replacement in case of failure. So we want to look for two 10-core CPUs, eight 16 GB memory modules, and so on.

How to do it...

Now it's time to do some research. Follow these steps:

1. Make a list of desired server vendors. This list may even be available from the infrastructure department, if our company has one.
2. For each vendor, check their available 1U and 2U products.
3. For each 1U or 2U server, remove from consideration any options that don't fulfill your minimum CPU requirements.
4. Repeat for RAM.
5. Repeat for RAID controller cards.
6. Repeat for network interface cards.
7. Fill in the actual selections, where appropriate, with unit prices.
8. Make corrections to the spreadsheet.

How it works...

While this is straightforward, it's highly time-consuming. The number of server variants available, even from a single vendor, can be staggering. This is one of the reasons we only consider 1U and 2U servers. The other reason is that 4U servers and larger are often designed for different use patterns related to vertical scaling, incorporating more CPUs, hard drives, and even multiple concurrent motherboards.

That is generally excessive for our purposes. When purchasing servers with the explicit intention to obtain multiple, redundant, and compatible examples, this becomes more difficult as the cost and complexity of the servers increase.

Although we have reduced our sample size, there is still more work to do. We can answer questions while considering CPU compatibility. If we want ten-core chips, and the motherboard only supports up to octa core chips, we can remove that option from consideration. This also applies to available memory slots and sizes. Yet there's an unwritten element to RAM: the maximum amount supported by the motherboard. If the motherboard only supports up to 768 GB, and our earlier calculations show we may eventually want 1 TB, we can immediately cross it off our list.

Since RAIDs and network cards must be plugged directly into the motherboard or an expansion daughter card, it's the number of these available slots that directly concerns us.

We need at least two to accommodate both cards, which could drastically reduce the contents of our motherboard list. In fact, higher expansion slot requirements may immediately exclude several 1U servers due to their limited expandability.

While performing this compatibility verification, it is difficult to ignore the prices listed next to each choice, or the total price changing with each selection. We might as well take advantage of that and fill in the rest of the spreadsheet and make a copy for each vendor or configuration. Some choices are likely to provide better complete matches overall, or offer more scalable future expandability or better price points, so tracking all of this is beneficial.

There's more...

RAID controllers and network interfaces are somewhat special cases. Some servers integrate these directly into the motherboard in order to reduce size. This is especially true when it comes to network modules. If at all possible, try to resist relying solely upon integrated components.

The entire server will require replacement if these fail. This makes it much more difficult and expensive to fulfill our redundancy requirement. Server-class motherboards without integrated network interfaces are rare, but we can use these as our backup path if their minimum speed matches what we've configured.

For instance, if we want a 10 **Gigabit Ethernet** (**GbE**) card and the motherboard has integrated a 10 GbE module, we can reduce the number of excess cards on our spreadsheet by one. It's very likely that the integrated version is of lower quality, but it can suffice until the bad card is replaced.

Redundancy doesn't have to be expensive.

See also

Here is a list of well-known server vendors we could consider while completing this section:

- Penguin Computing: `https://www.penguincomputing.com`
- Supermicro: `https://www.supermicro.com/en`
- Dell: `https://www.dell.com`
- HP: `https://www.hp.com`

Selecting a chassis

To round out our hardware selection phase, it's time to decide just what kind of case to order from our server vendor. This is the final protective element that hosts the motherboard, drives, and power supplies necessary to keep everything running. And like always, we place a heavy emphasis on redundancy.

For the purposes of this section, we will concentrate primarily on 1U and 2U rack-mounted servers. Why not 4U or larger? Our goal is to obtain at least two of everything, with similar or matching specifications in every possible scenario. The idea is to scale horizontally in order to more easily replace a failed component or server. As the size of the chassis increases, its cost, complexity, and resource consumption also rise. In this delicate balancing act, it's safer to err toward two smaller systems with respectable capabilities, than one giant server that's twice as powerful.

This recipe will provide a quick set of calculations we can perform to estimate how many server chassis we may need for a PostgreSQL cluster.

Getting ready

Since the server chassis and motherboard are generally a package deal, it's a good idea to refer to the *Managing motherboards* recipe. We will be using a very similar process to choose a server case. This time, we will focus on adequate room for hard drives and redundant power supplies.

How to do it...

Now it's time to do some more research. Follow these steps:

1. Refer to the final list of servers from our motherboard selection.
2. For our ideal count of active (not replacement) hard drives, remove any choice that doesn't have enough drive slots. Use this list if it's not immediately obvious:

   - The maximum number of 2.5" drives in a 2U server is 24.
   - The maximum number of 3.5" drives in a 2U server is 12.
   - The maximum number of 2.5" drives in a 1U server is 8.
   - The maximum number of 3.5" drives in a 1U server is 4.

3. Remove from consideration any chassis that does not support dual power supplies. This should happen rarely in server-class systems.

4. As the list dwindles, give higher priority to cases with more fans or lower average operating temperatures.

How it works...

This time, our job was much easier than considering motherboard constraints, as the drives themselves determine most of our decisions.

Hot-swappable hard drives are slightly larger than their standard brethren due to the swap enclosure. Yet cases exist than can hold up to 24 hot-swappable drives across the front. If we need that many storage devices, we save space by taking advantage of cases that can accommodate them. We also need to remember to reserve two drives for the operating system in a RAID-1, separate from our PostgreSQL storage. We can't diagnose problems on a server that is unable to boot.

Some cases reserve mounts inside, or at the rear, for operating system drives. They are harder to replace, but free more room for storage dedicated to PostgreSQL. Here, operating system drives are treated as an operating overhead without sacrificing case functionality.

If we need more drives than are available in any configuration, we should consider **Direct Attached Storage (DAS)**, **Network Attached Storage (NAS)**, or **Storage Area Network (SAN)**. Some vendors supply drive extension cages specifically to provide more hot-swap bays for specific server models. While we want to conserve space when possible, these are relatively inexpensive and much smaller than a NAS or SAN if we haven't progressed to requiring such a device.

The dual power-supply requirement is not negotiable. Many data centers provide two power rails per server rack. The intent is to deliver two separate sources of power to the server in case the server's power supply fails, or power is cut to one of the sources. Sometimes, these power sources even have separate generators. We're not the only ones interested in redundancy; data centers want to avoid outages too.

The final, more optional element involves investigating the case itself. Many server cases have several fans inside and along the rear, and are very loud as a consequence. This won't matter when the server is in the data center, but the number of fans and the shape of the airflow will directly affect the server temperature. Higher temperatures decrease system stability. It's not uncommon for vendors to list the maximum operating temperatures of each case, so try to gravitate toward the cooler ones if all else is equal.

There's more...

We use the word *vendor* frequently, and there's a reason for that. Short of outright accusing bare cases and motherboards of being faulty, they are simply not stable enough for our use. There are some great cases available that, in many ways, exceed the capabilities provided by established server providers.

We don't suggest the smaller vendors for a few reasons. Larger companies often have replacement policies for each server component, including the case and motherboard. Building a system ourselves may provide more satisfaction, but vendors presumably spend time testing for compatibility and failure conditions. They produce manuals hundreds of pages long detailing the viable parts, configurations, and failure conditions of the entire unit.

However, we could just as easily argue that redundant servers increase failure tolerance, as there's always an available backup. Bare cases and motherboards are usually cheaper, and user-serviceable besides. That is a completely valid path, and if your risk assessment suggests it's viable, try it out. Our particular recommendations and biases should not limit your choices.

Saddling up to a SAN

Those familiar with the industry may have encountered NAS as well. How exactly is that different, and how is it relevant to us?

It's subtle but important. While both introduce networked storage, only a SAN grants direct block-level access, as if the allocation were raw, unformatted disk space. NAS systems operate one level higher, providing a fully formatted filesystem such as NFS or CIFS. This means our PostgreSQL database does not have direct control over the filesystem; locks, flushes, allocation, and read cache management are all controlled by a remote server.

When building a highly available server, raw I/O and synchronization messages are very important, and NFS is more for sharing storage than extending the storage capabilities of a server. What must we consider when deciding upon utilizing a SAN, and when should we do this instead of adopting an inexpensive option such as DAS?

We won't be discussing how to evaluate a SAN, which vendors produce the best hardware, or even basic configuration strategies. There are scores of books dedicated to SAN management and evaluation that are far beyond the scope of our overview.

This recipe will only consider the when and why for incorporating SAN storage, not the how.

Getting ready

Because we're going to cover both SAN performance and storage allocation, we recommend referring to the *Having enough IOPS* recipe and the *Sizing storage* recipe. Just like physical disks, we need to know how much space we need, and roughly how fast it should be to fulfill our transaction and query requirements.

Do we need a SAN? We can ask ourselves a few questions:

- Do our IOPS or storage requirements demand more than 20 hard drives?
- Will the size of our database reach or exceed 3 TB within the next 3 years?
- Would the risk to the company be too high if we ever ran out of space?
- Is there already a SAN available for testing?

If we answer *yes* to any of these, a SAN might be in our best interests. In that case, we can determine whether it would fulfill our needs.

How to do it...

Follow these steps if possible:

1. Request a **Logical Unit Number** (**LUN**) from the infrastructure department with the necessary IOPS and storage requirements.
2. If a SAN isn't available, many SAN vendors will provide testing equipment to encourage purchases. Try to obtain one of these.
3. Have the infrastructure department format the allocation and attach it to a testing server. Keep note of the path to the storage.

4. Create a basic PostgreSQL testing database with the following command-line operations as the `postgres` user:

```
createdb pgbench
pgbench -i -s 4000 pgbench
```

5. Drop the system caches as a user capable of performing root-level commands, as follows:

```
echo 3 | sudo tee /proc/sys/vm/drop_caches
```

6. Test the storage read IOPS with one final command as the `postgres` user:

```
pgbench -S -c 24 -T 600 -j 4 pgbench
```

How it works...

The first part of our process is to decide whether or not we actually need a SAN at all. If the database will remain relatively small, capable of residing easily on local hard drives for several years, we don't need a SAN just yet.

While it might seem arbitrary, setting 3 TB as a cutoff for local storage comes with a few justifications. First, consider the local drives. Even if they were capable of saturating a 6 Gb/s disk controller, 3 TB would require over an hour to transfer to another local storage device. If that weren't a bottleneck, there is still the network. With a 10 Gb/s NIC and assuming no overhead, that's 40 minutes of transfer at full speed.

That directly affects the speed of backups, synchronization, emergency data restoration, and any number of other critical operations. Some RAID cards also require special configurations when handling over 4 TB of storage, to which 3 TB is uncomfortably close if we ever need an extension. SAN devices can often perform local storage snapshots for nearly instant data copies intended for other servers. There's no transfer overhead if the other server is also attached to the same SAN.

Remember that servers have limited local disk capacity, either due to the chassis itself, or by how many directly attached storage extensions they can accommodate. RAID devices allow online storage expansion, but they can't overcome physical limitations. SAN hardware does not have any of these inherent limitations and is one way to mitigate the risk of exhausting your maximum storage capacity.

If a SAN is ever available for testing, we're still not done. Operating performance is highly dependent on the configuration of the SAN or the storage allocation itself. It's a good idea to test SAN manufacturer claims before committing all of our storage to it.

A very easy way to do this is with a basic pgbench test. The pgbench command is provided by the PostgreSQL software, and can test various aspects of a server. For our uses, we want to focus on the disk storage. We start by creating a new pgbench database with createdb, so the pgbench command has somewhere to store its test data. The -i (init) option to pgbench tells it to initialize new test data, and the -s (scale) option describes the scale of test data we want.

A scale of 4000 creates a database of roughly 60 GB in size. We recommend adjusting this scale to be larger than the amount of available RAM. This will help guarantee that the server cannot cache all of the test data and taint our performance results by inflating the numbers.

After initializing a new test database, we can use a Linux command that instructs the server to drop all available cached data. This means none of our test data is in memory before we begin the benchmark. We don't want to inflate our results, otherwise the SAN looks more capable than it really is.

The test itself comes from pgbench again. The -S (select-only) option ensures we only analyze the performance of read operations. Furthermore, we tell the benchmark to launch 24 clients with the -c (client) parameter, and to run the test for a full 10 minutes with the -T (time) option. While we used 24 clients here, consider any amount up to three times the number of available processor cores. The final -j (jobs) flag merely launches 4 concurrent benchmark threads, preventing the test itself from reducing overall performance due to CPU throttling.

This process should reveal the true capabilities of the SAN, and whether or not our production database will be safe and offer good performance while relying on remote storage.

There's more...

Notice how we never ask for a specific number of disks when requesting a SAN allocation. Modern SAN equipment operates on an implied service level agreement based on installed components. In effect, if we need 6,000 IOPS and 10 TB of space, the SAN will combine disks, cache, and even SSDs if necessary, to match those numbers as closely as possible.

This not only reduces the amount of risky micromanagement we perform as **database administrators (DBAs)**, but acts as an abstraction layer between storage and server. In this case, it's possible to modify the storage in any number of ways. We can also enhance, adjust, or copy without affecting the database installation itself.

The main problem we encounter when using a SAN rather than several servers configured with local storage is that the SAN itself becomes a single point of failure. This is something to keep in mind as our journey to high availability progresses.

See also

Here is a list of several SAN vendors, from well-known companies to companies with great potential:

- EMC: https://www.emc.com
- NetApp: https://www.netapp.com
- VCE: https://www.vce.com
- Pure Storage: https://www.purestorage.com/

Tallying up

Now it's time to get serious. We have discussed all the components that go into a stable server for several pages, and have strongly suggested obtaining multiple spares for each. Well, that applies to the server itself. Not only does this mean having a spare idle server in case of a catastrophic failure, but it means having an online server as well.

Determining excess server inventory isn't quite that simple, but it's fairly close. This is where the project starts to get expensive, but high availability is never cheap; the company itself might depend on it.

Unlike the process we used in Chapter 1, *Architectural Considerations*, this recipe will focus on server hardware redundancy rather than cluster design. In many ways, this recipe can help augment architectural considerations.

Getting ready

We want to consider the overall state of the application architecture here. The database server doesn't exist in a vacuum. Work with the systems and application teams to get an idea of the other elements that may depend on our PostgreSQL server.

How to do it...

This won't be a very long list. In any case, follow these steps:

1. For every critical OLTP system, allocate one online replica.
2. For every two non-cached application or web servers, consider one online replica.
3. For every ten cached application or web servers, consider one online replica.
4. For every stage or QA database server analog, allocate one spare server.

How it works...

OLTP systems produce a very high transactional volume by their very nature. Any disruption to this volume is extremely visible and costly. The primary goal of running a highly available service, such as a database, is to minimize downtime. So for any database instance that is a critical component, there should be a copy of the server configured in such a manner that near-immediate promotion to production status is possible.

Any server that needs direct access to the database, whether it is a queue system, application server, or web frontend, is sensitive to database overload. One method for diffusing this risk is to create one database copy for every two to four directly connected servers. These copies are only usable for reading (rather than writing) data, but a properly designed application can accommodate this limitation. Not only does this reduce contention on the database instance that must handle data writes; but it also eliminates the likelihood of one misbehaving query disrupting the entire constellation of client-visible services.

The risk to the frontend is greatly reduced when a sophisticated cache is involved. Properly designed, a failed read from the database can default to a cached copy until reads can be re-established. This means we can subsist on fewer database replicas. If the application does not provide that kind of cache, our job as database advocates becomes one of working with appropriate technical leads until such a cache is established.

The extra QA resource may seem excessive at first, but it fulfills a critical role. While the testing teams may never touch the spare server, we can use it in their stead. It's not possible to safely configure a production system for online failover without first testing that configuration on two similarly equipped systems. To do otherwise risks failure of the automatic activation of alternate production servers, which is a *de facto* outage. We should always test all major actions before applying them to the production system. This means we should dry-run all database migrations, upgrades, resynchronization, backup restoration, and so on in the QA environment.

Without a second server, none of this would be possible.

There's more...

We have mentioned this tip previously, but this deserves special attention. PostgreSQL 9.2 and above now has the capability to stream replicated data from one database standby to another. Even with 10 GbE network cards, there is a limit to the amount of data our production server can or should transmit.

While there is still a limit to the number of replicas we can maintain with this new functionality, we also mitigate overall traffic, and therefore reduce risk. If our database is stuck on a version before 9.2, we may never realize these new benefits.

At the time of writing, PostgreSQL 12 is the latest release and versions lower than 9.4 are no longer supported. A crafty DBA can encourage the company to adopt a forward stance regarding upgrades by providing an upgrade proposal, procedural checklist, and deployment integration tests.

Now that `pg_upgrade` is a standard part of PostgreSQL, producing a robust upgrade plan and the associated compatibility tests is much easier than in the past. By pushing for upgrades early, we can use new features such as cascading replication, and with PostgreSQL, this can heavily influence our resulting architecture. Consider this when choosing your hardware.

The next chapter on zero downtime upgrades provides the recipes necessary to upgrade a PostgreSQL cluster without ever going offline. Consider this as a method for increasing server count, and for establishing a viable upgrade plan for abandoning older versions of PostgreSQL.

Protecting your eggs

Have we ever implied that mere server inventory was sufficient for high availability? The place where our servers live—the data center—also incorporates several redundancies. Extra network lines, separate power sources, multiple generators, air conditioning and ventilation—everything a server might require—are all part of most data center guarantees.

Yet some have joked that a common backhoe is the natural enemy of the internet. There is more truth to that statement than its apparent lack of gravitas might suggest. Data centers are geographically insecure. Inclement weather, natural disasters, disrupted network backbones, power outages, and of course, accidentally damaged trunk lines (from an errant backhoe?) and simple human error can all remove a data center from the grid. When a data center vanishes from the internet, our servers become collateral damage.

However, we've done everything right! We have duplicates of everything, multiple parts, cables, even whole servers. What can we possibly do about the data center?

It's somewhat complicated, but this recipe will help us in the final element of redundancy we need to always ensure that PostgreSQL remains online.

Getting ready

For this section, we will need a list of every database server in our proposed architecture and the desired role for each. Try to apply the recipes in the *Architectural Considerations* chapter before continuing.

How to do it...

This won't be a very long list. In any case, follow these steps:

1. For every critical OLTP operating pair, allocate at least one standby.
2. For every two online standby replicas, consider at least one standby.
3. For every other database instance, allocate one standby.

How it works...

This type of scenario is known as **disaster recovery**. In order to truly diffuse a data center outage, we need backups of every major database server, and even minor servers. The reasoning is simple: we don't know how long we have to operate at reduced capacity. At this point, even non-critical reporting services still need analogs; otherwise, business decisions that depend on activity analysis may not be possible.

We only really need half the amount of database servers. Most disaster recovery scenarios are severe enough for raised alertness, reduced refresh times, manually extended queue timeouts, and more. Not only is this less expensive than purchasing a copy of every server at the primary data center, but it also encourages closer monitoring until everything is fully restored. Larger companies can opt for complete parity between data centers, but this is not a requirement.

As DBAs, our scenario often resembles this:

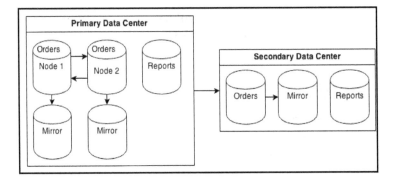

Notice that we didn't make any reservations for QA or development database servers. In the case of a disaster, the primary concern is ensuring the continued availability of the application platform. Further development or testing is likely on hold for the duration of the outage in any case.

There's more...

We cannot stress the importance of this section strongly enough. Some may consider an entire extra data center as optional due to the cost. It is not. Others may think a total of three servers for every primary system is too much maintenance overhead. Again, it is not. The price of a few servers must be weighed against the future of the company itself; it is the cost of admission into the world of high availability.

By the time we begin utilizing failover nodes, or any replicas in a separate data center, the damage has already been done. In the absence of these resources, a database crash can result in hours or even days of unavailability depending on the size of our database. This can exponentially compound the effects of the original problem.

With this in mind, all critical production systems the author designs always have a minimum of four nodes: two mirrored production systems, and two mirrored disaster recovery analogs. This ensures that the disaster recovery system location remains a viable failover target even while one node is offline for maintenance. Outages are unexpected, and we must always be prepared for them.

Minimizing Downtime 3

Every piece of software has bugs. All hardware eventually fails or becomes obsolete. No environment is perfect. As a consequence, even a perfectly healthy database will require downtime periodically. So, how do we reconcile this need with client expectations that demand data is always available no matter the circumstances?

As users ourselves, we can relate to the frustration associated with attempting to use an application or website that isn't responding. Perhaps the only impediment is a message indicating maintenance. No matter the cause, we have to remember to come back later and hope everything is working normally by then. Even with our knowledge about the complexity of software and databases, it is sometimes difficult to ignore an error message that prevents us from managing a bank account or making an online purchase.

Every day, users will be less understanding. Business owners and investors, who may be losing millions in potential sales and liabilities while a system is unavailable, are even less understanding. Yet there are several tools available that decrease the likelihood of outages, and others that help guarantee we're agile enough to handle them when outages, despite our best efforts, occur anyway.

As is often the case with high availability architecture, the trick is to plan ahead.

In this chapter, we will learn how we should react when outages inevitably occur and how to prepare ourselves for them. We will cover the following recipes in this chapter:

- Determining acceptable losses
- Configuration – getting it right the first time
- Configuration – managing scary settings
- Identifying important tables
- Defusing cache poisoning
- Terminating rogue connections
- Reducing contention with concurrent indexes
- Managing system migrations
- Managing software upgrades
- Mitigating the impact of hardware failure
- Applying bonus kernel tweaks

Determining acceptable losses

We know that the PostgreSQL database will be offline at some point in the future. Maybe we need an upgrade to remove a critical security vulnerability or address a potential data corruption issue. Perhaps a RAM module is producing errors and requires immediate replacement. Maybe the primary data center was struck by lightning.

No matter the reason, we need to make decisions quickly. A helpful way to ensure adaptability is to base our decision-making process on user expectations for various levels of liability and context. The QA department will not require the same response level as 10,000 shoppers who can't make a holiday purchase during a critically limited sale.

System outage and response escalation expectations are generally codified in a **service-level agreement (SLA)**. How long should the maintenance last? How often should planned outages occur? When should users be informed and to what extent? Who is included in the set of potential database users? All of these things, and more, should be defined before a production system is released. Otherwise, we risk alienating clients with unexpected and arbitrary downtime or outages that persist for hours.

Clients who have their trust broken may leave and never return. So, let's teach them when to expect short amounts of unavailability and set their minds at ease with prompt contact and status management.

Getting ready

Much of our work depends on knowing how much downtime the business is willing to tolerate and who uses the database and when. We also need to know how long the application can obscure a PostgreSQL outage through caches, queues, and connection management. Try to get a complete picture of the database's role before continuing. It's very likely we already performed some of these steps if we applied the recipes in Chapter 1, *Architectural Considerations*.

How to do it...

Try to answer all of these questions:

- Who uses the database? For each type of user, answer these questions:
  - When does this user access the database?
  - What is the maximum query timeout they will tolerate?
  - Will the user lose money during an outage?
  - Is the user likely to return later?
  - Should this user be included in maintenance notifications?
  - Should this user be included in emergency notifications?
- Can we get the user to agree to or even sign the SLA?
- What uptime percentage is expected? 99 percent? 99.9 percent? 99.99 percent? More?
- What are the company's official business hours?
- When should notifications be sent?
- How long can the platform operate without the database?
- How long should regular maintenance windows be?
- How often can maintenance occur?
- Which weekdays can we consider for maintenance?

- What constitutes an emergency?
- What situations require the activation of disaster recovery nodes?
- Can we get a lawyer to write all of these into a contract?

How it works...

That is a lot of questions, and the list isn't even complete. It is, however, a very good start. Notice how we want to know who (or what) is using the database on a regular basis. This is not the same as a user who connects to the database. In this context, we want to know the category of user. Is it a business department, another department, a critical application component, or even just a regular website user? Each of these will have different expectations, reactions, usage times, and impact.

The next question we need to answer is how uptime is defined. One frequently quoted value is the number of nines, referring to a percentage approaching 100 percent. Three nines, for example, would be 99.9 percent of a year, which is almost 9 hours. Four nines correspond to about 50 minutes. Keep in mind that we may design the SLA to include or exclude planned maintenance, depending on the audience. Unplanned outages definitely count, and remember that this is the total cumulative time for the entire year.

The next important aspect is the latest time a business is officially available. Maintenance should begin after this time and no sooner. Critical PostgreSQL nodes should not be taken offline if more than 5 percent of active users are utilizing the platform and database. It is not uncommon for regular maintenance windows to appear very late at night. Disaster recovery systems, standby nodes, and QA or development copies are all excellent candidates for updates following official business hours. We still want these systems to be available for developers and QA staff, or in the case of an unexpected production-level outage, so it pays to be a little more cautious.

The remainder of our checklist is a mix of important questions that need answers, the last of which implies the involvement of a lawyer. If possible, have the SLA in a contract form for all applicable clients and users. A signed agreement acts as a barrier to litigation and liability and sets very definite boundaries to user expectations early in the process.

Configuration – getting it right the first time

An important aspect of setting up a highly available database server is starting with a stable configuration that will not require a lot of future modifications. Even parameters that can be changed during the database operations can drastically alter its performance profile and behavior. Other settings may require a full database restart, which can lead to a short outage depending on the resiliency of the frontend application.

We want to avoid introducing instability into our PostgreSQL database from the very beginning. To that end, this recipe will explore common (and, perhaps, uncommon) configuration options to use in a highly available installation.

Getting ready

The PostgreSQL documentation describes all of the settings we will be discussing. We recommend that you visit the PostgreSQL website (https://www.postgresql.org/) and read the documentation regarding server configuration. There's probably too much to absorb before continuing with this section, but we recommend that you familiarize yourself with the settings presented here.

We will approach each setting in the order commonly encountered in a recent postgresql.conf file generated in a new database.

How to do it...

Find these settings in the postgresql.conf file for the desired PostgreSQL instance, and then perform the following steps:

1. Set max_connections to three times the number of processor cores on the server. Include virtual (hyperthreading) cores.
2. Set shared_buffers to 25 percent of RAM for servers with up to 32 GB of RAM. For larger servers, start with 8GB and then test for higher values in increments of 2 GB.
3. Set work_mem to 8MB for servers with up to 32 GB of RAM, 16MB for servers with up to 64 GB of RAM, and 32MB for systems with more than 64 GB of RAM. If max_connections is greater than 400, divide this by 2.

Systems with exceedingly large amounts of RAM (that is, 256 GB and higher) do not require artificially halving the final suggested value for `work_mem`.

4. Set `maintenance_work_mem` to 1GB.
5. Set `wal_level` to one of these settings:

   - Use `hot_standby` for versions prior to 9.4.
   - Use `logical` for versions 9.4 and higher.

6. Set `hot_standby` to `on`.
7. Set the minimum **write-ahead logging** (**WAL**) size to 10 percent of system RAM:

   - Divide this value by 16 and use the `checkpoint_segments` parameter for 9.4 and below.
   - Use `min_wal_size` for 9.5 and beyond. Then, double this value and use it to set `max_wal_size`.

8. Set `vacuum_cost_limit` to 2000.
9. Set `checkpoint_completion_target` to 0.9.
10. Set `archive_mode` to `on`.
11. Set `archive_command` to `/bin/true`.
12. Set `max_wal_senders` to 10.
13. Retain the necessary WAL files with these settings:
14. Set `wal_keep_segments` to 3 * `checkpoint_segments` for 9.3 and below. Set `replication_slots` to 10 for 9.4 and higher.

15. Set `random_page_cost` to 2.0 if you are using RAID or high-performance **storage area network** (**SAN**); 1.1 for SSD-based storage.
16. Set `effective_cache_size` to 75 percent of the available system RAM.
17. Set `log_min_duration_statement` to 1000.
18. Set `log_checkpoints` to `on`.
19. Set `log_statement` to `ddl`.

How it works...

The commonly accepted formula for estimating `max_connections` is to take the number of processor cores, multiply them by 2, and add disk spindles. With the relatively recent improvement of virtual cores, contributing factors such as SSD or other high-performance storage, we have a bit more freedom than before. In addition to this, even if we were to follow this estimation method, allowing a few extra connections can prevent highly visible connection rejections. Slightly lower performance is a small price to pay for availability.

The advice for `shared_buffers` is likely to be different from the accepted practice of simply setting it to a quarter of the available RAM. This is only really safe advice to follow for servers with relatively low amounts of RAM, that is, up to 32 GB. We must consider buffer flushing and the necessary synchronization time.

In the case of a forced checkpoint, an amount of RAM equal to `shared_buffers` could be flushed to disk. This kind of write storm can easily cripple even high-end hardware. Highly available hardware often has far more RAM that could easily be flushed to storage in an emergency. As such, be wary of using more than 8 GB unless it's known that the storage hardware is capable of directly absorbing higher amounts of buffer flushing.

> Depending on hardware capabilities, certain advancements in recent releases of PostgreSQL may benefit from higher amounts of `shared_buffers`. While we feel it's better to err on the side of caution, feel free to test larger values on servers equipped with 128 GB of RAM or more, provided the version of PostgreSQL is 10 or greater. Stop increasing the value once performance tests fail to improve.

The `work_mem` setting is the amount of memory used by several temporary operations, including data sorts. Thus a single query can consume multiple instances of this amount simultaneously. A good estimate is to assume that each connection will use up to four instances at a time. Setting this too high can lead to over-committed memory and cause the kernel to start killing processes until RAM is available. This can lead to PostgreSQL shutdown or a server crash, depending on what processes are stopped. Systems with very high connection counts (over 400) have increased risk of such a cascade, so we reduce `work_mem` in these cases.

The `maintenance_work_mem` setting is similar to the `work_mem` setting in that there can be multiple instances. However, this is reserved for background workers and maintenance such as *vacuum, analyze,* or *create index* activities. Starving these kinds of memory operations can drastically increase disk I/O, which can detrimentally affect query performance. For the cost of a few GBs of RAM, we get a more stable server.

The only reason we set `wal_level` to `hot_standby` or `logical` is that, in a highly available environment, we should have at least one online streaming standby. Other recipes will detail how we set these up, but this is the starting point. In the case of `logical`, we are using the most inclusive possible value to enable logical replication at a later date without needing to restart PostgreSQL. The related `hot_standby` setting ensures that any replicas we produce in the future will be available for reads while online.

The number of `checkpoint_segments` or the proper value for `min_wal_size` is not a simple thing to determine. The calculation we used assumes up to 10 percent of system memory, which could be in transit as checkpoint data, and each segment is 16 MB in size. This time, we are trying to avoid forced checkpoints because we ran out of segments during data acquisition. This also applies to `max_wal_size` for lucky users of 9.5 and above. This newer parameter also allows us to specify a more user-friendly value in GB or MB.

Vacuum activity is also critically important to server health. By increasing `vacuum_cost_limit`, we are making the background automatic vacuum more aggressive when it manages tables. We've found that the default value is not sufficient for larger and more active **online transaction processing** (**OLTP**) systems, and can threaten a dangerous scenario where the PostgreSQL transaction ID counter can exceed its 32-bit storage and result in data loss. PostgreSQL will preemptively shut itself down to prevent this, which is definitely a roadblock for achieving high availability.

We also want to reduce disk contention when possible, so we increase `checkpoint_completion_target` to `0.9`. We don't want to overwhelm the disk subsystem, and this setting will cause PostgreSQL to spread writes over 90 percent of the time specified by `checkpoint_timeout`. By default, `checkpoint_timeout` is set to 5 minutes, which should suffice until we start working with larger batches of data or a busy OLTP system.

Next, we enable `archive_mode` by setting it to `on`. This setting can only be changed by restarting PostgreSQL, which we want to avoid. It's possible we will be using WAL archiving in some respect, even if we don't yet know which method to use at this point. This means we also need to set `archive_command` to a command that always succeeds, or PostgreSQL will fill our logs with complaints that it couldn't archive old WAL files. By using `/bin/true` as a placeholder, we can alter it later should we choose an archiving method.

We increase `max_wal_senders` because it's necessary for certain synchronization and backup methods. 10 is a good starting point and is actually the default for PostgreSQL 10 and above. We can always decrease it later, and we definitely require a value greater than zero. Additionally, `wal_keep_segments` is set to a relatively high number in slightly older versions of PostgreSQL. In this case, we retain up to three multiples of `checkpoint_segments`, if a streaming standby falls behind. For newer versions, we set `replication_slots` to a starting value that should support at least 10 replica streams, and only retain as many checkpoints as strictly necessary.

 Astute readers may have noticed that `hot_standby`, `max_wal_senders` and `replication_slots` are already set properly if PostgreSQL is version 10 or higher. Thankfully, these parameters were altered frequently enough that the community decided to use more common defaults in newer releases.

For older systems that still use `wal_keep_segments`, a replica can fall permanently behind if this count of segments is exhausted before they can be processed. In this case, it can never catch up until the remaining WAL segments are provided with some other way or the standby is rebuilt. We'll discuss this more when it's time to discuss WAL archiving. This uses more disk space, so multiply the total number of these segments by 16 MB to estimate total disk usage.

The cost of reading a random disk block, as opposed to reading it sequentially, directly affects how the query planner decides to execute a query. By decreasing `random_page_cost`, we tell PostgreSQL that our storage's random read performance is very fast. A highly available server should have equally capable storage, so we lower this to something more reasonable. In the case of SSD- or PCIe-based storage, there is far less functional difference between a random or sequential read, so the setting should reflect this.

We did not use a value of 1.0 for `random_page_cost`, as that suggests solid-state storage is exactly as fast as RAM, and that simply isn't the case. Very low values should be sufficient for this setting, but should not be reduced beyond 1.1.

The last setting that modifies server behavior is `effective_cache_size`, which tells the query planner how much RAM is probably being used by the operating system to cache data. Generally, this makes PostgreSQL prefer indexes because it's likely that the indexed data is in memory. As most UNIX systems are fairly aggressive when caching, at least half of the available RAM on a dedicated database server will be full of cached data.

Finally, we want better logging. We increase the logging of slow queries by setting `log_min_duration_statement` to `1000`. This is in milliseconds, so any query that runs for over 1 second will be logged. This helps us to find slow queries without flooding the logs with thousands or even millions of entries by logging everything.

Similarly, we want `log_checkpoints` enabled because it provides extremely beneficial information on checkpoint activity. We can see how long they took, how frequently they ran, and also how much disk-sync time they required. We need to know if checkpoints start taking too long or occur too frequently so that some values can be adjusted. This setting really should be enabled in all PostgreSQL servers. Likewise, we set `log_statement` to `ddl` to at least log all database object changes (tables, indexes, and more). This is a security concern that we want to monitor.

There's more...

Many, if not most of these settings, show up frequently in the PostgreSQL mailing lists. As a result, we used many of the prescribed values or formulas. However, several of these settings show up very often; a tool is available to estimate them by analyzing the server hardware and by taking parameter hints. The `pgtune` program is a contributed utility for automatically estimating many system-dependent server settings, and there is a convenient online version.

We urge caution if you are relying primarily on this utility. It is extremely liberal when estimating `work_mem` and `shared_buffers`. Still, we feel that the values it produces are much better than the defaults for larger servers, so feel free to experiment.

See also

There are many more configuration settings that we haven't included. We recommend that you browse the PostgreSQL documentation to learn more. In addition to this, we've included a link to the `pgtune` utility, which may be useful for optimizing your `postgresql.conf` file:

- **PostgreSQL Server Configuration**: https://www.postgresql.org/docs/current/static/runtime-config.html
- **pgtune**: https://pgtune.leopard.in.ua/

Configuration – managing scary settings

When it comes to highly available database servers and configurations, a very important aspect is whether or not a changed setting requires a database restart before taking effect. While it is true that many of these are important enough that they should be set correctly before starting the server, sometimes, our requirements evolve.

If, or when, this happens, there is no alternative but to restart the PostgreSQL service. There are, of course, steps we can take to avoid this fate. Perhaps an existing server didn't need the WAL output to be compatible with hot standby servers. Maybe we need to move the log file, enable WAL archiving, or increase the number of connections.

These are all scenarios that require us to restart PostgreSQL. This recipe will demonstrate how we can avoid this by identifying these settings early on and paying special attention to them.

Getting ready

PostgreSQL has a lot of useful views for **database administrators (DBAs)** to gather information about the database and its current state. For this recipe, we will concentrate on the pg_settings view, which supplies a wealth of data regarding the current server settings, defaults, and usage context. We recommend that you peruse the PostgreSQL documentation for this view.

How to do it...

Follow these steps to learn more about PostgreSQL settings:

1. Execute the following query to obtain a list of settings that require a server restart and their current value:

```
SELECT name, setting
  FROM pg_settings
 WHERE context = 'postmaster';
```

2. Execute this query for a list of only those settings that are not changed from the default and require restart:

```
SELECT name, setting, boot_val
  FROM pg_settings
 WHERE context = 'postmaster'
   AND boot_val = setting;
```

3. Execute the following query for a list of all the settings and a translation of how each setting is managed:

```
SELECT name,
       CASE context
       WHEN 'postmaster' THEN 'RESTART'
       WHEN 'sighup' THEN 'Reload'
       WHEN 'backend' THEN 'Reload'
       WHEN 'superuser' THEN 'Reload / Superuser SET'
       WHEN 'superuser-backend'
            THEN 'Reload / Superuser Session'
       WHEN 'user' THEN 'Reload / User SET'
       END AS when_changed
  FROM pg_settings
 WHERE context != 'internal'
 ORDER BY when_changed;
```

How it works...

The first and simplest query merely identifies the name and value for each parameter, which may only be modified by restarting PostgreSQL. In relation to all of the available settings, this list is relatively short. However, there are a few notable settings that could affect us.

We already mentioned `wal_level`, `shared_buffers`, `max_connections`, and `max_wal_senders` in another recipe. However, this list also includes parameters related to **Secure Sockets Layer** (**SSL**) and WAL archiving. We will eventually discuss WAL archiving separately, so that leaves SSL. When provisioning a secure PostgreSQL server that encrypts connection traffic, we require a host SSL certificate. If this certificate is ever compromised, we need to regenerate it. Unfortunately, we can't simply tell PostgreSQL to reread the existing certificate; if we overwrite it, the entire database must be restarted.

The second query only shows the settings that we have not already changed but would require server restart. This list is potentially more interesting and concise, as we are presumably seeking further parameters to modify. Of course, the opposite can also be argued; we have only modified the settings we care about.

The final query is a bit more complicated as it uses a `CASE` statement, yet it also simplifies the contents of the view. First, consider the `WHERE` clause, which purges internal settings. We don't care about these specifically because they can only be set when compiling PostgreSQL itself. While such an action may be necessary to apply an emergency patch from the PostgreSQL developers, we cannot modify several of these parameters without rebuilding the entire contents of every affected database. These settings are for experts only, and these experts rarely even consider changing them.

Within the `SELECT` statement, we fetch the setting name as well as how it is modified. Note that all settings that require a server reload to take effect are found in `postgresql.conf`. Subsequent changes applied at the session level can also be overridden using the `SET` syntax, so we included that as well.

There's more...

Of course, the `pg_settings` view can provide more than just an insight into the parameters that require a server restart.

Distinct settings

A common request on the PostgreSQL mailing lists is for users to provide a list of settings they've changed. This helps everyone diagnose where a problem could originate or give us an idea of a database's usage pattern. Now that we know about this view, we can easily provide that data with the following query:

```
SELECT name, setting
  FROM pg_settings
 WHERE boot_val IS DISTINCT FROM setting;
```

The `IS DISTINCT FROM` clause isn't as well known as it should be. It can be easy to forget that `!=` or `<>` evaluates to `NULL` when either side of the equation is `NULL`. Thus, if the default `boot_val` value is `NULL`, we would fail to obtain the entire list of modified settings.

The `IS DISTINCT FROM` clause considers `NULL` as a distinct value instead of an unknown one, permitting direct comparisons.

More information

The `pg_settings` view also provides the `short_desc` and `extra_desc` columns. We can use these as shortcuts to remember why we might have changed a setting, without pulling up the PostgreSQL documentation.

See also

The `pg_settings` view has a lot more information than what we have presented here. You can refer to the following documentation for more details: `https://www.postgresql.org/docs/current/static/view-pg-settings.html`.

Identifying important tables

Another aspect of maintaining a highly available database is to know all of the important information about the contents of the database itself. In this case, we aim to focus on tables and indexes that receive the most activity. If any problems that might require maintenance or a restart arise, the most active portions are the likely origin.

What is activity? Inserts, updates, deletes, and selects are a good start. PostgreSQL collects statistics on all of this information, making it easy to collect and track. It also records how often indexes or tables are scanned and how many rows were affected by each. In addition to this, we can observe how much disk space any object consumes. Given the assistance of a couple of contributed tools, we can also calculate how much of this space is currently reusable.

Data like this identifies which tables and indexes are the most active, which objects have the highest row turnover, and which objects require copious disk I/O. Armed with these statistics, we can properly distribute tables to high-performance tablespaces, direct extra maintenance toward particularly active tables, or remove inefficient indexes.

All of these operations increase the stability, responsiveness, and throughput of a PostgreSQL database. This recipe will help us to accomplish all of those goals, and we begin by isolating our targets.

Getting ready

Many of these techniques rely on functions and views described in greater detail within the PostgreSQL documentation. In particular, we use a few system administration functions, such as pg_relation_size and pg_total_relation_size, and system views, such as pg_class, pg_index, pg_stat_user_tables, and pg_stat_user_indexes. We also make use of a contributed module named pgstattuple.

We strongly recommend that you become familiar with these functions and views in the PostgreSQL documentation before continuing. After we are finished, we hope to have successfully conveyed just how useful these views are and encourage further exploration. When you are building a highly available database, there is rarely such a thing as too much information about the database.

How to do it...

Follow these steps to learn a little about the database:

1. Use this query to retrieve a list of the top 20 largest tables in the current database:

```
SELECT oid::REGCLASS::TEXT AS table_name,
       pg_size_pretty(
```

```
              pg_total_relation_size(oid)
          ) AS total_size
    FROM pg_class
   WHERE relkind = 'r'
     AND relpages > 0
   ORDER BY pg_total_relation_size(oid) DESC
   LIMIT 20;
```

2. Use this query to obtain a list of the top 20 largest indexes in the current database and their parent tables:

```
SELECT indexrelid::REGCLASS::TEXT AS index_name,
       indrelid::REGCLASS::TEXT AS table_name,
       pg_size_pretty(
         pg_relation_size(indexrelid)
       ) AS total_size
  FROM pg_index
 ORDER BY pg_relation_size(indexrelid) DESC
 LIMIT 20;
```

3. Use this query to find the top 20 most active tables by determining which receive the most inserts, updates, or deletes:

```
SELECT relid::REGCLASS AS table_name,
       n_tup_ins AS inserts,
       n_tup_upd + n_tup_hot_upd AS updates,
       n_tup_del AS deletes
  FROM pg_stat_user_tables
 ORDER BY (n_tup_ins + n_tup_upd +
          n_tup_hot_upd + n_tup_del) DESC
 LIMIT 20;
```

4. Use this variant to obtain the top 20 tables with fetch activity by checking index and table scans:

```
SELECT relid::REGCLASS AS table_name,
       coalesce(seq_scan, 0) AS sequential_scans,
       coalesce(idx_scan, 0) AS index_scans,
       coalesce(seq_tup_read, 0) AS table_matches,
       coalesce(idx_tup_fetch, 0) AS index_matches
  FROM pg_stat_user_tables
 ORDER BY (coalesce(seq_scan, 0) +
    coalesce(idx_scan, 0)) DESC,
    (coalesce(seq_tup_read, 0) +
    coalesce(idx_tup_fetch, 0)) DESC
 LIMIT 20;
```

5. Use this query for the top 20 indexes with read activity in the current database:

```
SELECT indexrelid::REGCLASS AS index_name,
       coalesce(idx_scan, 0) AS index_scans,
       coalesce(idx_tup_read, 0) AS rows_read,
       coalesce(idx_tup_fetch, 0) AS rows_fetched
  FROM pg_stat_user_indexes
 ORDER BY (coalesce(idx_scan, 0) +
           coalesce(idx_tup_read, 0)) DESC
 LIMIT 20;
```

How it works...

Each of these queries offers a distinct piece of information about the database. Simply executing them in a vacuum offers very little insight. We must decipher the results of each to learn anything. In addition, all of the system catalog views only return statistics for the current database we're connected to.

If the PostgreSQL instance has dozens of databases and we're only connected to one, the statistics will only apply to that particular database. To obtain stats on every database in the instance, we would need to connect to each one and collect the information separately.

The first query returns the 20 largest tables in the database, including associated indexes and any **TOAST** (short for **The Oversize Attribute Storage Technique**) data. This way, if a table has a large amount of excessively long row data or several indexes, we still obtain its true size in relation to all of the other tables. We will likely make use of the `pg_size_pretty` function several times throughout this book. When given a size in bytes, it converts it to a more convenient and readable notation such as megabytes or gigabytes.

The next query returns the 20 largest indexes in the database. While it is very likely that these will be associated with the largest tables, this won't necessarily be the case. Indeed, large composite indexes, functional indexes, or bloated indexes will also be listed here. Indexes (which are not primary keys) that show up in this list are good candidates for optimization, either by substituting them with partial indexes or replacing them with a more efficient version.

After size, we move on to table activity. The third query returns the 20 most active tables based on writes. In many cases, this will immediately identify tables with high turnover that will frequently invoke `autovacuum` or `autoanalyze` and may require manual adjustment. Often, user session tables appear here due to the inefficient storage of web session data; identification provides ammunition for process revision. Overly active tables are bottlenecks and should be minimized if possible.

Then, we may wish to know the table select information. The fourth query is somewhat crude, but the intent is to return 20 tables that are most often read by user sessions. Again, it will likely identify tables with extremely inflated read activity in comparison to the database average. These cases can often be reduced by better frontend data caches, and identifying them is the first step down this path.

Finally, we can see the top 20 indexes reflecting elevated read activity. This can further isolate potential indexes that should be monitored. If we invert the sorting of this query, we can also identify indexes that are not producing many matches at all and are simply wasting space.

There's more...

Although we've already obtained a wealth of information from PostgreSQL, it still has a few tricks up its sleeve.

Reset stats

After executing these queries multiple times in a row, it's hard to ignore the fact that the numbers steadily increase, and there's no associated timestamp. Several statistics-tracking systems will tabulate the differences between readings and display this as the rate of change. If we're doing this by hand, we need another way to zero out statistics for ease of analysis. Use this function to reset all activity statistics to zero:

```
SELECT pg_stat_reset();
```

Of course, we suggest that you capture this data before resetting it.

Using pgstattuple

The `pgstattuple` extension is also useful for analysis by performing a deep scan of any supplied database object. It's best to use the extension to retrieve storage-related data regarding indexes or tables matched with the preceding queries. Since it interacts with the server filesystem, only superusers are allowed to install or invoke the function provided by this extension.

Execute this SQL query to install `pgstattuple`:

```
CREATE EXTENSION pgstattuple;
```

To use the extension, select from it as if it were a normal table or view. The only difference is that we use it as a function with the name of the table we want to analyze. For example, to obtain storage statistics on the `pg_class` table, we could execute this:

```
SELECT * FROM pgstattuple('pg_class');
```

Of particular interest is the `free_percent` column. If this is quite elevated, the table mostly consists of empty space and could benefit from `CLUSTER` or `VACUUM FULL`. In addition to this, we should tell developers if this table becomes bloated frequently, as it is possible that they can modify the application to use it more efficiently.

If this isn't possible, we can also set `autovacuum` to be more aggressive for each specific table if necessary.

See also

The tools discussed in this section have a lot of documentation and examples. Please refer to these sites for more information:

- **System administration functions**:
  https://www.postgresql.org/docs/current/static/functions-admin.html
- **The Statistics Collector**:
  https://www.postgresql.org/docs/current/static/monitoring-stats.html
- **pgstattuple**:
  https://www.postgresql.org/docs/current/static/pgstattuple.html

Defusing cache poisoning

Not every DBA has experienced disk cache poisoning. Those who have, recognize it as a bane to any critical OLTP system and a source of constant stress in a highly available environment.

When the operating system fetches disk blocks into memory, it also applies arbitrary aging, promotion, and purging heuristics. Several of these can invalidate cached data in the presence of an originating process change such as a database crash or restart. Any memory stored by PostgreSQL in shared memory is also purged upon database shutdown.

Perhaps the worst thing a DBA can do following a database crash or restart is to immediately make the database available to applications and users. Unless storage is based on SSDs or a very capable SAN, random read performance will drop by two or three orders of magnitude, as data is being supplied by slow disks instead of by memory. As a result, all subsequent queries will greatly oversaturate the available disk bandwidth. This delays query results and slows down the cache rebuild, potentially multiplying query execution times for several hours.

In a highly available system, we cannot ignore this kind of risk. Saturated disk bandwidth means random reads are spread very thin. We need to figure out how to reinstate the disk cache and possibly the PostgreSQL shared buffers before declaring that the database is usable. Otherwise, the claim of high availability becomes hollow indeed. Despite PostgreSQL being online, queries can often become so slow that applications will ignore results and return errors to users.

This recipe will provide a few strategies for mitigating those scenarios.

Getting ready

We recommend that you check the PostgreSQL documentation for system administration functions and views maintained by the statistics collector. We will be using the `pg_relation_filepath` function and the `pg_stat_user_tables` view.

We will also make use of a contributed utility named `pgFincore`. This utility is not included with standard PostgreSQL but is often packaged for popular Linux distributions. To install it on an Ubuntu server along with the PostgreSQL server, use this command:

```
sudo apt-get install postgresql-12-pgfincore
```

Afterward, activate it in the database with this query:

```
CREATE EXTENSION pgfincore;
```

Users of 9.4 and above also have the option of `pg_prewarm`. It can be installed with the following SQL statement:

```
CREATE EXTENSION pg_prewarm;
```

How to do it...

Begin by following these steps to create a static table that stores the top 20 active tables and indexes:

1. Execute the following query as a superuser and ignore any errors:

   ```
   DROP TABLE IF EXISTS active_snap;
   ```

2. Next, recreate the snapshot table by running this query as a superuser:

   ```
   CREATE TABLE active_snap AS
   (SELECT t.relid AS objrelid,
           s.setting || '/' ||
           pg_relation_filepath(t.relid) AS file_path
      FROM pg_stat_user_tables t, pg_settings s
     WHERE s.name = 'data_directory'
     ORDER BY coalesce(idx_scan, 0) DESC
     LIMIT 20)
   UNION
   (SELECT t.indexrelid AS objrelid,
           s.setting || '/' ||
           pg_relation_filepath(t.indexrelid) AS file_path
      FROM pg_stat_user_indexes t, pg_settings s
     WHERE s.name = 'data_directory'
     ORDER BY coalesce(idx_scan, 0) DESC
     LIMIT 20);
   ```

To restore the disk cache to the operating system easily for 9.4 systems and above with `pg_prewarm` available, merely execute this single SQL statement:

```
SELECT pg_prewarm(objrelid)
   FROM active_snap;
```

Otherwise, we need a slightly more manual route. For 9.3 and older, use these steps:

1. As a superuser in the database connected with `psql`, execute the following query in the critical OLTP database before shutting down the database:

```
COPY active_snap (file_path) TO '/tmp/frequent_tables.txt';
```

2. Shut down PostgreSQL.
3. Perform maintenance, updates, or recovery.
4. Execute these commands from the command line:

```
for x in $(tac /tmp/frequent_tables.txt); do
    for y in $x*; do
        dd if=$y of=/dev/null bs=8192
        dd if=$y of=/dev/null bs=8192
    done
done
```

5. Restart PostgreSQL.

If we're not comfortable with UNIX commands, this pure SQL method will work as well. Follow these steps instead:

1. Shut down PostgreSQL.
2. Perform maintenance, updates, or recovery.
3. Restart the database.
4. As a superuser in the database, execute the following SQL query in the critical OLTP database:

```
UPDATE pg_database
   SET datallowconn = FALSE
 WHERE datname != 'template1';
```

5. Next, execute the entire contents of this SQL block:

```
DO $$
DECLARE
    obj_oid oid;
BEGIN
    FOR obj_oid IN SELECT objrelid FROM active_snap
    LOOP
        PERFORM pgfadvise_willneed(obj_oid::regclass);
    END LOOP;
END;
$$ LANGUAGE plpgsql;
```

6. Finally, execute the following query to re-enable connections:

```
UPDATE pg_database SET datallowconn = TRUE;
```

How it works...

The first part of this recipe has two steps. We could perform this work at any time, so the table may have existed from our previous work. Therefore, the first step is to drop the active_snap table. None of the steps following this one remove this table, because, in the case of a crash, we want its contents as a starting point for restoring the cache contents.

After dropping the active_snap table, we recreate it with the top 20 tables and top 20 indexes, which are sorted by how often they're used in SELECT statements. This is only a close approximation based on the collected database statistics, but it's better than leaving the data entirely uncached.

After creating the list of the most accessed tables and indexes, we have one of two paths. In the first and simplest one, we merely preserve the file_path contents of the active_snap table, as this tells us exactly where the data files are located. After preserving the table, we can do anything we want, including restarting the database server.

After we're done with maintenance or crash recovery, we can actually restore the file cache before starting the PostgreSQL service. To do this, users of PostgreSQL 9.4 and above can simply rely on the pg_prewarm extension to do all of the hard work.

Otherwise, we require an imposing block of shell scripting. While it looks complex, it's actually just two loops to fetch a full list of every file that has a name similar to the ones we identified. As PostgreSQL objects exist in 1 GB chunks, there can be several of these that we may have to find. Then, we use the dd utility to read the file into memory twice. We do it twice because the first time it loads the data into memory, and the second time it encourages the filesystem to mark the blocks as frequently used so that the operating system is less likely to purge them.

Afterward, we can start PostgreSQL and enjoy a database that is much less likely to have problems retrieving frequently used data. If we don't have command-line access to the system where PostgreSQL runs, this process is a little more complicated but still manageable.

In the second scenario, we actually stop the database first. Any of our cache recoveries must come after the database is restarted. Until that time, we're free to perform any activity necessary to get the server or database contents in order. After we start the database, the *fun* begins.

We need to reject user connections while we load the database cache. The easiest way to do this without complicated scripts is to simply reject all connections that don't target the `template1` database. It's extremely unlikely that applications or users will connect to `template1` as it generally contains nothing and they have no permissions within it. For our use, it allows us to reconnect and re-enable connections from `template1` if, for some reason, we get disconnected.

Then, we can use the contents of our previously initialized `active_snap` table to tell the `pgFincore` module to load all of those tables and indexes into memory. After this is complete, we re-enable the database connections and our work is finished.

 Our `active_snap` table is pretty handy, but it depends on the existence of statistical data that might not be available in the case of a system crash. Be wary of using this approach if statistical information is not trustworthy or is missing.

See also

The tools discussed in this section have a lot of documentation and examples. Please refer to these sites for more information:

- **System administration functions**:
  https://www.postgresql.org/docs/current/static/functions-admin.html
- **The Statistics Collector**:
  https://www.postgresql.org/docs/current/static/monitoring-stats.html
- **pg_prewarm**: https://www.postgresql.org/docs/current/static/pgprewarm.html
- **pgFincore**: https://github.com/klando/pgfincore

Terminating rogue connections

There comes a time in every DBA's life when they must disconnect a PostgreSQL client from the server; for us, that time is now. There are varying degrees of escalation available for this purpose, and several system catalog views to provide viable targets. Why would we want to forcefully cancel a query or disconnect a user?

To prevent utter havoc; should a user forget an important clause, a query could require several hours to complete. During this time, it is consuming an entire CPU and saturating the storage bandwidth while doing so. A buggy application could start a transaction and stop responding, leaving an idle transaction potentially holding locks and causing a wait backlog.

There are many reasons to evict a connection, and most of them revolve around maintaining a regular flow of queries. If we're unable to maintain low latency and high throughput, our work in building a highly available environment is wasted. This recipe will help us to focus on dedicating resources primarily to active user sessions.

Getting ready

Luckily, PostgreSQL provides most of the tools we need. However, there is a more advanced command-line utility named `tcpkill` that we may need to use later. If it's not already installed, we recommend that you do so before continuing. Debian or Ubuntu-based systems can use this command as a root-capable user:

```
sudo apt-get install dsniff
```

For lucky users of 9.6 and above, we suggest setting the new `idle_in_transaction_session_timeout` parameter to `3600` or lower in `postgresql.conf`. This parameter will tell PostgreSQL to automatically cut any connection that is idle for longer than an hour.

How to do it...

The full escalation path starts very subtly to avoid major disruptive action. Perform these steps carefully, assuming `eth0` is the network interface that PostgreSQL is using:

1. Connect to the database as a superuser and execute the following query for PostgreSQL 9.2 and higher versions:

```
SELECT pid, client_port, state,
       now() - query_start AS duration, query
  FROM pg_stat_activity
 WHERE now() - query_start > INTERVAL '2 seconds'
   AND state != 'idle'
 ORDER BY duration DESC;
```

2. Use this query for 9.1 and lower versions:

```
SELECT procpid AS pid, client_port,
       now() - query_start AS duration, current_query
  FROM pg_stat_activity
 WHERE now() - query_start > INTERVAL '2 seconds'
   AND current_query != '<IDLE>'
 ORDER BY duration DESC;
```

3. Starting from the top, carefully examine the queries in this list. Make note of `pid` for any query that should be disconnected.

4. Stop the currently executing query for the selected `pid` variables with the following query:

```
SELECT pg_cancel_backend(pid);
```

5. Execute the first query again and check the results for the targeted `pid` variable.

6. If the query is still running, or if the state has switched to **idle in transaction**, execute the following query:

```
SELECT pg_terminate_backend(pid);
```

7. Execute the first query again and check the results for the targeted `pid` variable.

8. If the query is still running, disconnect from the database and connect to the server as a root-capable user.

9. Run the following command to terminate the client's network connection, using the contents of the `client_port` column:

```
sudo tcpkill -i eth0 -9 port client_port
```

10. Wait until the output from `tcpkill` resembles several identical lines.

How it works...

We begin the process by getting a list of every process ID, duration, and query currently running for longer than 2 seconds. Though 2 seconds is arbitrary, it helps filter out short and fast queries that we aren't interested in pursuing. If we examine the queries listed in these results, we may decide that one or more need to be canceled or disconnected. The results should resemble this output:

```
pid  | client_port |         state          |      duration    | query
------+-------------+------------------------+------------------+--------
5766 |          -1 | idle in transaction    | 00:03:53.894828  | BEGIN;
(1 row)
```

If this is the case, the `pid` column conveys important information necessary to target the client connection. We begin by invoking `pg_cancel_backend` in an attempt to terminate the currently running query. Often, this is enough to clear locks or stop a query from consuming excessive resources. It's important to rerun the status query to ensure that the command successfully stopped the client's activity.

If the target connection is still active, we need to escalate to the next step: disconnect the client from the database. For this, we use `pg_terminate_backend` instead. This is roughly equivalent to using an operating system utility to terminate the client process, but it is something we can do directly from PostgreSQL. Again, we check for success using the status query just in case.

In very rare cases, `pg_terminate_backend` can fail and the client connection will remain unscathed. So, how is this possible? Well, despite their apparent maturity, networks are notoriously unreliable. Misrouted packets, retransmissions, blocked sockets, timeouts, stalls, and more issues wait to disrupt the communication line between PostgreSQL and a connected client.

Sometimes, the network socket is in such a state that PostgreSQL was interrupted while writing output. In this case, PostgreSQL is waiting for the client to acknowledge the receipt of the data, or for the operating system to mark the network connection as broken. If this never happens, PostgreSQL will wait patiently forever until the client properly handles the terminate command.

This isn't ideal for us, as the process could be locking necessary tables or rows. If we can't get PostgreSQL to terminate the client, we need to use another approach. The tcpkill command gives us the ability to interrupt a network connection directly; this causes the operating system to close the network socket. When this happens, the PostgreSQL client exits automatically.

All we need to do is run tcpkill with the -i parameter, in order to tell it about the network interface the database is using, the port to focus on, and how aggressive to be. We know the port from the client_port column of our status query, and specifying -9 tells tcpkill to block all incoming and outgoing packets so that there's no ambiguity regarding our intent.

The output from a tcpkill command should look like this toward the end:

```
127.0.0.10:5432 > 127.0.0.1:37601: R 315492496:315490496(0) win 0
127.0.0.10:5432 > 127.0.0.1:37601: R 315492538:315490538(0) win 0
127.0.0.10:5432 > 127.0.0.1:37601: R 315492622:315490622(0) win 0
```

It's important to not be impatient. Sometimes, it can take a minute or two before the connection finally dies.

There's more...

If a connected application encounters a bug and goes haywire, it might be convenient to disconnect several clients simultaneously. PostgreSQL lets us run query results through functions, so we could kill all connections that were idle in the transaction for at least 2 minutes by running this query as a superuser:

```
SELECT pg_terminate_backend(pid)
  FROM pg_stat_activity
 WHERE now() - state_change > INTERVAL '2 minutes'
   AND state = 'idle in transaction';
```

The `pg_stat_activity` view offers a lot of characteristics to differentiate target queries. We could terminate only connections from a specific IP address or those that connected to the database over a week ago. There is a lot of opportunity here to maintain a highly available system through direct intervention.

Reducing contention with concurrent indexes

When administering a PostgreSQL installation, we will eventually need to create new tables and indexes. In the case of new indexes, the table is locked in *shared exclusive access* mode for the duration of the creation process, blocking any insert, update, or delete activity. This both prevents inconsistencies and allows the database to modify the table structure to reflect the new index.

Unfortunately, this process is fundamentally incompatible with maintaining a highly available server. While building the index, PostgreSQL needs to examine every valid table row, which means loading it from the disk into memory. For large or active tables, this can cause excessive strain on the system. Other database activities will reduce their available disk bandwidth, and the required lock will block all modifications of data in that table. Combined, this can lead to a table being locked for a very long time.

Ever since PostgreSQL 8.2, indexes could be created concurrently with other activities. This means PostgreSQL constructs the index in the background and only requests an exclusive lock that is long enough to attach it to the table. However, soon after its introduction, some DBAs felt reluctant to use it and have not changed their evaluation of its safety as it matured.

This may seem trivial, as the feature has now been around for over a decade by this point, but not enough new administrators know about this functionality. Using it properly and knowing the caveats can avert several DBA headaches. This recipe will provide a quick use case.

Getting ready

We just need to find an index to create. For the sake of this discussion, we may also want to create a small pgbench database for demonstration purposes. Execute the following commands as the postgres user to build a sufficient sample:

```
createdb pgbench
pgbench -i -s 200 pgbench
```

This will initialize (-i) a database with a table consisting of 2 million rows (-s 200), which we can leverage for the short recipe.

How to do it...

Follow these steps to test concurrent index creation:

1. Connect to the pgbench database and execute the following command as a superuser or the postgres user:

    ```
    CREATE INDEX CONCURRENTLY idx_account_bid
        ON pgbench_accounts (bid);
    ```

2. In another connection, attempt to execute the following INSERT command before the preceding command completes:

    ```
    INSERT INTO pgbench_accounts
    VALUES (50000000, 100, 15000, 'testing');
    ```

How it works...

By adding the CONCURRENTLY modifier, PostgreSQL will begin the process of building an index. While it does this, it also tracks the incoming insert, update, and delete activities to include them in the new index.

In the connection where we invoked the `CREATE INDEX` statement, we will not see a prompt again until PostgreSQL finishes building the index. So, how can we tell it apart from any regular index creation? Well, one of the reasons we built an example was to prove that concurrency is present. The `INSERT` statement in the second connection should succeed before the index is complete. The process is the same for a production PostgreSQL instance. Any incoming writes to a table undergoing a concurrent index creation will complete normally until the final lock is necessary.

There's more...

While concurrent indexes are very useful, they have some very important elements that we need to consider.

No transactions

Even as of PostgreSQL 12, concurrent index creation cannot take place inside a transaction. But why not? Well, remember that the process needs to look inside all of the incoming transactions that could modify the table being indexed. PostgreSQL normally never allows what most experienced DBAs know as *dirty* reads of uncommitted data. As a consequence, concurrent indexes must be built outside of a transaction by internal database mechanisms.

One at a time

As concurrent index creation is not transaction-safe, PostgreSQL will only build one at a time per table. Some enterprising DBAs have circumvented this limitation by building a queue system to send concurrent index-creation requests until the queue is empty. More advanced PostgreSQL installations may want to consider a similar system to utilize concurrent indexes extensively.

Dangers of OLTP use

Concurrent indexes are not a panacea; they still follow rules for lock acquisition. Specifically, PostgreSQL cannot acquire a lock to attach the index as long as any earlier transactions are still running. While it waits for the lock, any new transactions that need to modify the table contents will also wait. This feedback loop of waits can quickly consume all available client connections on an already busy OLTP system.

It's best to avoid this situation by following the normal index-creation protocol on OLTP systems: that is, only create indexes when the volume is low. We can also massively reduce the risk by avoiding long-running transactions that could potentially block the final lock request. OLTP systems should only have a few transactions in any case.

See also

PostgreSQL has an excellent manual page discussing indexes and concurrency. Please refer to this page for more information: `https://www.postgresql.org/docs/current/static/sql-createindex.html`.

Managing system migrations

As DBAs, it is likely that we will eventually preside over a server replacement. Whether this is to avoid failed hardware or due to system upgrades, our job is to move PostgreSQL from one system to the next.

Performing a server migration while simultaneously maintaining maximum availability is not simple. One of the easiest methods is limited to users of shared storage such as a SAN. Such storage can be reassigned to another server quite easily. Without a SAN or other means of shared storage, we need to utilize another method.

Luckily, PostgreSQL added streaming database replication in version 9.1. This recipe will explore how we can make a copy of the new server and then switch to it when we're ready.

Getting ready

For this demonstration, we will need another server or virtual machine to receive a copy of our database. Have one ready to follow along. We will also be using a PostgreSQL tool named `pg_basebackup`. Check the PostgreSQL documentation regarding this utility for more information.

If the donor server is configured as described in the *Configuration – getting it right the first time* recipe, modify its `pg_hba.conf` file and add the following line:

```
host      replication      rep_user      0/0      md5
```

Then, create a user to control replication with this SQL query issued as a superuser:

```
CREATE USER rep_user WITH PASSWORD 'rep_test' REPLICATION;
```

Finally, reload the server to activate the configuration line. If you are attempting this in a real production system, use a better password and replace `0/0` with the actual IP address of the new server.

How to do it...

Assuming `192.168.1.10` is our donor server, follow these steps to create a copy:

1. Connect to the new server as the `postgres` user.
2. Issue the following command to copy data from the donor system:

   ```
   pg_basebackup –U rep_user –h 192.168.1.10 –D /path/to/database
   ```

3. If using PostgreSQL 11 or earlier, create a file named `recovery.conf` in `/path/to/database` with the following content:

   ```
   standby_mode = 'on'
   primary_conninfo = 'host=192.168.1.10 port=5432 user=rep_user'
   ```

4. For PostgreSQL 12 or later, create a file named `standby.signal` in `/path/to/database`, and then add the following line to `postgresql.conf` directly:

   ```
   primary_conninfo = 'host=192.168.1.10 port=5432 user=rep_user'
   ```

5. Create a file named `.pgpass` in the home directory of the `postgres` user with the following line:

   ```
   *:5432:replication:rep_user:rep_test
   ```

6. Set the correct permissions for the `.pgpass` file with this command:

   ```
   chmod 0600 ~postgres/.pgpass
   ```

7. Start the new server using the following command:

```
pg_ctl -D /path/to/database start
```

8. Inform application owners to stop their applications or bring available services up with a maintenance message.

9. Issue the following command on the donor server to write any pending data to the database:

```
CHECKPOINT;
```

10. Connect to PostgreSQL on the donor server and issue the following query to check replication status:

```
SELECT sent_location, replay_location
  FROM pg_stat_replication
 WHERE usename = 'rep_user';
```

11. Periodically repeat the preceding query until `sent_location` and `replay_location` match.

12. Issue a command on the primary server to stop the database. This command should work on most systems:

```
pg_ctl -D /path/to/database stop -m fast
```

13. Issue this command on the new server:

```
pg_ctl -D /path/to/database promote
```

14. Inform application owners to start their applications or bring available services up normally configured in order to use the new database server address.

How it works...

We start the somewhat long journey on the new server by invoking the `pg_basebackup` command. When PostgreSQL introduced streaming replication, it also made it possible for a regular utility to obtain copies of database files through the client protocol. To create a copy of every file in the donor system, we specify its address with the -h parameter. Using the -U parameter, we can tell `pg_basebackup` to use the `rep_user` user we created specifically to manage database replication.

When PostgreSQL 11, or earlier, detects the presence of a recovery.conf file, it begins to recover as if it crashed. The value we used for the primary_conninfo setting will cause the replica to connect to the primary server. Once established, the replica will consume changes from the primary database server until it is synchronized. After starting the database, any activity that occurs in the primary system will also eventually be replayed in the copy.

PostgreSQL 12 introduces a new system where special files ending in .signal indicate how the server should start. In this case, we can still specify primary_conninfo in order to specify the upstream server, but we must also create a standby.signal file to tell PostgreSQL to treat this new instance as a data replica.

> Don't try to use the old recovery.conf standby method with PostgreSQL 12, as the server will refuse to start if that file is present.

As we created the replication user with a password, we need an automatic method to convey the password from the replica to the primary. PostgreSQL clients often seek .pgpass files to obtain credentials automatically; used in this context, the new server acts as a client.

Once we start the new server, everything should be ready, so we need all sources of new data in the database to stop temporarily. Once this has happened, we issue CHECKPOINT to flush the activity to disk. Afterward, we monitor the status of the replication stream until it is fully synchronized with the donor.

After the synchronization is verified with our replication lag query, we stop the source PostgreSQL database; its job is complete. All that remains is to promote the new database to full production status and tell various departments and application owners that the database is available at the new location. Before the introduction of replication, this was a far more complicated procedure.

There's more...

If you'd like to read ahead, in Chapter 4, *Proxy and Pooling Resources*, we explain how to simplify this even further. The process is the same until the final few steps, where applications reconnect to the database. If applications and users are using a virtual address instead of the actual server IP for the old database, they can continue to use the virtual location after the migration.

Simply detach the virtual IP from the old database server and attach it to the new one before informing the users that the migration is complete. As an added benefit, we can use the virtual IP address as a form of security. Until we create it, users will be unable to locate the database. We can take advantage of this and perform database checks before going fully online.

Once we have created the virtual IP address, any applications that were using the database before we started the migration will need to reconnect. However, even this necessity can be removed in certain circumstances; we will discuss this in a future chapter.

See also

System migrations are extremely complicated. This section only touches on a small number of concepts. Please refer to these PostgreSQL documentation links for a deeper exploration of the material we covered:

- **The pg_basebackup utility**:
  https://www.postgresql.org/docs/current/static/app-pgbasebackup.html
- **Log-Shipping Standby Servers**:
  https://www.postgresql.org/docs/current/static/warm-standby.html
- **Hot Standby**:
  https://www.postgresql.org/docs/current/static/hot-standby.html

Managing software upgrades

Software in the server space is normally fairly stable. However, elements such as security updates and bug fixes must be applied. Highly available servers can't be stopped often, but without important upgrades, they could crash or experience a breach, which would be far more serious.

So, how do we ensure that updates can be applied safely while maintaining consistent availability? Once again, this often comes down to preparation. We prepare by having duplicate online data copies and by abstracting access paths. With architecture like this in place, we can switch to a backup server while upgrading the primary server; thus, the database never actually goes offline.

We'll explore this scenario in this recipe, especially as it is a very common one.

Getting ready

For this section, we need at least one extra server with PostgreSQL installed. This server should be running a copy of our database. You can follow the *Managing system migrations* recipe to build a copy if you don't already have one available. We will also be using a very simple proxy technique to create a virtual IP address to simplify redirection. Reviewing these techniques now might be a good idea.

How to do it...

For this scenario, assume that we have two servers with the addresses of `192.168.1.10` and `192.168.1.20`, where `192.168.1.10` is currently the primary server. In addition, we have a virtual IP address of `192.168.1.30` on the `eth0` Ethernet device. To upgrade the PostgreSQL software on both nodes, follow these steps:

1. Stop the database copy on `192.168.1.20` as the `postgres` user using this command:

   ```
   pg_ctl -D /path/to/database stop -m fast
   ```

2. Perform any necessary software upgrades. For example, to upgrade a Debian or Ubuntu server to the latest PostgreSQL 12, use the following command as a root-capable user on `192.168.1.20`:

   ```
   sudo apt-get install postgresql-12
   ```

3. Start the database copy on `192.168.1.20` as the `postgres` user:

   ```
   pg_ctl -D /path/to/database start
   ```

4. As a root-capable user on `192.168.1.10`, stop the virtual IP address with the following command:

   ```
   sudo ip addr del 192.168.1.30/32 dev eth0
   ```

5. As a database superuser, issue a checkpoint to the database on `192.168.1.10`:

   ```
   CHECKPOINT;
   ```

6. Connect to PostgreSQL on `192.168.1.10` and issue the following query to check the replication status:

```
SELECT sent_location, replay_location
  FROM pg_stat_replication
  WHERE usename = 'rep_user';
```

7. Periodically, repeat the preceding query until `sent_location` and `replay_location` match.

8. As `postgres`, stop the PostgreSQL service on `192.168.1.10` with this command:

```
pg_ctl -D /path/to/database stop -m fast
```

9. As `postgres`, promote the PostgreSQL replica on `192.168.1.20` with this command:

```
pg_ctl -D /path/to/database promote
```

10. As a root-capable user on `192.168.1.20`, start the virtual IP address with the following command:

```
sudo ip addr add 192.168.1.30 dev eth0
```

11. If necessary, inform the developers and support staff to restart the application's database connection pools.

12. Repeat any necessary software upgrades on `192.168.1.10` as already performed on `192.168.1.20`.

13. Erase the existing database on `192.168.1.10` as the `postgres` user using the following command:

```
rm -Rf /path/to/database
```

14. Use `pg_basebackup` on `192.168.1.10` to make a copy of the upgraded database on `192.168.1.20`:

```
pg_basebackup -U rep_user -h 192.168.1.20 -D /path/to/database
```

15. If using PostgreSQL 11 or earlier, create a file named `recovery.conf` in `/path/to/database` with the following content:

```
standby_mode = 'on'
primary_conninfo = 'host=192.168.1.20 port=5432 user=rep_user'
```

16. For PostgreSQL 12 or later, create a file named `standby.signal` in `/path/to/database`, and then add the following line to `postgresql.conf` directly:

    ```
    primary_conninfo = 'host=192.168.1.20 port=5432 user=rep_user'
    ```

17. Start the newly created copy as the `postgres` user on `192.168.1.10` using the following command:

    ```
    pg_ctl -D /path/to/database start
    ```

How it works...

This entire process is very long, but we hope to illustrate that it is actually very straightforward. The first step is to upgrade the mirror copy of the database under the assumption that it is not actively utilized by applications or users. The role of the secondary node, in this case, is to act as an emergency backup for the primary database node. As it's not being used, we are able to stop the database, perform any necessary updates, and start it and allow it to synchronize again.

Afterward, we isolate the primary database node by disabling the virtual IP address. This allows the streaming replica to replay the last few active transactions so that it's fully synchronized before we make it the new primary database. We accomplish this by issuing CHECKPOINT and watching the replication status until it matches on both systems. When the replication status matches, we can stop the primary PostgreSQL server; its role in the process is complete.

As software upgrades may take some time to complete or require a server restart, we need to immediately make the secondary node available as the primary database. We start by promoting the replica to become the new primary server by sending the `promote` command to `pg_ctl`. Once the database is writable, we reinstate the `192.168.1.30` virtual IP address so that applications and users can reconnect safely.

This process of node switching is fairly quick, provided we already have a replica ready to take over. With the replica acting as a primary, the next step is to perform any necessary upgrades, just as we did on the secondary node. After the upgrades are finished, we cannot simply restart the primary database again, as the replica has been acting as a primary database for a period of time.

This means that we need to rebuild the primary database as a new replica. This makes both nodes ready for the next upgrade and maintains the two-node relationship. We start this process by erasing the old contents of the database and then use `pg_basebackup` to copy the current primary database.

Then, we create a new `recovery.conf` file for older versions of PostgreSQL and direct it to act as a new replica. PostgreSQL 12 and later requires a file named `standby.signal` along with changes to `postgresql.conf` instead, as noted in the *Managing system migrations* recipe.

Once the replica is started, we have the same configuration as we had earlier, but now the roles are reversed; `192.168.1.20` is the primary and `192.168.1.10` is the replica.

There's more...

Astute readers may have noticed that using `pg_basebackup` to copy the entire database following a minor upgrade is somewhat wasteful. We agree! In later recipes, we will make use of `rsync` or PostgreSQL-specific software to perform these tasks instead. This recipe was already pretty long, and setting up `rsync` properly for this operation would have added quite a bit more time. The point is to show you the switching process; feel free to substitute better methods you know for synchronizing data.

See also

In addition to `rsync`, a lesser-known utility named `pg_rewind` can make resetting replicas much easier. It is beyond the scope of this chapter, so we recommend that you read more about it here: `https://www.postgresql.org/docs/current/static/app-pgrewind.html`.

Mitigating the impact of hardware failure

Software can have bugs, and PostgreSQL is no exception. Flaws in the database software rarely, if ever, lead directly to data corruption. Hardware can fail too, but hardware problems are not always so straightforward.

Disk, CPU, or memory failures don't always cause the server to crash. In fact, these failures can persist for weeks or even months before their detection by a monitoring infrastructure. Disk failures are generally abstracted away by RAID or SAN devices, and these arrays are designed to readily handle online rebuilds. Other types of failures are more subtle.

CPU or memory problems can manifest in several different ways. In order for PostgreSQL to function, the data from disk must be read into memory to be processed by the CPU. During any of these transition states, a bad CPU or RAM module can inject an invalid checksum or data value that is inconsistent with the rest of the database. However, PostgreSQL generally assumes that the database is consistent and that the transaction logs have been faithfully recorded and applied.

When running a dual-node database where one node is always connected and synchronized with the other, a failure like this can corrupt data on both nodes nearly simultaneously. When both nodes contain invalid data, our promise of providing a highly available system is impossible. We have no backup to switch to and no alternate node to host the database while we repair the problem. Data corruption can require intricate investigative and mitigation efforts, which are much harder to complete while the database is online.

This recipe will explore some reasonable ways to prevent this type of scenario by exercising extreme caution and some extra preparation work.

Getting ready

We need to cover a few different scenarios here. One of the things we want to do is transfer files from one server to another. A popular way to do this is with the `rsync` command. On Debian or Ubuntu systems, we can install it as a root-capable user this way:

```
sudo apt-get install rsync
```

There's also a neat trick we can use to simplify the transferring of files to the WAL archive system. Create a file named `/etc/rsyncd.conf` and fill it with this content, assuming `/db/wal_archive` is where we want to send files:

```
[archive]
    path = /db/wal_archive
    comment = Archived Transaction Logs
    uid = postgres
    gid = postgres
    read only = true
```

We're now ready to protect our data from hardware problems.

How to do it...

The first thing we need to do is to secure the WAL stream. Follow these steps to build a semi-permanent copy of archived WAL data in the /db/wal_archive directory:

1. On the primary node, modify the postgresql.conf file to include the following setting:

   ```
   archive_command = 'cp -an %p /db/wal_archive/%f'
   ```

2. Create the /db/wal_archive directory as a root-capable user using the following commands:

   ```
   sudo mkdir -p -m 0700 /db/wal_archive
   sudo chown -R postgres /db/wal_archive
   ```

3. Reload the PostgreSQL service using the following command:

   ```
   pg_ctl -D /path/to/database reload
   ```

4. As a root-capable user, create a script, named del_archives, in the /etc/cron.daily directory and fill it with this content:

   ```
   find /db/wal_archive -name '0000*' \
       -type f -mtime +2 -delete
   ```

5. Make sure that the script is executable using the following command:

   ```
   chmod a+x /etc/cron.daily/del_archives
   ```

Next, we should create the /db/wal_archive folder elsewhere for safety. In this case, let's assume that the system is at 192.168.1.10 and we have another server set up specifically for WAL storage at 192.168.1.100.

Impose an hour's delay by following these steps:

1. On 192.168.1.100, create a /db/wal_archive directory as a root-capable user with these commands:

   ```
   sudo mkdir -p -m 0700 /db/wal_archive
   sudo chown -R postgres /db/wal_archive
   ```

2. Ensure that the server at `192.168.1.100` has the `rsync.conf` file we discussed earlier.

3. As a root-capable user on `192.168.1.10`, create a script named `sync_archives` in the `/etc/cron.d` directory with this content:

```
* * * * * postgres find /db/wal_archive -name '0000*' \
   -type f -mmin +60 | \
            xargs -I{} rsync {} 192.168.1.100::archive
```

How it works...

To ensure that WAL data is available for recovery or emergency restore, we need to secure it on a tertiary location away from the primary or secondary server. We start this by telling PostgreSQL to store the old WAL files instead of deleting them. The `cp` command we used to copy the files will not overwrite any existing archives due to the `-n` setting. This prevents accidentally corrupting the existing transaction logs.

Then, we need to create the directory where the files will reside. The `mkdir` command does this, and the `chown` command ensures that the PostgreSQL server can write to that directory. Once the directory is in place, we need to reload PostgreSQL because we changed `archive_command`.

Once a WAL file is no longer required by PostgreSQL, it's stored in our `/db/wal_archive` directory until it gets deleted. This is why we create the `del_archives` script. We only really need 2 or 3 days' worth of live WAL files. This allows us to send very old files to tape, and newer files are available for **Point-in-time recovery** (**PITR**) or restore. Once we make the script executable with the `chattr` command, we will not have to worry about accidentally filling the disks with WAL files.

The final steps might be the most important of all. We create a directory on a *completely different server* rather than on any of our existing database nodes. Once this directory is there, we create an automated `rsync` job on the database master that will run every minute and copy all WAL files older than 1 hour to the new storage area. Why only an hour? Well, current versions of PostgreSQL don't have the ability to delay the replay stream, so if we encounter a hardware problem, corrupt data will immediately synchronize to our spare server. This gives us up to an hour for monitors, maintenance, and logs to discover the problem before the corrupted WAL files pollute the tertiary storage server.

We could use PITR instead, at this point. However, an imposed 1-hour delay allows us to have live access to databases that obtain their WAL files from the tertiary server. Otherwise, we would have to restore from backup and apply WAL files to reach our desired point in time.

There's more...

In securing the WAL stream, there are a few other options available to us.

Copying WAL files more easily

If we have a version of PostgreSQL of 9.2 or above, there is a new command that, much like `pg_basebackup`, utilizes the replication mechanism for a new purpose. Assuming PostgreSQL is configured as described in the *Configuration – getting it right the first time* recipe, there should be several available replication streams. As we've planned ahead and have a dual-node cluster, we are already using at least one to create a copy of the database.

The next step is to focus on the safety of the WAL files, as they are critical to PITR. Instead of using `rsync` to copy these between nodes, we can simply pull them directly from the primary node. With `192.168.1.30` as the virtual database IP address and `rep_user` as the name of the replication user, we could use the following command to obtain WAL data:

```
pg_receivewal -h 192.168.1.30 -U rep_user -D /db/wal_archive
```

This command acts like a service. This means it will only copy from the replication stream while it is actually running. To use `pg_receivewal` effectively, it needs to be started as a background service and should be restarted if the virtual IP is moved or the server it's running on is ever restarted.

We should note that, prior to PostgreSQL 10, this utility was actually named `pg_receivexlog` instead. Otherwise, it acts exactly as described previously.

Built-in delay

When we said PostgreSQL has no way to delay applying WAL data to a streaming replica, we weren't quite telling the whole story. There actually is a setting in versions of PostgreSQL 9.4 and higher that will delay COMMIT of transactions from the upstream primary server.

If we wanted to use this with versions of PostgreSQL between 9.4 and 11, we could simply add this line to the standby's recovery.conf file to wait for an hour before committing data:

```
recovery_min_apply_delay = 3600
```

For PostgreSQL 12 or greater, we would simply add this to postgresql.conf instead.

This parameter acts very similarly to our cumbersome WAL marshaling, but with one key difference. All data in the replication stream is applied as quickly as possible, and only COMMIT is delayed. This means that any corrupt data on the upstream system could also be on the replica, but it would be invisible to us.

This isn't quite ideal since we want to avoid incorporating the bad data in the first place, but it's certainly easier to manage. Assuming we've secured the WAL files and have adequate backup coverage, this kind of delay may be an acceptable compromise.

Adding compression

PostgreSQL WAL files tend to be very compressible. As such, we can save quite a bit of space while storing them for long periods of time. Since PostgreSQL archive_command can be anything we wish, we can incorporate compression right into the process. For example, we could use this postgresql.conf setting instead:

```
archive_command = 'gzip -qc %p > /db/wal_archive/%f'
```

Now, whenever PostgreSQL moves a WAL file into the archive, it also compresses it.

Secondary delay

We have already discussed maintenance in the previous sections. What we never covered was self-imposed archival delay. If we're performing maintenance or the primary node crashes, it is a very good idea to either delete the `/etc/cron.d/sync_archive` script or comment out the `rsync` command itself until the maintenance is complete. This hour-long barrier helps us to avoid propagating corrupt data, but there's no reason to take excessive risks.

Some environments have another pair of servers in a different data center that acts as disaster recovery. If this is our setup, any running server on the disaster-recovery side should be stopped while we modify or rebuild the primary or secondary servers. The reasoning is the same: if there is a problem with the maintenance, we have an untainted copy of everything.

Feel free to re-enable all the synchronization after verifying that crash recovery or maintenance hasn't introduced invalid data.

See also

As we introduced the `pg_receivewal` utility, we would be remiss if we didn't include its helpful documentation as well. Follow this link for more information: `https://www.postgresql.org/docs/current/app-pgreceivewal.html`

Applying bonus kernel tweaks

Most operating system kernels are optimized for generalized use. While this does not preclude operation as a server, we can benefit greatly by altering a few settings to better utilize our available hardware. This isn't simply a series of configuration modifications meant to increase performance but critical kernel-related tweaks meant to prevent outages.

Though, while we're on the subject, there's no reason to not include purely performance-enhancing modifications. Getting the most out of our hardware prevents unnecessary operating strain on existing resources. A server running too close to its limits cannot be considered highly available; an unexpected increase in demand can render a server unusable under the right circumstances.

This recipe will cover several kernel changes that can keep our server online.

Getting ready

While the following settings are based on Linux servers, some of the concepts are universal. We'll try to provide enough information to illustrate this. However, keep that in mind for this recipe.

Otherwise, look for a directory named /etc/sysctl.d. Any system with this directory can be easily configured by adding a file that contains extra settings here. Otherwise, we need to find a file named /etc/sysctl.conf, which serves a similar purpose but requires direct modification.

The settings we are going to change include the following:

```
kernel.sched_migration_cost_ns = 5000000
kernel.sched_autogroup_enabled = 0
vm.dirty_background_bytes = 67108864
vm.dirty_bytes = 1073741824
vm.zone_reclaim_mode = 0
vm.swappiness = 1
```

How to do it...

If there's a /etc/sysctl.d directory, follow these steps to activate it:

1. Create a file named 30-postgresql.conf in the /etc/sysctl.d directory with the settings we mentioned earlier.
2. Execute this command as a root-capable user to activate:

   sudo sysctl --system

Otherwise, follow these steps:

1. Place the settings in /etc/sysctl.conf.
2. Execute this command as a root-capable user to activate:

   sudo sysctl -p

How it works...

In this case, it's all about the settings. Each of our two illustrated steps simply ensures that the settings are in a location where they become permanent parts of the server. Any future reboot will automatically apply these newly selected values instead of the defaults. The `sysctl` command activates them immediately, so we don't need to reboot to modify the system behavior.

The `sched_migration_cost_ns` setting is the total period of time the scheduler will consider a migrated process *cache hot*, and thus less likely to be migrated again. By default, this is 0.5 ms (or 500,000 ns). As the size of the process table increases, the complexity inherited by the process scheduler eventually results in high CPU overhead merely to assign processors to PostgreSQL tasks.

Depending on the count of database clients, we have observed overhead as high as 70 percent, greatly reducing database performance. Our suggested setting of 5 ms gives PostgreSQL enough time to process one or more queries before the task is eligible for migration and prevents the CPU task scheduler from being overworked.

The `sched_autogroup_enabled` setting causes the operating system to group tasks by origin in order to improve perceived responsiveness. On server systems, large daemons such as PostgreSQL are launched from the same system task. As they're all in the same large group, they can be effectively choked out of CPU cycles in favor of less important tasks. The default setting is 1 (enabled) on some platforms. By setting this to 0 (disabled), PostgreSQL query performance can be improved by up to 30 percent on databases with hundreds of user connections.

We modify `zone_reclaim_mode` to completely disable its operation by setting it to 0. According to the Linux kernel documentation, it may be beneficial to switch off zone reclaim when memory should be used for caching files from disk. Without this, the kernel aggressively balances memory between zones, causing excess overhead and reducing available memory for caching disk data.

The `dirty_background_bytes` setting is the amount of memory (in bytes) that can be marked as modified before the operating system begins writing data to disk in the background. It is closely tied to `dirty_ratio`, which is the amount of memory (in bytes) where the operating system blocks all other write activities and aggressively writes dirty memory until everything has been flushed. This kind of occurrence effectively stops all database activity until the flush is complete.

By setting the background bytes to such a low value of 64 MB, the constant background writes make it far less likely that we will reach that trigger point. A highly available server cannot afford long unplanned periods of stopped query handling. The constant writing actually slightly reduces performance, which is a risk we have to weigh against the stability of the server.

> Older kernels used `dirty_background_ratio` and `dirty_ratio` in place of `dirty_background_bytes` and `dirty_bytes`. These older settings are percentages of total memory and, as such, should not exceed 1 and 5, respectively, especially on systems with more than 64 GB of RAM. Doing otherwise risks large flushes that could over-saturate disk caches and cause I/O waits.

Lastly, we set `swappiness` to `1`; this all but disables memory swapping. When Linux runs low on memory, it normally starts moving *idle* processes to disk to free up RAM. We don't want to risk any of our PostgreSQL clients getting this treatment, so we tell Linux to only swap if there is no other option. This is common to dedicated servers such as a critical PostgreSQL system. We don't use zero here because that can cause strange effects in some cases, and heavily discouraging swap use is usually sufficient.

There's more...

Given that we're discussing kernel parameters pertaining to process scheduling and memory management, we would like to discuss some of these in more depth. Some of this involves version-dependent parameter names or explaining why we chose certain attributes for this recipe. We also need to introduce the critically important topic of **Transparent Huge Pages** (**THP**), which can drastically reduce PostgreSQL performance.

Some additional background

Some kernel settings have different names with different versions. For instance, `sched_migration_cost_ns` is renamed `sched_migration_cost` in the older kernel releases. In the most recent kernels, the setting is missing entirely. In addition, `dirty_background_ratio` and `dirty_ratio` have been replaced for a very good reason.

Imagine a server with 512 GB of RAM. Even with a setting of only 1 percent, up to 5 GB of memory could be dirty before the operating system writes anything to disk. In the event of an emergency flush, the disk subsystem may not be capable of handling such a large amount. The new settings allow us to use the same logic as before, but with bytes instead of percentages. In systems with more than 64 GB of RAM, we highly recommend upgrading to a more recent kernel to make use of `dirty_bytes` and `dirty_background_bytes`.

A good place to start for setting `dirty_background_bytes` is up to double the size of the RAID or disk controller cache. This ensures that there is never more memory waiting to be written than the controller can handle. Similarly, we can set `dirty_bytes` to 8 to 10 times the size of the controller cache. This prevents long flushing delays if the background writer ever falls behind. Our default of 1 GB should suffice for most modern systems.

As always, your mileage may vary. Some PostgreSQL servers may experience slightly faster writes with larger amounts of dirty memory buffers. However, the goal of this book is to reduce the overall risk, even if that's at the cost of some performance. Long periods of database timeouts due to an overwhelmed disk subsystem do not fit this model.

Be wary of THP

Addressing memory efficiently is sometimes very difficult, especially on large servers equipped with vast amounts of RAM. For the sake of efficiency, more modern Linux kernels might attempt to communicate with larger preallocated blocks of memory.

Normally, this would be extremely beneficial. However, handling such large contiguous memory segments requires regular maintenance procedures that can disrupt processes assigned to that portion of RAM. In the wrong circumstances, PostgreSQL services may be implicitly suspended for tens of seconds while memory is defragmented.

Due to this, we strongly recommend disabling these if possible. This can be done with the following commands:

```
echo never > /sys/kernel/mm/transparent_hugepage/enabled
echo never > /sys/kernel/mm/transparent_hugepage/defrag
echo no > /sys/kernel/mm/transparent_hugepage/khugepaged/defrag
```

If the third command results in an error, use this instead:

```
echo 0 > /sys/kernel/mm/transparent_hugepage/khugepaged/defrag
```

Unfortunately, as this is a kernel-level setting, it is applied during system boot and can't be enforced by a configuration file setting. Changing it permanently so that it persists between reboots is highly specific to the Linux distribution in use.

For Red Hat and CentOS variants, this command may permanently disable THP:

```
grubby --update-kernel=ALL --args='transparent_hugepage=never'
```

Debian and Ubuntu family systems are a bit more difficult. Modify the /etc/default/grub file and look for the GRUB_CMDLINE_LINUX variable. Once there, append the following to any string that variable might contain. Here's an example:

```
GRUB_CMDLINE_LINUX="transparent_hugepage=never"
```

Then, execute this command as a root-level user:

```
sudo update-grub
```

If further steps are necessary or distributions change how these settings are managed in the future, please find the most recent instructions and apply them. This setting is important to ensure a healthy PostgreSQL system.

4
Proxy and Pooling Resources

Abstraction can protect a database from even the busiest platform and also ensure that applications always contact an online database server. Previous chapters in this book have already emphasized the importance of masquerading the primary database node to enable maintenance and availability. Two tools that are very popular for this purpose are **virtual IP addresses** and **HAProxy** software.

Yet there's always more to the story; abstraction isn't merely about indirection.

Modern applications, microarchitectures, and web services often involve hundreds or even thousands of servers and **virtual machines** (**VMs**). If we follow a simple and naive development cycle where applications have direct access to the database, each of these servers may require dozens of connections per program. Should each of these applications maintain their own connection pool, then this can result in hundreds or thousands of direct connections to the database. But is this what we want? Consider the scenario illustrated in the following diagram:

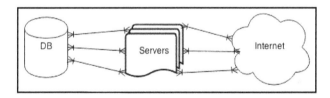

We need a way to avoid overwhelming the database with the needs of too many clients. As we suggested in `Chapter 3`, *Minimizing Downtime*, a PostgreSQL server experiences its best performance when the amount of active connections is less than three times the available CPU count.

With a thousand incoming client connections, we will need hundreds of CPU cores to satisfy that formula. Every incoming connection requires resources such as memory for query calculations and results, file handling and port allocations for network traffic, process management, and more. In addition to this, each connection is another process that the operating system has to schedule CPU time for. Very large servers are extremely capable, but resources are not infinite. Even if the database can handle thousands of connections, performance will suffer for each connection that is in excess of the design capacity. Therefore, we need to change the map to something slightly different, as shown here:

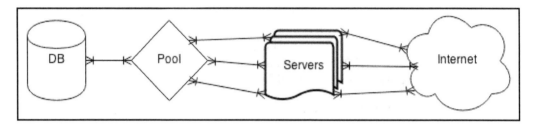

By inserting a connection pool in front of the database, hundreds of PostgreSQL server processes are reduced to just dozens. A database pool works by recycling database connections as soon as the client completes its current transaction or when its database work is complete. Instead of hundreds of mostly idle database connections, we maintain a specific set of highly active connections.

The principal tool that provides pooling capability for PostgreSQL is **PgBouncer**. We will explore data node abstraction as well as pooling resources in this chapter to fully maximize our availability and application responsiveness.

In this chapter, we will learn to combine and abstract connectivity to isolate and protect the database. We will cover the following recipes in this chapter:

- Exploring the magic of virtual IPs
- Obtaining and installing HAProxy
- Configuring HAProxy to load balance PostgreSQL
- Determining connection costs and limits
- Installing PgBouncer
- Configuring PgBouncer safely
- Connecting to PgBouncer
- Listing PgBouncer server connections

- Listing PgBouncer client connections
- Evaluating PgBouncer pool health
- Changing PgBouncer connections while online
- Enhancing PgBouncer authentication

Exploring the magic of virtual IPs

In Chapter 1, *Architectural Considerations*, we included a recipe on *Introducing Indirection*. One of the simplest methods for attaining indirect access to our data is by assigning a virtual network address to whichever server hosts our current primary PostgreSQL node.

Therefore, whenever a standby node is promoted to primary status, we can move the network address to the new server. No applications need to be reconfigured, no connections must be changed, and all connections are routed to the writable node in our cluster.

Another semi-popular method is to change the **Domain Name System** (**DNS**) to redirect network connections to the new server. The beauty of this technique is that it fully insulates the entire access path so that the reorganization of the entire network can include IP addresses. The main drawback of this approach is that DNS changes are slow, even with extremely low **time-to-live** (**TTL**) settings. It can take several minutes for DNS updates to fully propagate through various hardware, software, and caches.

Instead, we can tie the subdomain to an IP address that isn't associated with any particular server. Then, it's simply a matter of changing the server that claims it owns that IP address. If we assign a permanent DNS to that IP as well, we can still use DNS updates for major migrations at a later time. And, better yet, virtual IPs are something we can control directly.

Getting ready

We only need the `ip` and `arping` command-line tools to perform this process. These utilities may not be present by default, so install them before you continue.

If you are on a Debian or Ubuntu system, issue this command:

```
sudo apt-get install iproute arping
```

Red Hat and CentOS users can use this:

```
sudo yum install iproute iputils
```

 Previous versions of this recipe used the `ifconfig` tool instead. This has been deprecated in favor of `ip` based on recent Linux distribution trends.

How to do it...

For these steps, assume `eth0` is the primary network interface and `10.0.0.10` is the IP we are trying to claim. Follow these steps to move or create a virtual IP:

1. First, connect to the PostgreSQL node that had the IP address earlier. This is often the primary server.
2. Release the IP address with the following command:

   ```
   sudo ip addr del 10.0.0.10/32 dev eth0
   ```

3. Ping the desired IP address with the following command:

   ```
   ping -c 3 10.0.0.10
   ```

4. If the preceding command reaches a PostgreSQL server, connect to that system and repeat *step 2* to *step 3*.
5. Next, connect to the new server that should own the IP address.
6. Claim the IP address with the following command:

   ```
   sudo ip addr add 10.0.0.10/32 dev eth0 label eth0:pgvip
   ```

7. Tell the network about the location of the new IP address using this command:

   ```
   sudo arping -c 3 -A -I eth0 10.0.0.10
   ```

How it works...

If we haven't created a virtual IP yet, we can skip the first three steps. Otherwise, in order to use an IP address, it must be available. Setting up the same IP address on multiple servers can wreak havoc on network traffic routing.

It's important to never operate while two PostgreSQL servers claim the same IP address.

Next, we ping the desired address to ensure that there are no replies. This should prove that our IP address is free for use. It should end with something like this:

```
--- 10.0.0.10 ping statistics ---
3 packets transmitted, 0 received, +3 errors, 100% packet loss,
    time 2015ms
```

We want to see 100 percent packet loss. This means that the IP address is currently unclaimed. If this results in an active server, we need to repeat the command that we used to shut down the existing virtual IPs there as well.

Provided the address is available, we simply connect to the desired server and use `ip` to create a new virtual IP. We named the virtual IP `pgvip` and attached it to the `eth0` interface, using `10.0.0.10` as the target address to claim.

After this step, the IP address may only be visible on the local server, so we need to tell the upstream switches and routers that the IP is in use. The `arping` command does precisely this when passed to the `-A` parameter. We use the `-c` setting to send three gratuitous broadcasts to help ensure that at least one is accepted. Like `ip`, we need to tell `arping` to use `eth0` with the `-I` parameter; otherwise, traffic may be misrouted.

There's more...

This is really only a demonstration of virtual IP functionality. In the case of a server reboot, network assignments created directly through `ip` will disappear. For our purposes, this is actually the desired result. If a PostgreSQL server tried claiming a virtual IP address upon reboot and we had already assigned it to a different system, traffic could go to either system and result in severe consequences.

Would either database handle the requests? Would the misrouted network packets cause invalid data or some other result? Well, we don't know that network routing can affect any level of the communication process. The end result is that the database is unusable in this state.

Regardless, the process of maintaining virtual IP addresses is easily automated. Later in this book, we will discuss at least one tool that automatically assigns a virtual IP or some other indirection method to the current primary PostgreSQL server. Until then, this is still a very powerful tool to add to our arsenal.

Obtaining and installing HAProxy

Another great way of abstracting PostgreSQL is to place it behind a proxy to redirect traffic to the primary read/write node in our cluster. One of the most popular of these proxies is HAProxy, a generic proxy software that was originally designed for load balancing web servers.

It's also a highly versatile layer that we'll be using in several other recipes in this book. Not only does it ensure we always reach the primary node regardless of its location, but we can also leverage its functionality to spread read queries across multiple PostgreSQL replicas.

This recipe will explain the basic installation of this high-availability connection proxy, which we can then extend later on.

Getting ready

If this is a Debian-based system, begin by installing HAProxy from the standard system repository with the following `apt-get` command:

```
sudo apt-get install haproxy
```

For Red-Hat-based servers, use an equivalent `yum` command:

```
sudo yum install haproxy
```

While distribution-provided versions of HAProxy are fully functional, they're also extremely antiquated in many cases. If HAProxy appears to have an apparent bug, it may be necessary to build it from the source. We've found this isn't generally necessary for using PostgreSQL since we aren't using the more advanced or enterprise-enabled functionality.

How to do it...

For this recipe, we will need only one PostgreSQL server, and one server for HAProxy. We'll assume the PostgreSQL server is named pgha1, and the HAProxy is named pgha-proxy. In addition to this, the IP address for pg1 is 10.0.30.1, while pgha-proxy uses 10.0.30.20. Follow these steps to configure HAProxy on the pgha-proxy server:

1. Create a PostgreSQL database role on pgha1 by executing this SQL:

   ```
   CREATE ROLE haproxy_check;
   ```

2. Create or modify a file named haproxy.cfg in the /etc/haproxy directory with the following content:

   ```
   global
       maxconn 100

   defaults
       log       global
       mode      tcp
       retries 2
       timeout client 30m
       timeout connect 4s
       timeout server 30m
       timeout check 5s

   frontend ft_postgresql
       bind *:5432
       default_backend bk_db

   backend bk_db
       option pgsql-check user haproxy_check

       server postgresql_primary pgha1:5432 check
   ```

3. If this is an older Debian-based system, set the ENABLED variable to 1 in the /etc/default/haproxy file.

4. Start (or restart) HAProxy with the following command as a root-enabled user:

   ```
   sudo systemctl restart haproxy
   ```

5. Try to connect to pgha1 using psql from pgha-proxy:

   ```
   psql -h pgha-proxy -U postgres -c "SELECT inet_server_addr()"
   ```

How it works...

HAProxy has a very powerful configuration syntax, which is backed by hundreds of parameters. While this makes it quite versatile, trying to write a configuration file from scratch would be extremely difficult. In our case, the number of parameters we need to set is actually fairly minimal.

We start by creating a simple `role` named `haproxy_check` so HAProxy can attempt to connect to PostgreSQL and verify the server is responding. HAProxy uses its own connection method that has some compatibility problems if no username is specified. PostgreSQL roles are not allowed to connect to any database by default, but are sufficient to pass a connectivity *attempt*. Once HAProxy has attempted to connect to PostgreSQL and has received an expected response, it considers the server to be online. Using a role in this way is completely safe, though, somewhat unorthodox.

Next, we set the global connection limit to 100 connections. This is the number of connections HAProxy will manage before simply allowing them to queue in the kernel buffer. Generally, we would want to set this to the same value we use with `max_connections` in `postgresql.conf`, but it's not required.

We continue by configuring the `log` parameter to `global` so all HAProxy instances write to the same log output. HAProxy is an HTTP proxy system at heart, so we must ensure `mode` is set to `tcp`, so HAProxy doesn't try to interpret the actual traffic as though it were HTTP headers.

After these essentials are set, we also define a number of connection retry and timeout values. These are all subject to usage patterns, so feel free to modify them to better fit your cluster needs. Of special note are the `server` and `client` timeouts, which will break the connection if either the client or server is idle for over 30 minutes. We also set the `connect` timeout to 4 seconds so that HAProxy doesn't wait forever to establish a connection. And, finally, we set the `check` timeout to 5 seconds so that, once a connection is established, it isn't alive for much longer than is necessary before being disconnected.

 Databases that commonly host persistent connections may need to greatly increase `client` and `server` timeout values or set them to `0` to disable the feature altogether.

Once we've taken care of the default connection handling behavior, we must define frontend and backend actions. On the frontend, HAProxy will be handling incoming connections, so we create a new frontend named `ft_postgresql`.

Within this definition, we set `bind` to `*:5432` to listen to all available interfaces on port `5432` so it looks like just another PostgreSQL node. Then, we link the frontend to a backend that we'll name `bk_db`.

On the backend, HAProxy will be forwarding connections to our primary writable PostgreSQL server. To handle this, we create a new backend named `bk_db`, which we already referenced in the `frontend` configuration section. The only option we set here is `pgsql-check`, which is the method HAProxy should use to confirm server health. This is a special option built specifically for checking PostgreSQL servers.

The only other line in the `backend` section refers to our PostgreSQL server. Each server line comes in three distinct sections. First is the server name, second is the host and port for the service, and, third, is the further options for the definition. We chose rather boring server names such as `postgresql_primary` to make it obvious what is expected.

After starting the `haproxy` service on all of the cluster servers, it's a good idea to run a quick test to ensure the proxy is working as expected. To do this, we connect to `pgha1` through `pgha-proxy` and execute the `inet_server_addr` function to obtain the IP address of the server we've contacted. Since this is the port HAProxy is monitoring, we should have been redirected to `pgha1` and received `10.0.30.1` as the result. A successful result should resemble this output:

```
bones@pgha-proxy: psql -h pgha-proxy -U postgres -c "SELECT inet_server_addr()"

 inet_server_addr
------------------
 10.0.30.1
```

See also

HAProxy is available as an open-source product, but it also has an Enterprise Edition for more advanced functionality. We haven't used any of this here, but you may still find it useful. There is also other documentation available on how to use more advanced configuration. Take a look at the following for more information:

- **HAProxy**: `https://www.haproxy.com/`

- **HAProxy documentation**: `https://cbonte.github.io/haproxy-dconv/`

Configuring HAProxy to load balance PostgreSQL

Given that we're attempting to build a highly available cluster of PostgreSQL nodes, it's very likely we'll have a veritable horde of replicas for various purposes. Some will exist as dedicated standby nodes, one may be a quorum witness, others could be remote disaster-recovery alternates, and so on.

It would be a shame if all of these resources were not utilized in some manner. We've bought multiple servers, and strategically placed them in important locations while taking their dedicated roles into consideration.

Perhaps more importantly, not every application requires the ability to write to the database. Interactive applications are far more likely to present information obtained from the database multiple times before incorporating changes. If we facilitate that behavior by ensuring read requests are always available, we're one step closer to high availability.

Now it's time to extract the full value from the nodes so that they don't simply sit idly. This recipe will explain how to leverage HAProxy such that read requests are always served by one PostgreSQL node or another.

Getting ready

Since this recipe depends on the presence and operation of HAProxy, we recommend following the *Obtaining and installing HAProxy* recipe in this chapter before continuing. Otherwise, this procedure is fairly simple.

How to do it...

We will demonstrate this recipe by using three PostgreSQL servers and one server for HAProxy. We'll make these assumptions:

- There are three PostgreSQL servers with the following attributes:
  - pgha1 at 10.0.30.1
  - pgha2 at 10.0.30.2
  - pgha3 at 10.0.30.3
- There is a dedicated HAProxy node named pgha-proxy.

Follow these steps to configure HAProxy on the `pgha-proxy` server:

1. Add the following block near the end of the `/etc/haproxy/haproxy.cfg` file:

```
frontend ft_pg_ro
    bind *:5500
    default_backend bk_pg_ro

backend bk_pg_ro
    balance leastconn
    option pgsql-check user haproxy_check

    server postgresql_pgha1 pgha1:5432 check
    server postgresql_pgha2 pgha2:5432 check
    server postgresql_pgha3 pgha3:5432 check
```

2. Trigger HAProxy to reload the configuration file with the following command as a root-enabled user:

```
sudo systemctl reload haproxy
```

3. Try to connect to the new proxy using `psql` from `pgha-proxy`:

```
psql -h pgha-proxy -p 5500 -U postgres \
    -c "SELECT inet_server_addr()"
```

4. Repeat the previous step two or three more times to observe different connection targets.

How it works...

This recipe is simple but very powerful; it lets us leverage our other PostgreSQL replicas even if we originally intended only to use them for high availability. In this example, we will start with three PostgreSQL servers, which we can imagine to be the primary node and two standby systems.

Given that we already followed the *Obtaining and installing HAProxy* recipe, we already have a working HAProxy node that we can reuse for redirecting the database read traffic. This kind of dual-purpose use isn't something we could have done with a virtual IP address, especially given the load balancing we're about to enable.

Since HAProxy works in frontend/backend pairs, we begin by creating a second frontend named ft_pg_ro (for frontend, PostgreSQL, read-only) that utilizes the backend named bk_pg_ro (for backend, PostgreSQL, read-only). We also bind to port 5500 since the standard PostgreSQL port of 5432 is already used by the configuration we built for the primary node.

Then, we set up the bk_pg_ro backend itself by listing all of our PostgreSQL nodes. The trick here is that we set the balance algorithm to leastconn, which sends database sessions to whichever node has the least number of connections. If multiple nodes have the same amount, it reverts to simply assigning them in a round-robin manner. And, as in our previous recipe, we want to enable the pgsql-check feature so that HAProxy doesn't accidentally attempt to send connections to a node that isn't fully online.

Once our configuration is complete, we simply need to use systemctl to reload the HAProxy service itself so it integrates the changes we made. Then, we do something very interesting by connecting to the proxy server and specifying the read-only port designation. If we repeat this command several times, we should observe a different connection result each time, as shown in the following screenshot:

```
#> psql -h pgha-proxy -p 5500 -U postgres -c "SELECT inet_server_addr()"

 inet_server_addr
------------------
 10.0.30.1
(1 row)

#> psql -h pgha-proxy -p 5500 -U postgres -c "SELECT inet_server_addr()"

 inet_server_addr
------------------
 10.0.30.2
(1 row)

#> psql -h pgha-proxy -p 5500 -U postgres -c "SELECT inet_server_addr()"

 inet_server_addr
------------------
 10.0.30.3
(1 row)
```

This helps to illustrate that HAProxy is doing exactly as we asked. Now, if the application has a read-heavy component, we can configure it to utilize port 5500 and spread that workload to several systems. Due to the proxy, we can even create several more PostgreSQL replicas dedicated to this purpose to augment the members of the high-availability stack itself.

There's more

It is fairly obvious that the use of port `5500` isn't ideal. Our choice was arbitrary, and, therefore, there's a small amount of potential for misconfiguration in some other part of the application stack; some even expect defaults when possible.

To that end, we encourage the use of multiple HAProxy servers. Modern servers are often deployed as a low-resource virtual system, and proxy nodes are an especially good match for that approach. Proxy software doesn't require much overhead in the way of CPU, RAM, or storage bandwidth, so we can simply create more of them.

Always test HAProxy before introducing too many abstraction elements into a software stack. However, you may find that it's better to create a dedicated HAProxy node for each purpose, one for write traffic and another for read traffic. Perhaps we could even use one proxy node per subcategory of the application stack to target specific PostgreSQL nodes, or stay within a particular data center.

We've even seen situations where HAProxy is installed locally on each application server with a configuration like the one we shared here. This is especially prevalent in microarchitectures that want to minimize single-point-of-failure risks by duplicating everything. Architectures like this will simply rebuild the full application node if it misbehaves, and HAProxy is part of the total package. The database servers are on another layer, and HAProxy is no longer a node, but more of a pathfinder.

Determining connection costs and limits

Excessive database connections are not without risk. The level of risk we incur and what exactly qualifies as excessive are important to determine early. The company and our customers will find it extremely inconvenient if normal database activity exhausts system memory, causes timeouts due to increased context-switching, or overwhelms the kernel with an overly large process table.

To maintain a highly available server, we must know the full impact of every single connection in terms of required memory and CPU resources. Servicing several disparate applications from various external servers is difficult, so we must provide availability while simultaneously avoiding resource exhaustion. If we properly assess the ideal balance between connection count and performance early on, we can avoid costly emergencies.

Irrespective of whether we helped specify the hardware that will host our PostgreSQL installation, it's still our job to figure out how many clients it can comfortably support. Since this chapter is primarily focused on database pools, we can use this opportunity to choose a practical pool size as well.

Getting ready

We will make a few rough calculations in this section. If possible, obtain data regarding the number of CPU cores, available RAM, and the number of disk spindles in the storage pool.

Linux systems have a live filesystem that tracks most of this information. To obtain the number of CPUs, simply execute this at the command line, and add one to the highest value since indexing starts at zero:

```
grep ^processor /proc/cpuinfo
```

For the amount of RAM in kilobytes, use this command:

```
grep MemTotal /proc/meminfo
```

Finding the number of disk spindles can vary greatly between RAID and **storage area network** (**SAN**) implementations, so we suggest obtaining the number from the infrastructure department.

How to do it...

Start by calculating the number of connections that the RAM can accommodate by following these steps:

1. Begin the estimate with 8 MB used per connection.
2. Add four times the value of the `work_mem` PostgreSQL configuration setting in megabytes, for a per-client total.
3. Obtain the amount of RAM in megabytes.
4. Divide half of the RAM size by the per-client MB total.

Next, calculate the number of connections the CPU and disk resources can support by following these steps:

1. Obtain the CPU count in cores, including virtual if present.
2. Double the CPU core count.
3. Add the number of disk spindles.
4. If storage is SSD-based, add 100.

Use the lower of the two values as the final ideal connection count.

How it works...

To know how much RAM a connection may use, we start with a baseline of 8 megabytes. This accounts for the library overhead, the likelihood of using a temporary tablespace, and other various allocations necessary for a session to function. To that, we add four times the work_mem setting. PostgreSQL allocates an instance of work_mem for each join, sort, merge, and several other operations necessary to execute a query.

Why four? Well, large and complex queries will use more, while short and simple queries will use less, so we start with something in the middle. It's actually possible that this multiplier is somewhat pessimistic, so it trends toward assuming higher memory use. That's fine, since overestimating, in this case, is safer than running out of memory in the presence of several simultaneous complex queries.

With this total, we can see how many connections will use half of the available RAM. We only use half of the system RAM here, since the database itself needs memory. In addition, queries are much faster when tables are available in the operating system page cache. If too much RAM is reserved for client use, query performance can suffer considerably.

In the next set of calculations, we start with the CPU total and double this amount. The more disk spindles available, the less time each CPU spends waiting for results. By adding the number of disks, we get an approximation of how many connections our CPUs can actually support without excessive idling caused by insufficient storage performance. Every time the CPU must wait for storage IO, that's less time it's performing valuable work.

We also recognize modern hardware is likely to reside on solid-state storage. This can dramatically improve session responsiveness and thus increase our production throughput when handling innumerable connections.

By taking the lower of these two calculations (based on RAM, or CPU and IO capabilities), we account for whatever bottleneck will constrain system performance the most. This is our ideal connection count, and it works as a first approximation for the size of any connection pool we create.

There's more...

For an example of this in action, consider a system with 32 GB of RAM, 8 CPU cores, and 8 disk spindles. We used 8 MB for our `work_mem` setting, so this means we may need up to 40 MB per database connection. 16 GB of RAM can then safely support about 409 connections, assuming memory is our only resource limit.

Otherwise, our 8 CPUs and 8 disks can support up to 24 connections. This is quite a discrepancy! However, 24 is the safer of the two limits to prevent latency. If we find that a certain amount of latency is not overly disruptive, we can increase the connection count, but not higher than 400; otherwise, we risk actually exhausting the available RAM. The ideal value is likely to be between these two extremes and will require many rounds of testing to derive; database performance is highly dependent on data and query composition.

 Please keep in mind that the focus of this book is high availability at nearly all costs, and, as such, our formulas are extremely pessimistic. We encourage experimentation with these values; you may find a better balance than what we suggest here.

Installing PgBouncer

The first pooling resource we will explore is called **PgBouncer**. This is a very popular connection pool written by Skype developers in 2007. The project has been maintained by various developers in subsequent years, but its role in lowering the cost of connecting to PostgreSQL has never changed.

PgBouncer allows PostgreSQL to interact with enormous number of clients than is otherwise possible because its connection overhead is much lower. Instead of huge libraries, accounting for temporary tables, query results, and other expensive resources, it essentially just tracks each client's connection in a queue. Then, based on the configuration settings, it creates several PostgreSQL connections and assigns them to the connections on a first-come, first-served basis.

This means hundreds, or even thousands of database clients, can theoretically share a single PostgreSQL connection. Of course, we will never suggest implementing a ratio that absurd without testing it, yet this possibility presents several new opportunities for better resource allocation.

The first step for getting this exciting new functionality is the installation of the software. PgBouncer is popular enough for most Linux systems to package it along with other PostgreSQL tools, so we will cover some of the most popular distributions. For the sake of completeness, we also intend to cover pure source installations, which means we can utilize the latest release regardless of the distribution.

Getting ready

PgBouncer has recently been incorporated into the official PostgreSQL PGDG package distribution resource. As a result, we no longer recommend compiling from source as was done with previous revisions of this recipe. We suggest enabling the PGDG repository if this hasn't already been done.

Simply follow the instructions for the appropriate Linux distribution here: `https://www.postgresql.org/download/linux/`.

How to do it...

The steps necessary here are refreshingly short. Simply follow along:

1. To install in a Debian- or Ubuntu-based system, execute this command:

   ```
   sudo apt-get install pgbouncer
   ```

2. To install in a Red Hat, CentOS, Fedora, or another RHEL-based system, execute this command:

   ```
   sudo yum install pgbouncer
   ```

3. Optionally, make the configuration directory owned by the `postgres` system user:

   ```
   sudo chown postgres:postgres /etc/pgbouncer
   ```

4. Create a `pgbouncer` user in our primary PostgreSQL server with this SQL:

```
CREATE USER pgbouncer WITH PASSWORD 'whatever';
```

5. If it isn't already, add the service to system startup and shutdown:

```
sudo systemctl enable pgbouncer
```

How it works...

Before we start the recipe, we recommended installing the PostgreSQL **PGDG** (short for **PostgreSQL Global Development Group**) package repository. We did that because officially supported packages are often tweaked to work best in the Linux distribution where they're installed, much like packages from a certain vendor. The primary difference here is that these will always be the latest supported versions, rather than what the Linux vendor has decided they will maintain for that particular release.

Then, we simply use the appropriate package manager to install the `pgbouncer` set of packages. We understand this is somewhat anticlimactic, but it's certainly less effort than compiling from the source and allocating a custom initialization or startup script. It's also less error-prone since the PostgreSQL package maintainers work hard to ensure PgBouncer will work as well as a native installation, rather than any workaround this book could offer. This is especially true now that most mainstream distributions have switched to systemd.

 We understand that the assumed use of systemd commands such as `systemctl` or `journalctl` may be controversial. Regardless, the most commonly deployed distributions in the Linux server space are based on Debian and Red Hat. Both of these base distributions manage system services using systemd, so that will be the convention used here as well.

Then, we believe it's frequently useful to modify configuration files within the `/etc/pgbouncer` folder while we're working within the `postgres` user account. Therefore, we alter it to have that user as the owner. This is an entirely optional step, more for the sake of convenience than anything critical, so it may be skipped for security purposes.

At this point, we want to create a `pgbouncer` user that can log in to the server. We will want this for a secure authentication system later, so we should not skip this step. Whatever password is chosen here should be retained for later recipes.

Finally, we add PgBouncer to the list of other services that start or stop when the server is shut down or booted up. This ensures the service is always available, and we don't have to remember to start or stop it ourselves. The initial installation of PgBouncer may or may not be enabled depending on our Linux distribution, so we elect to enable it just in case.

See also

The PgBouncer site contains source downloads, documentation, and much more. Feel free to visit the site to learn more about the project at `https://pgbouncer.github.io/`.

Configuring PgBouncer safely

Once PgBouncer is installed, we need to configure it to honor our ideal pool size calculations. The settings included with the supplied configuration file are for demonstration purposes only and are unlikely to match our requirements. This situation is easy to rectify, but it requires a bit of research on our part.

Getting ready

The PgBouncer settings are explained in detail in the example configuration file. However, we suggest making full use of the service documentation while following this recipe. We will endeavor to explain important parameters, but there are more parameters available than we cover here.

When we installed PgBouncer, we suggested modifying the configuration directory to be writable by the `postgres` system user, which is the same user that owns the PostgreSQL service. For the sake of simplicity, we recommend using either this user or a root-capable user that can modify files on its behalf.

We also need the calculated pool size from the *Determining connection costs and limits* recipe, so keep it handy.

How to do it...

Presuming that our calculated pool size for our `pgha1` PostgreSQL server was 25, with a memory-imposed maximum of 350, follow these steps to properly configure PgBouncer:

1. Execute this query as the `postgres` user while connected to any database within PostgreSQL:

   ```
   COPY (
       SELECT '"' || rolname || '" "' ||
              coalesce(rolpassword, '') || '"'
         FROM pg_authid
   )
   TO '/tmp/userlist.txt';
   ```

2. Copy the `/tmp/userlist.txt` output file to the `/etc/pgbouncer` directory where PgBouncer is installed, and then remove `/tmp/userlist.txt`.

3. Open the `/etc/pgbouncer/pgbouncer.ini` file as the `postgres` system user.

4. Under the section labeled `[databases]`, create the following entry:

   ```
   * = host=pgha1
   ```

5. Under the section labeled `[pgbouncer]`, locate each of these entries and change them to the following:

   ```
   listen_addr = *
   auth_type = md5
   admin_users = postgres
   max_client_conn = 1000
   default_pool_size = 25
   reserve_pool_size = 5
   ```

6. Start the PgBouncer service by executing the following at the command line as a root-capable user:

   ```
   sudo systemctl start pgbouncer
   ```

How it works...

The first thing we do is create an authentication file that PgBouncer can use. As a third-party daemon, it does not have direct access to PostgreSQL authentication. Yet, it must still authenticate users before assigning pool resources. Unfortunately, this means we need to create a copy of the current users and their encrypted passwords that PgBouncer can use. This file should be regenerated any time new users are created or passwords are changed.

 Frequently regenerating this file will probably be extremely inconvenient in many environments. We recommend either automating this process or relying on **Lightweight Directory Access Protocol (LDAP)**, **Pluggable Authentication Modules (PAM)**, or some other service that PgBouncer can forward on behalf of the upstream PostgreSQL server.

The next thing we do is alter the pgbouncer.ini file where the configuration settings are stored. The first portion that concerns us is the [databases] section, which keeps track of every database that PgBouncer has mapped. This can be a one-to-one association or an alias that changes various connection parameters such as port, host, or username. Feel free to experiment. The value we used will simply map all of the connections to the pgha1 server.

All of the subsequent settings are to change the operation of PgBouncer. By changing listen_addr, PgBouncer will monitor all IP addresses assigned to this server. If we make use of virtual IPs, this is especially important. Later, we ensure that auth_type is set to md5 so that all of the encrypted passwords we exported are actually used. We set admin_users to postgres because PgBouncer has an administration console that we can use to control pooling behavior. For now, setting it to the superuser database is a good start.

The max_client_conn setting does not restrict PostgreSQL clients, but it does restrict PgBouncer clients. This is mainly to prevent clients from waiting too long before being assigned a connection. If throughput is generally good, feel free to increase this.

The `default_pool_size` setting and the `reserve_pool_size` setting are actually per-user and per-database. Therefore, even if we only have one primary database in our instance, every user can have 25 connections before PgBouncer puts them in the wait queue. If the number of PostgreSQL connections gets too high and starts affecting query throughput, we may need to reduce these settings. It may be best to reserve the pool for applications that need it, so we have better control of the PostgreSQL connections that it might create.

Once the settings are saved, we start PgBouncer. When we do that, it will watch port `6432` for new PostgreSQL connections. This is the default, just in case PgBouncer is installed on the same server as our database instance. If installed on a dedicated proxy node, it may make more sense to change this parameter to `5432`.

There's more...

Now that PgBouncer is running, there are a couple of things that require further explanation.

What about pool_mode?

Perceptive readers probably noticed the `pool_mode` configuration setting both in the documentation and in the example file. The possible options for this setting can essentially be summarized as follows:

- **Session**: A PostgreSQL setting is assigned to a client until the client disconnects. This is considered to be the safest method, but greedy applications can monopolize limited connections by never freeing them. This is the default, and we don't change it in our instructions.
- **Transaction**: Connections are assigned to clients until they complete a single transaction. Once the transaction is either committed or aborted, the connection re-enters the pool and is assigned to another client. This is a good setting to use for applications that insist on holding persistent database connections as it still enables connection cycling within the pool. Unfortunately, some applications that use cursors expect them to persist between transactions for fetching purposes. Since the connection is reset between every transaction, these cursors are also deallocated and the application will not function normally.

- **Statement**: After every single SQL statement completes, the connection re-enters the pool for reassignment to another client. There are few, if any, valid situations where this setting should be used. Only servers that never make use of features such as transactions, cursors, or prepared queries should use this value. Most PostgreSQL systems can avoid it completely.

Problems with prepared statements

Database applications and object-relational mappers that use prepared queries will have a problem if we enable transaction-level pooling. Once a statement is prepared for execution, it can be reused until it is deallocated. We know that connections are reset between sessions by default, so these prepared statements are lost. We can fix this by changing `server_reset_query` in `/etc/pgbouncer/pgbouncer.ini` to the following:

```
server_reset_query =
```

By setting a blank value, objects allocated between transactions can persist. However, this also means that the application should check for a prepared statement before creating it. Since the connections are recycled, the application may be assigned a connection where prepared statements are not in their expected states. This is a lot of extra work on the application side, so we generally don't suggest using transaction mode while prepared statements or cursors are present.

See also

Although our suggestions on proper configuration will get things working, there are more options available. We suggest reading the following documentation to learn more about PgBouncer:

- **PgBouncer configuration file**: `https://pgbouncer.github.io/config.html`
- **PgBouncer FAQ**: `https://pgbouncer.github.io/faq.html`

Connecting to PgBouncer

Once PgBouncer is installed, configured, and operational, we still need to utilize it. So, how do we connect to PgBouncer instead of PostgreSQL? Let's explore that next.

Getting ready

Make sure PgBouncer is configured and running. Take a look at the *Configure PgBouncer safely* recipe. Then, execute this at the command line to check for the service:

```
pgrep -alf pgbouncer
```

We should see a line similar to this:

```
21281 /usr/bin/pgbouncer -d /etc/pgbouncer/pgbouncer.ini
```

If this is not the case, we need help beyond the scope of this book. Feel free to check the PgBouncer mailing list for assistance. The community is willing to help too, so let them.

How to do it...

If our PgBouncer server is on `pgha-proxy`, we can connect to PgBouncer by using port `6432`. We can connect to the `postgres` database through PgBouncer with the `psql` command:

```
psql -p 6432 -h pgha-proxy postgres
```

With GUI or other utilities, we simply need to change our host target to the PgBouncer server, and the port should be `6432`.

How it works...

PgBouncer works like a simulated PostgreSQL server. Thus, any standard PostgreSQL client or driver should be fully compatible. The only difference is that the default port is `6432` instead of `5432`. Effectively, this makes PgBouncer a connection proxy, and it can be treated as such.

See also

After we connect to PgBouncer, we may want community assistance with common problems. While the PgBouncer-specific mailing list is no longer available, the PostgreSQL community lists are very active. For more information, you can refer to https://www.postgresql.org/list/.

Listing PgBouncer server connections

PgBouncer provides an administration console to view pool status or control the service. For now, we will focus on viewing the list of server connections that PgBouncer maintains. These connections are held for distribution to database clients as necessary, and they can tell us much more about the health of the pool. Let's explore the PgBouncer console a bit.

Getting ready

We need to know how to connect to PgBouncer instead of PostgreSQL, so check the *Connect to PgBouncer* recipe for a refresher. In this section, we will use something known as a pseudo-database. When in use, PgBouncer reserves the database name, pgbouncer, for its own internal purposes in order to access its administration console. This database does not actually exist, but it will still connect from the perspective of our PostgreSQL client.

In the highly unlikely event that the pgbouncer database actually exists within your PostgreSQL installation, we recommend renaming it to avoid confusion.

How to do it...

Follow these steps to get the status of PgBouncer connections to PostgreSQL on the pgha-proxy server:

1. Connect to the pgbouncer database on port 6432 of the pgha-proxy server as the postgres user.
2. Issue the following query:

```
SHOW SERVERS;
```

How it works...

By connecting to the pgbouncer database name on port 6432, we connect to PgBouncer using a simulated database that doesn't actually exist. This name tells PgBouncer that we want the administration console. If we configured PgBouncer according to the *Configure PgBouncer safely* recipe, the postgres user is the only database user allowed to use the console.

The author wishes that this information was also available as a view so that we could fetch only interesting fields, but the PgBouncer syntax is easier to type. By sending SHOW SERVERS as a query, PgBouncer responds with a list of every connection to PostgreSQL it is using to fulfill client requests. Fields of particular interest include the following:

- user: This column lists the users that are currently connected to the database. If we used advanced settings, this could differ from the user that connected to PgBouncer.
- database: This shows the database that the connection is attached to. A PostgreSQL server can host many databases, so this is very helpful information. Again, advanced settings can change this from the database name used to create the connection to PgBouncer.
- state: This column answers the following question: is the connection active, used, or idle? Connections are marked as active when they are assigned to a client. Connections marked as used have handled at least one query, but haven't been checked for validity. Used connections are still idle and available; they merely haven't been verified by PgBouncer. The idle status means the connection is verified as available, and it hasn't been used recently. On active servers, PgBouncer connections will almost never be marked as idle.
- connect_time: It displays the exact time PgBouncer created the connection to PostgreSQL. We can use this to determine connection freshness. If most of these are recent, it means that the connections are probably opening and closing too frequently. Connections to PostgreSQL are relatively expensive to allocate, and connection pools are partially meant to reduce this cost. We may need to consider changing some of the PgBouncer connection timeout settings based on the contents of this field.
- request_time: This column provides the last time the listed connection handled query activity. On busy servers, this should always be a very recent timestamp. Otherwise, we are potentially wasting server resources by maintaining unnecessary idle connections. In this case, we need to examine the pool size settings and consider reducing them. Alternatively, there may be a problem with the marked PostgreSQL connection, or the assigned client can be frozen. This indicates that we need to check the database health, or ask the development or support departments to investigate applications for normal operation.

Feel free to browse the PgBouncer documentation for other available fields.

There's more...

We like referring readers to external resources on occasion. Unfortunately, the PgBouncer documentation is incomplete in important ways. Our explanation of the **state** field is a good example of this. The interpretation we used for that field came from a post in the mailing list by one of the authors. Keep this in mind when seeking assistance not covered by this book. Mailing lists can fill a huge void left by Spartan documents meant to cover the bare necessities.

See also

We know that we've listed these documentation links before, but we're still working with complicated configuration settings and usage. We've listed them here again for convenience:

- **PgBouncer usage**: https://pgbouncer.github.io/usage.html
- **PostgreSQL mailing lists**: https://www.postgresql.org/list/

Listing PgBouncer client connections

In addition to PostgreSQL server connection status, PgBouncer's administration console can provide details regarding clients within its queue. Maintaining a healthy and active PgBouncer queue is the key to high throughput over limited resources. In this case, we artificially limited the number of server connections available to clients, which means that there is a potential for stubborn or broken clients to prevent connection turnover.

This will, of course, effectively remove the connections from the pool, creating a bottleneck that could lead to choking the transaction throughput. This recipe will explore the PgBouncer console in a bit more detail so that you can understand what it knows about the database clients attempting to communicate with PostgreSQL.

Getting ready

In this section, we will continue our previous exploration into the PgBouncer console. Check the *Listing PgBouncer client connections* recipe for a refresher. Remember to use the pgbouncer database name to enter the administration console.

How to do it...

Follow these steps to get the status of PgBouncer clients:

1. Connect to the `pgbouncer` database on port `6432` of the PostgreSQL server as the `postgres` user.
2. Issue the following query:

```
SHOW CLIENTS;
```

How it works...

As before, we connect to the `pgbouncer` database name on port `6432` to use the administration console. By sending `SHOW CLIENTS` as a query, PgBouncer responds with a list of every client using or waiting for a PostgreSQL connection. Fields of particular interest include the following:

- `user`: This displays the user that is currently connected to the database. If we used advanced settings, this could differ from the user that is connected to PgBouncer.
- `database`: This column indicates the database that the client is attached to. A PostgreSQL server can host many databases, so this is very helpful information. Again, advanced settings can change this from the database name used to create the connection to PgBouncer.
- `state`: This column shows whether the connection is active, used, waiting, or idle. Clients are marked as active when they are currently using a connection. If the client is queued prior to a connection becoming available, they are marked as waiting. The used and idle status assignments do not seem to actually be valid for the client state, so don't worry about them.
- `connect_time`: This provides the exact time PgBouncer created the connection to PostgreSQL. Although we specifically ask about the client status, this element is associated with the connection to PostgreSQL. Since connections are recycled, they can be hours or even days old. In determining health, we actually want slightly older connections in this list, as that suggests low connection turnover, and connection turnover can be expensive.

- `request_time`: This lists the last time the listed client transmitted query activity. On busy servers, this should always be a very recent timestamp. Otherwise, we are potentially wasting server resources by maintaining unnecessary idle connections. In this case, we need to examine the pool size settings and consider reducing them. Alternatively, there may be a problem with the marked PostgreSQL connection, or the assigned client could be frozen. This will indicate that we need to investigate the database health, poll the development, or support departments to check applications for normal operation.

Feel free to browse the PgBouncer documentation for other available fields.

There's more...

If this recipe looked familiar, that's because the important fields are exactly the same as those in the *Listing PgBouncer server connections* recipe. Though their interpretation is slightly different, and the list itself is probably more dynamic due to active client states, it's effectively the same data.

The primary difference is the waiting state that we discussed, which doesn't exist when listing server connections. If there are too many clients waiting for too long, it can be a sign of a potential issue. Perhaps the connection pool is too small, resulting in insufficient connection assignments. Maybe a client has gone haywire and is opening hundreds of connections and never closing them, which could lock up all of the available connections in the pool.

Whatever the case is, we look for regular state transitions between waiting and active. It is unfortunate that there is no field that details the connection assignment time. With this datum, we could readily discover the clients that are unfairly monopolizing database resources.

See also

We know that we've listed these documentation links before, but we're still working with complicated configuration settings and usage. We've listed them again for convenience:

- **PgBouncer usage**: `https://pgbouncer.github.io/usage.html`
- **PostgreSQL mailing lists**: `https://www.postgresql.org/list/`

Evaluating PgBouncer pool health

Though PgBouncer provides similar information regarding both server and client database connections, the status and health of each pool are also available. If we didn't already clarify, PgBouncer pools are separated by username, database name, and the server's hostname. Thus, each PostgreSQL server may have as many connection pools as there are different databases a user might access via PgBouncer.

PgBouncer supplies somewhat detailed information when seeking server or client status. However, these are not database views, so we can't summarize or aggregate the output to make it more usable. When running a highly available database server, we need to monitor aggregate values if possible to watch for potential patterns of misconfiguration or abuse.

Unfortunately, since PgBouncer acts as a proxy, we can't rely on the pg_stat_activity system view for summaries. This means PgBouncer and its administrative consoles are the main sources of debugging and status information. Thankfully, there is quite a lot of useful information.

This recipe will explore what information we can gather about our database pools and usage statistics.

Getting ready

As before, we continue to use the PgBouncer administration console, so we recommend following the *Listing PgBouncer client connections* recipe before continuing here. Remember to use the pgbouncer database name to enter the administration console.

How to do it...

Follow these steps to get the status of PgBouncer clients:

1. Connect to the pgbouncer database on port 6432 of the PgBouncer server as the postgres user.
2. Issue the following query for the pool status:

   SHOW POOLS;

3. Issue the following query for pool statistics:

```
SHOW STATS;
```

How it works...

Connecting to the `pgbouncer` database name on port `6432` connects us to PgBouncer using a simulated database that doesn't actually exist. This name tells PgBouncer that we want the administration console. If we configured PgBouncer according to the *Configure PgBouncer safely* recipe, the `postgres` user is the only database user allowed to use the console.

By sending `SHOW POOLS` as a query, PgBouncer responds with a row for every PostgreSQL database to which it is acting as a proxy. Each column is a summary for various client and server metrics, mainly related to activity or status. Here is a detailed summary of the columns:

- `cl_active`: This column shows the number of clients that are currently assigned to a server connection. This number should not exceed the value we get by adding `default_pool_size` and `reserve_pool_size` from the `pgbouncer.ini` configuration file. If the total is regularly below the maximum, we may consider reducing the pool size.
- `cl_waiting`: It denotes the number of clients waiting for a server connection. Since this is a snapshot of the current activity, the number can fluctuate drastically between checks. However, if it regularly remains above zero, and the `maxwait` column is increasing, the pools are probably too small.
- `sv_active`: This column details how many PostgreSQL server connections are assigned to the PgBouncer clients. These clients are not necessarily active, just associated with the connection. The `cl_active` and `sv_active` columns should always be equal.
- `sv_idle`: This column provides a count of PostgreSQL server connections that are not in use at all. PgBouncer marks connections as *idle* after it sends a reset query to clear out the allocated objects and settings. Thus, not only is the connection idle but it's also immediately ready for assignment. If there are several of these, it's because PgBouncer doesn't need them; think about reducing the pool size.

- `sv_used`: This indicates the count of *dirty* PostgreSQL server connections. These connections are actually idle, but they have not yet been reset by PgBouncer for reuse. This means we need to add `sv_used` to `sv_idle` to get the real count of idle connections for this database and user combination. As with `sv_idle`, a large number of used connections indicate reducing pool size limits.
- `maxwait`: This column outlines the maximum number of seconds a client has waited for a connection. Combined with the `cl_waiting` cumulative total, we can infer either an excess or shortage of throughput based on the connection availability. This statistic is constantly updated, so, if no clients are waiting, it will show zero. This kind of live feedback allows us to adjust our pool sizes to ideal levels.

By sending `SHOW STATS` as a query, PgBouncer responds with a row for every PostgreSQL database to which it is acting as a proxy. Each column is a summary of various network and time metrics. Here is a detailed summary of these columns:

- `total_xact_count`: This column represents the total number of transactions that PgBouncer has directed through the pool. As transactions are more expensive than simple queries, they can represent a larger ratio of excess work.
- `total_query_count`: SQL requests are summarized here, and this can help determine the average number of queries per transaction.
- `total_received`: This column tracks the total amount of data in bytes sent to PgBouncer through the network for this database and user combination. In order to have a healthy pool, we need to illustrate high throughput. Thus, we must also examine the next column.
- `total_sent`: This column tracks the total amount of data in bytes sent from PgBouncer to the clients accessing the database. The ratio of this value to `total_received` can indicate that PgBouncer is handling too many large queries, which reduces pool connection throughput. It's also possible that a misconfigured batch job is improperly accessing the database via PgBouncer.
- `total_query_time`: This is the amount of time in microseconds that PgBouncer has spent communicating with a client in this pool. This can be a particularly difficult column to read because it's cumulative, based on all clients accessing PostgreSQL connections. For now, we suggest ignoring it.
- `avg_req`: This column shows the average number of requests per second since the last stat update. As with `total_requests`, this is the number of transactions, not queries, handled by PgBouncer.

- `avg_recv`: This column details the average number of bytes sent to PgBouncer by each client since the last stat update. In low activity pools, this may reset to zero between samples.
- `avg_sent`: This column indicates the average number of bytes that PgBouncer has sent to each client since the last stat update. In low activity pools, this may reset to zero between samples. Along with `avg_recv`, we can again obtain a ratio of sent bandwidth versus received to look for potential excessive query output.
- `avg_query_time`: This column provides the average query duration in microseconds for all connections in this pool. This is a much more useful metric than `total_query_time` as it actually tells us the average throughput of the pool. If the average query time is 50 ms, for example, we can expect each PostgreSQL connection to handle 20 clients per second. This is valuable data to properly size the connection pools.
- `avg_wait_time`: This column maintains the average number of microseconds client sessions have waited before being assigned a server backend. Ideally we want this value to be extremely low or near zero. Higher values may indicate our pool settings are too low, or that we have too many slow queries that are limiting session reuse.

Feel free to browse the PgBouncer documentation for other available fields.

There's more...

We've mentioned adjusting pool size several times in this recipe. Since Pgpool acts as a single proxy for several database and user combinations, we can actually override the default in cases where pools require more direct management. For instance, suppose we change our entry in `/etc/pgbouncer/pgbouncer.ini` for the `postgres` database to this:

```
postgres = host=pgha1 pool_size=5
```

Then, no user connecting to the `postgres` database can use more than five connections, even if the default is 50 per pool. Keep this in mind when analyzing the pools, clients, servers, and other statistics that PgBouncer collects on our behalf. We will most likely need several adjustments before reaching an ideal state that won't overwhelm the PostgreSQL server, yet adequately supplies client requirements.

See also

We know we've listed these documentation links before, but we're still working with complicated configuration settings and usage. We've listed them again for convenience:

- **PgBouncer usage**: `https://pgbouncer.github.io/usage.html`
- **PostgreSQL mailing lists**: `https://www.postgresql.org/list/`

Changing PgBouncer connections while online

One potentially problematic aspect of PgBouncer is that each database mapping may only have one endpoint. That is, for each named server we add to its configuration, it can only represent a single PostgreSQL node.

That may seem like a strange concern on our part, but consider circumstances of advanced clusters with multiple Primary nodes. This is a completely valid configuration now that logical replication makes it possible to have two-way replication. Normally, when we reconfigure PgBouncer to send connections to a new database server, this change is absolute.

However, advances in PgBouncer versions after 1.9 make it possible to retain connections to the old PostgreSQL server, yet send new traffic to our new target. This allows for smooth transitions between servers, since transactions are allowed to complete rather than face an interruption due to our swap.

This recipe will explain how to accomplish this kind of transition bridge to deliver even better uptime for multi-master systems.

Getting ready

Since we're working with an advanced use-case of PgBouncer, we recommend either applying each of the previous PgBouncer recipes, or at least familiarizing yourself with their contents.

Secondly, the contents of this recipe only really apply to PgBouncer nodes configured in `session` pooling mode. If you're using `transaction` or `statement`, feel free to skip.

How to do it...

Imagine our PgBouncer server is on `pgha-proxy`, our *old* PostgreSQL server is `pgha1` with an IP address of `10.0.30.1`, and the *new* target is `pgha2` with an IP address of `10.0.30.2`. Follow these steps to switch servers:

1. Set the `server_fast_close` parameter in `pgbouncer.ini` to 1.

2. Make whatever changes are necessary to the `pgbouncer.ini` file. For example, we could change our global mapping to this:

   ```
   [databases]
   * = host=pgha2
   ```

3. Send the new `RECONNECT` command to PgBouncer:

   ```
   psql -U postgres -h pgha-proxy -p 6432 -c "RECONNECT;"
   pgbouncer
   ```

How it works...

We enable this functionality by setting the `server_fast_close` parameter in `pgbouncer.ini` to 1. This parameter causes PgBouncer to mark a server connection with a special `close_needed` attribute any time a session might be affected by a change to the `[databases]` section of the configuration file, or someone issues an explicit `RECONNECT`.

When this attribute is active, PgBouncer will terminate the server connection as soon as the current transaction completes. This prevents interrupting transactions that are in progress, such as long running jobs, or even any transactions in-flight from an extremely active application. It also means we don't need to wait until the client explicitly disconnects. The `server_fast_close` setting should always be enabled if you want this kind of functionality.

Next, we provide an example where we altered a connection mapping and redirected it from the `pgha1` server to `pgha2`. Once we've done this, we actually have two options. If we issue a `RELOAD` command to PgBouncer, it will detect that the server string has changed and set the `close_needed` attribute for us. If we use `RECONNECT`, it will set the `close_needed` attribute whether or not we changed anything. For this example, we simply used `RECONNECT`.

Once PgBouncer receives the RECONNECT command, we can actually connect to PgBouncer and check the status of the server backends and observe which connections will reconnect if they haven't already, as shown in the following screenshot:

```
pgbouncer=# SHOW SERVERS;

-[ RECORD 1 ]+-----------------------
type          | S
user          | postgres
database      | postgres
state         | active
addr          | 10.0.30.1
port          | 5432
local_addr    | 10.0.30.20
local_port    | 42822
connect_time  | 2019-10-08 01:33:39 UTC
request_time  | 2019-10-08 01:33:40 UTC
wait          | 0
wait_us       | 0
close_needed  | 1
ptr           | 0x17c0090
link          | 0x17b99d8
remote_pid    | 26299
tls           |
```

As we can see, PgBouncer is still connected to the old server IP address, and has marked the server as close_needed. Once that session has finished its transaction, PgBouncer will reallocate a new connection to pgha2.

There's more...

At this point, the RECONNECT command and related server_fast_close parameter probably seem extremely handy. However, the process for doing this is also completely asynchronous.

Imagine we want to perform some maintenance on pgha1 and have issued the RECONNECT command. How do we know all client sessions have finally been redirected to the new target server? We could connect to the pgbouncer admin database and repeatedly issue SHOW SERVER commands, but that's highly inconvenient.

Instead, we should use the new WAIT_CLOSE command. This command will not return until all connections have cleared their close_needed flag. This makes it a perfect tool to pause until all sessions have completed a transition from one PostgreSQL server to another. If we were to use it in a script to automate such server switches, it might look like this:

```
psql -U postgres -h pgha-proxy -p 6432 -c "WAIT_CLOSE;" pgbouncer
```

Now we could write a switchover script that moves connections from pgha1 to pgha2 and then waits until all transactions have completed before continuing to subsequent steps. This makes automation within a high availability context much more consistent.

See also

We know we've listed these links before, but these new commands are explained in greater depth in the PgBouncer documentation. We've listed them again for convenience:

- **PgBouncer configuration**: https://pgbouncer.github.io/config.html
- **PgBouncer usage**: https://pgbouncer.github.io/usage.html

Enhancing PgBouncer authentication

By default, PgBouncer is configured to maintain a file of all users that are allowed to connect. In a previous recipe, we even explain how to produce and maintain this file. However, as the amount of users increases, or, in the case where some part of the application creates users dynamically, this is highly inconvenient and potentially insecure.

Newer versions of PgBouncer improve this situation by implementing a new authentication procedure. This means we almost never need to manually update a list of users ever again. Not only does this mean we no longer maintain a list of usernames and encrypted passwords in a potentially insecure location, but we can use PostgreSQL itself to manage authentication through PgBouncer.

In this recipe, we will enable the new PgBouncer authentication system, and explore some of its other capabilities.

Getting ready

Since we're working with an advanced use-case of PgBouncer, we recommend either applying each of the previous PgBouncer recipes, or at least familiarizing yourself with their contents. Pay special attention to the *Configuring PgBouncer safely* recipe, as we'll be making further modifications to the `pgbouncer.ini` and `userlist.txt` files.

How to do it...

For this section, we will have a PgBouncer server on `pgha-proxy`, and a standard PostgreSQL server at `pgha1`.

Follow these steps to improve PgBouncer authentication:

1. Connect to `pgha1` as the `postgres` user to the `postgres` database, and execute this SQL:

   ```
   CREATE SCHEMA pgbouncer AUTHORIZATION pgbouncer;

   CREATE OR REPLACE FUNCTION pgbouncer.get_auth(p_usename TEXT)
   RETURNS TABLE(username TEXT, password TEXT) AS
   $$
   BEGIN
       RAISE NOTICE 'PgBouncer auth request: %', p_usename;
       RETURN QUERY
       SELECT usename::TEXT, passwd::TEXT
         FROM pg_catalog.pg_shadow
        WHERE usename = p_usename;
   END;
   $$ LANGUAGE plpgsql SECURITY DEFINER;

   REVOKE ALL ON FUNCTION pgbouncer.get_auth(p_usename TEXT)
     FROM PUBLIC;
   GRANT EXECUTE ON FUNCTION pgbouncer.get_auth(p_usename TEXT)
      TO pgbouncer;
   ```

2. Repeat the preceding step for any other databases where PgBouncer should be allowed to connect.

3. Remove all lines from `/etc/pgbouncer/userlist.txt` except for the entry for the `pgbouncer` user.

4. Open the `/etc/pgbouncer/pgbouncer.ini` file as the `postgres` system user.

5. Under the section labeled `[pgbouncer]`, locate each of these entries and change it to the following:

```
auth_user = pgbouncer
auth_query = SELECT * FROM pgbouncer.get_auth($1)
```

6. Reload the PgBouncer service by executing the following at the command line as a root-capable user:

```
sudo systemctl reload pgbouncer
```

How it works...

The first thing we need to do is create a secure method for PgBouncer to check passwords. PgBouncer knows how PostgreSQL stores passwords, so it can compare any value from a client authentication request with the encrypted information in the database. We merely need a way to retrieve it.

The `pgbouncer.get_auth()` function does this by retrieving a requested user and encrypted password from where PostgreSQL itself stores it. Normally it's not possible for regular users to view the `pg_shadow` table, but since we created the function as `SECURITY DEFINER`, it will execute as the user that created it. That means the `pgbouncer` user has indirect access to a secure resource since we ran this SQL as the `postgres` user.

We also secure this function by preventing any other user from executing it. By default, functions created by any user may be executed by any other user. Thus we want to be extra cautious and explicitly revoke permission from `PUBLIC`, while explicitly granting access to the `pgbouncer` user.

Don't forget to create the function on every database where PgBouncer may connect. If it can't find the function, no user will be able to authenticate.

Next we alter the `userlist.txt` file and remove every entry except for the encrypted password line for the `pgbouncer` user itself. PgBouncer will authenticate any user not listed in this file with the function we just created. By removing all other users, it can only authenticate itself locally, and all other users must be verified by PostgreSQL.

The next step is to essentially enable this functionality. We start by setting the `auth_user` to `pgbouncer`, since that's the user we want to use for authentication purposes. We can specify any user that exists in `userlist.txt` and is also allowed to execute our special function.

Then, we set the query that actually invokes the `pgbouncer.get_auth()` function into `auth_query`. This can really be any query to PostgreSQL, provided it always returns two columns where the first contains the username, and the second has the encrypted password. PgBouncer will use these results to verify any password a client attempts to provide.

The final step is simply to tell PgBouncer to reload the configuration file to incorporate our modifications. Once we've done this, we should be able to authenticate as any user we've previously created in the database instance, even though the user is not specified in `userlist.txt`.

There's more...

It may be desirable to make our function even more secure. Perhaps we want to avoid allowing superuser access through PgBouncer. Maybe we want to be even more draconian and only allow users assigned to a certain group. We can accomplish both of these by modifying the verification query to something like this:

```
SELECT u.rolname::TEXT, u.rolpassword::TEXT
  FROM pg_authid g
  JOIN pg_auth_members m ON (m.roleid = g.oid)
  JOIN pg_authid u ON (u.oid = m.member)
 WHERE NOT u.rolsuper
   AND g.rolname = 'use_proxy'
   AND u.rolname = p_usename;
```

Not only do we explicitly disallow superusers from connecting through the proxy, but now users need a supplementary GRANT statement before they're allowed to connect. If we want a new user `recent_hire` to connect through this specific proxy, we could manage the user this way:

```
CREATE USER recent_hire WITH PASSWORD 'foobar';
GRANT use_proxy TO recent_hire;
```

And, then, if this user moves to some other part of the company or no longer has access to this segment of the application, we can easily revoke access:

```
REVOKE use_proxy FROM recent_hire;
```

There really is quite a bit of potential for managing access by customizing the verification function.

See also

We know we've listed this link before, but these new parameters are explained in greater depth in the PgBouncer documentation. We've listed it again for convenience: https://pgbouncer.github.io/config.html

5
Troubleshooting

A **database administrator** (**DBA**) managing a highly available database server is charged with a huge responsibility. The amount of integration, speed of operations, and urgency behind resolving performance degradation can be extremely stressful. Some personalities thrive under this kind of pressure, while others will find it impossible to concentrate and will become paralyzed in fear.

We're not going to claim that every DBA in this position is a battle-weary veteran, typing furiously to save the day while disaster looms. This kind of scenario only exists in movies and often leads to compounding the original problem. In reality, a DBA's job includes many more calculated reactions even when managing a transaction-heavy database with a frightfully low tolerance for downtime. The best tip we can give—and the whole reason behind this book—is to have an expansive bag of tricks.

For the purposes of this chapter, our bag is full of common Linux utilities useful for troubleshooting. With them, we approach system malfunctions like scientists. Given the behavior of the database or the underlying operating system, it is our job to produce a hypothesis for the cause. The tools serve as our instruments, ready to measure and sample, to either prove or disprove until we successfully isolate and address the problem.

With enough practice, we can begin to expect a certain output, given PostgreSQL's behavior. Like a good mechanic who can diagnose an engine by its sound, we will hear the subtle tone of distress deep in the database cluster and have an answer. The first step toward this goal is to learn the tools.

In this chapter, we will learn several techniques to track sources of poor performance or stop potential outages before they occur. We will cover the following recipes in this chapter:

- Performing triage
- Installing common statistics packages

- Evaluating the current disk performance with iostat
- Tracking I/O-heavy processes with iotop
- Viewing past performance with sar
- Correlating performance with dstat
- Interpreting /proc/meminfo
- Examining /proc/net/bonding/bond0
- Checking the pg_stat_activity view
- Checking the pg_stat_statements view
- Deciphering database locks
- Debugging with strace
- Logging checkpoints properly

Performing triage

When things go wrong or begin to look strange to an experienced eye, it is time to investigate. But where do we start?

Is the **redundant array of independent disks (RAID)** running in parity mode, thereby drastically reducing the I/O throughput? Is the upstream switch saturated, robbing the database of bandwidth? Are we out of memory and swapping to disk, or are we causing memory reclamation threads to terminate processes? Has the operating system task scheduler gotten overloaded and spiraled into oblivion?

Maybe! We've seen all of these scenarios, and many more. We can't fix a problem that we are unable to locate. Any time that we spend analyzing an unlikely path is ultimately wasted, and it only increases downtime. We must take an inventory of the known symptoms and extrapolate this evidence into one or more avenues of investigation.

Anything less is simply guesswork. This recipe will explain how to quickly assess a situation to better direct subsequent forensics.

Getting ready

We do not need a spreadsheet for this. A computer with a network connection should be enough to quickly rule out several possibilities. Enough practice will render this process second nature and make some checks unnecessary.

How to do it...

When deciding how to analyze a possible system problem, consider the items in this checklist:

- Can `ping` reach the PostgreSQL server?
- Is it possible to use `ssh` to enter the server?
- Do simple commands such as `echo` immediately return a Command Prompt?
- Does `uptime` show the following:
    - A system load higher than the number of available CPUs?
    - Whether the server has rebooted recently?
- Can `psql` connect to PostgreSQL locally?
- Does the `free` command show the following:
    - Any swap space used?
    - Less free memory than used memory after accounting for the cache?
- Does the `df` command indicate that the database storage is:
    - Present and accounted for?
    - Used below 95 percent?

How it works...

With the exclusion of `psql`, all of the commands we use in this checklist are present on almost every Unix system. They do nothing more than provide a very general idea of the system's health.

If we can ping a server, that doesn't mean it is running. The network service is one of the first things that the operating system starts and one of the last things it stops. The server can be stuck somewhere in its boot process or, equally, frozen in a shutdown. It does indicate, however, that something is available for further checks.

The next thing we try is to `ssh` to the server. If this command hangs indefinitely or returns with any kind of error, the server is effectively unusable. At this point, we would request the infrastructure or server administration departments to attempt to log in through the local console. Unfortunately, a failed `ssh` attempt often means that the server requires a manual reboot and further analysis. If we have a replication server, now would be a good time to use it until we have a diagnosis.

The next thing we will check is shell responsiveness. Commands such as echo, ls, or cat are frequently used and should return control immediately after completing. If there is a significant delay, it's also likely that we experienced a long delay after logging in to the server. This is usually caused by an overloaded CPU, but extremely high I/O can also result in intermittent lag.

We can check the CPU tangentially, using the uptime command. Its output looks like this:

```
08:53:57 up 9 days, 4:07, 12 users, load average: 9.38, 8.01, 6.53
```

This particular system has been up for 9 days, indicating that it hasn't rebooted recently. If it had, this would be a sign that the system kernel might be at fault, since it can result in unexpected system crashes and reboots. The last three numbers indicate how stressed the CPU is at an average of 1, 5, and 15 minutes. If this server has only four CPUs, it is currently overloaded, and we should consider upgrading it or investigating what contributed to the excessive CPU use.

If we use psql while we are logged in to the server locally, we don't have to contend with network overhead. If the PostgreSQL service isn't running, we'll see output like this:

```
psql: could not connect to server: No such file or directory
       Is the server running locally and accepting
       connections on Unix domain socket "/tmp/.s.PGSQL.5432"?
```

Output like this would demand investigation, starting with the PostgreSQL logs. If we can connect, there are system views that we can analyze, which we will explain in the subsequent sections.

The free command is very inexpensive, and its output tells us a lot, as shown in the following example:

```
                  total    used    free   shared   buffers   cached
Mem:               2002    1559     443        0       153     1258
-/+ buffers/cache:          147    1855
Swap:              2043       0    2043
```

Invoked with the -m parameter, the free output is listed in **megabytes (MB)**. We can see that this system has 2 GB of RAM, and only 147 MB is used after we account for disk cache and buffers. We can also see that we are not using swap space. If the used column shows that more than 50 percent of the system memory is allocated or any swap is active, we don't have enough memory.

Finally, we use `df` to detail how much of our available storage space is consumed. Provided we know the source of the database storage, we can immediately see how much space is used. For example, this output suggests a problem:

```
Filesystem          Size  Used Avail Use% Mounted on
/dev/sda1           40G   5.6G 34.2G  14% /
/dev/sdc1            2T   1.9T   50M  97% /db
```

Invoked with the `-h` setting, the `df` output becomes *human-readable* instead of a very large number of **kilobytes** (**KB**). We can instantly see that our database mount is nearly full, and the amount of available space is so low that the database might actually be in danger.

There's more...

These types of *at-a-glance* commands are our first means of diagnosis. We need quick methods that do not require complex interpretation to assess the server. Given that a problem exists, one or more of these tests should show abnormal results right away. If not, more advanced techniques are necessary. We will endeavor to describe as many of these as possible.

Installing common statistics packages

There are several common data-gathering tools, and each of them has its own place. Several are already installed for extremely basic information, but for the purposes of this chapter, we need more depth.

For instance, we may want to know the exact distribution of CPU resources, aggregate views of memory paging volume, or disk I/O utilization. For more in-depth needs, we could analyze specific processes for storage interaction or resource locks. If we weren't watching at the exact time a problem occurred, we might want a historical record of various server performance metrics.

In order to have all these capabilities, we must first install the requisite tools. We might find it quite shocking that these tools are not installed by default, considering their role in server administration. This recipe will help ensure basic diagnostic tools are available for future recipes.

Packages installed in this recipe will be referenced in all the subsequent recipes, so please don't skip this!

How to do it...

Debian, Mint, or Ubuntu users can install the tools by executing this command as a root-level user:

```
sudo apt-get install dstat iotop sysstat
```

Red Hat, Fedora, CentOS, and Scientific Linux users can install the tools by executing this command as a root-level user:

```
sudo yum install dstat iotop sysstat
```

How it works...

Whether the servers in question are based on **RPM Package Manager** (**RPM**) or **Advanced Package Tool** (**APT**) packaging, these resources are commonly leveraged for diagnostic purposes. As such, modern distributions tend to include them. Once the software sources are accounted for, the only command we need installs all three statistics and monitoring tools simultaneously. Now comes the time to use them!

Evaluating the current disk performance with iostat

Due to the disparity in speed between storage and RAM, one of the first signs of distress that a DBA will observe is directly related to disk utilization. A badly written query, an unexpected batch-loading process, a forced checkpoint, overwhelmed write caches—the array of things that can ruin disk performance is vast.

The first step in tracking down the culprit(s) is to visualize the activity. The `iostat` utility is fairly coarse in that it does not operate at the process level. However, it does output storage activity by device and includes columns such as reads or writes per second, the size of the request queue, and how busy it is compared to its maximum throughput.

This allows us to see the devices that are actually slow, busy, or overworked. Furthermore, we can combine this information with other methods of analysis to find the activity's source. For now, this recipe will explore the `iostat` tool itself.

Getting ready

As `iostat` is part of the `sysstat` package, we should ensure that the statistics-gathering elements are enabled. Debian, Mint, and Ubuntu users should modify the `/etc/default/sysstat` file and make sure that the `ENABLED` variable resembles this line:

```
ENABLED="true"
```

Red Hat, Fedora, CentOS, and Scientific Linux users should make sure that the `SADC_OPTIONS` variable in `/etc/sysconfig/sysstat` is set to the following:

```
SADC_OPTIONS="-S DISK"
```

Once these changes are complete, restart the `sysstat` service with this command as a root-level user:

```
sudo systemctl restart sysstat
```

How to do it...

Leverage some sample `iostat` output by following these steps:

1. Obtain the statistics of the disk activity every second with this command:

   ```
   iostat -d 1
   ```

2. Show 10 seconds of disk activity in **megabytes per second** (**MBps**) with this command:

   ```
   iostat -dm 1 10
   ```

3. Show extended disk activity in MBps for the `sda` device with this command:

   ```
   iostat -dmx sda 1
   ```

How it works...

The `iostat` utility has a rather unique method of interpreting command-line arguments. If no recognized disks are part of the command, it simply shows information about all of them. After devices, it checks for timing statistics. To get a second-by-second status, we specify 1 second as the final argument. By providing the −d argument, we remove CPU utilization from the report.

The default output rate of `iostat` is in **kilobytes per second (kBps)**. Current hardware is often so fast that these results can be almost too high to easily compare, so we set the −m parameter in the second command to change the output to MBps. We also take advantage of the fact that the last two parameters are related to timing. The first parameter specifies the interval, and the second is the number of samples. So, the second command takes 10 samples at the rate of one per second.

The last command adds two more elements. First, we place a disk device (`sda`) before the timing interval. We can list as many devices as we want, and `iostat` will restrict the output to those specific resources. This is especially helpful in servers that can have dozens of disk devices, thus making it difficult to isolate potential performance issues. Then, we include the −x argument, which lists extended statistics.

Without extended statistics, the output is not very useful. For example, watching the `sda` device for 1 second will normally look like this:

Device:	tps	kB_read/s	kB_wrtn/s	kB_read	kB_wrtn
sda	806.59	3147.25	4742.86	5728	8632

The last two columns only list the cumulative activity for the sampling interval. This is of limited use. However, the first three columns display the number of **transactions per second (TPS)** and how much data was either read from or written to that device per second. Depending on the hardware we purchased, we might actually know its limits regarding these measurements, so we have a basic idea of how busy it might be.

If we enable extended statistics with the −x argument, we gain several extra fields, including the following:

- `r/s`: This column lists the number of reads per second from the device. This was previously aggregated into the `tps` field.
- `w/s`: This column shows the number of writes per second to the device. This was previously aggregated into the `tps` field.

- `avgqu-sz`: This column describes the number of requests in the disk's queue. If this gets very large, the disk will have trouble keeping up with requests.
- `await`: This column outlines the average time a request spends waiting in the queue and being serviced, in milliseconds. An overloaded disk will often have a very high value in this column as it is unable to keep up with requests.
- `r_await`: This column details the average time read requests spend waiting in the queue and being serviced, in milliseconds. This helps isolate whether or not the read activity is overloading the disk.
- `w_await`: This column depicts the average time write requests spend waiting in the queue and being serviced, in milliseconds. This helps isolate whether or not the write activity is overloading the disk.
- `%util`: This column represents the percentage of time the device was busy servicing I/O requests. This is actually a function of the queue size and the average time spent waiting in the queue. It's also an invaluable at-a-glance metric. If this is at or near 100 percent for long periods of time, we need to start analyzing the sources of I/O requests and think about upgrading our storage.

There's more...

Our examples of `iostat` always include the `-d` argument, to only show disk information. By default, it shows both CPU and disk measurements. The CPU data looks like this:

```
avg-cpu:  %user   %nice %system %iowait  %steal   %idle
           9.38    0.00   16.67   11.46    0.00   62.50
```

This can be useful for analysis as well, though there are several other tools that also provide this data. If we use the `-c` parameter instead of `-d`, we will see only the CPU statistics, and no information about disk devices will be included in the output.

See also

Always examine the manual for the tools that we use in these recipes. In this case, the manual for `iostat` is available by executing this command:

```
man iostat
```

Tracking I/O-heavy processes with iotop

Many DBAs and system administrators are familiar with the `top` command, which displays the processes that use the most CPU or RAM. However, this does not help us identify the processes that cause high amounts of system I/O.

Fortunately there is a command, much like `top`, that is designed specifically for displaying the processes that make storage requests. The `iotop` utility displays a continuously updated list of the processes and any I/O they are handling. Provided that the server is dedicated to PostgreSQL, we can use this information to almost instantly identify one or more database backends that accumulate disk requests.

Just like `top`, processes are sorted to the head of the list according to the volume of their I/O. This recipe will explain more about `iotop`, and how we can benefit from its functionality.

Getting ready

The `iotop` command can only be executed by root-level users, as it uses some kernel resources available only to superusers. Be ready with the `sudo` command!

How to do it...

Follow these steps to obtain a sample output from the `iotop` command:

1. Enter interactive mode with this command (exit by pressing *Q*):

   ```
   sudo iotop
   ```

2. Obtain batch output for 10 seconds with this command:

   ```
   sudo iotop -b -n 10
   ```

3. Restrict batch output to only active processes, include a timestamp, and suppress the headers with this command:

   ```
   sudo iotop -bot -qqq
   ```

How it works...

While it may be somewhat inconvenient to need superuser access to invoke `iotop`, we're willing to make that sacrifice in this case. Our first command simply starts `iotop` as we would use `top`, interactively. We can sort the output into different columns with the arrow keys, reverse the sort order by pressing the *R* key, and quit by pressing *Q*. Of the columns presented here, we may be interested in the following:

- `PID`: This column provides the **process ID** (**PID**) of process that makes I/O requests. This can be used to investigate or terminate the program.
- `DISK READ`: This column illustrates the number of bytes read per second by the listed process.
- `DISK WRITE`: This column details the number of bytes written per second by the listed process.
- `IO`: This column shows the percentage of time that the listed process spent issuing I/O requests.
- `COMMAND`: This column depicts the name of the process that handles I/O. If this is a master process, it might include command-line switches as well.

While this kind of use is informative for live troubleshooting, it's less applicable for historical applications. Thus, for the second command, we add the `-b` argument to put `iotop` in batch mode. This means that all the output is simply printed to the screen, which we can redirect to a file if desired. In addition, we used the `-n` parameter to only obtain 10 readings—one for each second—for later analysis.

Readers working along by trying these examples might notice that the amount of output in batch mode is overwhelming. By default, `iotop` lists every process it can see, whether or not it is actually utilizing disk resources. We can stop this behavior with the `-o` parameter, so only active processes are included in any output. By adding the `-t` argument, we also gain a timestamp that we can use to correlate disk activity across data-gathering techniques.

The `-q` argument acts to suppress excessive `iotop` output. By specifying it once, `iotop` only includes the column labels at the top of the output. If you specify it twice, it will never include the column labels. If you specify it a third time, it will also remove the summary data that `iotop` normally prints following every iteration. This type of output is ideal for importing into reporting tools or even analyzing by hand when searching for interesting time periods.

There's more...

While the `iotop` data is not actually part of the statistics gathered automatically by the `sysstat` package, we can log the data for posterity anyway. Follow these steps as a root-level user to log the `iostat` data:

1. Create a file named `iotop` at `/etc/cron.d/` and fill it with this line:

   ```
   * * * * * root iotop -boat -qqq -d 5 -n 2 >> /var/log/iotop
   ```

2. Reload the configuration files of the `cron` service with this command:

   sudo systemctl restart cron

3. If the previous command didn't work, try this:

   sudo systemctl restart crond

By adding the -a parameter, `iotop` will log the cumulative total of the I/O used between the readings instead of the I/O per second. We use the -d argument to add a 5-second delay between two readings, as specified by the -n parameter. Together, this means that we get a 5-second sample logged to `/var/log/iotop` every minute.

> If you don't know how `cron` works, the first five columns list the minute, hour, day, month, or day of the week when the program should run. Using a * character here means **all**, so this job runs every minute, every day, as the `root` user.

See also

Always examine the manual for the tools that we use in these recipes. In this case, the manual for `iotop` is available by executing this command:

```
man iotop
```

Viewing past performance with sar

While there are many tools to view or analyze the current server performance and behavior, how do we examine historical activity? Most Linux systems rotate log files in `/var/log` for varying periods of time. Unfortunately, these are programs and system logs, not performance measurements.

When we installed the `sysstat` package in a previous recipe, we gained the use of the `sar` utility. Some argue that `sar` is the Swiss Army knife of metric collection. A simple invocation can display past data regarding memory, CPUs, **interrupt requests (IRQs)**, disk devices, networks, or even **teletypewriters (TTYs)**.

When administering a highly available server, there are few things as helpful as performance trends. This recipe will explore historical trends available via the `sar` command.

Getting ready

As `sar` and `iostat` are both part of the `sysstat` package, we recommend that you review the *Evaluating current disk performance with iostat* recipe before continuing.

How to do it...

Collect some sample `sar` data by following these steps:

1. Display the default `sar` output with the following command:

   sar

2. Show the disk device status every 5 seconds with this command:

   sar -d 5

3. View memory usage between 4:00 A.M. and 6:00 A.M. today with this command:

   sar -r -s 04:00:00 -e 06:00:00

Examine the I/O statistics for any existing past dates by following these steps:

1. Find the appropriate `sysstat` log directory:

   - Red Hat, Fedora, CentOS, and Scientific Linux users should use the `/var/log/sa` directory.
   - Debian, Mint, and Ubuntu users should use the `/var/log/sysstat` directory.

2. List the contents of that directory and choose a file. Files are simply binary formats containing `sar` data for each retained date. Files are prefixed with sa. Thus, sa23 is the `sar` data for the 23rd of the month.

3. Execute the following command to view past I/O statistics for the 3rd of the month:

```
sar -f /var/log/sysstat/sa03 -b
```

How it works...

By default, `sar` operates in CPU mode. Simply using the command as named; we will receive CPU activity samples for every 10 minutes of the current day. Once `sar` produces this output, it exits. We must invoke it much as we did with `iostat` if we want the current data.

In our second example, we've chosen to emulate the `iostat` output by providing a summary of disk activity every 5 seconds until we cancel the command. The -d argument tells `sar` to display the disk statistics. Just like `iostat`, `sar` accepts two optional parameters for interval and count. As we didn't specify a count, `sar` will print disk performance every 5 seconds.

The third example is where we finally begin leveraging the real power of `sar`. If we had examined our PostgreSQL log and noticed a large number of idle queries between 4:00 A.M. and 6:00 A.M., we would need a method to obtain data for that time period. Well, `sar` has one argument (-s) to specify the start time of a data extract, and another argument (-e) to set the end time. These parameters must be written in HH:MM:SS format or `sar` will ignore them with an error. We also elected to use the -r argument to display memory usage data, just to illustrate another metric that `sar` can expose.

Our final example depends entirely on what Linux distribution we're using. Unfortunately, each distro stores its collected `sar` data in different areas within /var/log. With that said, the directory assigned to sysstat for data storage normally retains a default of 7 days' worth of historical information for analysis.

Every day, this data is collected in a file prefixed with sa and suffixed with the current month's day. On weeks that span 2 months, the count simply restarts with 01. Once again, we use a different output mode for `sar` and display the I/O activity.

There's more...

7 days may not be enough for some administrators. To increase this amount, modify `/etc/sysconfig/sysstat` or `/etc/sysstat/sysstat` and change the `HISTORY` setting to the desired amount of days to retain data for. For example, we could use this to keep 30 days of records:

```
HISTORY=30
```

See also

Always examine the manual for the tools that we use in these recipes. In this case, the manual for `sar` is available by executing this command:

```
man sar
```

This is especially true for `sar`, as it has so many different operating modes and display formats.

Correlating performance with dstat

Eventually, we will want to view multiple types of system activity simultaneously. While `sar` has many operating modes, its output is linear. Without a tool to interpret its exhaustive data, we are left with a lot of manual analysis of several `sar` invocations. While `iostat` and `iotop` are wonderful tools, they are rather limited in scope by comparison.

So, let's introduce `dstat`. While `dstat` can't access historical data like `sar`, it can display output from several different operation modes side by side. It also includes color coding to easily distinguish units. It's a very pretty command-line tool and summarizes several different metrics at a glance.

For servers that are of particular importance, we actually keep a Terminal window that displays the `dstat` results openly so that we get an early warning when numbers begin to look bad.

Getting ready

Unlike the `sysstat` package, `dstat` is ready to use immediately after being installed.

How to do it...

The output from `dstat` is very colorful. Obtain a few samples with these steps:

1. Display default information with this command:

```
dstat
```

2. Display only system load and network activity with this command:

```
dstat -n -l
```

3. Display CPU usage, I/O, and disk utilization averaged over 5-second intervals with this command:

```
dstat -c -r --disk-util 5
```

4. For the next 10 seconds, we can display the time, memory usage, interrupts and context switches, disk activity from only the `sda` device, and the process using the most I/O, in addition to capturing the results in a CSV file, all with this command:

```
dstat -tmyd -D sda --top-io --output /tmp/stats.csv 1 10
```

How it works...

We hope it's obvious by now that the number of combinations available for the `dstat` output is effectively infinite. By default, the `dstat` output resembles this:

```
----total-cpu-usage---- -dsk/total- -net/total- ---paging-- ---system--
usr sys idl wai hiq siq| read  writ| recv  send|  in   out | int   csw
  1   0  97   1   0   0|  81k  229k|   0     0 |   0     0 | 100   479
 17   4   2  75   0   2| 376k 1920k|   0     0 |   0     0 | 440  4335
 16   2  10  70   0   2| 320k 1344k|   0     0 |   0     0 | 382  3371
 19   3   1  73   0   3| 496k 1956k|   0     0 |   0     0 | 502  5574
 15   3   3  77   0   2| 320k 2320k|   0     0 |   0     0 | 449  3936
 17   2   9  71   0   1| 304k 1248k|   0     0 |   0     0 | 361  3481
 19   3   3  73   0   2| 496k 1816k|   0     0 |   0     0 | 513  6388
 18   5   0  74   0   2| 376k 2112k|   0     0 |   0     0 | 481  4988
```

The default output from `dstat` enables CPU, disk, network, memory paging, and system modules. In this particular example, we can see that the `wai` column is extremely high, suggesting that the server is currently I/O bound.

Another interesting thing about `dstat` is that it really only displays the exact modules we request. For the second example, the output becomes this:

```
-net/total- ---load-avg---
 recv  send| 1m   5m   15m
    0     0 |2.06 0.79 0.36
  236k  201k|2.06 0.79 0.36
  218k  186k|2.13 0.83 0.37
  265k  219k|2.13 0.83 0.37
  176k  157k|2.13 0.83 0.37
  120k  117k|2.13 0.83 0.37
```

In this second example, we've only enabled the network (-n) and system load (-1) modules, thus extremely reducing the output width. Yet simultaneously, this sparse format makes it very easy to combine several different metrics without absurdly wide Terminal windows.

The third sample begins using `dstat` plugins. By activating the `--disk-util` argument, `dstat` will show the utilization percentage for all active storage devices. This is in addition to the CPU stats (-c) and I/O (-r) that we already activated.

By adding the last parameter (5), we again take advantage of a common trend for system view utilities. The last two optional parameters are for a sample interval and count. In the case of `dstat`, any number printed while the interval is greater than 1 is actually the average of all the metrics collected during that time period. So, for our third example, these numbers are all 5-second cumulative averages.

For posterity, the output looks like this:

```
----total-cpu-usage---- --io/total- sda--sr0-
usr sys idl wai hiq siq| read  writ|util:util
  2   2  89   6   0   0|27.6  12.1 |8.56:0.00
  2  26   0  62   0   9| 156   169 |95.8:   0
  4  29   0  59   0   7| 147   190 |96.2:   0
  4  32   0  54   0  10| 134   203 |95.4:   0
  3  30   1  55   0  11| 134   249 |95.4:   0
  4  29   1  55   0  11| 119   258 |94.7:   0
```

This may be difficult to see, but the last line in this output is not bold like the rest. This means that this particular line had not yet reached the requested interval of 5 seconds. It's not an important detail, but it shows just how much attention the `dstat` developers paid to conveying information visually. We easily see a high percentage of CPU waits, and the `sda` device read and write utilization is over 90 percent. It looks like a visual presentation works pretty well.

For our fourth and final example, we try to include as many separate types of data as possible. In the beginning, we enable the -t, -m, -y, and -d switches. This adds timestamp, memory performance, interrupts and context switches, and device activity to the `dstat` output. We also take advantage of the -D parameter to limit disk statistics to the `sda` device. Default disk statistics are inclusive, but now, we can actually restrict the output to interesting devices.

Next, we add --top-io to list the process that's using the most I/O while `dstat` runs. Earlier, we needed `iotop` to get that data. Of course, `iotop` provides more depth and lists more than one culprit, but for quick identification, it's hard to beat `dstat`. Then, we use the --output parameter to send the `csv` output to /tmp/stats.csv so that we can potentially use a spreadsheet program to analyze or graph the data we gathered.

Finally, we take advantage of both the `interval` and `count` parameters so that we capture only 10 seconds of statistics. For all of that work, we're rewarded with this output:

```
----system---- ------memory-usage----- ---system-- --dsk/sda-- ----most-expensive----
     time      | used  buff  cach  free| int   csw | read  writ|    i/o process
15-10 18:08:11| 383M 9028k  298M 1311M| 561  3360 | 412k 1307k|postgres    1812k 1534k
15-10 18:08:12| 384M 9028k  301M 1306M| 627  6266 |3536k    0 |pgbench        0   424k
15-10 18:08:13| 384M 9028k  306M 1302M| 625  5973 |3560k   32k|pgbench        0   389k
15-10 18:08:14| 384M 9028k  309M 1298M| 776  6745 |3392k    0 |pgbench        0   397k
15-10 18:08:15| 384M 9028k  313M 1294M| 599  5670 |3720k    0 |pgbench        0   384k
15-10 18:08:16| 384M 9036k  317M 1291M| 561  5596 |3192k   24k|pgbench        0   354k
15-10 18:08:17| 384M 9036k  321M 1286M| 671  6438 |4128k    0 |pgbench        0   433k
```

Oh! It looks like all of the I/O and load we saw earlier was due to a pgbench test. How embarrassing!

See also

Always examine the manual for the tools that we use in these recipes. In this case, the manual for `dstat` is available by executing this command:

```
man dstat
```

Interpreting /proc/meminfo

Administrators familiar with the Linux `/proc` filesystem will know that it is a valuable source for both device status and performance information. The `meminfo` entry in this directory will always provide copious data regarding the status, contents, and state of the memory in our server.

We care about this as DBAs because file cache and write buffering can drastically affect disk I/O. We are not especially interested in analyzing PostgreSQL's memory usage itself at this point, except in the context of client connections, inode caches, and dirty page flushing.

On a modern Linux kernel, there are over 50 different lines of information in `/proc/meminfo`. Much of this data is not exceptionally useful to a DBA, so this recipe will focus on important fields only.

Getting ready

We will be using the `watch` and `grep` commands in this recipe. It will be a good idea to experiment with them and, perhaps, skim the `man` pages before continuing.

How to do it...

Follow these steps to capture an interesting memory status from `/proc/meminfo`:

1. Obtain basic memory states with the following command:

    ```
    grep -A3 MemTotal /proc/meminfo
    ```

2. Execute this command to extract dirty memory buffers and pending writes:

    ```
    grep -A1 Dirty /proc/meminfo
    ```

3. View the state of various memory caches with the following command:

```
grep -A1 Active /proc/meminfo
```

4. Show swap usage with the following command:

```
grep Swap /proc/meminfo
```

How it works...

The first command we execute is nothing but a basic summary of the current memory state. For a test system with 2 GB of RAM running PostgreSQL, it would resemble this:

```
MemTotal:        2050908 kB
MemFree:          840088 kB
Buffers:            9288 kB
Cached:          1102228 kB
```

This output is similar to what we would learn using the free command. The MemTotal row should speak for itself, as it is the total size of the memory in the system. The MemFree row is the total amount of completely unallocated system memory, including buffers or cache. The Buffers row in this context is mostly related to internal kernel bookkeeping, so we can ignore it. If we examine the value reported by the Cached row, we can see that over 1 GB of data is cached in memory.

The second command outlines dirty memory. Dirty memory, in this case, is the memory that is modified and awaiting synchronization to disk. On the same 2 GB test system, a long pgbench test might produce results like this:

```
Dirty:             29184 kB
Writeback:            40 kB
```

As we've said, the Dirty row details how much memory is waiting to be written to disk. On systems with very large amounts of RAM, this value can indicate that too much RAM is dirty. The consequences of this can include long query execution times or system stalls if the underlying storage is unable to quickly absorb that many disk writes. In practice, this should rarely be larger than the size of the disk controller's write cache.

However, what about the `Writeback` row? This field details how much of the dirty memory is currently being written to disk. When storage is overwhelmed, the amount reflected here will rise as the write-back buffer fills with more write requests. This is a definite sign that the system has encountered far more writes than it was designed to handle. In essence, each of these fields is a warning sign that the application must be modified to reduce write workload or that the database needs faster storage, with a bigger write cache.

With our next command, we examine the contents of the cache itself. Still using our 2 GB test system, the cache looks like this:

```
Active:           1105760 kB
Inactive:           32764 kB
Active(anon):      207696 kB
Inactive(anon):      9340 kB
Active(file):      898064 kB
Inactive(file):     23424 kB
```

We won't get into too much detail regarding how the kernel actually works, but we will note that all the fields named `Inactive` are something of a misnomer. Any time something is loaded into the cache, it first gets included in the `Inactive` list. Based on the subsequent amount and timing of requests for this data, it might be promoted into the `Active` set. Once it is in that list, various aging algorithms might eventually return it to the `Inactive` list. Inactive cache data is always a candidate for replacement with more important data.

In the context of PostgreSQL, we need to pay attention to the `Active(file)` entry. This is the number of disk pages in the cache. Disk reads are expensive, and as databases process data from disk, this is very important to us. We want as many disk pages as possible to be in the `Active(file)` list, but this doesn't mean we discount `Inactive(file)`. Remember, the inactive cache is still in memory and eligible for database use; it simply hasn't been promoted to the active list. Thus, we want the total amount of file cache to be as high as possible, reflecting the prioritization of disk reads for database processing.

We include `Active(anon)` and `Inactive(anon)` for one reason: database clients. Temporary data allocated to database clients is often assigned to an anonymous cache. This is good for the client program, but with enough of these, we lose valuable memory from use as a disk cache. One remedy for this is to buy more memory, but another more scalable solution is to utilize database connection pooling. That is why this book includes a chapter specifically dedicated to optimizing the connection count, as this helps preserve memory for data caching.

The last extract we obtain from `/proc/meminfo` is related to swap usage and looks like this:

```
SwapCached:              0 kB
SwapTotal:         2093052 kB
SwapFree:          2093052 kB
```

Again, we can get this kind of data using the `free` command as well. We mainly include it here in case any readers want to search for all of these fields with a single command, for monitoring purposes.

There's more...

The `watch` utility will execute any command and its arguments until it is canceled with *Ctrl* + *C*. Instead of using those `grep` statements every time we want to see interesting fields in the `/proc/meminfo` file, we can simply use `watch`. For example, to observe the state of dirty buffers waiting to be committed to disk, we can use the following command:

```
watch -n 5 grep -A1 Dirty /proc/meminfo
```

See also

The Linux kernel documentation is somewhat verbose. Nonetheless, more technically apt readers can find much more information regarding `/proc/meminfo` at this URL:
`https://www.kernel.org/doc/Documentation/filesystems/proc.txt`

Examining /proc/net/bonding/bond0

Highly available databases often come in pairs for redundancy purposes. These servers can have any number of procedures to keep the data synchronized, and this book suggests direct connections when possible. Direct connections between servers ensure fast communication between redundant servers, and it resembles the following network design:

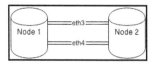

In some cases, it can be advantageous to connect the database servers to a general network fabric. Depending on the interaction of the upstream network devices, this can significantly increase the network packet's **round-trip time** (**RTT**). This is usually fine for PostgreSQL replication, but **online transaction processing** (**OLTP**) systems may be more sensitive. Block-level replication systems (such as **Distributed Regulated Block Device** (**DRBD**)) that operate beneath the filesystem fare even worse.

Each of our database servers should be equipped with at least two independent network interfaces. In order to prevent downtime, these interfaces must be linked with a bond. Network bonds act as an abstraction layer that can route traffic over either interface and, like many kernel-level services, bond status can be checked via the Linux /proc filesystem.

The health and current communication channel of the server network bond is surprisingly relevant to throughput. In order to rule out potential delays caused by upstream network hardware, this recipe will help understand how the bond is operating.

Getting ready

As we are going to examine the network bond on two paired PostgreSQL servers, connect to each before continuing. We don't need any special permissions or attributes for this recipe.

How to do it...

In order to check the status of the network bond, follow these steps:

1. Determine the current bonding method by executing this command:

   ```
   grep Mode /proc/net/bonding/bond0
   ```

2. Check the currently active interface with this command:

   ```
   grep Active /proc/net/bonding/bond0
   ```

How it works...

Surprised that it's so simple? Don't be. Much like `/proc/meminfo` and `/proc/cpuinfo`, the difficulty is not in obtaining the information we need, but in interpreting it. The first thing that concerns us is the bond mode. There are several modes, but only one is relevant to us for a dual-failover configuration. The mode should reflect some kind of an `active-backup` status; otherwise, it's combining the interfaces for bandwidth and throughput purposes. The line we want looks like this:

```
Bonding Mode: fault-tolerance (active-backup)
```

Next, we check the currently active interface. If the system was configured so that the network bond is in `active-backup` mode, only one is active at any one time. The other server acts as a backup in case the network connection or the interface itself fails. In an ideal situation, similar interfaces on both servers—for instance, `eth3`—are attached to the same switch. If not, we should talk to our network and server administrators to correct the setup.

We suggest that you use the same interface name on both the servers for one simple reason: it's difficult to diagnose network routes on bonded interfaces. For best throughput and RTT, our network should look like this:

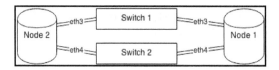

We hope it's clear from the diagram that this architecture introduces a possible source of network lag. As the servers cannot transfer data to each other directly, at least one extra switch that increases the RTT is involved. As our servers hopefully have two network interfaces, each server is communicating with the same two switches. However, if each server is currently working through a different switch, this actually adds at least two more jumps, as the switches must communicate with an upstream router. If we follow the dotted path, that unfortunate situation looks like this:

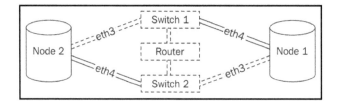

We've seen this scenario increase ping times from 0.03 milliseconds to 0.3 milliseconds. That may not seem like much, but when the network RTT is 10 times slower, replication and monitoring can suffer significantly. This is one of the few obscure troubleshooting techniques that can elude even experienced network administrators. Armed with this, we should be able to diagnose replication and idle-wait problems, using nothing more than `grep`.

Checking the pg_stat_activity view

Another source of valuable troubleshooting information is PostgreSQL itself. There are numerous views, tables, and functions dedicated to tracking and reporting various statistics and operating statuses for each hosted database. Principal among these is the `pg_stat_activity` view.

This view tells us what every database client is doing, where it is connected from, which user account it is operating under, and other important values. When administering a highly available database, we must have either iron control over what executes in the database or the ability to quickly and easily assess its execution state. Besides using this data to track suspicious activity, we can also cancel long-running queries or Cartesian products, or simply examine the connection turnover.

We probably use this view into the database more than any other, and it forms the backbone of several monitoring utilities as well. This recipe will explore just why this system catalog is so indispensable.

Getting ready

While any user can view the contents of the `pg_stat_activity` view, only a superuser can freely examine the contents of every column. To avoid security exploits, regular users cannot view the current query activity, any connection information, or fields related to query time or status.

To get the most out of this view safely, we want to grant elevated privileges to specific users dedicated to monitoring and status checks. In order to do this, we must first connect to the database as a superuser (such as the `postgres` user) for the duration of this recipe.

How to do it...

Perform the following steps to prepare pg_stat_activity for generalized use:

1. Execute this SQL statement as a database superuser to create a function:

```
CREATE OR REPLACE FUNCTION pg_stat_activity()
RETURNS SETOF pg_stat_activity AS $$
    SELECT * FROM pg_stat_activity;
$$ LANGUAGE sql SECURITY DEFINER;
```

2. Execute this SQL statement to secure the function we created:

```
REVOKE ALL ON FUNCTION pg_stat_activity() FROM PUBLIC;
```

3. Create a user dedicated to monitoring with this SQL statement:

```
CREATE USER db_mon WITH PASSWORD 'somepass';
```

4. Grant the monitoring user the ability to use our function with this SQL statement:

```
GRANT EXECUTE ON FUNCTION pg_stat_activity() TO db_mon;
```

5. Now, connect to PostgreSQL as the db_mon user and examine the contents of
pg_stat_activity by executing this SQL query:

```
SELECT * FROM pg_stat_activity();
```

How it works...

The pg_stat_activity view is a wealth of information for a DBA. Unfortunately, it is all but useless for monitoring due to the security measures that encumber it. Principally, some of these fields are obfuscated specifically to prevent system compromises and data leaks. Thus, we must protect the view while still loosening the security enough to enable better monitoring.

The first step we take is to create a function that is capable of returning a set of rows similar to the pg_stat_activity view itself. The SETOF modifier tells PostgreSQL that our function does exactly that. It's no coincidence that the body of our function is merely a SELECT statement on the pg_stat_activity view.

Why did we use a function to abstract the view? After all, it seems excessive to create a whole function for such a simple statement. The answer is in the SECURITY DEFINER function modifier that we added; it allows the function to execute as the user who created it. Thus, if we create the function as the postgres user, it runs as if the postgres user invoked it. As the postgres user is a superuser, the function can see all of the hidden columns, no matter who executes the function.

All new functions are available to all users by default. However, this function executes as a superuser and we don't want just anyone to execute it and view potentially sensitive query contents. So, we revoke all permissions from the PUBLIC context. At this point, only a superuser can call our function.

As we want to be able to monitor database status values, we create a user for this very purpose. We named our user db_mon, but any username works just as well. As long as it has a secure password or is only used locally, our security exposure is minimal. Then, we grant EXECUTE privileges on the pg_stat_activity function, and our work is complete. The db_mon user can now view all user queries. We can also grant EXECUTE privileges to other DBAs or support staff who may need it.

What data is available? Important fields include, but are not limited to, the following:

- pid or procpid: In versions of PostgreSQL 9.2 and above, this field is named pid; all older versions use procpid. This tells us the PID assigned to the backend server process by the operating system and is extremely valuable for debugging or connection-management purposes.
- usename: This displays the name of the user who owns this connection.
- backend_start: This provides the date and time when the connection was established.
- xact_start: This tracks the date and time when the current transaction started, if any.
- query_start: This reports the date and time of the last query submitted.

- `wait_event`: In versions of PostgreSQL 9.6 and higher, this labels the current lock event that is blocking the current query from continuing. There is a very detailed table in the documentation that further explains the labels used in this column. If there is nothing blocking this query, the value will be `NULL`.

- `waiting`: This column is only valid in PostgreSQL versions 9.5 and below. This tells us whether or not the connection is currently blocked by something, and will show either `t` for true or `f` for false.

- `state`: In versions of PostgreSQL 9.2 and higher, this column reports the current state of the connection. States marked as `active` are executing a query; the `idle` ones are not. If a connection is marked `idle in transaction`, look carefully at the `query_start` and `xact_start` fields for excessive delays. If a connection was in a transaction and encountered an error, it will report `idle in transaction (aborted)`; applications should catch errors and either roll back the transaction or disconnect, so `idle` aborted transactions are a possible source of trouble. Unfortunately, this field does not exist in older versions, so a certain context is lost during the investigation.

- `state_change`: This displays the last time the session state was altered. This could mean a query ended, or a new one started, or a new transaction began but the session is still idle, and so on. It's possibly one of the most important time-related fields because it lets us know how active the connection actually is. If this field is quite behind the current time, we know the session is still performing its last action, which is valuable diagnostic information.

- `query`: In versions of PostgreSQL 9.1 and above, this column contains most or all of the last known query this connection executed. This field does not exist in older versions.

- `current_query`: In versions of PostgreSQL 9.1 and below, this column contains most or the entire last known query that this connection executed. In newer versions, this field was split into the `state` and `query` fields to provide better insight into the connection activity during transactions.

There's more...

Mind the version! PostgreSQL versions below 9.2 do not have the `state` or `query` fields and supply only the `current_query` column. While it might be tempting to use `query` and `current_query` interchangeably, older PostgreSQL versions are strictly at a disadvantage.

 At the time of this edition, PostgreSQL versions older than 9.4 are no longer supported by the community. We've listed many fields in these older PostgreSQL versions, but if they are relevant to your installation, we strongly recommend upgrading.

Similarly, the way waits are displayed changed drastically in PostgreSQL 9.6. In older versions, the `waiting` column merely noted whether or not the query was blocked by some other process. The `wait_event` replacement makes it possible to actually see what is blocking a particular query. Previously obscured actions such as lock acquisitions, disk synchronization, or even background worker interaction, are now plainly visible. This amount of detail is far more useful for diagnostic purposes than a mere Boolean value.

In PostgreSQL 9.1 and below, queries are only reflected in the `pg_stat_activity` view while they are actually executing. As soon as the query finishes, the `current_query` column will be empty or report `idle in transaction` if the query was part of a transaction. This means we lose a lot of operating context unless we just happen to be logging every database query.

On very high-volume OLTP systems, recording every query is not feasible. We've personally administered databases that handle over 1 billion queries per day, at a rate of 60,000 per second. Even with a conservative query length of 50 characters, we would produce over 50 GB of logs every day.

Troubleshooting stuck, idle, or otherwise faulty connections is much easier in the newer versions of PostgreSQL. If at all possible, upgrade to 9.6 or above.

See also

PostgreSQL has extremely informative documentation regarding how it collects and maintains statistics. The `pg_stat_activity` view is described in more depth there, so take a look at `https://www.postgresql.org/docs/current/static/monitoring-stats.html`.

Checking the pg_stat_statements view

We mentioned in another recipe that logging every query on a highly available database that handles high volumes of query traffic is undesirable. DBAs often solve this problem by only logging slow queries, by setting `log_min_duration_statement` to a reasonable number of milliseconds in `postgresql.conf`. Later, only queries that cross this threshold are logged, along with binding parameters if the query was a prepared statement.

We strongly encourage this practice, as it is invaluable for catching outlying queries that could benefit from optimization. Unfortunately, faster queries are still invisible to us. Worse, queries that execute often probably have their data sources cached in memory, so it's unlikely that they contribute to I/O. The database could be executing an inefficient or redundant query thousands of times per second, and besides an elevated server load, we would never know.

This situation is not conducive to the long-term viability of a highly available database. Phantom queries like this don't simply gorge on valuable CPU resources; they can multiply unseen until the combined load requires more expensive hardware or the database buckles under the stress.

However, PostgreSQL can see everything, and now so can we, with `pg_stat_statements`. This recipe will explain how to install and utilize this valuable diagnostic tool.

Getting ready

Activating and using this extension requires us to modify the `postgresql.conf` configuration file and restart PostgreSQL. As usual, we need to ensure that we have access to a PostgreSQL superuser and a user capable of restarting the service, such as the `postgres` or `root` system users.

How to do it...

Begin by installing the `pg_stat_statements` module. Follow these steps:

1. Modify the `shared_preload_libraries` line in `postgresql.conf` to include the module, like this:

    ```
    shared_preload_libraries = 'pg_stat_statements'
    ```

2. If you are using PostgreSQL 9.1 or older, add this line to `postgresql.conf`:

```
custom_variable_classes = 'pg_stat_statements'
```

3. Restart PostgreSQL with a command similar to this:

pg_ctl -D /db/pgdata restart

4. Log in to PostgreSQL as a superuser into any database that should have access to `pg_stat_statements` and execute the following SQL statement:

```
CREATE EXTENSION pg_stat_statements;
```

Perform the following steps to prepare `pg_stat_statements` for generalized use:

1. Execute this SQL statement as a database superuser to create a function:

```
CREATE OR REPLACE FUNCTION pg_stat_statements()
RETURNS SETOF pg_stat_statements AS $$
    SELECT * FROM pg_stat_statements;
$$ LANGUAGE sql SECURITY DEFINER;
```

2. Execute this SQL statement to secure the function we created:

```
REVOKE ALL ON FUNCTION pg_stat_statements() FROM PUBLIC;
```

3. Create a user dedicated to monitoring with this SQL statement:

```
CREATE USER db_mon WITH PASSWORD 'somepass';
```

4. Grant the monitoring user the ability to use our function with this SQL statement:

```
GRANT EXECUTE ON FUNCTION pg_stat_statements() TO db_mon;
```

5. Now, connect to PostgreSQL as the `db_mon` user, and examine the contents of `pg_stat_statements` by executing this SQL statement:

```
SELECT * FROM pg_stat_statements();
```

How it works...

In our opinion, the first set of instructions should not be required. The `pg_stat_statements` module is so important that we feel everyone can benefit from its contents. In any case, the first thing we must do is add `pg_stat_statements` to the `shared_preload_libraries` configuration setting. Several PostgreSQL modules are only available after being added this way.

The next step is only necessary if we are running a version older than PostgreSQL 9.2. The `custom_variable_classes` setting allows us to further configure the `pg_stat_statements` module later. Current versions of PostgreSQL will handle this for us.

As the `pg_stat_statements` module depends on activating an external library, we must restart PostgreSQL for it to take effect. Once the module is loaded, there are necessary functions that access the module; we must also install these functions in any database where we want `pg_stat_statements` to be available. By executing the `CREATE EXTENSION` statement, we register these functions with the current database.

The next set of instructions focuses on making the `pg_stat_statements` module usable to non-superusers and mirrors the process we used in the *Checking the pg_stat_activity view* recipe. We begin by creating a function that runs as the user who defined it. As we created the function as a superuser, this means regular users can use it to examine the contents of `pg_stat_statements`.

To prevent any user from executing this elevated privilege function, we revoke all access from the `public` context. Then, if we don't already have a user set aside for monitoring database activity, we create one and then grant them access to execute `pg_stat_statements()`, because this is one of their acknowledged roles.

Newer versions of PostgreSQL add more fields to this view, seemingly with every release. Many of the new fields focus on the I/O related to disk timing and blocks being dirtied, so they are intended for more advanced usage. However, the columns we can count on include the following:

- `query`: This column displays up to 1,024 characters of the query being tracked.
- `calls`: This column contains the total number of times the SQL has been executed.

- `total_time`: This column provides the total time spent processing the query, in milliseconds.
- `rows`: This column lists the total number of rows ever returned by the query.

This is actually enough to perform quite a bit of investigation. We can divide `total_time` by `calls` to obtain the average execution speed. Perhaps we want to know the total ratio of INSERT statements to SELECT statements. Simply sorting the data by the `calls` column can reveal outliers that execute far more often than most queries. We used these ourselves to find a query that represented more than 50 percent of all the calls in the database. Our developers were very happy to cache the results of this query for us.

Modern versions of this view actually perform many of these calculations for us, along with a few we can't. One of the new fields is `sttdev_time`, and it's not possible to calculate standard deviations with only aggregate values. Given that standard deviations are a great tool for quantifying performance variance, this alone is a reason to upgrade.

There's more...

Of course, this extremely useful view has a few extra features that we want to explain.

Reset the status

Statistics stored in the `pg_stat_statements` view accumulate until they are forcefully reset. If we don't want to monitor value deltas between checks, we can simply reset the status of the module and cause it to erase the data it has collected. To do that, execute this SQL statement as a superuser:

```
SELECT pg_stat_statements_reset();
```

Catch more queries

By default, the `pg_stat_statements` module only tracks the first 5,000 queries it encounters during database operation (or 1,000 in older versions). Normally, this is enough, especially in versions of PostgreSQL above 9.1. Newer versions provide better aggregation because they remove SQL variables and constants from the query before including them in the view. However, older versions of databases that experience a high variance in query construction may want to increase this number. To do that, add this line to the `postgresql.conf` file:

```
pg_stat_statements.max = 10000
```

Then, we have to restart PostgreSQL again. Once this is finished, the `pg_stat_statements` module will track 10,000 queries instead of 1,000. Feel free to experiment with other values.

See also

We feel strongly that the `pg_stat_statements` view is indispensable, but we can only convey a tiny amount in a usage recipe. For an in-depth explanation of its contents and usage, please check the documentation at `https://www.postgresql.org/docs/current/static/pgstatstatements.html`.

Deciphering database locks

It's not uncommon for various elements of the database to block each other. Queries can lock shared resources, system maintenance can temporarily prevent a transaction from committing; the list is endless. As a result, a critical aspect of troubleshooting a PostgreSQL system is tracking down blocked sessions, and what might be preventing normal operation.

There are two very powerful ways to decipher locks within PostgreSQL in the `pg_locks` view and the PostgreSQL 9.6+ `pg_blocking_pids` function. This recipe will demonstrate why these approaches are so useful.

Getting ready

The `pg_locks` view needs no special access for use, and the `pg_blocking_pids` function can be called by any user. However, these resources are of limited utility without full access to `pg_stat_activity` as well. To proceed with this recipe, either connect to the database as a superuser (such as the `postgres` user) or refer to the *Checking the pg_stat_activity view* recipe to circumvent this limitation.

How to do it...

Create a blocking scenario with the following steps:

1. Connect to a database and create a test table, and then lock it with this SQL code:

   ```
   CREATE TABLE lock_test (junk INT);
   BEGIN;
   LOCK TABLE lock_test IN EXCLUSIVE MODE;
   ```

2. In a second connection, execute the following statement:

   ```
   INSERT INTO lock_test (junk) VALUES (42);
   ```

Next, investigate the problem with these steps (PostgreSQL 9.6 and above only):

1. Execute this query to obtain locking information:

   ```
   SELECT pid, locktype, mode, granted,
          relation::REGCLASS::TEXT AS locked_object
     FROM pg_locks
    WHERE relation IS NOT NULL
    ORDER BY relation, granted DESC;
   ```

2. Run this query to determine blocker sources:

   ```
   SELECT p.pid, p.query,
          s.pid AS blocker_pid, s.query AS blocker_query
     FROM pg_stat_activity p
     JOIN pg_stat_activity s ON (
             s.pid = ANY(pg_blocking_pids(p.pid))
          );
   ```

How it works...

The first set of steps is not strictly necessary if we have access to a particularly busy database. The lock tables are generally very active, and output in such a scenario is usually rather copious. Barring this, we need a way to purposefully demonstrate just how powerful the PostgreSQL lock debugging tools are.

Of the two queries that actually display PostgreSQL activity blocks, the first relies entirely upon the `pg_locks` view. After executing it, we should see this on an otherwise empty database:

```
 pid  | locktype |       mode        | granted | locked_object
------+----------+-------------------+---------+--------------
 3147 | relation | AccessShareLock   | t       | pg_locks
 3128 | relation | ExclusiveLock     | t       | lock_test
 3137 | relation | RowExclusiveLock  | f       | lock_test
```

What we can learn directly from the output is that there are two different PIDs that want to use the same object. We can see that one has a granted exclusive lock to `lock_test`, which means it is preventing any other process from modifying its contents. The other connection needs a lock to a specific row it can't obtain, and hence we have a lockup.

Yet this particular situation—and many like it—can only be implied by tracking resource conflicts between connections. There's no causal relationship other than what we might interpret based on the current state of the `pg_locks` view. There were third-party utilities that aimed to address this shortcoming, but none became particularly popular and the problem remained unresolved.

This is why PostgreSQL 9.6 added the `pg_blocking_pids` function. Given a single PID, it can gather a list of any other processes that are currently preventing it from proceeding. This is why our second query also makes use of `pg_stat_activity`. Including it allows us to directly witness the cause-and-effect relationship, as seen here:

```
-[ RECORD 1 ]-+----------------------------------------
pid           | 3137
query         | INSERT INTO lock_test VALUES (42);
blocker_pid   | 3128
blocker_query | LOCK TABLE lock_test IN EXCLUSIVE MODE;
```

Our demonstration is extremely simplified, yet the design of the query will capture any blocking activity due to our use of the ANY array conditional. The pg_blocking_pids function returns an array of all blocking processes, meaning our query should unroll and display an entire chain of locks right up to the original query.

There's more...

Astute readers may have noticed that the pg_locks and pg_stat_activity views both share the pid column. Since the pg_locks view only detailed information about the locks themselves, we can't tell when the lock might have been granted, or any other pertinent troubleshooting details. There is a very handy query that uses both of these views.

Users of PostgreSQL 9.5 and older can use this query:

```
SELECT l.pid, l.mode, l.granted, a.waiting,
       l.relation::REGCLASS::TEXT AS locked_object,
       a.datname, a.client_addr, a.usename,
       a.query_start, now() - a.query_start AS duration,
       substring(a.query, 1, 20) AS query_part
  FROM pg_locks l
  JOIN pg_stat_activity a USING (pid)
 WHERE l.relation IS NOT NULL
   AND now() - a.query_start > INTERVAL '10 minutes'
 ORDER BY a.query_start;
```

This query is more suitable for PostgreSQL 9.6 and above:

```
SELECT l.pid, l.mode, l.granted, a.wait_event,
       l.relation::REGCLASS::TEXT AS locked_object,
       a.datname, a.client_addr, a.usename,
       a.query_start, now() - a.query_start AS duration,
       substring(a.query, 1, 20) AS query_part
  FROM pg_locks l
  JOIN pg_stat_activity a USING (pid)
 WHERE l.relation IS NOT NULL
   AND now() - a.query_start > INTERVAL '10 minutes'
 ORDER BY a.query_start;
```

This query is large, but it also does a lot of work. First, it only returns results where locks have been held for at least 10 minutes so we're not overwhelmed. It also orders the rows based on when the queries started. In some cases, the best solution is to simply observe the number of resources the top queries might be locking, and terminate the connection to clear the jam. This is much easier when we can actually tell which queries started the problem.

Beyond this, we've included a good assortment of debugging columns such as database name, username, connection origin, and a fragment of the query itself. These details are indispensable when attempting to derive a requisite cause. If a script isn't operating normally, we want to know where it's running so a developer can fix the problem! If we can tell them where the query came from, its details, and the full list of locks, finding the problematic code will be far easier.

Of course, this is only one of many possible combinations of fields between these two views. Don't be afraid to mix and match!

See also

Read more about `pg_locks` and `pg_blocking_pids` in the PostgreSQL manual:

- **pg_locks**:
  `https://www.postgresql.org/docs/current/static/view-pg-locks.html`

- **System information functions**:
  `https://www.postgresql.org/docs/current/static/functions-info.htm l`

Debugging with strace

Sometimes, the only way to truly observe a server process is by using the kernel itself. This kind of data is invaluable for troubleshooting or research into PostgreSQL activity.

The Linux `strace` utility provides detailed system trace data for any process or service running on the server. For use with PostgreSQL, this utility means we can target the database itself or any of the background processes it uses for maintenance.

Perhaps more importantly, we can debug or examine any client connection. Is the network connection permanently hung? Is the client sending thousands of simple SQL requests instead of bulk-handling the results of a single large query? The `strace` command output is both intricate and verbose. This recipe will use `strace` to inspect our server and see what we can discover.

Getting ready

There are certain limitations to using `strace`. Because of its high-level access to process information, only root-level users are allowed to examine an application's activity. Make sure to have this capability before continuing.

As we want activity we can depend on, open a connection to PostgreSQL for us to locate later. We will be using this connection to generate debug output.

How to do it...

Follow these steps to examine the PostgreSQL processes in various ways:

1. In our PostgreSQL connection, execute the following query to find the PID of the server backend assigned to us:

   ```
   SELECT pg_backend_pid() AS pid;
   ```

2. As our root-capable user, attach `strace` to the preceding PID (`4200`, for example) with this command:

   ```
   sudo strace -p 4200
   ```

3. In our PostgreSQL connection, execute the following query to generate some activity:

   ```
   SELECT 1;
   ```

4. In the Terminal where `strace` is running, press *Ctrl* + *C* to disconnect.

5. Attach `strace` again, but collect the statistics with the following command:

   ```
   sudo strace -c -S calls -p 4200
   ```

6. Now, execute the following query to generate some complex activity:

   ```
   SELECT * FROM information_schema.columns;
   ```

7. In the Terminal where `strace` is running, press *Ctrl + C* to disconnect.
8. Attach `strace` a final time, but limit the output with the following command:

```
sudo strace -e recvfrom -p 4200
```

9. Execute the following query to generate a simple activity:

```
SELECT 1;
```

How it works...

We can connect to any process with `strace`, but for demonstrative purposes, we elect to control the environment by watching a connection we directly control. The `pg_backend_pid` function returns the PID of the backend process that serves our client, which then lets us monitor its activity on the server.

With the PID of the backend, we can monitor it with the -p parameter to `strace`, which watches the listed PID. As we don't want too much output, we elect to execute a very simple query that does not touch the tables, functions, or views. Our output should resemble this:

```
Process 4200 attached - interrupt to quit
recvfrom(11, "Q\0\0\0\16SELECT 1;\0", 8192, 0, NULL, NULL) = 15
sendto(11,
"T\0\0\0!\0\1?column?\0\0\0\0\0\0\0\0\0\0\27\0\4\377\377\377\377"...,
66, 0, NULL, 0) = 66
```

Once we press *Ctrl + C*, `strace` exits, and we can try a different combination of parameters. For example, the -c setting disables the normal output in favor of summarizing the kernel calls. If we use the -S parameter to change the sort column, we can focus on repeated calls. As counts will be boring with only a few columns, we've suggested a query that will touch on several database objects. Once we exit from the second `strace` command, the output looks like this:

% time	seconds	usecs/call	calls	errors	syscall
0.00	0.000000	0	93		lseek
0.00	0.000000	0	63		sendto
0.00	0.000000	0	17		brk
0.00	0.000000	0	2	1	recvfrom
0.00	0.000000	0	1		epoll_wait
100.00	0.000000		176	1	total

Finally, we would like to introduce the –e parameter, which limits the `strace` output to the calls listed. In our case, we chose `recvfrom`, which is a network-related call that the backend uses to await requests. When in this mode, `strace` will only print `recvfrom` calls, and nothing else.

The –e setting also provides several shortcuts. If the first keyword is `trace`, instead of a recognized call, we can specify a type of call to watch. For example, this revision of our last `strace` command would watch all network-related activities:

```
strace -e trace=network -p 4200
```

There's more...

Output from `strace` can be somewhat esoteric, especially as it limits the content length by default to increase readability. If we want to really capture a lot of data with extreme verbosity that will help a human make a diagnosis, we need to increase the string length. For `strace`, the parameter for that is –s. If we wanted to greatly extend the length of the string output, we can do that with this command:

```
sudo strace -p 4200 -s 2000
```

Then, we execute the following query:

```
SELECT 'This is a very long query to view.';
```

We would then see the following output:

```
recvfrom(11, "Q\0\0\0001select 'This is a very long query to
   view.';\0", 8192, 0, NULL, NULL) = 50
```

This would be instead of this output:

```
recvfrom(11, "Q\0\0\0001select 'This is a very long"..., 8192, 0,
   NULL, NULL) = 50
```

This is all that is required to monitor PostgreSQL, as even simple queries and data are truncated with default settings.

See also

Always examine the manual for the tools that we use in these recipes. In this case, the manual for `strace` is available by executing this command:

```
man strace
```

Logging checkpoints properly

Checkpoints are an integral part of a PostgreSQL server. Table data is not modified during query execution until modified rows, index pages, and other structures are committed to the **Write-Ahead Log** (**WAL**). WAL files are also known as checkpoint segments. When the cumulative size of these files exceeds `max_wal_size`—or the time since the last checkpoint exceeds `checkpoint_timeout`—the data files are modified to reflect the changes.

 In versions older than PostgreSQL 9.5, checkpoints were specified as a count of 16 MB files with the `checkpoint_segments` parameter, rather than a cumulative total size. The setting for `max_wal_size` in MB is roughly equivalent to `checkpoint_segments` * 16.

This decoupled writing approach ensures database integrity, at the cost of doubling the necessary disk writes. This is the main reason why some experienced PostgreSQL DBAs interested in performance may relocate the WAL location to a separate storage device. However, even moving the WAL files to another device may not sufficiently reduce write pressure. Database activity is variable in nature, and checkpoints only happen every few minutes or after a threshold of data modifications.

As PostgreSQL tries to avoid overwhelming the operating system, writes necessary to satisfy a checkpoint are spread evenly over the checkpoint interval. Unfortunately, the operating system may choose to buffer these writes unevenly, resulting in unexpected write spikes. A busy database might have saturated disk bandwidth already, thus tying up any resources necessary for writing data modifications.

The way we combat this is by logging all checkpoints and analyzing the output of our log for checkpoint activity. We may need to leverage tablespaces, storage improvements, or application revisions to really address resource collisions like this, so it's in our best interest to be proactive.

This recipe will demonstrate how and why checkpoint logging can help maintain a highly available PostgreSQL system.

Getting ready

You need to know where to find PostgreSQL logs. We usually suggest a few specific modifications to the `postgresql.conf` file for logging, including the following:

```
log_directory = 'pg_log'
log_checkpoints = on
```

This means logs will be found within our PostgreSQL data directory, in a subdirectory named `pg_log`. Some distributions use `/var/log/postgresql` instead. Regardless, determine where the logs are kept. To ensure access, examine these as the `postgres` user, who should either own the logs directly or have the necessary read access.

How to do it...

Assuming our logs are located at `/db/pgdata/pg_log`, follow these steps to examine the checkpoint activity:

1. Execute this command to find the most recent log file:

   ```
   ls -lt /db/pgdata/pg_log/postgres*.log | head -n 1
   ```

2. If the latest log is named `postgresql-2019-10-16.log`, view all the checkpoints in this log with the following command:

   ```
   grep checkpoint /db/pgdata/pg_log/postgresql-2019-10-16.log
   ```

3. Execute the following command to obtain the five longest disk syncs:

   ```
   grep 'checkpoint complete:' \
        /db/pgdata/pg_log/postgresql-2019-10-16.log \
        | sed 's/.* sync=/sync=/;' \
        | sed 's/total=[0-9.]* s; //; s/; dist.*//;' \
        | sort -n | tail -n 5
   ```

How it works...

We need to first find the most recent log file. The `ls` command's `-t` parameter will sort the data by the last modified time, which the `head` command limits to one line of results. Distributions that provide PostgreSQL may adhere to a log-rotation scheme instead. In these cases, the latest log file will reside in `/var/log/postgresql` and will always have the same name. Older logs will have a number appended until the retention period passes.

No matter how we locate the most recent log file, we use two relatively simple commands to examine its contents. These log files can be extremely useful, though we will focus on the checkpoint activity for now. Of those two commands, the first simply isolates all the checkpoint data in the order it occurred. One complete checkpoint will resemble these lines:

```
2019-10-16 23:02:53.108 UTC [34849] LOG:  checkpoint starting: time
2019-10-16 23:02:53.128 UTC [34849] LOG:  checkpoint complete:
wrote 129631 buffers (24.7%); 0 WAL file(s) added, 0 removed,
2 recycled; write=392.875 s, sync=1.789 s, total=394.667 s;
sync files=203, longest=1.004 s, average=0.008 s, distance=0 kB,
estimate=0 kB
```

This data is helpful in determining the time period of the checkpoint. Combined with other troubleshooting tools such as `sar`, we can correlate the checkpoint with disk activity. In the case of this example, we wrote 24.7 percent of a 4 GB buffer as well, which is quite a bit of data. However, these writes are spread over more than 6 minutes, reducing contention.

As useful as the raw log lines are, we can apply a few filters and sorting to expose the disk synchronization time. Our last command makes use of `grep` to isolate the checkpoints, `sed` to remove excess data, `sort` to focus on the longest syncs, and `tail` to restrict the output to the top five. Of these, the `sed` commands are the most complex. However, they merely remove all the content before the first `sync` field, the `total` field, and a couple of excess entries at the end, leaving only the data related to disk synchronization. Then, our top five most expensive checkpoints look like this:

```
sync=0.891 s, sync files=87, longest=0.470 s, average=0.010 s
sync=1.203 s, sync files=129, longest=0.302 s, average=0.009 s
sync=1.789 s, sync files=203, longest=1.004 s, average=0.008 s
sync=2.004 s, sync files=187, longest=1.031 s, average=0.010 s
sync=5.083 s, sync files=104, longest=3.076 s, average=0.048 s
```

The first four could be improved, but the last example is clearly much larger than we would normally expect or desire. Relatively few files were synchronized, yet the longest sync of over 3 seconds would likely adversely affect query performance. The disk synchronization duration exhibited here indicates a high level of contention. If we were to execute `sar` for the time periods indicated by the longest checkpoint, we would most likely see 100 percent disk utilization.

If this utilization is primarily data reads, we may be able to ignore it if the checkpoint time occurred outside of operational hours. In such cases, the cause is probably related to maintenance or voluminous batch jobs. Otherwise, we should expand our investigation to track the source of the disk activity until all the checkpoints are below a desirable threshold.

There's more...

Some checkpoint data is stored in a PostgreSQL view named `pg_stat_bgwriter`. This is more of a summary view of the checkpoint activity, but it is available to any user who can execute SQL statements in the database. Within this view, there are three fields related to this recipe that directly concern us:

- `checkpoints_timed`: This column provides the number of checkpoints that occur based on a schedule. These are normal checkpoints and indicate regular operation.
- `checkpoints_req`: This column stores the number of checkpoints that PostgreSQL has forced to occur in order to keep up with write activity. If there are too many of these, database performance can be extremely reduced and disk contention can have other adverse effects.
- `checkpoint_sync_time`: This column describes the total amount of time that the checkpoint system has spent in sync status, in milliseconds. This is basically a sum of all of the `sync` columns for all the checkpoints since the statistics were last reset. This is a good value to graph if you are monitoring the database, as a sudden spike in the elapsed sync time can indicate trouble.

See also

The WAL is integral to how PostgreSQL operates. We strongly recommend that you learn as much about its functionality as possible. The PostgreSQL documentation provides a great deal of depth in its explanation of how the WAL really works. Please make use of these links:

- **WAL Configuration**:
  `https://www.postgresql.org/docs/current/static/wal-configuration.html`
- **Write-Ahead Log**:
  `https://www.postgresql.org/docs/current/static/runtime-config-wal.html`
- **The Statistics Collector**:
  `https://www.postgresql.org/docs/current/static/monitoring-stats.html`

6
Monitoring

One aspect of PostgreSQL administration that is unfortunately ignored too frequently is system monitoring. Provisioning, constructing, and maintaining a high availability cluster is difficult by itself without the extra complications inherent in setting up yet more infrastructure.

Larger companies with an established **Network Operations Center** (**NOC**) probably have extremely mature incidence response and escalation procedures in place. Others may rely on a few basic monitors and alerts or ad hoc scripts set to trigger on certain thresholds. If we aren't part of the first group, we certainly can't include ourselves in the second and consider our cluster protected. When availability is important for business continuity, we should take the time to ensure that its activity is continuously reported, graphed, and summarized.

In this chapter, we will focus on what we should monitor, how often we should check system status, and how to present the data for easy consumption. When the database goes down, we need to know immediately. When the storage is higher than our projected limits, we need to plan accordingly. When database behavior is unexpected or abnormal, we should have a baseline for comparison. There are several tools available to do all of these things, and we're going to examine a stack of complementary services to automate everything.

There's no need to build any of our own tools. System monitoring is a very active field awash in mature software; we'd be wasting our time and needlessly putting our database architecture at risk. Let's protect our investment properly with professional tools vetted by hundreds or thousands of equally concerned and attentive **Database Administrators** (**DBAs**).

In this chapter, we will learn how to effectively monitor PostgreSQL's server status and database performance. Primarily, we will focus on using Nagios, Check_MK, `check_postgres`, Telegraf, InfluxDB, and Grafana; all of these tools excel at system monitoring. We will cover the following recipes in this chapter:

- Figuring out what to monitor
- Installing and configuring Nagios
- Configuring Nagios to monitor a database host
- Enhancing Nagios with Check_MK
- Getting to know check_postgres
- Installing and configuring Telegraf
- Adding a custom PostgreSQL monitor to Telegraf
- Installing and configuring InfluxDB
- Installing and configuring Grafana
- Building a graph in Grafana
- Customizing a Grafana graph
- Using InfluxDB tags in Grafana

Figuring out what to monitor

Modern servers have a lot of active hardware and software that can stop working at any time. A failure can start with the operating system, storage, database, network connectivity, heat, or several other sources.

So, which elements do we rank highest to ensure system availability? Which hardware needs the closest monitoring? What kind of tests should we use to ensure that the software is operating as expected?

When dedicating monitoring resources to check hardware and software, we must answer several questions to distribute effort efficiently. Every test takes time, uses network resources, and must save its results to a status file or another database. If our system checks are too frequent or numerous, we could end up overwhelming our monitor server. Failing to prioritize the alerting criteria can actually be more dangerous; if we become too accustomed to ignoring irrelevant alerts, legitimate system issues can propagate unchecked.

Hence, the first step in building a monitoring infrastructure is to decide what it will monitor and why. This recipe will guide our efforts in reaching that goal.

Getting ready

We're going to be building a spreadsheet. This spreadsheet will rank all of our hardware and software so that we know which systems deserve the most focus. Have a spreadsheet program available before starting.

How to do it...

Follow these steps to rank the priority and frequency of monitoring hardware and software:

1. Create a spreadsheet with six columns labeled `Monitor`, `Importance`, `Frequency`, `Warning Level`, `Critical Level`, and `Action`.
2. Under the `Monitor` column, list every relevant piece of hardware and software on the server.
3. Under the `Importance` column, rank every monitor at one of these three levels: `minor`, `major`, or `critical`.
4. Under the `Frequency` column, choose a monitoring interval. We suggest that you use one of these choices: `10 seconds`, `30 seconds`, `1 minute`, `1 hour`, `12 hours`, or `1 day`.
5. Under the `Warning Level` column, choose a threshold where the status of this resource should be considered a warning and might require further examination.
6. Under the `Critical Level` column, choose a threshold where the status of this resource should be considered critical and in need of immediate attention.
7. Under the `Action` column, pick an appropriate action that the monitor should take when a check triggers an alert. We suggest one of these choices: `ignore`, `email support`, `email DBAs`, and `panic`.

How it works...

The spreadsheet we're making requires only six columns to fit this recipe. Feel free to include any other relevant information when making your own spreadsheet. In fact, we suggest that you retain this document in source control for reference purposes and revisions. Its mere existence can prove beneficial as a necessary compliance document.

When we say to list every piece of hardware or software under the `Monitor` column, we expect a few to be forgotten. Part of this step is a mental filter; if we can't think of the resource, it probably isn't important enough to watch. There are limits to this, and we strongly suggest that you have at least two other objective people to verify that the list is complete.

For `Importance` and `Frequency`, we're really deciding how active this resource is and its likelihood to fail or require intervention. For example, consider a disk-space monitor. Usable disk space is a major concern, but it's not likely to grow quickly. We can safely check disk space every hour or even every day and remain completely covered.

There is a major caveat here. Servers that make extensive use of replication slots should closely monitor disk space in case replica systems become inactive. Under high WAL write volume, this could quickly exhaust disk resources and becomes a critical alert.

The `Warning Level` and `Critical Level` columns are essential to route the triggered alerts. A level of *warning* means a resource may need someone to double-check its status or acknowledge a problem for later review. If a resource reaches a *critical* status, every person interested in the server should be alerted immediately.

Mind the signal-to-noise ratio. Critical alerts should really only trigger under circumstances that require immediate and concerted attention. If this is not the case, the threshold is likely too low. Alerts that become too noisy are eventually ignored. Don't fall into this trap!

Finally, the monitoring software needs to know what action to take if an alert is triggered. If we ever choose *ignore,* we should simply disable that particular alert entirely. On the other hand, the support staff can usually solve simple resource problems or forward the alert to a DBA. At other times, we want the DBA to know immediately due to the importance or complexity of the hardware or software being monitored. As a last resort, the alert can merely *panic* and alert everyone in every contact list in the hope that at least one person is available to address the issue.

In the end, the first few lines of our spreadsheet may look something like this:

	A	B	C	D	E	F
1	Monitor	Importance	Frequency	Warning Level	Critical Level	Action
2	Disk Space of /db	major	1 hour	1.5TB	2TB	email support
3	PostgreSQL online	critical	10 seconds	N/A	no	email DBAs
4	Server Ping	critical	10 seconds	100ms	500ms	email support
5	OS User Count	minor	1 minute	10	20	ignore
6	/db Mount	critical	10 seconds	N/A	missing	panic

There's more...

If we have access to a collaborative spreadsheet tool such as Google Docs or an internal wiki, we should maintain this information there. Not only does this act as a central resource, but it ensures that all monitors have a logical reason to exist and have a predetermined escalation path. When problems arise, any time spent on deciding what to do or who to inform only serves to increase the overall amount of risk.

In the rare instance that management or business interests question our system monitoring policies, we have an immediate answer. As DBAs, we want our company to know that the database is in good hands, and a strict monitoring policy helps to accomplish this.

Installing and configuring Nagios

Nagios is a well-known monitoring tool. We won't make any claims that it is the best or most suitable tool for watching a highly available PostgreSQL installation. However, the community is large, the functionality is extensive and established, and interoperability with other tools and libraries is high. It was also one of the first to attain prominence and, as such, is a good way to learn how most monitoring systems function.

As an unfortunate consequence, the amount of installation prerequisites is rather lengthy. To get Nagios working properly, we need an HTTP server, Perl, and a mail daemon. Some plugins require PHP, while others need MySQL, **SNMP** (short for **Simple Network Management Protocol**) or any number of esoteric utilities and acronyms. There might be DBAs who also have strong skills as webmasters, but we can't depend on that. Getting Nagios installed with all of its foundation services is very complex, so we don't recommend that you do so.

Due to its history, the likelihood that Nagios is available on major Linux distributions is very high. Installing Nagios through the distribution will handle most, if not all, configuration and interoperability concerns. While an installation of this type only has minimal settings enabled and only monitors the monitoring server itself, it's a step in the right direction.

This recipe will focus on using distribution packaging tools such as yum or apt to install and configure a basic Nagios setup.

Getting ready

Red Hat-derived systems such as Fedora, RHEL, and CentOS have a prerequisite package that is not part of the included distribution repositories. To install Nagios, we need to add the **Extra Packages for Enterprise Linux** (**EPEL**) library. Red Hat systems can do this by obtaining the most recent EPEL package for their OS versions and architectures from https://fedoraproject.org/wiki/EPEL.

Look for the package file that begins with epel-release and download it to the monitoring server. Once the package is downloaded, it can be installed with this command as a root-level user:

```
sudo rpm -ivh epel-release-*.rpm
```

How to do it...

Follow these steps to install and configure Nagios on a Debian, Mint, or Ubuntu monitoring server:

1. Execute these commands as a root-level user to install Nagios and some useful plugins:

   ```
   sudo apt update
   sudo apt install nagios4 nagios-nrpe-plugin
   ```

2. Set the nagiosadmin password by executing this command as a root-level user:

   ```
   sudo htdigest -c /etc/nagios4/htdigest.users Nagios4
   nagiosadmin
   ```

3. Modify the `/etc/nagios4/apache2.conf` file and comment out the following lines:

```
#       Require ip ::1/128 [ignore the rest here]
#       <Files "cmd.cgi">
#       </Files>
```

4. Modify `/etc/nagios4/cgi.cfg` and set the following attribute:

```
use_authentication=1
```

5. Enable Nagios within Apache with this command:

```
ln -s /etc/nagios4/apache2.conf \
        /etc/apache2/sites-enabled/010-nagios.conf
```

6. Activate all necessary modules within Apache:

```
sudo a2enmod auth_digest authz_groupfile
```

7. Restart Apache with this command:

```
sudo systemctl restart apache2
```

8. Make the `ping` utility usable by Nagios:

```
sudo chmod u+s /bin/ping
```

Follow these steps to install Nagios on a Red Hat, Fedora, CentOS, and Scientific Linux monitoring server:

1. If it exists, open the `/etc/selinux/config` file and change the SELINUX parameter to match the following:

```
SELINUX=permissive
```

2. Execute the following command as a root-level user and ignore any errors:

```
sudo setenforce 0
```

3. Execute this command as a root-level user to install Nagios:

```
sudo yum install nagios nagios-plugins-all nagios-plugins-nrpe
```

4. Set the `nagiosadmin` password by executing this command as a root-level user:

```
htpasswd -c /etc/nagios/passwd nagiosadmin
```

5. Execute these commands as a root-level user to start Nagios on system boot:

```
sudo systemctl enable nagios
sudo systemctl enable httpd
```

6. Execute these commands as a root-level user to start Nagios:

```
sudo systemctl start httpd
sudo systemctl start nagios
```

7. Make the `ping` utility usable by Nagios:

```
sudo chmod u+s /usr/bin/ping
```

How it works...

Red Hat-based distributions focus primarily on system stability and lack many third-party utilities and daemons. Luckily, this is not a concern for us as groups exist to rectify this situation. One such group maintains EPEL, which we can exploit to simplify the process of installing Nagios.

Debian-based servers, for better or worse, are not so strict. Though they are often just as stable, the package repository is much more extensive. Hence, we can install Nagios with one invocation of `apt`. When installing the `nagios4` package, all of the necessary prerequisites are retrieved and installed as well. Unlike previous versions, however, authentication is not enabled by default so we must execute a few steps to manage that.

First, we actually create a password for the `nagiosadmin` user with the `htdigest` utility. Then, we must remove several lines from `apache2.conf`, which enable authentication only under limited circumstances. Finally, we modify `cgi.cfg` and explicitly enable authentication by setting `use_authentication` to 1.

Once we've done this, we need to tell Apache that it should serve the Nagios web management site. This is as simple as creating a symbolic link to the Apache `sites-enabled` directory where it looks for site configuration files. Afterward, we enable all modules within Apache that Nagios may use by calling the `a2enmod` utility. Finally, we simply restart Apache with `systemctl` to commit all of these changes.

Installing the `nagios` package on Red Hat-based systems is somewhat more complicated. RHEL servers will often enable **SELinux** by default for the sake of security. We choose to set SELinux in permissive mode so that it warns us of potential security problems but still allows basic functionality. Nagios makes use of external servers that SELinux would otherwise block. Using the `setenforce` utility, we also manually switch to permissive mode without rebooting the server. Due to our modification of `/etc/selinux/config`, future server reboots will leave SELinux in permissive mode.

With SELinux out of the way, we can install Nagios with `yum`, which should resolve and install any prerequisites for us. Unlike the Debian-based install, it will not automatically prompt us for a password for the `nagiosadmin` user. Hence, we must use the `htpasswd` utility to create one. To do so, we use the `-c` parameter to set the location of the password file we want to modify. Then, we set the second parameter to `nagiosadmin` as that's the name of the user for whom we are creating a password.

Next, we need to configure Nagios to start when the server starts. Modern Red Hat-based systems and Debian derivatives all use systemd for service management, so we use that to enable and start necessary HTTP and Nagios daemons.

And finally, since Nagios executes as a non-privileged system user, we need to modify the `ping` utility with `chmod` so it runs as the user who owns it. This means `ping` will execute as if launched by the `root` user. We used a quick-and-dirty approach, and there are generally better methods by using group memberships, but this should be OK for demonstration purposes.

There's more...

We know that Nagios is running by accessing its HTTP location. Provided we know the name or IP address of the monitor server, we can access Nagios via a web browser. Assuming that `10.0.30.51` is the IP of the server we're using to monitor PostgreSQL, the web interface would exist here on Red Hat systems:

```
http://10.0.30.51/nagios
```

Or it would exist here for Debian-based systems:

```
http://10.0.30.51/nagios4
```

Our default Nagios dashboard should resemble the following screenshot:

See also

As we mentioned earlier, installing Nagios is not easy due to all of the other resources it depends on. Please refer to the following links to learn more about installing and configuring Nagios. We've also included a link to a comparison of various monitoring tools in case you want to try one of the Nagios alternatives:

- **Nagios quickstart installation guides**:
  https://assets.nagios.com/downloads/nagioscore/docs/nagioscore/4/en/quickstart.html
- **Nagios Core documentation**:
  https://assets.nagios.com/downloads/nagioscore/docs/nagioscore/4/en/toc.html

Configuring Nagios to monitor a database host

Once Nagios is installed, it will automatically configure a few basic monitors directed toward its own server. If we click on the **Hosts** link in the web administration site, we are presented with this:

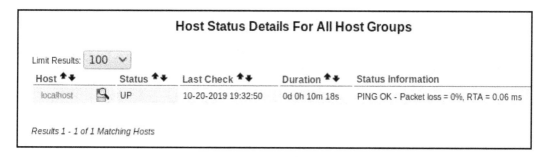

The local server is all that we are currently watching. This is useful to verify that Nagios is working as intended, but we need to monitor one or more database servers as well. In this recipe, we will learn how to watch external servers. By the end, we should see at least one more server listed by Nagios.

Getting ready

Initially, Nagios can only monitor remote servers by checking exposed services such as HTTP, FTP, or PostgreSQL. To check items such as CPU, RAM, or disk space, we need to rely on **Nagios Remote Plugin Executor** (**NRPE**) to forward system information to the monitoring server upon request. This means that NRPE must be installed on any server we want to monitor, including our PostgreSQL servers.

To install this on Debian-based servers, use the following command:

```
sudo apt-get install nagios-nrpe-server
```

Red Hat derivatives will need to use this command:

```
sudo yum install nrpe
```

Next, open /etc/nagios/nrpe.cfg and change the allowed_hosts setting to include the IP address or hostname of the monitor server. If 10.0.30.51 is the monitor server, it should look like this:

```
allowed_hosts=10.0.30.51
```

After this change is made, we must restart the NRPE service itself on Debian systems:

```
sudo systemctl restart nagios-nrpe-server
```

Red Hat derivatives will need to enable and start the service:

```
sudo systemctl enable nrpe
sudo systemctl start nrpe
```

How to do it...

Follow these steps on the monitoring system to watch the `10.0.30.1` server, which is the first node of our PostgreSQL cluster:

1. Use the following directory for Debian-based systems:

   /etc/nagios4

2. Use this directory for Red Hat derivatives:

   /etc/nagios

3. As a root-level user, create a file named `conf.d/db_conf.cfg` in the preceding path. It may be necessary to create the `conf.d` directory itself on some systems.

4. Make sure the following line appears in the `nagios.cfg` file on Debian-based systems:

   ```
   cfg_dir=/etc/nagios4/conf.d
   ```

4. Otherwise, make sure this line appears in `nagios.cfg` on Red Hat-based systems:

   ```
   cfg_dir=/etc/nagios/conf.d
   ```

5. In the `db_conf.cfg` file, define a `command` entry by adding this text:

   ```
   define command {
       command_name check_nrpe_1arg
       command_line $USER1$/check_nrpe -H $HOSTADDRESS$ -c $ARG1$
   }
   ```

6. In the `db_conf.cfg` file, define a `hostgroup` entry by adding this text:

   ```
   define hostgroup {
       hostgroup_name  pg-servers
       alias           PostgreSQL Servers
   }
   ```

7. In the `db_conf.cfg` file, define a `host` entry by adding this text:

   ```
   define host {
       use             generic-host
       host_name       pg-1
       alias           PostgreSQL Node 1
       address         10.0.30.1
   ```

```
        hostgroups              pg-servers
        max_check_attempts      10
        check_command           check-host-alive
    }
```

8. In the db_conf.cfg file, define a service entry by adding this text:

```
define service {
        use                     generic-service
        hostgroup_name          pg-servers
        service_description     Current Load
        check_command           check_nrpe_1arg!check_load
    }
```

9. Reload the Nagios configuration files on Debian-based systems:

   sudo systemctl reload nagios4

10. Red Hat-based servers should use this command:

    sudo systemctl reload nagios

How it works...

This recipe has a lot of moving parts, but it merely looks more complicated than it really is. We begin by finding the directory where supplementary configuration files are stored. Once this is located, we can create an entry to watch our PostgreSQL servers. To do this, we create a file named db_conf.cfg.

> You don't have to use db_conf.cfg. Nagios should recognize any file that ends with a .cfg extension. If you'd rather separate hosts, host groups, and services, feel free to do so.

The order of the elements that we are creating does not matter; Nagios has a very advanced parser that checks configuration entries all at once. Still, it's more logical to define things before they're used, so we've elected to begin with the check command we'll be using in this example.

Once that's defined, we define the PostgreSQL hostgroup so that we have a way of grouping all of our database servers together. This enables us to create dozens or hundreds of PostgreSQL servers and apply the same checks to all of them.

The next entry we create in our `db_conf.cfg` file tells Nagios that this is a host it should monitor. Older versions of Nagios would implicitly ping hosts, but now we must explicitly request the method of host check. In our case, the predefined `check-host-alive` operation is fine. Nagios will ping this server to ensure that it's online, and this will be the only check until we configure more.

The meaning of the `use` line may not be obvious. Nagios has several requirements to define a configuration entry. Instead of copying the same settings over and over again, we can create a template and then use it later. In this case, Nagios comes preconfigured with several basic templates, and we're making use of one for our newly created hosts.

The next entry we create in `db_conf.cfg` is a service we want to check. In this case, we are going to take advantage of NRPE to obtain the current system load. By setting `hostgroup-name` to `pg-servers`, Nagios will check the system load on all PostgreSQL servers; there's no need to create a service entry for each host.

`check-command` is probably somewhat opaque as well. Every service requires a command to execute. Commands are defined like other Nagios objects and must be named for reference. This is why we defined the `check_nrpe_1arg` command before using it here. Nagios separates commands from their parameters with an exclamation point. Therefore, in this example, we're invoking NRPE to check the system load on the remote server.

Finally, we tell Nagios to reload its configuration files. This causes Nagios to reread all configuration files, including the one we created. If everything goes well, clicking on **Host Groups** in the web interface should produce this summary:

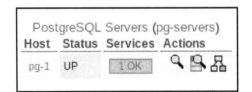

If we don't see this, it may be necessary to manually upgrade the NRPE service on each remote host. Nagios, backward compatibility in this area could stand to be improved, and Debian monitoring systems are especially prone to experience complications when communicating with older versions of NRPE.

There's more...

Wait a minute! We never added a check for PostgreSQL itself! As we can't allow PostgreSQL to remain unmonitored, create a user on our PostgreSQL server with the following command:

```
CREATE USER nagios;
```

Then, make an entry in the `pg_hba.conf` file to allow trusted checks from the monitoring server with this line:

```
host    template1    nagios    10.0.30.51/32    trust
```

Then, reload the PostgreSQL configuration with this command:

```
pg_ctl -D $PGDATA reload
```

Next, add a service entry to our `db_conf.cfg` file like this:

```
define service {
        use                     generic-service
        hostgroup_name          pg-servers
        service_description     PostgreSQL Status
        check_command           check_pgsql
}
```

Red Hat systems or others that do not supply `check_pgsql` as a standard definition may also need the command itself defined like this:

```
define command{
    command_name  check_pgsql
    command_line  $USER1$/check_pgsql -H '$HOSTADDRESS$' '$ARG1$'
}
```

After reloading our Nagios configuration files, click on the **Services** link in the web interface. It should now list two monitored services for the `pg-1` server, as seen here:

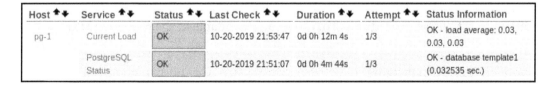

Host ↕	Service ↕	Status ↕	Last Check ↕	Duration ↕	Attempt ↕	Status Information
pg-1	Current Load	OK	10-20-2019 21:53:47	0d 0h 12m 4s	1/3	OK - load average: 0.03, 0.03, 0.03
	PostgreSQL Status	OK	10-20-2019 21:51:07	0d 0h 4m 44s	1/3	OK - database template1 (0.032535 sec.)

See also

Nagios configuration objects are fairly complicated. To use them properly, we strongly suggest that you browse the Nagios object manual located at `https://assets.nagios.com/downloads/nagioscore/docs/nagioscore/4/en/object definitions.html`

Enhancing Nagios with Check_MK

While Nagios is well established in the system administration community, it retains a few shortcomings due to its long legacy. This is not to suggest that Nagios is a bad platform! However, we can make it better for our own uses and for other administrators that help us to monitor our database clusters.

Check_MK is a popular extension to Nagios that provides a better interface, more built-in monitors, and—for those interested—a GUI management system. This management GUI is actually one of the main things we will cover in this recipe as it has some idiosyncrasies of its own. This recipe will present the basics of Check_MK and encourage you to experiment with some of its more powerful features.

Getting ready

To complete this recipe, we will need a configured Nagios installation. Please follow the steps in the *Installing and configuring Nagios* recipe. However, either skip the *Configuring Nagios to monitor a database host* recipe or follow these two steps:

1. Delete the `db_conf.cfg` file that we created for our database host.
2. Reload the `nagios` service.

We also need to install and configure the base packages. The creators of Check_MK published a comprehensive set of instructions on how to download the correct system packages for your distribution, as well as basic installation steps. They also provide follow-up activation procedures. This should be available at the following URL: `https://checkmk.com/cms_introduction_packages.html`.

For reference, when it comes to the `omd create` step, we chose to name our OMD server `pgmon`. You do not need to do this to follow along, but do consider naming it something general for the entire PostgreSQL cluster if Check_MK isn't already maintained by another server management department.

> Remember to download and install the Raw edition of Check_MK, unless you own a subscription to their Enterprise edition.

How to do it...

For this recipe, our database has a local hostname of `pg-1`, and the monitor server is named `monitor-server`. Start by following these steps to set up `pg-1` with a Check_MK resource agent:

1. Click on **Monitoring Agents** in the **WATO - Configuration** segment of the left sidebar.
2. Download the appropriate agent that matches the operating system being monitored. Assuming `pg-1` is a Debian system, we might download `check-mk-agent_1.6.0p5-1_all.deb`.
3. Install the agent via `yum`, `apt`, or any appropriate package manager.
4. Select and download any additional agent plugins you'd like to monitor. We recommend the `mk_postgres` plugin.
5. Install any chosen plugins into the following folder on `pg-1`:

   /usr/lib/check_mk_agent/plugins

6. Mark any downloaded plugins as executable so Check_MK can use them:

   sudo chmod a+x /usr/lib/check_mk_agent/plugins

Follow these steps to create and configure the host and service monitors for our PostgreSQL server:

1. Navigate to the monitor server in a web browser, to the `pgmon` URL (or the name you chose during `omd create`): `http://monitor-server/pgmon`.
2. Enter `cmkadmin` as the username and use the password generated during `omd create`.
3. Click on **Hosts** in the **WATO - Configuration** segment of the left sidebar.
4. Click on the **Create new folder** icon.
5. Name the folder `PostgreSQL Servers`, and click on **Save & Finish**.
6. Click on the `PostgreSQL Servers` folder.
7. Click on the **Create new host** icon.

8. Set the **Hostname** to pg-1 and the **Alias** to PostgreSQL Node 1, and click on **Save & Finish**.

9. Click on the highlighted **service discovery** link in the information box above the list of hosts. It will then begin scanning pg-1 for services.

10. Click on **Fix all missing / vanished** after the scan is complete.

11. Click on the orange icon that says there are **Changes**.

12. Click on **Activate Affected**.

13. Wait for five minutes, then click on **All services** in the **Views-Services** segment of the left sidebar.

How it works...

While we could have included instructions on installing Check_MK, they are actually very long and would have required several pages of explanation. The official site does an admirable job presenting the installation process, so why duplicate it? The abundant documentation is a great reason to use it.

Once we log in, we see a very large and somewhat imposing interface. However, for now, we are only interested in the left sidebar. What we're looking for is the **Web Administration Tool** (**WATO**) section, as seen here:

It's a good idea to quickly explain how to install Check_MK resource agents before we start monitoring anything. This will need to be done on any system that Check_MK is expected to monitor. Thankfully, it's very simple and Check-MK itself even provides the agents and any related plugins directly within the **Monitoring Agents** menu option.

All we must do is download an agent for the operating system of the server we're monitoring. Users of Red Hat-based or Debian-derived distributions can merely download and install the package and have a working resource agent. Installing plugins is equally simplified since we only need to download any plugins we want and deposit them into the /usr/lib/check_mk_agent/plugins folder. After a quick chmod command to make plugins usable, the agent is fully configured.

Otherwise, the interface for managing hosts is actually very friendly to new users. Once we click on **Hosts**, we can either create a new host right away or create a folder first. We recommend that you always group the servers in specific folders to make bulk actions easier. Hence, we click on this enticing icon:

Once we name and save the folder, we can enter the folder and create the new host. After creating the host and saving its configuration, we are presented with this notice:

Now you should do a service discovery in order to auto-configure all services to be checked on this host.

When Check_MK inventories a server, it attempts to automatically detect the services and resources it can monitor. Nagios definitely can't do this! Once we activate all of the changes we made, we need to wait for a minute or two for Check_MK to add the new checks and collect the status of each. After some time has elapsed, we can click on **All services** to see our newly monitored PostgreSQL server:

Local site pgmon, pg-1

STATE	SERVICE	ICONS	STATUS DETAIL	AGE	CHECKED	PERF-O-METER
OK	Check_MK		OK - [agent] Version: 1.6.0p5, OS: linux, execution time 0.6 sec	17 h	7.46 s	574 ms
OK	Check_MK Discovery		OK - no unmonitored services found, no vanished services found, no new host labels	17 h	60 m	
OK	CPU utilization		OK - Total CPU: 0.93%	17 h	6.47 s	0.93%
OK	Filesystem /		OK - 1.42% used (580.75 MB of 40 GB), trend: +122.57 kB / 24 hours	17 h	6.47 s	1.42%

On our particular test server, Check_MK found about 25 services it knew how to monitor, including those detected by the optional mk_postgres plugin. We don't have to select all of them of course, but adding the same services to Nagios would have been much more difficult.

There's more...

Check_MK doesn't just provide a handy web interface, but it actually has a very advanced command-line utility. For instance, if we stopped the recipe after creating the folder and server and then activated the changes, we could have performed the server inventory with these two commands:

```
su - pgmon
cmk -I pg-1
cmk -O
```

The first command checks the `pg-1` server for new services. The second saves the services it found and reloads so they show up in our **All services** menu option. The command-line tool makes a great companion to the web interface when handling several server clusters.

See also

We really like the Check_MK documentation. It's comprehensive, verbose, and full of examples. Check some of the following links for more information:

- **Getting Started with Monitoring**: `https://checkmk.com/cms_check_mk_getting_started.html`
- **Check_MK on the command line**: `https://checkmk.com/cms_cmk_commandline.html`
- **Catalog of Check Plug-ins**: `https://checkmk.com/cms_check_plugins_catalog.html`

Getting to know check_postgres

Our friends at Bucardo created a useful, general-purpose PostgreSQL checking utility. The `check_postgres` tool currently has an inventory of more than 50 checks to monitor PostgreSQL servers.

While this is an exceptionally useful tool, integrating it into our overall stack is necessary to fully take advantage of its capabilities. This recipe will cover the basic usage and integration with Nagios for easy PostgreSQL monitoring of large database clusters.

Getting ready

Though some Linux distributions package the check_postgres utility for easy installation, the versions that are included are usually quite antiquated. We recommend that you obtain a copy of the latest check_postgres source code. At the time of this book revision, the latest version is 2.24.0, released on November 5, 2018. Obtain the latest copy of the check_postgres source code from https://bucardo.org/check_postgres/.

As we want to use Nagios to execute the check_postgres, please follow the steps in the *Configuring Nagios to monitor a database host* recipe to produce a working installation with a basic database host configuration. We will be making further modifications to the db_conf.cfg file introduced there.

The check_postgres program also needs PostgreSQL command-line tools to invoke checks. So, we should at least install minimal packages on the monitoring server. Assuming we've already enabled the PostgreSQL PGDG repository, Debian systems can install them this way:

```
sudo apt install postgresql-client-12
```

Red Hat-derived distributions can use this:

```
sudo yum install postgresql12
```

How to do it...

Install check_postgres by following these steps:

1. Use these commands to extract the check_postgres source and enter the source directory:

   ```
   tar -xf check_postgres-2.24.0.tar.gz
   cd check_postgres-2.24.0/
   ```

2. Next, build and install the actual software with these commands:

   ```
   perl Makefile.PL
   make
   sudo make install
   ```

3. Repeat these steps on any servers where you wish to run check_postgres. It's a good idea to install it on any PostgreSQL servers in addition to the monitoring system.

As the `postgres` user on a PostgreSQL server, try using these commands to obtain database information:

1. Check the state of the database size with this command:

```
check_postgres.pl --action=database_size -w 100MB -c 200MB
```

2. Create a large table by executing this SQL as the `postgres` user in the `postgres` database:

```
CREATE TABLE bigtable AS
SELECT generate_series(1,1000000) AS vals;
```

3. Cause a critical alert by executing this command:

```
check_postgres.pl --action=table_size -w 10MB -c 20MB
```

Integrate `check_postgres.pl` into Nagios by following these steps:

1. Create a `command` section in the `db_conf.cfg` file with this content:

```
define command {
  command_name   check_pg
  command_line   /usr/local/bin/check_postgres.pl -H
$HOSTADDRESS$ --action $ARG1$ -w $ARG2$ -c $ARG3$
}
```

2. Create a `service` section in the `db_conf.cfg` file that looks like this:

```
define service {
  use                  generic-service
  hostgroup_name       pg-servers
  service_description  PostgreSQL Database Size
  check_command        check_pg!database_size!100MB!200MB
}
```

3. Reload the Nagios configuration files on Debian-based systems:

```
sudo systemctl reload nagios4
```

4. Red Hat-based servers should use this command:

```
sudo systemctl reload nagios
```

How it works...

This recipe comes in three parts because we're doing three distinctly different things. Installing `check_postgres` itself is actually very easy. The entirety of the utility is contained within a single file, so we can simply move `check_postgres.pl` to a suitable location in our PATH environment setting. However, we suggest that you use the standard installation process as we did.

> While executing `sudo make install`, look for this line near the end: `Installing /usr/local/bin/check_postgres.pl`.
>
> This will indicate where the `check_postgres.pl` script is located. Ours was installed in `/usr/local/bin`, but yours may be elsewhere.

Next, we try a couple of basic commands to ensure that `check_postgres` works. The first command makes use of the `database_size` action and alerts us if our database is larger than the warning (-w) or critical (-c) thresholds that we set. The `table_size` action performs a similar task but applies the thresholds to every table in the database. By default, `check_postgres` connects to the `postgres` database, so we placed a large table there to trigger a critical alert. The output is very large as it lists every table, but it should begin like this:

```
POSTGRES_TABLE_SIZE CRITICAL: DB "postgres" (host:pgha1) largest table
is "public.bigtable": 35 MB
```

As we have verified that the check works, we want Nagios to invoke it instead. This removes the need to create ad hoc invocations and allows us to search for large tables on all of the database servers that Nagios is monitoring.

We will start the process by adding a command to Nagios in the `db_conf.cfg` file we created for our single test server. Remember where `check_postgres.pl` was installed because we need to specify the full path to the script just in case it's not part of the standard PATH environment. We will set the first argument to the action we want to perform and reserve the second and third for the warning and critical levels respectively. By making our `check_pg` command so generic, we can use it for every action that `check_postgres` supports. Otherwise, we would have needed a separate `command` section for each check.

Then, we add a `service` check. We will need to add one of these for each `check_postgres` action that we want to activate. In our example, we only enabled the `database_size` check and applied the same thresholds that we used when manually invoking the script. By reloading the Nagios configuration files, it will incorporate the new PostgreSQL database size check and apply it to any server that we have in the `pg-servers` group.

There's more...

Though the documentation explains all of the actions available for `check_postgres`, it may be inconvenient to refer to it regularly. The `check_postgres.pl` script accepts the usual `--help` parameter, but it also has a more notable ability. If we specify the `--man` parameter instead, `check_postgres` will actually display the entire manual. This is similar to investigating the `check_postgres` man page like this:

```
man check_postgres
```

Sometimes, man pages don't get installed properly or are not available for one reason or another. The `--man` parameter should always work on any system that also contains the `perl` documentation package.

See also

As `check_postgres` is developed by Bucardo, their site contains various resources related to its operation. We recommend these links for more information:

- **The check_postgres site**: https://bucardo.org/check_postgres/
- **The check_postgres documentation**:
  https://bucardo.org/check_postgres/check_postgres.pl.html

Installing and configuring Telegraf

When monitoring multiple clusters of servers, we need a data collection method that's both scalable and configurable. The **Telegraf** daemon is a scalable statistics gathering service, perfect for large clusters as it operates in conjunction with InfluxDB in a client-server model. A common Telegraf + InfluxDB cluster may look like this, with Telegraf running on every PostgreSQL server:

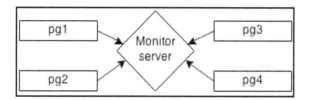

While Telegraf works best with InfluxDB, it's not required to start collecting information from the server and PostgreSQL itself. This recipe will explain how to install and configure Telegraf so we have basic performance monitoring at our fingertips.

Getting ready

We must prepare by obtaining a copy of the latest Telegraf package as distributed by influxdata. At the time of this edition, the latest version is 1.12.3, released on October 7, 2019. Download the latest copy
from `https://portal.influxdata.com/downloads/`.

Later, we simply need a root-capable user to install Telegraf as a system-wide service. Use `apt` or `yum` (or any relevant package management system) to install the package on any PostgreSQL server we want to monitor.

How to do it...

Assume that we have a PostgreSQL server named `pgha1`. Follow these steps on the server to enable basic monitoring:

1. Create a file named `pgha1.conf` in `/etc/telegraf/telegraf.d` and use the following contents:

```
[[inputs.postgresql]]
  address = "host=pgha1 user=postgres"
```

```
outputaddress = "pgha1"
max_lifetime = "0s"
databases = ["pgbench"]
```

2. Modify the `/etc/telegraf/telegraf.conf` file and add these two lines near the end:

```
[[outputs.file]]
files = ["/tmp/metrics.out"]
```

3. Then, restart the `telegraf` service:

`sudo systemctl restart telegraf`

4. Watch the `/tmp/metrics.out` file to see what Telegraf is doing:

`tail -f /tmp/metrics.out | grep postgres`

How it works...

Believe it or not, the first step is to create a configuration file for the local PostgreSQL installation so we can monitor every database that looks interesting. For now, we'll focus on a previously created `pgbench` database because it's easy to simulate database activity here.

There are really only four configuration elements we must actually set. We begin with `address`, which is a standard PostgreSQL connection string, and we've specified our `pgha1` server. Related to this is `outputaddress`, which acts as a label in any monitoring display and lets us identify the system specifically instead of using a default generated name.

Then, we set `max_lifetime` to `0s`, which indicates we want Telegraf to remain connected to PostgreSQL and simply submit queries after every waiting interval. If Telegraf loses the connection, it will simply re-establish it and continue operations.

And finally, we specify the databases where we actually want metrics. This is an array and we've limited it to `pgbench` as it's the only database currently in our installation. If there are more databases to monitor, we would add them here.

What we love about Telegraf is that it exists purely to poll other services, commands, or systems for performance data and then send it elsewhere for processing. Unfortunately for us, it's not so obvious what Telegraf is doing without some kind of way to examine what it's monitoring. So, to prove Telegraf is actually doing something, we enable the `file` output plugin so all collected metrics are written to `/tmp/metrics.out`.

We probably wouldn't write to a disk file on a real production system, but it's great for demonstration purposes. Once we've restarted Telegraf itself, it should immediately start writing to the metric file we specified. We can use a basic tail command to watch it poll PostgreSQL for status information at the default interval of 10 seconds.

See also

Telegraf is designed to communicate with many popular data aggregation, monitoring, and visualization systems. There are also copious plugins available for different methods of collecting data to send. As such, it has extensive documentation on configuring these. Check out this URL for more: `https://docs.influxdata.com/telegraf/`

Adding a custom PostgreSQL monitor to Telegraf

The primary reason we chose to install Telegraf stems from its ability to monitor arbitrary data points. Due to the existence of a PostgreSQL plugin for Telegraf capable of handling arbitrary SQL, we can actually collect data from the database itself. Monitoring PostgreSQL becomes as easy as writing a query!

Even though the *Installing and configuring Telegraf* recipe already used the PostgreSQL plugin, that particular extension only offers basic metrics. This recipe is going to introduce and explore the extensible PostgreSQL plugin instead.

We will include a few sample queries we developed for monitoring PostgreSQL servers through this recipe. Feel free to develop your own as we explain how to further leverage the Telegraf PostgreSQL module.

Getting ready

As the Telegraf PostgreSQL module needs to log in to a database within the cluster to gather its statistics, we should create a user specifically for this purpose. Execute these SQL queries to create a user with an appropriate password and all the necessary permissions to read all statistics:

```
CREATE USER perf_mon WITH PASSWORD 'testpw';
GRANT pg_read_all_stats TO perf_mon;
```

In addition, follow the instructions in the *Installing and configuring Telegraf* recipe so that there is a fully functional Telegraf data collector.

How to do it...

Assume that we have a PostgreSQL server named `pgha1`. Follow these steps on the server to enable more enhanced metrics:

1. Create or modify a file named `pgha1.conf` in `/etc/telegraf/telegraf.d`.

2. Start with the header section for the extensible metrics:

```
[[inputs.postgresql_extensible]]
  address = "host=pgha1 user=perf_mon dbname=postgres"
  outputaddress = "pgha1"
  max_lifetime = "0s"
  databases = ["pgbench"]
```

3. Continue by defining a query to monitor replication slot lag:

```
[[inputs.postgresql_extensible.query]]
  sqlquery="""
    SELECT slot_name,
           pg_wal_lsn_diff(
             pg_current_wal_insert_lsn(),
             restart_lsn
           )::BIGINT as restart_lsn_lag,
           pg_wal_lsn_diff(
             pg_current_wal_insert_lsn(),
             confirmed_flush_lsn
           )::BIGINT as confirmed_flush_lag
      FROM pg_replication_slots
  """
  version=940
  withdbname=false
```

```
    tagvalue="slot_name"
    measurement="postgresql.slot_lag"
```

4. Next, add a query to retrieve XID wraparound information:

```
[[inputs.postgresql_extensible.query]]
  sqlquery="""
    SELECT age(datfrozenxid) AS xid_age
      FROM pg_catalog.pg_database
     WHERE datname
  """
  version=900
  withdbname=true
  measurement="postgresql.xid"
```

5. Then, add a query to view session activity statistics:

```
[[inputs.postgresql_extensible.query]]
  sqlquery="""
    SELECT count(*) AS total,
           count(*) FILTER (
             WHERE state
               LIKE 'idle in%') AS trans_idle,
           count(*) FILTER (
             WHERE state = 'active') AS active,
           count(*) FILTER (
             WHERE wait_event
                IS NOT NULL) AS waiting,
           count(*) FILTER (
             WHERE state = 'active' AND
               now() - state_change >
                 INTERVAL '1s') AS slow
      FROM pg_stat_activity;
  """
  version=960
  withdbname=false
  measurement="postgresql.sessions"
```

6. Finally, restart the `telegraf` service:

   sudo systemctl restart telegraf

7. Watch the /tmp/metrics.out file to see what Telegraf is doing:

   tail -f /tmp/metrics.out | grep xid

How it works...

If we already applied the *Installing and configuring Telegraf* recipe, the first portion of the configuration probably looks familiar. We define a connection string and set `address` so our `perf_mon` user can connect and retrieve metrics. As before, we use `outputaddress` to provide a convenient system alias so we can find these statistics later. We also set `max_lifetime` to `0s` for persistent connections and databases to `pgbench` so we can focus on our primary database.

But that was something we already knew how to do. The exciting part lies within the `inputs.postgresql_extensible.query` sections. Telegraf will execute each of the queries we define every 10 seconds by default so we'll have a continuous stream of information. We already know how to write queries, so let's explore the other parameters for each query.

The first is the `version` specification. If we examine each query, we might see that they reflect a different version number every time. This is for compatibility purposes to prevent Telegraf from executing a query on a version of PostgreSQL that doesn't support it. It also means we can define the same query multiple times with different syntax if necessary, if we want to support multiple PostgreSQL versions.

In our case, we restricted each query to match system catalog columns or supported SQL syntax. Just remember that Telegraf expects versions to be reflected as `960` instead of `9.6.0` or it may not execute the queries at all.

Next comes the `withdbname` attribute, which is a way to restrict results to each database we specified in the `databases` parameter. All we need to do is assume Telegraf will append one or more database names at the end of the query. If we set this value to `true`, it will transform `WHERE dbname` into `WHERE dbname=pgbench`, for instance.

The `tagvalue` field can be misleading. It essentially means we should specify any columns that act as labels rather than metrics. This is why we only set it to `slot_name` for the first query for replication slot lag, as the first column specifies the name of the slot we want to monitor. This allows various monitoring systems to watch specific replication slots if desired.

Lastly, for each query, we define the name of `measurement` itself. Certain display systems for these metrics provide a convenient drill-down system where we can choose each element as separated by a period. So, for example, if we wanted to view XID wraparound information, we would first choose `pgha1`, then `postgresql`, and then `xid`.

Once we restart the Telegraf service itself, we can watch our previously defined output in /tmp/metrics.out for some of these values to prove everything is working properly.

 We also want to bring attention to the fact we used ::BIGINT casting in the second query for slot lag. This is necessary because the value is interpreted as text by default, which we won't be able to aggregate later. This is one good reason to check file output, as we can then ensure integer types show up correctly.

There's more...

The queries we defined earlier should not be considered the only things that should be monitored. We chose some very important elements, including the following:

- Replication lag when using slots can be extremely dangerous. Replication slots cause PostgreSQL to retain WAL files indefinitely until the downstream system indicates they are no longer required. In addition to monitoring disk space, this is important to watch over time because we can observe when the lag began to increase, how long the value was elevated, and other long-term activity. This is something Nagios or Check_MK won't do natively, so it's good to explicitly collect this data.

- The next query tracks transaction ID wraparound. PostgreSQL uses a 32-bit integer in tuple headers to indicate which transaction can see each row. Due to this limitation, it can only handle up to 2 billion transactions before cleanup is required. This cleanup is done during each VACUUM and the background autovacuum process. These both locate overridden rows to erase or set visible rows to a special value until an update overrides them. However, if this cleanup is blocked or falls behind, the XID age can climb until it reaches a maximum value that will cause the database to shut down to preserve data. It's always important to watch this value in any metric dashboard available.

- Finally, we watch general query activity. In this case, we just do the basics. Lots of sessions that are idle in a transaction can lead to lock contention or blocked DDL, so we want that to stay low. We also watch for queries that have been running for longer than one second, as a sharp increase here may indicate a resource bottleneck. Waiting is also important to observe since that's an easy indicator of row contention or a rogue lock.

However, there is always more to consider. We provided a query for watching slot lag, but not regular replication lag. Maybe we want to watch database size over time, the ten largest tables in the database, or the number of rows fetched from disk instead of shared memory. The PostgreSQL catalog is vast and we can retrieve and format much of it in a way that would present well in a monitoring dashboard.

We encourage browsing the web for more metrics and including them; information is power.

See also

We refer to both the Telegraf extensible PostgreSQL plugin and the PostgreSQL catalogs here. Refer to these resources to learn more:

- **The Telegraf postgresql_extensible plugin**:
  `https://github.com/influxdata/telegraf/tree/master/plugins/inputs`
  `/postgresql_extensible`
- **PostgreSQL System Catalogs**:
  `https://www.postgresql.org/docs/current/catalogs.html`

Installing and configuring InfluxDB

One critical component of a monitoring system is a data collection or aggregation layer. A very common design here is to use a client-server model so that multiple independent metric gathering services communicate with a centralized system for processing and interpretation.

InfluxDB is a time-series database designed specifically for efficiently ingesting performance metrics from varying sources. One of these just happens to be Telegraf, which we introduced in previous recipes. A common Telegraf + InfluxDB cluster may look like this, with InfluxDB running on a single monitoring server, as seen in this familiar diagram:

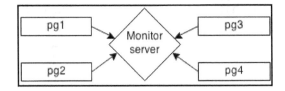

InfluxDB acts as a data-gathering and centralization repository so data visualization tools and trend analysis software can produce trend information, graphs, dashboards, alerts, and other useful elements for server management.

This recipe will explain how to install and configure InfluxDB so we can combine all of our Telegraf readings in a single location for interpretation.

Getting ready

We must prepare by obtaining a copy of the latest InfluxDB package as distributed by influxdata. At the time of this edition, the latest version is 1.7.8, released on August 21, 2019. Download the latest copy from
`https://portal.influxdata.com/downloads/`.

Later, we simply need a root-capable user to install InfluxDB as a system-wide service. Use `apt` or `yum` (or any relevant package management system) to install the package on any PostgreSQL server we want to monitor.

Don't forget to follow the instructions in the *Installing and configuring Telegraf* recipe and the *Adding a custom PostgreSQL monitor to Telegraf* recipe so that there is a fully functional Telegraf data collector. The custom PostgreSQL metric data may also be useful for demonstration purposes.

How to do it...

Assume that we have a monitoring server named `pgmon` and a PostgreSQL server named `pgha1` on which we installed Telegraf. Follow these steps on the server to enable basic monitoring:

1. Install the InfluxDB package downloaded from influxdata on `pgmon` as recommended by your Linux distribution's packaging system.
2. Enable and start InfluxDB with `systemctl`:

```
sudo systemctl enable influxdb
sudo systemctl start influxdb
```

3. Find the `[[outputs.influxdb]]` header in the `/etc/telegraf/telegraf.conf` file on `pgha1` and ensure it looks like this:

```
[[outputs.influxdb]]
  urls = ["http://pgmon:8086"]
```

4. Then, restart the `influxdb` service on `pgha1`:

```
sudo systemctl restart telegraf
```

5. Wait about 5-10 minutes to accumulate some data within InfluxDB.

6. Connect to InfluxDB with this command on `pgmon`:

```
influxdb –database telegraf
```

7. Write the following query, and make sure it's all on one line:

```
SELECT * FROM "postgresql.sessions" ORDER BY time DESC LIMIT 5;
```

How it works...

We don't go into too much detail when installing InfluxDB because influxdata offers several different types of packages for many operating systems and Linux distributions. Normally we focus on Debian/Ubuntu and Red Hat derivatives, but in this case, they made sure to make the software very widely available. It should be possible to simply install the package we downloaded at the beginning of this recipe so we can move on.

The true beginning of the recipe is starting InfluxDB itself. Note how we say *starting* and not *configuring*. Believe it or not, the default configuration is fine for demonstration purposes, and if you later determine you want to increase security, InfluxDB has excellent documentation for accomplishing that. So, we just need to use `systemctl` to first `enable` and then `start` the `influxdb` service, and we're ready to consume data.

With InfluxDB running on `pgmon`, we should turn our attention to the `pgha1` PostgreSQL server. We should already have Telegraf running there if we applied those recipes, so all we need to do now is modify the configuration there to send performance measurements to our `pgmon` server.

The default /etc/telegraf/telegraf.conf configuration has most likely already enabled the output plugin that communicates with InfluxDB. However, the default operating mode is to send data to the localhost while we want to use pgmon instead. InfluxDB offers many methods for data transmission, and the easiest of these is simple HTTP. So all we need to do is add one or more URLs so Telegraf sends data to the right location.

In this case, we can simply set the urls parameter array to include http://pgmon:8086, which is the host where our InfluxDB system is running, and its default port. Since we've modified the telegraf.conf configuration file, we must also restart Telegraf with systemctl to incorporate our changes.

At this point, it's best to wait a few minutes. The default Telegraf sampling rate is one reading every ten seconds, so we don't need to wait long. But why not go make a cup of coffee and relax while InfluxDB accumulates some data?

Connecting to InfluxDB is extremely simple. We simply need to use the influx command-line tool and specify the database we want to connect to by setting the – database parameter to telegraf. We should be able to connect immediately without any further authentication needed. This may seem insecure at first, but performance metrics are rarely sensitive. If they are, there are options for securing the InfluxDB database itself.

Note how we didn't actually create the telegraf database within InfluxDB. The InfluxDB Telegraf output plugin does that automatically when communicating with InfluxDB through HTTP—convenient!

Once connected, we can issue queries using a very similar SQL syntax that we, as PostgreSQL users, may recognize. However, there is one critical difference: newlines are not allowed unless they're part of the data itself. So, we can't use multi-line queries. Aside from that, we can view session information quite easily. The query we used in the instructions should return results that look like this:

```
name: postgresql.sessions
time                 active db       host  server slow total trans_idle waiting
----                 ------ --       ----  ------ ---- ----- ---------- -------
1571960210000000000 1             postgres pgha1 pgha1 0    12    0              0
1571960200000000000 1             postgres pgha1 pgha1 0    12    0              0
1571960190000000000 1             postgres pgha1 pgha1 0    9     0              0
1571960180000000000 1             postgres pgha1 pgha1 0    8     0              0
1571960170000000000 1             postgres pgha1 pgha1 0    9     0              0
```

There's more...

Unlike the handy `psql` command-line tool for PostgreSQL, InfluxDB's `influx` does not offer a ready supply of handy shortcuts for finding information about the database itself. Like MySQL, it uses `SHOW` syntax. InfluxDB was also designed from the ground up to track performance measurements. As such, it doesn't actually have tables but refers to collected data as measurements instead.

Hence, if we want to know what measurements are available for analysis, we can issue `SHOW MEASUREMENTS` and receive a list like this:

```
name: measurements
name
----
cpu
disk
kernel
mem
postgresql
postgresql.sessions
postgresql.slot_lag
postgresql.xid
processes
swap
system
```

Notice how all of our PostgreSQL measurements, including the custom ones, are visible here. If we want to see which fields are available in each measurement, we would have to use this query:

```
SHOW FIELD KEYS FROM "postgresql.sessions"
```

That statement would return something like this based on how we defined that measurement:

```
name: postgresql.sessions
fieldKey    fieldType
--------    ---------
active      integer
slow        integer
total       integer
trans_idle  integer
waiting     integer
```

It's not likely we'll be exploring InfluxDB this way since we'll be installing a GUI in subsequent recipes, but it's still fun to see how things work.

See also

Luckily, InfluxDB provides very thorough documentation. They cover everything from explicit installation instructions, influx syntax, and advanced configuration to security and supported communication plugins. You can find it all at this URL: `https://docs.influxdata.com/influxdb/v1.7/`

Installing and configuring Grafana

When viewing the collected data and statistics regarding our highly available database, we could simply settle for the raw numbers. They tell a story and include the precise measurements necessary for making decisions regarding architecture and incidence response. However, many would argue that this is much easier with graphs and charts, as they enable the identification of trends.

There are a lot of graphing libraries and tools, but relatively few of them are tailored to the needs of an agile monitoring team. The developers at Grafana Labs helped fill this role by contributing **Grafana**, which is an extremely versatile tool. Grafana makes visualizing the collected system statistics easy. Better yet, it's extremely easy to install and use.

This recipe will describe how to obtain and install Grafana and get it ready to receive data from InfluxDB.

Getting ready

We must prepare by obtaining a copy of the latest Grafana package as distributed by Grafana Labs. At the time of this edition, the latest version is 6.6.2, released on February, 2020. Download the latest copy from `https://grafana.com/grafana/download`.

This page also contains instructions for Debian, Ubuntu, Red Hat, and CentOS operating systems, which essentially recommends using `apt` or `yum` to install.

We also recommend following the instructions in the *Installing and configuring Telegraf, Adding a custom PostgreSQL monitor to Telegraf*, and *Installing and configuring InfluxDB* recipes so that there is a fully functional Telegraf and InfluxDB combination complete with fresh activity data from at least one PostgreSQL server.

How to do it...

Follow these steps to install, configure, and start Grafana on a dedicated monitoring server such as `pgmon`:

1. Install the Grafana package downloaded from Grafana Labs on `pgmon` as a root-enabled user as recommended by your Linux distribution's packaging system.
2. Enable and start Grafana with `systemctl`:

   ```
   sudo systemctl enable grafana
   sudo systemctl start grafana
   ```

3. Direct a browser to the default port (`3000`) on the monitor server to log in to the interface. For our example, this would be: `http://pgmon:3000/`.
4. Enter the user admin and password admin and click **Log In**.
5. Change the password as directed and click **Save**.
6. Click **Add data source**.
7. Select the **InfluxDB** option.
8. Enter `http://pgmon:8086/` as the **URL**.
9. Set the **Database** to `telegraf`.
10. Change the **HTTP Method** to `POST`.
11. Click **Save & Test**.

How it works...

Like most modern Linux software, Grafana Labs provides Grafana through prepared `.deb` or `.rpm` packages, though they also provide standard compiled binaries. This should be sufficient for Red Hat, CentOS, Debian, Ubuntu, and other similar distributions, as well as other systems. They also have more advanced installation instructions for situations where these won't work.

Unlike some system services, Grafana is not automatically enabled upon installation, so we do this ourselves with `systemctl`. Afterward, all we need is a browser to continue working with Grafana. Assuming we installed the package on a server named `pgmon`, this means Grafana will run on port `3000` by default. Once we direct a browser to `http://pgmon:3000/`, we should see this screen:

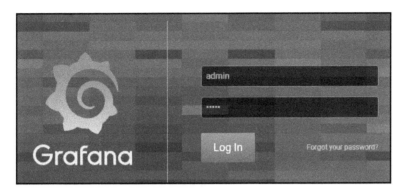

Since Grafana realizes it was freshly installed, it honors the default username of `admin` and password of `admin`. We can enter these to **Log In** for further configuration—well...almost. We must first change the password for the admin user before continuing. We're glad Grafana requires this, as it's good practice to enforce password management early and often. All we need to do here is enter a reliable and memorable password (or paste one from a password management system) and click **Save**.

If everything is successful, we should see the default dashboard, which helpfully shows us the next steps we should complete. It should look like this (though we've changed the default theme to make everything a bit more readable):

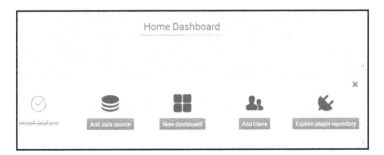

It's great that Grafana puts this on the dashboard for new installations. This makes it much easier to get fast and efficient historical data graphs and dashboards for our cluster. We then move on to adding the data source itself by choosing **Add data source**. Once we do that, we should see this screen:

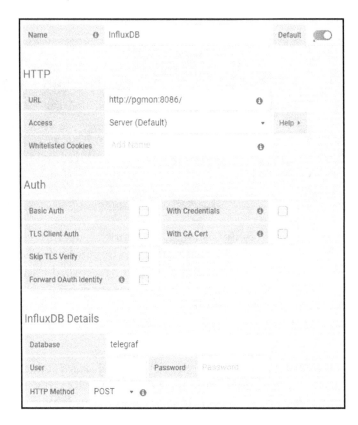

There are several options here, but we only need to set three of them. We start with the **URL** to our pgmon server and the default port where InfluxDB runs at 8086. Together, this makes http://pgmon:8086/. Next, we skip down to **InfluxDB Details** where we set the **Database** to telegraf and **HTTP Method** to POST. This will allow us to submit more complex queries if necessary, and if our InfluxDB server contains multiple databases, we can focus on the one installed by following the recipes in this book.

Once we click **Save & Test**, we want to see this output from Grafana:

At this point, we are ready to start adding Grafana dashboards to view our server activity.

See also

Grafana has rather extensive documentation. We suggest that you read further on these topics if possible. Use the following links for more information:

- Grafana Documentation: https://grafana.com/docs/
- **Download** Grafana: https://grafana.com/grafana/download
- **Installing Grafana**: https://grafana.com/docs/installation/

Building a graph in Grafana

The Grafana interface introduces several extensive capabilities. Grafana primarily displays information as a series of **dashboards** meant to group together interesting or related graphs. Dashboards contain **panels**, which are essentially customized views of our performance measurement data.

These panels can contain any number of things, from standard graphs to gauges, top-10 lists, logs, heat-maps, or even lists of other dashboards. There's a lot here to work with and, given all of these options, it's probably best to begin with a standard chart of values so we can understand how Grafana works with the most common use case.

This recipe will take you through the interface to create a graph within a Grafana dashboard. Finally, we can avoid extremely technical discussions for a while!

Getting ready

In this recipe, we will be combining the results of all of the previous recipes related to Telegraf, InfluxDB, and Grafana. We recommend that you have a functional monitor server configured as discussed in those recipes.

When we installed and configured Grafana, it should have asked us to provide a new password for the `admin` administrative user. This information will be necessary to log in to the interface.

How to do it...

We will mainly be exploring the web interface of the Grafana installation we created earlier, which should be located on our `pgmon` server at the `http://pgmon:3000/` URL. Please log in to the interface and follow these steps:

1. Click **New dashboard** to create a new dashboard:

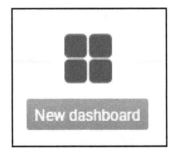

2. In **New Panel**, click **Add Query** to start creating the chart:

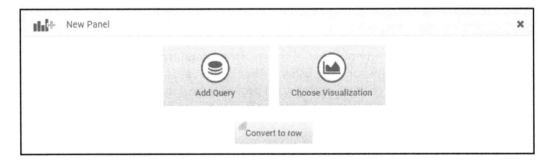

3. Click **Select measurement** and select `postgresql.sessions`.
4. Click on **value** within **field (value)** and choose `total`.
5. In the **SELECT** line, click the + icon and select **Aliasing - alias**.
6. Click the inside of **alias (alias)** and write `Total`.
7. In the **FORMAT AS** line, select `Table`.

8. In **Mean time interval**, write `10s`.
9. In the **SELECT** line, click the + and select **Fields - field**.
10. Modify the second **field** to monitor the `slow` field with an alias of `Slow`.
11. Repeat the last two steps to add a field for every data point so it resembles the following:

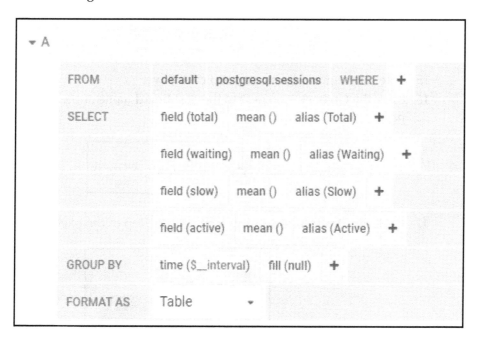

12. Click the gear icon on the left to select **General**:

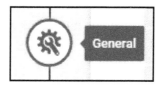

13. Change the **Title** to `Session Activity`.
14. Click the **Save dashboard** icon near the top of the page:

15. Enter any notes if necessary, and click **Save**.
16. Click the **Go back** icon next to the dashboard name at the top-left of the page:

17. Click the **Dashboard settings** icon near the top of the page:

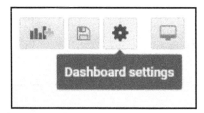

18. Change the **Name** to `PostgreSQL Cluster` and click the **Save** button.
19. Click the **Go back** icon one more time to return to the main dashboard view.

How it works...

While the Grafana interface is easy to navigate, some elements of it may seem non-intuitive, and many of the icon command descriptions are hidden within tooltips. So, just in case, we've provided instructions to click through each element of the interface and produce a graph within a custom dashboard.

We begin by clicking **New dashboard** to start the process. Since this is a new installation of Grafana, we even get a special link to do this that's on the main page. Normally, we have to use the left sidebar menu to do this, as shown in the following screenshot:

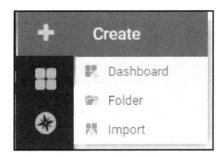

In the future, when we add more dashboards, we would want to use this procedure instead. Otherwise, every dashboard is composed of one or more panels that contain display information. We create one of these by choosing **Add query** within the default **New Panel** that exists for any new dashboard.

This will send us to a new page to configure the *query* for the data we want to display in the graph. To facilitate ease of use, this is primarily a point-and-click affair of picking what we want to display through several dialogs.

By clicking **Select measurement**, we should see a list of every metric within the Telegraf database we created within InfluxDB. Any more measurements we add to that database in the future will also be available here, and we can add them to any new graph we create. So, if we find new or better queries, this list should be a complete reference to what is available.

The fields themselves are managed by **field()** declarations. If we click inside the parentheses, Grafana will list only valid fields contained in the table we're trying to display. It's like writing a SELECT statement one field at a time and only being allowed to choose valid columns. And similarly, we can choose to add an **Alias** modifier to make the graph legends easier to interpret. Every time we click the + icon at the end of the line, we can add further items or transformations to our data.

Changing the **FORMAT AS** line to Table is technically optional, but we've done that here to simplify the display. By default, Grafana displays new data as a time series, which includes the full path to the data point in question. We don't particularly need that, so we'll treat the measurements as if they were from a table.

It's best for the **Mean time interval** to reflect the granularity of the measurements themselves, and since Telegraf defaults to collecting readings every ten seconds, we set this to `10s`. If we increase the interval, that will just average more readings together and potentially smooth some of the curves in our graph. If we don't need ten seconds of granularity, it's perfectly acceptable to increase to longer intervals.

We can optionally return to the field list and begin adding the remaining columns we want to incorporate into this graph. We wrote the query ourselves, so it makes sense to include all of them if possible. We also want to rename this panel to match what we're displaying, so we then switch to the **General** interface tab where we can change the **Title** to something descriptive such as `Session Activity`.

We're basically finished with adding the graph, so we can save the changes we made to the dashboard using the context menu at the top of the screen and exit back to the dashboard itself. We can edit the dashboard properties themselves by clicking the gear icon near the top of the screen. This allows us to change the **Name** of the dashboard to something more appropriate such as `PostgreSQL Cluster`. Afterward, we just **Save** and return to the main dashboard display.

If we did everything correctly, we should see something like this:

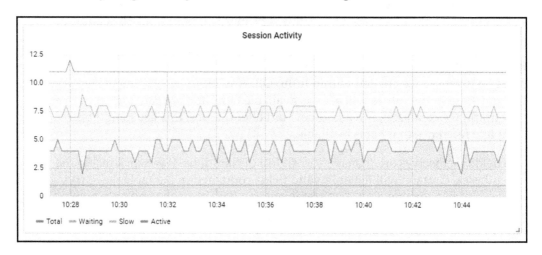

 For the sake of this demonstration, we kept `pgbench` running in the background while adding this data to Grafana. A real production system would likely be much more active.

It seems like a lot of steps, but with enough practice, it will become second nature. Besides that, we don't have to learn any new languages or syntax to monitor our PostgreSQL node and database performance, so we can immediately become productive.

See also

As we've mentioned before, Grafana has excellent documentation. Dashboards and panels are both described here, and we recommend reading more about them to truly leverage their available functionality:

- **Basic concepts**: `https://grafana.com/docs/guides/basic_concepts/`
- **Graph Panel**: `https://grafana.com/docs/features/panels/graph/`

Customizing a Grafana graph

Grafana panels are very helpful in their default form, even though they simply reflect the data they can access. One of the less obvious features that Grafana offers is data transformation. Grafana has several choices for line and background colors, legend names, and so on. Beyond simply making a chart more readable, sometimes this is necessary to properly interpret the data!

There is a lot of extra functionality available in Grafana, and only exploration will truly unveil much of it. We'll introduce a few basic examples in this recipe.

Getting ready

In this recipe, we will be combining the results of all of the previous recipes related to Telegraf, InfluxDB, and Grafana. We recommend that you have a functional monitor server configured as discussed in those recipes.

When we installed and configured Grafana, it should have asked us to provide a new password for the `admin` administrative user. This information will be necessary to log in to the interface.

How to do it...

Follow these instructions to apply several transformations to a simple graph:

4. Direct a web browser at the monitor server on port 3000.
5. Click the **Home** quick menu in the top left-hand corner and choose the **PostgreSQL Cluster** dashboard.
6. Choose the **Add panel** option from the context menu at the top of the screen:

7. Choose the **Add Query** option under **New Panel**.
8. Click **Select measurement** and select postgresql.
9. Set the new **field** to xact_commit.
10. In the **SELECT** line, click the + icon and select **Transformations - derivative**.
11. In the **SELECT** line, click the + icon and select **Math - math**.
12. Change the parameter to the **math()** function to /10.
13. In the **SELECT** line, click the + icon and select **Transformations - moving_average**.
14. In the **SELECT** line, click the + icon, select **Aliasing - alias**, and set the alias to Commit/s.
15. In the **FORMAT AS** line, select Table.
16. Select the **Visualization** icon to the left of the query area:

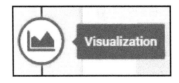

17. Under **Mode Options - Line Width**, select 2.

18. Click the button labeled **Add series override**.

19. Enter Commit/s in the box next to **alias or regex**.

20. Click the + icon next to **alias or regex**, select **Color - change**, and choose a new color for the graph line.

21. Toggle the **Avg**, **Current**, and **Max** options under **Legend - Values**.

22. Click the gear icon on the left to select **General**.

23. Change **Title** to TPS.

24. Save the dashboard and return to the general dashboard view.

How it works...

To explain how to customize a graph within Grafana, we should probably start by creating a new panel to contain it. Once we've logged into the interface, we must first navigate to the **PostgreSQL Cluster** dashboard we want to modify, and then add a new panel using the context menu at the top of the screen. As in the last recipe, this will create a **New Panel** where we can start the process by using **Add Query**.

The fun starts after we change **Select measurement** to postgresql and change the **field** to xact_commit as now we can start adding transformations. The first thing we do is add a **derivative** transformation. Why must we do this? We do so because many PostgreSQL catalog statistics consist of monotonically increasing values. The InfluxDB derivative() function calculates the rate of change over time, so it works so long as we have at least two measurements.

Next, we add a **Math** transformation to divide the total by 10. This is necessary because Telegraf only reads the data from PostgreSQL every ten seconds. This means the difference between the two readings will be ten times higher than the number of transactions per second we're trying to calculate. It also means if we modify the sampling rate within Telegraf, we'll want to change any graphs that may depend on that as well.

Finally, we add a moving_average transformation to smooth out the graph slightly. Instead of just the mean value, we're actually averaging the last ten readings together along a sliding window. This kind of filter may or may not be necessary, but this is mainly for demonstration purposes. What *is* necessary is adding a column, **Alias**, as we'll be using that later. We also set the **FORMAT AS** line to Table again for the sake of readability.

If we did everything correctly, our final query should look like this:

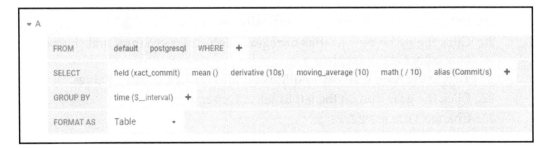

Next, we move to the visualization menu so we can change how the graph and lines appear on the screen. We begin our exploration by setting **Line Width** to 2 to make our chart line a bit thicker. This should immediately be reflected in the preceding graph, so feel free to experiment with other settings in the **Mode Options** section.

Now it's time to demonstrate how it's possible to change each field individually instead of for the entire graph. This is done by selecting **Add series override** for any field we desire to modify. When we click the + icon next to **alias or regex**, we are presented with a very long list of possible changes. For now, we just want to change the color to prove it works as advertised. The default color is green in our particular chart, so we changed it to blue.

We can also modify the legend that describes the chart itself. We feel it's always useful to include **Avg**, **Current**, and **Max** options since this is much more precise than the relative values presented in the chart itself. Once that's done, feel free to explore this menu further and play with the other visualization tweaks; there may be some other components that may prove useful.

Once we're satisfied that the chart has been adequately beautified, all that remains is to rename the panel to something more useful and save our changes. Since this chart is meant to display transactions per second, we named ours TPS. Assuming everything went well, we should see this new panel once we return to the PostgreSQL Cluster dashboard:

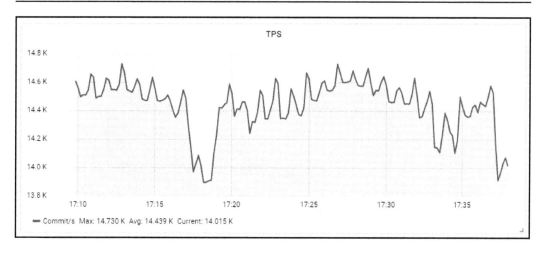

We can see a moderately busy server thanks to the `pgbench` we are running in the background. Nice, eh?

There's more...

Eagle-eyed readers may have noticed that our chart isn't quite complete. We're missing the number of rollback operations per second! If we click the top bar of the panel, we should see an **Edit** option. If we choose that, we can add the `xact_rollback` field and further customize the visualization appropriately.

This is probably important since we want the number of rollback operations per second to be extremely low if not zero. To help to reach that goal, we added the `xact_rollback` field, entered the **Visualization** menu, and set the color for that reading to `red`. We also changed the line width to 5 so we had a nice bold indicator of potential problems.

This is what we ended up with:

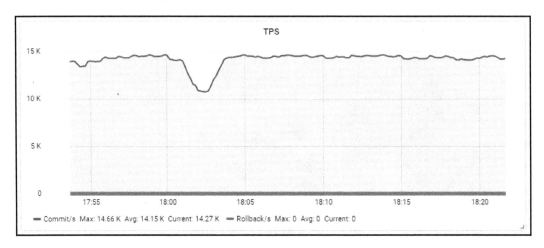

As we hoped, there are no rollbacks in our current database for the period of time we're watching.

See also

We haven't even really scratched the surface of what Grafana can do. Here are a few links to sections in the documentation that may provide some better insight about what customization options are available, along with more advanced use cases:

- **Graph Panel**: https://grafana.com/docs/features/panels/graph/
- **Using InfluxDB in Grafana**: https://grafana.com/docs/features/datasources/influxdb/
- **Time Range Controls**: https://grafana.com/docs/reference/timerange/

Using InfluxDB tags in Grafana

One thing we have not yet explored is using display tags or labels in presenting graph data within Grafana. This is critical as it is something we will do regularly, especially when charted data must be grouped by one or more column names.

This is also important when interacting with InfluxDB systems, as Grafana sends queries using its natively supported syntax. This means any query that is not quite understood by InfluxDB will also not display properly in Grafana. The output from Grafana is also not something we would recognize as users of PostgreSQL.

This recipe will explain how to set up one final Grafana panel that will track replication slot lag on two previously allocated replica nodes.

Getting ready

In this recipe, we will be combining the results of all of the previous recipes related to Telegraf, InfluxDB, and Grafana. We recommend that you have a functional monitor server configured as discussed in those recipes.

When we installed and configured Grafana, it should have asked us to provide a new password for the `admin` administrative user. This information will be necessary to log in to the interface.

How to do it...

Follow these instructions to add a replication slot lag graph to Grafana using display tags:

1. Direct a web browser at the monitor server on port `3000`.
2. Click the **Home** quick menu in the top left-hand corner and choose the **PostgreSQL Cluster** dashboard.
3. Choose the **Add panel** option from the context menu at the top of the screen.
4. Click **Select measurement** and select `postgresql.slot_lag`.
5. Set the new **field** to `restart_lsn_lag`.
6. In the **GROUP BY** line, click the **+** icon and select `tag(slot_name)`.
7. Enter `$tag_slot_name` in the box to the right of **ALIAS BY**.
8. Leave the **FORMAT AS** line as `Time series`.
9. Click the gear icon on the left to select **General**.
10. Change **Title** to `Replication Slot Lag`.
11. Save the dashboard and return to the general dashboard view.

How it works...

Assuming we've applied the previous recipes, much of this is the same procedure as they outlined. Log in to the interface, choose our favorite **PostgreSQL Cluster** dashboard, and select **Add panel**.

What's new here is how we write the query. Unlike previous recipes, after we use **Select measurement** to pick `postgresql.slot_lag` as our measurement and set the **field** to `restart_lsn_lag`, we skip the step of adding a column alias. As it turns out, we won't be needing it.

Instead, we move to the **GROUP BY** line and make sure to group by the tag we created when initially configuring Telegraf: `slot_name`. We also want to leave **FORMAT AS** alone because, this time around, we want to view the data as a time series.

So, how do we make the graph more readable? Grafana creates variables for many common substitutions. One of these, of course, is the name of any tag contained within the data it retrieves from InfluxDB. It prefixes these tags with `$tag_`, hence any tag we create should be available as `$tag_whatever_tag`. In this case, we want to use `$tag_slot_name` for the slot name.

Once we make the tag substitution change, the graph legend should immediately reflect the more readable slot name values. All that remains is to make any other changes we may desire and save the dashboard for our viewing pleasure.

For this chapter, we left `pgbench` running in the background on a PostgreSQL cluster containing two replica nodes. We then turned one of these off so replication lag would be non-zero. Here's what we ended up with:

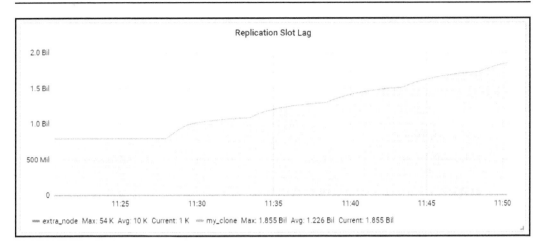

As we can see here, our `my_clone` node is the one that fell behind and probably requires intervention.

There's more...

The resulting graph isn't quite complete from our example. Note how the *y* axis simply says the units are in billions. Billions of what? We know the slot lag is represented in bytes, so we could edit the panel, enter the **Visualization** menu, and change the **Unit** to `bytes`. This makes the graph more representative of what's actually happening. As it turns out, the `my_clone` replica is really behind by about 2 GB of WAL data. Now we could add further advanced options such as setting alerts to avoid exhausting available storage space.

Don't forget to explore the Grafana documentation to really take advantage of its full range of capabilities. It's much easier to relate to metrics we can see and understand.

See also

We haven't even really scratched the surface of what Grafana can do. Here are a few links to sections in the documentation that may provide some better insight about interacting with InfluxDB, along with more advanced use cases such as creating alerts:

- **Graph Panel**: `https://grafana.com/docs/features/panels/graph/`
- **Using InfluxDB in Grafana**: `https://grafana.com/docs/features/datasources/influxdb/`
- **Alerting Engine and Rules Guide**: `https://grafana.com/docs/alerting/rules/`

PostgreSQL Replication 7

One element that is absolutely required for any highly available PostgreSQL installation is replication. It does not matter whether we have a **Storage Area Network** (**SAN**) that provides disk redundancy, nor is **Distributed Replicated Block Device** (**DRBD**) or other block-level replication sufficient to protect our investment. Duplicating and backing up data is always a good practice, but when it comes to availability, we need online copies of the database.

Similarly, if other departments need data that resides in our **Online Transactional Processing** (**OLTP**) database, how can we provide it safely? In ideal circumstances, we can supply a copy of the necessary tables. This way, we don't strain the primary database with ad hoc report-based queries. A new **Database Administrator** (**DBA**) might try to accomplish this by building a synchronization library or performing scheduled extracts and copies into a remote database. However, there are easier ways!

PostgreSQL gives us methods to build and maintain a fully online copy of our primary database. Furthermore, there are existing utilities to duplicate tables when we don't need a copy of the whole database. In this chapter, we will utilize PostgreSQL replication as well as third-party table-synchronization tools. Building the best stack requires familiarity with the tools available.

In this chapter, we will learn several methods to copy entire databases or individual tables. We will cover the following recipes in this chapter:

- Deciding what to copy
- Securing the WAL stream
- Setting up a hot standby
- Upgrading to asynchronous replication
- Bulletproofing with synchronous replication
- Faking replication with pg_receivewal
- Setting up Slony

- Copying a few tables with Slony
- Setting up Bucardo
- Copying a few tables with Bucardo
- Setting up pglogical
- Copying a few tables with pglogical
- Copying a few tables with native logical replication

Deciding what to copy

Before copying anything, we need to determine what to copy. In some instances, it might be necessary to copy the entire database for disaster-recovery purposes. At other times, such copying would waste resources. We need to differentiate between these two scenarios.

Once we've done this, we should decide what to do when we don't want to copy the whole database. We need to know which tables to copy and where to send them. To accomplish this, we will build a very small spreadsheet in this section to keep track of the resources we will need for all of our table and database replicas.

Getting ready

We're going to build a spreadsheet. This spreadsheet will specify the type of replica we want to maintain, as well as where it will reside. Have a spreadsheet program available before starting.

How to do it...

Follow these steps to determine replication resource requirements:

1. Create a spreadsheet with six columns labeled `Source Server`, `Target Server`, `Type`, `DB Name`, `Table`, and `Set`.
2. Under the `Source Server` column, list the role or name of the PostgreSQL server that provides the data.
3. Under the `Target Server` column, list the role or name of the PostgreSQL server that receives the data.
4. Under the `Type` column, select either `Replica` to copy the whole database or `Logical` to copy individual tables.

5. Under the `DB Name` column, enter the name of the database where tables reside on the source server. If you are using `Replica` for `Type`, enter `All` here.

6. Under the `Table` column, enter `All` for every table in the listed database, or enter a single table name. If you are copying multiple individual tables, create a single row for each table.

7. Under the `Set` column, enter a name for the set of tables being copied. Do this only if using `Logical` for the `Type` column.

8. Create at least one row in the spreadsheet for a **Disaster Recovery (DR)** copy of every source server in your PostgreSQL clusters.

How it works...

The spreadsheet we're making only requires six columns to fit this recipe. Feel free to include any other relevant information when making your own. In fact, we suggest that you retain this document for reference purposes and revisions.

We begin by listing the name or role of the server where all of the data will originate. This `Source Server` column will help us—and everyone else—to keep track of where the original data resides. If a server is listed too often in this column, we may want to reconsider removing some replicas so that we don't overwhelm it.

Next, we need to decide where to send the data. The `Target Server` column lets us define where the tables will reside after being replicated. This allows us to formally dictate how many copies will live in how many locations. There are some limitations based on the type we define for this replica entry.

We have only two options when listing the type of replication. We can either mirror the entire database as a `Replica` type or single tables in the case of a `Logical` copy. Any target server can only appear once if its value in the `Type` column is `Replica`. Otherwise, a server might receive several `Logical` sources.

Then, we need to list `DB Name` where we can find the table to copy. If we are copying the entire database as a `Replica` type, this value will always be `All`. Otherwise, we should list a single database name.

Next, we decide which table(s) to copy. In the case of a `Replica` type, this value will be `All`. Otherwise, should we copy the entire listed database or an inventory of specific tables? To mirror every table in the database, enter `All` here. Otherwise, use the name of the table that we want to include (including its schema).

Finally, if we are copying a list of individual tables or a named database, we should name the replica Set. Replication utilities commonly use these set names to address the objects being copied, so we can define any sets we plan to use.

The final step we've listed is to determine where we require at least one copy of the entire database. This replica will be an online copy that we can switch to in the case of server or data center failure. In a truly high-availability architecture, this is not optional.

With all of these entries, our spreadsheet might look something like this:

	A	B	C	D	E	F
1	Source Server	Target Server	Type	DB Name	Tables	Set
2	Trading	Trading DR	Replica	All	All	N/A
3	Trading	Trading Ad Hoc	Replica	All	All	N/A
4	Trading	Reporting	Logical	maindb	customer	orders
5	Trading	Reporting	Logical	maindb	order	orders
6	Trading	Reporting	Logical	maindb	product	orders

In this particular example, we have our DR copy of the database and another full replica for departments to query without disturbing the primary system. Then, we copy three tables to the reporting database for our **Business Intelligence (BI)** or marketing teams to integrate into their customer activity reports.

Securing the WAL stream

The primary mechanism that PostgreSQL uses to provide a data durability guarantee is through its **Write-Ahead Log (WAL)**. All transactional data is written to this location before ever being committed to database files. Once WAL files are no longer necessary for crash recovery, PostgreSQL will either delete or archive them. For a highly available server, we recommend that you keep these important files as long as possible. There are several reasons for this:

- Archived WAL files can be used for **Point-In-Time Recovery (PITR)**.
- If you are using streaming replication, interrupted streams can be re-established by applying WAL files until the replica has caught up.
- WAL files can be reused to service multiple server copies.

To gain these benefits, we need to enable PostgreSQL WAL archiving and save these files until we no longer need them. This recipe will address our recommendations for the long-term storage of WAL files when not using a WAL streaming backup mechanism such as Barman.

Getting ready

To properly archive WAL files, we recommend that you provision a server dedicated to backups or file storage. Depending on the transaction volume, an active PostgreSQL database might produce thousands of these daily. At 16 MB apiece, this is not an idle concern. For instance, for a 1 TB database, we recommend at least 3 TB of storage space.

Also, we will be using `rsync` as a daemon on this archive server. To install this on a Debian-based server, execute the following command as a root-level user:

```
sudo apt-get install rsync
```

Red Hat-based systems will need this command instead:

```
sudo yum install rsync xinetd
```

How to do it...

Our archive server has a 3 TB mount at the `/db` directory and is named `arc_server` on our network. The PostgreSQL source server resides at `pgha1`. Follow these steps for long-term storage of important WAL files on an archive server:

1. Debian-based systems will need to modify the `/etc/default/rsync` file and change the `RSYNC_ENABLE` variable to `true`.
2. Create a directory to store archived WAL files as the `postgres` user with these commands:

   ```
   sudo mkdir -p /db/pg_archived
   sudo chown postgres:postgres /db/pg_archived
   ```

3. Create a file named `/etc/rsyncd.conf` and fill it with the following contents:

   ```
   [wal_store]
       path = /db/pg_archived
       comment = DB WAL Archives
       uid = postgres
       gid = postgres
       read only = false
       hosts allow = pgha1
       hosts deny = *
   ```

4. Restart the `rsync` daemon on Debian-based systems with the following command:

```
sudo systemctl start rsync
```

Red Hat-based systems can start `rsync` with this command instead:

```
sudo systemctl start rsyncd
```

5. Change the `archive_mode` and `archive_command` parameters in `postgresql.conf` to read the following:

```
archive_mode = on
archive_command = 'rsync -aq %p arc_server::wal_store/%f'
```

6. Restart the PostgreSQL server with the following command on Debian-based hosts (assuming this is our `main` installation):

```
sudo systemctl restart postgresql@12-main
```

Red Hat-related distributions should use this command instead:

```
sudo systemctl restart postgresql-12
```

How it works...

The `rsync` utility is normally used to transfer files between two servers. However, we can take advantage of using it as a daemon to avoid connection overhead imposed by using SSH as an `rsync` protocol. Our first step is to ensure that the service is not disabled in some manner, which would make the rest of this recipe moot.

Next, we need a place to store archived WAL files on the archive server. Assuming that we have 3 TB of space in the `/db` directory, we simply claim `/db/pg_archived` as the desired storage location. There should be enough space to use `/db` for backups as well, but we won't discuss that in this recipe.

Following that, we create a file named `/etc/rsyncd.conf`, which will configure how `rsync` operates as a daemon. Here, we name the `/db/pg_archived` directory `wal_store` so that we can address the path by its name when sending files. We give it a human-readable name and ensure that files are owned by the `postgres` user as this user also controls most of the PostgreSQL-related services.

The next and possibly the most important step is to block all hosts but the primary PostgreSQL server from writing to this location. We set hosts deny to *, which blocks every server. Then, we set hosts allow to the primary database server's hostname so that only it has access. If everything goes well, we can start rsync with systemd, though Red Hat-related Linux systems may use the name rsyncd instead.

Then, we enable archive_mode by setting it to on. With archive mode enabled, we can specify a command that will execute when PostgreSQL no longer needs a WAL file for crash recovery. In this case, we invoke the rsync command with the -a parameter to preserve elements such as file ownership, timestamps, and so on.

In addition, we specify the -q setting to suppress output as PostgreSQL only checks the command exit status to determine its success. In the archive_command setting, the %p value represents the full path to the WAL file, and %f resolves to the filename. In this context, we're sending the WAL file to the archive server at the wal_store module we defined in rsyncd.conf. Once we restart PostgreSQL, it will start storing all of the old WAL files by sending them to the archive server.

If any rsync command fails because the archive server is unreachable, PostgreSQL will keep trying to send it until it is successful. If the archive server is unreachable for too long, we suggest that you change the archive_command setting to store files elsewhere. This prevents accidentally overfilling the PostgreSQL server storage. Make sure you're monitoring the pg_xlog or pg_wal folder with an alerting system, as discussed in Chapter 6, *Monitoring*.

There's more...

As we will likely want to use the WAL files on other servers, we suggest that you make a list of all of the servers that could need WAL files. Then, modify the rsyncd.conf file on the archive server and add this section:

```
[wal_fetch]
    path = /db/pg_archived
    comment = DB WAL Archive Retrieval
    uid = postgres
    gid = postgres
    read only = true
    hosts allow = host1, host2, host3
    hosts deny = *
```

Now we can fetch WAL files from any of the hosts in `hosts allow`. As these are dedicated PostgreSQL replicas, recovery servers, or other defined roles, this makes the archive server a central location for all of our WAL needs. Make sure this server is as fault-tolerant as possible; otherwise, it becomes a single-point-of-failure to lose all of the WAL files at once.

See also

For more details, refer to the following:

- We suggest that you read more about the `archive_mode` and `archive_command` settings on the PostgreSQL site. We've included a link here:

  `https://www.postgresql.org/docs/current/runtime-config-wal.html`.
- The `rsyncd.conf` file should also have its own manual page. Read it with this command to learn more about the available settings:

  man rsyncd.conf

Setting up a hot standby

It is a very good practice, if not an outright requirement, to have a second online copy of a PostgreSQL server in high-availability clusters. Without such an online server, recovery from an outage may require hours of incident response, backup recovery, and server provisioning. We have everything to gain by having extra online servers.

In addition, the process of setting up a hot standby acts as the basis for creating PostgreSQL streaming replicas. This means that we can reuse this recipe over and over again anytime we need to create PostgreSQL mirrors, provision extra backup copies, set up test instances, and so on.

All of this is made possible by the `pg_basebackup` command, which forms the basis of many other derived tools. This recipe will cover the basic usage of this backup command so we can leverage it for the rest of this book.

Getting ready

A hot standby server should have similar—if not exactly the same—specifications as the PostgreSQL server it is subscribed to. Try to accomplish this if possible. Due to our use of `rsync`, we recommend applying the *Securing the WAL stream* recipe to consume WAL files from the upstream system.

 The **log shipping** method we'll be using here has been deprecated for quite a while. However, this is a good opportunity to learn how things worked in the past and the benefits of newer approaches.

If this is a Red Hat or CentOS system, the new server will need some initial provisioning now that systemd is more prevalent. To run PostgreSQL in a non-default directory, we recommend executing this command:

```
systemctl edit postgresql-12
```

Then, enter the following contents to use `/db/pgdata` as the PostgreSQL data directory:

```
[Service]
Environment=PGDATA=/db/pgdata
```

This will ensure standard `systemctl` commands work as expected and the server is fully integrated with other system management tools.

How to do it...

For this scenario, the server at `10.0.30.1` is the primary PostgreSQL server, and `10.0.30.2` will be the new copy. On all PostgreSQL servers, our data directory should be located at `/db/pgdata`.

Follow these steps to build a PostgreSQL hot standby:

1. Ensure that the `pg_hba.conf` file on the primary server contains this line:

```
host    replication    rep_user    10.0.30.2/32    trust
```

2. Set the `wal_level` and `max_wal_senders` parameters in `postgresql.conf` to the following (or higher) values on the primary server:

```
wal_level = logical
max_wal_senders = 10
```

3. If these settings weren't already at or above these levels, restart PostgreSQL on the primary server. Debian-based systems can use a command like this:

```
sudo systemctl restart postgresql@12-main
```

4. Red Hat-based systems would need a command like this:

```
sudo systemctl restart postgresql-12
```

5. Create the replication user, if it doesn't already exist, with this SQL statement:

```
CREATE USER rep_user WITH REPLICATION;
```

6. On the new server replica, create the `/db/pgdata` directory with this command as a root-level user:

```
sudo mkdir -p /db/pg_archived
sudo chown -R postgres:postgres /db
```

7. Create a file named `/etc/cron.d/postgres` with the following contents in a single line:

```
* * * * * postgres flock /tmp/wal_sync rsync -aq --del
    arc_server::wal_fetch/ /db/pg_archived
```

8. Copy the primary server data with this command on the secondary server as the `postgres` user:

```
pg_basebackup -D /db/pgdata -h 10.0.30.1 -U rep_user
```

9. Users of PostgreSQL 12 should place the following single line in the `/db/pgdata/postgresql.conf` file on the new server copy:

```
restore_command = 'test -f /db/pg_archived/%f && cp -n
/db/pg_archived/%f %p'
```

10. PostgreSQL 12 will also need a file named `standby.signal` in the `/db/pgdata` directory:

    `touch /db/pgdata/standby.signal`

11. Older versions will require a file named `recovery.conf` and the following contents:

    ```
    standby_mode = 'on'
    restore_command = 'test -f /db/pg_archived/%f && cp -n
    /db/pg_archived/%f %p'
    ```

12. Ensure that the `postgresql.conf` file on the standby server contains the following setting:

    ```
    hot_standby = on
    ```

13. Start PostgreSQL on the new standby server on Debian-based systems like this:

    `sudo systemctl start postgresql@12-main`

14. Red Hat-based systems would need a command like this:

    `sudo systemctl start postgresql-12`

How it works...

The first thing we do with this recipe is to allow the new PostgreSQL server to retrieve data from the primary server. There are a few ways to do this, but for the sake of demonstration, we created a rule for the server at `10.0.30.2` to connect to the `replication` pseudo-database. This allows tools such as `pg_basebackup` to copy database files from the primary database when we initialize the replica.

In a related concern, we must ensure that the `wal_level` setting of the primary server is set to `hot_standby` and that `max_wal_senders` is a value greater than `0`. Earlier chapters on configuring PostgreSQL have already made this suggestion, but this recipe won't work at all if these parameters are set wrong. We restart PostgreSQL after modifying these settings to force it to use the new values. This also has the added benefit of integrating the changes to `pg_hba.conf` so `rep_user` has sufficient access to copy PostgreSQL data files.

Next, we should make sure that `rep_user` exists. Earlier chapters contained instructions to create this user, but it doesn't hurt to double-check. Regardless of what user we use to copy data, it must have the `replication` permission used in the `CREATE USER` syntax.

Once we've done that, the new child server needs the same data directory as its parent. We also want to have a location to synchronize WAL files so that the copy can process them and remain up to date. We set the permissions so that only the `postgres` user can view their contents. We should end up with something like this:

```
drwx------   2 postgres postgres 4096 Oct 22 15:25 pg_archived
drwx------  19 postgres postgres 4096 Oct 22 15:33 pgdata
```

With these two directories in place, it's time to copy WAL files from the archive server. To accomplish this, we create a file in `/etc/cron.d` that will execute an `rsync` command every minute. This `rsync` command will copy WAL files from the archive server to the `/db/pg_archived` directory. The `-a` parameter ensures that it will include file permissions and ownership, and `-q` will suppress non-error messages so it's easier to tell whether something went wrong. We have also added the `--del` setting, which will cause `rsync` to delete any files that don't exist on the archive server.

Why execute every minute? It prevents the hot standby from falling too far behind without making use of pure PostgreSQL replication. If you want to use this server as an insurance policy, it might be a good idea to delay it behind the source database by an hour. This way, mistakes will not appear on the standby for an hour, giving us a chance to fix problems before they taint database copies. To sync every hour, change the `* * * * *` portion of the `rsync` command to `0 * * * *`.

As we're launching `rsync` asynchronously, we use `flock` to create a temporary lock file in the `/tmp` directory. This way, if the primary server produced a large burst of WAL files, we won't have two conflicting `rsync` commands trying to synchronize the files to `/db/pg_archived` on the standby server.

Once we've established a ready supply of WAL files, we need to copy the actual database. For this, we use the pg_basebackup command itself. While pg_basebackup is primarily a backup utility, it serves a dual purpose. When launched with the -D parameter, it copies the server data files from the host indicated by the -h parameter and saves them to the indicated directory. Hence, our pg_basebackup command copied files from 10.0.30.1 to /db/pgdata. This produces a PostgreSQL data directory capable of hosting a running database. We also applied the -U setting to use the rep_user user that we created specifically for replication-related tasks.

Next, we want to start the PostgreSQL hot standby, but first, we need to tell it how to recover WAL files. Older versions of PostgreSQL require us to create a file named recovery.conf so PostgreSQL will enter recovery mode instead of normal operation, while versions 12 and beyond use a file named standby.signal. In this recovery mode, it expects to process WAL files until there are no more available. While modern versions of PostgreSQL do this automatically, versions 11 and older require us to set standby_mode to on in recovery.conf, which instructs it to wait forever under the assumption that more WAL files will arrive later. This is called **continuous recovery**, and this is what makes a hot standby work.

Another setting that we use is restore_command. Here, we use a simple cp command to regularly consume WAL files in the /db/pg_archived directory after using the test command to check whether the file exists. This prevents annoying log entries like this:

```
cp: cannot stat `0000000400000001000007E': No such file or directory
cp: cannot stat `0000000400000001000007E': No such file or directory
cp: cannot stat `0000000400000001000007E': No such file or directory
```

There are other ways to do this, such as the deprecated pg_standby utility, but the documentation is quite clear that these approaches are to be avoided.

There's one more thing to confirm before we start the PostgreSQL hot standby. Simply having a standby is useful, but having a readable standby is better. By enabling hot_standby in the postgresql.conf file, we can execute basic SELECT statements against the standby instance.

We should have a fully functional hot standby PostgreSQL server once we start the database on the replica.

See also

As this is such a common configuration, the PostgreSQL documents discuss it at great length. We also made extensive use of the `pg_basebackup` command. You can find out more information about these from the following URLs:

- **Log-Shipping Standby Servers**: `https://www.postgresql.org/docs/current/warm-standby.html`
- **Hot Standby**: `https://www.postgresql.org/docs/current/hot-standby.html`
- **pg_basebackup**: `https://www.postgresql.org/docs/current/app-pgbasebackup.html`

Upgrading to asynchronous replication

Since the release of PostgreSQL 9.0, DBAs have had access to asynchronous streaming replication. This means all modern supported versions anyone is likely to encounter have this feature.

Unlike the older hot standby methods used in earlier versions, replica servers can connect to an upstream PostgreSQL server and consume data modifications directly. With low network latency and fast transactions, this means that it is fairly common for streaming replicas to lag behind the master by only a few milliseconds.

In the context of high availability, this means we can scale horizontally by copying the database to multiple servers. Of course, this means that we need to copy the entire database to each server. For small-to-medium-sized database instances, this is a relatively minor requirement. This also means that we can produce up-to-date backups, perform ad hoc queries on practically live data, and aggregate information into reports without disrupting our primary database.

This recipe will explain how to set up a streaming asynchronous database replica and explore some of the hidden caveats of doing so.

Getting ready

We will be continuing the work we performed in the *Setting up a hot standby* recipe, so please refer to that recipe to build a working hot standby. We will alter the standby setup to include streaming replication and better security.

How to do it...

For this scenario, the server at 10.0.30.1 is the primary PostgreSQL server, and 10.0.30.2 will be the asynchronous replica. Follow these steps to build a PostgreSQL asynchronous replica:

1. Give the rep_user user a password with this SQL statement:

   ```
   ALTER USER rep_user WITH PASSWORD 'newpass';
   ```

2. On the primary server, modify the pg_hba.conf line and remove any references to the rep_user user. Then, add this line:

   ```
   host    replication    rep_user    10.0.30.2/32    md5
   ```

3. Reload the configuration files on the primary server with the following command as the postgres user:

   ```
   pg_ctl -D /db/pgdata reload
   ```

4. On the replica server, create a file named .pgpass in the postgres user's home directory with the following contents:

   ```
   10.0.30.1:*:replication:rep_user:newpass
   ```

5. Alter the .pgpass file to have the correct permissions with this command:

   ```
   chmod 600 ~/.pgpass
   ```

6. Add the following parameter in postgresql.conf (12+) or recovery.conf on the recovery server:

   ```
   primary_conninfo = 'host=10.0.30.1 user=rep_user'
   ```

7. Restart PostgreSQL on the streaming replica server on Debian-based systems like this:

   ```
   sudo systemctl restart postgresql@12-main
   ```

8. Red Hat-based systems would need a command like this:

   ```
   sudo systemctl restart postgresql-12
   ```

9. Confirm that the standby is connected by executing this SQL on the primary PostgreSQL server:

```
SELECT client_addr, usename, state
  FROM pg_stat_replication;
```

How it works...

Using trust authentication is not generally a recommended practice. It is one thing to copy the database without a password once, but quite another to leave a long-term security hole for all database replicas. This means it is time to ensure that the rep_user user has a password. We also need to change pg_hba.conf to reflect the fact that we want to use regular md5 authentication instead of trust. Once we reload the configuration files on the primary server, we move on to the streaming replica.

To get into the practice of using .pgpass files, we create one on the replica server for the rep_user user. The line we created in this file will send our desired password when the sections match; in this case, if we connect to 10.0.30.1 on any port to the replication database as the rep_user user, authentication will succeed automatically. If any of these are different, the PostgreSQL client libraries will not send a password, and the client will receive an error. This is a fairly easy way to automate password submissions securely. PostgreSQL will also ignore this file if the permissions are wrong, so we set the control flags with chmod so that only the postgres user can access it.

Next, we rewrite the contents of the recovery.conf file to include primary_conninfo. This line is used to specify the connection information for establishing streaming replication. Since our password is in the .pgpass file, we don't need to enter it here. We also removed pg_standby in favor of a regular cp command with the errors suppressed. Now that our primary method of WAL consumption is directly from another server, we only need WAL files from /db/pg_archived as a failback in case the stream is disrupted.

Why do we use .pgpass instead of entering the password in the recovery.conf file? It is very common for system automation tools to distribute configuration files to dozens or even hundreds of servers. Using .pgpass, we can settle on and redistribute passwords easily. Also, tools that build recovery.conf will not need to know the password for the replication user. Just make sure to protect this file well, as it's a potential attack vector since it contains several important database passwords.

Once we reload the standby server, it should become a streaming replica instead of a regular hot standby. We can confirm this with the SQL statement that checks the `pg_stat_replication` view on the primary server. We should get output similar to this:

```
 client_addr   | usename  |   state
---------------+----------+-----------
 192.168.56.20 | rep_user | streaming
```

Once we've got streaming replication working, generally, we recommend eventually disabling log shipping by removing `restore_command` from `recovery.conf` or `postgresql.conf`. Scenarios failing back to this old methodology are rare, given streaming's overall superiority.

There's more...

We unleash a whole universe of new functionality when we switch to asynchronous replication. As the versions of PostgreSQL have advanced over the years, this list becomes longer.

Cascading replication

If we have several streaming replicas, older versions of PostgreSQL required replica servers to connect directly to the primary server. PostgreSQL allows streaming replicas to subscribe to other replicas in versions 9.3 and above. We can further reduce strain on the primary database server by offloading replication duties to a topology of alternate servers using this capability.

This chaining includes backup features. The `pg_basebackup` tool puts PostgreSQL in backup mode by invoking the `pg_start_backup()` function. As this function writes to the database, it normally can't be used on a streaming replica because it's read-only. However, chaining replication makes it possible to use `pg_basebackup` on standby servers. This can greatly simplify the backup process and reduce overhead on the primary server.

Using replication slots

Relying on transaction log files is a risky endeavor. If the primary server deletes one before a replica can process it, we may need to rebuild the replica outright. If we're using PostgreSQL 9.4 or higher, we can prevent that kind of mishap by using replication slots instead.

We would need to create a replication slot on the primary server itself with this SQL:

```
SELECT * FROM pg_create_physical_replication_slot('pg2_slot');
```

Then, on the replica, we would add this line to its `postgresql.conf` (12+) or `recovery.conf` files before starting (or restarting) the instance:

```
primary_slot_name = 'pg2_slot'
```

Now our replica can't fall behind. We should be careful that replica outages are limited, otherwise, the primary could accumulate too many unnecessary transaction log files and run out of storage space. It may be necessary to remove unused replication slots so this doesn't happen. Use this SQL if a replica needs to be offline for long periods of time:

```
SELECT pg_drop_replication_slot('pg2_slot');
```

Viewing replication status on a replica

Beginning with PostgreSQL 9.6, we can view a lot of information about the replication stream from the replica server. In previous versions, there were only a couple of functions, and they only really told us which transaction log the replica had recently processed. Version 9.6 introduces a view named `pg_stat_wal_receiver` to solve that issue. Consider we have our `pg2` replica and it's using a replication slot named `pg2_slot`. We could use this query on the replica to learn a bit more:

```
SELECT status, latest_end_lsn, latest_end_time, slot_name
  FROM pg_stat_wal_receiver;
```

The output of this should resemble the following screenshot:

```
 status    | latest_end_lsn |         latest_end_time        | slot_name
-----------+----------------+--------------------------------+----------
 streaming | 0/BD000148     | 2019-11-02 16:40:57.529051+00  | pg2_slot
```

This tells us that the streaming is active and it's using the slot as expected, and it tells us the position in the transaction log it last replayed. We can also see the upstream time that position represents, making it much easier to determine replication lag visually.

Views like this help us to troubleshoot and monitor status from a replica's perspective. Remember the PostgreSQL catalog is available and is always growing with each new version.

See also

There are good resources within the PostgreSQL documentation regarding streaming replication. For more information, please visit these URLs:

- **Log-Shipping Standby Servers**:
  https://www.postgresql.org/docs/current/warm-standby.html
- **The Password File**:
  https://www.postgresql.org/docs/current/static/libpq-pgpass.html

Bulletproofing with synchronous replication

Sometimes, to provide acceptable data durability, a high-availability configuration must utilize synchronous commits. Beginning with PostgreSQL 9.1, database servers can now refuse to commit a transaction until the data is located on at least one alternate server. Unlike asynchronous replication, where this is optional, synchronous replicas enforce this requirement to a fault.

Past discussions in the PostgreSQL mailing list suggest that there is a long-standing misconception that synchronous replication is similar to RAID-1 operation. In RAID-1, the same exact data exists on two disks (or two disk sets), and if one of the pair fails, it continues to operate in degraded mode until the problem is addressed. This is absolutely not the case with PostgreSQL synchronous replication.

Unlike RAID-1, PostgreSQL replicas can exist on different servers, on different networks, or even in different countries. PostgreSQL synchronous replication is a guarantee that data is written to at least two servers. Despite the necessary increase in latency to confirm this, the guarantee is upheld at all times.

This recipe is for databases that need this kind of extreme durability.

Getting ready

We will be continuing the work we performed in the *Upgrading to asynchronous replication* recipe, so please refer to that section to build a working asynchronous replica. We will alter the standby setup to include synchronous streaming replication.

How to do it...

For this scenario, the server at 10.0.30.1 is still the primary PostgreSQL server. Follow these steps to change an asynchronous PostgreSQL server into a synchronous replica:

1. Revise the primary_conninfo parameter on the recovery server to add application_name:

   ```
   primary_conninfo = 'host=10.0.30.1 user=rep_user
   application_name=pgha2
   ```

2. Restart the streaming server with systemctl as standard:

   ```
   systemctl restart postgresql@12-main
   ```

3. Or alternatively, use the following:

   ```
   systemctl restart postgresql-12
   ```

4. Change the synchronous_standby_names and synchronous_commit settings in the postgresql.conf file on the primary server to read the following:

   ```
   synchronous_commit = 'on'
   synchronous_standby_names = 'pgha2'
   ```

5. Reload the configuration files on the primary server with the following command as the `postgres` user:

```
pg_ctl -D /db/pgdata reload
```

6. Confirm that the standby is connected by executing this SQL on the primary PostgreSQL server:

```
SELECT client_addr, state, sync_state, application_name
  FROM pg_stat_replication;
```

How it works...

Promoting an asynchronous standby server to synchronous mode is actually a fairly simple procedure. We begin by modifying the `primary_conninfo` setting in the standby's `postgresql.conf` (12+) or `recovery.conf` file to include the `application_name` value. PostgreSQL differentiates replicas by their stated application name, so if we change this, we can specifically target that particular replica. Any other synchronous standby nodes should be assigned different names.

Once we restart the PostgreSQL server on the streaming standby, it will reconnect to the primary server with the new `application_name` value that we assigned. From this point onward, we can refer to the standby server as `pgha2`. Hence, when we alter the `synchronous_standby_names` and `synchronous_commit` variables in the primary server's `postgresql.conf` file, we use the same name there.

Any time we want to change the `synchronous_standby_names` variable, we merely need to tell PostgreSQL to reload its configuration files. This should immediately cause the primary node to consider `pgha2` a synchronous standby server. Any transaction will only commit if it can write to this server as well as the primary one.

This last point is extremely important. If the synchronous standby becomes unavailable for any reason, the primary server will stop writing to the database as well! If you are performing maintenance on the secondary server, we suggest that you set `synchronous_standby_names` to a blank value and reload the PostgreSQL server. This will break the synchronous guarantee until the standby can be reconnected.

Once we have reloaded the primary server's configuration files, we can check the `pg_stat_replication` view again to observe how streaming is currently functioning. After executing the query, we should see something like this:

```
client_addr |   state    | sync_state | application_name
------------+-----------+------------+-----------------
10.0.30.2   | streaming | sync       | pgha2
```

As we can see in this example, the primary server sees `pgha2` as a synchronous streaming replica.

There's more...

Beyond the basics of synchronous replication, there are also a few other things we can do with this powerful feature.

Being less strict

We really want to confirm whether the streaming replication works as advertised. To do this, let's shut down the standby server with this command:

```
sudo systemctl stop postgresql-12
```

Then, try to write to the primary server. This simple SQL statement should wait indefinitely:

```
CREATE TABLE foo ( bar INT );
```

If we then restart the streaming replica using the following command, we should see the transaction complete:

```
sudo systemctl start postgresql-12
```

As you might imagine, this can be problematic in true high-availability architectures that handle thousands of transactions per second. As such, we don't actually recommend that you use synchronous replication on OLTP servers. As these comprise the bulk of highly available PostgreSQL clusters, opportunities to take advantage of this level of data durability are somewhat slim.

However, a synchronous commit is actually somewhat optional. If we want to try the experiment again, we can first issue this SQL statement before trying a basic write query:

```
SET synchronous_commit TO false;
```

This disables synchronous replication temporarily for the current session. Subsequent write queries in this connection should succeed normally as if the remote server was a standard asynchronous copy.

Being more strict

The `synchronous_commit` configuration parameter has another, more relevant setting for those interested in high availability. The default functionality of a synchronous standby is to consume transactions from the replication stream and acknowledge receipt. Yet this only means the data has been physically written to disk on the replica system. There's still the very slim chance that a crash of the synchronous standby might prevent transactions from reaching the actual data files on that system.

If we set `synchronous_commit` to `remote_apply`, however, the result is subtly different. This value is only available in PostgreSQL 9.6 and higher and it makes synchronous replication even more strict in its implementation. With this value in place, a transaction will not be committed on the primary node until it's written to a standby server and that standby has also processed the transaction. It's a slight but extremely important difference.

In the context of high availability, it means the replica is an exact copy of the upstream server at all times because the primary server can't even commit transactions without the standby also reflecting those changes. Unlike standard synchronous commits, there is no race condition between receipt and application.

Of course, we pay for this durability and availability with latency. It's important to know when to decide between the two extremes.

Enabling extreme durability

PostgreSQL 9.6 also introduces another important component to a highly available cluster of servers commonly found in the NoSQL world. Of course, we're talking about committing writes to several replicas simultaneously. Version 9.6 changes the syntax for synchronous_standby_names so that it's now possible to specify multiple standby servers as well as how many should be active at once. If we had two replicas, rep1 and rep2, and needed both to always be in sync with the primary, we would modify the parameter accordingly:

```
synchronous_standby_names = '2 (rep1, rep2)'
```

We could also have five replicas in the list, and enable three of them or any similar combination. Again, we trade latency for better durability, but in some cases, that's a perfectly valid transaction. This level of paranoia is rarely necessary, but it's nice to have the choice.

See also

There are good resources within the PostgreSQL documentation regarding streaming replication. For more information, please visit these URLs:

- **Log-Shipping Standby Servers**:
  https://www.postgresql.org/docs/current/warm-standby.html
- **Write-Ahead Log**:
  https://www.postgresql.org/docs/current/runtime-config-wal.html

Faking replication with pg_receivewal

Some built-in tools deserve a special mention. The pg_receivexlog command was introduced with PostgreSQL 9.2. With this utility, PostgreSQL can transmit transaction logs to a remote system without the need for a dedicated PostgreSQL server. This also means that we can avoid ad hoc tools such as rsync when maintaining an archive server to save old WAL files.

This allows us to set up any server to pull transaction logs directly from the primary PostgreSQL server. For highly available servers, PostgreSQL no longer needs to fork an external command to safeguard transaction logs into an archive location. Also, we can monitor the state of the transmission through the `pg_stat_replication` system view.

In effect, we remove quite a bit of overhead from our PostgreSQL server and offload it to a less sensitive system. This recipe will provide a quick outline for using this utility.

Getting ready

Before starting with this recipe, ensure that you have a good understanding of how PostgreSQL replication works. To do this, follow the *Upgrading to asynchronous replication* and *Bulletproofing with synchronous replication* recipes.

 Can't find `pg_receivewal`? This utility was named `pg_receivexlog` until PostgreSQL 10 imposed a naming revision of several internal systems related to WAL management. If you're using one of these older installations, use that command name instead. It should work the same!

How to do it...

For this scenario, the server at `10.0.30.1` is still the primary PostgreSQL server, and `10.0.30.20` will be our archive server. Follow these steps to save WAL data remotely:

1. Ensure that the `pg_hba.conf` file on the primary server contains this line:

   ```
   host    replication    rep_user    10.0.30.20/32    md5
   ```

2. Ensure that the `wal_keep_segments` and `archive_mode` settings in `postgresql.conf` are set as follows on the primary server:

   ```
   wal_keep_segments = 1000
   archive_mode = off
   ```

3. Restart the configuration files on the primary server with the following command:

   ```
   sudo systemctl restart postgresql@12-main
   ```

4. Alternatively, restart with this command:

```
sudo systemctl restart postgresql-12
```

5. On the archive server, create the `/db/pg_archived` directory with these commands as a root-enabled user:

```
sudo mkdir -p -m 0700 /db/pg_archived
sudo chown postgres:postgres /db/pg_archived
```

6. Start the `pg_receivewal` utility on the archive server with the following command as the `postgres` user:

```
pg_receivewal -h 10.0.30.1 -U rep_user \
              -D /db/pg_archived -v \
              &> /db/pg_archived/wal_archive.log &
```

How it works...

First, we need to ensure that the archive server at `10.0.30.20` can connect to the primary server to receive the transaction log traffic. Next, unlike other recipes that depend on `archive_mode` to be enabled on the primary server, we want to disable it this time. We are going to rely on `pg_receivewal` instead.

One setting that we change might seem a bit odd at first. The `wal_keep_segments` parameter defines how many transaction logs PostgreSQL should keep after it no longer needs them. Normally, it would delete old files or call the `archive` command to process them if `archive_mode` is on. By setting it to `1000`, we are telling it to always have at least 1,000 extra files. This helps to avoid lost WAL archives if there's a network problem or we have to restart `pg_receivewal`.

> Are 1,000 files too many? At 16 MB each, this accounts for 16 GB of space. Providing this much space should be very easy with modern storage devices. This many files should account for several hours of activity on all but the most active databases. It may actually be prudent to increase the limit further, depending on database activity.

Once these settings are in place, we need to restart PostgreSQL to disable WAL archival. At this point, the primary server will no longer save or transmit old WAL files anywhere. To make up for this, we make sure that the archive server has a location to store these files and that the `postgres` user can write to it. To continue with our examples, we will continue to use the `/db/pg_archived` directory.

Finally, we start the `pg_receivewal` tool itself. We pass the `-h` parameter to connect to the primary database and use `-U` to enforce the replication user, `rep_user`. The `-D` parameter is required, and we use it to save WAL files to the `/db/pg_archived` directory we created.

Then, we enable verbose output with `-v` just so that we are always informed about what `pg_receivewal` is doing. We direct all output to a file named `wal_archive.log` and consider our work complete. The final `&` character launches the command in the background so that it functions even if we disconnect from the server.

If everything goes well, our `/db/pg_archived` directory should soon have some WAL files and a log inside it, as shown in the following screenshot:

```
-rw------- 1 postgres postgres 16777216 Oct 22 16:19 000000010000000000000007
-rw------- 1 postgres postgres 16777216 Oct 22 16:20 000000010000000000000008
-rw------- 1 postgres postgres 16777216 Oct 22 16:20 000000010000000000000009
-rw------- 1 postgres postgres 16777216 Oct 22 16:20 00000001000000000000000A.partial
-rw-rw-r-- 1 postgres postgres      242 Oct 22 16:20 wal_archive.log
```

The file that ends in `partial` is a WAL transfer that is currently in progress.

There's more...

Starting with PostgreSQL 9.5, `pg_receivewal` is also fully compatible with synchronous replication. If we wanted to enable this capability, we could modify the final launch command to look something like this:

```
pg_receivewal -h 10.0.30.1 -U rep_user \
              -D /db/pg_archived -v --synchronous \
              &> /db/pg_archived/wal_archive.log &
```

Normally, `pg_receivexlog` only flushes to disk periodically. With the `--synchronous` parameter enabled, it will flush all transactions upon receipt, as well as sending an acknowledgment to the upstream primary. Now, we don't necessarily need a full copy of our database everywhere. Perhaps we could leverage this feature on a server that simply accumulates transaction logs in a secure location.

Being available isn't always a matter of never going offline; it also means our data is safe. Transaction logs are a critical source of PITR functionality and crash recovery. Having transaction logs written immediately to a tertiary location without database overhead conveys a certain amount of high availability to the files themselves.

See also

The `pg_receivewal` / `pg_receivexlog` utility has more extensive documentation on PostgreSQL's site. Visit these URLs to learn more:

- **pg_receivewal**: https://www.postgresql.org/docs/current/app-pgreceivewal.html
- **pg_receivexlog**: https://www.postgresql.org/docs/9.6/app-pgreceivexlog.html

Setting up Slony

While there are a few logical asynchronous replication systems for PostgreSQL, **Slony-I** (Slony, in short) was the first to gain wide adoption. Why would we use Slony when PostgreSQL already has physical and logical replication? PostgreSQL versions prior to 10 could only copy the entire installation.

The only option for those systems is to copy every database, schema, table, and user at the binary level. In effect, streaming replication creates perfect clones of PostgreSQL servers. So what happens if we want to upgrade from one of these antiquated versions to something more modern without shutting down PostgreSQL itself? Sometimes this requires tooling designed back when those versions were more predominant.

Slony accomplishes exactly that goal. It is designed to copy tables only, capturing changes on a provider server and sending them to one or more subscribers. This recipe will provide a basic installation and configuration designed for one provider and one subscriber.

Getting ready

If we've already installed the official PostgreSQL PGDG repositories, we already have access to this replication utility. At the time of this book revision, the latest version available is 2.2.8.

Slony can be installed on Debian or Ubuntu systems with this command:

```
sudo apt install postgresql-12-slony1-2 slony1-2-bin
```

And Red Hat-derived systems can use this:

```
sudo yum install slony1-12
```

Once this is done on all intended provider and subscriber nodes, continue with the recipe to configure and use Slony.

How to do it...

For these instructions, 10.0.30.1 (pgha1) is the provider PostgreSQL node, and 10.0.30.2 (pgha2) is our desired subscriber. Follow these instructions to activate Slony on the postgres default database:

1. Provide the rep_user database user with superuser capabilities by running this SQL statement on both PostgreSQL nodes:

   ```
   ALTER USER rep_user WITH SUPERUSER;
   ```

2. Enter the following line in the .pgpass file for the postgres OS user on both nodes:

   ```
   *:*:postgres:rep_user:passwordhere
   ```

3. Ensure that the following line exists within the pg_hba.conf file on the master node:

   ```
   host    postgres    rep_user    10.0.30.2/32    md5
   ```

4. Ensure that the following line exists within the pg_hba.conf file on the subscriber node:

   ```
   host    postgres    rep_user    10.0.30.1/32    md5
   ```

5. Reload the PostgreSQL service on both nodes with the following command as the postgres user:

   ```
   pg_ctl -D /db/pgdata reload
   ```

6. Find the Slony configuration directory. In Debian and Ubuntu systems, this is simply /etc/slony1 while Red Hat derivatives use /etc/slony1-12.

7. Create a symbolic link from the preceding directory to /etc/slony as in this Debian example:

   ```
   sudo ln -s /etc/slony1 /etc/slony
   ```

8. Create a file named `nodes.slonik` in the Slony configuration directory of the provider node with the following contents:

```
cluster name = replication;
define master 'dbname=postgres host=pgha1
            user=rep_user';
define sub1 'dbname=postgres host=pgha2
            user=rep_user';
node 1 admin conninfo = @master;
node 2 admin conninfo = @sub1;
```

9. Create a file named `init.slonik` in the `/etc/slony` directory of the master node with the following contents:

```
include </etc/slony/nodes.slonik>;
init cluster (id=1, comment = 'Master');
store node (id=2, comment = 'Subscriber', event node=1);
store path (server = 1, client = 2, conninfo = @master);
store path (server = 2, client = 1, conninfo = @sub1);
```

10. Install Slony on both nodes by executing the following command as the `postgres` user on the provider node:

```
slonik < /etc/slony/init.slonik
```

11. Start Slony on the provider node with this command as the `postgres` user:

```
slon replication \
    'dbname=postgres host=10.0.30.1 user=rep_user' \
    &> /var/log/postgresql/slony.log &
```

12. Start Slony on the subscriber node with this command as the `postgres` user:

```
slon replication \
    'dbname=postgres host=10.0.30.2 user=rep_user' \
    &> /var/log/postgresql/slony.log &
```

How it works...

Once installed, we need to ensure that our `rep_user` user, which we've used in the past, has PostgreSQL superuser capabilities. Slony performs many tasks that are only available to superusers, so this step is not optional. Then, we modify the `postgres` user's `.pgpass` file to allow the `rep_user` database user to connect from either node. While we're making user changes, we also alter `pg_hba.conf` on both nodes so that each server can connect to the other. Once we reload the PostgreSQL configuration files, the user setup is complete.

> We should note that more advanced installations will probably have a specific user for streaming replicas and a completely separate user for logical replication solutions such as Slony due to the superuser requirement. That wasn't entirely necessary for this book, but do consider it when using tools such as Slony.

With our preliminary work complete, we create a basic configuration file (in the directory that we've linked to `/etc/slony` for convenience) named `nodes.slonik`. This file describes the name of the cluster as well as each node and its connection parameters. We create this file because it is a preamble commonly used in all Slony-related commands—why not save some typing effort?

Next, we create the `init.slonik` file to initialize the Slony cluster. We start by including the `nodes.slonik` file we created earlier, and then initialize node 1 as the master node. After the cluster is created, we store the node for our subscriber. The two `store path` commands are necessary so that each node knows how to communicate with the other.

We should create two path entries for each subscriber node that we create, as each channel is unidirectional. Slony communicates like this, where each Slony box represents one path:

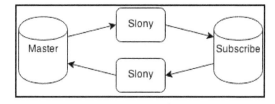

With our configuration files created, we need to install Slony on both nodes. We do this by sending the contents of our `init.slonik` file to the `slonik` command. The `slonik` tool has its own language and interprets our configuration files as instructions. For now, these instructions tell it to initialize a cluster named `replication` with one node, one subscriber, and two communication paths.

Now that Slony is installed on both the master and subscriber nodes, we need to start the `slon` utility. This tool does all of the actual work of the Slony software. It copies data to the subscriber, schedules and executes internal events, performs maintenance, and so on. It acts like a multipurpose daemon but does not fork or run in the background by itself. Hence, we send the output to a log file in `/var/log/postgresql` and tell it to run in the background by specifying `&` at the end of the command. Once again, we have to specify connection information for these daemons to work properly.

There's more...

Only Debian variants are supplied with a systemd-compatible service control file, mainly because it is adapted from the deprecated `/etc/init.d/slony1` file included with the package. As a consequence, we chose to start Slony manually to demonstrate how this is done. On Debian systems, you can do this instead:

```
sudo systemctl enable slony1
sudo systemctl start slony1
```

We're not quite sure why the PGDG packagers of Red Hat and CentOS don't include a similar file for these distributions but suspect it's partially due to the fact Slony itself has been deigned a historic curiosity. Indeed, we'll soon learn that all trigger-based replication systems are considered antiquities.

See also

The Slony documentation is extremely extensive and includes a tutorial similar to this one. It also includes much more in-depth explanations of the process. Please refer to these resources for more:

- **Slony-I 2.2.8 Documentation**: http://www.slony.info/documentation/2.2/index.html
- **Replicating Your First Database**: http://www.slony.info/documentation/2.2/tutorial.html

Copying a few tables with Slony

Once Slony is installed and running on both nodes, we can actually make use of it and copy tables to a remote database. For high-availability PostgreSQL servers, making data available to external systems means long-running and potentially disruptive ad hoc queries no longer execute locally. It also means that reporting environments have direct copies of relevant tables and do not need to retrieve this data from our OLTP systems.

While OLTP servers can act as OLAP systems as well, these workloads are quite different. For the best performance possible and the least risk of outages, each server should be specialized. This recipe will use Slony to copy individual tables so we can decouple these two use cases.

Getting ready

We will be continuing where we left off in the *Setting up Slony* recipe. Please make sure to have completed that recipe before continuing. As we need tables to test Slony, we should create some. The pgbench utility can do this quickly. Execute this command on the primary PostgreSQL server as the postgres user:

```
pgbench -i postgres
```

How to do it...

For this recipe, pgha1 is our provider and pgha2 will remain our subscriber. Follow these instructions on the provider node (unless told otherwise) to copy the pgbench tables and all future changes from pgha1 to pgha2:

1. Extract the table creation statements from the primary database with the following command as the postgres user:

   ```
   pg_dump -s -t 'pgbench*' postgres > /tmp/tables.sql
   ```

2. Create the empty tables on the subscriber node by executing this command as the postgres user on the primary node:

   ```
   psql -U rep_user -h pgha2 -f /tmp/tables.sql postgres
   ```

3. Confirm that the tables exist on the subscriber node by executing the following SQL statement on the subscriber node:

```
SELECT schemaname, tablename
  FROM pg_tables
 WHERE tablename LIKE 'pgbench%';
```

4. Create a file named pgbench_set.slonik in the /etc/slony directory with the following contents:

```
include </etc/slony/nodes.slonik>;
create set (id=1, origin=1, comment='pgbench Tables');
set add table (set id=1, origin=1, id=1,
    fully qualified name = 'public.pgbench_accounts');
set add table (set id=1, origin=1, id=2,
    fully qualified name = 'public.pgbench_branches');
set add table (set id=1, origin=1, id=3,
    fully qualified name = 'public.pgbench_tellers');
```

5. Create a file named subscribe_pgbench.slonik in the /etc/slony directory with the following contents:

```
include </etc/slony/nodes.slonik>;
subscribe set (id = 1, provider = 1, receiver = 2,
    forward = no);
```

6. Create the pgbench subscription set with this command:

```
slonik < /etc/slony/pgbench_set.slonik
```

7. Subscribe our secondary node to the new pgbench set with this command:

```
slonik < /etc/slony/subscribe_pgbench.slonik
```

8. Execute the following SQL on the subscriber node to confirm that data is being copied:

```
SELECT count(*) FROM pgbench_accounts;
```

How it works...

Before we can copy any data, we need to begin by building the necessary table structures to receive the data. Slony only copies data and assumes that the source and target tables have the exact same columns. Therefore, we use pg_dump to obtain a schema-only (-s) extract of any table that begins with pgbench (-t 'pgbench*'). Using the -h parameter, we can execute the resulting SQL statement on the subscriber database and create all of the pgbench tables as empty shells.

Before attempting to create the Slony set, we should first confirm that the tables exist on the subscriber. We can check the pg_tables view and should see these records:

```
schemaname |     tablename
-----------+-------------------
public     | pgbench_accounts
public     | pgbench_branches
public     | pgbench_history
public     | pgbench_tellers
```

Once we've done this, we can continue by creating a slonik script that will create the Slony subscription set itself. Sets are sent to any node that requests a subscription and only includes tables in that set. This lets us group tables by content if necessary. Observant readers may notice that we didn't add the pgbench_history table to the subscription set. This is because Slony only copies tables with primary keys by default.

 Slony table IDs are assigned manually and must be unique across all sets. We recommend skipping IDs between sets in case tables are added later. An easy rule is to add 100 or 1,000 between each set. Hence, if we created another set, its table IDs could start at 100 to provide a sufficient buffer.

Next, we create one more slonik script for the subscription command itself. As this is our first set, its id is 1. Though Slony supports chained table replication, we don't need that for our setup, so we disable it by setting forward to no.

To send table contents to the remote server, we simply need to create the table set on the primary node and subscribe the secondary node to the new set. This is one reason that we created the two slonik scripts. Another reason is due to the chance that we might need to rebuild this Slony replication cluster in the future. By having all of these scripts, we can do this in a few quick steps by executing all of the slonik scripts.

Provided there were no errors returned by the `slonik` commands, we can confirm that data is being sent to the subscriber with a single SQL query. We should see this:

```
postgres=# SELECT count(*) FROM pgbench_accounts;
 count
--------
 100000
```

Remember that we only extracted and copied the table definitions to the remote server. If we see any rows there, they must have come from Slony.

There's more...

Slony operates by attaching triggers to both the source and target tables. Due to this, creating a Slony set on a very active database can cause locking contention. Why does it need triggers? The triggers on the source system capture *insert*, *update*, and *delete* activities and forward them to the remote system. On subscriber nodes, the triggers block any insert, update, or delete activity that does not originate from Slony itself.

The triggers also make it possible to switch between which node is the subscriber and which is the origin without any further table locks. Keep this in mind when copying data via Slony, or the locks could cause query timeouts and customer complaints. Try to schedule new sets and set modifications during maintenance periods or low-usage periods.

See also

The Slony documentation is extremely extensive and includes a tutorial similar to this one. It also includes much more in-depth explanations of the process. Please refer to these resources for more:

- **Slonik Meta Commands**:
  http://www.slony.info/documentation/2.2/metacmds.html
- **Slonik Preamble Commands**:
  http://www.slony.info/documentation/2.2/hdrcmds.html
- **Configuration and Action commands**:
  http://www.slony.info/documentation/2.2/cmds.html

Setting up Bucardo

Bucardo is another popular logical replication engine that actually seems to have originated earlier than Slony, in 2002. Like Slony, it also uses triggers to perform its synchronization activity, but its syntax is much simpler. Furthermore, it also provides multi-master capabilities; this means that changes made in either the primary or secondary node will appear in both copies of a replicated table.

There is something to be said for tools that encourage simplicity when maintaining a complex high-availability architecture. Let's explore Bucardo further.

Getting ready

If we've installed the official PostgreSQL PGDG repositories, we already have access to this replication utility. At the time of this book revision, the latest version available is 5.5.0.

Bucardo can be installed on Debian or Ubuntu systems with this command:

```
sudo apt install bucardo
```

And Red Hat-derived systems can use this:

```
sudo yum install bucardo_12
```

Once this is done on all intended provider and subscriber nodes, continue with the recipe to configure and use Bucardo.

How to do it...

For these instructions, `10.0.30.1` (pgha1) is the provider PostgreSQL node, and `10.0.30.2` (pgha2) is the subscriber. Follow these instructions on the provider system (unless informed otherwise) to activate Bucardo:

1. Enter the following line in the `.pgpass` file for the `postgres` user:

   ```
   *:*:*:bucardo:passwordhere
   ```

2. Ensure that the following line exists within the `pg_hba.conf` file on both` systems:

   ```
   host    all    bucardo    10.0.30.1/24    md5
   ```

3. Reload the PostgreSQL service on both nodes with the following command as the postgres user:

```
pg_ctl -D /db/pgdata reload
```

4. Next, create a bucardo user in the database by executing the following command as the postgres user:

```
CREATE USER bucardo WITH PASSWORD 'newpass' SUPERUSER;
```

5. Create a bucardo database with this command as the postgres user:

```
createdb -O bucardo bucardo
```

6. Create the default Bucardo configuration file and make it owned by the postgres user:

```
sudo touch /etc/bucardorc
sudo chown postgres:postgres /etc/bucardorc
sudo chmod 644 /etc/bucardorc
```

7. As the postgres system user, complete the Bucardo installation with this command, making sure to follow the configuration prompts:

```
bucardo install
```

8. Add the postgres database with these commands as the postgres user:

```
bucardo add db pgha1 dbname=postgres host=pgha1
bucardo add db pgha2 dbname=postgres host=pgha2
```

9. Then, ensure the necessary /var/run and /var/log directories can be written by the postgres user:

```
sudo mkdir /var/run/bucardo /var/log/bucardo
sudo chown postgres:postgres /var/log/bucardo
sudo chown postgres:postgres /var/run/bucardo
```

10. Finally, start the Bucardo service by executing this command as the postgres user:

```
bucardo start
```

How it works...

Bucardo has a lot of prerequisites, and its installation and configuration process has become somewhat cumbersome. Yet it also provides a proper daemon control utility in bucardo once the onerous installation is complete. Once Bucardo is installed on the primary server, we merely have to invoke bucardo with the install parameter to finish the process.

For Bucardo to be installed, it needs a user named bucardo and a database named bucardo. The bucardo user acts like the rep_user user we created for replication, so it must be a PostgreSQL superuser. As such, we need to ensure that we use a superuser for the User configuration setting during the installation process. This is why we recommend that you run the bucardo utility as postgres when possible. Here's what our installation screen looked like:

```
Current connection settings:
1. Host:          pgha1
2. Port:          5432
3. User:          bucardo
4. Database:      bucardo
5. PID directory: /var/run/bucardo
Enter a number to change it, P to proceed, or Q to quit:
```

Once we press *P* and hit *Enter*, Bucardo is installed. This means the only steps that remain involve starting the Bucardo service itself.

A lot of our preparatory work in creating the bucardo user and database are only necessary because we didn't use trust authentication in pg_hba.conf. Normally the bucardo install command does all of this for us. Unfortunately, it also contains a lot of reconnection magic and is very easy to disrupt with unexpected settings. It's easier to simply circumvent a large portion of its installation by doing it ourselves.

To do this, we need to prepare the /var/run/bucardo and /var/log/bucardo directories so that Bucardo can create files there. As we are going to launch it as the postgres user, the postgres system user needs to own these directories as well.

Next, we configure Bucardo itself by adding an internal alias for the postgres database on each server. The bucardo command has a lot of operation modes, but for now, all we need to do is add the postgres database itself. After doing so, we can start Bucardo by calling bucardo with the start parameter.

If everything goes well, we can call bucardo with the status parameter and see that it's running, as shown in the following screenshot:

```
PID of Bucardo MCP: 18941
No syncs have been created yet.
```

See also

Bucardo has an easy-to-follow documentation page with instructions on installation and basic configuration. To learn more, please visit their site for these resources:

- **Bucardo Installation**: https://bucardo.org/Bucardo/Installation.html
- **The Bucardo command-line tool**: https://bucardo.org/Bucardo/bucardo.html

Copying a few tables with Bucardo

Bucardo provides a very capable control mechanism in the bucardo command-line tool. Unlike Slony, which depends on an arcane programming language to create new replication sets and subscriptions, Bucardo is much more straightforward. As with Slony, we still want to copy data to other servers to avoid overwhelming our primary server.

In this recipe, we will utilize bucardo to create what Bucardo refers to as a **dbgroup** and **relgroup**. A Bucardo dbgroup consists of multiple databases in a provider-subscriber relationship, and a relgroup contains one or more tables. These are the basis of its synchronization system.

Getting ready

We will be continuing where we left off in the *Setting up Bucardo* recipe. Please make sure that you have completed that recipe before continuing. As usual, we will use the pgbench utility to create an initial set of tables. Execute this command on the primary PostgreSQL server as the postgres user if you haven't already done so:

```
pgbench -i postgres
```

How to do it...

As with all of the previous recipes, pgha2 will remain our replication subscriber. Execute all commands in this recipe on the provider system (pgha1) as the postgres system user. Follow these steps to copy the sample pgbench tables:

1. Extract the table creation statements from the primary node with the following command:

    ```
    pg_dump -s -t 'pgbench*' postgres > /tmp/tables.sql
    ```

2. Create the empty tables on the subscriber node by executing this command on the primary node:

    ```
    psql -U rep_user -h pgha2 -f /tmp/tables.sql postgres
    ```

3. Add all of the pgbench tables to Bucardo with these commands:

    ```
    bucardo add table pgbench_accounts db=pgha1
    bucardo add table pgbench_branches db=pgha1
    bucardo add table pgbench_tellers db=pgha1
    ```

4. Confirm tables are being tracked by executing this command:

    ```
    bucardo list tables
    ```

5. Create a Bucardo database group with this command:

    ```
    bucardo add dbgroup pgbench pgha1:source pgha2:target
    ```

6. Create a Bucardo relation group by executing this command:

    ```
    bucardo add relgroup pgbench pgbench_accounts \
        pgbench_branches pgbench_tellers
    ```

7. Execute the following commands to add a synchronization set to Bucardo:

    ```
    bucardo stop
    bucardo add sync pgbench dbgroup=pgbench \
            relgroup=pgbench onetimecopy=1
    bucardo start
    ```

8. Finally, execute this command to view the status of Bucardo:

    ```
    bucardo status
    ```

How it works...

As with Slony, we need to begin by duplicating table structures to the subscriber. Bucardo only copies data and assumes that the source and target tables have the exact same columns. Therefore, we use pg_dump to obtain a schema-only (-s) extract of any table that begins with pgbench (-t 'pgbench*'). Using the -h parameter, we can execute the resulting SQL on the subscriber database and create all of the pgbench tables as empty shells.

After copying the table definitions, we can use the bucardo tool for all of the remaining steps. The first of these include configuring Bucardo to recognize each table we want to replicate. The add table parameter does this. By adding the db=pgha1 segment, we explicitly state which database owns the table we're adding. In this case, pgha1 is the alias we created for the origin server during the installation of Bucardo.

To prove that Bucardo added these tables to its configuration, we can check with the list tables parameter. The output from bucardo should resemble this:

```
1. Table: public.pgbench_accounts  DB: pgha1  PK: aid (integer)
2. Table: public.pgbench_branches  DB: pgha1  PK: bid (integer)
3. Table: public.pgbench_tellers   DB: pgha1  PK: tid (integer)
```

This relation group is the equivalent of a Slony table set. Like a relation set, we also need to define a database group. This database group will represent the source and target relationships for all of the tables we plan to synchronize. We state this relationship explicitly as pgha1:source and pgha2:target so there is no ambiguity regarding how these two databases are related within Bucardo.

With a database group defined, it's time to give directions to our relation group by utilizing the bucardo tool again. This time, we send the add sync parameter and a few other elements. The relgroup parameter tells Bucardo which table set we will be copying, and the dbgroup parameter denotes which database relationship we wish to involve. Bucardo defines groups this way because it's entirely possible for tables to exist in multiple databases. Were we to declare multiple different database groups, we could assign the same relation group to any or all of them.

These tables are empty on the target, and this is not the behavior we want. So, we also set the onetimecopy value to 1, indicating that it should fill the tables before keeping them updated.

This behavior is much different from how Slony works. If the source and target tables already contain data, Slony will truncate the target and copy all data from the source. If a table has already been synchronized before adding it to a replication set, this redundant copying can be very expensive. Bucardo only copies all data if it is told to do so with the onetimecopy parameter, which is a major benefit when running a sensitive high-availability cluster.

Bucardo maintains separate child processes for each replication set so that it can handle multiple synchronization sets simultaneously. However, notice that we temporarily stopped the bucardo service before adding the synchronization set. This is because we noticed an intermittent bug regarding the onetimecopy parameter.

If a new sync set is added while Bucardo is running, there's a chance the current table contents won't be copied to the target database even though we asked for an initial copy. Even if this bug has been fixed, it's good to be precautious.

After Bucardo is restarted, we should view the sync status to confirm that it is active and copying our cluster properly. The status output from bucardo should look like this:

```
PID of Bucardo MCP: 16211
 Name        State       Last good     Time      Last I/D     Last bad      Time
=========+========+============+========+===========+===========+=======
 pgbench | Good    | 22:28:56    | 7m 41s | 0/0         | none       |
```

From this output, we can see that the pgbench synchronization set is in a Good state and hasn't encountered any events that would adversely affect replication.

See also

Bucardo has more capabilities than we've covered here. To learn more, please visit their site: https://bucardo.org/Bucardo/bucardo.html

Setting up pglogical

PostgreSQL 9.4 introduced a feature called replication slots. This essentially makes it possible to decode the transaction log and extract database write traffic for remote replay at a logical level. Unlike standard replication, which requires the primary and replica to be identical, slots can be mined for specific information relevant to user needs.

One of the first PostgreSQL extensions to make use of replication slots is **pglogical** by 2ndQuadrant. Like Slony and Bucardo, pglogical can copy individual tables from one database to another. Unlike those other pieces of software, it does so without encumbering tables with performance-robbing triggers and does not rely on an external daemon to coordinate data copy streams.

This recipe will explain how to install and configure pglogical for easy table copies.

Getting ready

The latest community version of pglogical at the time of writing this book is 2.2.2. 2ndQuadrant conveniently maintains packages for most major Linux platforms and makes them available as a public repository. They provide instructions for subscribing at this URL: https://dl.2ndquadrant.com/default/release/site/.

Rather than editing several files and importing keys, 2ndQuadrant has a script that handles this automatically. Debian variants can use these commands to install the repository and pglogical for PostgreSQL 11:

```
curl https://dl.2ndquadrant.com/default/release/get/deb | sudo bash
sudo apt install postgresql-11-pglogical
```

Red Hat or CentOS fans would add a repository and pglogical for PostgreSQL 11 with these commands:

```
curl https://dl.2ndquadrant.com/default/release/get/11/rpm | sudo bash
sudo yum install postgresql11-pglogical
```

Note that RPM/yum-managed distributions must include the version in the repository subscription.

At the time we were updating this chapter, pglogical didn't yet support PostgreSQL 12. As such, all instructions and demonstrations will assume PostgreSQL 11. This may have changed by the time of publication, so we recommend checking the repository at this URL for the target platform and PostgreSQL version: `https://dl.2ndquadrant.com/default/release/browse/`.

How to do it...

As usual for these instructions, `10.0.30.1` (pgha1) is the provider PostgreSQL node, and `10.0.30.2` (pgha2) is the subscriber. Follow these steps to install pglogical:

1. Ensure that the `pg_hba.conf` file on the provider and subscriber servers contains these lines:

```
host    all              rep_user    10.0.30.1/24    md5
host    replication      rep_user    10.0.30.1/24    md5
```

2. Ensure that the `wal_level`, `max_replication_slots`, and `shared_preload_libraries` settings in `postgresql.conf` are set as follows on the provider server:

```
wal_level = logical
max_replication_slots = 10
shared_preload_libraries = 'pg_stat_statements, pglogical'
```

3. Ensure the `shared_preload_libraries` setting is set as follows on the subscriber server:

```
shared_preload_libraries = 'pg_stat_statements, pglogical'
```

4. Debian-based distributions should restart PostgreSQL with this command:

```
sudo systemctl restart postgresql@11-main
```

5. Red Hat-based distributions should restart PostgreSQL with this command:

```
sudo systemctl restart postgresql-11
```

6. Create the replication user on both nodes if it doesn't already exist with this SQL statement:

```
CREATE USER rep_user WITH REPLICATION SUPERUSER PASSWORD
'newpass';
```

7. On both servers, create a file named .pgpass in the postgres user's home directory with the following contents:

```
*:*:*:rep_user:newpass
```

8. Alter the .pgpass file to have the correct permissions with this command:

```
chmod 600 ~/.pgpass
```

9. Execute these statements in the postgres database on the provider server:

```
CREATE EXTENSION pglogical;
SELECT pglogical.create_node(
    node_name := 'origin',
    dsn := 'host=pgha1 dbname=postgres user=rep_user'
);
```

10. Finally, execute these statements in the postgres database on the subscriber node:

```
CREATE EXTENSION pglogical;
SELECT pglogical.create_node(
    node_name := 'target',
    dsn := 'host=pgha2 dbname=postgres user=rep_user'
);
```

How it works...

We start by changing a handful of configuration settings. The two lines in pg_hba.conf ensure that the rep_user user can connect to both the replication stream on the origin server, along with any database we might want to use as a source for table replication.

The other settings are for `postgresql.conf`, and if you followed the *Configuration – getting it right the first time* recipe in `Chapter 3`, *Minimizing Downtime*, on configuration, you should already have all of these set properly. We change `wal_level` to `logical` because that's a requirement to use logical replication in PostgreSQL. The previous `replica` setting is only suitable for standard streaming replication.

We also need to increase `max_replication_slots` if it is a low or zero value so logical replication works as expected. And finally, we must include `pglogical` in the list of shared libraries to load on server start. By restarting PostgreSQL, we activate all of these modifications, and this step is required because we introduced a new shared library.

The next steps create a `rep_user` user to actually manage the replication stream, with a password saved in `.pgpass` so the stream is at least relatively secure. Note that we included both `SUPERUSER` and `REPLICATION` modifiers to provide this user with appropriate privileges.

The last two steps simply install the `pglogical` extension in the primary and subscriber databases and create a node to represent each. By naming any nodes involved in replication, we can use them in multiple replication streams if we so desire.

See also

To learn more about pglogical and PostgreSQL logical replication, refer to the following resources:

- **The pglogical documentation**:
  `https://www.2ndquadrant.com/en/resources/pglogical/pglogical-docs/`
- **Logical Decoding Concepts**:
  `https://www.postgresql.org/docs/current/logicaldecoding-explanation.html`

Copying a few tables with pglogical

Once we've installed the pglogical extension, we have access to any of the functionality it provides. For now, we're going to focus on the basic table replication features. More advanced capabilities are available, but we won't be needing them for this recipe.

An important difference between pglogical and every other current logical replication system is that it does not use triggers to capture changes to table contents. With the addition of logical replication slots, pglogical actually intercepts table changes as transactions are committed. This makes it a perfect match for OLTP database systems that require high availability and don't want to sacrifice performance. The transaction log is a standard part of PostgreSQL, so why not leverage it for logical replication now that such a thing is possible?

This recipe will demonstrate how to copy tables with this useful extension.

Getting ready

We will be continuing where we left off in the *Setting up pglogical* recipe. Please make sure that you have completed that recipe before continuing. As usual, we will use the pgbench utility to create an initial set of tables. Execute this command on the primary PostgreSQL server as the postgres user if you haven't already done so:

```
pgbench -i postgres
```

How to do it...

As with all of the previous recipes, pgha1 is our origin server and pgha2 will remain our replication subscriber. Execute all commands in this recipe as the postgres system user on the provider node unless stated otherwise. Follow these steps to copy the sample pgbench tables:

1. Extract the table creation statements from the primary node with the following command:

```
pg_dump -s -t 'pgbench*' postgres > /tmp/tables.sql
```

2. Create the empty tables on the subscriber node by executing this command on the primary node:

```
psql -U rep_user -h pgha2 -f /tmp/tables.sql postgres
```

3. Execute this SQL on the primary server to create a replication set:

```
SELECT pglogical.create_replication_set(
    set_name := 'pgbench',
    replicate_insert := TRUE, replicate_update := TRUE,
    replicate_delete := FALSE, replicate_truncate := FALSE
);
```

4. Add the pgbench tables to the replication set with the following SQL on the primary server:

```
SELECT pglogical.replication_set_add_table(
    set_name := 'pgbench', relation :=
'public.pgbench_accounts'
);
SELECT pglogical.replication_set_add_table(
    set_name := 'pgbench', relation :=
'public.pgbench_branches'
);
SELECT pglogical.replication_set_add_table(
    set_name := 'pgbench', relation :=
'public.pgbench_tellers'
);
```

5. Execute the following SQL on the subscriber node to begin replicating the set:

```
SELECT pglogical.create_subscription(
    subscription_name := 'pgbench',
    replication_sets := ARRAY['pgbench'],
    synchronize_data := TRUE,
    provider_dsn := 'host=pgha1 dbname=postgres user=rep_user'
);
```

6. Check the health of our subscription with this SQL statement executed on the subscriber node:

```
SELECT subscription_name, status, provider_node,
       replication_sets
  FROM pglogical.show_subscription_status('pgbench');
```

How it works...

After the last few extensions, using pglogical is almost refreshingly easy. As usual, we start by copying the `pgbench` table definitions from the origin node to the subscriber. Once that is done, the provider node has only one job: to create a subscription set.

The subscription set we create is named `pgbench` to fit the theme of copying multiple `pgbench` tables. When defining a replication set with the `create_replication_set` function, we actually have a few options that the other replication systems did not offer. We elected to only replicate `INSERT` and `UPDATE` statements in this example. In such a scenario, the origin server can delete records from the table or truncate it entirely, and the records on the subscriber will remain. The only other step is to add all of the tables we want in that replication set with the `replication_set_add_table` function.

We only need to execute a single command on the subscriber! We've already created the tables themselves, so why complicate matters? By invoking the `create_subscription` function, we specify the name of the subscription itself, the replication set we want, and the provider of the table contents. We don't need to state the `synchronize_data` parameter since it defaults to `TRUE` already, but it's important to know the option is available.

If we execute the final statement on the subscriber, we should be able to determine whether our data stream is working properly. The output from the provided SQL statement should look something like this:

```
 subscription_name |   status    | provider_node | replication_sets
-------------------+-------------+---------------+------------------
 pgbench           | replicating | origin        | {pgbench}
```

The `pglogical` extension works by utilizing background workers, a feature added in PostgreSQL 9.4. Since these background workers are a part of PostgreSQL itself, they're running while our database instance is online. This is the reason pglogical does not require a daemon to manage subscriptions or data transfers; PostgreSQL handles it automatically.

There's more...

Remember in *step 3* how we defined the replication set to only forward INSERT and UPDATE statements? The primary reason to do something like this is that we're sending data to some kind of archival system. Since these types of databases tend to accumulate data for months or even years, they're also commonly partitioned. The pglogical extension is perfectly compatible with this approach, but there is one caveat.

Before PostgreSQL 10 introduced native partitioning, partitions were usually managed via a trigger and a complicated series of constraints to distribute data based on inheritance rules. Reporting or other data accumulation systems that use this approach rely on this trigger to ensure data is deposited in the correct partition.

To ensure data gets where we need it to go, we need to modify that trigger slightly so it's compatible with pglogical. For example, if our trigger is named pgbench_accounts_part_trig, we would need to execute this SQL:

```
ALTER TABLE pgbench_accounts
ENABLE ALWAYS TRIGGER pgbench_accounts_part_trig;
```

Once we've done that, we could have a single partition or hundreds, and incoming data from pglogical will reach its appropriate destination. If we already have data in our tables, we also need to set synchronize_data to FALSE during the subscription phase, or we might end up with multiple copies of the origin data. This is due to limitations PostgreSQL inheritance-based partitions have regarding primary keys.

The preceding caveat only applies to inheritance-based partitions. Partitions created using the native PostgreSQL 10+ (CREATE TABLE ... PARTITION OF ...) syntax are implemented much differently. As a consequence, pglogical is not able to insert into native PostgreSQL partitions.

The base table in these cases is not really a table, but more of a redirection object and pglogical operates at an API level that does not follow the redirection. Hence, pglogical will attempt to insert into the base partition table, which does not really exist.

See also

Again, we strongly recommend visiting the following documentation to learn more about pglogical and logical replication slots:

- **The pglogical documentation**:
  https://www.2ndquadrant.com/en/resources/pglogical/pglogical-docs/
- **Logical Decoding Concepts**:
  https://www.postgresql.org/docs/current/logicaldecoding-explanation.html

Copying a few tables with native logical replication

Starting with version 10, PostgreSQL natively supports logical replication using **publication** and **subscription** structures. These are directly managed by the PostgreSQL syntax parser as native SQL, and create objects in the system catalog that are managed just like everything else.

This makes it almost trivial to create lists of tables to transmit to recipient PostgreSQL servers located elsewhere. It also means standard PostgreSQL tools can interact with the subscription and table sets in ways that extensions cannot reproduce.

This recipe will create a basic table set and explain a bit about the limitations of this type of logical replication.

Getting ready

Unlike the other software we've discussed previously, there's nothing to install. So long as we're using PostgreSQL 10 or greater, we already have this functionality. Simply follow along with the recipe!

Otherwise, we will use the pgbench utility to create an initial set of tables. Execute this command on the primary PostgreSQL server as the postgres user if you haven't already done so:

```
pgbench -i postgres
```

How to do it...

As with all of the previous recipes, pgha1 is our origin server and pgha2 will remain our replication subscriber. Execute all commands in this recipe as the postgres system user on the provider node unless stated otherwise. Follow these steps to copy the sample pgbench tables:

1. Extract the table creation statements from the primary node with the following command:

    ```
    pg_dump -s -t 'pgbench*' postgres > /tmp/tables.sql
    ```

2. Create the empty tables on the subscriber node by executing this command on the primary node:

    ```
    psql -U rep_user -h pgha2 -f /tmp/tables.sql postgres
    ```

3. Execute this SQL on the primary server to create a replication set:

    ```
    CREATE PUBLICATION pgbench
        FOR TABLE pgbench_accounts, pgbench_branches,
                  pgbench_tellers, pgbench_history;
    ```

4. Execute the following SQL on the subscriber node to begin replicating the set:

    ```
    CREATE SUBSCRIPTION pgbench CONNECTION 'host=pgha1
    dbname=postgres user=rep_user' PUBLICATION pgbench;
    ```

5. Check the health of our subscription with this SQL statement:

    ```
    SELECT slot.slot_name, slot.slot_type, slot.active,
           stat.application_name, stat.state, stat.client_addr
      FROM pg_replication_slots slot
      JOIN pg_stat_replication stat ON (stat.pid =
    slot.active_pid);
    ```

How it works...

That was much easier than expected! Without any extra software to install, there's very little in the way of setup. All we need to do is create the publication and the subscription and our tables are immediately in transit.

Still, we need something to replicate, so we used `pg_dump` to extract the tables we want to copy. Similarly, PostgreSQL will not automatically create recipient tables on the subscriber, so we must bootstrap them as empty shells with `psql` by importing the `tables.sql` file we extracted previously.

Unlike Slony, Bucardo, or pglogical, however, we don't need to first create node records before copying tables. PostgreSQL itself is the node, and it has its own records, which it manages internally. Hence, we can jump straight to using `CREATE PUBLICATION` to publish the list of tables we want to provide to other nodes. We could have specified `FOR ALL TABLES` here instead, but we like being explicit.

Next, we invoke `CREATE SUBSCRIPTION` on the recipient node, and in this case, we only need to name our subscription and list the provider DSN and the fact we want to obtain the pgbench `PUBLICATION` set. Since a listed provider may publish multiple sets, this is a fairly logical operation.

Once we've done all of that, we can inquire as to the state of the subscription by executing a query on the provider node. If everything went well, we should see this:

```
 slot_name | slot_type | active | application_name |   state   | client_addr
-----------+-----------+--------+------------------+-----------+------------
 pgbench   | logical   | t      | pgbench          | streaming | 10.0.30.2
```

From here, we can see that PostgreSQL explicitly names the slot after the subscription, and the connecting server does the same via `application_name`. This makes it much easier to track which publications are being sent to which subscribers.

There's more...

Despite how easy native replication is to manage, there are some elements we believe are important to share.

No sequences

Unlike Slony, Bucardo, or pglogical, native logical replication does not support sequences. We didn't explain how to copy sequences in those recipes, but the functionality is provided. This means if we want to use PostgreSQL native logical replication to upgrade between major versions, we would need to manually dump the most recent sequence values from the origin node and import them in the subscriber.

This isn't too difficult to accomplish manually but should be a consideration before expecting the sequences to automatically reflect the proper values.

Tool integration

We mentioned that PostgreSQL native logical replication is highly integrated into the database system and included tools. The best way to demonstrate this is to use the `\d` command from within `psql` to describe one of the tables we're copying:

```
postgres=# \d pgbench_accounts

                 Table "public.pgbench_accounts"
  Column   |     Type      | Collation | Nullable | Default
-----------+---------------+-----------+----------+---------
 aid       | integer       |           | not null |
 bid       | integer       |           |          |
 abalance  | integer       |           |          |
 filler    | character(84) |           |          |
Indexes:
    "pgbench_accounts_pkey" PRIMARY KEY, btree (aid)
Publications:
    "pgbench"
```

As we can see here, `psql` reported that this table is part of a publication. This is also very handy when browsing through the database objects in our system.

Keys required for UPDATE and DELETE

Observant readers may have noticed we added the `pgbench_history` table to the publication. We've already explained why other logical replication solutions do not allow this, but we felt it would be a good demonstration. PostgreSQL did not complain about this when we created the publication, but watch what happens when we try to delete a value from the table:

```
postgres=# DELETE FROM pgbench_history WHERE tid=1 AND bid=5;

ERROR:  cannot delete from table "pgbench_history" because
it does not have a replica identity and publishes deletes
HINT:  To enable deleting from the table, set REPLICA IDENTITY
using ALTER TABLE.
```

This means PostgreSQL native logical replication has the same limitation as other implementations. This makes perfect sense though, as it would be impossible for the recipient system to safely delete or update a record without a unique identifying characteristic. Hence, it's always a good practice to add some kind of key to any tables to facilitate replication at a later time.

See also

PostgreSQL native logical subscription sets are extremely useful for basic replication needs. For more information, check out the PostgreSQL documentation:

- **CREATE PUBLICATION**: `https://www.postgresql.org/docs/current/sql-createpublication.html`
- **CREATE SUBSCRIPTION**: `https://www.postgresql.org/docs/current/sql-createsubscription.html`
- **Logical Replication**: `https://www.postgresql.org/docs/current/logical-replication.html`

8
Backup Management

A proper database backup is probably the most important component of a true high availability stack. Inadequate backups can lead to or even compound data loss by providing a false sense of security in the face of a catastrophe.

In the chapter where we explained architecture, we provided a recipe that explained the 3-2-1 backup rule. This is a good start but is more of a design and resource allocation consideration. Truly managing PostgreSQL backups means having the right software, configuring it optimally, and testing both the backup and recovery procedures.

We've written this chapter to apply the architecture lessons we learned at the beginning of this book, and expand upon it with a solid foundation by focusing on the Barman backup software. In our experience, this is the most reliable approach for constructing a fully integrated high availability stack because it's designed from a server management perspective. Most backup tools merely focus on one instance of PostgreSQL, despite the fact most larger installations consist of multiple independent clusters that require coordination.

Yet other tools still serve a valuable purpose. Sometimes a one-off backup really is the best approach, and other tools work better for synchronizing data to dedicated cloud servers. This is why this chapter also covers the proper usage of the popular pgBackRest and WAL-E backup systems. All that we really ask is that nobody ever depends on `pg_dump` for anything beyond occasional partial extracts; it is not a backup tool.

This chapter will help to ensure backups not only fulfill their stated role but are also reliable, fast, and efficient. Disk space is getting cheaper every day, but it still isn't free. Let's make our backups a true pillar that supports the availability of our data.

In this chapter, we will learn where to turn when backing up large PostgreSQL clusters becomes a concern. We will cover the following recipes in this chapter:

- Deciding when to use third-party tools
- Installing and configuring Barman
- Backing up a database with Barman
- Restoring a database with Barman
- Obtaining Barman diagnostics and information
- Sending Barman backups to a remote location
- Installing and configuring pgBackRest
- Backing up a database with pgBackRest
- Restoring a database with pgBackRest
- Installing and configuring WAL-E
- Managing WAL files with WAL-E

Deciding when to use third-party tools

Managing PostgreSQL backups need not be difficult or require third-party software tooling. In many small or even medium-size environments, it may be perfectly acceptable to rely on the provided `pg_basebackup` utility.

Yet this assumption rapidly breaks down upon the introduction of even small amounts of complexity. Creating a one-time backup is only a tiny portion of backing up a **Relational Database Management System (RDBMS)**. A complete backup solution will also manage WAL files to orchestrate **Point-In-Time Recovery (PITR)**, restore a backup to a remote location, and target multiple servers if necessary. There's a lot of room for accidents, and any mistake can result in a useless backup or a lost production environment.

While much of this can be scripted, why reinvent the wheel? These tools exist because someone took the time to solve the problem of backup management beyond the basics. This recipe will act as a worksheet to assess the PostgreSQL clusters and what environments they represent. This will help us to determine how many backups we should have and perhaps how best to automate using more advanced software.

Getting ready

We will be filling out a very short spreadsheet inventory of our PostgreSQL server clusters. In this context, a cluster is an independent combination of primary nodes and associated standby or replica systems. Some organizations have several of these, so we must have a record of them all to ensure each can be replaced in the case of a total server loss. Even if we choose not to use more advanced backup software, this will serve as a valuable source of inventory and documentation for our database infrastructure.

Be sure to have access to a spreadsheet program before continuing. We also strongly recommend a diagram of all PostgreSQL servers for each segment of your database architecture. This will likely include production and **Disaster Recovery** (**DR**) environments, but may also include user acceptance testing, staging/QA, and development depending on how critical these are to the organization.

How to do it...

Follow these steps to determine the extent of necessary backup tooling:

1. Create a spreadsheet with the following columns: `Cluster Name`, `Environment`, `Streaming`, `Logical`, `DC`, `Size (GB)`, `PITR`, and `Backup`.
2. Create a row for each server indicating its `Cluster Name` based on the primary focus of the data.
3. For each row, set the corresponding attribute column as follows:
   - For `Environment`, use `Production`, `Disaster Recovery`, `UAT`, `QA`, or any other common internal indicator.
   - Specify the number of physical streaming replica nodes in the cluster.
   - If applicable, list the number of logical replica nodes; any node that may exist as a write target counts here.
   - If there are multiple data centers, list how many the cluster inhabits in the `DC` column.
   - Indicate the amount of storage required for the largest node in the cluster.
   - Specify either `TRUE` or `FALSE` in the `PITR` column if PITR is desired when restoring from a backup.

4. Enter the highest value between the `DC` and `Logical` columns in the `Backup` column.

5. Consider using a backup management platform if any of these are true:
   - Any environment contains three or more clusters.
   - Three or more environments are involved.
   - Three or more nodes in a cluster may provide a source for a backup.
   - Three or more nodes are logical in nature.
   - The total number of backups across all clusters is greater than three.
   - `PITR` is `TRUE` for any cluster.
   - Any cluster is greater than 1 TB in size.

How it works...

The idea behind this spreadsheet is to describe the environments in our architecture sufficiently so that we can track where the backups originate and how many there should be. Once we have a definitive number, it may be apparent that it's too much to manage with a series of ad hoc scripts and scheduled backup or WAL archival maintenance events.

This example spreadsheet represents part of our architecture in the introduction:

	A	B	C	D	E	F	G	H
1	**Cluster Name**	**Environment**	**Streaming**	**Logical**	**DC**	**Size (GB)**	**PITR**	**Backup**
2	Trading	Production	3	3	3	800	TRUE	3
3	Trading	DR	3	3	3	800	TRUE	3
4	Trading	UAT	2	2	2	200	FALSE	2
5	Gameworld	Production	4	0	2	4489	TRUE	2
6	Gameworld	DR	2	0	2	4489	TRUE	2
7	Gameworld	QA	1	0	2	1242	FALSE	2
8	Gameworld	Dev	0	8	2	350	FALSE	8

When we say `Cluster Name`, we really mean the primary focus of the data itself. If the application stack is a stock trading system, we might call it **Trading**. If it's a complex game engine based on many interactions, it could be a **Gameworld** instead. The point is to be descriptive of the collective PostgreSQL nodes where the data resides.

The `Environment` column has another goal related to physical separation. In many systems, it's not uncommon to duplicate every server in multiple tiers. Some may exist in case of a system outage, others for quality assurance, and more for development. Each may be separated from the others by strict firewall rules to prevent cross-contamination. Some may be built as a restoration from another.

It's important to know how many PostgreSQL nodes exist as `Streaming` replicas mainly because any of them may become a source of our backup data. In the event a primary server goes offline permanently, we may need to reconfigure the backup system to use the new server as a target.

Next, we want to know how many logical nodes there are in the cluster. What is a *logical* node? Any node that can receive writes qualifies here. This could be a reporting or archival server that ingests and accumulates data for long-term analysis, or any writable node in a multi-master cluster, or even horizontally scaled shards managed by some complex data federation mechanism. Whatever the case, all writable nodes have data that is not represented on another node, and hence should be backed up.

The number of **data centers** (`DC`) is important mainly as a data isolation case. Backup systems are usually physically located in the same data center as the nodes they back up. This data may be exported later, but the first iteration is usually local. What happens if we have two data centers and only back up one of them? That's fine until we lose that data center in a catastrophic event, at which point we have no backups at all! The truly paranoid will want a backup in every data center as a failsafe.

The reason we care about the `Size (GB)` of each node is based on backup duration. Physical storage performance has generally not been keeping pace with data growth rates in larger organizations. The author has personally administered a 60 TB cluster and designed a backup system specifically to manage its size in a reasonable time. This required several weeks of development and debugging, and while the end result worked as desired, it's entirely custom-made. That makes it fragile and lacking in support. Many custom backup solutions have these attributes, and database size tends to amplify problems. It's much harder to diagnose or restart a failed 60 TB backup than one that's only 200 GB.

Finally, we must consider whether or not we want to use PITR when performing a database restoration. Not all environments will require this, as indicated in the example spreadsheet. However, managing PITR means keeping track of every WAL file produced from every writable server between each backup. It means those files must be managed, backed up, and retrieved individually. This can be complex on its own and becomes much more difficult as server count increases.

From all of this, we can produce a rough (and likely inflated) estimate of how many backups we could need to safeguard the cluster. Each of these is a moving part that we don't want to mix with others, which may exist in multiple environments and consist of several mutually-exclusive targets. Orchestrating this manually or using bespoke scripts is possible, but extremely error-prone even when designed by experts in the field.

The recommendations we listed for choosing to use backup software should not be considered exhaustive. Attentive readers may have noticed that we used the number **3** frequently, and we did so to gently suggest anything greater than a mere pair of servers likely requires augmented management.

Consider the **Dev** environment of the **Gameworld** example we provided. Each developer likely has their own sample data, working set, portion of the engine, patch level, and any number of variables. If that PostgreSQL resource were lost, that could result in hours or even days of lost productivity. This means even development environments can contribute to backup complexity, as in this example we would need to manage eight separate backups for each PostgreSQL system being used by a different developer.

Installing and configuring Barman

Though PostgreSQL provides a very capable tool in `pg_basebackup`, it's not really a complete backup management system. Barman is a backup and recovery manager developed by 2ndQuadrant to remedy that situation.

Unlike included utilities, Barman can receive WAL archives, produce and restore database backups, list available backups, control backup retention policies, and more. With a single command, we can manage backups of any PostgreSQL server we've configured Barman to recognize. Further, we can accomplish this from the backup server itself with no need to perform any local post-installation tasks on any PostgreSQL servers.

However, before we can get any of these abilities, we must first install and configure Barman. This recipe will walk you through this process as simply as possible.

Getting ready

At the time of writing this book, the most recent version of Barman is 2.9. Because of 2ndQuadrant's close interaction with the PostgreSQL community, it is available within the PostgreSQL package repositories. If you are using a Debian- or Ubuntu-based system, follow the instructions at this URL to add the PostgreSQL repository to the system that will be running Barman: `https://wiki.postgresql.org/wiki/Apt`.

Otherwise, Red Hat-based systems should add the PostgreSQL repository by installing the derivative-appropriate RPM located at this URL: `https://yum.postgresql.org/repopackages.php`.

We recommend that you use repositories only, as the repository-provided packages perform tasks other than software installation, such as user creation.

Please note that Barman 2.9 is the first version that supports PostgreSQL 12 and above. If you are using such a PostgreSQL installation, ensure the Barman version meets or exceeds this minimum.

How to do it...

For this procedure, we will need two servers. The backup server will be named `pg-backup`, and our primary PostgreSQL server will be named `pg-primary`. Make sure to have the password for the `barman` system user and the `postgres` database user. As usual, our database is located at `/db/pgdata`.

Follow these steps:

1. For Red Hat-based servers, use the following command:

    - Install the Barman toolkit as a root-capable user:

        ```
        sudo yum install barman
        ```

    - Debian-based systems should use this command instead:

        ```
        sudo apt-get install barman
        ```

2. On the `pg-backup` server as the `barman` user, execute the following commands for direct SSH access to `pg-primary` as the `postgres` user:

```
ssh-keygen -t rsa -N ''
ssh-copy-id postgres@pg-primary
```

3. Execute this SQL on the `pg-primary` server to create a user for `barman`:

```
CREATE USER barman WITH REPLICATION SUPERUSER
        PASSWORD 'mypasshere';
```

4. Ensure that the following lines exist in the `pg_hba.conf` file on pg-primary:

```
host    all          barman    pg-backup    md5
host    replication  barman    pg-backup    md5
```

5. Enter the following line in the `.pgpass` file for the `barman` user on pg-backup:

```
*:*:*:barman:barman-password
```

6. Reload the PostgreSQL service on `pg-primary` with the following command as the `postgres` user:

```
pg_ctl -D /db/pgdata reload
```

7. Create a file named `pg-primary.conf` in the `/etc/barman.d` folder, and use the following contents:

```
[pg-primary]

description = "Primary PostgreSQL Server"
conninfo = "host=pg-primary user=barman dbname=postgres"
streaming_conninfo = "host=pg-primary user=barman"
ssh_command = "ssh postgres@pg-primary"
backup_method = rsync
archiver = off
streaming_archiver = on
slot_name = barman
backup_options = exclusive_backup
```

8. If this is a Debian-based system, include this line in `pg-primary.conf`:

```
path_prefix = /usr/lib/postgresql/12/bin
```

For Red Hat-based distributions, include this line in `pg-primary.conf`:

```
path_prefix = /usr/pgsql-12/bin
```

9. As the `barman` user on `pg-backup`, execute the following commands to bootstrap the WAL-streaming process:

```
barman receive-wal pg-primary --create-slot
barman cron
barman switch-wal pg-primary --force
barman archive-wal pg-primary
```

10. As the `barman` user on `pg-backup`, execute the following command to check the primary server's configuration entry:

```
barman check pg-primary
```

How it works...

Our first step is to install Barman itself. As this book focuses on Red Hat-based and Debian-based Linux systems, this process is very simple. Barman is available in the PostgreSQL repositories for either platform, making the first step the easiest. Unfortunately, we have quite a few more steps to complete.

For Barman to work properly, it must be able to retrieve PostgreSQL files from the `pg-primary` server. To facilitate this, we generate an SSH key on `pg-backup` with `ssh-keygen`. We set the key type to RSA with the `-t` parameter and set the passphrase to a blank value with `-N`. This allows Barman to communicate with the `pg-primary` system without a password, yet do so securely. The `ssh-copy-id` command sends the public key to the desired server. This is why we need the `postgres` system user password if possible.

Then, we create a `barman` user so Barman can log into the `pg-primary` instance to invoke backup commands, attach to the replication stream, and perform other high-level administrative actions. Because we do both of these things, we create the user with SUPERUSER and REPLICATION privileges.

Next, we need to modify `pg_hba.conf` on the `pg-primary` server to allow the barman database user to connect from `pg-backup` to the replication stream and other databases as well. We also update the `.pgpass` file for the `barman` user so it sends the password when requested. Once we reload PostgreSQL with `pg_ctl`, we are finished making changes on the `pg-primary` server.

When we install the Barman packages, they should create a /etc/barman.d directory. To manage our pg-primary server, we create a pg-primary.conf file to specifically manage its backup settings. We can do this for as many systems we want to back up.

The first is a label for the section so that Barman knows pg-primary refers to the pg-primary PostgreSQL server. By setting conninfo, Barman can use internal Python libraries to perform management functions that require direct database access. The streaming_conninfo setting is similar, but necessary only for streaming replication in case we want to use a different user or DSN here. And ssh_command tells Barman how to access files on the pg-primary server as the postgres system user.

Then, we set backup_method to rsync because this is one of the most efficient procedures and takes advantage of our ssh_command earlier as well. This type of backup makes use of filesystem hard links to make it possible to produce differential backups, something PostgreSQL doesn't natively support.

We set archiver to off and streaming_archiver to on because we want to explicitly prefer WAL streaming rather than rely on PostgreSQL to transmit WAL files to a directory Barman watches for that purpose. This isn't strictly necessary but removes any ambiguity as to how this backup should be handled.

The last meaningful parameter we change is the slot_name option, setting it to barman so if Barman is ever disconnected from pg-primary for any extended duration, it can resume fetching WAL files once the connection is re-established. This ensures PITR is as up to date as replication allows.

Lastly, we explicitly set backup_options to exclusive_backup. Currently, Barman supports both exclusive and concurrent backups and will produce a warning if we don't choose one or the other. The default here could change in the future, so we set it here just to avoid unexpected behavior when or if that happens.

Barman is fully configured at this point, but we're still not quite done. Because we want to use WAL streaming, we need to kickstart the process manually. This procedure tends to proceed in this order with the commands listed:

1. Create the replication slot Barman expects.
2. Make sure Barman background processes are launched.
3. Tell PostgreSQL to switch to another WAL file so Barman can archive one.
4. Archive the captured WAL file so it is reflected in the WAL inventory.

Technically, only the first step is required. When Barman gets installed, it includes a file that should automatically invoke `barman cron` every minute. That command automatically includes steps to archive any incoming WAL files and to launch the background WAL retrieval thread. However, if our PostgreSQL server isn't very active, we could end up waiting quite a long time before a WAL switch occurs naturally.

That's a lot of preliminary work, but if everything goes well, the Barman command-line tool will be fully functional. We can test this by checking the status of the server that we've configured under the `pg-primary` label. It's important that we use `barman` with the `check pg-primary` parameters because it doesn't just check the server status—it also creates various directories and tracking files that it uses to manage the PostgreSQL server backups. If everything goes as expected, server status should resemble this output:

```
Server pg-primary:
    WAL archive: OK
    PostgreSQL: OK
    is_superuser: OK
    PostgreSQL streaming: OK
    wal_level: OK
    replication slot: OK
    directories: OK
    retention policy settings: OK
    backup maximum age: OK (no last_backup_maximum_age provided)
    compression settings: OK
    failed backups: OK (there are 0 failed backups)
    minimum redundancy requirements: OK (have 0 backups, expected at least 0)
    ssh: OK (PostgreSQL server)
    not in recovery: OK
    pg_receivexlog: OK
    pg_receivexlog compatible: OK
    receive-wal running: OK
    archiver errors: OK
```

See also

Barman has a very clean and concise website, which includes basic documentation on installation and usage. For further reading, we recommend these URLs:

- **Barman**: https://www.pgbarman.org/
- **Barman Manual**: https://docs.pgbarman.org/

Backing up a database with Barman

After Barman is installed, we should be able to leverage any of its capabilities using the Barman command-line tool. For now, we will focus entirely on creating a backup, verifying that the new backup exists, and examining its contents.

Barman doesn't just produce backups—it also catalogs them extensively. We will use this to our advantage in this recipe to prove that Barman works as advertised.

Getting ready

This recipe depends on Barman being installed on a backup server. Please follow the *Installing and configuring Barman* recipe before continuing.

How to do it...

All steps should be executed as the `barman` system user on the `pg-backup` server that we were using in the previous recipe. Follow these steps to create, verify, and examine a Barman backup:

1. Create the first backup with this command:

   ```
   barman backup pg-primary
   ```

2. Examine the list of backups with this command:

   ```
   barman list-backup pg-primary
   ```

3. View the metadata of the most recent backup with this command:

   ```
   barman show-backup pg-primary latest
   ```

4. View all of the files in the most recent backup with this command:

   ```
   barman list-files pg-primary latest
   ```

How it works...

Creating a backup is extremely easy. To do so, we merely need to invoke the barman command with the backup parameter and specify pg-primary as the label we want to back up. When activated, Barman contacts the pg-primary server and tells it to enter backup mode. It then retrieves all database files over SSH and saves them in its backup catalog. We can view the contents of the catalog in several ways.

The first way to examine the catalog is by using the list-backup parameter. On our test server, we would expect to see output similar to this:

```
barman@pg-backup:~$ barman list-backup pg-primary
pg-primary 20191109T172344 - Sat Nov  9 17:23:49 2019 - Size: 54.8 MiB - WAL Size: 0 B
```

Backups are listed from the least to most recent. The first column is the name of the server that Barman backed up. The second column details the unique ID of the backup and is composed primarily of the time and date the backup started. All further commands need this ID, as it tells Barman which backup we want to view.

> Barman provides a few convenient shortcuts to avoid needing the backup IDs. The latest keyword, for example, always resolves to the ID of the most recent backup.

We won't show the output of the next two commands because they're somewhat overwhelming and can fill several screens. However, we can explain what they would display. In the case of the show-backup parameter to barman, we get to see the metadata of the backup itself. Metadata may include the start and stop time of the backup, the timeline the server was on, the range of WAL files produced during the backup, and so on.

We can also observe the full contents of the backup. If we invoke barman with the list-files parameter and pass the ID of the backup we want to view, it sends a list of every file that it has stored. This includes any WAL files necessary to restore this particular backup.

There's more...

There are, however, a couple of extra points we'd like to make.

Retention policies

We referred to retention policies at the beginning of this recipe. This means that we can configure Barman to only retain a certain number of backups to avoid exhausting disk space. We begin by adding this line to the `pg-primary.conf` file under the `pg-primary` label:

```
retention_policy = RECOVERY WINDOW OF 1 WEEK
```

This tells Barman to delete any backup files or WAL archives that are not necessary to restore backups less than one week old. To perform this maintenance, execute the following command regularly:

```
barman cron
```

Since we installed from distribution packages, this command should already be part of our Barman server. In case it isn't, we recommend ensuring it is launched from the system or user `crontab` regularly.

Parallel backup

One great feature of Barman is that it can launch several simultaneous `rsync` threads to help to accelerate the backup process. This is disabled by default to avoid overloading the backup server, but if the system has a lot of CPUs available and high disk throughput, we can make backups complete even faster. Simply include a line like this in the server configuration such as `pg-primary.conf`:

```
parallel_jobs = 8
```

All future PostgreSQL backup jobs will start eight simultaneous file transfer threads when backing up the `pg-primary` server. In some cases, this can drastically reduce backup times!

See also

For more details, refer to the following:

- The `barman` command tool has a manual that we can view locally. Use this command to learn more about what it can do:

  ```
  man barman
  ```

- We would also like to recommend the Barman documentation again. It really does a very good job of describing some of the more advanced functionality. For reference, use this URL: `https://docs.pgbarman.org/`.

Restoring a database with Barman

As you might expect, Barman does not just create backups—it can also restore them. This functionality can be used to restore the current server, but its real power lies in its ability to restore data remotely. With this capability and a little bit of preparation, we can clone a PostgreSQL backup any number of times without straining the primary database server.

This recipe will explore Barman's recovery aptitude and the steps necessary to start a PostgreSQL server cloned by Barman.

Getting ready

This recipe depends on Barman being installed on a backup server and at least one backup registered in the backup catalog. Please follow the *Installing and configuring Barman* recipe and the *Backing up a database with Barman* recipe before continuing.

How to do it...

We will need one new server for this procedure. The backup server will remain pg-backup, but we need a target server for the restore. This server will be named pg-clone. Make sure to have the password for the postgres system user on this server. As usual, our database will be located at /db/pgdata:

1. On the pg-backup server as the barman user, execute the following command for direct SSH access to pg-clone as the postgres user:

   ```
   ssh-copy-id postgres@pg-clone
   ```

2. Ensure that the target restore directory is empty on pg-clone with this command executed as the postgres user:

   ```
   rm -Rf /db/pgdata
   ```

3. Transmit the backup to `pg-clone` by running this command as `barman` on the `pg-backup` server:

```
barman recover \
        --remote-ssh-command "ssh postgres@pg-clone" \
        pg-primary latest /db/pgdata
```

4. As the `postgres` user on `pg-clone`, start the PostgreSQL service with the following command:

```
pg_ctl -D /db/pgdata start
```

How it works...

As with our Barman installation process, we need to ensure that Barman can communicate directly with the PostgreSQL clone system. Once more, we rely on `ssh-copy-id` to transmit the necessary SSH key to the `pg-clone` server.

The next step is to erase any existing PostgreSQL files on the target server. This step should not be necessary on a new server, but it never hurts to double-check. Assuming that the `postgres` user has permission to write to `/db directory`, we are now ready to recover the backup to the `pg-clone` server.

At this point, we want to invoke the `barman` command with its `recover` operand. Remember, the default recovery system is the local server. As we're executing commands from `pg-backup`, that's not entirely useful to us. Instead, we want to send the data to `pg-clone`. We do this using the `--remote-ssh-` command parameter and by specifying the `ssh` command necessary to reach the `pg-clone` server. This is why we copied Barman's public RSA key to `pg-clone`.

The next parameter to `barman` includes the label of the backup we want to restore, the ID of the specific backup, and the directory where the files should be located. In this case, we are restoring the `pg-primary` database using the latest backup and restoring it to the `/db/pgdata` directory. We want the output of this command to look like this:

```
Starting remote restore for server pg-primary using backup 20191109T172344
Destination directory: /db/pgdata
Remote command: ssh postgres@pg-clone
Copying the base backup.
Copying required WAL segments.
Generating archive status files
Identify dangerous settings in destination directory.

Recovery completed (start time: 2019-11-09 17:39:11.715072, elapsed time: 5 seconds)

Your PostgreSQL server has been successfully prepared for recovery!
```

If any parameters could be dangerous to the cluster upon starting the cloned server, Barman will warn us of them in this output. However, we should give a cursory look at `postgresql.conf` to ensure that the server will run properly on `pg-clone`. For example, Barman will disable the `archive_command` setting on a newly restored server. We don't want the new server polluting our WAL archive with invalid files!

The final step is to start the PostgreSQL server on the new `pg-clone` server with `pg_ctl`.

There's more...

There are, however, a couple of extra points we'd like to make.

Streaming replicas

Barman does not have a mode to initialize the newly restored server as a streaming replica of the original. This would require setting `primary_conninfo` in either `recovery.conf` or `postgresql.conf` of the newly restored system. However, Barman only knows how to connect to the backup source as the user we've configured for backup purposes.

Since this could be considered a security exploit, it's up to us to specify the correct DSN necessary to transform the new server to a streaming replica. Barman does, however, provide a parameter named `--standby-mode`, which will set create a `standby.signal` file in Postgres 12 and above, or add the equivalent `standby_mode` setting to `recovery.conf` for older installations.

Still, we need to supply the appropriate `primary_conninfo` parameter in `postgresql.conf` for PostgreSQL 12 and above, or `recovery.conf` otherwise, like this:

```
primary_conninfo = 'host=pg-primary user=postgres'
```

If you've followed the recipes in the previous chapters, you may also consider using the `rep_user` user instead, as we created it specifically for replication purposes.

RPO zero

RPO zero is an industry term that stands for **Recovery Point Objective** of zero. In the context of a backup, it means we've lost zero committed transactions and can recover to full operating capacity as if nothing had happened.

Unlike most other backup management suites, Barman provides the capability of obtaining transaction data directly from the PostgreSQL replication stream as we demonstrated in this recipe. It's also important to understand that Barman supports synchronous replication as well.

To begin, we check the `pg-primary` server to find the name Barman assigns:

```
barman show-server pg-primary | grep archiver_name
```

The result of this command will be the value we use for `synchronous_standby_names` in `postgresql.conf`. It would also be necessary to enable `synchronous_commit`, as seen in this example:

```
synchronous_commit = 'on'
synchronous_standby_names = 'barman_receive_wal'
```

Now, all committed transactions must be acknowledged by Barman before they can complete on the upstream server. When a Barman backup is restored, it has access to these streamed transactions as well.

It's important to note that WAL files are not archived by Barman until the next is started. This is the reason we use the `switch-wal` routine in the installation recipe. That means incomplete or *partial* WAL files are stored in a temporary holding area. Once again, we can obtain that information by using the `show-server` sub-command:

```
barman show-server pg-primary | grep streaming_wals_directory
```

The result of this command is a directory where any partially transferred WAL files may exist for the indicated server. If there is a file there named with a .partial extension, this means there's either an ongoing WAL stream or the upstream server has crashed.

For ongoing streams, this is normal and expected since Barman is still receiving data for that file. If the upstream server has crashed, we would want to use this file to replay those last few transactions that were committed before the system became unrecoverable. Barman doesn't currently perform this task automatically, but this is an expected feature in Barman 2.10 or 2.11.

Otherwise, we can simply perform our backup restore and manually move the .partial WAL file into the pg_wal folder before starting PostgreSQL. We would also need to remove the .partial extension for PostgreSQL to recognize it.

This is a feature no other PostgreSQL backup solution provides and is one of the reasons we chose to feature Barman prominently in this book.

See also

For more details, refer to the following:

- The barman command tool has a manual we can view locally. Use this command to learn more about what it can do:

  ```
  man barman
  ```

- To get the more immediate output of the restore mode parameters, execute this command:

  ```
  barman recover
  ```

Obtaining Barman diagnostics and information

Simply storing backup data in a series of directories is of limited use. With PostgreSQL especially, it's important to know the WAL positions when the backup started and ended so a backup restore recovers properly.

There are other important and relevant questions as well. How many servers are we managing? How many backups exist for each of these? What are the names and dates for each backup? What about the synchronization status of Barman while retrieving WAL files? What if we need product support and need to provide diagnostic data? Where does Barman store files? What about other settings we didn't specify during installation?

We could go on and on with endless questions like this. Instead, this recipe will focus on a handful of the most useful forensic information commands and explain how they work.

Getting ready

This recipe depends on Barman being installed on a backup server and at least one backup registered in the backup catalog. Please follow the *Installing and configuring Barman* recipe and the *Backing up a database with Barman* recipe before continuing.

How to do it...

All steps should be executed as the `barman` system user on the `pg-backup` server that we were using in the previous recipe. Follow these steps to obtain diagnostic and other information about Barman server and backups:

1. Show the list of all servers Barman is managing with this command:

   ```
   barman list-server
   ```

2. View a basic summary of all backups with this command:

   ```
   barman list-backup all
   ```

3. Show all configuration settings for a particular server with this command:

   ```
   barman show-server pg-primary
   ```

4. Display the current replication status of a server with this command:

   ```
   barman replication-status pg-primary
   ```

5. Show the full status of the Barman installation, including all servers, backups, and WAL archives with this command:

```
barman diagnose
```

How it works...

One of the first things we may need to do upon logging in to a new Barman server is to figure out what it's backing up. We could check the /etc/barman.d folder for a list of files, but this isn't always the best approach. Why not just ask Barman itself with the list-server parameter? We created another server on our test system and can see them both listed here:

```
barman@pg-backup:~$ barman list-server
pg-primary - Primary PostgreSQL Server
pg-reports - Trade Reporting Server
```

Now that we have a list of servers, we can dig into each individually if necessary. Barman also provides an all keyword, which substitutes for a server name in any command that expects this information. Hence, we could either list all backups that exist for one server in particular or all at once. By executing the command as written, we saw this on our test server:

```
barman@pg-backup:~$ barman list-backup all
pg-primary 20191109T193859 - Sat Nov  9 19:39:05 2019 - Size: 54.8 MiB - WAL Size: 16.0 MiB
pg-primary 20191109T172344 - Sat Nov  9 17:23:49 2019 - Size: 54.8 MiB - WAL Size: 80.0 MiB
pg-reports 20191109T193739 - Sat Nov  9 19:37:44 2019 - Size: 54.8 MiB - WAL Size: 48.0 MiB
```

At this point, we could use barman show-backup to show extended information about any of the backups listed in this output. That would tell us how big the backup was on disk, how long the backup took, WAL files required, and so on.

How is each server actually configured within Barman? There are a lot of possible configuration parameters we didn't change in `pg-primary.conf`, so those are some defaults that are unknown to us. With that in mind, we can invoke the `show-server` command on a particular server, as we did with the `pg-primary` system in this output:

```
barman@pg-backup:~$ barman show-server pg-primary
Server pg-primary:
    active: True
    archive_timeout: 0
    archiver: False
    archiver_batch_size: 0
    backup_directory: /var/lib/barman/pg-primary
    backup_method: rsync
    backup_options: BackupOptions(['exclusive_backup'])
    bandwidth_limit: None
    barman_home: /var/lib/barman
    ...
```

Consider that this particular output is truncated because it includes dozens of settings that would require several pages to display. Still, we can see many important values, including `barman_home`, which is where backups and WAL files are actually stored. We could use this information to change or introspect any parameter Barman offers.

It's also important to know the replication state of Barman itself. Not only is observable lag relevant, but so are the connected user and host and anything that may be related here. This is what we see for replication status on our very basic `pg-primary` server:

```
barman@pg-backup:~$ barman replication-status pg-primary
Status of streaming clients for server 'pg-primary':
  Current LSN on master: 0/D000140
  Number of streaming clients: 1

  1. Async WAL streamer
     Application name: barman_receive_wal
     Sync stage      : 3/3 Remote write
     Communication   : TCP/IP
     IP Address      : 10.0.30.1 / Port: 45836 / Host: -
     User name       : barman
     Current state   : streaming (async)
     Replication slot: barman
     WAL sender PID   : 38424
     Started at      : 2019-11-09 16:34:02.578519+00:00
     Sent LSN   : 0/D000140 (diff: 0 B)
     Write LSN  : 0/D000140 (diff: 0 B)
     Flush LSN  : 0/D000000 (diff: -320 B)
```

What we see here is a healthy replication connection that shows no lag, meaning Barman is perfectly up to date with the upstream system.

We saved the biggest and most thorough command for last. If we execute `barman diagnose`, Barman will supply us with all of the preceding information, and quite a bit more just in case. The command was designed to show all Barman settings, server settings for each server, full diagnostic data for every backup, known WAL ranges, and much more, all exported as a single JSON object.

This can either be imported into a monitoring system to watch for important changes or trends such as backup sizes and durations or to send to a consulting company for support. The output of the `diagnose` command is basically everything necessary to troubleshoot a misbehaving or misconfigured Barman server.

Sending Barman backups to a remote location

Previous chapters emphasized the importance of storing backups in a remote offsite location in case of catastrophic site loss. Often, this is handled manually by exporting the backup mount or its contents using software or hardware-level filesystem synchronization features.

Beginning with Barman 2.6, it's possible to configure a server to act merely as an offsite storage location for Barman backup data. This can be done on a per-server basis in case it's necessary to follow certain distribution criteria. Not every enterprise has access to sophisticated or expensive distributed SAN snapshots and scripting is sometimes temperamental. Why not use Barman?

This recipe will explain how to configure a passive server that acts merely as an offsite backup holding area.

Getting ready

This recipe depends on Barman being installed on a backup server and at least one backup registered in the backup catalog. Please follow the *Installing and configuring Barman* recipe and the *Backing up a database with Barman* recipe before continuing.

How to do it...

For this procedure, we will need two servers. The backup server will be named pg-backup and our offsite backup server named pg-offsite. Make sure to have the password for the barman system user or at least access to the account via sudo. As usual, our database is located at /db/pgdata.

Follow these steps:

1. Install Barman packages on pg-offsite as if it were another Barman server.

2. On the pg-offsite server as the barman user, execute the following commands for direct SSH access to pg-backup as the barman user:

```
ssh-keygen -t rsa -N ''
ssh-copy-id barman@pg-backup
```

3. If the barman system user on pg-backup has no password, use sudo to access the account. Then, create a file named authorized_keys in the .ssh folder with the contents of the .ssh/id_rsa.pub file from pg-offsite.

4. Create a file named sync-primary.conf in /etc/barman.d on pg-offsite with the following contents:

```
[pg-primary]

description =  "Offsite Copy of Primary PostgreSQL Server"
primary_ssh_command = "ssh barman@pg-backup"
```

5. Wait while the contents from pg-backup synchronize to pg-offsite.

6. Execute the following command on pg-offsite to list synchronized data:

```
barman list-backup pg-primary
```

How it works...

We begin the recipe with a very familiar procedure: installing Barman. Any passive Barman server is just another Barman system that subscribes to other Barman servers. Since this is handled through configuration files, this means we could even have a Barman server that both handles PostgreSQL backup directly and subscribes to some other Barman system.

One good application of this concept is to have one Barman server in each of the two data centers. The Barman server that is local to one data center can back up all PostgreSQL servers at that location and subscribe to the Barman server in the other location. This would ensure both Barman servers have offsite equivalents to protect their backups.

Next, we can repeat the usual process of creating an SSH key for the `barman` user on the `pg-offsite`. Then, we copy that key to the `barman` user on `pg-backup` to allow passwordless SSH access between the systems. This is mainly required so `pg-offsite` can use `rsync` to retrieve backup and WAL files from `pg-backup`.

Just as we had to configure `pg-primary` on `pg-backup` to actually back up that PostgreSQL server, we must produce an equivalent configuration on `pg-offsite`. This is easily done by starting with a section named for the PostgreSQL server we want to synchronize (`pg-backup`) and then setting `primary_ssh_command` to connect to `pg-backup` via SSH. This is why the (`pg-primary`) section header matches the one we created on `pg-backup`.

Once this configuration exists, `barman cron` will eventually run and launch a process that synchronizes data from `pg-backup`. Depending on the size of our backup directories, this could take a while to complete. After that process has finished, we can execute any of the same diagnostic commands as we would on `pg-backup`. This includes `barman list-backup`.

Installing and configuring pgBackRest

It may not always be necessary to maintain a cluster-wide PostgreSQL backup management server. Sometimes we just want to back up a single instance quickly and efficiently. While `pg_basebackup` provides at least this much functionality, it doesn't provide WAL management, backup inventories, retention expiration, automatic PITR capabilities, and so on.

pgBackRest is a command-line tool that provides all of the aforementioned features and more, including inline compression, checksum verification, data encryption, and offsite storage. While not really meant to manage an army of PostgreSQL servers, it is more than capable of handling a local installation with aplomb.

This recipe will help to install and bootstrap pgBackRest as simply as possible.

Getting ready

At the time of writing this book, the most recent version of pgBackRest is 2.18. Because of Crunchy Data's close involvement and interaction with the PostgreSQL community, it is available within the PostgreSQL package repositories. If you are using a Debian- or Ubuntu-based system, follow the instructions at this URL to add the PostgreSQL repository to any system that will be running pgBackRest: `https://wiki.postgresql.org/wiki/Apt`.

Otherwise, Red Hat-based systems should add the PostgreSQL repository by installing the derivative-appropriate RPM located at this URL: `https://yum.postgresql.org/repopackages.php`.

 Please note that pgBackRest 2.18 is the first version that supports PostgreSQL 12 and above. If you are using such a PostgreSQL installation, ensure the pgBackRest version meets or exceeds this minimum.

How to do it...

For this procedure, we will need one server, our primary PostgreSQL server, which will be named `pg-primary`. As usual, our database is located at `/db/pgdata`.

Follow these steps to install and configure pgBackRest:

1. Install the pgBackRest toolkit as a root-capable user:

   - For Red Hat-based servers, use the following command:

     ```
     sudo yum install pgbackrest
     ```

   - Debian-based systems should use this command instead:

     ```
     sudo apt-get install pgbackrest
     ```

2. Modify `/etc/pgbackrest.conf` to reflect the following contents:

   ```
   [main]
   pg1-path=/db/pgdata
   [global]
   repo1-path=/var/lib/pgbackrest
   repo1-retention-full=1
   start-fast=y
   ```

3. Ensure the following parameter is set in `postgresql.conf`:

```
archive_command = 'pgbackrest --stanza=main archive-push %p'
```

4. If it isn't there already, add this line near the top of the `pg_hba.conf` file:

```
local    all    postgres    peer
```

5. Reload PostgreSQL using `pg_ctl` as the `postgres` user:

```
pg_ctl -D /db/pgdata reload
```

6. Create the cluster definition within `pgBackRest` as the `postgres` user:

```
pgbackrest --stanza=main \
           --log-level-console=info stanza-create
```

7. Check that WAL archival is working properly with this command as the `postgres` user:

```
pgbackrest --stanza=main \
           --log-level-console=info check
```

8. Retrieve information about pgBackRest as the `postgres` user to verify installation:

```
pgbackrest info
```

How it works...

As usual, we start by installing the software itself using `apt` or `yum`. PgBackRest itself doesn't actually consist of many files but requires several Perl libraries that will also be installed. Try not to be alarmed by the list of dependencies.

Next, we need to modify the `pgbackrest.conf` file and configure it to know the path to our local PostgreSQL installation by setting `pg1-path` to `/db/pgdata`. We don't set any other parameters because pgBackRest works well locally by calling commands as the `postgres` user. The reason the path variable is named `pg1-path` is due to pgBackRest support for managing multiple databases, so they introduced variable indexing in version 2.

Note the [global] section is meant to contain settings that would apply to all possible PostgreSQL systems it manages. Due to that, we've set the storage location of the pgBackRest repository to /var/lib/pgbackrest since we want to keep all backups in the same directory. Additionally, we specify that there must be at least one full backup at all times by setting repo1-retention-full. Further, every backup should force an immediate CHECKPOINT with start-fast to prevent potentially waiting for several minutes for a backup to begin.

Since pgBackRest relies on archive_command to collect WAL files from PostgreSQL, we must set that parameter to use the archive-push option. Depending on how our installation is secured, we may also need to modify pg_hba.conf to include a peer line. This will allow the local Postgres OS user—provided we're logged into that account—to connect as the postgres PostgreSQL user without a password.

One reason previous chapters recommended setting archive_mode to on is that changes to archive_command only require a reload of the PostgreSQL service rather than a full restart. Once we perform this step, we will activate any authentication changes as well and should be able to start executing pgBackRest commands.

 We'll note that not every pgBackRest command requires specification of the relevant configuration stanza, but most do. This is why almost every command in this recipe includes -- stanza=main as a preamble. We also include --log-level- console=info or most commands would produce no output at all. We like to know what's on!

The first of these is to initialize a pgBackRest stanza. While we may think of PostgreSQL clusters based on functions such as trading or reporting, pgBackRest approaches these from the perspective of sections within the configuration file. Because we're only working with a single cluster at the moment, we named our stanza main, and the stanza-create command bootstraps pgBackRest with all expected path locations for saving WAL and backup files.

Next, we must test a WAL transfer to pgBackRest. Just as Barman will not back up a database until it can verify at least one successful WAL retrieval, we want an unbroken chain of custody between PostgreSQL and pgBackRest. The check command performs this task for us, forcing PostgreSQL to switch to a new WAL file and archive the previous one into the pgBackRest repository.

Our final step is to verify the `pgBackRest` repository reflects some record of our stanza. If we use the `info` command, we should see all stanza and backup information contained in the repository. Right now we only have the main stanza and no backups at all, so we should see something like this:

```
postgres@pg-primary:~$ pgbackrest info

stanza: main
    status: error (no valid backups)
    cipher: none

    db (current)
        wal archive min/max (11-1): 000000010000000000000018/000000010000000000000018
```

As we can see here, the WAL file we archived while running the `check` command is listed in this output.

There's more...

If we inadvertently implied that pgBackRest cannot function from an external centralized backup server, that is not actually the case. However, setting it up to operate in this manner is actually somewhat complicated. Unlike Barman, which leverages `rsync` and PostgreSQL streaming replication, pgBackRest uses its own communication protocol between systems.

This means it must be installed in a client to server model, where pgBackRest is installed on both systems and configured separately on either. The configuration itself is not especially difficult, but this kind of configuration is beyond the scope of this particular chapter. The pgBackRest documentation actually has a comprehensive explanation of how this model works and provides adequate instruction on implementation as well.

See the section entitled *Dedicated Backup Host* in the pgBackRest user guide for more information.

See also

PgBackRest has a dedicated concise website that includes basic documentation on installation and usage. For further reading, we recommend these URLs:

- **pgBackRest**: `https://pgbackrest.org/`
- **pgBackRest Command Reference**: `https://pgbackrest.org/user-guide.html`

Backing up a database with pgBackRest

Once we've configured pgBackRest to our satisfaction, producing a backup is actually very simple using the `pgbackrest` command-line tool. As with Barman, we will focus entirely on creating a backup, verifying that the new backup exists, and examining its contents.

Part of the point of such backup tools is the fact they maintain an extensive catalog of backup and WAL information. This recipe will leverage that information to prove pgBackRest works as advertised.

Getting ready

This recipe depends on pgBackRest being installed on a PostgreSQL server. Please follow the *Installing and configuring pgBackRest* recipe before continuing.

How to do it...

For this procedure, we will need one server, our primary PostgreSQL server, which will be named `pg-primary`. As usual, our database is located at `/db/pgdata`. Follow these steps to create, verify, and examine a pgBackRest backup:

1. Create a full backup with this command:

```
pgbackrest --stanza=main --type=full \
        --log-level-console=info backup
```

2. Examine the metadata of the most recent backup with this command:

```
pgbackrest --stanza=main info
```

3. Retrieve the list of files in the most recent backup with this command:

```
pgbackrest ls backup/main/latest --recurse
```

How it works...

It should be no surprise that we begin the recipe by creating a backup of our main PostgreSQL instance. What may not be so obvious is that we could have dispensed with the unnecessary extra options such as `--type=full`. While normally this will force a full backup rather than an incremental one, pgBackRest requires the first backup to be a full backup anyway. As such, we could have used this command instead:

```
pgbackrest --stanza=main backup
```

The reality is that pgBackRest commands are not as verbose as they first appear. We're simply being thorough and explicit, which isn't always required. Either way, we can verify the backup exists and has completed successfully by checking the backup inventory using the `info` command. We should see something like this:

```
postgres@pg-primary:~$ pgbackrest --stanza=main info

stanza: main
    status: ok
    cipher: none

    db (current)
        wal archive min/max (11-1): 000000010000000000000001A/000000010000000000000001A

        full backup: 20191110-163055F
            timestamp start/stop: 2019-11-10 16:30:55 / 2019-11-10 16:31:09
            wal start/stop: 000000010000000000000001A / 000000010000000000000001A
            database size: 38.9MB, backup size: 38.9MB
            repository size: 3.6MB, repository backup size: 3.6MB
```

One thing that's interesting from this output is that the repository size is listed separately. This is because pgBackRest automatically enables compression of files as they're processed. Also, note that we used the `--stanza` parameter here to ensure we only see results for the main stanza. This isn't required, but if we were backing up multiple PostgreSQL instances, it would be better to focus on one at a time.

Finally, we included a command that will produce a list of every file in the pgBackRest file inventory. The `ls` command expects a parameter that essentially maps to the contents of the repository itself. We can list archive (WAL) or backup files, and search further by adding a slash and a subdirectory name to see more information.

For the sake of this recipe, we used the shortcut that represents the latest backup in the main repository. We also added the `--recurse` option to see all files, including those in subdirectories. Feel free to experiment with this command to see what else it can do.

There's more...

There are, however, a couple of extra points we'd like to make.

More backup types

pgBackRest actually supports three types of backup. We only used fully because this is a demonstration of a single backup, but this is what the documentation has to say about all of them:

- `full`: All database cluster files will be copied and there will be no dependencies on previous backups.
- `incr`: This is incremental from the last successful backup.
- `diff`: This is like an incremental backup but always based on the last full backup.

Incremental backups only contain differences since the last successful backup, hence creating a chain of much smaller backups than we'd expect from storing every PostgreSQL file. Consider what happens when we take an incremental backup and check the repository:

```
incr backup: 20191110-163055F_20191110-170534I
    timestamp start/stop: 2019-11-10 17:05:34 / 2019-11-10 17:05:43
    wal start/stop: 000000010000000000000001C / 000000010000000000000001C
    database size: 38.9MB, backup size: 8.3KB
    repository size: 3.6MB, repository backup size: 494B
    backup reference list: 20191110-163055F
```

If we compare that to the full backup we started with, it's much smaller at less than 500 bytes! Of course, our test database is essentially idle, but this should prove that only modified files are being backed up incrementally.

Use full regularly

Barman performs incremental backup by using filesystem hard links for files that haven't changed, hence ensuring every backup always has a full file listing. pgBackRest simply skips unmodified files.

The end result is very similar except that pgBackRest incremental backups become fully dependent on previous full backups. If a pgBackRest full backup is removed, all subsequent incremental and differential backups become invalid. Hence, pgBackRest has safeguards to ensure at least one full backup exists at all times and recommends creating new ones regularly, such as once per week.

Keep this in mind when scheduling backups and choosing which type to use!

See also

pgBackRest has a dedicated concise website that includes basic documentation on installation and usage. For further reading, we recommend these URLs:

- **pgBackRest**: https://pgbackrest.org/
- **pgBackRest Command Reference**: https://pgbackrest.org/command.html

Restoring a database with pgBackRest

Like all good backup management suites, pgBackRest is also well equipped to restore data from its backup repository. We can either restore the latest backup for a specific stanza or choose one of the specific backups in the inventory. There are also settings we can use to restore to a different directory than where the data originated.

It's also important to understand that pgBackRest is a pull-based system. This means only the repository itself may be considered remote. Hence, if we want to build a new PostgreSQL clone system, we have to install pgBackRest and configure it to request files from the backup server. This is a stark contrast to Barman, which assumes all commands are initiated from the backup server itself.

This recipe will explore pgBackRest's recovery aptitude and the steps necessary to start a PostgreSQL server restored by pgBackRest.

Getting ready

This recipe depends on pgBackRest being installed on a remote PostgreSQL server. Please follow the *Installing and configuring pgBackRest* recipe before continuing.

How to do it...

We will need one new server for this procedure. The primary PostgreSQL server will remain pg-primary, but we need a target server for the restore. This server will be named pg-clone. Make sure to have the password for the postgres system user on this server. As usual, our database will be located at /db/pgdata:

1. Install the pgBackRest toolkit as a root-capable user on pg-clone:

    - For Red Hat-based servers, use the following command:

        sudo yum install pgbackrest

    - Debian-based systems should use this command instead:

        sudo apt-get install pgbackrest

2. On the pg-clone server as the postgres user, execute the following command for direct SSH access to pg-primary as the postgres user:

    ssh-copy-id postgres@pg-primary

3. Ensure that the target restore directory is empty on pg-clone with this command executed as the postgres user:

    rm -Rf /db/pgdata

4. Modify the /etc/pgbackrest.conf file on pg-clone and fill it with these contents:

    ```
    [main]
    pg1-path=/db/pgdata

    [global]
    repo1-host=pg-primary
    ```

```
repo1-host-user=postgres
repo1-path=/var/lib/pgbackrest
repo1-retention-full=1
start-fast=y
```

5. Transmit the backup from `pg-primary` by running these commands as `postgres` on the `pg-clone` server:

```
mkdir -p 0700 /db/pgdata
pgbackrest --stanza=main \
           --log-level-console=info restore
```

6. As the `postgres` user on `pg-clone`, start the PostgreSQL service with the following command:

```
pg_ctl -D /db/pgdata start
```

How it works...

pgBackRest operates under the assumption that repositories act as central storage locations for all WAL and backup file contents, and that these repositories may be located remotely. This means we must install pgBackRest on any server that requires access to the repository. So, our first step is to install the software itself, allowing us to use the `pgbackrest` command-line utility.

To facilitate remote repository access, we need to ensure that pgBackRest can communicate directly with the `pg-primary` server as the `postgres` user since that is the user that owns the backup files on that system. Once more, we rely on `ssh-copy-id` to transmit the necessary SSH key to the `pg-primary` server.

The next step is to erase any existing PostgreSQL files on the `pg-clone` server. This step should not be necessary on a new server, but it never hurts to double-check. Assuming that the `postgres` user has permission to write to the `/db directory`, everything should be ready for the restoration procedure.

Before we can do that, however, we must configure pgBackRest to understand it needs to rely on a remote repository. To do this, we actually begin with a very similar configuration file as we used in the *Installing and configuring pgBackRest* recipe. The primary difference here is that we also specify the `repo1-host` and `repo1-host-user` parameters to target the `pg-primary` server as the `postgres` user. When these settings are provided, pgBackRest will operate by retrieving information from the remote repository via SSH.

Once we create the /db/pgdata directory, it's safe to invoke the pgbackrest command with its restore operand. As written in the instructions, this will produce a high volume of output as files are transferred and decompressed to the proper locations. Since we didn't specify which backup we wanted to restore, pgBackRest will default to the latest available.

After the restore is complete, pgBackRest will helpfully configure restore_command in postgresql.conf for PostgreSQL 12 and above, or recovery.conf otherwise. It sets this parameter to use the archive-get command to fetch WAL files from the archive. This will retrieve WAL files in recovery mode until there are no more available.

We want the output of restore_command to end with output telling us the process was successful, as in this example:

```
2019-11-10 21:22:15.108 P00   INFO: restore global/pg_control (performed last to ensure
aborted restores cannot be started)
2019-11-10 21:22:15.419 P00   INFO: restore command end: completed successfully (11260ms)
```

As usual, we should give a cursory look at postgresql.conf to ensure that the server will run properly on pg-clone before starting the service. For example, don't forget to either comment out the archive_command parameter or to set it to something safe such as /bin/true. Otherwise, we could end up transmitting WAL files from the restored database to the existing WAL archive!

The final step is to start the PostgreSQL server on the new pg-clone server with pg_ctl. If we modified systemctl properly to use our nonstandard directory, we could also use sudo systemctl start instead.

There's more...

pgBackRest has a somewhat unconventional feature that allows it to restore into an existing PGDATA directory. Most backup and restore utilities steadfastly refuse to operate within a live PostgreSQL installation, but pgBackRest sees this as an opportunity for efficiency.

Imagine for instance we dropped the pgbench_accounts table from our test database and that's the only action we've taken since the last backup. It would be silly to restore the entire database, which could be hundreds of GB or even TB in size. Why not just restore only the files that have changed since the backup occurred?

pgBackRest calls this type of a restore a delta, and we can invoke such a restore with this variant of the `restore` command:

```
pgbackrest --stanza=main --delta \
        --log-level-console=info restore
```

By specifying `--delta`, we tell pgBackRest that we want to restore directly into the PostgreSQL data directory of our specified stanza and only want to restore files that changed since the last backup. If we omit this option and try to restore into a pre-existing data directory, pgBackRest will refuse to overwrite any files.

Installing and configuring WAL-E

WAL-E is a tool designed specifically for interacting with various cloud services and PostgreSQL. Cloud services are often designed to require complex API calls before accepting read or write commands. This makes it somewhat difficult to send them arbitrary files such as PostgreSQL transaction logs we wish to save in a secure location.

The principal benefit of keeping WAL files in a remote cloud location is the same as maintaining offline backups. By moving transaction logs to an external server, we can use them in emergencies or complete data center disasters. It's a different form of high availability where we trade the expense and latency of involving distant servers for a major increase in geographical diversity.

WAL-E supports transmitting and retrieving files through several cloud vendors and APIs:

- Amazon S3 (`https://aws.amazon.com/s3/`)
- Microsoft Azure Blobs (`https://azure.microsoft.com/en-us/`)
- Google Storage (`https://cloud.google.com/storage/`)
- SWIFT (`https://wiki.openstack.org/wiki/Swift`)

While creating accounts with these services and managing their resources is beyond the scope of this book, several Packt books do an admirable job in our stead. If you are unaccustomed to managing cloud-based systems, we recommend becoming familiar with at least one of these environments before attempting to implement this recipe.

This recipe will explore the process of integrating WAL-E into our PostgreSQL environment.

Getting ready

Before storing our WAL files in the cloud, we'll need somewhere to put them. Create an account with one of the supported WAL-E services and create a storage location for files we'll be transmitting. For example, in Amazon AWS, we would select **S3** and **Create Bucket**, and fill out a form like this:

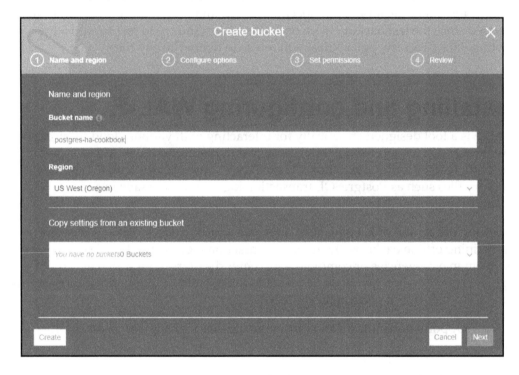

We also strongly encourage setting up specific authentication credentials for this location to avoid unnecessary distribution of critical users or passwords for other portions of the application layer.

After this, we need to install some prerequisite libraries. WAL-E depends on Python 3 and is easiest to install with `pip`. With that in mind, Debian-based systems would use this `apt-get` command to prepare:

```
sudo apt-get install python3-pip lzop
```

Red Hat-based systems need to install the EPEL package for the appropriate Red Hat platform from the following URL: `https://fedoraproject.org/wiki/EPEL`.

Then, execute this command to get `pip` running:

```
sudo yum install python36-setuptools lzop
```

How to do it...

For this recipe, we'll be using an Amazon S3 user account with associated access key identified as key-ID and key-value. We've also created a bucket we will refer to as `bucket-path`, which is located in the `aws-region` zone. Follow these steps to install and configure WAL-E on a PostgreSQL server:

1. As the `postgres` user, use `pip3` to install WAL-E and a complementary environment utility:

   ```
   pip3 install --user wal-e envdir
   ```

2. Install the necessary WAL-E cloud driver (Amazon, in our case) as the `postgres` user with this command:

   ```
   pip3 install --user boto
   ```

3. Create a configuration directory as the `postgres` user to contain environment variables:

   ```
   mkdir -m 0700 -p ~/env
   ```

4. As the `postgres` user, install several environment variables with these commands:

   ```
   cd ~/env
   echo 'key-id' > AWS_ACCESS_KEY_ID
   echo 'key-value' > AWS_SECRET_ACCESS_KEY
   echo 'bucket-path' > WALE_S3_PREFIX
   echo 'aws-region' > AWS_REGION
   ```

5. Test WAL-E by retrieving a list of existing backup files:

   ```
   envdir ~/env wal-e backup-list
   ```

How it works...

We begin by using `pip3` to actually install WAL-E using Python version 3. As with most Python software, now that Python 2 has been deprecated, WAL-E requires Python 3 to function. Some older Linux distributions may still make it difficult to side-load Python 3, so be wary of this requirement.

While each cloud service has its own necessary driver, we don't need to install all of them. The appropriate driver should be described in the WAL-E requirements, but a failed attempted transmission will also tell us which one we need if it isn't already installed. If we were missing the necessary driver, we would receive an error like this:

```
postgres@pg-primary:~$ envdir ~/env wal-e backup-list
wal_e.main   INFO    MSG: starting WAL-E
        DETAIL: The subcommand is "backup-list".
        STRUCTURED: time=2019-11-11T16:46:17.386417-00 pid=25245
wal_e.main   ERROR   MSG: AWS support requires module "boto"
        HINT: Try running "pip install boto".
        STRUCTURED: time=2019-11-11T16:46:17.388675-00 pid=25245
```

Next, we create a directory to keep configuration files for WAL-E. This part isn't strictly necessary, but WAL-E depends on quite a bit of sensitive information. It needs to authenticate with the cloud storage server for every interaction. The safest way to do this is to maintain several files that are only readable by the `postgres` system user. The only other alternative is calling the `wal-e` command by manually passing these values.

The final step is configuring our authentication, connection, and storage path information with files in the directory we prepared. In the case of Amazon S3, this means we need an access key ID and an associated secret access key saved into similarly named files for WAL-E.

In the case of the `WALE_S3_PREFIX` variable, it's important to only use the path to the bucket we created earlier and, optionally, a directory. If we named our bucket `postgres-ha-cookbook` and added a `wal` directory, we would use `s3://postgres-ha-cookbook/wal` for `WALE_S3_PREFIX`.

When we created our bucket, we were allowed to select a region where the Amazon servers would actually store our data. `WAL-E` needs to know where those servers are, so at least in the case of Amazon S3, we need to set the `AWS_REGION` variable. The default region is `us-east-1`, but the correct region for our bucket should be listed in the AWS S3 interface.

We can't actually test sending a WAL file just yet but can verify whether or not WAL-E can communicate with our cloud resource. The `backup-list` command will retrieve a list of backups previously uploaded by the `wal-e` utility. We don't have any of those, but any response other than an error should be considered a successful test.

 Given how cloud service API needs may vary, we strongly recommend learning about cloud services in general before attempting this recipe. It's far easier to understand what WAL-E expects if we're comfortable working with cloud servers.

See also

WAL-E is also available on GitHub, along with all of its documentation. Please use the following resource to learn more: `https://github.com/wal-e/wal-e`.

Managing WAL files with WAL-E

With WAL-E installed, we can now use it to transmit transaction WAL files to and from our cloud service of choice. Remember, by keeping WAL files in a remote location, they're isolated from natural disasters, data center outages, being overwritten, and any number of unplanned events. Consider cloud storage as a form of long-term archival of our transaction logs.

Why is this important? Remember our mantra: outages are unavoidable. We can take multiple steps to avoid them, but sometimes the situation is beyond human intervention. Sometimes, we simply need to rebuild. Offsite backup of WAL files means we can apply PITR to a recent backup and reach the last known stable state of our data. Since WAL-E integrates directly into the PostgreSQL transaction log archival process, the WAL files we preserve are as fresh as possible.

This recipe will explore see how offsite WAL management works with WAL-E.

Getting ready

Before continuing with this recipe, please complete the steps in the *Installing and configuring WAL-E* recipe.

How to do it...

Assuming we have a server that should be archiving transaction logs, follow these steps to store them in a cloud service using WAL-E:

1. Edit the `postgresql.conf` file to reflect these parameter settings:

    ```
    archive_command = 'envdir ~postgres/env wal-e wal-push %p'
    archive_timeout = '60'
    ```

2. Reload the PostgreSQL service with the following command as the `postgres` user:

    ```
    pg_ctl -D /db/pgdata reload
    ```

3. Connect as the `postgres` user and force it to switch transaction logs with this SQL if using PostgreSQL 10 or above:

    ```
    SELECT pg_switch_wal();
    ```

4. Users of PostgreSQL 9.6 and below should use this SQL instead:

    ```
    SELECT pg_switch_xlog();
    ```

5. Watch the end of the PostgreSQL log file for transmission success. Use a command similar to this to capture WAL-E-specific information:

    ```
    tail -f /var/log/postgresql/postgresql-12-main.log \
      | grep "DETAIL"
    ```

How it works...

WAL-E is generally easy to use once it has been installed. In this case, we merely need to modify the `postgresql.conf` configuration file and reload PostgreSQL to change the `archive_command` parameter. Assuming our installation of WAL-E is working properly, there really are no more steps. However, it's always a good idea to verify.

Regarding the changes we made to `postgresql.conf`, only two are different than those we dictated in the *Configuration – getting it right the first time* recipe of `Chapter 3`, *Minimizing Downtime*.

We begin by setting `archive_command` to invoke the `wal-e` utility. The `wal-push` parameter tells it to transmit the specified file to our cloud storage and to assume it's a WAL file. It performs some cursory checks before and after it does this, so we can't use it as a general tool to send miscellaneous files to the cloud.

Next, it's a good idea to set `archive_timeout` to some value other than zero. This recipe uses a value of 60 seconds as a guide, but to determine the appropriate value, it's important to consider what the parameter actually does. When `archive_timeout` is set to a non-zero value, it will rotate transaction logs after that many seconds have elapsed, regardless of need.

This matters because PostgreSQL usually only switches the current transaction log after the number of changes inside exceeds about 16 MB. On low-volume systems, this may take minutes or even hours. As a result, there could be up to 16 MB of data that hasn't yet been archived and would be lost in the case of a catastrophic outage. By forcing PostgreSQL to switch transaction logs more frequently, we produce a type of heartbeat that implies the server is alive so long as transaction logs keep appearing in our cloud storage. We could argue any highly available PostgreSQL server should always utilize this parameter.

The last thing we do before checking our log file is to simply invoke the `pg_switch_wal` or `pg_switch_xlog` function to manually switch to a new WAL file. This effectively triggers an immediate archival of the previous WAL file and, hence, WAL-E. There's a lot more output than we're watching for, but if everything went well, we should see something like this in the logs:

```
DETAIL: Uploading "pg_wal/000000010000000000000001F" to
"s3://postgres-ha-cookbook/prod-db/wal_005/000000010000000000000001F.lzo".
DETAIL: Archiving to "s3://postgres-ha-cookbook/prod-db/wal_005/000000010000000000000001F.lzo"
complete at 149.161KiB/s.
```

There's more...

WAL-E has a lot of other functionality we don't have time to fully describe. There are, however, a couple of extra points we'd like to make.

Recovering WAL files

Every good command has an analog, right? We can send WAL files, so we must also be able to receive them. Imagine we have a replica system or a backup we've recently pulled from a tape archive. Now we want to use our safe and secure WAL files previously stored in the cloud. Like all good PostgreSQL restores, we need to start with a properly prepared `recovery.conf` file.

To use WAL-E to restore remotely stored transaction logs to a recovered database, start with something like this:

```
restore_command = 'envdir ~postgres/env wal-e wal-fetch "%f" "%p"'
```

Of course, this would cause our PostgreSQL server to constantly spam the cloud service with file requests. This is fine so long as there are files to retrieve, but if we've reached the end of available files it's just excess traffic against our cloud quotas. We can avoid that by using `recovery_target_name`, `recovery_target_time`, or `recovery_target_xid` to stop recovery once it reaches our chosen destination.

If it's not possible to obtain a specific recovery target, we recommend watching the log file during recovery until messages start repeating. If WAL-E repeatedly fails to obtain the next transaction log in the sequence, it's probably time to promote the server so it stops recovering.

Backing up the database

WAL-E can also act as a backup solution. We don't generally recommend this as backing up to a remote location is usually a rather expensive proposition. It isn't simply a matter of monetary cost; we should also consider time and latency. It might not be a good idea to back up a 1 TB database using WAL-E, but a smaller system that doesn't exceed a few GB may be a perfect fit.

The best thing about this capability is that it's easy to invoke. Here's how we would back up our database using WAL-E:

```
envdir ~postgres/env wal-e backup-push /db/pgdata
```

And here's the command we would use to restore the same database:

```
envdir ~postgres/env wal-e backup-fetch /db/pgdata LATEST
```

These two commands make a great pair if we have no other recourse or want to test offsite recovery. In highly available systems, it's always good to have prepared alternatives standing by.

Removing old files

Of course, we might not need to retain transaction logs forever. WAL-E also provides a simple command for purging old WAL files that have served their purpose. We're mainly concerned with high availability, so being able to restore from a backup taken several weeks ago probably isn't necessary. We can use a command like this to remove these old files:

```
envdir ~postgres/env wal-e delete --confirm retain 2
```

This would remove all but WAL files for the two most recent backup operations. The `--confirm` flag commits the change; otherwise, WAL-E errs on the side of caution and considers the command a dry run.

Unfortunately, this only really works if we have performed a backup with WAL-E. If our database is too large for this to be feasible, we would need another clean-up method. We hope a future release of WAL-E will allow specifying a time target instead of assuming all WAL files are related to a backup in some way.

See also

WAL-E is also available on GitHub, along with all of its documentation. Please use the following resource to learn more:

- WAL-E: `https://github.com/wal-e/wal-e`

High Availability with repmgr 9

repmgr is a replication management tool developed by 2ndQuadrant. Originally, it was mainly intended to simplify the management of streaming replicas but has since evolved into a full failover management suite.

Up until now, we've performed a great deal of preliminary work. We know the proper settings, we can create replicas in our sleep, and we have all the skills necessary to troubleshoot and fix a misbehaving server or two. Yet we're still missing at least one critical element to truly achieve high availability: automation.

Many of the recipes in previous chapters cover utilities that are *almost* automated. We learned how to manage access abstraction in Chapter 4, *Proxy and Pooling Resources*, for example. Chapter 7, *PostgreSQL Replication*, got us even further, giving us the necessary tools to maintain a veritable army of alternate servers for primary substitution at a moment's notice.

But we still need manual intervention. Only one of the backend nodes is writable, so we have a virtual IP address, or CNAME, that needs to be reassigned to whichever node is acting as the primary. What we need is some kind of daemon that will watch the state of the cluster and use a consensus algorithm to manage voting so that we always have only one primary node. That daemon could also manage shared resources and ensure a single-access path to the sole writable server.

From the three PostgreSQL servers and the concepts that we learned in previous chapters, we know that the best stack we could produce with the aforementioned tools would look like this:

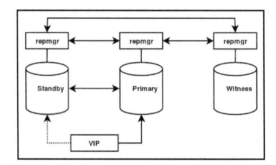

This arrangement of servers definitely combines the lessons we've learned from this book so far. There is a minimum of two nodes for maintenance purposes, and a witness system to maintain voting quorum. We also have a floating virtual IP address for abstract application access, and everything is managed by the repmgr software.

Use of repmgr provides a cluster with the following capabilities:

- Various tools for building and maintaining nodes
- Automatic election of a replacement in the case of node failure
- Quorum management to prevent erroneous or unintentional node promotion
- Robust split-brain protection
- Recovered primary nodes can rejoin the cluster as replicas

In this chapter, we will discuss all of these capabilities and more so that we can construct a fully automated high availability stack. Let's get started!

 Past editions of this book focused mainly on using repmgr as a replica-management tool, but there are far more capabilities that remained unexplored. This new chapter explains how to use repmgr to achieve high availability with no other necessary software.

This chapter is dedicated to building a fully automated high availability stack using the repmgr replica and cluster-management tools by 2ndQuadrant. We will cover the following recipes in this chapter:

- Preparing systems for repmgr
- Installing and configuring repmgr

- Cloning a database with repmgr
- Incorporating a repmgr witness
- Performing a managed failover
- Customizing the failover process
- Using an outage to test availability
- Returning a node to the cluster
- Integrating primary fencing
- Performing online maintenance and upgrades

Preparing systems for repmgr

The repmgr has a few dependencies necessary for it to function optimally, and systems should be provisioned with certain minimal capabilities. This recipe will discuss what these dependencies are and how the servers themselves should be prepared to best facilitate repmgr communication and node management.

Let's get this part done so we can proceed to the really interesting stuff!

Getting ready

At the time of writing this book, the most recent version of repmgr is 5.0. As with Barman, repmgr is available within the PostgreSQL package repositories. If you are using a Debian- or Ubuntu-based system, follow the instructions at `https://wiki.postgresql.org/wiki/Apt`. This link will provide instructions to add the PostgreSQL repository to any system that will be running as a repmgr server or client.

Otherwise, Red Hat-based systems should add the PostgreSQL repository by installing the derivative-appropriate RPM located at `https://yum.postgresql.org/repopackages.php`.

We recommend that you use repositories only, as the repository-provided packages perform tasks other than software installation, such as user creation.

Additionally, repmgr works best when it can communicate via passwordless SSH between nodes. Several commands leverage this capability, and we recommend setting this up to get the most out of repmgr. We'll explain one method of doing this, but the best approach is to manage server keys through configuration management, such as Ansible, Puppet, or Salt.

This recipe also assumes the use of systemd on modern Linux systems. Consequently, the PostgreSQL service is named and maintained differently on each of the major distributions. Debian-based systems name the service `postgresql@[version]-[name]`, while Red Hat systems usually name it `postgresql-[version]`.

The examples in this recipe will assume that you are using a Debian or an Ubuntu system, but you should always use the appropriate and correct value that corresponds to your Linux distribution.

Finally, one of the utilities used to manage the VIP resource is not considered standard and may not be installed. Debian-based systems should use this command to install the potentially missing resource:

```
sudo apt-get install arping
```

Red Hat derivatives should install this package:

```
sudo yum install iputils
```

How to do it...

For this recipe, we will need at least three PostgreSQL servers. For demonstration purposes, we'll assume that they are named `pgha1`, `pgha2`, and `pgha3`. We will also need a dedicated IP address to use for the VIP location, such as `10.0.30.50`.

Follow these steps on all three servers:

1. Debian-based systems should use the following `apt-get` command to install the base repmgr software:

```
sudo apt-get install postgresql-12-repmgr
```

   Red Hat-based systems will need to use this `yum` command instead:

```
sudo yum install repmgr12
```

2. Execute the following commands for direct SSH access to the `postgres` user to all nodes:

```
ssh-keygen -t rsa -N ''
ssh-copy-id postgres@pgha1
ssh-copy-id postgres@pgha2
ssh-copy-id postgres@pgha3
```

3. Repeat the preceding step for pgha2 and pgha3.

4. Prepare a file named `nodes.txt` and fill it with each known node name, FQDN, and IP address for all cluster nodes. The following is an example for our cluster:

```
pgha1
pgha2
pgha3
10.0.30.1
10.0.30.2
10.0.30.3
```

6. Execute the following command on all hosts as the `postgres` user:

```
ssh-keyscan -H -f nodes.txt >> ~/.ssh/known_hosts
```

7. Create a file named `/etc/sudoers.d/postgres` and use the following contents:

```
Defaults:postgres !requiretty
postgres ALL = NOPASSWD: \
 /bin/systemctl stop postgresql@12-main, \
 /bin/systemctl start postgresql@12-main, \
 /bin/systemctl restart postgresql@12-main, \
 /bin/systemctl reload postgresql@12-main, \
 /sbin/ip addr add 10.0.30.50/32 dev eth0 label eth0\:pg, \
 /sbin/ip addr del 10.0.30.50/32 dev eth0 label eth0\:pg, \
 /usr/sbin/arping -b -A -c 3 -I eth0 10.0.30.50
```

How it works...

Since repmgr works as both a PostgreSQL extension and a service daemon, we've chosen to differentiate between installing the software packages and installing repmgr components in the next recipe. To that end, we've provided both `apt` and `yum` commands to install the appropriate repmgr package for prominent supported Linux distributions.

Since repmgr uses a PostgreSQL extension, it is version dependent, so make sure that you install the version that matches your PostgreSQL installation.

Once the package itself is installed, we merely need to ensure that every node can communicate via passwordless SSH through the `postgres` user. This is a fairly common configuration, so it's possible that this has already been done. Regardless, we begin by generating an RSA token with a public key.

This key should be added to the `.ssh/authorized_keys` file on every cluster node, which can be done via the `ssh-copy-id` command. We transmit this to all nodes, as repmgr does not assume that it is being invoked from one of our PostgreSQL nodes. This will allow it to connect to all servers via SSH, including the local system. If we don't have the `postgres` user password necessary to use `ssh-copy-id`, simply cut and paste the contents of the `.ssh/id_rsa.pub` file into the `.ssh/authorized_keys` file manually on all nodes.

Once we've accomplished this step for each node in the cluster, every node should be able to communicate via SSH as the `postgres` user in a reciprocal manner. This symmetric design will ensure that any node can operate as the primary node and that we can connect to any system and execute repmgr commands without worrying whether or not they will succeed.

Next, we create a file named `nodes.txt` that contains every possible known name for each of these nodes. We simply use the hostname and IP address for the systems in our example, but it's best to include any name and alias used to connect to the servers via SSH. This is in case the SSH utilities prompt us to add hosts to the `.ssh/known_hosts` file if they are not already listed.

If repmgr encounters one of these prompts while operating, the requested command will fail, and so we use the `ssh-keyscan` utility to retrieve the SSH signature from each name listed in `nodes.txt` to preallocate entries in `.ssh/known_hosts`. Provided that we also perform this procedure on every node, there should be no disruption of repmgr commands that require SSH.

Lastly, we create a definition for `sudoers` so that the `postgres` user can invoke certain commands through `sudo`. This will allow us to start, stop, or restart PostgreSQL, as well as administer the VIP as necessary. Only these exact commands are allowed, so this isn't considered a vulnerability, and all of these commands will prove useful for high-availability automation.

With these steps completed, we should be able to proceed to repmgr activation.

Installing and configuring repmgr

Installation of the repmgr software package is only the beginning of activating repmgr itself. The repmgr keeps track of the cluster state within the PostgreSQL cluster nodes. Each cluster change is reflected in the stored metadata, and command-line tools compare this information to the current cluster state in order to detect inconsistencies that require intervention.

This recipe will focus on activating repmgr within PostgreSQL and configuring the command-line tool and daemon to manage each node.

Getting ready

One important requirement of this recipe is that we know where certain PostgreSQL binaries are found. Locate the directory where PostgreSQL binaries are installed—for example, most Debian-based systems use /usr/lib/postgresql/12/bin while Red Hat systems use /usr/pgsql-12/bin instead.

One way to do this is to obtain the information from the package manager itself. Debian systems can use this command to find PostgreSQL binaries:

```
dpkg -L postgresql-12 | grep bin
```

Red Hat and similar systems can use this command instead:

```
rpm -ql postgresql12 | grep bin
```

Other package managers may have different methods of collecting this information.

How to do it...

For the purposes of this recipe, we will need one server named pgha1. As always, the /db/pgdata path will be our default data directory. Follow these steps:

1. Connect to PostgreSQL and execute the following commands to create a user and database for managing repmgr:

   ```
   CREATE USER repmgr WITH SUPERUSER REPLICATION;
   CREATE DATABASE repmgr OWNER repmgr;
   ```

2. Modify the `postgresql.conf` file and set the following parameters:

```
shared_preload_libraries = 'pg_stat_statements, repmgr'
wal_log_hints = 'on'
```

3. Modify the `pg_hba.conf` file and add the following lines:

```
host    all           repmgr    10.0.30.0/24    trust
host    replication   repmgr    10.0.30.0/24    trust
```

4. Restart the PostgreSQL service with this command on Debian-based systems

   sudo systemctl restart postgresql@12-main

   Red Hat derivatives should restart PostgreSQL with this command instead:

   sudo systemctl restart postgresql-12

5. Create a file named `/etc/repmgr.conf` with the following contents:

```
node_id = 1
node_name = 'pgha1'
conninfo = 'host=pgha1 port=5432 dbname=repmgr user=repmgr'
data_directory = '/db/pgdata'
pg_bindir = '/path/to/postgres/bin'
use_replication_slots = 'yes'

log_level = 'DEBUG'
log_file = '/var/log/postgresql/repmgr.log'
monitoring_history = 'true'

failover = 'automatic'
primary_visibility_consensus = 'true'

promote_command = 'repmgr standby promote'
follow_command = 'repmgr standby follow -f /etc/repmgr.conf -W
--upstream-node-id=%n '

service_start_command = 'sudo systemctl start postgresql@12-
main'
service_stop_command = 'sudo systemctl stop postgresql@12-
main'
service_restart_command = 'sudo systemctl restart
postgresql@12-main'
service_reload_command = 'sudo systemctl reload postgres@12-
main'
```

On Red Hat and CentOS systems and similar, use the appropriate configuration path instead. This will likely be `/etc/repmgr/12/repmgr.conf` or similar.

6. Register this node as the primary with the following command as the `postgres` user:

```
repmgr primary register
```

7. Debian-based systems will need to modify the `/etc/default/repmgrd` file and set the following variables:

```
REPMGRD_ENABLED=yes
REPMGRD_CONF="/etc/repmgr.conf"
REPMGRD_OPTS="--daemonize=false"
```

8. Enable and restart the `repmgrd` daemon with the following commands as a root-level user:

```
sudo systemctl enable repmgrd
sudo systemctl restart repmgrd
```

If the preceding commands do not work, try these instead:

```
sudo systemctl enable repmgr12
sudo systemctl restart repmgr12
```

9. Examine the `repmgr` logfile with `tail`:

```
tail -n 5 /var/log/postgresql/repmgr.log
```

How it works...

Though this recipe focuses on a single PostgreSQL node to initialize the cluster, only the first step must be performed on our initial primary node. For setting up subsequent replica nodes, we only need to begin with the configuration file.

This first step is to provide a location where repmgr can maintain its metadata regarding the cluster status and configuration. To do this, we create a `repmgr` user and a `repmgr` database to make the association obvious. As repmgr itself is a PostgreSQL extension, we must also modify `postgresql.conf` to include `repmgr` in the `shared_preload_libraries` parameter.

Without this step, the repmgr command-line tool and daemon will be unable to initialize or operate. We also enable `wal_log_hints` as recommended by the PostgreSQL documentation so that repmgr can take advantage of tools such as `pg_rewind` when rejoining old primary nodes.

Next, we add two lines to the `pg_hba.conf` file to allow the `repmgr` user to connect to any database, including the `replication` pseudo database. To follow our example, we allow these connections to originate from anywhere within the `10.0.30.0` subnet.

> Though our example uses `trust` authorization, we suggest that real production systems utilize `.pgpass` files and `md5` authentication instead. Unless the PostgreSQL servers can communicate directly on a private firewalled network, this setup allows any user on these servers to clone our database.

To finish our configuration duties, we create a single file named `repmgr.conf` in the `/etc` directory. All repmgr configuration files technically only require us to modify four parameters, and these are the most critical.

The first of these is the `node_id` parameter, which we set to 1 to indicate that this is the first node. The ID for a node can be any value, so long as it is unique for every node in the cluster. Since this is our only cluster, we can rely on incremental values such as 1, 2, and 3 for subsequent nodes.

Next comes the `node_name` parameter, which we set to `pgha1` to reflect the hostname. There really are no requirements here other than using a distinct and memorable name within the cluster.

Then we move on to specifying the `conninfo` parameter. This is the PostgreSQL connection string that repmgr will use when interacting with its metadata. As a consequence, connection information needs to match our previous entries in `pg_hba.conf` and use the `repmgr` database that we created specifically for this purpose.

The final required element is the `data_directory` parameter, which we've set to our standard parameter of `/db/pgdata`. Some repmgr commands require this to produce replicas, or to rewind an old primary node so that it can be reattached as a standby.

Next, we set `pg_bindir` so that repmgr always knows where to find certain PostgreSQL binaries. Some of these include `pg_rewind`, `psql`, `pg_basebackup`, and others. Many Linux distributions place these in nonstandard directories that are not included in any system `PATH` specification, meaning that repmgr will not operate normally if this setting is omitted.

The last change that we need to make is to set the `use_replication_slots` parameter to `true`. When repmgr creates new replicas, it will automatically produce the appropriate `conninfo` entry in `recovery.conf` or `postgresql.conf`, depending on the PostgreSQL version. When slots are enabled, it will also create and manage associated replication slots so that replicas cannot fall behind during extended outages. While this is not required, we strongly recommend keeping this parameter enabled to avoid potentially lengthy and frequent rebuilds of replica nodes.

We then take the opportunity to make the output more verbose for demonstration purposes by setting `log_level` to `DEBUG`. Similarly, we set the `monitoring_history` parameter to `true` so that cluster events are all recorded in the `repmgr.monitoring_history` table for debugging purposes. We also set `log_file` to an appropriate location because `journald` only captures a small fraction of the debugging output, and we want to see everything.

> You may find the `log_level` output of `DEBUG` too verbose once we've established a working system. If this is the case, feel free to comment out this line to revert to the default value of `INFO`.

The next few parameters pertain specifically to daemon operation. We first set `failover` to `automatic` so that the daemon can manage failovers without manual intervention. Next, we enable the slightly more obscure `primary_visibility_consensus` so that there must be consensus from remaining nodes that the primary node is unreachable before the promotion is allowed. This helps specifically to prevent split-brain in uneven network disruptions.

The `promote_command` value is used when repmgr decides that a specific node should be promoted to primary status. In simple cases like this, simply using `repmgr standby promote` is usually sufficient. This will cause the repmgr process running on the elected node to execute that command as if we had done so from the command line.

Similarly, the `follow_command` parameter is used to inform other existing replicas to follow the newly promoted primary. In this case, we specify the standard `repmgr standby follow command`, the `-W` parameter to indicate that it should wait for the primary to become available, and `--upstream-node-id` to be explicit about which node to follow.

While our examples show `repmgr standby promote` and `repmgr standby follow` without specifying the full path to these binaries, this is only because Debian-based systems create a `/usr/bin/repmgr` wrapper, which is likely to be in most system paths. Any other Linux distribution (or otherwise) that does not share this attribute should always specify the full path to the `repmgr` binary in these parameters.

The `pg_bindir` parameter is not prepended to `promote_command` or `follow_command`, as either command may refer to an executable script in any location. When in doubt, or if things aren't working as expected, specify the entire path.

The `--upstream-node-id` option is not technically required to follow the current primary node. If replication is working normally, repmgr will obtain the correct target from the metadata database; however, in limited circumstances, the state of this metadata can be ambiguous, such as in witness nodes that merely copy the metadata periodically. We can prevent this by explicitly specifying the upstream node, which should be correct unless the node record itself was changed.

The final components of our configuration file pertain to how repmgr manages the PostgreSQL service. Each of the `service_*_command` parameters correspond to the operation we would need repmgr to perform automatically in our stead. In this case, we rely on `systemctl` to invoke these commands via `sudo`. This is one reason we configured `sudoers` in the *Preparing systems for repmgr* recipe; be sure to use the same commands that we specified there.

Now that everything is prepared, we can finally register the primary node and complete the installation process by creating various database objects. These steps are all performed by the `repmgr` command, provided that we specify the `primary register` parameters. Our output should look something like this:

```
postgres@pgha1:~$ repmgr primary register

INFO: connecting to primary database...
NOTICE: attempting to install extension "repmgr"
NOTICE: "repmgr" extension successfully installed
NOTICE: primary node record (ID: 1) registered
```

We're almost done! The repmgr system comes with a daemon that manages communication and controls behavior between other repmgr nodes. If we start this daemon, then repmgr will run in the background and process node communication, the consensus model, elections, and node promotions, among other elements.

Debian systems need to modify the /etc/default/repmgrd file and enable the daemon itself by setting REPMGRD_ENABLED to yes, and by specifying the location of the repmgr configuration file with REPMGRD_CONF. While /etc/repmgr.conf is the default location, Debian systems require this to be set explicitly before operating. And perhaps most importantly, we must ensure that REPMGRD_OPTS is set to --daemonize=false so that systemd properly tracks the repmgrd process ID and can successfully stop or restart the service.

 This has been a long-standing bug ever since repmgr changed the default for the --daemonize option to true in version 4.1 back in early 2018. We're not quite sure why the PGDG packagers still haven't corrected this issue.

Once we enable and start the repmgr daemon using the distribution-appropriate command, we can examine the log. We should see the initial startup messages there, as shown in the following screenshot:

```
[2019-11-23 22:42:58] [NOTICE] repmgrd (repmgrd 5.0.0) starting up
[2019-11-23 22:42:58] [INFO] connecting to database "host=pgha1 port=5432 dbname=repmgr user=repmgr"
[2019-11-23 22:42:58] [NOTICE] starting monitoring of node "pgha1" (ID: 1)
[2019-11-23 22:42:58] [INFO] "connection_check_type" set to "ping"
[2019-11-23 22:42:58] [NOTICE] monitoring cluster primary "pgha1" (ID: 1)
```

See also

The official repmgr site maintains current documentation and sources, along with version announcements. Please use these resources for more information:

- **repmgr**: https://repmgr.org/
- **repmgr documentation**: https://repmgr.org/docs/current/index.html
- **repmgr GitHub**: https://github.com/2ndQuadrant/repmgr

Cloning a database with repmgr

As repmgr is a client/server PostgreSQL management suite, we need at least two nodes involved before we're really using it. We can perform the tasks outlined in this recipe as many times as we wish, creating several clones and registering them with repmgr. Of course, this book is only for demonstration purposes, so we'll leave the larger clusters to you. With multiple nodes involved, the chances of data loss or system outages decline, which is excellent for our goal of attaining high availability.

This recipe will focus on the process necessary to add a node to an existing repmgr cluster. The existing cluster in our case is the one that we established on pgha1 in the previous recipe.

Getting ready

This recipe depends on repmgr being installed on both a primary server and the clone that we will use. Please follow the *Installing and configuring repmgr* recipe before continuing.

How to do it...

For the purposes of this recipe, pgha1 will remain our primary node, and the replica will be pgha2. As always, the /db/pgdata path will be our default data directory.

All of these commands should be executed from pgha2. Follow these steps to produce a fully functional repmgr replica:

1. Create a repmgr.conf file as described in the *Installing and configuring repmgr* recipe on pgha2, but make the following changes to the stated parameters:

   ```
   node_id = 2
   node_name = 'pgha2'
   conninfo = 'host=pgha2 port=5432 dbname=repmgr user=repmgr'
   ```

2. Clone the pgha1 node with the following command as the postgres user. Executed this command on pgha2:

   ```
   repmgr standby clone -h pgha1 -U repmgr -d repmgr
   ```

3. Start the new replica as the `postgres` user with `systemctl` on Debian systems:

   `systemctl start postgresql@12-main`

   On Red Hat-based systems, use the following command:

   `systemctl start postgresql-12`

4. Register `pgha2` with `pgha1` as the `postgres` user:

   `repmgr standby register`

5. Start the `repmgrd` daemon with the following command as a root-level user on Debian systems:

   `sudo systemctl start repmgrd`

   Use this command for Red Hat variants:

   `sudo systemctl start repmgr12`

6. Connect to the `repmgr` database on `pgha1` and view the sync status of `pgha2` with this SQL statement:

   `SELECT standby_node_id, standby_name, replication_lag`
   `FROM repmgr.replication_status;`

How it works...

One good thing about the *Installing and configuring repmgr* recipe is that it applies to any and all repmgr nodes, except for a few settings that must be distinct on each. These include the `node_id`, `node_name`, and `conninfo`. This makes sense, as each node should have a uniquely identifiable ID and name, and the `conninfo` parameter should always be set to the local node managed by repmgr.

Once the `repmgr.conf` configuration file is properly defined, we can clone `pgha1` with the `repmgr` command-line tool. Because no PostgreSQL instance exists on `pgha2` yet, this should be a safe operation. Since the new node has no metadata, we must specify the upstream host that we're cloning with `-h` and the name of the metadata database itself with `-d`. All other settings, such as the PostgreSQL data directory, are derived from our `repmgr.conf` file.

Assuming that there were no errors, the command should produce a lot of extremely verbose output, with the following at the end (we've removed the debugging output for readability):

```
NOTICE: destination directory "/db/pgdata" provided
DETAIL: connection string is: host=pgha1 dbname=repmgr
DETAIL: current installation size is 31 MB
NOTICE: checking for available walsenders on the source node (2 required)
NOTICE: checking replication connections can be made to the source server (2 required)
NOTICE: starting backup (using pg_basebackup)...
HINT: this may take some time; consider using the -c/--fast-checkpoint option
NOTICE: standby clone (using pg_basebackup) complete
NOTICE: you can now start your PostgreSQL server
HINT: for example: sudo systemctl start postgres
HINT: after starting the server, you need to register this standby with "repmgr standby register"
```

If we follow the advice in the last line and start PostgreSQL with `systemctl`, then the clone should immediately connect to pgha1 and begin replication. We can do this because repmgr knows all of the connection information necessary to establish a streaming replication connection with pgha1. During the cloning process, repmgr automatically sets the `primary_conninfo` and `primary_slot_name` parameters in `recovery.conf` or `postgresql.auto.conf` as necessary to start directly in replication mode.

With everything up and running, we should be able to register the new clone similar to the process that we used to register the primary. The `repmgr` command-line tool offers several useful operations. For now, we will settle with `standby register` to inform repmgr that it should track pgha2 as part of the new cluster.

Once we start the `repmgrd` daemon, all nodes should become aware of each other and the current status of each one. We can confirm this by checking the `replication_status` view on any node. If we execute the supplied SQL statement, we should see this:

```
standby_node_id | standby_name | replication_lag
----------------+--------------+----------------
              2 | pgha2        | 0 bytes
```

The `replication_status` view has other useful columns, but for now, we can see that the cluster considers pgha2 the only standby node, and it's not lagging behind the current primary at all.

There's more...

Cloning to expand our cluster is only the beginning of the story. Once we have more than one node, it also makes sense to start viewing the cluster itself. We can even clone from Barman backups as well! Let's learn about these additional features in more detail.

Viewing the cluster

There is another way to obtain the cluster status. The `repmgr` command can also report how it perceives the cluster from any active node, given the `cluster show` parameter. Here is the entire command as executed by the `postgres` user:

```
repmgr cluster show
```

The result of this command as executed on `pgha2` is as follows:

```
postgres@pgha2:~$ repmgr cluster show

ID | Name  | Role    | Status    | Upstream | Location | Priority | Timeline | Connection string
---+-------+---------+-----------+----------+----------+----------+----------+--------------------------------------------------
1  | pgha1 | primary | * running |          | default  | 100      | 1        | host=pgha1 port=5432 dbname=repmgr user=repmgr
2  | pgha2 | standby |   running | pgha1    | default  | 100      | 1        | host=pgha2 port=5432 dbname=repmgr user=repmgr
```

The `repmgr cluster show` command also accepts a handy `--csv` option to indicate the online status of each node ID and whether or not it is replicating. This is presented in CSV format for easy programmatic interpretation if desired.

Cloning from Barman

Since repmgr and Barman are both developed by 2ndQuadrant, they have been designed to be integrated if this is what is wanted. One reason that we might decide to do this is to reduce I/O strain on the primary node when creating a new clone. It's also very easy to configure.

Assuming that we've already explored the recipes in the chapter on backup management, we could add these two settings to `repmgr.conf` and clones would be constructed from a backup rather than the primary node:

```
barman_host='barman@pg-backup'
    barman_server='pg-primary'
```

Since repmgr knows the parameters that Barman expects, it can invoke all the commands necessary to recover the latest backup on the local node. Of course, this assumes that we have already configured passwordless SSH from the new node to the backup server as the `barman` user, and from the backup server to the new node as the `postgres` user.

Keep these reciprocal SSH expectations in mind, as several PostgreSQL tools rely upon them.

See also

The official repmgr site maintains current documentation and goes into more depth on how these commands work. Please use these resources for more information:

- **repmgr standby clone**: https://repmgr.org/docs/current/repmgr-standby-clone.html
- **repmgr standby register**: https://repmgr.org/docs/current/repmgr-standby-register.html
- **repmgr cluster show**: https://repmgr.org/docs/current/repmgr-cluster-show.html
- **Cloning a standby from Barman**: https://repmgr.org/docs/current/cloning-from-barman.html

Incorporating a repmgr witness

As we discussed in `Chapter 1`, *Architectural Considerations*, it is incredibly important to include an odd number of nodes in most cluster designs. Generally, this is necessary to guarantee that a voting quorum can be established in the case that the primary node becomes unavailable. We must choose one existing standby system to promote and take over the cluster.

We must also consider the possibility of split-brain and network partitions. Witness nodes help protect us from these scenarios by acting as an objective third party. If they are located in the same data center as the current primary, then the network partitions will prevent it from voting at all, and we will be protected from network partitions. If it's in a tertiary data center away from either the current primary or standby, there will be two independent routes to verify whether or not the primary node is actually offline or unreachable.

Essentially, a witness node must agree with the remainder of the cluster to form a majority and trigger a failover event. This recipe will focus on the process necessary to add a witness to an existing repmgr cluster.

Getting ready

This recipe depends on repmgr being installed on both a primary server and the witness that we will use. Please follow the *Installing and configuring repmgr* and *Cloning a database with repmgr* recipes before continuing.

How to do it...

For the purposes of this recipe, pgha1 will remain our primary node and the witness will be pgha3. As always, the /db/pgdata path will be our default data directory.

All of these commands should be executed from pgha3. Follow these steps to produce a fully functional repmgr witness:

1. Create a new and empty PostgreSQL instance using initdb as the postgres user:

   ```
   initdb -D /db/pgdata
   ```

2. Modify the postgresql.conf file and set the following parameter:

   ```
   shared_preload_libraries = 'repmgr'
   ```

3. Modify the pg_hba.conf file and add the following line:

   ```
   host      all      repmgr      10.0.30.0/24      trust
   ```

4. Start the PostgreSQL service with this command on Debian-based systems:

   ```
   sudo systemctl start postgresql@12-main
   ```

   Red Hat derivatives should restart PostgreSQL with this command instead:

   ```
   sudo systemctl start postgresql-12
   ```

5. Connect to PostgreSQL and execute the following to create a user and database for managing repmgr:

```
CREATE USER repmgr WITH SUPERUSER REPLICATION;
CREATE DATABASE repmgr OWNER repmgr;
```

6. Create a file named /etc/repmgr.conf with the following contents:

```
node_id = 3
node_name = 'pgha3'
conninfo = 'host=pgha3 port=5432 dbname=repmgr user=repmgr'
data_directory = '/db/pgdata'
pg_bindir = '/path/to/postgres/bin'
log_level = 'DEBUG'
log_file = '/var/log/postgresql/repmgr.log'
monitoring_history = 'true'
primary_visibility_consensus = 'true'
```

7. On Red Hat and CentOS systems and similar, use the appropriate configuration path instead. This will likely be /etc/repmgr/12/repmgr.conf or similar.

8. Register this node as the witness with the following command as the postgres user:

```
repmgr witness register -h pgha1 -d repmgr
```

9. Debian-based systems will need to modify the /etc/default/repmgrd file and set the following variables:

```
REPMGRD_ENABLED=yes
REPMGRD_CONF="/etc/repmgr.conf"
REPMGRD_OPTS="--daemonize=false"
```

10. Enable and restart the repmgrd daemon with the following commands as a root-level user:

```
sudo systemctl enable repmgrd
sudo systemctl restart repmgrd
```

If the preceding commands do not work, try these instead:

```
sudo systemctl enable repmgr12
sudo systemctl restart repmgr12
```

11. Verify that the witness can see the cluster using the following command as the `postgres` user:

```
repmgr cluster show
```

How it works...

In many ways, creating a witness node is very similar to starting a new repmgr cluster. Since the witness only needs to act as a voting member and observe the primary node, it does not need a full copy of our operational data. In fact, it only needs a very small PostgreSQL installation to track the repmgr cluster metadata.

To that end, we can use `initdb`, `pg_createcluster`, or whatever tool is provided by our Linux distribution to start with an empty database. The important thing is that we make the same modifications that we made when we initialized the primary node.

Principally, this means adding the `repmgr` shared library to `shared_preload_libraries` in `postgresql.conf` and modifying `pg_hba.conf` to allow connections; however, unlike a full member node, we don't need to allow replication streaming; this node will never act as a primary, and is not a candidate for promotion.

With the PostgreSQL configuration complete, we should be able to start the database service. Just like our primary node, we must also create the `repmgr` user and database to store the cluster metadata.

Once PostgreSQL is running and the `repmgr` user and database exist, we can focus on configuring repmgr as a witness node. As with all `repmgr.conf` files, we include the `node_id`, `node_name`, and `conninfo` parameters and modify them to reflect `pgha3` in all respects. We also specify the same `data_directory`, `pg_bindir`, `log_level`, `log_file`, and `monitoring_history` entries as our other recipes for consistency.

And that is where the configuration ends. Unlike regular nodes that expect to be promoted, we don't need promotion or follow commands. There's no reason for the daemon to start, stop, reload, or restart the PostgreSQL service. In this case, the repmgr daemon merely exists to vote and watch the rest of the cluster and nothing more.

With the configuration complete, we should be able to register the new witness in a similar way to the process that we used to register the first standby. Since witness nodes are treated differently, they also have their own syntax. In this case, we use `witness register` to inform repmgr that it should track `pgha3` as a cluster witness.

Note that, much like `repmgr standby clone`, we also provide the host (-h) and database (-d) options while registering. This is because we're not cloning the node, but we still need the cluster metadata. One of the jobs of the repmgr daemon on a witness node is to regularly refresh the contents of the metadata from the appropriate primary system. But we must get at least one copy to bootstrap the process. To do this, when we register a witness node, we tell it where that information resides.

At this point, we can enable and start the `repmgrd` daemon with `systemctl`. Since the witness node depends on a copy of the cluster metadata rather than streaming it directly via replication, one of the best ways to demonstrate proper operation is with `repmgr cluster show`, as shown here:

```
postgres@pgha3:~$ repmgr cluster show
 ID | Name  | Role    | Status    | Upstream | Location | Priority | Timeline | Connection string
 ---+-------+---------+-----------+----------+----------+----------+----------+---------------------------------------------
 1  | pgha1 | primary | * running |          | default  | 100      | 1        | host=pgha1 port=5432 dbname=repmgr user=repmgr
 2  | pgha2 | standby |   running | pgha1    | default  | 100      | 1        | host=pgha2 port=5432 dbname=repmgr user=repmgr
 3  | pgha3 | witness | * running | pgha1    | default  | 0        | 1        | host=pgha3 port=5432 dbname=repmgr user=repmgr
```

Note how the witness is identified specifically by its role, and that the upstream is `pgha1`. This means that it is currently copying metadata regularly from `pgha1`. In the event of a switchover or failover, this will necessarily change.

See also

The official repmgr site maintains current documentation and goes into more depth on how these commands work. Please use these resources for more information:

- **repmgr witness register**: https://repmgr.org/docs/current/repmgr-witness-register.html
- **Using a witness server**: https://repmgr.org/docs/current/repmgrd-witness-server.html

Performing a managed failover

Creating a PostgreSQL clone can be surprisingly dangerous. When using a utility such as `rsync`, accidentally transposing the source and target can result in erasing the source PostgreSQL data directory. This is especially true when swapping from one node to another and then reversing the process. It's all too easy to accidentally invoke the wrong script when the source and target are so readily switched.

We've already established how repmgr can ease the process of clone creation, and now it's time to discuss node promotion. There are two questions we will answer in this recipe: how do we swap from one active PostgreSQL node to another, and how do we then reactivate the original node without risking our data? The second question is perhaps more important because of the fact that we will be at reduced capacity following node deactivation.

This recipe will explore how to keep our database available through multiple node swaps.

Getting ready

This recipe depends on repmgr being installed on a primary server, and the possession of at least one standby and a witness. Please go through all previous recipes before continuing.

How to do it...

For the purposes of this recipe, pgha1 will start as our primary node and pgha2 will start as a physical standby. Follow these steps to promote pgha2 to be the new cluster primary:

1. Pause the repmgr daemon on all nodes by executing this command as the postgres user on any system:

   ```
   repmgr service pause
   ```

2. As the postgres user on pgha2, invoke the following command to promote it to become the new primary:

   ```
   repmgr standby switchover --siblings-follow
   ```

3. Check the cluster status as the postgres user on any node:

   ```
   repmgr cluster show
   ```

4. Unpause the repmgr daemon on all nodes by executing this command as the postgres user on any system:

   ```
   repmgr service unpause
   ```

How it works...

To start the process, we must first temporarily disable the automated repmgr daemon with `repmgr service pause`. This is extremely important, as repmgr is currently configured to detect an outage, trigger an election, and automatically promote a node. If we manually invoke commands that alter the cluster state, the daemon could also start issuing commands and we may end up with an inoperable cluster.

It's extremely important to always pause the service when using repmgr commands that reassign, modify, or disable the current primary node. If we fail to do this, repmgr may start trying to "fix" the cluster while we're still making manual changes. Consider this a standard part of any kind of maintenance of a cluster operating under repmgr.

Next, we invoke the `repmgr` tool from `pgha2` with `standby switchover` parameters. This tells repmgr that the current node should be the new primary and that the previous primary should be converted into a standby.

By including the `--siblings-follow option`, we explicitly request that all other standby or witness nodes follow the new primary. This is not done automatically in the case of temporary maintenance procedures, where nodes will be reverted to their old roles once complete. It can also be a good idea to omit this option in clusters that make extensive use of cascading replication; otherwise, all nodes will follow the promoted standby system.

We can actually observe the entire procedure in the output from the command, which even without debugging enabled, is extremely verbose. We hope the output ends with these messages:

```
NOTICE: starting server using "sudo systemctl start postgresql@12-main"
NOTICE: replication slot "repmgr_slot_2" deleted on node 1
NOTICE: NODE REJOIN successful
DETAIL: node 1 is now attached to node 2
NOTICE: executing STANDBY FOLLOW on 1 of 1 siblings
INFO:  node 3 received notification to follow node 2
INFO: STANDBY FOLLOW successfully executed on all reachable sibling nodes
NOTICE: switchover was successful
DETAIL: node "pgha2" is now primary and node "pgha1" is attached as standby
NOTICE: STANDBY SWITCHOVER has completed successfully
```

From this output, we can not only see that the switchover was successful, but we can also see some of the subcommands that repmgr used to accomplish that end goal. We can also see that it cleaned up any unused replication slots, since `pgha1` should be streaming from `pgha2` rather than vice versa.

We can further verify the state of the cluster by using the `repmgr cluster show` command, as seen in this example:

```
postgres@pgha2:~$ repmgr cluster show

ID | Name  | Role    | Status      | Upstream | Location | Priority | Timeline | Connection string
---+-------+---------+-------------+----------+----------+----------+----------+-----------------------------------------------
1  | pgha1 | standby |   running   | pgha2    | default  | 100      | 2        | host=pgha1 port=5432 dbname=repmgr user=repmgr
2  | pgha2 | primary | * running   |          | default  | 100      | 2        | host=pgha2 port=5432 dbname=repmgr user=repmgr
3  | pgha3 | witness | * running   | pgha2    | default  | 0        | 1        | host=pgha3 port=5432 dbname=repmgr user=repmgr
```

What we want to see here is that both the old primary and the witness are both following the newly promoted node. We also want to see that pgha2 is running as the primary node for the cluster. The `cluster show` command tends to notice inconsistencies, and these will appear in the output as something that could warrant investigation or corrective measures.

Once we've verified that the cluster is operating as expected, we unpause the repmgr service with `repmgr service unpause` so that future failovers will work normally.

There's more...

There are, however, a couple of extra points that we'd like to make.

Always watching

Remember the witness node? Pausing the repmgr service only prevents the daemons from taking action when they detect an outage. Each will continue to watch the other nodes, especially the upstream primary. If we check the witness node logs, we have an objectively uninvolved history of the manual switchover we demonstrated previously.

Here is an example of that activity:

```
[2019-11-25 19:37:03] [WARNING] unable to ping "host=pgha1 port=5432 dbname=repmgr user=repmgr"
[2019-11-25 19:37:03] [DETAIL] PQping() returned "PQPING_NO_RESPONSE"
[2019-11-25 19:37:03] [INFO] checking state of node 1, 1 of 6 attempts
[2019-11-25 19:37:03] [DETAIL] PQping() returned "PQPING_NO_RESPONSE"
[2019-11-25 19:37:03] [INFO] sleeping 10 seconds until next reconnection attempt
[2019-11-25 19:37:13] [INFO] checking state of node 1, 2 of 6 attempts
[2019-11-25 19:37:13] [NOTICE] node 1 has recovered, reconnecting
[2019-11-25 19:37:13] [INFO] connection to node 1 succeeded
[2019-11-25 19:37:13] [INFO] original connection no longer available, using new connection
[2019-11-25 19:37:13] [NOTICE] reconnected to upstream node after 10 seconds
[2019-11-25 19:37:13] [NOTICE] current upstream node "pgha1" (ID: 1) is not primary, restarting monitoring
[2019-11-25 19:37:13] [INFO] witness monitoring connection to primary node "pgha2" (ID: 2)
```

It's apparent that the witness node noticed the connection from pgha1, and that triggered six 10-second checks where it would have declared that node as unreachable. This would determine how the witness would vote if we hadn't paused the daemon cluster management.

Since the cluster recovers before the full timeout period, the witness reconnects and then notices that some other node is the new primary. Since witness nodes only maintain a copy of the cluster metadata, it realizes it must connect to pgha2 to maintain the current information.

If this had not been a manual switchover or some kind of other test, we would have seen far more output pertaining to a node election, selection, and so on.

Testing the waters

Several repmgr commands also accept the --dry-run argument. When supplied to an operation, repmgr will invoke the process normally, but will only produce debugging output, and will skip elements that would modify the cluster state. It's a way of verifying that there are no unexpected problems that would definitely disrupt the switchover.

This is especially important here, as a switchover actually performs several actions:

- Stops the current primary node
- Promotes the standby on the selected node
- Converts the old primary into a new standby
- Connects to any other nodes in the cluster and changes their streaming connection

This is not an exhaustive list, as each of the preceding steps may consist of further granular operations. It's important to use the dry run option before triggering such potentially dangerous tasks.

Useful shortcuts

Since the introduction of repmgr 4.2, repmgr standby switchover will automatically pause the service to prevent it from interfering in the procedure. While we still recommend pausing the service explicitly to prevent accidents in case other commands are involved, it's permissible to omit this in this circumstance.

However, repmgr will not automatically unpause the daemons at the end of a switchover. After all, the repmgr service may have been paused before we invoked the switchover process. Therefore, if we want to both automatically pause *and* unpause the repmgr service during a switchover, we can use this command instead:

```
repmgr standby switchover --siblings-follow --repmgrd-force-unpause
```

See also

The official repmgr site maintains current documentation and goes into more depth on how these commands work. Please use these resources for more information:

- **repmgr standby switchover**: `https://repmgr.org/docs/current/repmgr-standby-switchover.html`
- **repmgr service pause**: `https://repmgr.org/docs/current/repmgr-service-pause.html`
- **repmgr service unpause**: `https://repmgr.org/docs/current/repmgr-service-unpause.html`
- **Pausing the repmgrd service**: `https://repmgr.org/docs/current/repmgrd-pausing.html`

Customizing the failover process

Very few out-of-the-box installations adequately represent the needs of every potential user. As a result, repmgr relies more on command invocation than on configuration parameters.

As a result, repmgr functions in far more environments than it normally would. There are organizations that use a VIP to always track the current primary node, as we will soon demonstrate. There are others that prefer reconfiguring PgBouncer hosts instead. Still others rely on F5 load balancers, CNAME assignment, or any number of other abstraction techniques.

Rather than dictate which is the preferred method, repmgr allows all of these to flourish as necessary based on user needs. In fact, repmgr offers quite a few parameters that accept a script or another kind of command to manage cluster operations. There's even an event handler to act as a routing engine for more advanced use cases.

This recipe, however, will focus on explaining the `promote_command` parameter necessary to allocate a VIP that follows our current primary node.

Getting ready

This recipe depends on us having a fully operational repmgr cluster. Please go through all recipes up to and including *Incorporating a repmgr witness*. Pay special attention to the *Preparing systems for repmgr* recipe, which defines the `/etc/sudoers.d/postgres` definition that allows the `postgres` user to invoke specific root-level commands.

How to do it...

For the purposes of this recipe, pgha1 will remain our primary node, and the standby will be pgha2. Follow these steps on pgha1 and pgha2, unless otherwise specified:

1. Create a file named `repmgr_promote_self.sh` in the `/usr/local/bin` folder and specify the following contents:

```
#!/usr/bin/env bash

VIP=10.0.30.50
IFACE=eth0
PATH=/usr/pgsql-12/bin:$PATH
VIP_CONF="${VIP}/32 dev ${IFACE} label ${IFACE}:pg"

ssh -o StrictHostKeyChecking=no \
    -o UserKnownHostsFile=/dev/null \
    -o ConnectTimeout=5 \
    -o ServerAliveInterval=1 \
    postgres@${VIP} sudo ip addr del ${VIP_CONF}

sudo /sbin/ip addr add ${VIP_CONF}
sudo /usr/sbin/arping -b -A -c 3 -I ${IFACE} ${VIP}

repmgr standby promote
exit 0
```

2. Mark the script as executable with this command as a root-level user:

```
sudo chmod a+x /usr/local/bin/repmgr_promote_self.sh
```

3. Modify `repmgr.conf` and make sure that `promote_command` is set to use the new script, including the full path, as shown here:

```
promote_command = '/usr/local/bin/repmgr_promote_self.sh'
```

4. Restart repmgr using `systemctl` on Debian systems with this command:

```
sudo systemctl restart repmgrd
```

Red Hat-based servers should use this command instead:

```
sudo systemctl restart repmgr12
```

5. Issue the following commands on `pgha1` as the `postgres` user to bootstrap the VIP:

```
sudo ip addr add 10.0.30.50/32 dev eth0 label eth0:pg
sudo arping -b -A -c 3 -I eth0 10.0.30.50
```

How it works...

The focus of this recipe is on operational customization. We begin by defining a script that performs several actions on our behalf.

Say that we want a VIP to always be located on the current primary node. In the event of a switchover or failover, this means that the VIP must be moved. The easiest (but perhaps not the safest) way to do this is to connect to the VIP itself and invoke a command that destroys it.

Our `ssh` command does just that, and we use the `ConnectTimeout` and `ServerAliveInterval` options to ensure that our connection doesn't get stuck because we terminate the VIP while still connected to it. The reason for specifying `StrictHostKeyChecking` and `UserKnownHostsFile` is less obvious. We do this because the VIP is used by at least two systems, and if each server has a unique host key, the key will change every time we move it. To avoid worrying about that, we simply avoid tracking the host key entirely, but only when manipulating the VIP itself.

The `StrictHostKeyChecking` and `UserKnownHostsFile` flags are not necessary if all hosts share the same host key. This can happen if a single key pair is generated with `ssh-keygen` and copied to the `~postgres/.ssh` folder on all known hosts. This is not an uncommon configuration, but this recipe can't work with this example. If your environment reflects this design, feel free to remove these SSH options.

Next, we use the `ip addr` command to add the `10.0.30.50` VIP address to our `eth0` interface. To be safe, we also use what is known as a gratuitous ARP with `arping` to broadcast the fact that we arbitrarily claimed the IP address. This will inform listening hosts to treat us as the owner of that address since we were the last ones seen communicating on it.

At the end of the script, we issue a standard `repmgr standby promote`, which is always required of a promotion event. This will act as a trigger to repmgr that it should promote the local standby and modify dependent metadata for the sake of consistency. In reality, we are merely augmenting the `repmgr standby promote` event to include extra steps. In this case, we destroy a remote VIP claim and issue our own.

As always, any executable script should be assigned the proper operating system flags; that's our last step to make the script usable. Once we modify the `promote_command` parameter in `repmgr.conf` to invoke the script on any failover event, repmgr should use our new script instead of `repmgr standby promote`.

We're technically done with the process after restarting the repmgr daemon. At that point, failure of the primary node will trigger an election that will elect the current (and only) standby. Then repmgr will execute the `repmgr_promote_self.sh` command, which will ensure that the VIP only exists on the promoted node.

However, just to ensure that the cluster is fully operational, it's in our interest to create the VIP on the current primary node. This is likely to be `pgha1`, but if it is `pgha2`, that is perfectly fine. The cluster should be symmetrical thanks to the witness.

There's more...

Don't think that our VIP takeover script is the only thing that is possible to accomplish here. In fact, we hope you don't even use our example at all. There are no safeguards that verify that the VIP no longer works after attempting to deactivate it; in fact, there aren't any other kinds of error checking at all. A real production-quality script would, for example, ensure that the VIP could be claimed before finally calling `repmgr standby promote`.

In fact, the script can do basically anything that doesn't affect the cluster until finally triggering the promotion step itself. Provided that each of these steps includes some kind of verification or exception handling, all it takes to abort the whole process is to either return a nonzero status or simply to avoid invoking `repmgr standby promote`.

Remember, in a high-availability cluster, it's not just the uptime that we must consider. In an event where we can't verify that no other server is still presenting the VIP, our attempt to create it locally could result in a split-brain scenario. It's better to be cautious, even if that means that we don't get an automatic failover if something isn't working as expected.

An inoperable failover system is merely annoying and can be fixed relatively painlessly. A situation where two nodes are listening on the same IP address, perceived differently from various application servers, where nobody knows where data may have been committed, is much more troublesome.

But it's not all doom and gloom. Since the script is arbitrary, it really can do anything. It may make sense to transmit an email with machine or cluster details by embedding `repmgr cluster show` before and after the failover.

The script doesn't even need to be written in a shell language. So long as it executes `repmgr standby promote` at some point and exits with 0 upon success, it could be written in any language—even C.

See also

The official repmgr site maintains the current documentation and goes into more depth on how these commands work. Please use this resource for more information: `https://repmgr.org/docs/current/repmgrd-basic-configuration.html`

Using an outage to test availability

It's always considered good practice to test a failover procedure to prove that it functions as designed. There are a lot of moving parts in the cluster design discussed in this chapter, and an errant setting in PostgreSQL, repmgr, SSH, the VIP, network hardware, or any number of other influences can impact automation.

Testing helps reveal potential problem areas in a procedure, demonstrates average event durations, and serves as practice for when unexpected outages actually occur. The easiest way to test a cluster is to stop PostgreSQL on the primary server, which should trigger repmgr on other nodes to hold an election and promote the standby.

This recipe will demonstrate a simple failover procedure caused by stopping PostgreSQL, but also more advanced techniques to test operation during a network outage.

Getting ready

This recipe requires us to have a fully operational repmgr cluster. Please complete all of the recipes up to and including *Incorporating a repmgr witness*. You should also complete the *Customizing the failover process* recipe so that we have a functional VIP established.

How to do it...

For the purposes of this recipe, pgha1 will remain our primary node, the standby will be pgha2, and our witness is pgha3. The VIP is 10.0.30.50. Follow these steps to test the failover process:

1. Issue the following command on pgha1 to stop PostgreSQL on a Debian system:

    ```
    sudo systemctl stop postgresql@12-main
    ```

    Red Hat derivatives should use this command to stop PostgreSQL instead:

    ```
    sudo systemctl stop postgresql-12
    ```

2. Watch the repmgr logs on pgha2 as the postgres user:

    ```
    tail -f /var/log/postgresql/repmgr.log
    ```

3. Watch the state of the cluster on `pgha3` with this command as the `postgres` user:

```
watch -n 1 repmgr cluster show
```

4. Once `pgha2` assumes the primary role, execute this command to check the state of the VIP on `pgha2`:

```
ip addr show dev eth0 label eth0:pg
```

How it works...

Finally, an easy recipe! Our first (and really only) step is to stop PostgreSQL on the primary node. Our second step is to watch the aftermath. One quick call to `systemctl` to stop PostgreSQL, and we want to watch the other two nodes to see the state of the cluster change, and how it happens.

The first of these observations is on the standby node, which will presumably be promoted. We set the log location to `/var/log/postgresql/repmgr.log` in the *Installing and configuring repmgr* recipe. This allows us to watch the log as the repmgr daemon begins to perform the failover process.

The first thing that happens is that `pgha2` loses contact with `pgha1` and begins a series of checks to verify that this wasn't an errant reading. We can see this in the following log extract:

```
[2019-11-26 15:28:58] [WARNING] unable to ping "host=pgha1 port=5432 dbname=repmgr user=repmgr"
[2019-11-26 15:28:58] [DETAIL] PQping() returned "PQPING_NO_RESPONSE"
[2019-11-26 15:28:58] [WARNING] unable to connect to upstream node "pgha1" (ID: 1)
[2019-11-26 15:28:58] [INFO] checking state of node 1, 1 of 6 attempts
```

The default check interval of ten seconds is defined by the `reconnect_interval` parameter in `repmgr.conf`. The default number of six checks before considering the primary node failed is defined by the `reconnect_attempts` parameter. These two attributes combine to a default of 60 seconds to allow for transitory events, after which an election will follow. In our case, the outage window will be a minimum of one minute.

Once the checks have all been exhausted, we can see the election occur in the `pgha2` logs as well, as shown here:

```
[2019-11-26 15:29:48] [WARNING] unable to reconnect to node 1 after 6 attempts
[2019-11-26 15:29:48] [INFO] 1 active sibling nodes registered
[2019-11-26 15:29:48] [INFO] primary and this node have the same location ("default")
[2019-11-26 15:29:48] [INFO] local node's last receive lsn: 0/89A0C10
[2019-11-26 15:29:48] [INFO] checking state of sibling node "pgha3" (ID: 3)
[2019-11-26 15:29:48] [INFO] node "pgha3" (ID: 3) reports its upstream is node 1, last seen 52 second(s) ago
[2019-11-26 15:29:48] [INFO] node 3 last saw primary node 52 second(s) ago
[2019-11-26 15:29:48] [INFO] visible nodes: 2; total nodes: 2; no nodes have seen the primary within the last 4 seconds
[2019-11-26 15:29:48] [NOTICE] promotion candidate is "pgha2" (ID: 2)
[2019-11-26 15:29:48] [NOTICE] this node is the winner, will now promote itself and inform other nodes
```

Interestingly, we can actually see that `pgha3` reports its visibility of `pgha1` as well. This means that if the witness node could still interact with the primary, the election would have been aborted at that point. The assumption here is that a transient network disruption occurred, and we would not want to promote `pgha2` under those circumstances. In this instance, we can see that all requirements for promotion have passed and that `pgha2` will begin the promotion step by executing whatever command is specified in the `promote_command` parameter.

We already discussed the script that manages the VIP in the previous recipe, where the VIP is moved to the new server before the node promotes itself. Assuming that things went as expected, we should see something like this:

```
NOTICE: promoting standby to primary
DETAIL: promoting server "pgha2" (ID: 2) using pg_promote()
NOTICE: waiting up to 60 seconds (parameter "promote_check_timeout") for promotion to complete
NOTICE: STANDBY PROMOTE successful
DETAIL: server "pgha2" (ID: 2) was successfully promoted to primary
[2019-11-26 15:29:56] [INFO] 1 followers to notify
[2019-11-26 15:29:56] [NOTICE] notifying node "pgha3" (ID: 3) to follow node 2
INFO:  node 3 received notification to follow node 2
[2019-11-26 15:29:56] [INFO] switching to primary monitoring mode
[2019-11-26 15:29:56] [NOTICE] monitoring cluster primary "pgha2" (ID: 2)
[2019-11-26 15:30:02] [NOTICE] new witness "pgha3" (ID: 3) has connected
```

What's interesting about the promotion process is that we not only observe more potential timeout areas but that the witness daemon automatically followed the rightly elected primary node. Remember, we're watching the logs on `pgha2`, which is the standby node being elected, not the witness node itself. Yet these messages are relevant from the perspective of the primary node since the witness plays a critical observational role, so it's important to know its status.

Speaking of the witness node, we should have a connection to that server from which we were also watching the state of the cluster as it evolved. At the end, when `pgha2` is the new primary, we should see the following as the final result of `repmgr cluster show`:

```
ID | Name  | Role    | Status    | Upstream | Location | Priority | Timeline | Connection string
---+-------+---------+-----------+----------+----------+----------+----------+------------------------------------------
1  | pgha1 | primary | - failed  |          | default  | 100      | ?        | host=pgha1 port=5432 dbname=repmgr user=repmgr
2  | pgha2 | primary | * running |          | default  | 100      | 4        | host=pgha2 port=5432 dbname=repmgr user=repmgr
3  | pgha3 | witness | * running | pgha2    | default  | 0        | 1        | host=pgha3 port=5432 dbname=repmgr user=repmgr

WARNING: following issues were detected
 - unable to connect to node "pgha1" (ID: 1)
```

We can see from this output that `pgha2` is the only running primary node. But why are there two primary nodes listed in this output? Until `pgha1` rejoins the cluster as a standby, it still is technically a primary node. Another way to look at the situation is that any node that is writable could be considered primary in nature, even if it's not the dedicated primary of the repmgr cluster itself.

This is why it's important to strictly control access paths to our PostgreSQL nodes. If any applications can connect directly to `pgha1`, they could erroneously insert data that would be lost unless we check before converting the node to a standby. To that end, we want to verify that the VIP properly relocated to `pgha2`.

The `ip` command reports all network devices and assigned addresses, and we can use the `show` operation to specifically find the VIP itself among those claimed on `pgha2`. To be safe, we would also want to repeat the command on `pgha1` in order to confirm that the VIP is not active there.

There's more...

Stopping PostgreSQL isn't the only way to test how failover systems work. One common method is to force a network break instead of a true outage. This helps to demonstrate how systems work when only one path of communication is disrupted.

For example, assuming that `pgha2` is using IP `10.0.30.2`, we could instruct `pgha1` to ignore all traffic from that location with a command such as this:

```
sudo iptables -A INPUT -s 10.0.30.2/32 -j DROP
```

Since network barriers such as this don't immediately break established connections, it may take some time to affect `pgha2`. Once it does, `pgha2` will attempt to trigger an election. However, there will be one critical difference in the result, as shown here:

```
[2019-11-26 17:40:53] [INFO] checking state of sibling node "pgha3" (ID: 3)
[2019-11-26 17:40:53] [INFO] node "pgha3" (ID: 3) reports its upstream is node 1, last seen 2 second(s) ago
[2019-11-26 17:40:53] [NOTICE] node 3 last saw primary node 2 second(s) ago, considering primary still visible
[2019-11-26 17:40:53] [INFO] 1 nodes can see the primary
[2019-11-26 17:40:53] [DETAIL] following nodes can see the primary:
 - node "pgha3" (ID: 3): 2 second(s) ago
[2019-11-26 17:40:53] [NOTICE] cancelling failover as some nodes can still see the primary
[2019-11-26 17:40:53] [NOTICE] election cancelled
```

This outcome is due to the fact that we enabled the primary_visibility_consensus parameter. If we had not done this, then repmgr would have considered a simple node majority sufficient to continue the election. In that case, pgha2 would have won and promoted itself.

As a result, we consider that parameter paramount in any production repmgr configuration. Had we omitted visibility consensus and continued, the cluster would have reflected two online and operational primary nodes! In fact, we believe the parameter should be enabled by default for this very reason.

In any case, when we are done testing, we can remove the firewall rule like this:

```
sudo iptables -D INPUT -s 10.0.30.2/32 -j DROP
```

Returning a node to the cluster

Any time one primary PostgreSQL node is superseded by another, either because of a crash or planned switchover, it becomes necessary to return the node to the cluster as a standby. This returns the cluster to a fully symmetric pair so that the node can operate as a candidate in future migration events.

Rather than manually using pg_rewind, rsync, or some other intervention method, repmgr has a dedicated command that should be sufficient for returning the cluster to fully operational status. This recipe will explain how to return a node to the cluster and what limitations there might be while doing so.

Getting ready

This recipe requires us to have a fully operational repmgr cluster. Please complete all recipes up to and including *Using an outage to test availability*. This means that pgha2 rather than pgha1 will likely be operating as the primary.

How to do it...

For the purposes of this recipe, `pgha2` will be our primary node, and the old primary will be `pgha1`. Follow these steps to reincorporate `pgha1` into the repmgr cluster:

1. If this wasn't a planned switchover event, check the PostgreSQL logs for any anomalies that could explain the outage. Likewise, gather forensic and diagnostic evidence, as this information will likely be destroyed once the node is reintroduced to the cluster.

2. If it is not already stopped, stop PostgreSQL on `pgha1` with this command on Debian-based systems:

   ```
   sudo systemctl stop postgresql@12-main
   ```

   Red Hat variants should use this command instead:

   ```
   sudo systemctl stop postgresql-12
   ```

3. Issue the following command on `pgha1` as `postgres` to test the rejoin process:

   ```
   repmgr node rejoin -h pgha2 -U repmgr -d repmgr --force-rewind
   --dry-run
   ```

4. If the output explains that prerequisites are met, repeat the previous command without the `--dry-run` option—for example:

   ```
   repmgr node rejoin -h pgha2 -d repmgr --force-rewind
   ```

5. Check the state of the cluster as the `postgres` user on any node:

   ```
   repmgr cluster show
   ```

How it works...

One thing we must remember before attempting to rejoin a node to the cluster is that doing so will necessarily eliminate potential diagnostic information from the node. In the event that `pgha2` becomes the primary because `pgha1` failed, we would want to investigate to gather information, and potentially try to recover data if there was evidence of a split-brain state.

Assuming that this is not the case, or that we've otherwise decided that the old primary is reusable, we must then ensure that PostgreSQL has been stopped. The repmgr rejoin process only works if PostgreSQL is not running. This is because several base files will require modification, and the `primary_conninfo` streaming parameter requires a service restart in any case. One call to `systemctl` later, and we're ready for the fun part.

To reintroduce an old primary to an established repmgr cluster, we only need to invoke the `repmgr node rejoin` operation. As with `standby clone` and `witness register`, we need to specify the upstream hostname (`-h`) and metadata database name (`-d`) in order to stream from the correct target. Remember, repmgr can manage tens or even hundreds of PostgreSQL nodes, and any may have become the primary since the rejoining node went offline. We need the latest information to safely join the cluster once more.

We also specify the `--dry-run` option to test the procedure before executing it. Similarly to `standby switchover`, it's always a good idea to test a dangerous command before you commit to executing it. As a rejoin process can modify the underlying files and reconfigures PostgreSQL, we definitely want to ensure that everything will work before we start making changes.

Here is an example of a successful dry run:

```
postgres@pgha1:~$ repmgr node rejoin -h pgha2 -d repmgr --force-rewind --dry-run

INFO: replication connection to the rejoin target node was successful
INFO: local and rejoin target system identifiers match
DETAIL: system identifier is 6762559643146339444
INFO: prerequisites for using pg_rewind are met
INFO: pg_rewind would now be executed
DETAIL: pg_rewind command is:
  /usr/lib/postgresql/12/bin/pg_rewind -D '/db/pgdata'
  --source-server='host=pgha2 port=5432 dbname=repmgr user=repmgr'
INFO: prerequisites for executing NODE REJOIN are met
```

This applies especially to our case since we've also decided to include the `--force-rewind` parameter. The `pg_rewind` utility was designed to essentially revert WAL changes, allowing a node to resynchronize with an upstream system without copying every single file. This is generally much faster than using `rsync` or some other data copy utility, but has certain prerequisites. It also means that we may only be able to perform the operation one time. Performing a dry run first suggests, but does not guarantee, that the rewind will likely succeed.

Assuming that the dry run was successful, a node rejoin should have very similar output, as shown here:

```
postgres@pgha1:~$ repmgr node rejoin -h pgha2 -d repmgr --force-rewind

NOTICE: executing pg_rewind
DETAIL: pg_rewind command is "/usr/lib/postgresql/12/bin/pg_rewind -D '/db/pgdata'
        --source-server='host=pgha2 port=5432 dbname=repmgr user=repmgr'"
pg_rewind: servers diverged at WAL location 0/E004F50 on timeline 5
pg_rewind: no rewind required
NOTICE: 0 files copied to /db/pgdata
NOTICE: setting node 1's upstream to node 2
WARNING: unable to ping "host=pgha1 port=5432 dbname=repmgr user=repmgr"
DETAIL: PQping() returned "PQPING_NO_RESPONSE"
NOTICE: starting server using "sudo systemctl start postgresql@12-main"
NOTICE: NODE REJOIN successful
DETAIL: node 1 is now attached to node 2
```

In this case, we didn't need to rewind at all because this was a controlled test where we gracefully stopped `pgha1`. This won't always be the case.

The last thing we want to do when everything is complete is to examine the state of the cluster. Again, we rely on `repmgr cluster show` for this and should see output similar to the following:

```
 ID | Name   | Role    | Status    | Upstream | Location | Priority | Timeline | Connection string
----+--------+---------+-----------+----------+----------+----------+----------+-------------------------------------------------
 1  | pgha1  | standby |   running | pgha2    | default  | 100      | 5        | host=pgha1 port=5432 dbname=repmgr user=repmgr
 2  | pgha2  | primary | * running |          | default  | 100      | 5        | host=pgha2 port=5432 dbname=repmgr user=repmgr
 3  | pgha3  | witness | * running | pgha2    | default  | 0        | 1        | host=pgha3 port=5432 dbname=repmgr user=repmgr
```

As expected, the cluster is operating with `pgha2` as the current primary node, and `pgha1` is seen as the sole standby system.

There's more...

There are limited circumstances where a node cannot be recovered, rewound, or rejoined. In these instances, it becomes necessary to essentially rebuild the node. When this happens, we can basically follow the procedure outlined in the *Cloning a database with repmgr* recipe to reintroduce the node to the cluster. If we're brave, we can even truncate the procedure to these commands as the `postgres` user on the failed node:

```
sudo systemctl stop postgresql@12-main
rm -Rf /db/pgdata
repmgr standby clone -h pgha2 -d repmgr
sudo systemctl start postgresql@12-main
```

In past engagements, the author has even written scripts that attempt to use `node rejoin`, and if that command returns a nonzero exit code, it rebuilds the node, as shown previously.

In fact, it may be a good idea to wrap many of these recipe examples as scripts in any case. It's probably much easier to type `do_rejoin.sh` rather than the command offered in this recipe, provided that the script automatically derives the correct upstream and builds the expected command line. Sometimes it's the best way to ensure that optimal parameters are always specified, and helps us avoid accidentally typing in the wrong targets.

See also

The official repmgr site maintains the current documentation and goes into more depth on how these commands work. Please use these resources for more information:

- **repmgrd configuration**: `https://repmgr.org/docs/current/repmgrd-basic-configuration.html`
- **repmgr node rejoin**: `https://repmgr.org/docs/current/repmgr-node-rejoin.html`

Integrating primary fencing

An important concept of high availability is node fencing, or physically disabling or separating a node from the cluster under specific circumstances. A somewhat common related method of accomplishing this is to **shoot the other node in the head (STONITH)**.

We technically utilize an aspect of this in other recipes when we connect to the VIP in order to destroy it before establishing it on the local node. One critical flaw in STONITH is the assumption that it's possible to contact the remote system in order to disable it. This may not be possible in cases of network disruption, leaving us with no assurance that the remote primary is actually offline or otherwise disabled.

This is why version 4.4 of repmgr introduced a workaround for this scenario. It is now possible to specify a certain amount of connected child nodes (either standby or witness) must exist. The assumption here is that the primary can become isolated from a quorum amount of remaining nodes, and that those nodes will then elect a new primary. At that point, repmgr can invoke a script that is presumably designed to disable the node and thereby prevent a split-brain scenario.

This recipe will explain how to safely enable this mode of operation, and discuss other strengths that it can impart to a healthy repmgr-enabled HA cluster.

Getting ready

This recipe requires us to have a fully operational repmgr cluster. Please complete all recipes up to and including *Incorporating a repmgr witness*. This will ensure that a full cluster exists to demonstrate how quorum majority exclusion works.

How to do it...

For the purposes of this recipe, `pgha1` will remain our primary node, the standby will be `pgha2`, and the witness will be `pgha3`. Follow these steps on `pgha1` and `pgha2` unless otherwise specified:

1. Alter the `repmgr.conf` file and add the following parameter settings:

   ```
   child_nodes_connected_min_count = 1
   child_nodes_connected_include_witness = 'true'
   child_nodes_disconnect_command =
   '/usr/local/bin/repmgr_fence_node.sh'
   ```

2. Create a file named `repmgr_fence_node.sh` in /usr/local/bin with the following contents:

   ```
   #!/usr/bin/env bash

   VIP=10.0.30.50
   IFACE=eth0
   PATH=/usr/pgsql-12/bin:$PATH
   VIP_CONF="${VIP}/32 dev ${IFACE} label ${IFACE}:pg"

   sudo /sbin/ip addr del ${VIP_CONF}

   psql -c "UPDATE pg_database SET datconnlimit=0" postgres
   ```

```
sudo systemctl stop postgresql@12-main
exit 0
```

3. Mark the script as executable:

    chmod a+x /usr/local/bin/repmgr_fence_node.sh

4. Restart repmgr on Debian-based systems with this command:

    sudo systemctl restart repmgrd

5. Red Hat variants should use this command instead:

    sudo systemctl restart repmgr12

How it works...

This recipe essentially comes in two parts, consisting of three configuration changes and a management script. All of the configuration settings related to standby disconnection handling are prefixed with child_. There are several of these, but for a cluster of this design where there is one primary, one standby, and one witness, we only really need to modify three of them.

The first two parameters are fairly closely related. We begin by setting the child_nodes_connected_min_count option to 1, which reflects our desire for at least one node to always be connected to the primary. However, witness nodes are not considered part of this count unless we also enable the child_nodes_connected_include_witness option. In a cluster of three nodes, this means that either the standby or witness (or both) should be connected at all times.

Given maintenance and other common tasks, we would expect periodic node communication disruptions. Safe guidelines suggest that we should coordinate efforts to avoid disabling multiple nodes simultaneously. So in the case that both of the other nodes disconnect from the primary system, it should be relatively safe to assume that the other nodes are still operating, but are unable to communicate with the primary. In such an event, they would hold an election and promote the standby.

 Always use repmgr service pause to temporarily disable the repmgr daemon during maintenance work. This will prevent automated failover until the maintenance is complete and automation is resumed with repmgr service unpause.

The final parameter we must provide is `child_nodes_disconnect_command`, which, like `promote_command` or `follow_command`, specifies an arbitrary program or script to invoke when certain criteria are met. In this case, repmgr will execute the command if fewer than one child node is connected for over 30 seconds by default.

The script itself is relatively simple in our example. It begins by dismantling the VIP, thereby preventing connections through that resource. Because of the fact that it is possible to declare a VIP from anywhere, two or more nodes may be broadcasting availability for that address. By having the primary destroy its own VIP address, the only other possible source is the other standby node.

The script continues by manipulating the `pg_database` PostgreSQL catalog table and setting the `datconnlimit` column to `0` for all databases. The purpose of this is to disallow any connections except for superusers. This facilitates investigation of the node, including data extraction in case any transactions committed before the network split occurred. It also excludes applications or other connections from further introducing new data.

The final step that the script performs is to physically stop the PostgreSQL service. Again, this is a precaution that fulfills two goals: disconnect previously established connections and disallow PostgreSQL from ingesting any further data at all. We can't have a split brain if it's literally impossible to write to the old primary.

Once we mark the new management script as executable, the only remaining step is to restart the repmgr daemon with `systemctl`. The repmgr service will apply child monitoring once it restarts, but that won't be immediately evident from the log until we start disconnecting nodes.

A great benefit from the approach that we've used in this example is that any changes we make to the PostgreSQL configuration are immediately reverted once we execute `repmgr node rejoin` and add the old primary to the cluster once more. If the standby was unable to promote itself before communication was re-established, we can simply start the primary and execute the following SQL to restore the default connection limits:

```
UPDATE pg_database SET datconnlimit=-1;
```

Setting `datconnlimit` to `-1` means that there's no limit other than `max_connections`. We would also want to rebuild the VIP connection manually since it was removed without some other node taking over. A very easy way to do this is to manually invoke the `repmgr_promote_self.sh` command.

There's more...

If we use firewall rules, we can even watch the fencing process in action. In our cluster, the IP addresses `10.0.30.2` and `10.0.30.3` correspond to the standby and witness respectively. We can block all traffic from those nodes with these commands:

```
sudo iptables -A OUTPUT -s 10.0.30.2/32 -j REJECT
sudo iptables -A OUTPUT -s 10.0.30.3/32 -j REJECT
sudo iptables -A INPUT -s 10.0.30.2/32 -j REJECT
sudo iptables -A INPUT -s 10.0.30.3/32 -j REJECT
```

Then we would want to observe the primary's reaction by watching the log like this:

```
tail -f /var/log/postgresql/repmgr.log
```

After a few seconds, the primary will notice that communication to both the standby and witness is no longer possible. This is what the logs look will like at this point:

```
[2019-11-26 22:53:09] [NOTICE] witness node "pgha3" (ID: 3) has disconnected
[2019-11-26 22:54:10] [NOTICE] standby node "pgha2" (ID: 2) has disconnected
[2019-11-26 22:54:10] [NOTICE] 0 (of 2) child nodes are connected, but at least 1 child nodes required
[2019-11-26 22:54:10] [INFO] most recently detached child node was 2 (ca. 2 seconds ago),
                    not triggering "child_nodes_disconnect_command"
[2019-11-26 22:54:10] [DETAIL] "child_nodes_disconnect_timeout" set to 30 seconds
```

Once `pgha1` detects that `pgha2` and `pgha3` have disconnected, there's a chance that it could be outvoted by the remaining two nodes. The default child disconnection timeout is 30 seconds because that is half as long as the default necessary to elect a new primary. This ensures that `pgha1` will disable itself before another primary node exists in the same cluster.

Once the timeout elapses, `pgha1` decides that communication has been sufficiently disrupted and that it should invoke the disconnection script. We can see that decision and the result in the logs as well:

```
[2019-11-26 22:54:40] [INFO] most recently detached child node was 2 (ca. 32 seconds ago),
                    triggering "child_nodes_disconnect_command"
[2019-11-26 22:54:40] [INFO] "child_nodes_disconnect_command" is:
  "/usr/local/bin/repmgr_fence_node.sh"
[2019-11-26 22:54:41] [INFO] "child_nodes_disconnect_command" successfully executed
[2019-11-26 22:54:41] [ERROR] unable to determine if server is in recovery
[2019-11-26 22:54:41] [DETAIL]
FATAL:  terminating connection due to administrator command
server closed the connection unexpectedly
    This probably means the server terminated abnormally
    before or while processing the request.
```

Remember, one of the actions of the fencing script is to shut down PostgreSQL. This would mean that `repmgrd` can no longer perform checks on the database. This is as it should be, since we haven't yet investigated the situation.

If we do decide to start PostgreSQL again, we can take advantage of the fact that only superuser accounts are allowed to connect. This will help us investigate the node or export data if necessary before stopping it again and applying the *Returning a node to the cluster* recipe.

See also

The official repmgr site maintains the current documentation and goes into more depth on how these commands work. Please use these resources for more information:

- **Monitoring standby disconnections on the primary node**: https://repmgr.org/docs/current/repmgrd-primary-child-disconnection.html
- **repmgrd configuration**: https://repmgr.org/docs/current/repmgrd-basic-configuration.html

Performing online maintenance and upgrades

Once repmgr is in charge of a fully online PostgreSQL cluster consisting of multiple nodes, we need to account for server maintenance. Whether we need to apply a security patch to PostgreSQL or replace server hardware, it is inevitable that we will perform at least one switchover over the lifetime of the cluster.

What else must we consider when performing maintenance on a PostgreSQL cluster managed by repmgr? What about upgrading repmgr itself? This recipe will answer those questions to round off the chapter.

Getting ready

This recipe requires us to have a fully operational repmgr cluster. Please complete all recipes up to and including *Incorporating a repmgr witness*. We will need a working cluster to demonstrate various transient states and log messages.

How to do it...

For the purposes of this recipe, we will rely on the standard three nodes of pgha1 as the primary node, pgha2 as the physical standby, and pgha3 as the dedicated witness. Follow these steps to carry out maintenance on the repmgr primary server:

1. Begin by pausing the repmgr service on all nodes by executing this command as the postgres user on any system:

   ```
   repmgr service pause
   ```

2. Verify that all repmgr services are suspended by executing this command as the postgres user on any system:

   ```
   repmgr service status
   ```

3. As the postgres user on pgha2, invoke the following command to test the switchover process:

   ```
   repmgr standby switchover --siblings-follow --dry-run
   ```

4. Check the dry-run output for errors, and if all messages are successful, invoke the following commands to promote pgha2 to become the new primary:

   ```
   repmgr standby switchover --siblings-follow
   /usr/local/bin/repmgr_promote_self.sh
   ```

5. Check the cluster status as the postgres user on any node:

   ```
   repmgr cluster show
   ```

6. Perform the necessary maintenance on pgha1, including software upgrades, server reboots, and other items.
7. Test the rejoin process for pgha1 to the cluster with the following command as the postgres user:

   ```
   repmgr node rejoin -h pgha2 -d repmgr --force-rewind --dry-run
   ```

8. Check the dry-run output for errors, and if all messages are successful, rejoin pgha1 to the cluster:

   ```
   repmgr node rejoin -h pgha2 -d repmgr --force-rewind
   ```

9. Unpause the repmgr service on all nodes by executing this command as the `postgres` user on any system:

```
repmgr service unpause
```

10. Check the cluster status as the `postgres` user on any node:

```
repmgr cluster show
```

How it works...

Observant readers probably noticed that this recipe can essentially be summarized as a combination of the *Performing a managed failover* and *Returning a node to the cluster* recipes. In many ways, this is true; it's also the purpose here to emphasize the importance of pausing the repmgr service.

We can't state how important this is: always pause the repmgr daemons before executing potentially disruptive commands. The last thing we want is for the repmgr service to start trying to promote a node while we're tinkering with anything within the cluster. This could produce unexpected results, including service outages!

So after pausing the daemon, it's a good idea to verify that the daemons are paused. Sometimes network disruptions or other events may prevent the `pause` command from working normally. This is an example of a paused cluster that is otherwise functioning without error:

```
postgres@pgha3:~$ repmgr service status

 ID | Name  | Role     | Status      | Upstream | repmgrd | PID   | Paused? | Upstream last seen
----+-------+----------+-------------+----------+---------+-------+---------+--------------------
 1  | pgha1 | standby  |   running   | pgha2    | running | 7655  | yes     | 0 second(s) ago
 2  | pgha2 | primary  | * running   |          | running | 12074 | yes     | n/a
 3  | pgha3 | witness  | * running   | pgha2    | running | 22420 | yes     | 0 second(s) ago
```

Once we've established that repmgr will no longer interfere with our work, we can carry out the switchover. We've already mentioned in the switchover recipe that the `repmgr standby switchover` command should automatically pause the daemons by default; however, it's always a good idea to explicitly control some elements of cluster management—for example, we may not want a switchover if we are performing maintenance on the standby node. Pausing the service ensures that no matter what kind of work is required, the cluster is safe.

As such, we also changed our instructions slightly to always include the `--dry-run` argument. This allows us to verify that the switchover event should conclude without significant problems. A failed switchover could leave our cluster without a primary node, so it's important to dry run before executing the standard command that actually performs the transfer.

Since the `repmgr standby switchover` operation is a command-line action, and the repmgr service is disabled, we also need to manually move the VIP to the new node. Remember that the `repmgr_promote_self.sh` script is only invoked during an automatic failover, so this means that we must perform this task ourselves during maintenance.

Once pgha2 is promoted and the VIP is no longer running on pgha1, we can do whatever we want to the node. We can reboot it, install new hardware, upgrade software, or even totally replace the entire operating system. So long as we don't erase the PostgreSQL data and configuration files for repmgr, it should be possible to reconnect pgha1 to the cluster.

Having completed the maintenance, it will be time to rejoin the node to the cluster. As with the switchover, we test this procedure with `--dry-run` to avoid any unexpected complications. This isn't as critical as it is when performing a switchover, but it could save us from a time-consuming node rebuild in the case that pgha1 encounters rejoin problems that can't be resolved.

Finally, assuming that everything went smoothly, we can unpause the repmgr service and then check to make sure that the cluster appears healthy. While we have shown it at the end here, don't be afraid to run `repmgr cluster show` frequently to see the status of the cluster. One way to react quickly to a situation is to be highly familiar with the results. If we know what the cluster looks like at each point of our maintenance, we can avoid panic and costly or unnecessary lost time trying to decipher the status output.

There's more...

What about upgrading repmgr itself? It's important to understand that repmgr operates both as a PostgreSQL extension and as a piece of software that includes a management daemon. The procedure outlined here also applies to upgrading repmgr itself, but there's an important caveat.

Between major versions, from 4.4 to 5.0 for example, it's possible that incompatibilities may have been introduced that affect the PostgreSQL extension. When this happens, it becomes necessary to manually upgrade the extension within the repmgr metadata database. It can also only be done on the primary node since we must write to that database.

We can use the following steps to accomplish this goal:

1. Stop repmgrd on all nodes using systemctl.
2. Explicitly disable the repmgrd service to prevent restarting—for example:

   sudo systemctl disable repmgrd

3. Upgrade the repmgr packages on all nodes using yum, apt, make, and so on.
4. Restart PostgreSQL on each node. This will load the newest version of the repmgr shared library.
5. Connect to PostgreSQL on the primary node and execute this statement to commit any pending writes, thereby reducing service restart time:

   CHECKPOINT;

5. Restart PostgreSQL using systemctl to reload the updated shared library.
6. Connect to PostgreSQL on the primary and witness nodes as the postgres user to the repmgr database and execute this statement:

   ALTER EXTENSION repmgr UPDATE;

7. Use the following systemctl command to update the daemon service file:

   sudo systemctl daemon-reload

8. Re-enable the repmgr service with systemctl—for example:

   sudo systemctl disable repmgrd

9. Start repmgrd on all nodes using systemctl.

This procedure is outlined in more detail within the repmgr documentation, and is a bit different than what we explained in the recipe. This is because we're changing how repmgr itself works, and that can be more invasive than other kinds of maintenance because it operates with PostgreSQL itself.

This is the one exception where we must suffer a slight amount of downtime that can't be eliminated by switching to another node.

See also

The official repmgr site maintains the current documentation and goes into more depth on how these commands work. Please use these resources for more information:

- **repmgr service pause**: https://repmgr.org/docs/current/repmgr-service-pause.html
- **repmgr service unpause**: https://repmgr.org/docs/current/repmgr-service-unpause.html
- **repmgr standby switchover**: https://repmgr.org/docs/current/repmgr-standby-switchover.html
- **repmgr node rejoin**: https://repmgr.org/docs/current/repmgr-node-rejoin.html
- **Upgrading repmgr**: https://repmgr.org/docs/current/upgrading-repmgr.html

10
High Availability with Patroni

Patroni is a high-availability management software developed by Zalando for orchestrating and automating several aspects of a PostgreSQL cluster. Unlike repmgr, it requires a series of other components and interacts with them as a series of layers to produce the end result of high availability.

We learned how to manage access and abstraction in `Chapter 4`, *Proxy and Pooling Resources*. `Chapter 7`, *PostgreSQL Replication*, took us even further, giving us the necessary tools to maintain a veritable army of alternative servers for primary substitution at a moment's notice. Much of what we discussed while describing a repmgr-driven cluster, is that Patroni takes the last few steps necessary to automate failover and other elements of a healthy PostgreSQL cluster.

In this chapter, we will learn how to build a quick, yet adaptable, high-availability stack to keep our PostgreSQL servers online. In order to do that, we will cover the following recipes:

- Preparing systems for the stack
- Installing and configuring etcd
- Installing and configuring HAProxy
- Installing and configuring Patroni
- Performing a managed switchover
- Using an outage to test availability
- Returning a node to the cluster
- Adding additional nodes to the mix
- Replacing etcd with ZooKeeper
- Replacing etcd with Consul
- Upgrading while staying online

Before we dive into the recipes, let's learn a bit more about Patroni and its assistant components of HAProxy and etcd.

Understanding more about Patroni and its components

The reason Patroni works as a series of software layers is to reduce the reliance on any single point of failure. There's always a consensus management element and a pooling resource. Each portion of the stack is designed to operate on all candidate servers. Due to this, we no longer need to rely upon a virtual IP address or **Canonical Name Record** (**CNAME**) that must be reassigned to a promoted replica.

In the end, Patroni should deliver a cluster with the following capabilities:

- It can automatically elect a replacement in the case of failover.
- It can redirect write-capable connections to a newly elected primary node.
- Newly provisioned nodes can add themselves to the cluster.
- Recovered primary nodes can rejoin the cluster as replicas.

Luckily, our new stack is capable of satisfying all of those requirements.

Why HAProxy?

Part of improving our stack is to understand its weaknesses. Even our repmgr design called for the use of a virtual IP address. The primary complication here is that a virtual IP can be declared from anywhere and, if not properly managed, can lead to a split-brain scenario.

HAProxy doesn't have that limitation because every IP address acts as if it were the primary node. So, as long as we connect through the proxy port we choose during configuration, we're communicating with whichever node is the primary at that specific moment. HAProxy acts as a routing layer, rather than a single floating resource.

Why etcd?

In order to build our stack, we will need a reliable message-passing layer. Some enterprising students at Stanford University came up with a consensus algorithm, which they named **Raft**. There's a lot of theory regarding how it works, but the end result is that a key-value pair stored within a Raft-based layer remains internally consistent across all servers and is generally resistant to network partitions and split-brain. Unlike repmgr, which implements the algorithm directly, Patroni makes this a modular component.

The default software Patroni uses for Raft is **etcd**. This is crucially important because we will be using etcd to store the location of the primary Postgres server. Provided we have a service that can connect to etcd, any one of our Postgres servers will immediately know the location of the primary system. This makes it trivial to alter replication sources when the primary system changes.

Why Patroni?

Patroni is the glue that binds these pieces together. It acts as a master coordinator and serves a number of roles. This is the process it uses on every PostgreSQL server:

1. It checks for the presence of an existing primary server in the Raft layer.
2. If no primary server is found, it inserts a key in the Raft layer claiming the primary role.
3. If this server is the primary, it signals the HAProxy layer to use it as the new redirection target.
4. If a primary server is found, it performs several checks and attempts to transform the current server into a replica.

Patroni repeats these steps every few seconds on every server where it is installed. As a consequence, some outages may result in race conditions where multiple replicas will attempt to become the new primary server. The Raft layer ensures that only one will win this race, and Patroni takes care of the rest.

This also allows each Postgres server to operate independently, so there is no single point of failure. Since replicas redirect themselves to the new primary server in parallel, the whole cluster becomes a self-healing swarm.

The stack

By the time we're finished with this chapter, our complete architecture diagram will be far different from what we might normally expect:

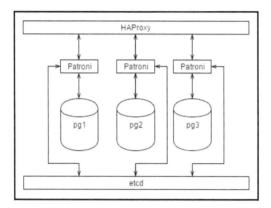

We can see that each Patroni element only communicates with its own local Postgres instance. It also communicates with etcd and HAProxy in order to maintain the cluster in a healthy state. Because each of these vertical elements operates independently, we could continue adding Postgres nodes with managing Patroni elements almost indefinitely.

But first, we have to build it.

You can refer to the following links for more information:

The Raft Consensus Algorithm: https://raft.github.io/
HAProxy: http://www.haproxy.org/
etcd: https://github.com/coreos/etcd
Patroni: https://github.com/zalando/patroni

Preparing systems for the stack

Patroni, etcd, and HAProxy have a number of dependencies that they need to function. Most of these can be easily obtained, so the amount of work in this recipe should be relatively minimal.

Let's get this part done so that we can proceed to the really interesting stuff!

Getting ready

This recipe depends on a few potentially supplementary packages that are missing from many Linux distributions. Red Hat-based systems need to install the EPEL package for the appropriate Red Hat platform from the following URL:
`https://fedoraproject.org/wiki/EPEL`.

Users of Debian-based distributions should be able to follow this recipe as written.

How to do it...

For this recipe, we will need at least three PostgreSQL servers. For demonstration purposes, we'll assume they are named `pgha1`, `pgha2`, and `pgha3`. Follow these steps on all three servers:

1. Debian-based systems should use the `apt-get` command to install as many distribution-provided packages as possible:

   ```
   sudo apt-get install python3-psycopg2 python3-pip python-yaml
   ```

2. Red Hat-based systems will need to substitute this `yum` command instead:

   ```
   sudo yum install python3-psycopg2 python3-pip PyYAML
   ```

How it works...

We begin by ensuring multiple popular libraries are available. After following so many recipes in this book, it's extremely likely that many (or even all) of these libraries are already installed. That said, it never hurts to be certain!

First in the list is Python's `psycopg2` Postgres interface layer. Patroni uses this to connect to Postgres for various operations, and, because it is so commonly used, it's already packaged by our distribution. Python libraries tend to evolve extremely quickly, so this isn't always possible.

Next, we install `pip`, a Python-specific installation utility that can download and install Python packages from the **Python Package Index** (**PyPI**). This is very similar to the PostgreSQL Extension Network, but for popular Python packages. We'll need it to continue with this recipe as well as Patroni's own installation routine.

YAML stands for **Yet Another Markup Language**. It's a format that some projects use to define configuration files. Patroni happens to be among these projects. The Python API that interacts with these files is actually named PyYAML, but Debian-based systems rename it to `python-yaml` to fit their chosen naming scheme. Red-Hat systems tend to use the provided package name.

With all of these elements installed, we should be able to construct the rest of the stack fairly easily.

See also

- **psycopg2**: `http://initd.org/psycopg/`
- **PyPI**: `https://pypi.org/`
- **PyYAML**: `https://pyyaml.org/`

Installing and configuring etcd

In order for Patroni to reliably determine or define the identity of the primary PostgreSQL instance, we need a distributed key-value layer. In this recipe, we'll be installing etcd to fulfill that role.

The etcd maintainers appear to have designed it to operate primarily in nameless virtual containers. This means that we just need to download it and place some binaries in appropriate locations. It's not an ideal installation with reliable configuration files and other expected components, but that's easily rectified if we decide to rely on etcd in the long term.

So, let's get started.

Getting ready

The `etcd` service does seem to be a commonly provided package in many Linux distributions, but it commonly lags behind the latest patches. The project itself moves rapidly as well; in fact, the version changed four times while this book was being written. As such, we recommend obtaining the latest stable release provided at `https://github.com/etcd-io/etcd/releases`.

While we will use 3.3.18 as the version number in our instructions, don't worry if the version you use is slightly different.

How to do it...

For this recipe, we will need at least three PostgreSQL servers. For demonstration purposes, we'll assume they are named pgha1 (10.0.30.1), pgha2 (10.0.30.2), and pgha3 (10.0.30.3). Follow these steps on all three servers except where indicated:

1. Extract the files in the etcd binary distribution and install the necessary files with the following commands as a root-capable user:

   ```
   tar -xf etcd-v3.3.18-linux-amd64.tar.gz
   sudo cp etcd-v3.3.18-linux-amd64/etcd* /usr/local/bin
   ```

2. Create a storage directory for etcd with these commands as a root-level user:

   ```
   sudo mkdir /db/etcd
   sudo chown postgres:postgres /db/etcd
   ```

3. Create a file named /etc/etcd.conf on the pgha1 server with the following content:

   ```
   name: pgha1
   data-dir: /db/etcd
   initial-advertise-peer-urls: http://pgha1:2380
   listen-peer-urls: http://0.0.0.0:2380
   listen-client-urls: http://0.0.0.0:2379
   advertise-client-urls: http://pgha1:2379
   initial-cluster:
   "pgha1=http://pgha1:2380,pgha2=http://pgha2:2380,pgha3=http://
   pgha3:2380"
   ```

4. Create a file named /etc/etcd.conf on the pgha2 server with the following content:

```
name: pgha2
data-dir: /db/etcd
initial-advertise-peer-urls: http://pgha2:2380
listen-peer-urls: http://0.0.0.0:2380
listen-client-urls: http://0.0.0.0:2379
advertise-client-urls: http://pgha2:2379
initial-cluster:
"pgha1=http://pgha1:2380,pgha2=http://pgha2:2380,pgha3=http://
pgha3:2380"
```

5. Create a file named /etc/etcd.conf on the pgha3 server with the following content:

```
name: pgha3
data-dir: /db/etcd
initial-advertise-peer-urls: http://pgha3:2380
listen-peer-urls: http://0.0.0.0:2380
listen-client-urls: http://0.0.0.0:2379
advertise-client-urls: http://pgha3:2379
initial-cluster:
"pgha1=http://pgha1:2380,pgha2=http://pgha2:2380,pgha3=http://
pgha3:2380"
```

6. Start the etcd daemon by executing this command as the postgres user:

```
etcd --config-file /etc/etcd.conf
&>/var/log/postgresql/etcd.log &
```

7. As the postgres user on pgha2 and pgha3, execute the following command but replace NUM with the node number:

```
ETCDCTL_API=3 etcdctl put ha-cookbook-NUM "Hello World!"
```

8. As the postgres user on pgha1, execute the following command:

```
ETCDCTL_API=3 etcdctl get ha-cookbook-1 ha-cookbook-9
```

How it works...

We start by downloading and installing etcd so that we have a distributed communication layer for Patroni to use. The file we download should contain the documentation as well, but we only need to install etcd and etcdctl. These two command-line utilities either launch etcd or send it arbitrary instructions while it's running.

Much like PostgreSQL, etcd also uses a **write-ahead log** (**WAL**) for data durability. Therefore, we need a storage location for this WAL data. By default, etcd will create a subdirectory from where it was launched, which we don't really want if our intent is to establish and interact with the same etcd cluster every time.

Now, we must configure etcd on all of the PostgreSQL servers that comprise the Patroni cluster. We start by naming the node with the `name` parameter, and then define the WAL directory we discussed earlier with the `data-dir` parameter.

The `etcd` service maintains a peer-to-peer network for nodes to communicate among themselves. By default, this network operates on port `2380` on each node where etcd is running, but we want to explicitly state the hostname to ensure that we can accept outside connections. The `initial-advertise-peer-urls` setting defines the name and port that other etcd nodes should use when communicating with this system.

Likewise, the `listen-peer-urls` parameter provides an analogous behavior by defining which host and port to monitor for connections. Essentially, we're binding to local resources in this case, and, according to the documentation, it's not valid to specify a hostname here. So, we've used `0.0.0.0` in order to bind to any addresses used by the host where etcd is running. This should be fine as long as no other services are using port `2380`.

Beyond internal communications, clients usually connect to etcd on port `2379` to store and retrieve key-value pairs. By setting the `listen-client-urls` parameter to listen on both the node name and `0.0.0.0`, we've ensured Patroni can set values locally, and any node in the cluster can also communicate with etcd in case their local etcd service is unavailable. Similarly to peer advertisement, each node announces itself with the value in the `advertise-client-urls` parameter, so we use the node name for external communication.

Finally, we can launch the etcd service itself and redirect its output to a log file. Normally, etcd operates explicitly through command-line flags or environment variables, but these are somewhat inconvenient compared to the stability of a configuration file. Therefore, we set the --config-file flag to our /etc/etcd.conf file to prevent that behavior.

To prove everything went as expected, and that the keys set in one node are available on all nodes, we used etcdctl to set a value. The reason we also set the ETCDCTL_API environment variable to 3 is due to the fact that etcdctl is only compatible with the version 2 API by default. We wanted to specifically demonstrate that the get parameter can fetch a whole range of keys if we so desire. Here's what the get output should look like on pgha1:

```
postgres@pgha1:~$ ETCDCTL_API=3 etcdctl get ha-cookbook-1 ha-cookbook-9

ha-cookbook-2
Hello World
ha-cookbook-3
Hello World
```

There's more...

We don't provide a standard Linux init script to control the etcd service because most Linux distributions have migrated to systemd as a service control mechanism. If we wanted to control etcd in this way, we would create a file named etcd.service in the /etc/systemd/system directory with the following content:

```
[Unit]
Description=etcd key-value store
Documentation=https://github.com/etcd-io/etcd
After=network.target

[Service]
User=postgres
Type=notify
ExecStart=/usr/local/bin/etcd --config-file /etc/etcd.conf
Restart=always
RestartSec=10s
LimitNOFILE=40000

[Install]
WantedBy=multi-user.target
```

Then, we could enable, start, and stop etcd using the following `systemctl` commands:

```
sudo systemctl enable etcd
sudo systemctl start etcd
sudo systemctl stop etcd
```

Additionally, our log output would be available via the `journalctl` command:

```
journalctl -u etcd
```

This is much easier than the old process of writing a shell script to manage these actions. Consider using this approach for other services or daemons installed in the recipes of this book.

See also

The etcd configuration flags: `https://etcd.io/docs/v3.4.0/op-guide/configuration/`

Installing and configuring Patroni

Patroni is the primary coordinating component of our stack. As we can see from diagram in The *stack* subsection, it is involved in every element of the stack to some degree. Although it ties all of the stack elements together, we're installing it next specifically because of how tightly it integrates with the key-value layer and PostgreSQL.

If a PostgreSQL server is already running, Patroni will adopt it. If not, Patroni will create a new instance based on how it's configured. We've already established that the key-value store distributes the same information across the entire cluster, so the first established server also becomes the primary node for the cluster. Any subsequent Patroni instance will start as, or transform itself into, a replica.

This means that it's critically important to get this part right. So, pay special attention to this recipe!

Getting ready

This recipe depends on multiple libraries and services. Please follow the *Preparing systems for the stack* and *Installing and configuring etcd* recipes before continuing.

While some distributions make Patroni available, including PGDG, distribution packages are not yet consistent. As of writing this book, the latest version of Patroni is 1.6.3, which released on December 5th, 2019.

The latest version of Patroni should be available for installation using the `pip` utility. However, some of the requirements to run Patroni are not listed. Therefore, we recommend downloading and extracting the source for the `requirements.txt` file it contains. The latest release can be found at `https://github.com/zalando/patroni/releases`.

Extract the package and note the `requirements.txt` file we will use in the recipe.

How to do it...

For this recipe, we will need at least three PostgreSQL servers. As before, we'll assume they are named `pgha1`, `pgha2`, and `pgha3`, all of which exist on the `10.0.30.x` subnet. Follow these steps on all three servers except where indicated:

1. Use `pip` to install Patroni by running the following commands as a root-capable user:

```
sudo pip3 install -r /path/to/requirements.txt
sudo pip3 install patroni
```

2. Execute this command to find where the PostgreSQL binaries are stored:

```
pg_config --bindir
```

3. Now, create a configuration directory for Patroni, which is owned by the `postgres` user:

```
sudo mkdir /etc/patroni
sudo chown postgres:postgres /etc/patroni
```

4. As the `postgres` user, continue by creating a file named `stampede.yml` in the `/etc/patroni` directory with the following content. Replace all instances of `pgha1` with the appropriate server name on each node:

```
scope: stampede
name: pgha1

restapi:
  listen: pgha1:8008
  connect_address: pgha1:8008

etcd:
  host: pgha1:2379

bootstrap:
  dcs:
    ttl: 30
    loop_wait: 10
    retry_timeout: 10
    maximum_lag_on_failover: 1048576
    postgresql:
      use_pg_rewind: true
      use_slots: true
      parameters:
        wal_level: logical
        wal_log_hints: "on"

  initdb:
  - encoding: UTF8
  - data-checksums

  pg_hba:
  - host replication rep_user 10.0.30.1/24 md5
  - host all 10.0.30.1/24 md5
  - host all 10.0.30.1/24 md5

  users:
    admin:
      password: adminpass
      options:
        - createrole
        - createdb

postgresql:
  listen: pgha1:5432
  connect_address: pgha1:5432
  data_dir: /db/pgdata
```

```
bin_dir: [VALUE FROM STEP 2]
pgpass: /tmp/pgpass0
authentication:
  replication:
    username: rep_user
    password: newpass
  superuser:
    username: postgres
    password: newpass
parameters:
  unix_socket_directories: '/var/run/postgresql'
  external_pid_file: '/var/run/postgresql/12-main.pid'
  logging_collector: "on"
  log_directory: "/var/log/postgresql"
  log_filename: "postgresql-12-main.log"
```

5. As the `postgres` user, modify the readability of the `stampede.yml` file with this command:

```
chmod 600 /etc/patroni/stampede.yml
```

6. Starting with `pgha1`, execute the following command as the `postgres` user to start Patroni on each server:

```
patroni /etc/patroni/stampede.yml \
        &> /var/log/postgresql/patroni.log &
```

How it works...

As with all good recipes, we begin with the primary ingredients. Several projects written with Python are often distributed via PyPI and the associated `pip` installation tool. If we invoke `pip3` (for Python version 3) with the `install` parameter, we should be able to obtain any software available in the package index. We're particularly interested in the `patroni` and `patronictl` utilities, as well as the associated requirements.

This is why we recommended downloading the Patroni source. Patroni is somewhat terse with its exception handling, and rather than explain a missing dependency, it simply fails and emits a jumbled heap of debug output. To avoid this, we simply install all the basic requirements as defined by the source, even if this is more than we may strictly need.

Then, we need to locate the PostgreSQL binaries, and the easiest way to do that is to invoke the `pg_config` utility with the `--bindir` parameter. This is especially necessary if we're using a Linux distribution that has a nonstandard binary directory that might affect a cluster operation. We will be using this value later in the configuration file, so keep it for later.

> Debian-based distributions will likely use `/usr/lib/postgresql/[version]/bin` as the binary path, while Red Hat-variants will use `/usr/pgsql-[version]/bin` instead. Try to use these first to save some time.

Our next job is to create a configuration file for Patroni. This file will define how a new cluster definition is initialized, the current operation parameters, and the existing structure of the `patronictl` command-line tool. We start by creating a file named `stampede.yml` in the `/etc/patroni` directory and ensure it's owned by the `postgres` user. This allows us to potentially add password information and ensure it remains confidential and secure within our cluster.

This configuration file is defined in YAML format and can be considered in five distinct sections. We define the cluster and node name in the first section. We chose the name `stampede` due to its relation to the PostgreSQL mascot, but feel free to choose something better suited to the cluster's purpose. The node name should reflect the name of the server to keep things simple, but, again, this is not a requirement.

> Anywhere you see `pgha1` in the configuration file, remember to change it to `pgha2`, `pgha3`, and so on, on each system. This file needs to be distinct for each PostgreSQL instance being managed by Patroni, and we've elected to have one Patroni + instance pair per server.

In the `restapi` section, we define two parameters. We set `listen` to `pgha1:8008` so Patroni watches port `8008` on the named node. This URL can be used to obtain or define configuration information, or for determining the current primary server. We set `connect_address` to the same value so that Patroni can access its own REST API if necessary. These parameters are distinct in case of scenarios where they must differ, but in most cases this isn't necessary.

After `restapi` is the `etcd` section. This is where we define the location of our key-value store. Due to its relative simplicity, we're only required to set the `host` parameter to `pgha1:2379`, the same client interface and port we defined for etcd.

Next, we define the `bootstrap` section, and it contains several sub-elements. All of the parameters we define within these subsections are used to initialize a new cluster. If we attach Patroni to an existing PostgreSQL instance, only the `dcs` section remains relevant and is saved to the key-value store for further use.

The `dcs` portion corresponds to the cluster definition. We begin by setting `ttl` to `30`, meaning the primary node must reclaim its status every 30 seconds, or potentially trigger a failover to another node. By setting `loop_wait` to `10`, a replica should notice a missing master in 10 seconds or less. Setting the `retry_timeout` parameter to `10` essentially prevents stalled connections during operations, that is, if the servers vanish due to network issues. And finally, we set `maximum_lag_on_failover` to the byte equivalent of 1 MB, which is a minimum threshold that replicas must satisfy before being considered failover candidates.

After the basic `dcs` elements, we define how PostgreSQL is handled by Patroni. If we're using PostgreSQL 9.5 or higher, we can set `use_pg_rewind` to `true` as a faster method for transforming a former primary into a new replica without the need for a data resync. We also recommend using replication slots in PostgreSQL 9.4 and greater when possible to prevent irrecoverable replica lag, and setting `use_slots` to `true` makes that explicit to Patroni.

The `parameters` subsection is merely a series of values commonly found in `postgresql.conf`. Versions of PostgreSQL older than 12 can also specify a `recovery_conf` section, which corresponds to the `recovery.conf` file used to define replica recovery operations. These are specifically supplementary values, meaning we only add them if we want to override Patroni defaults or define any configuration elements we consider to be critical to the cluster operation. Normally, we would restrict such additions to replication requirements, or for necessary WAL file management.

After the `dcs` section comes the `initdb` section, which is basically used to handle parameters to PostgreSQL's `initdb` utility. In this case, we've elected to enable data checksums and ensure a newly initialized database uses the `UTF8` character encoding. Specifying this latter value may not seem necessary, but we've encountered `ASCII` encoded databases, and it's very difficult to fix these once they're established. This can sometimes happen if the machine's locale is not properly bootstrapped, as is sometimes the case in Docker or LXC containers.

Then there's a pg_hba section for additional entries in newly created pg_hba.conf files. In this case, we've elected to allow the rep_user account to utilize the replication pseudo-database, and all other accounts can connect within our limited subnet. This is where you would place any necessary pg_hba.conf entries for the basic cluster operation within an application stack.

Next, we have the users section, where we may create as many user accounts for a newly instantiated cluster as we need. In our case, we opted for a single admin account with the ability to generate further roles and databases. This section is also the reason we want the file to be owned by the postgres system user. We want as little password exposure as possible!

The last section in the configuration file is postgresql, which determines the operating state of each local PostgreSQL instance. Like the restapi section, this also has listen and connect entries for defining connection targets. This is also where we define data_dir as the PostgreSQL data may reside in different locations on each server.

The reason we set bin_dir explicitly to the full path of the PostgreSQL binaries is due to the possibility of servers hosting multiple PostgreSQL versions, or using nonstandard installation directories. This is where we use the value we obtained with pg_config earlier.

The pgpass and authentication sections essentially go together. The first defines a location for a temporary password file, and the second declares both the replication and superuser. Since proper authentication is necessary for newly provisioned replicas to bootstrap themselves and begin replication, these sections ensure that the process always succeeds.

And finally, we can provide as many arbitrary postgresql.conf values in the parameters subsection as we desire. Unlike those within the bootstrap section, these are only applied to the instance the current Patroni node is managing. While not likely, there are occasions where certain nodes will require specific settings to function properly.

Fortunately, the Patroni configuration file is the most difficult part of using it. Once we make the configuration file readable only to the postgres user, we can start Patroni on each node bypassing the full path of the configuration file to the patroni command.

Even if the data directory of each new replica was completely empty, we should see something like this in the Patroni logs shortly after starting the service:

```
2019-12-08 22:32:33,663 INFO: Lock owner: pgha1; I am pgha2
2019-12-08 22:32:33,663 INFO: does not have lock
2019-12-08 22:32:33,663 INFO: establishing a new patroni connection to the postgres cluster
2019-12-08 22:32:33,703 INFO: no action.  i am a secondary and i am following a leader
```

This is because Patroni will use pg_basebackup to initialize new replicas that have no existing data.

There's more...

Once Patroni is installed, we can view the cluster status to understand how it's running. There are some additional modifications we can also make to better integrate Patroni with the operating system.

Cluster status

We can also view the full status of the cluster from any existing node. To do this, we need to pass the list parameter and the path to our configuration file to the patronictl command-line tool. We also need to specify which cluster we want information about. This is because there are multiple methods for obtaining cluster information.

If we use the -c parameter to detail a configuration file, our results should look like this:

```
postgres@pgha1:~$ patronictl -c /etc/patroni/stampede.yml list stampede

+----------+--------+-------+--------+---------+----+-----------+
| Cluster  | Member | Host  | Role   | State   | TL | Lag in MB |
+----------+--------+-------+--------+---------+----+-----------+
| stampede | pgha1  | pgha1 | Leader | running | 12 |           |
| stampede | pgha2  | pgha2 |        | running | 12 |         0 |
| stampede | pgha3  | pgha3 |        | running | 12 |         0 |
+----------+--------+-------+--------+---------+----+-----------+
```

The patronictl command also accepts the location of the distributed keystore system. So, we could get the same summary status by passing -d pgha1:2379 instead, for example.

We want to note that, in this example, pgha3 was the same node designated as our witness in Chapter 9, *High Availability with repmgr*. Such nodes are not streaming replicas; Patroni saw that this node was invalid and, as a result, rebuilt it. This is what Patroni was designed to do, that is, to automate as much as possible.

Better service management

As with etcd, we can manage Patroni via systemd if we create a file named patroni.service in the /etc/systemd/system directory with the following content:

```
[Unit]
Description=Patroni PostgreSQL Cluster Service
Documentation=https://github.com/zalando/patroni
After=etcd.service

[Service]
User=postgres
Type=simple
ExecStart=/usr/local/bin/patroni /etc/patroni/stampede.yml
Restart=always
RestartSec=10s
LimitNOFILE=40000

[Install]
WantedBy=multi-user.target
```

Note that we want to start after etcd, and that we set the Type field to simple, which indicates the patroni process should be running for the service to be considered active.

Then, we could enable, start, and stop etcd using these systemctl commands:

```
sudo systemctl enable patroni
sudo systemctl start patroni
sudo systemctl stop patroni
```

Additionally, our log output would be available via the journalctl command:

```
journalctl -u patroni
```

While there are legitimate complaints regarding how `systemd` handles certain elements, it's hard to argue against how quickly we integrated this service into our server. It's certainly cleaner than relying on `pkill` to stop Patroni, or using output redirection and `&` to fork a process manually.

 The remaining recipes in this chapter will assume that a `patroni.service` file is in place to encourage reliable cluster management.

See also

YAML configuration settings:
`https://github.com/zalando/patroni/blob/master/docs/SETTINGS.rst`

Installing and configuring HAProxy

The final element on the stack is HAProxy. Patroni uses this to redirect traffic to the primary read/write node in our PostgreSQL cluster. Technically, we don't strictly need this component since Patroni will operate without it. However, if we want the capability to always reach the primary node regardless of its location, then this recipe is essential.

This recipe will introduce HAProxy to act as a high-availability connection proxy for Patroni.

Getting ready

This recipe depends on some necessary libraries and services. Please follow the *Preparing systems for the stack* and *Installing and configuring Patroni* recipes before continuing.

If this is a Debian-based system, begin by installing HAProxy from the standard system repository with the `apt-get` command:

```
sudo apt-get install haproxy
```

For Red Hat-based servers, use an equivalent yum command:

```
sudo yum install haproxy
```

How to do it...

For this recipe, we will need atleast three PostgreSQL servers. As usual, we'll assume they are named pgha1, pgha2, and pgha3. In addition, assume that the IP address of pgha1 is 10.0.30.1. Follow these steps on all three servers except where indicated:

1. Create a file named haproxy.cfg in the /etc/haproxy directory with the following content:

   ```
   global
       maxconn 100

   defaults
       log       global
       mode      tcp
       retries 2
       timeout client 30m
       timeout connect 4s
       timeout server 30m
       timeout check 5s

   frontend ft_postgresql
       bind *:5000
       default_backend bk_db

   backend bk_db
       option httpchk

       server postgresql_pg1 pgha1:5432 check port 8008
       server postgresql_pg2 pgha2:5432 check port 8008
       server postgresql_pg3 pgha3:5432 check port 8008
   ```

2. If this is an older Debian-based system, set the ENABLED variable to 1 in the /etc/default/haproxy file.

3. Start HAProxy with the following command as a root-enabled user:

   ```
   sudo systemctl restart haproxy
   ```

4. Execute the following command as the postgres user on any node:

   ```
   psql -h localhost -p 5000 -c "select inet_server_addr();"
   ```

How it works...

HAProxy has a very powerful configuration syntax backed by hundreds of parameters. While this makes it quite versatile, trying to write a configuration file from scratch would be extremely difficult. In our case, the number of parameters we need to set is actually fairly minimal.

We start by setting the global connection limit to 100 connections. This is the number of connections HAProxy will manage before simply allowing them to queue in the kernel buffer. Generally, we would want to set this to the same value we use with `max_connections` in `postgresql.conf`, but it's not required.

Next, we set the `log` parameter to `global` so all HAProxy instances write to the same log output. HAProxy is an HTTP proxy system at heart, so we must ensure the `mode` parameter is set to `tcp` so HAProxy doesn't try to interpret the actual traffic.

After these essentials are set, we also define a number of connection retry and timeout values. These are all subject to usage patterns, so feel free to modify them to better fit your cluster needs. Of special note are the `server` and `client` timeouts, which will break the connection if either the client or the server is idle for over 30 minutes. We also set the `connect` timeout to 4 seconds so HAProxy doesn't wait forever to establish a connection. And finally, we set the `check` timeout to 5 seconds so that once a connection is established, it isn't alive much longer than necessary before being disconnected.

 Databases that commonly host persistent connections may need to greatly increase the `client` and `server` timeout values or set them to 0 in order to disable the feature altogether.

Once we've taken care of the default connection handling behavior, we must define the frontend and backend actions. On the frontend, HAProxy will be handling incoming connections, so we create a new frontend called `ft_postgresql`. Within this definition, we set `bind` to `*:5000` to listen to all of the available interfaces on port 5000. Then, we link the frontend to a backend that we'll name `bk_db`.

On the backend, HAProxy will be forwarding connections to our primary writable PostgreSQL server. To handle this, we create a new backend named `bk_db`, which we already referenced in the `frontend` configuration section. The only option we set here is `httpchk`, the method HAProxy should use to confirm server health.

All of the other lines in the `backend` section refer to one of our PostgreSQL servers. Each server line comes in three distinct sections. First comes the server name, then the host and port for the service, and finally further options for the definition. We chose rather boring server names such as `postgresql_pg1` to make it obvious what is expected.

Aside from the `host:port` combination for each server, we also defined `check port 8008`. This option tells HAProxy to connect to port `8008` to determine server health, and this is also where Patroni is performing some magic. When HAProxy connects to a server on port `8008`, it is actually connecting to Patroni.

Since each local Patroni node knows whether or not it is the primary system, HAProxy is actually asking each node whether or not it is the primary. It's an ingenious way to leverage a proxy health check. With these configuration values in place, any incoming connection to port `5000` on any HAProxy host will be forwarded to whichever server passed the backend health check. Due to this, there's no need for a virtual IP address or a CNAME definition; we'll always be sent to the correct system.

After restarting the `haproxy` service with `systemctl` on all of the cluster servers, it's a good idea to run a quick test to ensure that the proxy is working as expected. To do this, we connect to port `5000` on any server and execute the `inet_server_addr` function to obtain the IP address of the server we've contacted. Since this is the port HAProxy is monitoring, we should have been redirected to `pgha1` and get `10.0.30.1` as the result. A successful result should resemble this output:

```
postgres@pgha2:~$ psql -h localhost -p 5000 -c "select inet_server_addr();"

 inet_server_addr
-------------------
 10.0.30.1
```

See also

The HAProxy documentation: `https://cbonte.github.io/haproxy-dconv/`

Performing a managed switchover

Managing a Patroni cluster is relatively easy as long as it's operating normally. The primary reason for this is the provided `patronictl` command-line tool. Beyond simply displaying the cluster status, it also manages several other helpful operations.

In particular, we can use it to force the primary node to step down and allow one of the replicas to take its place. In a high-availability context, this is a great way to perform system upgrades. We merely need to switch to another primary, upgrade the old system, and repeat. We're done when every node is the latest PostgreSQL version. During this process, the database is never offline. This procedure also works for regular system maintenance.

This recipe will demonstrate the process to change the primary node using Patroni.

Getting ready

This recipe depends on the presence of the entire stack. Please complete all of the previous recipes in this chapter before continuing.

How to do it...

For this recipe, we should already have three PostgreSQL servers. As usual, we'll assume they are named `pgha1`, `pgha2`, and `pgha3`. If `pgha1` is the current primary, follow these steps to promote a different node to primary status:

1. Execute the following command as the `postgres` user to initiate a failover:

   `patronictl -d pgha1:2379 switchover stampede`

2. Answer the presented prompts as directed.
3. Wait a few seconds before running this command as the `postgres` user:

   `patronictl -d pgha1:2379 list stampede`

How it works...

We were serious when we said this recipe would be fairly simple. By calling `patronictl` with the `failover` parameter, we're telling it that we definitely want to promote another node to primary status.

The −d flag allows us to specify etcd as a configuration source and is usually the safer option since it should always reflect the current state of the cluster.

Our example targeted the pgha1 server on the etcd port of 2379, but we could have used any of the cluster systems. Since the distributed key-value system may play host to any number of clusters, we must also specify stampede as the name of the cluster we want to manage.

Once we invoke the failover command, Patroni asks multiple questions to verify the process to make absolutely certain before altering the cluster state. Most of these choices are defaults that do not require an answer. We could choose any one of the replicas to promote, but if we do not, Patroni will select one on our behalf.

After we confirm the final prompt, Patroni will present the status output like this:

```
2019-12-09 23:36:08.82135 Successfully switched over to "pgha2"
+----------+--------+-------+--------+---------+----+-----------+
| Cluster  | Member | Host  | Role   | State   | TL | Lag in MB |
+----------+--------+-------+--------+---------+----+-----------+
| stampede | pgha1  | pgha1 |        | stopped |    |   unknown |
| stampede | pgha2  | pgha2 | Leader | running | 12 |           |
| stampede | pgha3  | pgha3 |        | running | 12 |         0 |
+----------+--------+-------+--------+---------+----+-----------+
```

Note that pgha1 is now marked as stopped and pgha2 is the new cluster leader. This state is actually only temporary. We never removed pgha1 from the cluster, so Patroni will modify it to act as a replica. If we wait for a few seconds and check the cluster status with the list parameter to patronictl, we will see evidence of the transition:

```
+----------+--------+-------+--------+---------+----+-----------+
| Cluster  | Member | Host  | Role   | State   | TL | Lag in MB |
+----------+--------+-------+--------+---------+----+-----------+
| stampede | pgha1  | pgha1 |        | running | 13 |         0 |
| stampede | pgha2  | pgha2 | Leader | running | 13 |           |
| stampede | pgha3  | pgha3 |        | running | 13 |         0 |
+----------+--------+-------+--------+---------+----+-----------+
```

The procedure for reclaiming a previous master and converting it to a replica normally requires several commands. We would need to manually invoke pg_rewind or rsync, find the location of the new leader, modify recovery.conf, and restart the instance with pg_ctl. Patroni performs all of these steps automatically.

Patroni delivers a very hands-off self-healing approach that is actually fairly difficult to defeat, even on purpose. That's exactly what we want from a high-availability solution.

There's more...

We were not exaggerating when we said Patroni was difficult to defeat. If a system operator was ignorant of Patroni's presence, they might attempt to stop the PostgreSQL service with `pg_ctl` or some other system-level script. Upon noticing the outage, Patroni would immediately restart the database instance.

If the outage was on the primary node, Patroni would promote another node to leader status and begin the process of converting the old leader into a replica. It's extremely likely that this cycle will complete before the system administrator is able to even verify that the PostgreSQL service was stopped.

Patroni considers itself the true arbiter of the PostgreSQL systems it manages. So, the only way to actually prevent the comical scenario here is to temporarily defer cluster management. We can do that by invoking `patronictl` with the `pause` parameter, as shown in this command:

```
patronictl -d pgha1:2379 pause stampede
```

While paused, Patroni will not detect outages, invoke automated failovers, or enact any other kind of high-availability actions. To revert the cluster to its standard managed state, we would use the `resume` parameter, as shown in this command:

```
patronictl -d pgha1:2379 resume stampede
```

Using an outage to test availability

Every high-availability cluster must possess the capability to detect and route around server failures. Hardware faults, virtual instance crashes, mistyped commands, and any number of potential disasters lurk around every corner. The best way to determine the true resilience of our stack is to test it by breaking something.

This recipe will explore what happens when attacking Patroni directly.

Getting ready

This recipe depends on the presence of the entire stack. Please complete all of the recipes up to *Installing and configuring HAProxy* before continuing.

How to do it...

For this recipe, we should already have three PostgreSQL servers. As usual, we'll assume they are named `pgha1`, `pgha2`, and `pgha3`. If `pgha2` is the current primary, follow these steps to simulate a server failure:

1. Execute the following command as a root-enabled user on `pgha2`:

   sudo systemctl stop patroni

2. Follow the Patroni log on `pgha1` or `pgha3` with this command:

   sudo journalctl -u patroni

How it works...

This recipe relies on a dirty trick to avoid the long and irritating process of rebooting a server. The `patroni` daemon considers itself the solitary coordinator of the PostgreSQL service. Just as it will restart the PostgreSQL services that we stop without its permission, it will also stop the PostgreSQL service if we end the `patroni` service itself.

Since we set up Patroni as a system service, we can use the `systemctl` command to stop the `patroni` daemon. We need to stop Patroni on the server currently acting as the primary node. Without Patroni running on this server, the lock on the primary node pointer in the key-value layer will expire. Upon the next internal status iteration, both `pgha1` and `pgha3` will notice there's no registered leader and attempt to claim the position.

Only one node can win this race. If we invoke the `tail` command with the `-f` (follow) flag on either `pgha1` or `pgha3`, or both, we can actually watch the takeover. This is what it should look like on the new primary window:

```
2019-12-09 23:49:14,769 INFO: promoted self to leader by acquiring session lock
server promoting
2019-12-09 23:49:14,776 INFO: cleared rewind state after becoming the leader
2019-12-09 23:49:15,799 INFO: Lock owner: pgha3; I am pgha3
```

There's more...

Relying on the `tail` command is an old standby method that's frequently useful for watching logs. Unfortunately, we also need to know which server won the leadership race to know which logs to observe. We could use the `list` parameter for `patronictl`, yet the takeover process relies on several timeouts. The authors of Patroni considered this and added a `-w` flag to *watch* the command by running it upon a configurable interval.

This means we could observe the failover and takeover as it happened with a command like this:

```
patronictl -d pgha1:2379 list -w 5 stampede
```

Of course, this isn't really a novel feature. It's extremely likely that most Linux systems have the `watch` command installed, and it fills the same role. We could get the same result with this command:

```
watch -n 5 patronictl -d pgha1:2379 list stampede
```

Still, it's less typing. If we know about the `-w` flag, we're likely to use it when interacting with the `patronictl` command simply due to convenience.

Returning a node to the cluster

Recovering systems after a major crash or outage is not an enjoyable experience. We must reboot or restore one or more servers, perform forensics to determine the root cause of the failure, and attempt to repair or replace corrupt data files.

This is no less true on systems that rely on Patroni as their high-availability solution. However, Patroni automates the more annoying portions of recovering a damaged PostgreSQL database.

This recipe will show how to recommission a previously damaged or offline PostgreSQL node within a Patroni cluster.

Getting ready

This recipe depends on the presence of the entire stack. Please complete all of the previous recipes in this chapter before continuing.

We also need a broken server. The easiest way to do this is to break it ourselves. Execute these commands on any system to simulate an unrecoverable server crash:

```
pkill -9 patroni
pkill -9 postgres
find /db/pgdata -name '*r*' -o  -name '*0*' -delete
```

This will cause an unclean shutdown of both Patroni and PostgreSQL and remove several necessary files for the PostgreSQL service to operate.

How to do it...

For this recipe, we should already have three PostgreSQL servers. As before, we'll assume they are named pgha1, pgha2, and pgha3. Follow these steps to fix the broken system:

1. Remove the contents of the corrupt cluster by running the following command as the postgres user on the broken system:

    ```
    rm -Rf /db/pgdata
    ```

2. Start a new patroni daemon with this command as a root-enabled user:

    ```
    sudo systemctl start patroni
    ```

3. Follow the Patroni log with this command:

    ```
    sudo journalctl -u patroni -f
    ```

How it works...

Do, or do not; there is no try. If the system outage is serious enough, we do not know the full extent of the damage to system files. If our database was not initialized with file checksums, it might be weeks before the corruptions make themselves known. If a crashed server takes over as a primary before that happens, these corruptions could eventually be replicated to other systems.

It's safer to simply start from scratch. Therefore, our first step is to erase the
`/db/pgdata` directory itself. With no old files to lead Patroni astray, it will rebuild
the data by invoking `pg_basebackup` and configuring the instance that we specified
in `/etc/patroni/stampede.yml`. We can even watch this happen by following the
logs.

This is what we should see when recreating a node with an empty data directory:

```
2019-12-10 00:01:27,855 INFO: Lock owner: pgha3; I am pgha2
2019-12-10 00:01:27,868 INFO: trying to bootstrap from leader 'pgha3'
2019-12-10 00:01:33,964 INFO: replica has been created using basebackup
2019-12-10 00:01:33,966 INFO: bootstrapped from leader 'pgha3'
2019-12-10 00:01:34,617 INFO: postmaster pid=1106
2019-12-10 00:01:35,752 INFO: Lock owner: pgha3; I am pgha2
2019-12-10 00:01:35,752 INFO: does not have lock
2019-12-10 00:01:35,753 INFO: establishing a new patroni connection to the postgres cluster
2019-12-10 00:01:35,779 INFO: no action.  i am a secondary and i am following a leader
2019-12-10 00:01:35,810 INFO: Lock owner: pgha3; I am pgha2
```

This seems too easy, but that really is all we need to do. Erase the old data and start
Patroni. The simpler a procedure is, the more difficult it is to make mistakes. Once
that step is complete, we can utilize `journalctl` to follow the logs as the node is
rebuilt and rejoins the cluster.

There's more...

Of course, this process does not lend itself well to extremely large database
installations. Beyond a few hundred gigabytes, erasing all of the data and
resynchronizing is extremely time, network, and I/O intensive. For these scenarios,
we recommend a different technique. Before starting Patroni, we can manually
synchronize the data files with `rsync`.

These are the commands we might use when rebuilding `pgha2` from the contents of
`pgha1` if we have **Secure Shell (SSH)** keys in place:

```
psql -U rep_user -h pgha1 \
    -c "SELECT pg_start_backup('resync', TRUE);" postgres
rsync -av --delete-after postgres@pgha1:/db/pgdata /db
psql -U rep_user -h pgha1 -c "SELECT pg_stop_backup();" postgres
rm /db/pgdata/postmaster*
```

Some more experienced DBAs might recognize this as the *old* process for obtaining a
PostgreSQL backup before `pg_basebackup` became a standard utility. Though
somewhat antiquated by today's standards, there's really no replacement for `rsync` to
minimize the amount of synchronizing with an existing set of files.

We hope that PostgreSQL will eventually integrate partial file transfers into `pg_basebackup` so it's possible to *patch* a replica from a donor system. Until then, we always have `rsync`.

Adding additional nodes to the mix

Eventually, we may decide to expand our cluster of PostgreSQL servers to accommodate more traffic, further increase availability, or retire an old system. Once we've established an etcd + HAProxy + Patroni stack, how difficult is the process of adding further nodes?

We wish it were possible to follow the previous recipes and consider ourselves finished. Unfortunately, modifying an operating cluster stack requires a small amount of finesse. Luckily, the extra steps are somewhat minimal, and our reward is an adaptable architecture. Let's get started.

Getting ready

This recipe is somewhat unique. It depends primarily on the *Installing and configuring etcd*, *Installing and configuring Patroni*, and *Installing and configuring HAProxy* recipes. However, we must stress that they should not be followed exactly. The steps outlined here will explain necessary deviations, so pay close attention.

How to do it...

For the purposes of this recipe, we are going to be adding a new `pgha4` server to the stack. As in all of the other recipes, we already have `pgha1`, `pgha2`, and `pgha3` operating. Follow these steps to fully integrate `pgha4` into the cluster:

1. Follow the steps in the *Installing and configuring etcd* for `pgha4` until you are asked to start etcd, but do not start the service.
2. Execute the following command as the `postgres` user on any one of `pgha1`, `pgha2`, or `pgha3`:

```
etcdctl member add pgha4 http://pgha4:2380
```

3. Modify the `/etc/etcd.conf` configuration file on `pgha4` and make sure it includes these lines (take note not to copy line wrapping from the book here):

```
initial-cluster-state: existing
initial-cluster:
"pgha4=http://pgha4:2380,pgha1=http://pgha1:2380,pgha2=http://
pgha2:2380,pgha3=http://pgha3:2380"
```

4. Start the `etcd` daemon as a root-enabled user with the following command on `pgha4`:

`sudo systemctl start etcd`

5. Follow the steps in the *Installing and configuring HAProxy* recipe.
6. Modify the `/etc/haproxy/haproxy.conf` configuration file on all of the servers and ensure it includes this line in the `backend bk_db` section:

```
server postgresql_pg4 pgha4:5432 maxconn 100 check port 8008
```

7. Reload the `haproxy` daemon on all of the servers by executing the following command as a root-enabled user:

`sudo systemctl reload haproxy`

8. Follow the steps in the *Installing and configuring Patroni* recipe.
9. On any server, execute the following command as the `postgres` user to obtain the new cluster status:

`patronictl -d localhost:2379 list stampede`

How it works...

As with most things, we start at the beginning. To integrate a new node, we need to add each necessary component of the stack. In this case, etcd is the first, and most complicated, portion. Generally, we can follow the installation process as outlined in the *Installing and configuring etcd* recipe, but we absolutely *must not* start the `etcd` service just yet.

When we first bootstrapped etcd, we specified the `initial-cluster` parameter in the original configuration file. This parameter did not include `pgha4` when the cluster was established, so etcd will not acknowledge its attempts to join. We can modify the cluster definition by invoking the `etcdctl` command with the `member add` parameter. We only need to supply the name of the member and its peer connection information so that etcd knows how to connect to it.

Then, we need to add `pgha4` to the list of servers in the `initial-cluster` parameter in its own configuration file. This allows `pgha4` to join the cluster in a similar manner as the original members when it was newly established. The only difference is that we also need to set the `initial-cluster-state` parameter to `existing` so that the `etcd` daemon on `pgha4` joins the current cluster instead of creating a new one.

Once we've added `pgha4` to the `etcd` cluster in the proper way, it is safe to start the `etcd` service. After this, the remaining steps to integrating `pgha4` practically complete themselves.

> In circumstances where there is already a ring of consensus etcd servers, it may not be necessary to create local installations specifically for Patroni. Check with your infrastructure department to see whether they already have a key-value set of servers that Patroni can utilize. Then, we can skip the entire process up to this point.

To that end, we can install and configure HAProxy just as we did on the other nodes. We can even start the daemon without worry. It just won't connect to any services on the new node until we add the necessary `server` configuration line in the `backend bk_db` section of the configuration file on all nodes. Once we reload the `haproxy` service so it integrates the changes we've made to the configuration file, we're ready to complete the cluster expansion.

The easiest step is to install and start Patroni on `pgha4`. As we've learned from previous recipes, Patroni handles most of the difficult elements in bootstrapping a PostgreSQL server. It will connect to the current leader, create a new data directory by cloning the contents of the primary node, and automatically add it to the Patroni layer.

After Patroni is installed and running, we can view the current operational nodes bypassing the `list` parameter to `patronictl`. If everything went as expected, we should see this:

```
postgres@pgha4:~$ patronictl -d localhost:2379 list stampede

+-----------+--------+-------+--------+---------+----+-----------+
| Cluster   | Member | Host  | Role   | State   | TL | Lag in MB |
+-----------+--------+-------+--------+---------+----+-----------+
| stampede  | pgha1  | pgha1 |        | running | 16 |         0 |
| stampede  | pgha2  | pgha2 |        | running | 16 |         0 |
| stampede  | pgha3  | pgha3 | Leader | running | 16 |           |
| stampede  | pgha4  | pgha4 |        | running | 16 |         0 |
+-----------+--------+-------+--------+---------+----+-----------+
```

There's more...

The analogous process of adding a node to the cluster stack is to remove one. That procedure is considerably easier, in general. For example, we could execute these commands as a root-level user in order to remove pgha2 from our Patroni cluster:

```
sudo systemctl stop patroni
export MEMBER=$(etcdctl member list | grep pgha2 | cut -d ':' -f 1)
etcdctl member remove $MEMBER
```

Since the etcd layer is persistent across all nodes, pgha2 is permanently removed from all of them unless we add it again by following this recipe. Once Patroni is stopped and etcd no longer considers the pgha2 part of the key-value layer, we can safely recycle the server without worry.

We also need to remove references to pgha2 from the HAProxy configuration file, but that isn't critical.

Hopefully, you're making use of configuration management tools such as Ansible, SaltStack, Puppet, or Chef. In larger clusters, these types of management tools are essential for modifying configuration files and restarting services. With these tools, we could remove pgha2 from the HAProxy configuration file, transmit it to every node in the cluster, and restart the haproxy service without logging into each individual system. They also greatly simplify bootstrapping new servers with mostly configured software and settings based on predefined profiles.

See also

The etcd runtime reconfiguration: https://etcd.io/docs/v3.4.0/op-guide/runtime-configuration/

Replacing etcd with ZooKeeper

It's common for server stacks to already partially exist, often using components we don't have the privilege of choosing. Servers and related software can be around for years before we adapt them to our needs. Therefore, it's possible an infrastructure department already uses a distributed key-value storage system such as etcd for its own purposes.

ZooKeeper is one of these alternative key-value storage layers. Patroni is fully capable of utilizing this instead of etcd, provided we make some changes to how it is configured.

This recipe will explain how to leverage an existing ZooKeeper installation to our advantage!

 Please note that installing ZooKeeper itself is beyond the scope of this recipe. The intention here is to make changes to Patroni that make it compatible with an existing ZooKeeper installation. This can happen when an infrastructure already incorporates ZooKeeper, allowing us to leverage it as well. If there is no pre-existing set of ZooKeeper nodes, feel free to skip this recipe.

Getting ready

This recipe depends on the presence of the entire stack, as well as an existing installation of ZooKeeper. Please complete all of the recipes up to *Installing and configuring HAProxy* before continuing.

How to do it...

For this recipe, we should already have three PostgreSQL servers. As usual, we'll assume they are named pgha1, pgha2, and pgha3. If pgha1 is the current primary, follow these steps to switch to ZooKeeper:

1. Locate the myid file in the ZooKeeper configuration directory for each server. This is usually /etc/zookeeper/conf. It should contain a single-digit number. Keep this for reference.

2. Assuming the server number in myid corresponds to the server name we've assigned (pgha1 and so on), ensure the zoo.cfg configuration file on each server contains the following lines:

   ```
   server.1=pgha1:2888:3888
   server.2=pgha2:2888:3888
   server.3=pgha3:2888:3888
   ```

3. If necessary, reload the ZooKeeper configuration file with the following command:

   ```
   sudo systemctl reload zookeeper
   ```

4. Execute this command as a root-enabled user on all nodes to stop Patroni, ensuring the cluster leader is stopped last:

   ```
   sudo systemctl stop patroni
   ```

5. Remove these two lines from /etc/patroni/stampede.yml on each server:

   ```
   etcd:
     host: ...
   ```

6. Add these two lines to /etc/patroni/stampede.yml on each server:

   ```
   zookeeper:
     hosts: pgha1:2181,pgha2:2181,pgha3:2181
   ```

7. Beginning with the former leader (pgha1), start Patroni on all servers with this command:

   ```
   sudo systemctl start patroni
   ```

How it works...

Since these servers presumably already have ZooKeeper installed and configured, it's likely the configuration files reflect the settings we want. However, it's always a good idea to perform due diligence. This also gives us the opportunity to see the full list of available ZooKeeper servers as listed in the configuration file. It may mean there is a large constellation of additional systems available for our PostgreSQL cluster.

Of special note is the `myid` file. ZooKeeper can maintain a cluster of up to 255 nodes, and each is assigned an arbitrary number in this file. Our small sample setup can easily align these ID values to the server name we've assigned, but this is probably not the case in a real environment. Make special note of these ID values when checking the ZooKeeper configuration file for the `server.x` entries we need for our own uses.

If we modified the ZooKeeper configuration file, we need to reload the `zookeeper` service so that it incorporates our changes. Afterward, we must stop Patroni on all hosts where it is installed for our cluster. This is one of the rare instances where we have no choice but to accept downtime within our cluster. The key-value layer is a critical component to Patroni, and switching it requires temporarily disabling the entire stack.

Moving from etcd to ZooKeeper is actually fairly easy. We start by removing the etcd and associated `host` entries from the `stampede.yml` configuration file for the cluster. Then, we add equivalent lines for `zookeeper`, which requires the entire list of `hosts` in `host:port` format for the cluster.

Once we start Patroni, the alterations are complete and we are now using ZooKeeper as our key-value layer instead of etcd. We can verify this by examining the Patroni log output. Here's what the primary node logs should contain after it has been launched:

```
2016-11-13 14:57:11,164 INFO: Connecting to pg3:2181
2016-11-13 14:57:11,337 INFO: Zookeeper connection established, state: CONNECTED
2016-11-13 14:57:11,589 WARNING: Postgresql is not running.
2016-11-13 14:57:11,610 INFO: Lock owner: None; I am pg1
2016-11-13 14:57:11,611 INFO: starting as a secondary
2016-11-13 14:57:21,414 INFO: establishing a new patroni connection to the postgres cluster
2016-11-13 14:57:21,445 INFO: cleared rewind flag after becoming the leader
2016-11-13 14:57:21,860 INFO: promoted self to leader by acquiring session lock
```

There's more...

Since we changed the location of the key-value layer of our cluster, we should also alter the host:port value to the -d parameter when invoking the patronictl command. If we wanted to temporarily disable cluster management while relying on ZooKeeper, we could invoke this command on any node:

```
patronictl -d pgha3:2181 pause stampede
```

See also

The ZooKeeper Getting Started Guide:
https://zookeeper.apache.org/doc/current/zookeeperStarted.html

Replacing etcd with Consul

Consul is another key-value layer we can use instead of etcd. As with ZooKeeper, it's possible that an infrastructure department has already decided on the official software for several dedicated roles. If this is the case and Consul is the chosen key-value store within the company, it would be silly to maintain another without some overriding reason.

There may be reason to prefer one key-value layer over another, but that conversation is far beyond the scope of this book. Instead of initiating an argument on the finer points of leader election algorithms, let's convert our stack to Consul in place of etcd.

 Please note that installing Consul itself is beyond the scope of this recipe. The intention here is to make changes to Patroni that make it compatible with an existing Consul installation. This can happen when an infrastructure already incorporates Consul, allowing us to leverage it as well.

Getting ready

This recipe depends on the presence of the entire stack. Please complete all of the recipes up to *Installing and configuring HAProxy* before continuing.

How to do it...

For this recipe, we should already have three PostgreSQL servers. As usual, we'll assume they are named pgha1, pgha2, and pgha3. If pgha1 is the current primary, follow these steps to switch to Consul:

1. Execute this command as the postgres user on all nodes to stop Patroni, ending with the cluster leader:

```
sudo systemctl stop patroni
```

2. Remove these two lines from /etc/patroni/stampede.yml on each server:

```
etcd:
  host: ...
```

3. Add these two lines to /etc/patroni/stampede.yml on each server, remembering to substitute the proper server name:

```
consul:
  host: pgha1:8500
```

4. Beginning with the former leader (pgha1), start Patroni on all servers with this command:

```
sudo systemctl start patroni
```

How it works...

Unfortunately, our first order of business is to break the entire cluster. The key-value layer is essential to storing the cluster definition, as well as ensuring that only one PostgreSQL server ever wins the leadership race. It's one element that is not optional, and, as a result, we must shut down all of our Patroni instances in order to swap out all key-value references at once.

 While we suggest stopping the leader node last, this is not entirely essential. However, avoiding needless failovers is always beneficial to cluster health.

Next, we need to remove the etcd and corresponding `host` line from the Patroni `stampede.yml` configuration file. We can then add equivalent `consul` and `host` lines that inform Patroni to use Consul instead. It's important that we specify `8500` for the port element, as Patroni uses the HTTP protocol for all interactions. By default, Consul monitors port `8500` for incoming HTTP connections.

Our last step is to merely start the `patroni` service. Since we stopped the primary node last, we should start it before the others. It likely has the most up-to-date database state, and since we stopped all normal cluster operations, there's a slight chance the replica nodes are at least slightly behind the leader.

If we examine the Patroni logs after starting the `patroni` service, we should see something like this on the primary system:

```
2019-12-13 00:40:42,790 INFO: Lock owner: None; I am pgha1
2019-12-13 00:40:42,839 INFO: starting as a secondary
2019-12-13 00:40:42,845 INFO: Lock owner: None; I am pgha1
2019-12-13 00:40:42,845 INFO: not healthy enough for leader race
2019-12-13 00:40:42,864 INFO: restarting after failure in progress
pgha1:5432 - accepting connections
2019-12-13 00:40:43,197 INFO: establishing a new patroni connection to the postgres cluster
2019-12-13 00:40:43,244 INFO: promoted self to leader by acquiring session lock
server promoting
2019-12-13 00:40:43,250 INFO: cleared rewind state after becoming the leader
2019-12-13 00:40:44,267 INFO: Lock owner: pgha1; I am pgha1
```

Not very interesting, eh? Unlike etcd and ZooKeeper, Patroni doesn't tell us if it has connected to a Consul.io Raft cluster. We're not sure why this is, but we can still see that it has established a lock and promoted `pgha1` to be the cluster leader.

There's more...

Since we changed the location of the key-value layer of our cluster, we should also alter the `host:port` value to the `-d` parameter when invoking the `patronictl` command. If we wanted a list of cluster nodes from `pgha2` while relying on Consul, we would execute this command:

```
patronictl -d pgha2:8500 list stampede
```

See also

For more details on Consul, refer to the following links:

- **Consul – Bootstrapping a Datacenter**:
  `https://www.consul.io/docs/guides/bootstrapping.html`
- **Consul – configuration**:
  `https://www.consul.io/docs/agent/options.html`

Upgrading while staying online

We've all encountered this scenario: PostgreSQL recently released version 12.1 and we need to upgrade to protect ourselves from potential data corruption. Or perhaps it isn't PostgreSQL that requires an upgrade, but the system kernel or another critical element of the operating system.

Regardless of the reason, we must accommodate the procedure somehow. Upgrading software while remaining online is the ultimate aspiration of maintaining a high-availability stack. This recipe will demonstrate how we can reach that goal by leveraging Patroni's functionality.

Getting ready

This recipe depends on the presence of the entire stack. Please complete all of the recipes up to *Installing and configuring HAProxy* before continuing.

How to do it...

For this recipe, we should still have three PostgreSQL servers. As usual, we'll assume they are named `pgha1`, `pgha2`, and `pgha3`. If `pgha1` is the initial leader, follow these steps to perform an in-place system upgrade:

1. Start a status monitor on `pgha3` with the following command executed as the `postgres` user:

```
patronictl -d localhost:2379 list -w 5 stampede
```

2. Execute the following command on any node as the `postgres` user to initiate a switchover from pgha1 to pgha2:

```
patronictl -d localhost:2379 switchover \
    --master pgha1 --candidate pgha2 \
    --scheduled now --force stampede
```

3. Verify that pgha2 has assumed the cluster leadership role. The status screen should eventually resemble this output:

```
+-----------+----------+---------+----------+-----------+-----+-------------+
| Cluster   | Member   | Host    |  Role    |  State    | TL  | Lag in MB   |
+-----------+----------+---------+----------+-----------+-----+-------------+
| stampede  | pgha1    | pgha1   |          | running   | 28  |          0  |
| stampede  | pgha2    | pgha2   | Leader   | running   | 28  |             |
| stampede  | pgha3    | pgha3   |          | running   | 28  |          0  |
+-----------+----------+---------+----------+-----------+-----+-------------+
```

4. As a root-enabled user on pgha1, stop Patroni with this command:

```
sudo systemctl stop patroni
```

5. Perform any necessary upgrades to the system software, reboot the pgha1 server, or apply a minor PostgreSQL update.

6. When the upgrades are complete, start Patroni on pgha1 with the following command:

```
sudo systemctl start patroni
```

7. Verify that the `Lag in MB` column in the status report for pgha1 reaches 0.

8. Execute the following command on any node as the `postgres` user to initiate a switchover from pgha2 to pgha1:

```
patronictl -d localhost:2379 switchover \
    --master pgha2 --candidate pgha1 \
    --scheduled now --force stampede
```

9. Verify that pgha1 has resumed the cluster leadership role. As it was with the pgha2 switchover, it should show `Leader` under the `Role` column in the status report.

10. As a root-capable user on pgha2, stop Patroni with this command:

```
sudo systemctl stop patroni
```

11. Perform any necessary upgrades to the system software, reboot the `pgha2` server, or apply a minor PostgreSQL update.

12. When the upgrades are complete, start Patroni on `pgha2` with the following command:

```
sudo systemctl start patroni
```

13. Repeat the previous three steps for `pgha3`.

How it works...

Before we explain the steps of this recipe, we want to mention that none of this process is actually necessary except for killing the `patroni` daemon on the node we're upgrading. If we stop Patroni on `pgha1`, the cluster will eventually notice and elect a new leader without our direct intervention. However, depending on our timeout settings, the cluster may remain without a leader for several seconds. This recipe ensures the cluster is never without a primary server and is always writable.

Otherwise, our first step is to start a monitor on `pgha3` since it will be upgraded last. This allows us to see which node is the current leader and any transition states while we upgrade the other two systems. This is important since `pgha1` and `pgha2` will both spend time in a leadership position.

Our next step is to actually invoke a switchover. We already did this in the *Performing a managed switchover* recipe, but this time we've added a few extra flags to the `patronictl` command. We use `--master` to show that `pgha1` is the current leader, `--candidate` to specifically select `pgha2` as the failover target, `--scheduled` to `now` so the failover happens immediately, and `--force` because we are skipping verification prompts.

If we return to `pgha3` to watch the transition status, the whole process should finish relatively quickly. Once we're satisfied that the cluster is stable again, we can stop the `patroni` service and then do whatever we want with `pgha1`. After the upgrades or other maintenance processes have finished, we just need to start Patroni on `pgha1` and wait for it to catch up with the other nodes. Again, we can watch this happen on `pgha3`.

Now we revert the earlier transition with another managed failover. This time, `--master` is `pgha2` and `--candidate` is `pgha1`. All we have to do is watch the monitor on `pgha3` and wait until the cluster is stable once more. Then, `pgha2` and `pgha3` are both safe to upgrade as we did with `pgha1`. After stopping Patroni on the node we want to upgrade, we have carte blanche to make software modifications.

There's more...

Do not confuse a major PostgreSQL upgrade with a minor one. While we can use the steps in this recipe to upgrade from 12.0 to 12.1, for example, we cannot use it to move from 11.4 to 12.0 or 12.1.

This is because an upgrade of that magnitude currently requires `pg_upgrade`, `pg_dump`, or some clever application of logical replication. In any of these cases, the newly upgraded PostgreSQL instance is actually a copy of the old database, rather than a binary compatible update.

Patroni relies on the PostgreSQL physical replication system to synchronize nodes. Since it's not possible to replicate between major PostgreSQL versions, Patroni can't integrate nodes with large version mismatches.

If we tried a similar tactic as outlined in this recipe and used `pg_upgrade` after moving the cluster leader to `pgha2`, `pgha1` could never rejoin the cluster. As such, we could never revert the leadership role back to `pgha1`. It would forever be excluded from our existing Patroni cluster.

While unfortunate, a full major-version upgrade for a Patroni cluster still requires a full outage window as of PostgreSQL 12. Technically, there is a method for addressing this shortcoming, and we'll provide further details of this in `Chapter 15`, *Zero-downtime Upgrades*.

11
Low-Level Server Mirroring

So far in this book, we've discussed quite an array of functionality and methodology dedicated to keeping PostgreSQL systems online. By now, we have a burgeoning menagerie of replication utilities, system monitoring tools, connection pooling layers, failover and cluster automation frameworks, and even a handful of troubleshooting tips.

We then moved on to combining several of these techniques and a few others to create a software stack that automates and protects a PostgreSQL cluster. However, despite the power demonstrated in these chapters on repmgr and Patroni, they still rely primarily on PostgreSQL replication to safeguard replicated data. If we have an extremely high transaction throughput, even PostgreSQL replication may be too slow to fully resist data loss in the event of a server outage.

So, what tools can we use to safeguard our critical data beyond the guarantees that are granted by PostgreSQL? Where do we go next?

Well, as it turns out, merely installing PostgreSQL on a server can be done too early.

In this chapter, we will learn how to build and manipulate a fault-tolerant, high-performance foundation for our PostgreSQL clusters. We will cover the following recipes in this chapter:

- Preparing systems for volume mirroring
- Getting started with the **Logical Volume Manager** (**LVM**)
- Adding block-level replication
- Incorporating the second LVM layer
- Verifying a **Distributed Replicated Block Device** (**DRBD**) filesystem
- Correcting a DRBD split brain
- Formatting an XFS filesystem
- Tweaking XFS performance
- Maintaining an XFS filesystem

- Using LVM snapshots
- Switching live stack systems
- Detaching a problematic node
- Building and attaching a new node

Understanding our chosen filesystem components

Presuming that we have all of the hardware and software we discussed earlier, our servers are still missing the following three things:

- The ability to synchronize data to two servers simultaneously
- The capacity to freeze data to prevent changes for backup purposes
- A durable filesystem designed for multiprocessing I/O

There are several solutions for each of these missing elements, yet we've settled on three in particular: DRBD, LVM, and XFS. Let's explore a bit about each of these technologies and discuss why we've chosen them for mirroring data at the server level.

Why DRBD?

DRBD stands for **Distributed Replicated Block Device**. DRBD is meant to operate below the filesystem layer, mirroring the contents of one server's storage to another at the block level. This means the operating system doesn't even know that its data is located on another server as well. Having trouble imagining how it works? Well, the following diagram will help:

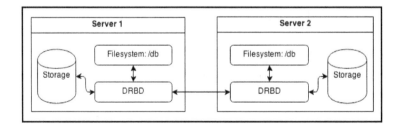

As you can see here, DRBD acts as an abstraction from the disk device that normally hosts our PostgreSQL database. The primary benefit we gain from this situation is that data is always located on at least two servers at all times. If one server crashes and its storage is rendered unusable, we have a backup available.

Why not use streaming replication instead? Default PostgreSQL synchronous streaming replication only guarantees that transactions are written to the standby, not replayed within the actual database. So, even if we use the `remote_apply` setting for the `synchronous_commit` parameter, we've merely increased our transaction commit latency.

As we've already discussed, streaming replication means that the primary node will halt on commit if there isn't at least one replica available at all times. With DRBD, the other server has a copy of the block written to disk, which is identical in all aspects. Any block written to one server is always available on the other.

There's also a dirty little secret that most people don't know about PostgreSQL synchronous replication: it's not really synchronous! Remember, PostgreSQL streaming replication works by transmitting **write-ahead logging** (**WAL**) events to recipient nodes. Well, consider the fact that COMMIT is a WAL event. This means it must be written in the WAL before it can be sent to another server.

In practice, all **synchronous replication** does is prevent the current PostgreSQL session from accepting further commands until COMMIT succeeds. The data has already been written to the WAL, and the transaction is already applied locally. If the primary server then crashes, technically, some committed transactions could be lost.

Since the application never received an acknowledgment for the COMMIT message, it would most likely try again after some failover process. This isn't always the case, however, and in less robust designs, it could ultimately result in data loss due to assumptions on data synchronicity. DRBD distinctly lacks this weakness.

Why LVM?

LVM is the **Logical Volume Manager**. Like DRBD, LVM is another abstraction layer that sits between the filesystem and the underlying disk devices. Why is this necessary? Well, LVM allows us to dynamically manage disk devices as one single continuous piece of storage that we can arbitrarily extend, group, freeze, or reorganize—all while remaining online.

Have you ever wanted to simply add storage to a filesystem without messy symbolic links or a server reboot? What about moving data from one device to another after an upgrade? With LVM, all of this is easily accomplished. Using a modern server with hot-swappable disks or a **storage area network** (**SAN**), we never even have to reboot the server to completely reconfigure its disk devices.

Through the entire process of almost any LVM change, PostgreSQL can remain online and service requests. This is the ultimate in high availability.

Why XFS?

XFS stands for **Extents File System**. Some may consider this a somewhat controversial selection, given that **ext4** performs perfectly well and is the current default for all of the major Linux distributions. Both XFS and ext4 are journaling filesystems; they provide online growth, LVM freezing, and numerous maintenance and repair tools.

However, XFS still has something that ext4 does not: allocation groups. ext4, like all of its predecessors, has a single file allocation table for the entire formatted device. XFS, on the other hand, can split the allocation table into several segments so that multiple independent CPU processes can write to the disk simultaneously. The end result of this is that large servers with many CPUs and random writes, such as a PostgreSQL database, can perform better on an XFS-formatted device.

 If you are using **Red Hat Enterprise Linux** (**RHEL**) and have a support contract with Red Hat, be wary of using XFS. Red Hat considers XFS enterprise-grade storage and distributes it separately as a paid extension. If this becomes a problem, please feel free to use ext4 and ignore the XFS-related sections of this chapter.

The stack

At the end of this chapter, we will have a software stack that looks like the following diagram:

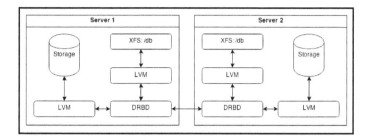

Each of the following layers represents one enhancement necessary for the best long-term high availability:

- The first LVM layer (starting at the storage) protects DRBD from inheriting device-specific block sizes and allows for online resizing or migration to new devices.
- The DRBD layer replicates data to another server for immediate use.
- The second LVM layer provides snapshot capabilities and other potentially useful LVM functionality to the filesystem.
- The XFS layer is the last element where data resides and is available for direct manipulation by programs such as PostgreSQL.

The recipes we provide in this chapter should make this easier to understand, despite its advanced nature.

 The layers in our stack do come at a cost, however. Since each is an abstraction above the raw storage device, performance will decrease slightly. We believe this trade-off is worth the security and availability the stack provides.

Preparing systems for volume mirroring

Before we can use LVM, DRBD, or XFS on our servers, we must take some preliminary steps. We've never encountered a Linux system that has been optimized for this kind of advanced usage directly after installation. In this recipe, we will modify several configuration files and even reboot the server.

We're trying to put each system in a standard state that we will use for all future database servers. This means that LVM needs to ignore some devices to prevent disrupting DRBD. The initial RAM disks during boot should reflect this same allocation, and device performance shouldn't be lost between abstraction layers. We also need all of the tools that we will use throughout this chapter.

This recipe will guarantee that these criteria are true, so be prepared!

Getting ready

The only things we should need at this point are the ability to run commands as root and a device dedicated to database storage. However, if you are running an RHEL system (not a derivative such as CentOS or Scientific Linux), you may need to contact Red Hat to obtain the necessary licenses and packages to add XFS functionality. Thus, we will approach this recipe under the assumption that packages are available on Debian-based servers and RHEL derivatives.

How to do it...

To keep things simple, we will assume that each server we prepare has a device named /dev/sdb for database storage. Follow these steps as root:

1. Install the xfsprogs package with apt-get or yum.
2. Install drbd-utils with apt-get on Debian-based systems, or drbd with yum on Red Hat derivatives.
3. In the devices section of /etc/lvm/lvm.conf, change the filter setting so that it reads like so:

   ```
   filter = [ "a|/dev/sd.*|", "a|/dev/drbd.*|", "r|.*|" ]
   ```

4. In the devices section of /etc/lvm/lvm.conf, set this parameter to disable the caching of the write state:

   ```
   write_cache_state = 0
   ```

5. In the global section of /etc/lvm/lvm.conf, set this parameter to disable the caching of device metadata:

   ```
   use_lvmetad = 0
   ```

6. Remove the existing LVM cache file with the following command:

   ```
   rm /etc/lvm/cache/.cache
   ```

7. Execute the following command to validate our LVM changes:

```
lvmconfig --validate
```

8. Update the kernel's list of available devices with the following command:

```
update-initramfs -u
```

9. Create a file named `/etc/udev/rules.d/20-postgresql.rules` with the following contents:

```
ACTION=="add|change", KERNEL=="sd[a-z]",
ATTR{queue/read_ahead_kb}="4096"
ACTION=="add|change", KERNEL=="drbd[0-9]",
ATTR{bdi/read_ahead_kb}="4096"
```

10. Finally, reboot the server using the following command:

```
reboot
```

How it works...

In order for the stack to work properly, we need to get the server ready. For now, this means installing basic toolkits such as `xfsprogs` for XFS maintenance tools and `drbd-utils` for DRBD administrative scripts. Once this is complete, we move on to preparing LVM.

Since LVM is so highly integrated into the system, we need to perform several steps. The first is to modify the primary `lvm.conf` file so that it only watches certain devices, and while it does so, it never caches the result. Due to the way Linux is designed, there are several different aliases and paths that point to the same device in the `/dev` filesystem. To remove these extra paths, we set a very strict `filter` that only includes `/dev/sd*` devices and `/dev/drbd*` devices.

We want LVM to avoid caching devices by setting `write_cache_state` to 0 because the DRBD devices may disappear or reappear based on their statuses. It's equally important to set `use_lvmetad` to 0, as this activates a daemon that caches the device state. We don't want an invalid cache poisoning the active device list. Just to make sure there are no stale LVM caches, we remove the existing `/etc/lvm/cache/.cache` file so that all readings are current.

Before we commit to these configuration changes, we absolutely must validate the configuration file with `lvmconfig`. If we reboot the server while there are mistakes in the LVM configuration file, it might not boot successfully! By invoking `update-initramfs` with the `-u` parameter, it generates a new device map that will be used when the system boots. This ensures that devices are consistent at all availability levels in case we need emergency access.

Before we venture further, we need to address performance. In the book *PostgreSQL 10 High Performance, Packt Publishing by Gregory Smith, Et al*, he suggests that we increase the `read_ahead_kb` setting for every block device to `4096` kilobytes or higher. Unfortunately, due to the transient nature of our devices, there is no static method we can use that would survive a device appearing after boot. This is where the `udev` filesystem comes in. It watches as various system devices change state, appear, or reappear. Thanks to this, we can give it parameters to use when new storage devices appear, such as our DRBD or LVM devices.

The two lines we added to `20-postgresql.rules` tell the `udev` filesystem to set the `read_ahead_kb` value to `4096` any time a new device is added or modified. In our case, we are specifically interested in the `sdb` and `drbd0` devices, but we include all `sd` or `drbd` devices for future expansion purposes if necessary. This ensures that we'll always have a large read buffer for good PostgreSQL performance, no matter how many abstraction layers we place between the device and the database.

The last thing we do is reboot the server. This gives us a fresh slate, with a cleanly generated device map based on the changes we made.

There's more...

The version of DRBD you receive with these instructions may vary depending on the age of your distribution. Though DRBD 9.0 is the latest official release, DRBD 8.4 is the most recent stable version included with many distributions at the time of writing this book. As such, all the recipes in this chapter assume that this is the installed version. To check whether you are using 8.4, execute `drbdadm` with the `-V` parameter and examine the `DRBD_KERNEL_VERSION_CODE` output.

If this value doesn't include `8040` or greater, please consider upgrading to a more recent distribution or kernel that includes a recent DRBD 8.4 module. Otherwise, it may be necessary to obtain the module source and build manually. The DRBD source is available from the Linbit site at `https://www.linbit.com/en/drbd-community/drbd-download/`.

If you complete this chapter and feel brave enough to try using DRBD 9.0, Linbit has a useful guide that you can refer to at `https://docs.linbit.com/docs/users-guide-9.0/`.

We should note that DRBD 9.0 is treated like a flagship piece of supported software. Linbit will only provide RPM and DEB packages to paying customers. Without these packages, installation is much more complicated and includes integrating a new Linux kernel module. We don't recommend this process unless you are comfortable with these types of procedures.

See also

For more details, refer to the following:

- **The DRBD User's Guide**: `https://docs.linbit.com/docs/users-guide-8.4/`
- **PostgreSQL 10 High Performance, Packt Publishing, by Gregory Smith, Et al**:
  `https://www.packtpub.com/big-data-and-business-intelligence/postgresql-10-high-performance`

Getting started with the LVM

The **LVM** is something of an optional master control panel for Linux storage devices. It can combine several devices into one, allows arbitrary storage grouping, which is far more granular than simple partitions, and provides functionality such as data snapshots and reorganization. It's very powerful and, in the right hands, greatly improves potential server uptime.

It is also the first layer above the raw storage device in our stack. We start with LVM instead of DRBD, because DRBD at the device level is extremely messy. So, what do we gain by insulating DRBD from the raw storage device? Take a look at the following:

- We can easily add storage to the LVM device group assigned to DRBD.
- DRBD can be resized while in an online state.
- We can perform storage migrations without taking PostgreSQL offline.

None of this is possible unless LVM is the first layer. For a high-availability server, this is extremely desirable. Follow along to see how it works.

Getting ready

At this point, all we need is a single unformatted device to use for database storage. In addition, make sure you've prepared the system as described in the *Preparing systems for the stack* recipe of Chapter 10, *High Availability with Patroni.*

How to do it...

For the purposes of this recipe, we will assume that the /dev/sdb device has been dedicated to PostgreSQL use. Follow these steps as the root user *on two servers* to create the first LVM layer:

1. Create and verify a single LVM partition on the device with these commands:

   ```
   parted /dev/sdb mklabel gpt
   parted /dev/sdb mkpart primary 1 100%
   parted /dev/sdb set 1 lvm on
   parted /dev/sdb print
   ```

2. Register /dev/sdb1 as an LVM physical device with this command:

   ```
   pvcreate /dev/sdb1
   ```

3. Create a single volume group to contain /dev/sdb1 with this command:

   ```
   vgcreate VG_DRBD /dev/sdb1
   ```

4. Create a single logical volume as 100% of the outer volume group with this command:

   ```
   lvcreate -n LV_DATA -l 100%VG VG_DRBD
   ```

5. Verify that the new volume exists and is available with this command:

   ```
   lvdisplay VG_DRBD/LV_DATA | grep LV
   ```

How it works...

Before we can use LVM safely, we should create at least one partition on the raw device. For this, we use `parted`, which is a more advanced partition editor than `fdisk`. We need `parted` because it can set the partition table type as `gpt`, which allows filesystems greater than 2 TB. This is what the first invocation of `parted` does, with the `mklabel` parameter set to `gpt`.

To create the partition itself, we call `parted` with the `mkpart` parameter. By using `mkpart`, we also need to specify the type of partition we want and its starting and ending positions. We keep things simple by starting at the beginning of the device and using `100%` of the available storage.

Finally, we set the LVM flag to `true` by invoking `parted` with the `set` parameter. The `set` parameter requires a partition number, the flag we want to set, and the value. In our case, we are using the first partition and setting the `lvm` flag to `on`.

It's always a good idea to verify our creations, and `parted` has a `print` setting to output the current partition table for a specified disk device. Here is `/dev/sdb` on our test system:

```
Model: QEMU QEMU HARDDISK (scsi)
Disk /dev/sdb: 34.4GB
Sector size (logical/physical): 512B/512B
Partition Table: gpt
Disk Flags:

Number  Start    End     Size    File system  Name     Flags
 1      1049kB   34.4GB  34.4GB               primary  lvm
```

As you can see, the test device we've used for this example is fairly small, at just around 32 GB. However, you can also see that the partition table is `gpt`, and the `lvm` flag is set as expected.

Now, we can start with LVM itself. The first step is to use `pvcreate` to create a physical LVM device. This allows LVM to manage the device and only requires us to name `/dev/sdb1` as the device we're adding.

Next, we need a volume group. Volume groups can be comprised of multiple physical volumes and be split into several logical volumes. By calling `vgcreate`, we need to name the group with the first parameter. Every subsequent parameter is a device that should be part of the new group. In our case, we only have the `/dev/sdb1` device, so that becomes our last parameter.

Since the volume group can host several logical volumes, we need to create at least one. Unlike `vgcreate`, the `lvcreate` command does not assume that the first parameter is the volume name. Therefore, we need to specify the `-n` parameter to name the volume. By using the `-l` parameter, we can specify a percentage of the volume group as the size of our volume. For the base volume, we want to use all available storage space (`100%VG`) since DRBD will be the next layer. The last parameter for `lvcreate` is the name of the volume group we are using for this logical volume.

The last thing we do is verify that the logical volume has the elements we expect. We can get this with the `lvdisplay` command, as follows:

```
LV Path                /dev/VG_DRBD/LV_DATA
LV Name                LV_DATA
LV UUID                HlfjLd-Knw7-X9Nb-k4WR-XRy6-8vRg-VKB4u1
LV Write Access        read/write
LV Creation host, time pgdrbd1, 2019-12-14 16:49:02 -0600
LV Status              available
LV Size                <32.00 GiB
```

From this, we can see that the new logical volume is `32.00 GiB` in size and is `available` for use. We can also observe that LVM created a new device path at `/dev/VG_DRBD/LV_DATA`. This path will be how we address the storage in the future. It can be formatted, mounted, or treated just like any other Linux storage device.

As we'll discuss in the next recipe, this new `/dev` location can be used as the target device for another resource, such as DRBD.

There's more...

We hope you noticed the naming scheme that's inherent in all of the LVM commands. Commands prefixed with `pv` are meant for physical volume management. Similarly, `vg` is used for volume groups, and `lv` is for logical volumes. This greatly simplifies the management of LVM devices.

We used `pvcreate`, `vgcreate`, and `lvcreate` in this recipe. However, it shouldn't surprise you that there are also analogous `pvremove`, `vgremove`, and `lvremove` commands as well. There are also commands to retrieve information about volumes and groups: `pvdisplay`, `vgdisplay`, and `lvdisplay`.

This is one of the reasons we enjoy working with LVM; we rarely have to guess at commands.

See also

- LVM itself is a conceptual architecture. To understand more about how it works, we recommend the **Linux Documentation Project** discussion on the topic at `http://tldp.org/HOWTO/LVM-HOWTO/`.
- In addition to this, all of the LVM commands have their own `man` page. We highly recommend at least viewing the man page for each utility before using it; for example, consider the following:

```
man lvextend
```

Adding block-level replication

DRBD is the next component of our software stack. Unlike LVM, it requires at least two servers to function normally. One server acts as the **Primary** data server, and the other acts as a **Secondary**. These roles can be switched at any time, depending on which server is running PostgreSQL.

This recipe will focus on configuring and activating DRBD as part of our stack.

Getting ready

By now, we hope you've followed the steps in the *Getting started with the LVM* recipe for *two servers* with `/dev/sdb` as the physically identical pieces of storage on each server. While DRBD can operate in standalone mode on a single server, this is actually a more advanced usage. The steps in this recipe are best applied on both of the servers simultaneously, that is, unless noted otherwise.

How to do it...

For the purposes of this recipe, we will assume that the `/dev/VG_DRBD/LV_DATA` device already exists. The two PostgreSQL nodes for this example are named `pg1` and `pg2` and are located on the `10.0.30.0` subnet. Follow these steps as the `root` user *on each server* to add DRBD:

1. Create a file named `/etc/drbd.d/pg.res` with the following content:

```
resource pg {
  device minor 0;
```

```
disk /dev/VG_DRBD/LV_DATA;
meta-disk internal;
on pg1 {
  address 10.0.30.101:7788;
}
on pg2 {
  address 10.0.30.102:7788;
}
}
```

2. Allocate the DRBD storage with this command:

   drbdadm create-md pg

3. Enable and start the DRBD service:

   systemctl enable drbd
   systemctl start drbd

4. Use drbdadm on pg1 to invalidate the data on pg2:

   drbdadm invalidate-remote pg

5. View the status of DRBD from any node using this command:

   cat /proc/drbd

6. Run this command on pg1 to declare it as the primary node:

   drbdadm primary pg

How it works...

We begin by creating a configuration file for DRBD with the least amount of information necessary. In the pg.res file, we define a DRBD resource named pg for our PostgreSQL data. DRBD resource numbers start at zero, so we use the define keyword to set the DRBD minor device number to 0. This means our DRBD device will be named /dev/drbd0.

After setting the device number, we specify which storage volume this DRBD resource should use with the disk keyword. The meta-disk keyword allows us to define a device to store DRBD metadata. To keep things simple, we've used the internal setting so that metadata is stored on the same device as the data we are synchronizing.

The last thing we do in the resource configuration file is to define each host involved in the replication. The on keyword expects a hostname that matches our PostgreSQL nodes, followed by a block of parameters. The only attribute we actually need is the IP address of the server we name, followed by a port, which DRBD should use for communication and transfer purposes. A common port number is 7788, as shown in our example, but really, this can be any arbitrary, unused value.

Once we have a valid configuration file, we need to initialize the DRBD device. When we invoke drbdadm with the create-md parameter, it allocates metadata for the named DRBD resource. Since pg is the name of our resource, we specify that here as well. We could have also used all, which applies the command to any configured resources.

Depending on the default debugging parameters, this may produce quite a bit of output, but should look like the following near the end:

```
initializing activity log
initializing bitmap (1024 KB) to all zero
Writing meta data...
New drbd meta data block successfully created.
```

With the metadata in place, we can enable and start (or restart) the DRBD service. Once we do this, DRBD will attempt to connect both nodes named in our resource definition file. This is why DRBD should be started on both nodes consecutively, or the running node will wait indefinitely for the other to start as well.

DRBD is connected at this point, but it doesn't know the state of the underlying storage data. Due to this, we must invalidate one of the nodes so that DRBD considers the other node up to date. When we use drbdadm with invalidate-remote, we tell DRBD to consider local data valid, and all data on any other node in need of replacement.

If we examine the contents of /proc/drbd at this moment, we should see synchronization taking place:

```
version: 8.4.10 (api:1/proto:86-101)
srcversion: 15055BDD6F0D23278182874
 0: cs:SyncSource ro:Secondary/Secondary ds:UpToDate/Inconsistent C r-----
    ns:20784 nr:0 dw:0 dr:20784 al:8 bm:0 lo:0 pe:0 ua:0 ap:0 ep:1 wo:f oos:33528492
    [>....................] sync'ed:   0.1% (32740/32760)M
    finish: 3:08:03 speed: 2,968 (2,968) K/sec
```

The top line of this output actually provides most of the DRBD status information. The section labeled `ro` stands for **roles**, and the slash always separates the current node from the remote node. By default, both DRBD systems report their role as a `Secondary` node. Similarly, `ds` represents **disk states** and tells us the status of data on each node. Based on this, we can see that the current node is `UpToDate`, while the remote is `Inconsistent`. We invalidated the data on `pg2` from `pg1`, so this is exactly what we should expect.

Once synchronization is complete, it is time to declare one of the nodes as the primary resource. For this task, we run `drbdadm` with the `primary` parameter. The only difference we should see is a change in the `ro` reading in `/proc/drbd`. It should reflect `Primary/Secondary` when viewed from `pg1` and `Secondary/Primary` when viewed from `pg2`. At this point, DRBD is working, and any data we save on one node should automatically exist on the other as well.

See also

For more details, refer to the following:

- The DRBD documentation is extremely detailed. We strongly recommend browsing this URL to truly understand how DRBD works: `https://docs.linbit.com/docs/users-guide-8.4/`.
- In addition to this, the `drbdadm` tool that administers almost all DRBD functionalities has a `man` page:

```
man drbdadm
```

Incorporating the second LVM layer

In this recipe, we are going to create the second of our two LVM abstraction layers. While the first layer provides an elastic base for DRBD, this one will provide most of the LVM functionality that we will actually use on a regular basis.

Tasks such as creating filesystem snapshots or reorganizing data are within the domain of the second layer. This is because we create the filesystem on top of this second LVM definition. We can mount or otherwise manipulate a snapshot like any other filesystem. If we tried to create a snapshot with the first LVM layer, we would still have a snapshot, but it would be of an unreadable DRBD binary blob.

With that in mind, this recipe will explain how to add an LVM layer necessary for filesystem manipulation.

Getting ready

Please follow all the previous recipes before starting.

How to do it...

Perform these steps only on `pg1` as the `root` user:

1. Register `/dev/drbd0` as an LVM physical device using this command:

   pvcreate /dev/drbd0

2. Create a single volume group to contain `/dev/drbd0` using this command:

   vgcreate VG_POSTGRES /dev/drbd0

3. Create a single logical volume as `95%` of the outer volume group using this command:

   lvcreate -n LV_DATA -l 95%VG VG_POSTGRES

4. Verify that the new volume exists and is available using this command:

   vgdisplay VG_POSTGRES | grep Size

How it works...

Do these steps seem familiar? They should! With a few minor exceptions, this is almost the same as the steps we used in the *Getting started with the LVM* recipe. Unlike the other instructions, we don't need to partition the `/dev/drbd0` device and can immediately add it to LVM with `pvcreate`.

Following this, we use `vgcreate` to define a new volume group named `VG_POSTGRES`, containing `/dev/drbd0` as its only device. The definition for this volume group actually exists on the `/dev/drbd0` device itself, meaning it is replicated by DRBD to the other node. This is why we only need to execute these commands on `pg1`.

Next, we use `lvcreate` with the -n parameter to create a logical volume named LV_DATA within the VG_POSTGRES group. This time, we use the -l parameter to set the volume size at 95%VG instead of 100%VG. This means LV_DATA will contain 95 percent of the total available space within the VG_POSTGRES volume group.

Why did we neglect to allocate the remaining 5 percent? Snapshot space. We can use snapshots for backups, risky temporary work, or simply as a placeholder. If you never plan on using filesystem snapshots, feel free to use 100 percent of the VG_POSTGRES group instead.

Instead of verifying the allocation of our logical volume, our last command retrieves some of the information about the volume group. On our testing system, it looks like the following:

```
VG Size              31.99 GiB
PE Size              4.00 MiB
Alloc PE / Size      7780 / 30.39 GiB
Free  PE / Size      410 / 1.60 GiB
```

We can see that the volume group is 31.99 GiB in size, that 3.79 GiB is allocated, and that 208.00 MiB is free. Based on this information, we can presume 30.39 GiB is allocated to the LV_DATA volume, leaving us with 1.60 GiB for allocating snapshots. We are glad this is only an example, as 1.60 GiB is not very much free snapshot space!

There's more...

Is 5 percent too much space to set aside for snapshots, especially in multi-terabyte volumes? Probably! Unfortunately, the only other mechanism available to define the volume size is the -L parameter for `lvcreate`, which only works with absolute measurements. Yet we know the size of our devices, and we are free to make loose estimates.

For example, imagine we have a 4 TB storage device, and we only want to leave around 50 GB for snapshots instead of 200 GB. This `lvcreate` command specifies the size of our device in GB:

```
lvcreate -n LV_DATA -L 3950G VG_POSTGRES
```

See also

As before, we strongly recommend examining the LVM documentation and `man` pages to fully leverage LVM's capabilities. We recommend using this URL from the *Linux Documentation Project* to learn more: `http://tldp.org/HOWTO/LVM-HOWTO/`.

Verifying a DRBD filesystem

A semi-common maintenance concern regarding synchronized devices is verification. The question we should always ask ourselves in a high-availability scenario is how confident we are that the data on both nodes match.

The `drbdadm` utility provides a parameter specifically for addressing this need. However, there are some caveats to consider when using it, which we will explain in this recipe.

Getting ready

Follow the recipes defined in all of the previous sections before starting here. At the very least, we need a fully operational DRBD node pair to follow this recipe.

How to do it...

Follow these steps as the `root` user on `pg1`:

1. Add this block of text inside the `resource` section defined in `/etc/drbd.d/pg.res`:

    ```
    net {
      verify-alg md5;
    }
    ```

2. Run this command to make DRBD reread its configuration files:

    drbdadm adjust pg

3. Begin verification with this command:

    drbdadm verify pg

4. Monitor /proc/drbd until verification is complete:

```
watch cat /proc/drbd
```

5. Disconnect and reconnect the DRBD resource:

```
drbdadm disconnect pg
drbdadm connect pg
```

How it works...

Our first job is to define what we mean by verify. DRBD is somewhat minimal by design, and it has no default for the algorithm it should use for checksum comparisons. The verify-alg setting is a network-oriented attribute and defines how DRBD should compare data segments. We also know md5 is a widely used checksum algorithm. Therefore, we set the verify-alg in a net block within the resource definition for pg.

Afterward, we need to reread the configuration files so that the verify-alg setting is defined for the verification step. By invoking drbdadm with the adjust parameter, it will read and apply any valid changes we made to /etc/drbd.d/pg.res. When we're ready, we can launch the verification process by calling drbdadm with the verify parameter.

Due to the CPU overhead of md5, this will be noticeably slower than a full device synchronization. We can watch its progress by paying attention to /proc/drbd:

```
version: 8.4.10 (api:1/proto:86-101)
srcversion: 15055BDD6F0D23278182874
 0: cs:VerifyS ro:Primary/Secondary ds:UpToDate/UpToDate C r-----
    ns:33549698 nr:0 dw:422 dr:39337064 al:9 bm:0 lo:0 pe:0 ua:0 ap:0 ep:1 wo:f oos:0
        [==>................] verified: 17.3% (27116/32760)M
        finish: 0:11:18 speed: 40,924 (29,052) want: 41,000 K/sec
```

We can see that our example verification is 17.3% complete, with an estimated completion time of just over 11 minutes. The estimate is produced based on network speed, md5 speed, and the amount of remaining data. These details can fluctuate frequently, as writes to the DRBD device slow down the verification process.

The last step is to disconnect and then reconnect the pg resource from the DRBD network. During verification, DRBD marks blocks that have unmatched md5 checksums but does not resend them until a new connection is established. We can't speculate about the reason for this step, but it is required to correct errors.

The last step is only required if any block failed verification. Errors (that is, bad blocks) will be located in the kernel log according to the DRBD documentation. We recommend checking for `drbd0` messages in `/var/log/syslog`, `/var/log/messages`, and `/var/log/kern.log`, depending on your distribution.

There's more...

When we're done with this recipe, it's important to ensure the configuration files on each system match. Since we added the `net` block to `/etc/drbd.d/pg.res` on `pg1`, we should do the same on `pg2`. After making any changes to a DRBD configuration file, run this command to enable them:

```
drbdadm adjust pg
```

See also

The DRBD documentation explains online verification in more detail than we do. Please refer to this URL for a full discussion of the process of invoking online verification: `https://docs.linbit.com/docs/users-guide-8.4/#s-use-online-verify`.

Correcting a DRBD split brain

One looming danger when running any replication system is that of node status conflicts. This happens when more than one node has been the primary, and we want to reestablish the previous mirror state. This can happen in many ways, but a common scenario can occur if the existing primary node experiences a sudden failure and the remaining secondary node is promoted to primary status.

In the case where we repair the old primary node, we can't simply reattach it to the DRBD network and expect successful synchronization. In cases where the last status for each node is that of a primary, DRBD will not resolve this conflict automatically. It is our job to manually choose the best primary node from our available choices, and reattach the other node.

In this recipe, we'll explore the steps necessary to reattach a malfunctioning node to an existing DRBD architecture. We can't have a highly available PostgreSQL cluster with only one functional node.

Getting ready

Since we're working with DRBD and need a fully established mirror, please follow the steps in all of the recipes up to *Adding block-level replication* before continuing. In addition to this, we need to simulate a split brain. A very easy way to do this is to put both nodes in the primary state while disconnected from each other.

Assuming that we have nodes pg1 and pg2, where pg1 is the current primary node, follow these instructions as the root user to cause a split brain:

1. On both nodes, disconnect from DRBD with this command:

   ```
   drbdadm disconnect pg
   ```

2. On pg2, execute this command to force it into primary status:

   ```
   drbdadm primary --force pg
   ```

If we were to use drbdadm to attempt to connect the nodes now, we would see the following message in the system logs:

```
Split-Brain detected but unresolved, dropping connection!
```

How to do it...

Follow these instructions as the root user to repair a split-brain scenario:

1. First, decide which node should be the new primary. This should be relatively easy, since some event likely precipitated the node mismatch. For the remainder of this recipe, we will assume pg2 should be the new primary node.

2. Prepare each server by assuring that each is disconnected from the other:

   ```
   drbdadm disconnect pg
   ```

3. Disable the VG_POSTGRES volume with vgchange on pg1:

   ```
   vgchange -a n VG_POSTGRES
   ```

4. Use `drbdadm` to downgrade `pg1` to `secondary` status:

   drbdadm secondary pg

5. Execute this command on `pg1` to connect while discarding metadata:

   drbdadm connect --discard-my-data pg

6. Execute this command on `pg2` to connect to DRBD:

   drbdadm connect pg

How it works...

The first step is clearly the most critical. We need to determine which node has the most recent valid data. In almost all cases, there should be sufficient logs to make this determination. However, in some network disruption scenarios coupled with automated failover solutions, this may not be obvious. Unfortunately, resolving this step is too varied to adequately express in a simple guide.

 If you are unsure of how to continue following an extremely complicated failure scenario, we strongly recommend contacting Linbit, which maintains the DRBD software. Their support information is available at `https://www.linbit.com/en/support/`.

For our example, we manually promoted the `pg2` node, so it should be the new primary. With that in mind, there are many states DRBD could have right now, and we want one in particular: `StandAlone`. By disconnecting both nodes, we don't have to worry about aborted or premature connection attempts disrupting our progress. We want both nodes to report `StandAlone` in `/proc/drbd` as the connection state (`cs`), as shown in this screenshot:

```
version: 8.4.10 (api:1/proto:86-101)
srcversion: 15055BDD6F0D23278182874
 0: cs:StandAlone ro:Primary/Unknown ds:UpToDate/DUnknown    r-----
    ns:0 nr:0 dw:33549698 dr:33549276 al:8 bm:0 lo:0 pe:0 ua:0 ap:0 ep:1 wo:f oos:0
```

Our next step is actually related to LVM. If DRBD status is primary on a node, the second LVM layer is probably active as well. Since LVM uses the underlying DRBD device, we can't demote this node to secondary status until we use `vgchange` to set the active (`-a`) state of `VG_POSTGRES` to no (`n`).

Given that there are no other elements connected to /dev/drbd0, we can set its status to secondary with drbdadm. While in the secondary state, we can attempt to connect to the DRBD network with drbdadm connect. Since both nodes were primary at one point, each was maintaining a different map of modified blocks; these maps will not match. If this happens, DRBD will refuse to connect to the network, and it will revert to the StandAlone status.

To prevent that, we add --discard-my-data to the connect operation. This option acknowledges the situation, and it tells the secondary node to ignore its own change map in favor of what the primary node may contain. If the secondary node is too out of date for the updated map, DRBD will simply resynchronize all data on the device.

Of course, none of this will happen until we invoke drbdadm connect from the new primary node. We do this last because we can always change our minds and abort the process. If we did this before connecting the secondary node, previously existing storage maps would have already been discarded, and resynchronization would be taking place.

See also

DRBD addresses this exact scenario in their documentation. We recommend reading through this URL for a different perspective on manual split-brain recovery: https://docs.linbit.com/docs/users-guide-8.4/#s-resolve-split-brain.

Formatting an XFS filesystem

The next and last part of our stack is the filesystem layer. This is where the PostgreSQL data will reside, so we need to ensure it's allocated properly. Unlike the underlying LVM layers, the filesystem is not so easily modified.

In this recipe, we will discuss some common formatting options and why we recommend them in addition to the necessary commands.

Getting ready

Since this is the last layer in our complete stack, we strongly suggest following all of the recipes up to *Incorporating the second LVM layer* before starting here.

How to do it...

Assuming `pg1` is our current primary node, follow these steps as the `root` user:

1. Activate the second LVM volume with this command:

   ```
   lvchange -a y VG_POSTGRES/LV_DATA
   ```

2. Count the number of CPUs on the primary node.
3. Multiply the CPU count by four.
4. If the total in the previous step is less than 256, use 256.
5. Use this command to find the Linux kernel version:

   ```
   uname -r
   ```

6. For kernel versions `3.0` and above, format the XFS filesystem with this command, setting `agcount` to the value derived in the preceding steps:

   ```
   mkfs.xfs -d agcount=256 /dev/VG_POSTGRES/LV_DATA
   ```

7. For kernels below `3.0`, format with this command:

   ```
   mkfs.xfs -d agcount=256 -l size=128m -l lazy-count=1 \
            -i attr=2 /dev/VG_POSTGRES/LV_DATA
   ```

How it works...

We begin by activating (`-a y`) the `VG_POSTGRES/LV_DATA` volume with `lvchange`. This is like `vgchange`, but only affects the named volume, instead of every volume in the named group. We used this command merely to demonstrate that either command will work for our stack, especially since there is only one volume to activate.

The next three steps involve a simple calculation, but it deserves some explanation. The main feature we want to exploit here is the count of allocation groups. Each allocation group can be addressed independently when making filesystem modifications. Presumably, this enhances performance in several different categories since it reduces allocation table contention.

To reach our desired number, we start with the total CPU count on our primary server. This is the maximum number of concurrent processes that can touch the filesystem simultaneously. However, we live in a world where upgrades are frequent and CPU core counts are only increasing. Thus, we suggest multiplying the current CPU count by four, because we only get one chance to create the XFS layer once it contains data. We want to keep time-consuming data migrations to a minimum if possible.

With this calculated allocation group count in hand, we can begin formatting. The mkfs.xfs utility supplied by xfsprogs will perform this step for us. The command we used contained several parameters, separated into data (-d), log (-1), and inode (-i) settings. Here is a quick summary of what these options do:

- The agcount setting defines how many allocation groups XFS should create. Our example uses 256, but you may have more.

 Because our sample device is only 4 GB, it's too small for an agcount value of 256. If you've been following along and created a similarly tiny device, use a setting of 128 instead.

- We set the log's size to 128m for a 128 MB journal. Journaling filesystems are not new, but we need a sufficient size in order to track many concurrent changes on active databases. On kernels at and above 3.0, this value is calculated based on the device size, so we don't need to set it.
- By setting lazy-count to 1, we get the full power of our agcount setting. Though there are several allocation groups, there is still a master superblock that tracks some universal counters. By enabling this, XFS uses other techniques to maintain these values, avoiding sequential superblock access. On kernels 3.0 and higher, this is set to 1 by default.
- The attr inode setting configures an internal mechanism to store inline attributes. This is more of an implementation detail, but version 2 is more efficient. On kernels above 2.6.16, this is set to 2 by default.

XFS has recently incorporated **discard** mechanics to interact better with SSD devices. However, this can introduce extreme delays while waiting for discard processing. For the initial filesystem formatting, it may be beneficial to add the -K parameter to disable this feature. This can significantly reduce formatting time.

While this is a lot to digest, it should be clear by now that newer kernels make it much easier to use XFS. Instead of all these other options, we merely need to set agcount and format the filesystem. If everything works as expected, we should see the following output from the mkfs.xfs command:

```
meta-data=/dev/VG_POSTGRES/LV_DATA isize=512    agcount=256, agsize=31120 blks
         =                         sectsz=512   attr=2, projid32bit=1
         =                         crc=1        finobt=1, sparse=1, rmapbt=0
         =                         reflink=0
data     =                         bsize=4096   blocks=7966720, imaxpct=25
         =                         sunit=0      swidth=0 blks
naming   =version 2               bsize=4096   ascii-ci=0, ftype=1
log      =internal log           bsize=4096   blocks=3890, version=2
         =                         sectsz=512   sunit=0 blks, lazy-count=1
realtime =none                    extsz=4096   blocks=0, rtextents=0
```

From this, we can see that our agcount value is indeed set to 256, lazy-count is set to 1, and attr is set to 2.

See also

A definitive source of current XFS documentation is oddly difficult to find. Instead, we recommend that you examine the mkfs.xfs manual provided by man for more information:

```
man mkfs.xfs
```

Tweaking XFS performance

When it comes to performance optimization on XFS filesystems, allocation groups are only the beginning. To maintain a high-availability PostgreSQL server, we want to get the most out of XFS. For us, this means using specific mount options.

Thankfully, unlike formatting, mount options can be changed frequently and require very little downtime. Though it isn't essential that we apply these values immediately, the options discussed in this recipe are our recommendations for this stack.

Getting ready

In order to mount an XFS filesystem, we need one to exist. Please follow the steps contained in the *Formatting an XFS filesystem* recipe before continuing.

How to do it...

Assuming pg1 is our current primary node, follow these steps as the root user:

1. Use this command to find the Linux kernel version:

   ```
   uname -r
   ```

2. Create a mount location by executing this command:

   ```
   mkdir /db
   ```

3. For kernel versions 3.0 and above, mount the filesystem with this command:

   ```
   mount -t xfs -o noatime,nodiratime \
       -o logbsize=256k,allocsize=1m \
       /dev/VG_POSTGRES/LV_DATA /db
   ```

4. For kernels below 3.0, mount with this command:

   ```
   mount -t xfs -o noatime,nodiratime \
       -o logbufs=8,logbsize=256k,attr2 \
       -o allocsize=1m /dev/VG_POSTGRES/LV_DATA /db
   ```

5. Execute this command to confirm a successful mount:

   ```
   df /dev/mapper/VG_POSTGRES-LV_DATA
   ```

How it works...

Our first step is to find our current kernel version as this will dictate which settings have been defaulted to our desired values. Then, we continue with the mount command and specify -t to set the filesystem type to xfs. The last two parameters to the mount command define the device we are mounting and which directory it should be attached to. In this case, we use our /dev/VG_POSTGRES/LV_DATA device and the /db directory that we've discussed throughout this book.

All of the parameters prefixed with -o are options that mount should apply during the mounting process. These options define how certain aspects of the filesystem behave. Here is a quick overview of the options we selected and what they mean:

- We use noatime to prevent file metadata from reflecting the last time the file was accessed. In a PostgreSQL database, storage files are likely constantly being accessed and modified, so tracking this information is a waste of time and incurs unnecessary writes.
- We use nodiratime for a similar reason regarding directory access times.
- By ensuring logbufs is set to 8, we get the maximum number of available buffers for the filesystem data journal. On kernels 3.0 and above, this is set to 8 by default.
- The maximum value for logbsize is 256k. This is a very small amount of memory, and it ensures good performance for file deletion operations.
- The attr2 option reflects the attr=2 value that we set when formatting XFS, and it produces more efficient inode tables. On kernels 3.0 and above, this is enabled by default.
- The allocsize setting is extremely important. It defines the amount of space associated with each newly created file. It's meant to prevent excessive file fragmentation by preallocating larger amounts than requested. By setting this to 1m, these allocations are limited to 1 MB in size.

In 3.0 kernels and above, XFS implemented a dynamic allocation calculation that will often use values above 256 MB *per file*. Due to aggressive kernel caching, these larger allocations may not be released for hours or even days, causing a mismatch between used and free space in the filesystem. This can result in 0 percent free space, even if the usage percentage is very low. Never forget this setting in newer kernels.

A successful mount will return no output, so we need to confirm that the space is available some other way. The df command will report the amount of used and free space on a device, and we can pass it the -h parameter to make the output human-readable. This is what we see on our test system:

```
Filesystem                       1K-blocks  Used Available Use% Mounted on
/dev/mapper/VG_POSTGRES-LV_DATA 31851320 77856  31773464   1% /db
```

There's more...

There is one final important mount option that we have not yet discussed—nobarrier. Write barriers insert a flush operation between a filesystem write and disk sync to prevent inadvertent data reordering. Some storage devices contain a battery-backed disk cache such as high-end RAID solutions, SANs, and some solid-state disks with on-board capacitors. This kind of hardware can survive sudden power loss and does not require explicit barrier-imposed data flushing.

Without this excessive data flushing, write performance can improve noticeably. To use this setting, merely include nobarrier in the list of mount options; for example, consider the following:

```
mount -t xfs -o noatime,nodiratime,logbsize=256k \
       -o allocsize=1m,nobarrier /dev/VG_POSTGRES/LV_DATA /db
```

Do not use this setting on any other device, as data corruption would be the likely result.

See also

For more details, refer to the following:

- The XFS FAQ contains a lot of information related to performance and tweaking XFS in general. You can view this information at https://xfs.org/index.php/XFS_FAQ.
- Otherwise, the mount manual provided by man has a section specifically pertaining to XFS mount options:

    ```
    man mount
    ```

Maintaining an XFS filesystem

Conventional wisdom regarding Linux filesystems suggests that file defragmentation is not a necessary task. While this is true in general, file fragmentation isn't something we should allow to spiral out of control. PostgreSQL storage files are limited to 1 GB in size, yet we configured XFS to preallocate no more than 1 MB at a time.

This introduces the potential for data fragmentation on **Online Transactional Processing** (**OLTP**) systems or any database cluster where several tables experience high turnover. To prevent this from adversely affecting sequential scans, and to promote good filesystem health in general, we need to track and potentially correct overly fragmented files.

XFS provides two tools suited to this activity. The first is xfs_db, which provides information about an XFS filesystem. The second is xfs_fsr, which allows us to defragment XFS while it is still mounted and active. This recipe will cover the basic usage of these tools to keep our high availability server performing well.

Getting ready

For this recipe, we want a formatted and active XFS filesystem. Follow the steps in the *Formatting an XFS filesystem* recipe before continuing. It may also be a good idea to set up a dummy database where you mounted XFS. This way, you can run a pgbench test to create a lot of database write activity so that there is a small amount of data fragmentation. This is not required to follow along with this recipe.

How to do it...

Assuming pg1 is our current primary node and /dev/VG_POSTGRES/LV_DATA is the device we formatted with XFS, follow these steps as the root user:

1. Examine the current fragmentation status with this command:

   xfs_db -f -c frag /dev/VG_POSTGRES/LV_DATA

2. Defragment the filesystem with xfs_fsr:

   xfs_fsr -t 600 /dev/VG_POSTGRES/LV_DATA

3. Afterward, view the real-time fragmentation status:

   xfs_db -f -c frag -r /dev/VG_POSTGRES/LV_DATA

How it works...

We begin with the xfs_db utility to view the current fragmentation status of the filesystem. The -c parameter lets us specify a command that xfs_db should invoke. In this case, we want it to check the fragmentation status, so we set -c to frag. We set the -f parameter as it allows us to use xfs_db on a mounted filesystem.

The fragmentation status is calculated by counting the number of non-contiguous extents on all files and comparing that number to the total amount of files. To prepare for this, we continuously invoked pgbench to cause a high level of fragmentation. Here is the fragmentation on our system:

```
actual 4690, ideal 2847, fragmentation factor 39.30%
Note, this number is largely meaningless.
Files on this filesystem average 1.65 extents per file
```

As you can see, our filesystem is 39.30% fragmented. To correct this, we need to use xfs_fsr to reorganize any fragmented files. To do this, we only need to call xfs_fsr with either the device path or the path where the device is mounted. For the sake of consistency, we chose the former.

We can also limit the amount of time XFS spends fixing fragmentation with the -t parameter, which sets the runtime in seconds. We chose 600 seconds for an even 10 minutes, but larger systems might require an hour or longer. By setting the -t parameter, we can run xfs_fsr regularly as a maintenance item so that fragmentation is regularly kept in check.

XFS defragmentation proceeds on a file-by-file basis. Therefore, if the xfs_fsr command is canceled, or does not defragment every file before it exceeds our time limit, no progress is lost.

If we examine the filesystem again with xfs_db, our fragmentation should be significantly reduced. Let's consider the following screenshot:

```
actual 2868, ideal 2851, fragmentation factor 0.59%
Note, this number is largely meaningless.
Files on this filesystem average 1.01 extents per file
```

Now, our fragmentation is down to 0.59%, which is well within the tolerances for good sequential access performance. However, you might have noticed that we added an -r parameter just after the -c frag declaration.

Remember when we said that XFS maintains an internal database? Well, due to caching and update intervals, parts of the XFS database are not always accurate. The `-r` option to the `-c frag` command tells XFS that we want real-time information about the filesystem, and not what is currently stored in the tracking database.

There's more...

While we use the `xfs_db` command to obtain file fragmentation information, it can actually do much more. XFS maintains a small internal database that `xfs_db` can view or manipulate. Unfortunately, modifying XFS metadata can render the filesystem corrupt or otherwise unusable. We highly recommend never using `xfs_db` for anything but checking fragmentation statuses or obtaining other forensic information.

Only experts should ever use `xfs_db` command parameters other than `frag`.

See also

Both the `xfs_db` and `xfs_fsr` commands have fairly extensive manual pages. We recommend using these to learn more about the other functionalities these tools provide:

```
man xfs_db
man xfs_fsr
```

Using LVM snapshots

One of the reasons we created a second layer of LVM on top of DRBD was to provide filesystem snapshot capabilities. When we create a snapshot, all the files on a particular volume will appear static on that snapshot until one of the following two things happens:

- We destroy the snapshot.
- The changes to the source volume are larger than the space we reserved for the snapshot.

This is the primary reason we left 5 percent space unused within our PostgreSQL volume group. If we create a snapshot, up to 5 percent of the database can change before we have to remove it. For larger storage devices, this should give us a lot of time to perform emergency restores, create byte-stable backups, or any other operation that requires consistent data.

In this recipe, we'll learn how to properly allocate, use, and remove an LVM snapshot.

Getting ready

For this recipe, we want a formatted and active XFS filesystem. Please follow the steps in the *Formatting an XFS filesystem* recipe before continuing.

How to do it...

This procedure will assume `pg1` is our current primary node and `VG_POSTGRES/LV_DATA` is the principal data volume. Follow these steps as the `root` user to create and use an LVM snapshot:

1. Create the snapshot with `lvcreate`:

   ```
   lvcreate -l 100%FREE -s -n snap VG_POSTGRES/LV_DATA
   ```

2. Create a directory to mount the snapshot on using this command:

   ```
   mkdir /mnt/db_snap
   ```

3. Mount the snapshot as a regular XFS filesystem using this command:

   ```
   mount -t xfs -o nouuid /dev/VG_POSTGRES/snap /mnt/db_snap
   ```

4. Enter the snapshot `pgdata` directory using this command:

   ```
   cd /mnt/db_snap/pgdata
   ```

5. Examine snapshot information with `lvdisplay`:

   ```
   lvdisplay VG_POSTGRES/snap | grep snap
   ```

Follow these steps as the `root` user to unmount and remove an LVM snapshot:

1. Unmount the snapshot with this command:

   ```
   umount /mnt/db_snap
   ```

2. Destroy the snapshot with `lvremove`:

```
lvremove VG_POSTGRES/snap
```

How it works...

We can use the same `lvcreate` utility that helped us provision the PostgreSQL volume. We start the command with the `-l` parameter set to `100%FREE` to use any unallocated space in the `VG_POSTGRES` volume group. While we can specify sizes in MB or GB with the `-L` setting, we really only need to do this if we plan on creating multiple snapshots.

The `-s` parameter makes this volume a snapshot, which causes LVM to base its contents on those of another volume. Thus, we specify `VG_POSTGRES/LV_DATA` as the origin volume group and volume we want to use for the snapshot. We also use the `-n` parameter to set the name of the new volume to `snap`, making our intentions more obvious.

With the volume created, we simply need to mount it to access the contents. A quick `mkdir` later, we have a location in `/mnt/db_snap`, where we can find the files after mounting.

The `mount` command itself contains the basic parts necessary to use the filesystem and nothing more. We set the type to `xfs` with `-t`, while the last two parameters dictate the device and the location where it should be mounted.

Since we are using an XFS filesystem, we also need to provide the `nouuid` mount option. By default, XFS will not allow the same filesystem to be mounted more than once. The `nouuid` option skips this check, allowing us to mount the snapshot.

At this point, the files in the `/mnt/db_snap/pgdata` directory will be the same as those in `/db/pgdata`. The primary difference between the two lies in the fact that `/db/pgdata` is our live database instance, and it has continued changing. The files at `/mnt/db_snap/pgdata` are frozen in time from when the `lvcreate` command was completed. If we view the snapshot volume with `lvdisplay`, we can see this in action:

```
LV Path                /dev/VG_POSTGRES/snap
LV Name                snap
LV snapshot status     active destination for LV_DATA
Allocated to snapshot  10.34%
```

Notice that LVM tells us that this is a snapshot volume and what the source volume is. We can also see that 10.34% of the snapshot space is used. This means that files have changed on the source volume, and the snapshot responded by storing the original blocks locally. When all of its space is consumed, the snapshot will be marked as invalid by LVM. Periodic checks with `lvdisplay` are important to determine the validity of the files we are using that reside on a snapshot.

When we are finished with the snapshot, it's good practice to destroy it. We start this process by unmounting the snapshot volume from `/mnt/db_snap`. Afterward, we can use `lvremove` for the first time to destroy the snapshot volume. The `lvremove` command only requires the name of the volume we want to destroy, and it will confirm our intent before doing so. Once a volume has been removed, there's no way to restore it.

Be careful with keeping snapshots around too long or creating them during business hours. Depending on the underlying device, performance can suffer significantly due to the extra writes necessary to maintain the snapshot.

See also

The Linux Documentation Project has a very simple example of snapshot usage. Feel free to browse the example at `http://www.tldp.org/HOWTO/LVM-HOWTO/snapshots_backup.html`.

Switching live stack systems

At this point, we have our data located simultaneously on two servers. The second system can fulfill many possible roles. It can replace the current node in case of hardware failure, or allow us to perform server maintenance or upgrades with very little downtime.

Regardless of our intent, properly utilizing the second system is the key to a highly available database server. In this recipe, we'll discuss the proper method for activating the second server in a two-node pair so that we can make changes to one or both nodes.

Getting ready

By now, we need the full stack and probably a fully active database server as well. Follow all the recipes up to *Tweaking XFS performance* before starting here.

How to do it...

For this recipe, we will need two PostgreSQL servers, pg1 and pg2, where pg1 is the currently active node. Follow these steps as the root user on the system indicated to move an active PostgreSQL service from one node to another:

1. Stop the PostgreSQL service on pg1 on Debian-based systems:

   ```
   sudo systemctl stop postgresql@12-main
   ```

2. Red Hat derivatives should use the following command instead:

   ```
   sudo systemctl stop postgresql-12
   ```

3. Unmount the /db filesystem on pg1:

   ```
   umount /db
   ```

4. Mark the VG_POSTGRES group as inactive using vgchange on pg1:

   ```
   vgchange -a n VG_POSTGRES
   ```

5. Demote DRBD status to secondary with drbdadm on pg1:

   ```
   drbdadm secondary pg
   ```

6. Promote DRBD status to primary with drbdadm on pg2:

   ```
   drbdadm primary pg
   ```

7. Mark the VG_POSTGRES group as active using vgchange on pg2:

   ```
   vgchange -a y VG_POSTGRES
   ```

8. Mount the /db filesystem on pg2:

   ```
   mount -t xfs -o noatime,nodiratime \
      -o logbsize=256k,allocsize=1m \
      /dev/VG_POSTGRES/LV_DATA /db
   ```

9. Start PostgreSQL on `pg2` on Debian-based systems:

```
sudo systemctl start postgresql@12-main
```

Red Hat derivatives should use this command instead:

```
sudo systemctl start postgresql-12
```

How it works...

There is actually very little in this recipe that we have not done in this chapter. What we have actually done here is formalized the steps necessary to tear down and build up an active stack. We start the process by stopping the PostgreSQL service with `systemctl`, as we clearly can't move the data while it's still in use.

Next, we use `umount` to decouple the `/dev/VG_POSTGRES/LV_DATA` device from the `/db` directory. With no locks on the storage volume, we can use `vgchange` with the -a parameter set to n to deactivate any volume in the `VG_POSTGRES` group. Since the `VG_POSTGRES` group actually resides on the DRBD device, it can only be active on one node at a time.

Once the volumes are no longer active, we can set the DRBD status to `secondary` with `drbdadm`. After we perform this step, the `/dev/VG_POSTGRES` directory and any corresponding device will actually disappear. This is because a DRBD device in the secondary status is only active within DRBD. Here is what DRBD shows us in `/proc/drbd` regarding this situation:

```
version: 8.4.10 (api:1/proto:86-101)
srcversion: 15055BDD6F0D23278182874
 0: cs:Connected ro:Secondary/Secondary ds:UpToDate/UpToDate C r-----
    ns:2057 nr:128504 dw:71521568 dr:33556387 al:11 bm:0 lo:0 pe:0 ua:0 ap:0 ep:1 wo:f oos:0
```

DRBD sees the device as `Secondary` on both nodes; currently, neither node can access our PostgreSQL data. From this point, we merely reverse the process to reactivate all of these resources on `pg2` instead.

We begin reactivating PostgreSQL by promoting the storage to the `primary` status with `drbdadm` on the `pg2` node. This causes the requisite `VG_POSTGRES` volume group to appear on `pg2`, making it a candidate for activation with `vgchange`.

Then, we simply reuse the `mount` command that we discussed in the *Tweaking XFS performance* recipe on the `pg2` node, making the data available to us once again. If we start PostgreSQL with the `systemctl` control system, our database will begin running as if it were still on the `pg1` node. PostgreSQL does not know anything has changed.

There's more...

Since data can switch nodes arbitrarily as demonstrated here, upgrades and maintenance to server hardware are much easier. What can we do with the extra node? We can reboot it, apply firmware or kernel updates, apply security patches, or even update the database software to a bug-fix release.

Following any required or suggested changes to the secondary node, we merely promote it to run PostgreSQL in place of the current server. Then, we can repeat modifications on the other node. With this, we can limit outages to a matter of seconds while still providing high uptime guarantees, all without skipping system maintenance.

In fact, this process is so standardized that we will be exploring it in great detail in the next chapter. Once this teardown and buildup procedure is automated, maintaining or replacing servers is even easier.

Detaching a problematic node

There's one last thing we need to cover before ending this chapter. If a server is causing problems, there's a good chance that the infrastructure department will want to reclaim, rebuild, or replace it. Simply stopping the broken server is a possible solution, but there is a safer way to decouple DRBD from another system.

In this recipe, we'll quickly cover partially dismantling a running DRBD system without disrupting the active server.

Getting ready

By now, we need the full stack and probably a fully active database server as well. Follow all the recipes up to *Tweaking XFS performance* before starting here.

How to do it...

For this recipe, we will need two PostgreSQL servers: pg1 and pg2, where pg1 is the currently active node. Follow these steps as the root user on the system indicated to permanently remove pg2 from the DRBD cluster:

1. Execute this command on both pg1 and pg2 to disconnect DRBD:

    drbdadm disconnect pg

2. Invalidate the data on the remote node with drbdadm on pg1:

    drbdadm invalidate-remote pg

3. Invalidate the data on the current node with drbdadm on pg2:

    drbdadm invalidate pg

How it works...

This recipe is one of the easiest in our list, but it is equally important. We begin by using drbdadm to disconnect each node from the communication link DRBD uses to copy data between servers.

Then, we use drbdadm again to doubly invalidate the data on the bad node. First, we use the invalidate-remote parameter on pg1 to ensure it sees pg2 as unusable. Then, we use the invalidate parameter on pg2, so it sees its own data as incorrect. We can see what this looks like by examining the contents of /proc/drbd again:

```
version: 8.4.10 (api:1/proto:86-101)
srcversion: 15055BDD6F0D23278182874
 0: cs:StandAlone ro:Secondary/Unknown ds:Inconsistent/DUnknown   r-----
    ns:2057 nr:128504 dw:71521568 dr:33556387 al:11 bm:0 lo:0 pe:0 ua:0 ap:0 ep:1 wo:f oos:33549276
```

As you can see here, DRBD considers the data on the current node as **Inconsistent**, meaning it cannot be used as the source data for a new DRBD pair. At this point, we can release pg2 to its fate, no matter what that might be.

There's more...

Some might claim that any data invalidation is excessive. DRBD has its own safeguards to protect against inadvertent data copies. While true, server pools are not always cleaned up properly. Invalidating the data on pg2 does more than protect pg1 from being adversely affected if or when pg2 reconnects. We've effectively ensured pg2 cannot contribute data to any other DRBD cluster as a primary node.

However, we can go even further. We can actually physically destroy all traces of DRBD data on the decommissioned node. These commands on pg2 will do the work for us:

```
drbdadm down pg
drbdadm wipe-md pg
dd if=/dev/zero of=/dev/VG_DRBD/LV_DATA bs=1024 count=1024
```

The first `drbdadm` command stops the DRBD device itself. The second command erases its metadata. Why then, do we need the third?

The `dd` utility is absurdly dangerous because it can write arbitrary blocks to any device on a server with almost no restrictions. We set the input file (`if`) to `/dev/zero`, and the output file (`of`) to `/dev/VG_DRBD/LV_DATA`, which we know as the device DRBD was using. Then, we set the block size (`bs`) to `1024`, and write a count of `1024` blocks to the device. Essentially, we just overwrite the first megabyte of data on the DRBD device with zeros.

We did this because metadata can be extracted from other nodes and reapplied. Theoretically, this means pg2 can be salvaged with enough expertise. By corrupting the data on the device itself, this is no longer possible. Furthermore, if we use `drbdadm` with `create-md` later, then there is no existing data to interfere with the new metadata.

See also

Linbit, the maker of DRBD, has very extensive documentation on system troubleshooting. Refer to this URL for more information:

https://docs.linbit.com/docs/users-guide-8.4/#ch-troubleshooting.

12
High Availability via Pacemaker

Almost everything that we've discussed so far has led directly to this chapter. By now, we have multiple servers, redundant alternates, backup, synchronization, and much more. If we combine all of these techniques, management becomes more difficult with each component we add.

In the previous chapter, we covered all of the elements for a robust and elastic storage structure. Even then, we noted the arduous nature of moving a running server from one node to another. Typing commands safely takes time, as does referring to a checklist and verifying commands before running them in a production environment. We would never recommend anything less.

Finally, we will learn how to configure two linked nodes to manage themselves. It's not entirely foolproof, yet the process we are about to undergo is robust and implemented safely by many enterprises. Instead of a dozen commands to move an active PostgreSQL instance to another server, we will need only one. Furthermore, the software can detect several failure scenarios and relocate PostgreSQL on our behalf if something goes wrong.

The safest cluster in a high availability architecture is one that requires the least amount of manual intervention. To that end, this chapter will cover **Corosync** and **Pacemaker** and the steps to manage dual-node servers with this software. By the end of this chapter, we should have something similar to this diagram:

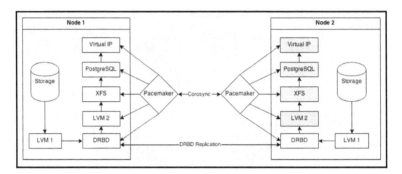

All of the components shown here are installed on both nodes, but the grayed-out ones are unavailable on **Node 2**. Yet, we could use Pacemaker to reverse the graph so that **Node 2** is the active server instead of **Node 1**. Those are a lot of changes to make manually.

In this chapter, we will learn how to automate cluster management and ensure high availability. We will cover the following recipes in this chapter:

- Installing the components
- Configuring Corosync
- Preparing start up services
- Starting with base options
- Adding DRBD to cluster management
- Adding LVM to cluster management
- Adding XFS to cluster management
- Adding PostgreSQL to cluster management
- Adding a virtual IP to proxy the cluster
- Adding an email alert
- Grouping associated resources
- Combining and ordering related actions
- Performing a managed resource migration
- Using an outage to test migration

Before we begin...

Before we spend any more time on this chapter, we should ask ourselves a question: is automation necessary? It's certainly nice to have, but is it required? Will we benefit from the admittedly esoteric incantations needed to install and configure these tools?

The answer is not always so straightforward. While exceedingly powerful, Pacemaker is infamously difficult to use and even a little overzealous in applying its rules. Both repmgr and Patroni are far more forgiving in this regard. An improperly built Pacemaker cluster might produce a database that moves to another node at the slightest provocation. Much like Patroni, Pacemaker enforces its current status and can actively thwart management attempts it didn't personally invoke.

We won't lie; the learning curve is immense and should extend far longer than what this chapter teaches. If this is too much for now, skip this chapter with our best regards. Both repmgr and Patroni are comparatively easier to use, and arguably more modern given today's clustering needs and the popularity of container-based servers. Some already rely on Pacemaker though, making it critically important to how this stack functions in those environments.

Otherwise, we want you to know that this chapter is only the beginning. We will guide you through the creation of a functional Pacemaker-managed system, but we strongly recommend experimenting frequently on a pair of virtual servers capable of managing filesystem mounts. This gives you a safe area to make mistakes, break Pacemaker in all kinds of interesting ways, and learn more about the material we present here.

None of this content is easy, but we promise it's worth the time to absorb. We will introduce this material slowly to aid the process.

Installing the components

The two main components of the software we use in this chapter are Corosync and Pacemaker. Each of these is comprised of or depends on several other elements and prerequisites. For now, we'll simply refer to the entire suite as Pacemaker, as it encompasses the bulk of how we will control the failover system.

This recipe should be relatively short, as we will only discuss the installation of Corosync and Pacemaker, not their configuration.

Getting ready

Red Hat-based systems such as Fedora, CentOS, and Scientific Linux will already have Pacemaker in their repositories. Debian and its derivatives, such as Ubuntu, also include Pacemaker as an optional install from standard repositories. **Red Hat Enterprise Linux (RHEL)** itself, however, only offers the software as a paid add-on, available at this URL: `https://www.redhat.com/en/store/all-products`.

Whatever choice you make, it shouldn't be necessary to compile Pacemaker from source on most Linux distributions.

How to do it...

Follow these quick steps to install Pacemaker and Corosync on all PostgreSQL server pairs:

1. Install the main packages and all dependencies with this command as a root-capable user for Debian-based systems:

   ```
   sudo apt-get install corosync pacemaker crmsh
   ```

2. Red Hat-based operating systems should use this command instead:

   ```
   sudo yum install corosync pacemaker
   ```

3. Stop the cluster software and disable Pacemaker from starting on system boot:

   ```
   sudo systemctl stop corosync
   sudo systemctl disable pacemaker
   sudo systemctl stop pacemaker
   ```

How it works...

This short recipe consists of three steps:

1. Install Corosync, Pacemaker, and cluster resource management tools.
2. Stop Corosync and Pacemaker.
3. Disable Pacemaker on server boot.

The first step makes sense since we need the software to build the cluster. The second step is necessary while we modify the configuration file in the next recipe. But why the last step? When running a highly available cluster, caution is a beneficial attribute. A server may reboot for any number of reasons, and many of those include crashes that require further investigation.

Were Pacemaker to start immediately following a server reboot, we could potentially lose valuable diagnostic information. More importantly, a rebooted server should be considered in an unknown or potentially damaged state until it is examined by an experienced system administrator. We don't want a misbehaving server as part of our critical infrastructure.

Corosync is the communication layer between each Pacemaker node, but it does not actually contribute to managing cluster services. Hence, it is safe to leave this enabled but not started while we modify its configuration in a later recipe.

There's more...

If you believe we are being too wary, simply skip the last step in our recipe. However, it's important to remember that services are easy to start on Linux servers. This command, for instance, will start Pacemaker normally even while disabled:

```
sudo systemctl start pacemaker
```

If the server was rebooted as result of maintenance, the preceding commands will return the system to normal operation. Otherwise, a few cursory checks through server logs may determine that the cause of the system crash does not adversely affect PostgreSQL data. If so, once again, it is easy to start Corosync and Pacemaker and re-establish the dual-node cluster.

What we have done here is a very rudimentary form of **STONITH**, which means to **Shoot The Other Node In The Head**. Dedicated STONITH hardware may power a server off completely or remove it from the network, making it inaccessible through anything other than console emulation or direct access. Truly high-availability systems cannot afford to introduce unknown entities into a carefully crafted and manicured architecture. To do so invites undefined behavior across the spectrum of database services that could lead to outages or data loss.

If we claim that our data is important and our uptime is essential, we need to adopt a similar stance toward crashed or damaged servers. We haven't gone so far as to completely disable the server in this recipe; we only prevent it from rejoining a functioning Pacemaker pair. In a true STONITH-enabled organization, our measures would be much more drastic.

See also

The ClusterLabs website (`https://clusterlabs.org/`) is a repository of all things related to Pacemaker. It has several relevant tutorials, examples, and copious documentation. If you had trouble installing with our recipe, try an alternative listed at this URL: `https://wiki.clusterlabs.org/wiki/Install`

Configuring Corosync

Once Corosync and Pacemaker are installed, we only need to modify a single configuration file to activate them. As we mentioned earlier and showed in the introduction diagram, Corosync is the conduit that Pacemaker uses for communication. Corosync also binds itself to services that rely on its channels, so it will also launch Pacemaker on our behalf.

This recipe will explain how to create a simple configuration for Corosync that will establish a secure Pacemaker cluster.

Getting ready

We have already installed everything we need, but if we are running an older Debian-based system such as Ubuntu or Mint, we have one more step. Before Corosync will work properly, we need to enable its start up script. Open the `/etc/default/corosync` file and make sure it contains this line:

```
START=yes
```

Without it, Corosync won't run even if we start it manually. We removed it from system boot time, but that doesn't mean we never want it to run at all!

How to do it...

For this recipe, we have two PostgreSQL nodes: pg1 and pg2, which are assigned IP addresses of 10.0.30.101 and 10.0.30.102. Follow these steps as a root-capable user:

1. On pg1, run this command to generate an authorization key file:

   corosync-keygen

2. If this doesn't return quickly, open another connection to pg1 and perform several activities to generate sufficient entropy until corosync-keygen completes. A good source of random events is software compilation, for example.

3. Copy the resulting /etc/corosync/authkey file to pg2.

4. Ensure the totem section of corosync.conf in /etc/corosync on both pg1 and pg2 resembles the following:

   ```
   totem {
           version: 2
           cluster_name: pgha
           crypto_cipher: aes256
           crypto_hash: sha256
           transport: knet
   }
   ```

5. Ensure the nodelist section of corosync.conf in /etc/corosync on both pg1 and pg2 resembles the following:

   ```
   nodelist {
      node {
              name: pg1
              nodeid: 1
              ring0_addr: 10.0.30.101
      }

      node {
              name: pg2
              nodeid: 2
              ring0_addr: 10.0.30.102
      }
   }
   ```

6. Start Corosync on both `pg1` and `pg2` with this command:

```
sudo systemctl restart corosync
sudo systemctl start pacemaker
```

7. Show the status of Pacemaker with the `crm` utility on `pg1`:

```
sudo crm status
```

How it works...

The first step involves securing our Corosync communication channel. The `corosync-keygen` utility will generate a 2,048-bit key that helps Pacemaker nodes to securely communicate with each other, but doing so may require a lot of random input. This random input must come from the server itself, so simply typing gibberish in the console while we wait will not suffice.

We can generate entropy by making the server perform tasks. If the server is otherwise idle, we may need to execute commands, test SQL, or compile basic software. Given enough server activity, the `corosync-keygen` command will eventually exit and save a file named `authkey` in the `/etc/corosync` configuration directory. As we want this file to be the same on all nodes, we also copy it from `pg1` to `pg2`.

There are two critical sections of the configuration we must modify. The first of these is the `totem` section, which acts as a kind of bootstrap for the cluster itself. The `version` portion is likely already in the existing configuration and, for now, can only be set to 2. Then, we set `cluster_name` to something informative like `pgha`, but use any descriptive name that best fits your environment.

Then, we need to change three more lines in the `totem` section to suit our needs. First, we change `crypto_cypher` and `crypto_hash` to one of the many supported protocols to enable secure and encrypted communication between nodes. The manual lists several, so choose an encryption algorithm that fits your security requirements. When using encryption, the `transport` attribute must be set to `knet`, completing this section of the configuration file.

Next, we must specify each node that is allowed to participate in this cluster within the `nodelist` section. Each node must provide `name`, `nodeid`, and `ring0_addr` to correspond with the hostname, node number, and IP address. It's very important that the name matches the actual hostname of each server, or Pacemaker will consider each node unhealthy and may not operate properly.

These configuration file instructions differ greatly from previous editions of this book. Version 3.0 of Corosync introduced a new configuration format and section requirements. We're not sure why they didn't change the `version` attribute to reflect this, however. The old instructions will not work with the newer versions of this software.

When this is done on both nodes, we can start Corosync and then Pacemaker with the `systemctl` command.

To verify that the Pacemaker cluster exists, we can use the `crm` command. What is `crm`? It stands for **cluster resource manager** and will be the command we use for all Pacemaker interactions from now on. The status parameter displays the current state of the cluster, and for our test systems, it looks like this:

```
root@pg1:~# crm status
Stack: corosync
Current DC: pg2 (version 2.0.1-9e909a5bdd) - partition with quorum
Last updated: Tue Dec 17 19:09:00 2019
Last change: Tue Dec 17 18:39:42 2019 by hacluster via crmd on pg2

2 nodes configured
0 resources configured

       : [ pg1 pg2 ]

No resources
```

As we can see, Pacemaker can communicate with both nodes, so it lists them as `Online`. The rest of the information presented here regarding `quorum` and `votes` can be ignored for now, but we'll cover it soon enough.

See also

For more details, refer to the following:

- As mentioned earlier, the ClusterLab site (`clusterlabs.org`) should be considered the ultimate resource regarding Corosync and Pacemaker. To learn more about the process we used here, proceed to this URL: `https://wiki.clusterlabs.org/wiki/Initial_Configuration`.
- Otherwise, the `corosync.conf` file actually has its own extensive manual page available via the `man` utility. It's extremely useful to create more advanced clusters. Use the following command:

```
man corosync.conf
```

Preparing start up services

A common interpretation of a functional server is one that runs on its own recognizance. After being rebooted, it starts all necessary services and does its job as configured. It might be hard to believe, but we want to fight that inclination for two important reasons:

- Pacemaker is a state machine.
- Pacemaker needs total control of any service it manages.

Pacemaker wants to start services itself so it knows that the current status is the one it created. It will perform tests to obtain this information, but for things such as DRBD, this isn't always reliable. It's generally safer to start from scratch. Beyond this, if a service that isn't supposed to be running starts, Pacemaker will only have to stop it anyway.

In this recipe, we'll quickly cover which services to disable on each of our PostgreSQL nodes.

Getting ready

As we're continuing to configure Corosync and Pacemaker, make sure you've followed all of the previous recipes of this chapter.

How to do it...

For this recipe, we will use the same two PostgreSQL nodes: `pg1` and `pg2`. We will also continue to assume that our PostgreSQL data is located at `/db/pgdata`:

1. Prevent PostgreSQL or DRBD from starting on system boot on Red Hat-based systems by executing these commands on both servers as a root-capable user:

    ```
    sudo systemctl disable postgresql-12
    sudo systemctl disable drbd
    ```

2. Debian-based systems should use the following commands to disable PostgreSQL and DRBD instead:

    ```
    sudo systemctl disable postgresql@12-main
    sudo systemctl disable drbd
    ```

How it works...

All we really want to do here is remove PostgreSQL and DRBD from the list of services that start at system boot time. These are the only two services that are controlled via system start up scripts, so our work here is very short indeed.

One critically important element is that systemd-equipped Linux distributions are fully compatible with the **Linux Standard Base** (**LSB**) set of expected status codes. Pacemaker uses this information to always know the result of an action. Stopped services return different codes than running ones when checked with `systemctl status`, for example. It's possible to manage PostgreSQL and DRBD without systemd, but be aware that LSB codes must be used properly for Pacemaker to operate normally.

Previous editions of this book also included a PostgreSQL start up script designed to ensure LSB exit codes expected by Pacemaker. This was because some Linux distribution control scripts didn't always return the proper exit codes, and this caused Pacemaker to act in unexpected ways. Modern Linux systems using systemd don't have this problem, so we've chosen to omit the extra script.

Otherwise, the main focus of this recipe is to ensure that only Pacemaker is allowed to fully control and manage the PostgreSQL and DRBD services. Since Pacemaker is a state machine, it also knows the expected status of every service it manages on each node. If PostgreSQL should not be running, but the service is configured to start on boot, Pacemaker would merely stop it again.

The point of this recipe is to be 100% certain that that doesn't happen.

There's more...

If you have another test server with PostgreSQL installed and running, try some of these tests to confirm it works as described:

1. Start PostgreSQL and confirm the exit status is 0 for success with this command:

```
sudo systemctl start postgresql@12-main
echo $?
```

2. Stop PostgreSQL and confirm the exit status is 0 for success with this command:

```
sudo systemctl stop postgresql@12-main
echo $?
```

3. Finally, check the status of PostgreSQL while it is stopped and confirm the exit value is 3, indicating the service isn't running, with this command:

```
sudo systemctl status postgresql@12-main
echo $?
```

The $? variable represents the exit status of the previous command. It's an easy way to visualize the exit code, which is normally only used by other utilities. Any script that does not return these three exit codes for these specific conditions cannot be used with Pacemaker.

See also

The Linux Standard Base specification for initialization scripts is fully documented. We recommend referring to the following URL to learn more about LSB exit codes: https://refspecs.linuxbase.org/LSB_5.0.0/LSB-Core-generic/LSB-Core-generic/iniscrptact.html

Starting with base options

As a cluster resource manager, Pacemaker has some defaults that we are interested in changing. Pacemaker is very powerful, so it makes several assumptions about the composition of cluster resources and nodes it controls. One of which is that there are several nodes and not just two.

This works well for large cooperative networks of web servers or independent services that can operate transiently. However, we have two nodes that are very much dependent on shared storage that can only be used by one node at a time. So, this recipe is going to perform three tasks:

1. Disable STONITH because we don't currently have STONITH-enabled hardware.
2. Disable cluster quorum because two systems cannot produce a meaningful vote.

3. Enable resource stickiness to prevent disruptive automated node swaps.

Getting ready

As we're continuing to configure Corosync and Pacemaker, make sure you've followed all previous recipes.

How to do it...

For this recipe, we will use the same two PostgreSQL nodes: `pg1` and `pg2`. Perform the following steps on either server as the `root` user:

1. Disable STONITH with this `crm` command:

   ```
   crm configure property stonith-enabled=false
   ```

2. Ignore quorum voting with this `crm` command:

   ```
   crm configure property no-quorum-policy=ignore
   ```

3. Increase the default resource stickiness with this `crm` command:

   ```
   crm configure rsc_defaults resource-stickiness=100
   ```

4. Finally, view the current state of the cluster configuration with this command:

   ```
   crm configure show
   ```

How it works...

This recipe differs from those in the previous sections in that we can execute these steps from any server. Commands issued by the `crm` utility are sent to the cluster itself, so any node will transmit them successfully and Pacemaker will act accordingly. In the case of our configuration changes, the only action that Pacemaker takes is to alter its stored settings.

The first thing we do is disable STONITH by calling `crm` with the `configure property` parameter for `stonith-enabled`. While STONITH is an amusing acronym, there are actual devices on the market that fill this role. These devices can isolate a node from a network in several ways, and Pacemaker is capable of interacting with them by default. As we don't have one right now, it's best to tell Pacemaker that it shouldn't expect such functionality.

Our next step includes shutting down our fledgling democracy by disabling quorum verification. We only have two nodes, and votes comprised of only two voters are entirely meaningless because they will always result in a tie. Without an odd number of nodes, no quorum (agreement) can be reached. This time, we configure `property` for `no-quorum-policy` and set it to `ignore`. This essentially means that the nodes will continue to vote, but we don't care unless they can reach a quorum. As two servers can't reach a quorum, resources will run where we tell them to run, and they have no say in the matter.

The last setting we change with `configure rsc_defaults` is `resource-stickiness`. As we mentioned earlier, Pacemaker is really built for transient services that act as independent agents. If an HTTP daemon moves from one node to another, nobody really cares or notices. If PostgreSQL acted similarly, there would be several broken applications and irritated users.

By changing this setting to `100`, we give every resource a default weight, so it sticks to whichever server it started on. Unless there's a crash or forced migration, it will stay there indefinitely.

Our last step is to view our handiwork by issuing `crm` with `configure show`. Pacemaker stores its configuration as XML, and while this is somewhat human-readable, it's hardly concise. On our test cluster, it produces this output:

```
root@pg1:~# crm configure show
node 1: pg1
node 2: pg2
property cib-bootstrap-options: \
        have-watchdog=false \
        dc-version=2.0.1-9e909a5bdd \
        cluster-infrastructure=corosync \
        cluster-name=debian \
        stonith-enabled=false \
        no-quorum-policy=ignore \
rsc_defaults rsc-options: \
        resource-stickiness=100
```

As we can see, both `pg1` and `pg2` are each labeled as `node`. In addition, `stonith-enabled`, `no-quorum-policy`, and `resource-stickiness` are all set as we described in the recipe.

We're well on our way to building a Pacemaker cluster.

There's more...

The `crm` command is actually a fully functional pseudo-shell. If executed without parameters, it presents a prompt and waits for valid `crm` commands. These commands include `help` for every level chosen. For example, to see what options are available when putting `node` into `standby`, we can type this input while in a `crm` shell:

```
node help standby
```

Then, we can use what we learned previously and put the node into standby state until it is rebooted and Corosync is started again, like this:

```
node standby pg1 reboot
```

This is extremely helpful as Pacemaker has a lot of commands, and it's easy to forget the proper syntax.

See also

The `crm` shell has undergone a lot of changes in the last few years, including splitting from the Pacemaker project itself. As such, its documentation is somewhat fragmented. The new `crm` shell maintainers have information that is mostly compatible with versions packaged with Debian and Red Hat-based systems at this URL: `https://crmsh.github.io/man/`

Adding DRBD to cluster management

DRBD is actually one of the most difficult resources to manage with Pacemaker. Unlike a regular service that is started or stopped depending on where it is active, DRBD is always active. The only thing that changes between two nodes running DRBD is the `Primary` or `Secondary` state ascribed to each.

Due to this complication, DRBD is not one resource but two:

- A DRBD resource to manage starting and stopping DRBD
- A master/slave resource to control which node acts as `Primary`

In this recipe, we'll allocate both of these resources so that Pacemaker can manage DRBD properly.

Getting ready

As we're continuing to configure Pacemaker, make sure you've followed all previous recipes.

How to do it...

In the previous chapter, we created a DRBD resource named `pg`. With this in mind, follow these steps as the `root` user to add DRBD to Pacemaker:

1. Create a basic Pacemaker primitive for DRBD with this command:

```
crm configure primitive drbd_pg ocf:linbit:drbd \
    params drbd_resource="pg" \
    op monitor interval="15" role="Master" \
    op monitor interval="20" role="Slave" \
    op start interval="0" timeout="240" \
    op stop interval="0" timeout="120"
```

2. Create a master/slave resource with this command:

```
crm configure ms ms_drbd_pg drbd_pg \
    meta master-max="1" master-node-max="1" \
    clone-max="2" clone-node-max="1" notify="true"
```

3. Clean up any errors that might have accumulated with `crm`:

```
crm resource cleanup drbd_pg
```

4. Display the status of our new resources with `crm`:

```
crm resource status
```

How it works...

Most of the resources we create in subsequent sections are called primitives. These should be considered the base resource element that Pacemaker controls as they have a one-to-one relationship with each service. The first one we create is for our DRBD service.

When creating new configuration entries with `crm`, we declare them with `configure primitive`, and then we must supply a name. To keep things simple, we named this resource `drbd_pg`. After the name, we must supply a resource agent to actually manage this service. Pacemaker is shipped with several, but we are specifically interested in the `ocf:linbit:drbd` agent, as it was written by the makers of DRBD themselves.

Next, we can configure the resource agent by specifying `params`, followed by the options it recognizes, labeled with `op`. Among these options, we define `monitor interval` for the master server and one for the slave that isn't quite as frequent. Finally, we override `start timeout` and `stop timeout` so that they match the minimum values expected by Pacemaker. It will complain if we use values lower than this, but feel free to increase them.

At this point, we create the master/slave resource that controls how Pacemaker views the `drbd_pg` resource. Instead of adding and configuring a primitive, this time we `configure` a master/slave resource (`ms`) and name it `ms_drbd_pg`. After naming our `ms` resource, we designate `drbd_pg` as the primitive to treat as a master or slave service. All of the entries after the `meta` designation are somewhat confusing and arbitrary, so we hope these pointers help:

- By setting `master-max` to 1, we tell Pacemaker that only one node in the cluster can ever be promoted to master for this service.
- Similarly, setting `master-node-max` to 1 limits Pacemaker to a single copy of this resource per server.
- The `clone-max` setting actually describes the number of active copies for this resource, which is 2 in our case.
- Oddly enough, the `clone-node-max` setting means basically the same thing as `master-node-max`. We set this to 1 as well to safeguard the DRBD resource from potential Pacemaker bugs or future changes in default settings.
- Finally, the `notify` setting effectively transmits master/slave notices to all nodes so that Pacemaker knows the new status of the shared resource everywhere it is running.

What do we mean by a resource *copy*? Internally, Pacemaker stores resources as defined roles. If a single resource has two roles, it actually exists as two items within Pacemaker. In Pacemaker lingo, these are referred to as **clones**. The crm system hides these details from us, but they're still very real and difficult to manage.

The values we chose for all of the meta options are actually Pacemaker defaults. We could have omitted them, but a high-availability system cannot remain safe while it is at the mercy of malleable defaults. We set these in stone now to prevent Pacemaker upgrades from potentially causing problems in the future.

When adding new resources, sometimes Pacemaker enters an undefined state and lists errors that aren't actually valid. We can clear these out using the resource cleanup parameter to target the drbd_pg primitive. It's always a good idea to keep the Pacemaker status clean to avoid possible conflicts later.

Our final job is to view the status of all configured resources by calling crm with resource status. Our test system showed this output:

```
root@pg1:~# crm resource status
 Clone Set: ms_drbd_pg [drbd_pg] (promotable)
     Masters: [ pg1 ]
     Slaves: [ pg2 ]
```

Even though we created two primitive resources, we only see one entry: ms_drbd_pg. Note, however, that it represents the drbd_pg resource. We can also see Masters and Slaves for this set, though there should never be more than one of each with the configuration we used.

There's more...

In Pacemaker, resource agents can be viewed separately with the crm program, and many are available. To get a list of all of the LSB resource agents (scripts in /etc/init.d or services available via systemd) Pacemaker can see, use this command:

```
crm ra list lsb
```

For a list of Pacemaker-specific agents, use this command:

```
crm ra list ocf
```

This information isn't entirely helpful by itself. Knowing that the agents exist does not tell us what parameters they have. To see this, we need to view the `meta` information for the agent. We used the `ocf:linbit:drbd` agent in this recipe, and we can view its usage information with this command:

```
crm ra meta ocf:linbit:drbd
```

If this is not convenient enough, we can actually use the `man` command for most agents as well. If we know the class, provider, and name of an agent, we can view its Unix manual. For example, to see the manual for the `ocf:heartbeat:nginx` agent, we could use this command:

```
man ocf_heartbeat_nginx
```

See also

Some of this information is also available within the DRBD documentation at this URL: `https://docs.linbit.com/docs/users-guide-8.4/#s-pacemaker-crm-drbd-backed-service`.

Adding LVM to cluster management

To avoid potential conflicts, we will continue to add resources to Pacemaker in the same order as if we were starting them manually. After DRBD, there comes our second LVM layer. The primary purpose of Pacemaker in this instance is to activate or deactivate the `VG_POSTGRES` volume group that we created in the previous chapter.

This is necessary because DRBD cannot demote a primary resource to secondary status as long as there are any open locks. Any LVM volume group that contains active volumes can cause these kinds of locks. Also, we cannot utilize a volume group that has no active volumes when DRBD is promoted on the second node.

This recipe will explain the steps necessary to manage our `VG_POSTGRES/LV_DATA` data volume with Pacemaker.

Getting ready

As we're continuing to configure Pacemaker, make sure you've followed all of the previous recipes.

 Users of some Debian-derivative systems, such as Ubuntu, need to beware! To avoid potential issues, it may be necessary to delete the `/lib/udev/rules.d/85-lvm2.rules` file if it exists. Some versions of this file automatically mount LVM devices when they appear; such actions can interfere with Pacemaker LVM management.

How to do it...

Perform these steps on any Pacemaker node as the `root` user:

1. Add an LVM `primitive` to Pacemaker with `crm`:

   ```
   crm configure primitive pg_lvm ocf:heartbeat:LVM \
       params volgrpname="VG_POSTGRES" \
       op start interval="0" timeout="30" \
       op stop interval="0" timeout="30"
   ```

2. Clean up any errors that might have accumulated with `crm`:

   ```
   crm resource cleanup pg_lvm
   ```

3. Display the status of our new LVM resource with `crm`:

   ```
   crm resource status
   ```

How it works...

As with the previous recipe, we begin by adding a primitive to Pacemaker. For the sake of consistency and simplicity, we name this resource `pg_lvm`. To manage LVM, we also need to specify the `ocf:heartbeat:LVM` resource agent.

Remember, to see the list of parameters for a resource agent, use the `ra meta` command to the `crm` shell. For the LVM agent, this invocation would display usage information: `crm ra meta ocf:heartbeat:LVM`.

The only parameter (`params`) that concerns us regarding the LVM resource agent is `volgrpname`, which we set to `VG_POSTGRES`. The other options we set are more advisory minimum values, which reflect the number of seconds we should wait before considering an operation as failed.

In our case, we wait 30 seconds before declaring a start or stop status check as a failed action. If Pacemaker is unable to start LVM, it will attempt to do so on other available nodes. In the event that Pacemaker can't stop LVM, it will report an error and perform no further actions until the error is cleared or corrected.

Speaking of clearing errors, it's a good practice to perform `resource cleanup` after adding a new resource to Pacemaker. While not strictly required, this keeps the status output clean and ensures that Pacemaker will add the next resource as expected. Sometimes, Pacemaker will refuse to perform further actions if the error list contains any entries.

As we will do with all of the recipes in this chapter, our last action is to view the status of the resources to prove that the new addition is listed. Our test server shows that it is:

```
root@pg1:~# crm resource status
 Clone Set: ms_drbd_pg [drbd_pg] (promotable)
     Masters: [ pg1 ]
     Slaves: [ pg2 ]
 pg_lvm (ocf::heartbeat:LVM):    Started
```

In addition to the `ms_drbd_pg` resource that represents `drbd_pg`, we can see the new `pg_lvm` resource. Pacemaker also checked the status of LVM and displays it as `Started`.

There's more...

If you're tired of always checking the status of Pacemaker manually, there is a tool we can use instead. Much like `top`, which displays the current list of running processes, the `crm_mon` command monitors the status of a Pacemaker cluster and prints the same output as `crm status`. For our cluster in its current state, it looks like this:

```
Stack: corosync
Current DC: pg2 (version 2.0.1-9e909a5bdd) - partition with quorum
Last updated: Thu Dec 19 17:17:02 2019
Last change: Thu Dec 19 17:11:19 2019 by root via cibadmin on pg1

2 nodes configured
3 resources configured

Online: [ pg1 pg2 ]

Active resources:

 Clone Set: ms_drbd_pg [drbd_pg] (promotable)
     Masters: [ pg1 ]
     Slaves: [ pg2 ]
pg_lvm  (ocf::heartbeat:LVM):   Started pg1
```

This will refresh regularly and makes it easy to watch live transition states as Pacemaker performs actions related to cluster management. Feel free to keep this running in another Terminal window for the sake of convenience.

Adding XFS to cluster management

Next in our list of resources to manage with Pacemaker is the filesystem. As with LVM and DRBD, Pacemaker needs the ability to start and stop the resource arbitrarily to clear locks or enable activation. In addition, filesystems are somewhat more complex than LVM simply due to the number of necessary parameters required to use them.

For Pacemaker to manage a filesystem, we need to tell it about the device it's mounting, which directory the mount should target, the type of filesystem, and any extra options we want to use. While DRBD and LVM encode metadata within reserved storage areas on the device, filesystem mounts require explicit parameters.

This recipe will explain the steps necessary to manage our XFS filesystem with Pacemaker.

Getting ready

As we're continuing to configure Pacemaker, make sure you've followed all of the previous recipes.

How to do it...

Perform these steps on any Pacemaker node as the `root` user:

1. Export our list of XFS mount options to avoid long lines by executing these commands:

   ```
   export OPS=noatime,nodiratime,logbufs=8,logbsize=256k
   export OPS=$OPS,attr2,allocsize=1m
   ```

2. Add an XFS primitive to Pacemaker with `crm`:

   ```
   crm configure primitive pg_fs ocf:heartbeat:Filesystem \
       params device="/dev/VG_POSTGRES/LV_DATA" \
               directory="/db" \
               fstype="xfs" \
               options="$OPS" \
       op start interval="0" timeout="60" \
       op stop interval="0" timeout="120"
   ```

3. Clean up any errors that might have accumulated with `crm`:

   ```
   crm resource cleanup pg_fs
   ```

4. Display the status of our new XFS resource with `crm`:

   ```
   crm resource status
   ```

How it works...

Due to the limited format of this book, we wanted to avoid excessive line wrapping in the commands we present. Hence, the first step simply saves all of the XFS mount options from the previous chapter in a variable named `OPS` that we can reference when adding the Pacemaker primitive.

Regarding the primitive itself, we continue our preferred naming scheme and label it pg_fs (for the PostgreSQL filesystem). As usual, we need a resource agent to facilitate Pacemaker management, and the ocf:heartbeat:Filesystem agent fills that role nicely.

As with all agents, to see the list of parameters for a resource agent, use the ra meta command to the crm shell. For the Filesystem agent, this invocation would display usage information: crm ra meta ocf:heartbeat:Filesystem.

We highly recommend that you use this command in each recipe, if only to verify that the parameters act as we claim they do.

This time, the list of parameters (params) we set for the resource agent is somewhat longer than what we used for LVM. Here's a short explanation of each:

- The device parameter tells Pacemaker which device it should try to mount. From the previous chapter, this is /dev/VG_POSTGRES/LV_DATA.
- The directory specifies where the device should be mounted. Following the example set by our previous chapter, this is the /db directory.
- By setting fstype, we explicitly tell Pacemaker we are attempting to mount an xfs filesystem. Modern mount commands can often determine the filesystem automatically, but we advocate a more cautious approach.
- Finally, we set the mount options. Our list of options was very long, so we stored it in the $OPS variable, which we used here.

The other options (op) we set are more advisory minimum values that reflect the number of seconds we should wait before considering an operation as failed. The timeouts to start and stop a filesystem are somewhat longer than an LVM device because filesystems can have direct users. A filesystem user includes any Terminals currently located in a mounted directory, automated tasks using it as a file target, or files held open by a running process—any one of these can prevent a filesystem from being unmounted.

As usual, we perform `resource cleanup` on the `pg_fs` device to clear out any invalid errors. Afterward, we can view the clean resource status with `crm`, which looks like this on our test system:

```
root@pg1:~# crm resource status
 Clone Set: ms_drbd_pg [drbd_pg] (promotable)
     Masters: [ pg1 ]
     Slaves: [ pg2 ]
 pg_lvm (ocf::heartbeat:LVM):    Started
 pg_fs  (ocf::heartbeat:Filesystem):    Started
```

As expected, we can see that `pg_fs` has joined our growing list of Pacemaker resources.

Adding PostgreSQL to cluster management

By now, we've fulfilled a fairly long series of prerequisites simply to add PostgreSQL to the list of services managed by Pacemaker. We're over halfway through this chapter and are just now getting to the parts relevant to a PostgreSQL DBA. If you're new to DBA work, this might come as quite a shock, but it comes with the territory.

Once we add this resource, Pacemaker will be capable of starting and stopping everything necessary to run a PostgreSQL server. We'll still need to add several more elements to control factors such as start order and associated services, but we've reached a critical juncture. We are very close to having a highly-available PostgreSQL cluster.

In this recipe, we'll discuss the steps required to add PostgreSQL itself to Pacemaker control.

Getting ready

As we're continuing to configure Pacemaker, make sure you've followed all of the previous recipes.

How to do it...

Perform these steps on any Pacemaker node as the `root` user:

1. Add a PostgreSQL primitive to Pacemaker with `crm`:

```
crm configure primitive pg_service systemd:postgresql@12-main \
    op monitor interval="30" timeout="60" \
    op start interval="0" timeout="60" \
    op stop interval="0" timeout="60"
```

2. Clean up any errors that might have accumulated with `crm`:

```
crm resource cleanup pg_service
```

3. Display the status of our new PostgreSQL resource with `crm`:

```
crm resource status
```

How it works...

The next primitive that we add to Pacemaker will need to use systemd to manage PostgreSQL. As we'd mentioned at the beginning of this chapter, this ensures Pacemaker receives expected LSB status codes when performing actions. Hence, when we call `crm` with the `configure primitive` parameters, we name the new primitive `pg_service` to remain consistent. We also use the `systemd:postgresql@12-main` resource agent, which targets our specific PostgreSQL instance.

One consequence of this is that our resource agent is not fully integrated into Pacemaker and has no configurable parameters. The only things we can change are the generic options (`op`) such as monitor intervals and start or stop timeouts. For this agent, we've set all of the timeouts to 1 minute, but you may need to adjust these based on your PostgreSQL usage.

We set the monitor interval to 30 seconds and the timeout to 60 seconds for one reason: system overload. If a checkpoint causes enough write activity, PostgreSQL may fail to respond quickly enough, even though it is still running. If this happens frequently, we strongly recommend that you look into the problem and correct it.

However, Pacemaker compounds this problem slightly. If a monitor action fails, Pacemaker assumes that the service is dead, and it will try to restart it. If that fails, it will move everything over to the alternate node. This can cause an outage seemingly at random, which is not good in a high-availability environment.

Following this, we continue our usual steps of clearing out any invalid errors and viewing the Pacemaker cluster status. On our test system, the status shows this output:

```
root@pg1:~# crm resource status
 Clone Set: ms_drbd_pg [drbd_pg] (promotable)
     Masters: [ pg1 ]
     Slaves: [ pg2 ]
 pg_lvm (ocf::heartbeat:LVM):    Started
 pg_fs  (ocf::heartbeat:Filesystem):    Started
 pg_service    (systemd:postgresql@12-main):    Started
```

As expected, we can see that pg_service is Started.

Until we add a few more rules, Pacemaker isn't very smart. On our test system, Pacemaker repeatedly attempted to start PostgreSQL on the pg2 node, even though it was already running on pg1. Of course, this failed, and it eventually checked pg1 to reach the preceding output. We were not kidding when we said Pacemaker considers resources transitory until told otherwise! Be wary of this behavior in the next few recipes.

There's more...

Though we used systemd to manage PostgreSQL, the resource-agents repository package installed with Pacemaker contains a resource agent specifically designed for PostgreSQL. However, its usage is far more complicated. It can also monitor PostgreSQL by querying it instead of simply using a process ID test. If you want to use this agent instead, follow these steps as root:

1. Set the path of pg_ctl with this command:

```
export CTL=$(pg_config --bindir)/pg_ctl
```

2. Add the pgsql resource agent as primary with this command:

```
crm configure primitive pg_agent ocf:heartbeat:pgsql \
    params pgctl="$CTL" \
```

```
                 pgdata="/db/pgdata" \
    op monitor interval="30" timeout="60" \
    op start interval="0" timeout="60" \
    op stop interval="0" timeout="60"
```

To get the full benefit of this resource agent, you'll also want to set the `monitor_user` and `monitor_password` agent parameters. To see the full list of parameters for this agent, use this `crm` command:

```
crm ra meta ocf:heartbeat:pgsql
```

Alternatively, view the `man` page:

```
man ocf_heartbeat_pgsql
```

Adding a virtual IP to proxy the cluster

We discussed virtual IP addresses earlier; now, it's time to leverage them in a more automated fashion. A virtual IP is not a service in the traditional sense, but it does provide functionality that we need in a high-availability configuration. In cases where we also have control over DNS resolution, we can even assign a name to the virtual IP address to insulate applications from future changes.

For now, this recipe will limit itself to outlining the steps required to add a transitory IP address to Pacemaker.

Getting ready

As we're continuing to configure Pacemaker, make sure you've followed all of the previous recipes.

How to do it...

We will assume that the `10.0.30.150` IP address exists as a predefined target for our PostgreSQL cluster. Users and applications will connect to it instead of the actual addresses of `pg1` or `pg2`.

Perform these steps on any Pacemaker node as the `root` user:

1. Add an IP address `primitive` to Pacemaker with `crm`:

```
crm configure primitive pg_vip ocf:heartbeat:IPaddr2 \
    params ip="10.0.30.150" \
        iflabel="pgvip" \
    op monitor interval="5"
```

2. Try to view the IP allocation on `pg1` and `pg2`:

```
ip addr | grep -A1 :pgvip
```

3. Clean up any errors that might have accumulated with `crm`:

```
crm resource cleanup pg_vip
```

4. Display the status of our new IP address with `crm`:

```
crm resource status
```

How it works...

This call to `crm` with `configure primitive` allows us to associate an arbitrary IP address with our Pacemaker cluster. Once again, we follow the simple naming scheme and label our resource `pg_vip`. As we always require a resource agent, we need one that is designed to handle network interfaces. There are actually two that fit this role: `IPaddr` and `IPaddr2`. Though we can use either, the `IPaddr2` agent is designed specifically for Linux hosts, so we might as well use it for maximum compatibility.

The minimum parameters (`params`) we need for this resource agent include the IP address (`ip`) and a label for network management (`iflabel`). We chose to set these to the IP address that we set aside earlier (10.0.30.150). We also chose a descriptive label to associate with the interface (`pgvip`). Due to the nature of IP addresses, it's a good idea to check the interface on both machines to see that it is properly listed. Our test system looks like this:

```
root@pg2:~# ip addr | grep -A1 :pgvip
    inet 10.0.30.150/16 brd 10.0.255.255 scope global secondary ens18:pgvip
        valid_lft forever preferred_lft forever
```

We check both `pg1` and `pg2` because Pacemaker still starts resources independently, and the new IP address might be on either node. We'll be resolving this soon, so don't worry if the IP address is allocated to the wrong node, as it was in our case!

As usual, we run `resource cleanup` and then display the `resource status` of the cluster. No matter where `pgvip` is running, we should see output similar to this:

```
root@pg1:~# crm resource status
 Clone Set: ms_drbd_pg [drbd_pg] (promotable)
     Masters: [ pg1 ]
     Slaves: [ pg2 ]
 pg_lvm (ocf::heartbeat:LVM):    Started
 pg_fs  (ocf::heartbeat:Filesystem):     Started
 pg_service     (systemd:postgresql@12-main):    Started
 pg_vip (ocf::heartbeat:IPaddr2):        Started
```

As expected, the `pg_vip` Pacemaker resource is `Started` and part of our growing list of resources.

Adding an email alert

The last thing we are going to add should be considered a requirement when building a high-availability PostgreSQL cluster. Any time the status of Pacemaker changes, we can have it transmit an email alerting us to the activity. Not only is this possible with Pacemaker, but it's also relatively easy to set up.

This recipe will outline the steps necessary to add an email alert to Pacemaker.

Getting ready

As we're continuing to configure Pacemaker, make sure you've followed all of the previous recipes.

How to do it...

Perform these steps on any Pacemaker node as the `root` user:

1. Add an email primitive to Pacemaker with `crm`:

```
crm configure primitive pg_mail ocf:heartbeat:MailTo \
    params email="dbas@mycompany.com" \
        subject="Pacemaker\ cluster\ status\ changed:\ "
```

2. Clean up any errors that might have accumulated with `crm`:

   crm resource cleanup pg_mail

3. Display the status of our new email alert with `crm`:

   crm resource status

How it works...

To add an email alert, we need to `configure` another `primitive` with `crm`. We name this resource `pg_mail` so that it fits in with the other services that we've configured so far. As always, we need a resource agent for Pacemaker to invoke when necessary, and the `ocf:heartbeat:MailTo` agent works well for our use case.

The `MailTo` agent is not a regular resource, as it does not represent any actual system service. It's more of a defined action that Pacemaker should invoke while managing *other* cluster resources. This means it's essentially useless until we associate it with another Pacemaker primitive.

The `MailTo` agent also has two parameters (`params`) we are interested in setting. We begin by setting `email` to an email address for a recipient tasked with monitoring the PostgreSQL cluster. In most cases, this is either a single DBA or the entire team. In any case, we strongly suggest that you transmit these alerts to anyone associated with the PostgreSQL database in case one or more members of the team are unavailable.

> If you don't already have one, speak with the infrastructure team or whoever is in charge of setting up email lists at your company. Using a generic address that reaches everyone in the team, Pacemaker won't need to be changed whenever you hire or fire a DBA.

The next setting that concerns us is the subject of the message. If we don't set this, Pacemaker uses a suitable default, but it's good to have more control over the messages in case we want to set up email rules or filters. Use any message you like, but there are a couple of important notes:

- Spaces must be escaped by a backslash (\). Otherwise, Pacemaker will print out a lot of errors and refuse to add the primitive.
- The subject is more of a prefix. Pacemaker will add more detail to the subject and body of the email when the message is sent.

With that said, we are now ready to clean up and view our list of resources. Let's see the output of `resource status` on our test system:

```
root@pg1:~# crm resource status
 Clone Set: ms_drbd_pg [drbd_pg] (promotable)
     Masters: [ pg1 ]
     Slaves: [ pg2 ]
 pg_lvm (ocf::heartbeat:LVM):    Started
 pg_fs  (ocf::heartbeat:Filesystem):    Started
 pg_service    (systemd:postgresql@12-main):    Started
 pg_vip (ocf::heartbeat:IPaddr2):    Started
 pg_mail        (ocf::heartbeat:MailTo):    Started
```

We can see from this output that `pg_mail` is listed as `Started`, even though it doesn't do anything by itself. We'll be fixing this soon enough.

Grouping associated resources

Defining all of the critical resources within Pacemaker is a good start. However, Pacemaker is not concerned with keeping related services operating together. It is designed to facilitate service management for any series of resources over a large array of servers. This is a recurring theme in this chapter and one we have to overcome to fully leverage Pacemaker's abilities.

One way we can do this is by creating a **group** of related resources. When we do this, the group represents every member as a whole and must run on one server or another. This prevents the problems we had in the previous recipes, such as the possibility of new resources being started on the wrong node.

We'll create a group in this recipe and discuss other important caveats.

Getting ready

As we're continuing to configure Pacemaker, make sure you've followed all of the previous recipes.

How to do it...

Perform these steps on any Pacemaker node as the `root` user:

1. Add `group` to Pacemaker with `crm`:

```
crm configure group PGServer pg_lvm pg_fs pg_service pg_vip
```

2. Display the status of our new group with `crm`:

```
crm resource status
```

How it works...

For the first time in this chapter, we are not configuring a primitive, but a group. Unlike primitives, which describe each resource we want to manage, a group tells Pacemaker how. In this case, any resource listed in the group must share a few new attributes:

- Resources must reside on the same node.
- Resources must be started in the specified order.
- Resources must be stopped by reversing the specified order.

We named the group `PGServer`, and now we can address every member as a cohesive unit using that name. The resource order mirrors the order in which we defined the primitives, which is the logical order necessary to start (and stop) a PostgreSQL server.

When `PGServer` is started, Pacemaker will activate LVM, followed by XFS, then PostgreSQL, and finally, it will add our virtual IP address. We didn't add the email alert, because there's no logical place for it within the group. If we list it at the beginning, we'll only get an alert if everything is shut down. We can't place it at the end, or we won't see changes in DRBD.

DRBD has a related complication: it's only a single entry but represents two states. We can't target specific states in the grouping, so we must omit it from the group. However, there is a solution to associate the mail and DRBD resources with our new group; we'll cover this in the next recipe.

Until then, we can view the group with our usual `resource status` command. Here's what we have on our test system:

```
root@pg1:~# crm resource status
 Clone Set: ms_drbd_pg [drbd_pg] (promotable)
     Masters: [ pg1 ]
     Slaves: [ pg2 ]
 pg_mail         (ocf::heartbeat:MailTo):        Started
 Resource Group: PGServer
     pg_lvm      (ocf::heartbeat:LVM):    Started
     pg_fs       (ocf::heartbeat:Filesystem):    Started
     pg_service (systemd:postgresql@12-main):    Started
     pg_vip      (ocf::heartbeat:IPaddr2):       Started
root@pg1:~#
```

Now we see a new `Resource Group` named `PGServer`. We can also see that all of the items within the group are indented, making the association more obvious.

Combining and ordering related actions

There are two final pieces of the puzzle that will produce a fully functional Pacemaker cluster. At this point, we have three independent base-level entries in Pacemaker: DRBD, the `PGServer` group, and the email alert. They are independent because Pacemaker may start or stop them on any server in the list of active nodes.

We can fix this by defining a **colocation** between related resources. When we create a colocation, we are effectively stating that wherever this service goes, this other service should follow. Of course, this by itself is not sufficient. We also need to declare the expected **order** necessary for the services to start.

In this recipe, we'll finish our Pacemaker setup by creating necessary colocation entries, and define a service start order.

Getting ready

As we're continuing to configure Pacemaker, make sure that you've followed all of the previous recipes.

How to do it...

Perform these steps on any Pacemaker node as the `root` user:

1. Add `colocation` for DRBD to Pacemaker with `crm`:

```
crm configure colocation col_pg_drbd \
    inf: PGServer ms_drbd_pg:Master
```

2. Add `colocation` for the email alert with `crm`:

```
crm configure colocation col_pg_mail \
    inf: pg_mail PGServer
```

3. Add a resource `order` to Pacemaker with `crm`:

```
crm configure order ord_pg \
    Mandatory: ms_drbd_pg:promote PGServer:start
```

4. Display the configuration of our cluster with `crm`:

```
crm configure show
```

How it works...

As with all of our changes to Pacemaker, we `configure` the item we're adding. For this first step, we are adding a `colocation` named `col_pg_drbd` to represent the dependency between the `PGServer` group and the `ms_drbd_pg` master/slave resource. To do this, we need three elements. They are as follows:

- **The strength of the relationship, expressed as a score**: We used `inf:` to represent infinity, meaning that these two items should always be associated.
- **The name of the resource we are trying to colocate**: We use the group name `PGServer`, as we want all Pacemaker resources to follow it to the same node.
- **The name of a resource this entry should be colocated with and is dependent upon**: By setting this to `ms_drbd_pg:Master`, we are telling Pacemaker that the `PGServer` group must be on the same server where DRBD is the master node, wherever that might be.

We then repeat this process with the email alert. This time we name the colocation `col_pg_mail` to express it as a colocation of the `pg_mail` resource. The score remains at `inf:` for infinity, and we make one final and very important change. When defining a colocation, the order is extremely important. In fact, all colocation entries should be read as: *resource a depends on resource b.*

With the email alert colocation, we now have what amounts to a dependency chain. The email alert depends on the state of the `PGServer` group, and the `PGServer` group depends on the DRBD master server. Yet, colocations are rules, so Pacemaker is still free to execute these resources independently of each other, as long as the final result matches the defined state we dictated.

As colocations have no inherent order, we need to impose one. We create one final `configure` entry by defining an order named `ord_pg`. This time we state that the relationship should be `Mandatory:`, which tells Pacemaker that the order of services is not optional or a mere suggestion. When we define the order of our resources, we can also dictate an action that Pacemaker should take, separated by a colon.

The order we defined tells Pacemaker that it should `promote` the `ms_drbd_pg` resource before it is allowed to `start` the `PGServer` group. Why didn't we add the email alert to our order definition? We didn't do so because its order doesn't matter. By being a colocation, it is associated with the `PGServer` group, but since it has no imposed order, any change to the group or to DRBD will trigger an email alert.

One `crm` command we haven't used until now is `configure show`. Colocation and order definitions don't alter the outward appearance of resource status, so we needed another way to prove Pacemaker incorporated our changes. This is what we see on our test system:

```
root@pg2:~# crm configure show | egrep "colocation|order"
colocation col_pg_drbd inf: PGServer ms_drbd_pg:Master
colocation col_pg_mail inf: pg_mail PGServer
order ord_pg Mandatory: ms_drbd_pg:promote PGServer:start
```

Notice that we ran this command on the `pg2` server, and we were still shown the current Pacemaker configuration. Pacemaker also takes it upon itself to remove all of our formatting for these particular entries. If we were to remove the `egrep` statement, we'd see the entire Pacemaker configuration for our cluster, containing all of the additions we've made in this chapter.

Performing a managed resource migration

Now that we have a working Pacemaker cluster-management system, we should put it to use. There are a lot of scenarios where we might need to manually change the active PostgreSQL node. Doing this with Pacemaker is much easier than the process we outlined in the previous chapter. That was a long process composed of several manual steps, each of which we would want to confirm in a perfect world.

With Pacemaker, we can change the active system by issuing a single command from any node in the cluster. There are some safeguards we'll also need to discuss and possibly a caveat or two to consider, but this will be our first use of Pacemaker as a piece of functional software. We've done a lot of work setting everything up!

Let's make Pacemaker do some work on our behalf for a change.

Getting ready

To migrate resources from one node to another, we need a fully functional Pacemaker cluster that manages all of our software layers. Make sure you've followed all of the previous recipes before continuing.

How to do it...

This recipe will assume pg1 is currently the active node, and we want to move PostgreSQL to pg2. Perform these steps on either Pacemaker node as the root user:

1. Initiate the migration with crm:

   ```
   crm resource migrate PGServer pg2
   ```

2. Remove the continued forced migration with this command:

   ```
   crm resource unmigrate PGServer
   ```

3. Use crm to display the currently active node:

   ```
   crm resource status PGServer
   ```

How it works...

The process is as simple as we claimed. We can launch a migration by specifying `resource migrate` as our primary `crm` arguments. There are only two remaining parameters for us to define: the resource we want to migrate and the target location. The `PGServer` group represents PostgreSQL and all of its prerequisite storage elements, so that is our third parameter.

The last parameter is the target node, and as `pg2` is the only other node in this Pacemaker configuration, it's an easy choice. What happens during a migration? The following is a screenshot of `crm_mon` during a migration:

```
Online: [ pg1 pg2 ]

Active resources:

 Clone Set: ms_drbd_pg [drbd_pg] (promotable)
     Masters: [ pg2 ]
     Slaves: [ pg1 ]
pg_mail (ocf::heartbeat:MailTo):         Started pg2
 Resource Group: PGServer
     pg_lvm     (ocf::heartbeat:LVM):     Started pg1
     pg_fs      (ocf::heartbeat:Filesystem):    Started pg1
     pg_service (systemd:postgresql@12-main):   Stopped
     pg_vip     (ocf::heartbeat:IPaddr2):       Stopped
```

As you can see, Pacemaker is doing just as we claimed in the previous section and is shutting down `PGServer` resources in reverse order. It has already stopped `pg_vip` and `pg_service` and will shortly proceed to the rest of the services. In fact, here is a full ordered list of what Pacemaker does during a migration with our configuration:

1. Create a rule with an infinite score that the `PGServer` group should be running on `pg2`.
2. Stop the `pg_mail` alert on `pg1`, causing an email alert.
3. Start the `pg_mail` resource on `pg2`.
4. Stop the `pg_vip` resource on `pg1`.
5. Stop the `pg_service` resource on `pg1`.
6. Stop the `pg_fs` resource on `pg1`.
7. Stop the `pg_lvm` resource on `pg1`.
8. Demote `ms_drbd_pg` to `Secondary` on `pg1`.
9. Promote `ms_drbd_pg` to `Primary` on `pg2`.

10. Start the `pg_lvm` resource on `pg2`.
11. Start the `pg_fs` resource on `pg2`.
12. Start the `pg_service` resource on `pg2`.
13. Start the `pg_vip` resource on `pg2`.

We hope you can see the obvious linear progression Pacemaker is following; it mirrors the process we used when we performed these tasks manually. After the migration is over, we call `unmigrate` to remove the infinite score that Pacemaker added. This will allow `pg1` to retain the `PGServer` group when it returns to that system at a later date.

Our final step is to examine `resource status` of the `PGServer` group itself. If we did our job right, we should see this output:

```
root@pg1:~# crm resource status PGServer
resource PGServer is running on: pg2
```

Pacemaker reports that `PGServer` is running on `pg2`, just as we asked.

There's more...

When we call `crm resource migrate`, Pacemaker merely makes a simple configuration change. As the `PGServer` resource is running on `pg1` and we set stickiness to `100`, any score higher than that will override the current (and preferred) node.

When we ask for a migration, Pacemaker sets the node score for `pg2` at infinity, the highest value possible. The next time the resource target evaluation system runs, it sees that the score has changed and starts reorganizing the cluster to match. It's actually quite elegant. Unfortunately, it means that we need to remove the score or we could be in trouble later.

When we `unmigrate` the `PGServer` group, Pacemaker removes the infinite score assigned to `pg2`, leaving it with a regular score of `100`. This is enough to keep `PGServer` attached to `pg2`, but nothing more. This is important because the score is absolute.

Imagine if the rule was still in place and Pacemaker vastly preferred pg2 over pg1. In the event pg2 crashes, Pacemaker will dutifully move PostgreSQL over to pg1. This is exactly what we want. However, what happens after we fix pg2 and reattach it to Pacemaker? That's right; the infinite score means Pacemaker will move it to pg2 immediately. Oh, no!

We can't overstate how important this is. Never invoke a resource migration without using unmigrate as the second step. Failure to do so can result in unplanned outages, which is not something we want in a highly available PostgreSQL cluster.

Using an outage to test migration

While planned migrations are always preferred, sometimes hardware failures or server instability will introduce an aspect of surprise. If we had not used Pacemaker, a server crash would be a catastrophic event. Even if we had followed every chapter in this book this far and had Nagios, the full TIG monitoring stack, and email alerts galore, a DBA would need to be available to activate the alternate node.

If an outage occurred at night when everyone was sleeping, we would be faced with a worst-case scenario. The necessary personnel might not hear the alert for several minutes, and more time would be lost on triage and activation steps. Such an outage could extend from a few minutes to over an hour. So much for our high availability!

Yet at this point, we don't know whether Pacemaker would negate the preceding scenario. While we've tested how Pacemaker handles an expected and safe migration, what happens when a node disappears entirely? Will Pacemaker cover us in the event that there is an outage when nobody is immediately available?

In this recipe, we'll attempt to answer all of those questions and test Pacemaker with a server reboot.

Getting ready

For this final recipe, we need a complete and tested Pacemaker stack before causing an automated migration. Make sure you've followed all of the previous recipes before attempting this.

How to do it...

This recipe will assume pg1 is currently the active node and pg2 is acting as the standby. Perform these steps on the Pacemaker node indicated as the root user:

1. Start crm_mon on pg2.
2. Kill the corosync service on pg1:

   ```
   pkill -f -9 corosync
   ```

3. Reboot pg1 with this command:

   ```
   reboot
   ```

4. Watch Pacemaker start all services on pg2.

How it works...

We've made use of crm_mon before; it's an easy way to view the current status of all Pacemaker cluster resources. By starting this monitor on pg2, we can watch what happens when pg1 shuts down. Unfortunately, simple reboots are too safe. The server will call the Pacemaker shutdown script, which will cause it to migrate to pg2 like it did in the previous recipe.

By calling pkill with the -9 argument on the corosync service, Pacemaker can no longer interfere. The Linux kernel will end the corosync process, negating any safeguards that Pacemaker might try to impose when pg1 reboots. We should return to pg2 to watch the output of crm_mon while pg1 is offline.

The final result should look something like this:

```
Online: [ pg2 ]
OFFLINE: [ pg1 ]

Active resources:

 Clone Set: ms_drbd_pg [drbd_pg] (promotable)
     Masters: [ pg2 ]
pg_mail (ocf::heartbeat:MailTo):          Started pg2
 Resource Group: PGServer
     pg_lvm      (ocf::heartbeat:LVM):    Started pg2
     pg_fs       (ocf::heartbeat:Filesystem):   Started pg2
     pg_service (systemd:postgresql@12-main):   Started pg2
     pg_vip      (ocf::heartbeat:IPaddr2):      Started pg2
```

Note that pg1 shows up as OFFLINE, and pg2 is the only server in the Online list.

There's more...

There's one final way to force a migration, and it's one we actually suggest for almost all cases. One of the arguments we can pass to `crm node` is the desired state of the node. Instead of killing the `corosync` service and rebooting pg1, we could run this command:

```
crm node standby pg1
```

This tells Pacemaker that pg1 should no longer be considered a valid target for resources. This also causes Pacemaker to migrate `PGServer` and any dependencies over to pg2. No matter what the state of Pacemaker is, pg1 will always be listed as `Standby` in the cluster by `crm status`.

This is an easy way to perform maintenance that might require multiple reboots or other potentially disruptive changes. To bring pg1 online once again, we would use this command:

```
crm node online pg1
```

The effect on Pacemaker is the same as a `migrate` command followed by an `unmigrate` operation. The pg1 node is simply added to the list of possible target nodes, and the cluster remains on pg2. The principal difference is that we've removed any chance of pg1 interfering with pg2. A standby Pacemaker node cannot participate in the cluster, and we can see at a glance that it's undergoing maintenance until we change it back to `online` status.

13
High Availability with Multi-Master Replication

Multi-master replication is a relatively new concept within the PostgreSQL world that allows more than one node to accept writes and all nodes to contain the same data regardless of origin. The concept of how the multi-master approach works is generally easy to understand if we examine the workflow of how it is implemented between two nodes.

This chapter will explore the inherent limitations of multi-master database technology as applied to PostgreSQL, as well as how to best utilize it to maximize application availability.

In this chapter, we will learn how multiple writable PostgreSQL nodes affect the concept of high availability. We will cover the following topics in this chapter:

- Deciding whether multi-master is right for you
- Obtaining and installing BDR
- Starting with a single BDR node
- Creating an additional BDR node
- Testing DDL replication on each node
- Using sequences safely
- Configuring HAProxy for the multi-master approach
- Combining PgBouncer with HAProxy
- Performing a managed node switchover
- Improving failover speed
- Performing a major-version online upgrade

Overview of multi-master

Consider the following diagram:

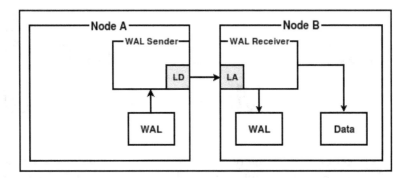

We can see in preceding diagram that there are two PostgreSQL nodes: **Node A** sends data from the WAL to **Node B** via **WAL** streaming, a feature that has been available since PostgreSQL 9.0.

The primary divergence here from regular streaming replication is the element labeled **LD**, which in this case stands for **logical decoder**. **Node B** contains a similar additional element that we've labeled **LA** for **logical apply**.

In standard streaming replication, WAL is transmitted unchanged and applied to the data files exactly as it is received. While fast and efficient, this meant that every streaming replica was required to be an exact copy of the upstream system. This is fine for distributing read traffic, but is somewhat limited in application since we can't simply copy a few tables, import only some data, and so on.

When logical streaming became available with PostgreSQL 9.4, it was suddenly possible to consume the writes themselves rather than how they were represented on disk when written on the upstream system. Those familiar with logical replication already know how this works.

The trick here is that the multi-master approach introduces a second logical channel and LA/LD combination so that the process is bidirectional. Consider the following diagram:

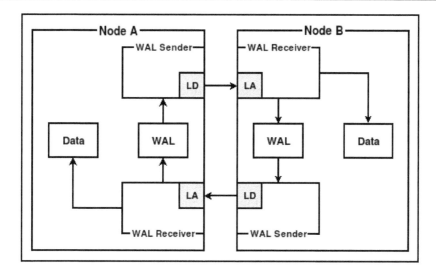

Now each node decodes, transmits, receives, and applies data from its local WAL to the other node.

However, this is much easier to describe with a couple of simplified diagrams than it is to build correctly. As a consequence, there is only one commercially available product that performs this kind of dual-channel logical replication for PostgreSQL. This product is called **bidirectional replication** (**BDR**), and has existed in some form or another since PostgreSQL 9.4 when it first became theoretically possible. So far, this is the only multi-master PostgreSQL platform available.

No matter how the multi-master approach is achieved, it presents a lot of exciting possibilities. Do we have databases on two or three continents? Instead of waiting 200–500 ms per transaction simply because of network transfer times, we can write all data locally, and it will reach other nodes eventually. And at a smaller scale, we no longer need to wait for the promotion of a physical standby if the primary node ever becomes unavailable; we can simply redirect the application to any other writable node. In extreme scenarios, this can even be done per connection.

Once this happens, we no longer need failover management frameworks. Node promotion is no longer necessary. Node maintenance is as simple as reconnecting the application layer to another writable node. While not a panacea, in many ways it seems too good to be true.

Deciding whether multi-master is right for you

Multi-master PostgreSQL promises many exciting benefits that are hard to ignore. Despite this, there are some inherent limitations that could potentially prevent safe adoption within the application stack. Failure to account for these before deploying multi-master PostgreSQL could result in data loss or disruption of the cluster itself.

Consider, for example, what happens if two nodes accept a write for the same tuple. How should the conflict be resolved? Are there any necessary changes to the schema, or the application itself, before the adoption of the multi-master approach is safe? What else must we plan for?

While not an exhaustive resource, this recipe will attempt to answer many pressing concerns related to multi-master PostgreSQL. Some of these are based on theoretical cluster concepts.

Getting ready

In some ways, this recipe can be considered advanced reading. For now, it's best to try to understand the full application stack and how it interacts with PostgreSQL. We will be asking several questions that should be answered before the multi-master approach is even considered as a possible solution.

How to do it...

Answer these questions about your application stack and PostgreSQL schema and databases:

1. Does our application use autoincrement or sequential surrogate keys?
2. Is the most recent modification an acceptable way to resolve conflicts?
3. Do we use any columns as data aggregates?
4. Which is more important: latency or immediate constancy?
5. Will cross-cluster DDL locks disrupt the application?

How it works...

There are several considerations we should make when evaluating multi-master PostgreSQL, but these are some of the most important. These are decisions we must make or changes that must be incorporated into the application itself before it is safe for distribution across multiple nodes.

We begin with an obvious one: incremental fields. If we rely on sequences and have two nodes, then there's potential for conflict if the nodes do not account for this. Say that Node A assigns ID 5 to a new row, and Node B does the same; this would result in one row being lost. One way of preventing this is to integrate the node number into the sequence and skip increments. So Node A could assign ID 5, 15, 25, and so on, while Node B uses 6, 16, 26, and so on.

However, that solution tends to require local node modification, which introduces the possibility of accidentally forgetting to make such changes after node allocation. Even automation may not totally solve this, depending on how sequences are tracked. It's better to use IDs that are physically unable to produce conflicts, such as UUIDs. BDR, in particular, offers multiple cluster-aware sequence configuration settings that handle ID values properly, though one requires the target field to be defined as a BIGINT.

 This is one example of how the schema itself may require modification or simply not be easily compatible. UUID use isn't common, and BIGINT isn't quite as frequent as we would like. Many of the questions we ask in this recipe will end this way, with some kind of compromise that is necessary for full compatibility.

The next question is related to how conflicts should be handled, should they arise. If two nodes operate on the same tuple, we can only retain one row or the other, not both. PostgreSQL logical replication works by sending the entire row to the recipient system, not merely any changed values. This means that merging is only possible under limited and highly advanced scenarios.

The main consequence of this is that the default algorithm for resolving conflicts is **last update wins**, which uses the transaction commit timestamp to determine which of the conflicting rows should be represented across the cluster. BDR does offer a method of performing column-level conflict resolution to accomplish a kind of merge operation, but this requires enabling timestamp tracking on a per-row and -column basis, which can result in quite a bit of overhead storage and processing.

It's best to answer this question about conflict resolution by perhaps asking a second question: can we avoid conflicts? A great way to do this is to simply avoid allowing multiple nodes to write to the same rows. This can be done through data hashing, sticky sessions that ensure that applications don't disruptively swap arbitrarily between nodes. There are other strategies, but these two tend to address the largest sources of unwanted data conflicts.

A somewhat related concern is how aggregate columns affect the multi-master approach. Since PostgreSQL can only substitute one column or the other (even when using BDR column-level conflict resolution), we could potentially lose data if that column value differs between the nodes.

A way of visualizing this is a situation that involves simple updates:

- **Node A**: `UPDATE tab_a SET val=val + 10 WHERE id=1;`
- **Node B**: `UPDATE tab_a SET val=val + 100 WHERE id=1;`

If `val` started at `100`, then we either have a value of `110` or `200`, and we can only store one. Even though this is a simple integer field, we are treating it as an aggregate value, since it accumulates data rather than being set directly. This applies equally to arrays that are appended, JSON objects that are modified, and so on. Any time we have a column that had a previous value that we modified and replaced would necessarily trigger a conflict if two nodes assign different values.

In many cases, the way forward is identical to the approach used in the previous question: avoid conflicts if possible. BDR does provide a data type known as a **conflict-free replicated data type** (**CRDT**) that can address this to an extent. There are several of these, and they all have different theoretical frameworks for which works best in certain situations. Once again, we're faced with a choice that may involve modifying the schema or application layer itself, should conflicting updates be a cause for concern.

The next question is more subtle: do we care more about latency or consistency? Those familiar with the **CAP** theorem know that it describes the relationship between **consistency**, **availability**, and **partition tolerance** within a cluster context. What is less commonly discussed is **PACELC**, a conceptual extension to CAP. Simply put, it says that in the case of a distributed cluster, it's only possible to have availability and consistency or latency and consistency, not both.

What this means in practice is that we must make a choice: do we want immediate transaction responses, or should the cluster's consensus management layer use distributed locking within a quorum of nodes to prevent any possibility of data conflict. The latter option is much slower, sometimes by more than an order of magnitude, but solves the preceding problems of having to manage row- or column-level conflicts.

The default for BDR is to prefer minimized latency, and hence high availability. It provides a configuration setting that implements a quorum-based consensus model instead, for those where slower transaction rates are preferable to eventual consistency. Either way, we must choose whichever is appropriate for our application stack.

Finally, we address the impact of DDL within the cluster. If we modify the database schema, it's safest to apply that same change to every node simultaneously. This prevents a row from one node being unable to replay on another node, such as in situations where there is a missing column. BDR does this by intercepting DDL statements and replaying them through the consensus layer to other participating nodes. The local transaction won't complete until other nodes can replay the DDL, and have done so.

Naturally, this introduces a potential problem for a DDL that requires an exclusive lock, such as table modifications or even index creation. We may have to wait for every node to allow pending transactions to complete before the lock is granted, then every node must wait until the change is applied before the global lock is released. In a busy application, this is likely to be unacceptable.

This is a harder problem to solve since the fabric of the replication system itself depends on schema compatibility. If Node B can't replay a row from Node A because a column is missing, then replication cannot progress at all on that channel. This may mean that we have to implement tiered deployment, where changes are made to each node manually but the column remains unused until all nodes reflect all modifications. BDR offers more advanced streaming triggers that can modify the tuple being applied, thereby implementing complex internode versioning transforms during DDL transitions.

No matter how we progress, the matter of DDL management should be addressed early. Some applications, such as reporting systems or applications that do not require 24/7 availability, can likely tolerate long DDL locks. But this book is about high availability, and so if our focus is on implementing high availability systems, then we're more likely dealing with a busy OLTP system. DDL changes in these situations are difficult enough when only one node is involved; it becomes much more difficult as the amount of writable nodes increases.

There are solutions. We simply want to emphasize that these should all be considered before a PostgreSQL cluster is deployed into a multi-master context. It would be a nasty surprise otherwise, especially if we can avoid problems through careful planning.

See also

As we've mentioned before, we covered several theoretical frameworks in this recipe. Please refer to the following resources to learn more:

- **CAP theorem**: `https://robertgreiner.com/cap-theorem-revisited/`
- **Consistency Tradeoffs in Modern Distributed Database System Design**: `https://www.cs.umd.edu/~abadi/papers/abadi-pacelc.pdf`

Obtaining and installing BDR

BDR is the first (and currently the only) multi-master solution for PostgreSQL. Once installed on two or more nodes, it allows database writes to occur on any node, and the changes will then be copied to the remainder of the cluster. This allows for immediate writes in any node within a distributed PostgreSQL cluster without any need for a failover.

BDR has existed as an open-source product since the introduction of logical replication in PostgreSQL 9.4, but required a specially patched version to operate. A later proprietary version worked as an extension to community PostgreSQL 9.6. At the time of writing, both of these implementations have been deprecated in favor of a new approach that we'll describe in the recipe itself.

This recipe will show you how to obtain and install BDR, including the necessary steps to integrate it into PostgreSQL so that all necessary background processes activate.

Getting ready

BDR is currently the only method of getting applying the multi-master approach to PostgreSQL, and it is only available as a proprietary extension to PostgreSQL 10 and 11. This may change in the future, but for now, this means that BDR will act as our demonstration platform for the multi-master approach. It will be necessary to obtain BDR directly from its vendor, 2ndQuadrant.

The BDR product page is available at `https://www.2ndquadrant.com/en/resources/postgres-bdr-2ndquadrant/`.

It will be necessary to sign up for a 60-day trial before continuing with this recipe, or indeed the remainder of this chapter.

While 2ndQuadrant supports a cloud-based option, Docker images and Debian- or Red-Hat-based packages obtained from their private repositories, we will focus on using the packages in this recipe.

At the time of writing this chapter, the latest version of BDR is 3.6.12. BDR follows a similar numbering scheme as versions of PostgreSQL before version 10. As a result, the current major version is 3.6. We recommend installing the latest version available when evaluating BDR.

How to do it...

Follow these steps to install BDR in a PostgreSQL 10 database node, assuming that it is located on the `10.0.30.1` subnet:

1. For Debian-based systems, install the following packages as a root-enabled user:

```
sudo apt install postgresql-10-dbgsym
sudo apt install postgresql-10-bdr-plugin \
                 postgresql-10-bdr-plugin-dbg \
                 postgresql-10-pglogical \
                 postgresql-10-pglogical-dbg
```

2. Red Hat systems should use the following commands instead:

```
sudo yum install postgresql10-debuginfo
sudo yum install postgresql10-pglogical \
                 postgresql10-pglogical-debuginfo \
                 postgresql10-bdr \
                 postgresql10-bdr-debuginfo
```

3. Modify `postgresql.conf` and ensure that the following parameters are set to these values:

```
wal_level = 'logical'
shared_preload_libraries = 'pglogical, bdr'
track_commit_timestamp = 'on'
```

4. Connect to PostgreSQL and create a user to manage BDR connectivity:

```
CREATE USER bdr_user WITH SUPERUSER REPLICATION
        PASSWORD 'changeme';
```

5. Modify `pg_hba.conf` and include the following two lines:

```
host      all           bdr    10.0.30.0/24    md5
host      replication   bdr    10.0.30.0/24    md5
```

6. Add `bdr_user` to the Postgres OS user's `.pgpass` file—for example:

```
*:*:*:bdr_user:changeme
```

7. Restart the PostgreSQL service on Debian systems with the following command:

```
sudo systemctl restart postgresql@10-main
```

Red Hat systems will need to use this command instead:

```
sudo systemctl restart postgresql-10
```

How it works...

The primary purpose of this short recipe is to install BDR on any PostgreSQL node that will participate in a BDR cluster. Primarily, this means installing the actual packages, modifying a few configuration files, and restarting the service itself. This is a universal recipe that applies equally to any BDR node, so keep that in mind for later, as we'll be referring to it frequently.

To that end, our first step is to install the packages themselves. We will assume that you either have a BDR 60-day trial or are a 2ndQuadrant support customer, giving you direct access to their private package repositories. Note that this step also recommends installing debugging packages as well. The reason for this is very simple: BDR is complicated. In the event that something goes wrong, diagnostic and forensic information is invaluable. Debug symbols make it possible to track problems down to the function level and even further in some cases. Given how tightly integrated BDR and PostgreSQL are, this is often necessary to track down problems that are caused by a bug or unhandled edge case.

Also note that even though this chapter is about BDR, we recommend that you install `pglogical` as well. This is because BDR itself works in conjunction with `pglogical`, which acts as the logical replication management layer. This way, `pglogical` can still act as a logical replication solution, and BDR can leverage that functionality rather than duplicating it. The two are tightly integrated, and BDR will often call `pglogical` APIs directly, so make sure both of these are available.

Next, there are three settings that we must change. It's very likely that we already set `wal_level` to `logical` as suggested in `Chapter 3`, *Minimizing Downtime*; however, we wanted to explicitly list this requirement, as BDR will not function without logical WAL settings enabled.

Next, we include `pglogical` and `bdr` in `shared_preload_libraries`. In this particular example, they are the only two enabled modules, but they need not be the only ones in the list; we did recommend adding `pg_stat_statements`, after all. Just make sure that they appear in the order that we described, as the BDR shared library depends on `pglogical` symbols being available before it will load properly.

Then we enable `track_commit_timestamp` to add commit timestamp information to the WAL. Remember how we explained that BDR uses the commit timestamp of each transaction to manage conflict resolution? This setting is necessary for BDR to tell that rows from one BDR node are newer than rows from another, and allows data to remain consistent across all nodes.

At this point, we can make a decision. Our instructions recommend creating a user specifically for managing BDR. This makes it easier to debug and also track events that happen in the cluster, assuming they were caused by BDR. So the next few steps involve creating a `bdr_user` superuser and ensuring that it is allowed to connect to all databases and the replication stream for logical streaming purposes.

However, this is not required. We could use the `postgres` user as we have many times throughout the book and everything would still work normally. If you are simply exploring BDR, it may even be easier to do just that. Just make sure that there are no password prompts, and that a superuser is involved.

 Why does BDR require a superuser? While some BDR functionality may be delegated to a non-superuser role for various purposes, BDR itself requires superuser capabilities for one major reason: user masquerading. Rows are applied according to table ownership, and the only way to do that is to become the user making the change. Currently, this is a capability restricted only to PostgreSQL superuser accounts.

Finally, we restart PostgreSQL itself, thereby activating the `pglogical` and `bdr` shared library modules. This will also launch a number of related background workers necessary for managing the cluster.

There's more...

Believe it or not, logical replication (and therefore BDR) is fully compatible with synchronous mode. If we wanted to enable this, we would need to bootstrap the entire cluster first. Afterward, we could define these two parameters in `postgresql.conf`:

```
synchronous_commit = 'remote_write' synchronous_standby_names = 'ANY 1
(sync_slot_1, sync_slot_2)'
```

In this case, `sync_slot_1` or `sync_slot_2` would be the name of the synchronization slot used by the downstream system. BDR has a particular naming scheme, so it would be something like `bdr_db_cluster_origin_target`, but it does work as expected. Any `COMMIT` will be held until the synchronous requirements are met, just as if we were using synchronous physical replication.

This way, we can use BDR nodes to act as synchronous targets for other BDR nodes. Assuming we have a cluster of more than two nodes, this is even fairly resilient, as it is unlikely that multiple nodes will fail simultaneously.

Starting with a single BDR node

Once the software is physically installed on the server and configured to launch with PostgreSQL, we must start building our cluster. Despite how strange it might seem to have a cluster of only a single node, that's exactly how every BDR cluster begins.

We can think of our first BDR node as a seed from which the remainder of the cluster will grow. This node is very likely the current writable node used by our application stack. Thus, this recipe is a sort of conversion procedure, where we will explain how to transform a standard PostgreSQL database into the first node of a BDR cluster.

Let's begin!

Getting ready

This entire procedure is dependent on BDR software being installed on your system. Please follow the *Obtaining and installing BDR* recipe before continuing.

How to do it...

Follow these steps as the bdr_user PostgreSQL user to activate BDR on an active database named myapp on the pgha1 host:

1. Execute the following SQL to create the BDR extension:

   ```
   CREATE EXTENSION bdr CASCADE;
   ```

2. Initialize the current node with the following SQL:

   ```
   SELECT bdr.create_node(
     node_name := 'chicago',
     local_dsn := 'dbname=myapp host=pgha1 user=bdr_user'
   );
   ```

3. Create the BDR cluster definition with the following SQL:

   ```
   SELECT bdr.create_node_group(
     node_group_name := 'megacorp'
   );
   ```

4. Run the following function to wait for everything to complete:

   ```
   SELECT bdr.wait_for_join_completion();
   ```

How it works...

Creating our first node basically consists of three steps. We start by creating the `bdr` PostgreSQL extension using the `CASCADE` keyword. This also creates the `pglogical` extension required for BDR to function. Alternatively, we could create the `pglogical` extension explicitly before doing the same for `bdr`. Either way, the presence of the extensions provides us with a wealth of function calls and metadata for building and introspecting our BDR cluster.

The second step is the creation of the node itself. Every BDR node definition is a pair comprised of a name and a connection DSN, both of which we set by supplying them to the `bdr.create_node` function. The node name must be unique across the cluster, so we recommend choosing something descriptive of the role this node should play or its location or perhaps both. We recommend using a consistent naming scheme for all nodes before creating them to prevent issues in the future.

Once we have an initial node, we can define the cluster itself by invoking the `bdr.create_node_group` function. There are a lot of advanced parameters we could supply, but the only one that really matters is the cluster name. This is where we give our BDR cluster a unique name that it will use for several metadata elements. It will also use this text string within replication slot names and other identifiers within PostgreSQL. Each BDR cluster can only have one name, so make this one count!

Finally, we have the generally optional step of waiting for the cluster creation steps to complete. The `bdr.wait_for_join_completion` function blocks until any asynchronous events related to node status have finished. Creating the node group carries the implicit step of joining the local node to that group. If we do this quickly enough, there is a slim chance that calling subsequent BDR functions could fail. This is extremely unlikely, but the function is there to prevent this from happening.

At this point, we have a fully functional BDR cluster by the strictest definition; however, we still don't have a multi-master cluster. Let's follow the next recipe to fix that.

There's more...

If we use `\dx+ bdr` within our database, we should see every function, table, and view available for interacting with the extension. Among these is the `bdr.node_summary` view that reflects the current join state and several other attributes of all nodes in the cluster.

Let's run the following query in the `myapp` database really quickly to see how it looks with a single node:

```
SELECT node_seq_id, node_id, node_name, node_group_name,
peer_state_name FROM bdr.node_summary;
```

We should see something like this:

```
node_seq_id |   node_id   | node_name | node_group_name | peer_state_name
------------+-------------+-----------+-----------------+----------------
          1 | 4152250112  | chicago   | megacorp        | ACTIVE
```

While BDR itself assigns a sequential node ID to each node as it joins the cluster, it also assigns an absolute `node_id` as part of the `create_node` function call. Various node attributes are combined to produce this number so that it will always be unique across the cluster. This way, there will be no conflicts when new nodes join the overall group.

We can also see that our node and group names are faithfully represented here and our node is listed as `ACTIVE`. This should not be viewed as a live or online status of the node, but the status of its current role as a cluster member. Nodes may be in the process of joining or they may have been parted (removed) from the cluster or several other states between these. This lets us see how all of the nodes are interacting, and how each may contribute to quorum votes, for instance.

There are a lot of tables and views here, so feel free to explore them to learn more.

Creating an additional BDR node

Once we've established the BDR cluster seed node, we can begin by adding one or more additional nodes to establish multi-master functionality. This is where things start to get exciting!

This recipe is also very simple and will focus on adding any new node to an established BDR cluster. We should be able to run through the recipe as many times as we want, using as many nodes as we desire, to create a large cluster.

Don't get too carried away, however, as BDR only supports up to 1,024 nodes!

Getting ready

We need at least one BDR node within an activated cluster, so make sure that you follow the *Starting with a single BDR node* recipe before beginning. Additionally, since this is a new node, make sure that you apply the *Obtaining and installing BDR* recipe here as well.

How to do it...

Follow these steps as the `bdr_user` PostgreSQL user to create another BDR node on an active database named `myapp`, on the `pgha2` host:

1. Execute the following SQL to create the BDR extension:

   ```
   CREATE EXTENSION bdr CASCADE;
   ```

2. Initialize the current node with the following SQL:

   ```
   SELECT bdr.create_node(
     node_name := 'tokyo',
     local_dsn := 'dbname=myapp host=pgha2 user=bdr_user'
   );
   ```

3. Create the BDR cluster definition with the following SQL:

   ```
   SELECT bdr.join_node_group(
   join_target_dsn := 'dbname=myapp host=pgha1 user=bdr_user',
   wait_for_completion := True
   );
   ```

4. Obtain the status of the cluster nodes with the following query:

   ```
   SELECT node_seq_id, node_id, node_name,
          node_group_name, peer_state_name
     FROM bdr.node_summary;
   ```

How it works...

Just as we did when we created the initial node, we always start by creating the `bdr` extension itself. This is a prerequisite to making all BDR-related functions available for our use.

Next, we perform the same step as the previous recipe by using `bdr.create_node` to establish metadata for this node before it joins the cluster. Perhaps it seems silly to create a node with no context for where it belongs since it's not associated with any cluster. The true role of the `create_node` function is to establish node metadata within BDR and `pglogical`. This information will be exchanged with any cluster we try to join.

> It's also the reason why the `node_id` value is generated to be unique across the cluster. This ensures that any new node is fully defined before it attempts to join our cluster.

The real work begins when we invoke the `bdr.join_node_group` function. Assuming we've started with a fresh, empty database, this function does several things:

- Contacts the upstream node specified by `join_target_dsn`
- Creates a replication slot on the upstream system
- Exchanges metadata information with the cluster
- Obtains schema definitions for the current database
- Copies any data from the node it's joining through
- Creates replication slots to and from all other BDR nodes
- Sets the node as `ACTIVE` once it joins the cluster successfully

There are other intermediate steps involved here, but these are the important ones. In the end, we've transformed an empty database into a fully qualified member of the BDR cluster with a single function call.

Though we set the `wait_for_completion` parameter to `True` explicitly, this parameter is enabled by default. We just wanted to demonstrate that the function will block until the entire `join` procedure is complete.

> Note that the `join_node_group` function is atomic. If it fails for some reason, or the node ends in a state other than `ACTIVE`, then the node generally cannot join the cluster. This is because BDR performs the entire `join` procedure within a transaction on the remote node. This ensures that the new node has retrieved all data up to that transaction and can then subscribe to a replication slot to obtain the remainder. If this fails for any reason, we recommend parting and dropping the failed node and trying again after fixing the error that prevented a successful join.

Once the node has joined, we can check with the `bdr.node_summary` view to see how our cluster looks with two nodes. Here's an example:

```
node_seq_id |   node_id   | node_name | node_group_name | peer_state_name
-------------+-------------+-----------+-----------------+-----------------
          2 | 1500522812  | tokyo     | megacorp        | ACTIVE
          1 | 4152250112  | chicago   | megacorp        | ACTIVE
```

In our case, we executed the query from `pgha2`, so we can see that the local record comes first. This output demonstrates that metadata from `pgha1` arrived safely, and at least as far as BDR is concerned, the nodes in the cluster should be fully operational.

There's more...

One difficulty associated with using the `bdr.join_node_group` function is that it relies on PostgreSQL logical replication semantics to transfer data from the remote node. The associated overhead makes this a fairly slow process, and for larger databases may mean days or even weeks of data synchronization. Assuming a single function call can survive for that long is a very risky proposition.

As a result, BDR also provides a command-line tool that can convert a physical replica into a BDR node. Using the same node DSNs and names as in the recipes, converting `pgha2` would work like this:

```
bdr_init_physical -D /db/pgdata \
    --node-name=tokyo \
    --remote-dsn='dbname=myapp host=pgha1 user=bdr_user' \
    --local-dsn='dbname=myapp host=pgha2 user=bdr_user'
```

Since the data already exists locally, the only things BDR needs to do is add the missing metadata and create BDR-specific replication slots between the new node and the rest of the cluster.

This is the most efficient way to add a BDR node, since there are numerous methods for copying data between servers. Unlike a single PostgreSQL transaction, these are events that can also be resumed if interrupted, making it much less likely that creating a cluster of VLDB BDR nodes will end in failure.

Testing DDL replication on each node

One of the potential roadblocks of multi-master replication is the fact that schemas must be compatible on all nodes. Any node that does not have the same columns and types on tables risks being unable to consume data from the upstream node that generated the incompatible tuple.

As a result, a hallmark feature of BDR (and likely any other multi-master system that emerges in the future) is that DDL is transparently replicated. This ensures that the schemas are always compatible with all nodes, and prevents costly delays in replication caused by stuck data.

This recipe will be a short proof of concept to prove that DDL is transparently replicated and serves as a good check to try on any new BDR cluster to ensure that it's working correctly.

Getting ready

In order to apply this recipe, we should begin with at least two functional BDR nodes. Please follow all recipes up to *Creating an additional BDR node* before continuing.

How to do it...

Assuming that we have two nodes in `pgha1` and `pgha2` and a BDR-enabled database named `myapp`, follow these steps to test the DDL replication:

1. Execute the following SQL on `pgha1`:

   ```
   CREATE TABLE event_log (
     event_id   BIGSERIAL PRIMARY KEY,
     event      VARCHAR(100) NOT NULL,
     event_dt   TIMESTAMPTZ NOT NULL DEFAULT now()
   );
   ```

2. Execute the following SQL on `pgha2`:

   ```
   CREATE INDEX idx_event_log_event_dt
       ON event_log (event_dt);
   ```

3. Examine the table on `pgha1` by using this command in `psql` (for example):

   ```
   \d event_log
   ```

How it works...

We start by creating `event_log` as our first table on `pgha1`. Those of you who are familiar with logical replication know that DDL is not part of the replication stream; however, it is possible to intercept DDL within PostgreSQL itself and trigger the actions afterward.

As a result, BDR captures DDL events and adds them to the replication stream as part of the logical output. The receiving node understands that this isn't standard replicated data and applies the DDL locally. Assuming that everything worked properly, we should see this table appear on `pgha2` as well.

Next, we create an index on the `event_dt` column because we want to be able to quickly locate events by date. The only difference here is that we applied the change from `pgha2`. This DDL should replay on `pgha1` much like the original table creation. We test for this by using the `\d` syntax within `psql` to describe the `event_log` table while on `pgha1`.

This is what we see on our test system:

```
myapp=# \d event_log
                                      Table "public.event_log"
    Column   |            Type            | Collation | Nullable |                 Default
-------------+----------------------------+-----------+----------+-----------------------------------------
 event_id    | bigint                     |           | not null | nextval('event_log_event_id_seq'::regclass)
 event       | character varying(100)     |           | not null |
 event_dt    | timestamp with time zone   |           | not null | now()
Indexes:
    "event_log_pkey" PRIMARY KEY, btree (event_id)
    "idx_event_log_event_dt" btree (event_dt)
```

As expected, the new index on `event_dt` shows up on this node as well. We now have proof that we have a two-node multi-master cluster.

There's more...

Not all DDL statements are equally safe. Say that we want to alter the `event` column and change the type to `TEXT`. Watch what happens if we attempt that directly:

```
myapp=# ALTER TABLE event_log ALTER event TYPE TEXT;
ERROR:  ALTER TABLE ... ALTER COLUMN TYPE may not affect replicated tables on a BDR node
CONTEXT:  in pglogical plugin bdr in the preprocess_ddl callback
```

The risk here is that certain type conversions would cause a full table rewrite on not just the node being altered, but every node in the cluster. This could lead to a long-duration exclusive lock everywhere, and could eventually cause major problems.

As an alternative, BDR recommends this process:

1. Add a new column:

```
ALTER TABLE event_log
   ADD event_new TEXT;
```

2. Create a trigger function that keeps the columns synchronized:

```
CREATE FUNCTION f_copy_event ()
RETURNS TRIGGER AS
$$
BEGIN
  NEW.event_new := NEW.event;
  RETURN NEW;
END;
$$ LANGUAGE plpgsql;

CREATE TRIGGER t_copy_event_b_iu
BEFORE INSERT OR UPDATE
    ON event_log
   FOR EACH ROW
       EXECUTE PROCEDURE f_copy_event ();
```

3. Copy all current data into the new column in small to medium batches:

```
UPDATE event_log
   SET event_new = event
 WHERE event_new IS NULL
   AND id BETWEEN 1 AND 1000000;
```

4. Once the new column is populated, add the NOT NULL constraint:

```
ALTER TABLE event_log
      ALTER event_new SET NOT NULL;
```

5. Finally, swap the column names and drop the old column and management trigger in a transaction:

```
BEGIN;
ALTER TABLE event_log RENAME event TO event_old;
ALTER TABLE event_log RENAME event_new TO event;
ALTER TABLE event_log DROP COLUMN event_old;
DROP TRIGGER t_copy_event_b_iu ON event_log;
COMMIT;
```

If that seems like a lot of work to make what should be one simple change, that's because it is. But consider the alternative if this procedure isn't followed. BDR would lock the table in exclusive mode on every node, PostgreSQL would entirely rebuild the table using a process that could take hours, and only then would the change finally be available.

Even if you are not using BDR, this is a better method for applying such invasive DDL changes while remaining highly available. The only difference is that BDR requires this approach because of the implications of cross-cluster locks.

There are some other DDL restrictions like this that should be considered, especially if the application relies on automated DDL deployment scripts. All of these will require auditing and very likely testing in another BDR-enabled environment to ensure that they will work as expected.

This is yet another factor that is part of embracing a full multi-master PostgreSQL cluster. While all standard PostgreSQL functionality is enabled, converting an application or stack isn't a trivial affair.

Using sequences safely

Sequences and identity columns within a multi-master context are especially prone to complications. PostgreSQL itself is essentially unaware of the presence of other PostgreSQL nodes that may refer to the same sequences, and each node operates independently of the others in that regard.

As a result, each new incremental value from a standard sequence is arbitrary and could result in duplicate values on nodes. This would be a disaster if we are using them for a primary key, as any conflicts here would result in lost data.

This recipe will demonstrate how to safely use sequences with BDR and prevent any node from producing conflicting values.

Getting ready

In order to apply this recipe, we should begin with at least two functional BDR nodes. Please follow all recipes up to *Creating an additional BDR node* before continuing.

How to do it...

Assuming we have two nodes in pgha1 and pgha2 and a BDR-enabled database named myapp, follow these steps to manage and use sequences:

1. Execute the following statement on any BDR node before using any DDL that contains BIGSERIAL or SEQUENCE:

   ```
   SET bdr.default_sequence_kind = 'timeshard';
   ```

2. Create a SEQUENCE and check the results as follows:

   ```
   CREATE SEQUENCE myseq;
   SELECT nextval('myseq');
   ```

3. Create a BIGSERIAL table and insert a test record as follows:

   ```
   DROP TABLE IF EXISTS event_log;
   CREATE TABLE event_log (
     event_id  BIGSERIAL PRIMARY KEY,
     event     VARCHAR(100) NOT NULL,
     event_dt  TIMESTAMPTZ NOT NULL DEFAULT now()
   );

   INSERT INTO event_log (event) VALUES ('Testing');
   SELECT * FROM event_log;
   ```

4. Use the following query to check the status of sequences tracked by BDR:

   ```
   SELECT * FROM bdr.sequences;
   ```

How it works...

Since the earliest incarnation of BDR 3, the timeshard sequence type has existed to prevent sequential ID collisions. It works using an algorithm pioneered by Instagram that uses bit packing to overload a 64-bit integer with identifying information. Each ID actually contains the BDR sequential node ID, a timestamp, and the local sequence value.

There are basically two ways to ensure that all new sequences generate values according to this approach. We can either do as the instructions suggest and set bdr.default_sequence_kind to timeshard before creating any kind of sequence, or we can set the same parameter in our postgresql.conf file. Whatever we decide, it's best to be consistent to avoid accidentally creating any of the wrong types on different nodes.

 The bdr.default_sequence_kind parameter is a local setting that takes effect once the sequence is created. Since the parameter itself is not replicated, we recommend setting it in the postgresql.conf file on all nodes. Alternatively, the parameter may be enforced by using a preamble that sets it after any connection is established.

Once the parameter is set, it should remain in effect until we disconnect our session. With that in mind, the first test of this functionality is to specifically create a sequence and then obtain one value to prove it's working.

Once we call nextval, we should see something like this:

```
myapp=# SELECT nextval('myseq');

       nextval
---------------------
 1718952888841027585
```

We can perform a similar feat using a BIGSERIAL type when creating a table. This produces an implicit sequence that BDR intercepts and modifies to use the timeshard algorithm.

We can check that our sequences are properly generated by selecting rows from the table. We should see something like this when doing so:

```
myapp=# SELECT * FROM event_log;

      event_id       | event   |          event_dt
---------------------+---------+------------------------------
 1718957700949229569 | Testing | 2020-01-05 19:53:22.783038+00
```

As we can see, these values are extremely and arbitrarily large. While they will not conflict, they're very likely a drastic departure from whatever sequence methodology may have been in use previously.

Due to the fact that the algorithm uses bit packing and assumes a 64-bit integer, this only works with `BIGINT` or `BIGSERIAL` column types. Using this approach may require us to modify the existing schema before implementation. In fact, BDR will report an error if `timeshard` is enabled and a table is created using `SERIAL` rather than `BIGSERIAL`.

Regardless, one cool trick we can perform after setting our sequence types is introspecting from the BDR metadata. At this point, we should see the following sequence settings:

```
myapp=# SELECT * FROM bdr.sequences;

 nspname |        relname        |  seqkind
---------+-----------------------+-----------
 public  | myseq                 | timeshard
 public  | event_log_event_id_seq | timeshard
```

We can use this to track all sequences on a BDR-enabled database.

There's more...

Managing sequences is a very important topic. As such, BDR has more functionality for managing them, which we will explore in the following section.

Global allocation sequences

As we've already seen, the values produced by `timeshard` sequences may not be desirable. In some cases, frontend languages may not even be compatible. JavaScript, for example, is not compatible with such large values by default. So what can we do instead?

Another valid setting for the `bdr.default_sequence_kind` parameter is `galloc`, for global allocation. Rather than arbitrarily producing large values, each node actually requests a range of values from the consensus layer. Once this range is exhausted, the node obtains another, and so on.

This approach may result in more latency on each sequence range boundary, but is otherwise compatible with more common INTEGER and SERIAL types. Look at the following SQL:

```
SET bdr.default_sequence_kind = 'galloc';
CREATE SEQUENCE galloc_test;
SELECT nextval('galloc_test');
```

If we were to execute this, then pgha1 would use values 1 through 1 billion, pgha2 would use the next billion values, and so on. If we used a SERIAL type while creating a table, the blocks would each be sized at 1 million instead.

Timeshard introspection

Remember how we mentioned that timeshard sequence fields are bit-packed 64-bit integers? Well, BDR includes functions that make it possible to unpack a value to obtain the information it contains.

Let's try this by using the following query to unpack the event_id field in the event_log table:

```
SELECT event_id,
    bdr.extract_nodeid_from_timeshard(event_id) AS node_id,
    bdr.extract_localseqid_from_timeshard(event_id) AS seq_val,
    bdr.extract_timestamp_from_timeshard(event_id) AS stamp FROM
event_log;
```

If we insert one or two more rows from each of our nodes, we should see something like this:

event_id	node_id	seq_val	stamp
1718957700949229569	1	1	2020-01-05 19:53:22.783+00
1719002262879109121	2	1	2020-01-05 20:37:38.881+00
1719004101762646018	2	2	2020-01-05 20:39:28.487+00

With this technique, we can actually see which nodes inserted which values. We can also see that the local sequences would have generated conflicting values if we hadn't used some kind of sanitized sequence approach. It should also be obvious from this output that even sequential seq_val values do not produce sequential results; bit-packing makes the results somewhat arbitrary.

Either way, this is a great source of diagnostic information, and we can even use it to compare node activity since we can aggregate these fields to determine which nodes generate the most rows.

See also

For more details on Sharding and IDs at Instagram, refer to the following link: `https://instagram-engineering.com/sharding-ids-at-instagram-1cf5a71e5a5c`.

Configuring HAProxy for the multi-master approach

Though we already have an entire chapter on proxy and load balancing techniques `Chapter 4`, *Proxy and Pooling Resources*, some of these concepts change slightly in a multi-master context.

Consider the implications of attempting to use simple round-robin query distribution. If our application reconnects for each operation and inserts data into Node A, but then selects from Node B, this is an implicit race condition that may not be satisfied at that specific time.

This can also produce strange effects if the application is stateless and performs `SELECT-UPDATE` pairs regardless of which node it is communicating with. In the presence of high latency for any reason, this could result in two different sequential incremental updates on the same base value.

This recipe will explain how to alter our previous HAProxy configuration to better adapt to a multi-master environment.

Getting ready

In order to apply this recipe, we should begin with at least two functional BDR nodes. Please follow all recipes up to *Creating an additional BDR node* before continuing. We also recommend following the recipes in `Chapter 4`, *Proxy and Pooling Resources*, that are related to HAProxy so that both BDR nodes are included.

How to do it...

Assuming `pgha-proxy` is the proxy server, and `pgha1` and `pgha2` are the BDR nodes, follow these steps to make HAProxy more compatible with BDR:

1. Add the following to the `global` section of the `haproxy.cfg` file:

```
global
    stats socket /var/run/haproxy/sock level admin
```

2. Ensure that the `bk_db` section of the `haproxy.cfg` file looks like this:

```
backend bk_db
    option pgsql-check user haproxy_check

    stick-table type ip size 1
    stick on dst

    server bdr_chicago pgha1:5432 check
    server bdr_tokyo pgha2:5432 backup check
```

3. Trigger HAProxy to reload the configuration file with the following command as a root-enabled user:

```
sudo systemctl reload haproxy
```

How it works...

This recipe actually performs two tasks. First, we enable `stats socket` in the `global` section in `admin` mode so we can retrieve information from HAProxy and send commands if necessary. We will be using this capability later, so it's a good time to do this since we're modifying the configuration anyway.

The next thing we do essentially converts HAProxy into more of a stateful connection arbitrator. We actually add only two things to the `bk_db` configuration to accomplish this. The first is an IP-based `stick-table` that stores the HAProxy `dst` (destination) field.

HAProxy stick tables determine where new connections will be directed when they are established. The reason we used the destination rather than the source is that the source is unreliable. It could be a legitimate application host system or a single address if connections are filtered through a PgBouncer node.

Using the destination gives us the capability of preferring one BDR node over another. In this case, the conceit is that this proxy node is closer to the Chicago data center than Tokyo, so we'd rather send application connections to the local database than the remote location.

That is also the reason we added the `backup` tag to the `server bdr_tokyo` line. If the state of HAProxy is ever reset, such as during a service restart, the Tokyo BDR node will be considered only a backup node if the Chicago location is not reachable.

The stick table also performs another important role: semi-permanence. In the event that the Chicago node goes offline and traffic is redirected to Tokyo, traffic remains in that configuration even if the Chicago node returns. This is to prevent frequent and unnecessary connection switching in the event a node is experiencing intermittent failures or there is some kind of network communication issue.

Restarting HAProxy activates these settings and resets any other stateful information that it may have been tracking. This gives our cluster a fresh starting point with our preferred architecture.

There's more...

One of the reasons we enabled the HAProxy stats socket is so we can send commands to the service. Some of these are diagnostic, while others are commands to manage the backends themselves.

Rather than connecting and then using the `inet_server_addr` function to determine which PostgreSQL node we're connecting to as we have done in the past, we can simply ask HAProxy. If we have `socat` installed, all it takes is this command to show the state of the stick table:

```
echo "show table bk_db" | socat /var/run/haproxy/sock -
```

Assuming that the HAProxy service was freshly restarted, we should see something like this:

```
root@pgha-proxy:~$ echo "show table bk_db" | socat /var/run/haproxy/sock -

# table: bk_db, type: ip, size:1, used:1
0x5575dfe908e0: key=127.0.0.1 use=0 exp=0 server_id=1 server_name=bdr_chicago
```

HAProxy numbers server backends sequentially, so the `server_id` of 1 is the expected result. More importantly, HAProxy also directly reports the `server_name` that corresponds to the current traffic target, which shows that `bdr_chicago` is where all new connections are being sent.

See also

For more details on HAProxy Unix Socket Commands, refer to the following: `https:/ /cbonte.github.io/haproxy-dconv/2.0/management.html#9.3`.

Combining PgBouncer with HAProxy

HAProxy fulfills an important role in a highly available multi-master stack by ensuring that we always reach one writable node in a manner that prevents server flapping. Despite this, we have no way of politely managing traffic without another component. PgBouncer is that missing piece.

Beyond the pooling functionality that PgBouncer provides, the elements we really want to exploit are the `RECONNECT` and `WAIT_CLOSE` operations. By combining these two operations, we can put a BDR node into maintenance mode and allow any pending transactions to complete before working on the server.

This recipe will explain how to combine PgBouncer with HAProxy in a way that will ensure that there is literally no interruption in application traffic.

Getting ready

In order to apply this recipe, we should begin with at least two functional BDR nodes and a suitable HAProxy managing them. Please follow all recipes up to *Creating an additional BDR node* and *Configuring HAProxy for the multi-master approach* before continuing. We also recommend following the recipes in Chapter 4, *Proxy and Pooling Resources*, that are related to PgBouncer, particularly *Installing PgBouncer*, *Configuring PgBouncer safely*, and *Enhancing PgBouncer authentication*.

How to do it...

These steps will assume that we've installed PgBouncer on `pgha-proxy`, the same node as our HAProxy service. Follow these instructions to tightly couple PgBouncer and HAProxy:

1. Alter the `haproxy.cfg` file so that the `ft_postgresql` section resembles the following:

   ```
   frontend ft_postgresql
       bind *:5433
       default_backend bk_db
   ```

2. Modify the `[databases]` section in the `pgbouncer.ini` file and ensure that it contains the following line:

   ```
   * = host=pgha-proxy port=5433
   ```

3. Modify the `[pgbouncer]` section in the `pgbouncer.ini` file and change the following entry:

   ```
   listen_port = 5432
   ```

4. Restart the HAProxy and PgBouncer services in the following order:

   ```
   sudo systemctl restart haproxy
   sudo systemctl restart pgbouncer
   ```

How it works...

This recipe is essentially a mild reconfiguration of both HAProxy and PgBouncer. We start by reconfiguring HAProxy to `bind` to port `5433` rather than our earlier recommendation of `5432`. We do this because HAProxy isn't going to be the only component between the application and the PostgreSQL nodes.

Next, we have to slightly modify two sections of the `pgbouncer.ini` file in order to work with HAProxy. Rather than configuring which backend PgBouncer connects to, we simply connect to the HAProxy node itself. This can either be the local server or the hostname of the proxy server; either way, PgBouncer should no longer directly contact any PostgreSQL nodes.

The connection target should always be handled by HAProxy since it can automatically detect which server is online and preferred based on the active stick table. Now we no longer need to modify the `pgbouncer.ini` file and reload the service any time we want to use one BDR node over another. We also need to change the connection port so that it uses the same target that HAProxy is monitoring: `5433`.

Then we move on to the port that PgBouncer itself binds to with the `listen_port` parameter. By setting this to `5432`, the `pgha-proxy` server becomes a transparent component that masquerades as whichever BDR node is currently the preferred target.

Finally, we restart the HAProxy and then the PgBouncer services—in that order—to cleanly reserve the correct and expected ports. From this point on, any connection through the proxy node should target the most appropriate BDR node based on availability.

 Given how simple this procedure is, we could have combined it with the next recipe; however, we feel having a separate set of instructions for node maintenance is better for reference purposes.

Performing a managed node switchover

HAProxy and PgBouncer are an ideal combination for performing high-availability node maintenance in a multi-master context. The reason for this is related to the fact HAProxy uses its detection mechanism to automatically direct traffic to any online node. Since all BDR nodes are writable, this means that any switch from one node to another will allow full application functionality. We can either allow this to happen automatically or we can take direct control.

When we added PgBouncer, this gave us the added capability of transaction management. Before we can stop a PostgreSQL node, it's considered polite to allow any executing transactions to complete their work. By combining the `RECONNECT` and `WAIT_CLOSE` operations of PgBouncer with the seamless redirection of HAProxy, we can decommission any BDR node without the application ever knowing.

This recipe will explain how to operate PgBouncer with HAProxy to safely remove a multi-master node from the cluster and how to return it to service.

Getting ready

This recipe requires the full BDR, HAProxy, and PgBouncer stack. Please follow all recipes necessary for completing the *Combining PgBouncer with HAProxy* recipe before continuing.

How to do it...

These steps should be performed on the PgBouncer and HAProxy nodes, which will be referred to as `pgha-proxy`. Follow these instructions to disable the `bdr_chicago` node and then return it to service:

1. Begin by disabling the Chicago server within HAProxy:

   ```
   echo "disable server bk_db/bdr_chicago" | \
       socat /var/run/haproxy/sock -
   ```

2. Then tell `PgBouncer` to reconnect after transactions are complete and to wait until all connections have been reestablished:

   ```
   psql -h pgha-proxy -U pgbouncer pgbouncer -c "RECONNECT"
   psql -h pgha-proxy -U pgbouncer pgbouncer -c "WAIT_CLOSE"
   ```

3. Perform whatever maintenance is necessary on the Chicago node.
4. Execute the following HAProxy command to re-enable the Chicago server:

   ```
   echo "enable server bk_db/bdr_chicago" | \
       socat /var/run/haproxy/sock -
   ```

How it works...

The focus of this recipe involves actively moving connections away from the preferred Chicago node. This requires three commands that could easily be scripted.

We start by disabling the `bdr_chicago` server using the HAProxy socket. This has the effect of preventing HAProxy from sending new connections to this server. Existing connections are not terminated! This is important for the next steps.

Then we issue a RECONNECT command to the pgbouncer pseudo database. This will mark all existing connections as requiring reconnection as soon as the current transaction has completed. Once the current transaction completes, the backend will be discarded and a new connection will be established. Thanks to HAProxy, this will be the Tokyo server.

Finally, we send a WAIT_CLOSE command to the pgbouncer pseudo database. This lets us poll for when the pending transactions have all committed and new connections have replaced the old ones. Once this happens, the Chicago node should be completely idle and safe to maintain.

Once that process is complete, we are free to mangle the Chicago server as we desire. When we want to reintroduce it to the cluster, we simply reverse the process and use socat to send an enable command to HAProxy for the bdr_chicago server.

Thanks to our stick table, this will not cause a disruptive reconnection event by itself. All connections will remain in Tokyo until we repeat the migration procedure on that node as well.

There's more...

All of these socat commands are highly cumbersome since they require pipes and the physical location of the command socket. Thankfully, there is a nonstandard utility named haproxyctl that simplifies many of these operations. Debian derivatives should have access to this within standard repositories, but Red-Hat-related systems may need to visit the Git repository.

However it is obtained, this utility transforms the management of HAProxy into something that's much easier to understand and perform:

```
haproxyctl disable server bk_db/bdr_chicago
haproxyctl enable server bk_db/bdr_chicago
```

We definitely feel that this is a major improvement! We only wish all Linux distributions packaged it as readily as HAProxy, or that the HAProxy project itself adopted it internally.

See also

The HAProxyCTL tool really is very useful. Please use the following resource to learn more or obtain it for unpackaged platforms: `https://github.com/flores/haproxyctl`.

Improving failover speed

Once we've completed a multi-master failover stack, there's really only one task remaining to prove that it does as we claim. We need to both test the failover process and also modify one or two settings to get it as low as possible, while also doing so safely and avoiding disruptive flapping between nodes.

This recipe will explain what tests we can perform on our cluster to do this and which settings we can modify to wring as much failover performance out of a multi-master environment as possible.

Getting ready

This recipe requires the full BDR, HAProxy, and PgBouncer stack. Please follow all recipes necessary for completing the *Combining PgBouncer with HAProxy* recipe before continuing.

How to do it...

This recipe will assume that we have two PostgreSQL BDR servers as `pgha1` and `pgha2` and a PgBouncer and HAProxy server as `pgha-proxy`. Follow these steps to observe and improve cluster failover time:

1. Start the following command on `pgha-proxy` in a terminal window:

   ```
   while [ true ]; do \
       psql -qAt -U postgres myapp \
           -c "SELECT inet_server_addr(), now()"; \
   done
   ```

2. Open a terminal connection to both `pgha1` and `pgha2` with the rights to start and stop the PostgreSQL service.

3. Observe the IP address returned while step 1 operates, and stop PostgreSQL on that server. Debian-related systems can use the following command:

```
sudo systemctl stop postgresql@10-main
```

4. Red Hat systems will need to stop PostgreSQL in the following way:

```
sudo systemctl stop postgresql-10
```

5. Return to pgha-proxy and wait until the connections resume, and then stop the loop with *Ctrl + C*.
6. Restart PostgreSQL on the system where it was stopped.
7. Modify the pgbouncer.ini configuration file on pgha-proxy, and modify these two parameters:

```
server_connect_timeout = 1
server_login_retry = 1
```

8. Reload the PgBouncer service on pgha-proxy:

```
sudo systemctl reload pgbouncer
```

9. Repeat *step 1* to *step 6* and note the difference in failover times.

How it works...

The goal of this recipe is to observe how quickly PgBouncer will switch from one server to another. HAProxy handles most of this work already, but PgBouncer has its own series of checks and safeguards that could artificially increase the failover time necessary to reassign server connections.

So the first thing we want to do is observe the process in action using the default settings. If we start an endless loop that simply reports the IP address of the server we're contacting, we accomplish two goals. The first is that we connect as quickly as possible to PgBouncer so that we have a timeline, and we also learn the IP address of the current BDR server, which should correspond to pgha1 or pgha2.

Then we will want a connection to both of our BDR servers, as we'll be stopping and starting PostgreSQL at least once on each server. By stopping the PostgreSQL service, HAProxy will quickly notice that it is offline and begin redirecting traffic to the other node. PgBouncer, however, will require quite a bit longer.

If we return to `pgha-proxy` after stopping PostgreSQL, we should see a long pause where there is no output, as `psql` can no longer connect to a database. PgBouncer still thinks its pool of connections is valid and doesn't really understand that HAProxy has changed targets. This is what we observed during our local test:

```
10.0.30.1|2020-01-08 23:29:25.118004+00
10.0.30.1|2020-01-08 23:29:25.187169+00
10.0.30.2|2020-01-08 23:29:40.677083+00
10.0.30.2|2020-01-08 23:29:40.824378+00
```

Once we have these results, it's safe to start PostgreSQL on `pgha1` or `pgha2` so that the cluster is fully operational again. We'll be repeating this process, so both nodes should be online and functional before we continue.

Note that it took just over 15 seconds for PgBouncer to begin making new connections to the currently active server. It turns out that there's a reason for this particular result: PgBouncer has two parameters in `pgbouncer.ini` that control how it interprets connection problems.

The first of these is `server_connect_timeout`, which we set to 1. Each new connection to PgBouncer is assigned a connection from the pool. If this connection does not respond, PgBouncer will try to establish a new one. The default time of 15 seconds means that the first failure requires 15 seconds before PgBouncer will connect to the new target HAProxy that was chosen.

The second relevant parameter is `server_login_retry`, which we also set to 1. If we've separated the authentication and pool systems as recommended in Chapter 4, *Proxy and Pooling Resources*, then PgBouncer will attempt to validate the login with PostgreSQL before assigning a backend. This is technically a separate timeout and is treated differently than a connection timeout. As a result, we also need to set this to a low value to minimize failover time.

Once we've changed these two attributes, we simply need to reload the PgBouncer service so that it incorporates them. After that step completes, we can repeat the entire process one more time. Since HAProxy has moved the connection target to the other server, we'll need to stop PostgreSQL on that node instead.

Following the same procedure as before, we should stop PostgreSQL on `pgha1` or `pgha2`, whichever is the active node. If we watch the `psql` loop on `pgha-proxy`, we should again see when connections switch from one target to the other. This is what we saw on our systems:

```
10.0.30.2|2020-01-08 23:35:26.230442+00
10.0.30.2|2020-01-08 23:35:26.305077+00
10.0.30.1|2020-01-08 23:35:28.664761+00
10.0.30.1|2020-01-08 23:35:28.805541+00
```

Now our failover process only required about 2.3 seconds, which is quite an improvement, and far better than any promotion-based stack could deliver. It doesn't matter whether we used repmgr, Patroni, or Pacemaker: there is no way to get a failover this fast using conventional means.

Generally, we don't want to go lower than this anyway. HAProxy has various settings that can make it more aggressive for marking a server as offline and switching traffic, but even a short network blip can last longer than 2–3 seconds. If we switch BDR nodes every time that happens, we may end up disrupting our database and actually lower our overall uptime.

Performing a major version upgrade online

One of the most sought-after features of a PostgreSQL high availability cluster is the ability to upgrade between major versions while still remaining online. By this, we mean upgrading from PostgreSQL 10 to 11, for instance.

Until the advent of logical replication, such a procedure was a literal impossibility. Even though `pg_upgrade` was a vast improvement over the previous dump and restore process, it still required a short outage to rebuild the database catalog and copy or link the data files. In a time-sensitive environment, even such a truncated outage of a few minutes can be disruptive and expensive.

A multi-master design changes literally everything in a way that's difficult to truly believe. Because of the use of logical replication, it's possible to mix different PostgreSQL versions within the same cluster. This makes upgrading between major PostgreSQL versions nearly trivial.

This recipe will demonstrate how the multi-master approach, and BDR in particular, makes such an upgrade possible. Why do you think we wrote this chapter using the older PostgreSQL 10 for all of the previous recipes?

Getting ready

This recipe requires the full BDR, HAProxy, and PgBouncer stack. Please follow all recipes necessary for completing the *Combining PgBouncer with HAProxy* recipe before continuing. We will also need a third PostgreSQL server with PostgreSQL 11 installed, rather than PostgreSQL 10.

How to do it...

For a cluster that includes PostgreSQL servers pgha1 and pgha2 and a pgha-proxy proxy server, follow these steps on the server indicated to integrate pgha3 to replace pgha1:

1. Bootstrap an empty PostgreSQL instance on pgha3 using initdb as the postgres user:

    ```
    initdb -D /db/pgdata
    ```

2. Copy the postgresql.conf and pg_hba.conf from pgha1 to pgha3.
3. Copy the .pgpass file from pgha1 to pgha3.
4. Follow the instructions in the *Obtaining and installing BDR* recipe, but substitute 11 anywhere 10 is used. This applies to package installation names, systemctl service names, and so on.
5. Dump all global objects on pgha1 from pgha3 as the postgres user:

    ```
    pg_dumpall -g -h pgha1 -U bdr_user \
        -f global_objects.sql -d postgres
    ```

6. Import all global objects in pgha3 as the postgres user:

    ```
    psql -f global_objects.sql
    ```

7. Create the empty myapp database as the postgres user on pgha3 for the BDR setup:

    ```
    createdb myapp
    ```

8. Follow the *Creating an additional BDR node* recipe for pgha3.

9. Examine the state of the cluster with the following query on any node:

```
SELECT node_seq_id, node_id, node_name,
       node_group_name, peer_state_name
  FROM bdr.node_summary;
```

10. Modify the haproxy.cfg file on pgha-proxy and add a new entry for pgha3. The bk_db section should now look like this:

```
backend bk_db
    option pgsql-check user haproxy_check

    stick-table type ip size 1
    stick on dst

    server bdr_chicago pgha1:5432 check
    server bdr_tokyo pgha2:5432 backup check
    server bdr_dubai pgha3:5432 check
```

11. Reload the haproxy service on pgha-proxy:

```
sudo systemctl reload haproxy
```

12. Follow the *Performing a managed node switchover* recipe, but do not re-enable pgha1 on the last step.

13. Repeat all steps for any remaining version 10 nodes.

How it works...

At its heart, this recipe is really just a combination of three other recipes:

- *Obtaining and installing BDR*
- *Creating an additional BDR node*
- *Performing a managed node switchover*

The beauty of the multi-master approach is that so long as the nodes can communicate, we have completed our upgrade process by simply adding another node of a higher version. We can either retain the node we're replacing or remove it from the cluster as part of a full upgrade and replace procedure.

As a result, the first few steps merely involve creating a fresh and empty PostgreSQL instance on pgha3 to receive the data from our cluster. While doing this, we want to copy any existing global objects from the existing cluster, such as users and roles. We also want to copy any configuration files and the .pgpass file we've been maintaining up to this point. It contains the bdr_user authentication information, and potentially other important users as well.

Then we apply the *Obtaining and installing BDR* recipe on pgha3, but make sure that you substitute the target version number where necessary. This means that packages named postgresql-10 will be postgresql-11, and the systemctl service will be named postgresql@11-main or postgresql-11 here as well. At the end of everything, we should have an empty instance with all libraries installed, up and running and ready for BDR.

At this point, we create the database for our app, which was myapp in our case. This is where BDR should be activated to synchronize data from the cluster. We can do this by simply following the *Creating an additional BDR node* recipe for the new pgha3 node. In our particular case, we named the new node after Dubai, to go along with Chicago and Tokyo.

If we examine the cluster at this point, it should show the new node as expected. This is what we see in our test system:

```
 node_seq_id |   node_id   | node_name | node_group_name | peer_state_name
-------------+-------------+-----------+-----------------+----------------
           3 | 1074906797  | dubai     | megacorp        | ACTIVE
           2 | 1500522812  | tokyo     | megacorp        | ACTIVE
           1 | 4152250112  | chicago   | megacorp        | ACTIVE
```

So far, none of this should be surprising. We added a new node and it shows up. The next part of the recipe is to add the new node to HAProxy so that it is a full member of the cluster. This only requires one more line to haproxy.cfg for the new pgha3 server. Note that we didn't use the backup keyword here. This is because our intent is to replace pgha1 with pgha3 so that it won't be an alternative connection target from pgha-proxy.

Once we reload the HAProxy configuration file, we merely need to move any existing connections elsewhere in the cluster. We can do this by following the *Performing a managed node switchover* recipe. This conveniently moves all traffic away from pgha1 to pgha3, and then we choose to leave pgha1 offline.

At this point, we can either change our mind and restart pgha1 or go through further steps to permanently remove it from the cluster, as if our upgrade were being performed on a node-by-node basis.

Then we simply need to apply the same procedure over and over again for each node in the cluster. Once we've incrementally replaced all PostgreSQL 10 nodes with new version 11 nodes, our upgrade is complete. By invoking manual node switchovers using PgBouncer, the application would never even realize an upgrade took place.

 BDR will support PostgreSQL 12 by the time this book is published, or a few months afterward, making it possible to upgrade to the most recent version without any downtime at all.

There's more...

So how would we permanently remove pgha1 from the cluster so that pgha3 replaces it entirely? We really only need to perform a handful of steps:

1. Remove pgha1 from haproxy.cfg and reload the HAProxy service.
2. Remove pgha1 from the cluster by executing the following command from either pgha2 or pgha3:

    ```
    SELECT bdr.part_node('chicago');
    ```

3. Purge the pgha1 metadata from the cluster by running the following SQL on both pgha2 and pgha3:

    ```
    SELECT bdr.drop_node('chicago');
    ```

4. Verify that the node has been removed with the following query:

    ```
    SELECT node_seq_id, node_id, node_name,
           node_group_name, peer_state_name
      FROM bdr.node_summary;
    ```

The first step should be obvious. We don't want HAProxy to send traffic to a node we're decommissioning.

But then we *part* pgha1 using bdr.part_node, which in BDR parlance means that we are removing the node from cluster communication. Any associated replication slots are removed from all nodes, any background associated workers are stopped, and so on. This only affects BDR and does not damage the contents of pgha1 in any way. It also means that the node cannot ever rejoin the cluster. It will be treated as if it has diverged because, without the replication slots, there's no way to know what data it has compared to the contents of the other nodes.

If we check the status of the cluster at this point, it will look like this:

```
node_seq_id |   node_id    | node_name | node_group_name | peer_state_name
------------+--------------+-----------+-----------------+----------------
          2 | 1500522812   | tokyo     | megacorp        | ACTIVE
          1 | 4152250112   | chicago   | megacorp        | PARTED
          3 | 1074906797   | dubai     | megacorp        | ACTIVE
```

As we can see here, our Chicago node is marked as **PARTED**, which means that the cluster still knows it exists, but will also refuse to communicate with it. This is because a node may be parted even when it is offline, in case it was damaged, for example. So in the rare case that an offline node returns to the cluster, it won't be allowed to exchange data and potentially cause corruption.

Then if we really want to remove a node, we would run bdr.drop_node to purge any remaining metadata from the cluster. The reason this is not done automatically when the node is parted is because of the handshake process and quorum system. Nodes across the cluster may be in up or down states and need to have matching metadata. This means that purging node metadata must be a manual procedure, and should be performed on each individual node. In this case, we're sincerely stating that we want all references to the old node to be totally destroyed.

One benefit of dropping the node after parting it is that we can reuse the node name later. If we decide to replace the Chicago node as a new entry, we may do so since it will be joining as an empty database or through bdr_init_physical, just as any other node did.

We want to emphasize that the old node cannot ever rejoin the cluster once parted, so long as it contains data, although it would be possible to drop and recreate the myapp database to reuse the physical instance.

Generally, parted nodes are only good for reference purposes. Only empty nodes or transformed physical replicas are allowed to join a BDR cluster.

14
Data Distribution

Every business has the goal of being successful. The consequence of having a successful business when there's a database involved is increasingly high volume. This volume can be composed of query activity, data accumulation, or both. A PostgreSQL database that is not prepared for vast amounts of data or transaction load will slowly falter until the platform suffers.

Customers notice bad performance just as readily as outages. If our database is struggling to service queries, we have three options:

- Spend time optimizing the platform to reduce database interaction
- Buy a more capable database server
- Store data on several PostgreSQL servers

Indeed, we should probably always implement the first option in any case. Yet there is a limit to what can be optimized. If the platform is using **object-relational mapping (ORM)**, then making query changes can be difficult because they are generated from the framework. Frontend caching can prevent a vast amount of database accesses, but we need to consider cold caches, refreshes, and write volume. Writes must touch the database regardless of the cache state, so we need a solution that does not involve optimization.

We can also buy a newer, bigger, and better server. We can add CPUs, memory, and storage to a single expensive server until we saturate its available slots and ports. If we've maximized the most expandable server currently manufactured, we have a problem if the database volume continues to increase. What can we do?

A good platform architect will see this potential disaster before it strikes. We must make the assumption that our business and software will be successful beyond our wildest dreams and act accordingly. If we were Facebook, Instagram, or Skype, we would recognize the necessity of using multiple database servers early, enabling horizontal growth. It just so happens that PostgreSQL has a rich interface for database federation that we can leverage.

That will be the focus of this chapter. A highly available PostgreSQL cluster isn't only online and responding now, it does so in the future as well. Whether we accomplish horizontal distribution through assigned regions, associated groups, or at random, we need the infrastructure in place to facilitate this type of access. We will use PostgreSQL features to split up our data and ensure that the platform can run for years to come for the millions of users that will follow.

The features we will discuss in this chapter rely on the PostgreSQL foreign data wrapper, which wasn't introduced until PostgreSQL 9.3. We want to emphasize that at the time of the writing of the current edition of this book, PostgreSQL 9.4 is the oldest community-supported version.

We strongly recommend upgrading any old PostgreSQL clusters to 9.4 or higher when possible if you foresee a future need for widely distributed data. They will not be able to implement many of the ideas discussed here until then. This also ensures compatibility with other techniques in this book that require logical replication.

In this chapter, we will learn how clever data management can increase uptime even further. We will cover the following recipes in this chapter:

- Identifying horizontal candidates
- Setting up a foreign PostgreSQL server
- Mapping a remote user
- Creating a foreign table
- Using a foreign table in a query
- Optimizing foreign table access
- Transforming foreign tables into local tables
- Creating a scalable nextval replacement
- Building a sharding API
- Talking to the correct shard
- Moving a shard to another server

Identifying horizontal candidates

Before we can really decide how to spread our data across several database servers, we need to find appropriate candidates. To do this, we should start at the database level for databases that are extremely active. What qualifies as extremely active? Databases that fit any of the following criteria are a good start:

- The database experiences more than 10 million transactions per day
- The database handles more than 100 million queries per day
- The database writes more than 100 million tuples per day

Once we've chosen a database for horizontal scalability, we need to look at its tables and decide which should be distributed. Tables that make good choices are those that fit one or more of the following criteria:

- Tables that contain more than 10 million rows
- Tables that experience more than 1 million writes per day
- Tables that are larger than 10 GB

This recipe will discuss some easy ways to find prospective tables for further study.

Getting ready

This recipe uses an existing database for concrete numbers. If you do not have one of these, create it with pgbench using the following commands as the postgres user:

```
createdb pgbench
pgbench -i -s 200 pgbench
```

The -i flag initializes a new series of benchmark tables and the -s flag specifies the scale of the data. We started with a scale of 200, so our largest table has 20 million rows and is about 3 GB in size. Feel free to use a higher scale for demonstrative purposes.

We will also be using the pg_stat_statements extension that we discussed in the *Checking the pg_stat_statements view* recipe from Chapter 5, *Troubleshooting*. Make sure that it's installed in every database with the following SQL statement:

```
CREATE EXTENSION pg_stat_statements;
```

How to do it...

As the `postgres` user on a suitable PostgreSQL cluster, follow these steps to find horizontal scalability candidates:

1. Execute the following query while connected to any database:

```
WITH db AS (
  SELECT d.datname AS database_name,
         d.xact_commit + d.xact_rollback AS transactions,
         d.tup_inserted + d.tup_updated
                        + d.tup_deleted AS writes,
         sum(s.calls) AS queries
    FROM pg_stat_database d
    LEFT JOIN pg_stat_statements s ON (s.dbid = d.datid)
   WHERE d.datname NOT IN (
           'template0', 'template1', 'postgres'
         )
   GROUP BY 1, 2, 3
)
SELECT *
  FROM db
 WHERE db.transactions > 10000000
    OR db.writes > 100000000
    OR db.queries > 100000000;
```

2. Create the following view in the candidate database with this SQL statement:

```
CREATE OR REPLACE VIEW v_shard_candidates AS
 SELECT c.oid::regclass::text AS table_name,
        c.reltuples::NUMERIC AS num_rows,
        pg_total_relation_size(c.oid) / 1048576 AS size_mb,
        t.n_tup_ins + t.n_tup_upd + t.n_tup_del AS writes
   FROM pg_class c
   JOIN pg_namespace n ON (n.oid = c.relnamespace)
   JOIN pg_stat_user_tables t ON (t.relid = c.oid)
  WHERE n.nspname NOT IN ('pg_catalog',
                          'information_schema')
    AND c.relkind = 'r'
    AND (c.reltuples > 10000000
         OR
         t.n_tup_ins + t.n_tup_upd + t.n_tup_del > 1000000
         OR
         pg_total_relation_size(c.oid) / 1048576 > 10240);
```

3. Use the following query to check that the view matches the tables:

```
SELECT *
  FROM v_shard_candidates
 ORDER BY size_mb DESC;
```

How it works...

The first step checks the `pg_stat_database` system view. This provides various global statistics about all databases in the PostgreSQL database cluster. This is a very easy way to obtain a list of extremely active databases that we can break into smaller pieces. The query gives us all three numbers that we want regarding database statistics.

Our example database isn't quite busy enough, so we omitted the entire WHERE clause to show the `pgbench` database statistics:

database_name	transactions	writes	queries
pgbench	449077	20094597	589424

To get specific table measurements, we need to connect to any databases named by the database activity query. Then we create a view that will always provide a list of tables that match our three criteria. This will probably be used much more often than the database query, so it's handy to have it defined at all times.

 If you create the view in the `template1` database, then all future databases created within this cluster will automatically have the view defined.

The view itself isn't too complicated but deserves some explanation. The `pg_total_relation_size` function provides the size of the table, including all indexes and TOAST data. This is important because the full impact of a table is much more than the data it contains. The `pg_total_relation_size` function returns results in bytes, so we transform it into megabytes so that it's more useful to us.

We restrict `relkind` to r because this only matches relations, which is how PostgreSQL identifies tables. The last thing we do is apply our three conditions for candidate tables so that any criterion is enough for the table to appear on our list. The last query simply invokes the view and orders the results nicely for us.

Our `pgbench` database contained a single matching table, as shown in the following:

```
    table_name    | num_rows | size_mb |  writes
------------------+----------+---------+----------
 pgbench_accounts | 20000000 |    2993 | 20023044
```

We can see that the `pgbench_accounts` table contains 20000000 rows and is 2993 MB in size.

There's more...

Growth rates are also important. We recommend creating a scheduled task that checks these results at the end of every day and either emails them to a responsible DBA or saves them into a table for further examination. After the statistics are checked and logged, call the following two functions to reset them to zero:

```
SELECT pg_stat_statements_reset();
SELECT pg_stat_reset();
```

Any tables that are growing quickly are even more critical to identify early.

See also

We used quite a few system views in this recipe. Please use the following URLs to PostgreSQL documentation that provides further depth regarding statistic tables and system catalogs:

- **The Statistics Collector**:
  https://www.postgresql.org/docs/current/monitoring-stats.html
- **pg_stat_statements**:
  https://www.postgresql.org/docs/current/pgstatstatements.html
- **pg_class**:
  https://www.postgresql.org/docs/current/catalog-pg-class.html

Setting up a foreign PostgreSQL server

The first requirement of data federation is the ability to connect to remote databases. With this capability, we can read or write to a remote PostgreSQL database table as if it were local. By doing so, certain query elements can be offloaded to the other server. We can also access metadata that is stored in a central location that acts as a shared resource for all database servers.

This recipe will describe how to create a foreign PostgreSQL server and will be the basis for several of the upcoming sections.

Getting ready

Before we can use the PostgreSQL foreign data wrapper functionality, we need to add the postgres_fdw extension to the database that will use it. Execute the following SQL statement as the postgres user in the database that will be contacting foreign servers (pgbench, for example):

```
CREATE EXTENSION postgres_fdw;
```

How to do it...

For this recipe, we have two servers: pg-primary as our main data source and pg-report as a reporting server. As with the previous recipe, we will use pgbench as our sample database. Follow these steps to create a connection from pg-report to pg-primary within pgbench.

1. Connect to pgbench on the pg-report PostgreSQL server as the postgres user.
2. Execute the following SQL statement:

   ```
   CREATE SERVER primary_db
       FOREIGN DATA WRAPPER postgres_fdw
       OPTIONS (host 'pg-primary', dbname 'pgbench');
   ```

3. Execute the following SQL statement to check for the foreign server entry:

   ```
   SELECT srvname, srvoptions
     FROM pg_foreign_server;
   ```

How it works...

We start by connecting to the database where we will be accessing remote data. As our test database is pgbench, this is where the foreign server will reside.

The server creation itself consists of a server name, a foreign-data wrapper, and options for the foreign-data wrapper. For the server name, we used primary_db to keep things simple, but anything relatively descriptive is a good choice.

The CREATE SERVER statement can use several available foreign data wrappers, but to contact a PostgreSQL server, we need postgres_fdw. This data wrapper will accept many standard PostgreSQL connection parameters, including host, dbname, port, and so on.

We only used the dbname and host settings because we don't want to force this server connection to always use any specific user or password combination. This allows us to map one or more local users to users on the remote database. When new connections are created to the foreign server, each user will access the remote data as themselves. This is a much more secure usage pattern.

Finally, we check the pg_foreign_server view to make sure that PostgreSQL registered it with the options we specified. Once this is verified, we can move on to the next step. Here is our test server's output:

```
pgbench=# SELECT srvname, srvoptions
pgbench-#   FROM pg_foreign_server;

  srvname   |             srvoptions
------------+------------------------------------
 primary_db | {host=pg-primary,dbname=pgbench}
```

There's more...

Foreign data servers have a couple more pieces of functionality that we should discuss.

Altering foreign servers

Assume for a moment that we need the definition of the `primary_db` foreign server to change. For instance, what if we integrated `PgBouncer` to reduce user contention and we need to use the non-default port of `6432`? Here's how we would add the `port` option:

```
ALTER SERVER primary_db OPTIONS (ADD port '5433');
```

If we need to change this again later, we would use the following syntax instead:

```
ALTER SERVER primary_db OPTIONS (SET port '5444');
```

We must admit that this difference in syntax is something of an oddity. To PostgreSQL, `SET` only modifies attributes that were specified when we called `CREATE SERVER`. We must use `ADD` to override a default, even though `SET` could have been overloaded to perform both actions. This merely means that `SET` might fail with an error, noting that the option isn't found. If this happens, simply use `ADD` instead.

Dropping foreign servers

If we no longer want a foreign server, we can drop it along with all dependent objects. This use case is probably the only one that will work unless we simply never referenced the foreign server at all. Use the following SQL statement as a database superuser:

```
DROP SERVER primary_db CASCADE;
```

See also

The PostgreSQL foreign data wrapper has quite a bit of documentation available. The `CREATE SERVER` statement has its own entry as well. Please refer to the following URLs for more information:

- **postgres_fdw**:
  https://www.postgresql.org/docs/current/postgres-fdw.html
- **CREATE SERVER**:
  https://www.postgresql.org/docs/current/sql-createserver.html
- **pg_foreign_server**:
  https://www.postgresql.org/docs/current/catalog-pg-foreign-server.html

Mapping a remote user

Database users and the permissions they are granted may vary between PostgreSQL clusters. This is especially true if we do not directly administer the remote server. The role of user mappings is to overcome this obstacle by linking a local database user with a remote database user.

User mappings must be created for any local user that is going to utilize the remote server. Furthermore, these mappings are only valid for the remote server for which they're defined. This can be somewhat inconvenient in situations where all or most local users will be accessing remote data; however, this is a small price to pay for the security inherent in such a design.

In this recipe, we will create a user mapping to access our remote server.

Getting ready

As we will be using a foreign server in this recipe, please follow the *Setting up a foreign PostgreSQL server* recipe in this chapter before proceeding.

How to do it...

For this recipe, we will continue to use two servers: pg-primary as our main data source and pg-report as a reporting server. We will keep pgbench as our sample database. Follow these steps to create and map a user from pg-report to pg-primary within pgbench:

1. Execute the following SQL statement on both PostgreSQL servers as the postgres user:

   ```
   CREATE USER bench_user WITH PASSWORD 'testing';
   ```

2. Connect to pgbench on the pg-report PostgreSQL server as the postgres user.

3. Execute the following SQL statement to create the mapping:

   ```
   CREATE USER MAPPING FOR bench_user
       SERVER primary_db
       OPTIONS (user 'bench_user', password 'testing');
   ```

4. Execute the following SQL statement to check for the foreign server entry:

```
SELECT u.rolname AS user_name,
       s.srvname AS server_name,
       um.umoptions AS map_options
  FROM pg_user_mapping um
  JOIN pg_authid u ON (u.oid = um.umuser)
  JOIN pg_foreign_server s ON (s.oid = um.umserver);
```

How it works...

The first thing we need is a user that we know exists on both servers. While we can link a local user with any remote user, this is easiest when they have the same name. This prevents confusion or connection problems in the future. If we are linking to a remote server that we don't administer, then this may not be possible. For now, however, we have control over both systems, so we can create the bench_user safely with a simple password for testing purposes.

Next, we create the user mapping itself. As with the server, we need to fill in three sections: a local user name, the server to use, and options for the mapping. We just created bench_user, so this will be our local user that we will associate with the mapping. Then we specify the primary_db server that we created in the previous recipe. Finally, we set the options for the mapping, which consists of the name of the remote user and their password.

> The password option is required for non-superusers. This is not noted in the documentation for foreign servers, user mappings, or foreign tables. The PostgreSQL developers included it as a security precaution to prevent mapped users from accessing unauthorized entries in .pgpass files or other automated password entry systems.

As a last step, we want to verify that PostgreSQL is storing the user mapping with the options we specified. It's always good to visualize database changes whenever possible, if only to put our minds at ease. The query we use gets its data from pg_user_mapping, though we do perform a couple of joins to transform meaningless IDs into useful information. Here's how it looks on our test server:

```
 user_name  | server_name |               map_options
------------+-------------+------------------------------------------
 bench_user | primary_db  | {user=bench_user,password=testing}
```

As we can see, the `bench_user` is properly associated with the `primary_db` server and shows the correct remote `user` mapping name and associated `password`.

There's more...

As we said in the introduction, every user must have a mapping if they are to access the remote data. This is rather onerous to do manually, so we can use PostgreSQL anonymous blocks to make things easier. The following SQL statement, for instance, will map all local users under the assumption that the remote system has the same users:

```
DO $$
DECLARE
  user_name VARCHAR;
BEGIN
  FOR user_name IN
      SELECT usename FROM pg_user
  LOOP
    EXECUTE
      'CREATE USER MAPPING FOR ' || user_name || '
      SERVER primary_db
      OPTIONS (user ' || quote_literal(user_name) || ')';
  END LOOP;
END;
$$ LANGUAGE plpgsql;
```

Feel free to modify the `SELECT` phrase that we used to only target certain groups of users. This isn't the only way PostgreSQL anonymous blocks make maintenance easier. Learn more about them at `https://www.postgresql.org/docs/current/sql-do.html`.

Keep in mind that you will need to either use a non-password authentication system in `pg_hba.conf` on the remote server or simply use `trust` authentication. By not specifying passwords, PostgreSQL will refuse to check any local password source, making authentication impossible otherwise.

See also

The CREATE USER MAPPING statement has good documentation in the PostgreSQL manual, as does the pg_user_mapping view. Please refer to the following URLs for more information:

- **CREATE USER MAPPING**:
  https://www.postgresql.org/docs/current/sql-createusermapping.html

- **pg_user_mapping**:
  https://www.postgresql.org/docs/current/catalog-pg-user-mapping.html

Creating a foreign table

The last step in initializing foreign data access is the creation of the foreign table itself. While doing so, we are limited to specifying column names, types, default values, and whether or not each column is nullable. This table skeleton helps the PostgreSQL query planner interact with the remote data as efficiently as possible.

In this recipe, we will create a foreign table and make it ready for use by our mapped user.

Getting ready

As we will be using a foreign server and a user mapping in this recipe, please follow all the previous recipes before proceeding.

How to do it...

For this recipe, we will perform all actions on the pg-report PostgreSQL server in the pgbench database. Follow these steps as the postgres user to create a table in pg-report that refers to a table on pg-primary within pgbench:

1. Create a user mapping for the postgres user with the following SQL statement:

```
CREATE USER MAPPING FOR postgres
    SERVER primary_db
    OPTIONS (user 'postgres', password 'changeme');
```

2. Drop any existing `pgbench_accounts` table with the following SQL statement:

   ```
   DROP TABLE IF EXISTS pgbench_accounts;
   ```

3. Execute the following SQL statement to create the foreign table:

   ```
   CREATE FOREIGN TABLE pgbench_accounts
   (
       aid         INTEGER NOT NULL,
       bid         INTEGER,
       abalance    INTEGER,
       filler      CHAR(84)
   )
   SERVER primary_db
   OPTIONS (table_name 'pgbench_accounts');
   ```

4. Analyze `pgbench_accounts` to create local statistics:

   ```
   ANALYZE pgbench_accounts;
   ```

5. Grant `bench_user` access to `pgbench_accounts` with the following SQL statement on both `pg-primary` and `pg-report`:

   ```
   GRANT ALL ON pgbench_accounts TO bench_user;
   ```

6. Describe the contents of the `pgbench_accounts` table with `psql`:

   ```
   psql pgbench -c '\d pgbench_accounts'
   ```

How it works...

In the first step, we create a user mapping for the `postgres` user. This is primarily a security step; remote tables should be as locked down as possible under the assumption that their contents are untrusted or otherwise sensitive. This allows us to create the foreign table as the `postgres` database superuser, preventing any unauthorized use of the remote server.

Next, we drop the local copy of the `pgbench_accounts` table on the `pg-report` server. This is both the largest table created by `pgbench` and the table we identified as a potential candidate for remote access of some kind. We drop it because we are going to replace it with a foreign table that refers to the same table on `pg-primary`.

To create the foreign table itself, we can look at the table definition of pgbench_accounts and ignore things such as primary keys, indexes, and other types of constraint. By issuing a CREATE FOREIGN TABLE statement instead of CREATE TABLE, PostgreSQL looks for some additional table-specification settings. As with user mappings, we set the SERVER to primary_db. For OPTIONS, we simply need to name the remote table that this foreign table represents: pgbench_accounts.

The next step is not strictly necessary, but one that we strongly recommend taking. PostgreSQL knows very little about the contents of the remote database or the table we've just created. The PostgreSQL query planner makes much better decisions when it is fully informed of the table contents. By running ANALYZE on pgbench_accounts, PostgreSQL fetches enough data to perform statistical analysis and stores that information in pg_stats for query-planning purposes.

Then the bench_user user mapping we created needs specific access to be granted before it can use the new table. If we simply granted access locally, then the remote bench_user would still not be able to use the table, so we would receive an error by doing so. Any grants for foreign tables must be equivalent on both of the servers involved.

Finally, we use psql to examine the foreign table structure. The following is what PostgreSQL sees when a foreign table is used in a query. Our test server provided the following output:

```
pgbench=# \d pgbench_accounts
                 Foreign table "public.pgbench_accounts"
  Column   |     Type      | Collation | Nullable | Default | FDW options
-----------+---------------+-----------+----------+---------+-------------
 aid       | integer       |           | not null |         |
 bid       | integer       |           |          |         |
 abalance  | integer       |           |          |         |
 filler    | character(84) |           |          |         |
Server: primary_db
FDW options: (table_name 'pgbench_accounts')
```

PostgreSQL makes it fairly clear that this is a Foreign table. The FDW options column lists any column options that we might have attached, though it's empty in this case. We can see that this table resides on the primary_db server and that it corresponds to the pgbench_accounts table on that system. All of this allows us to see that this isn't a regular table; it also allows us to see where its data is actually stored.

There's more...

While creating foreign tables is a good start, there are a couple more tricks remaining for this PostgreSQL feature.

Creating all tables for a foreign schema

This recipe provides an example of the creation of a single foreign table, though in an actual production system, this process could be quite cumbersome. Do we really want to create dozens or even hundreds of tables one by one? In PostgreSQL 9.5 and later, we can actually import the entire foreign schema.

The test data we're using is the default set of tables created by the pgbench tool. This means that all of the tables exist in the public schema. With this knowledge, we could substitute this command for the CREATE FOREIGN TABLE step in our recipe:

```
IMPORT FOREIGN SCHEMA public
  FROM SERVER primary_db
  INTO public;
```

Of course, importing the public schema is not a recommended practice. Yet it's clear that we can utilize this syntax to greatly simplify mirroring remote schemas from other PostgreSQL systems. Also note that we can import from one schema but place the new foreign tables somewhere else entirely. While it's good practice to maintain consistent schema names across a cluster, there are scenarios where we can benefit from renaming them.

Consider a series of PostgreSQL servers that each hosts one or more shards. We could link the servers together using foreign tables and name remote schemas based on the shards they reference. In essence, we would have access to all of our data from any node. How's that for high availability?

Dropping foreign tables

PostgreSQL enforces foreign table statements everywhere. For instance, let's try to drop this table using a regular DROP TABLE statement:

```
DROP TABLE pgbench_accounts;
```

The server would quickly respond with the following output:

```
pgbench=# DROP TABLE pgbench_accounts;
ERROR:  "pgbench_accounts" is not a table
HINT:   Use DROP FOREIGN TABLE to remove a foreign table.
```

Similarly, if we checked the `relkind` column in the `pg_class` catalog table, its type would be listed as `f` for foreign table instead of `r` for relation. PostgreSQL saves several hints and other breadcrumbs so that there is never any question as to the nature of foreign tables. Doing so prevents bugs and can even produce better performance, as remote access is taken into consideration before it selects the most efficient query plan. The more you use foreign tables, the more of these reminders you'll encounter.

See also

Refer to the following links for more details:

- **CREATE FOREIGN TABLE**:
  https://www.postgresql.org/docs/current/sql-createforeigntable.html
- **IMPORT FOREIGN SCHEMA**:
  https://www.postgresql.org/docs/current/sql-importforeignschema.html

Using a foreign table in a query

Foreign tables exist as empty shells on the local database, lending merely their structure for query-planning and data-fetching purposes. The foreign-data wrapper transforms data requests into something the remote server can understand and presents it in a way that PostgreSQL will recognize.

As we're using the `postgres_fdw` wrapper, the situation is simplified. A PostgreSQL server should have less trouble communicating with another PostgreSQL server than an Oracle server, for instance. Though this means less transformation, there are still limitations to what functionality a foreign table might provide compared to a local table.

In this recipe, we'll use a foreign table in a few scenarios and examine how it performs in each. We'll also explore some of the common caveats involved in foreign table access.

Getting ready

As we will be using the `pgbench_accounts` foreign table in this recipe, please complete all of the previous recipes before proceeding.

How to do it...

All queries in this recipe should be performed by the `bench_user` mapped user in the `pgbench` database on the `pg-report` PostgreSQL server. Follow these steps:

1. Execute the following simple query to view a remote query plan:

```
EXPLAIN VERBOSE
SELECT aid, bid, abalance
  FROM pgbench_accounts
 WHERE aid BETWEEN 500000 AND 500004;
```

2. Execute the following SQL statement to examine how PostgreSQL handles remote aggregates:

```
EXPLAIN VERBOSE
SELECT sum(abalance)
  FROM pgbench_accounts
 WHERE aid BETWEEN 500000 AND 500004;
```

3. Execute the following SQL statement to see a query plan involving a `JOIN`:

```
EXPLAIN VERBOSE
SELECT a2.aid, a2.bid, a2.abalance
  FROM pgbench_accounts a1
  JOIN pgbench_accounts a2 USING (aid)
 WHERE a1.aid BETWEEN 500000 AND 500004;
```

How it works...

The first query is very simple. We only fetch the five inclusive records from 500000 to 500004. We chose these values because they are so far into the table that scanning to find them would be very slow. This encourages the remote system to use the index on the `aid` column, and we can easily tell if it does not.

As we used `EXPLAIN VERBOSE`, PostgreSQL reports the query that it would have performed on the remote server as well. This is how the full explanation looks on our test server:

```
Foreign Scan on public.pgbench_accounts
        (cost=100.00..628351.08 rows=4 width=12)
  Output: aid, bid, abalance
  Remote SQL: SELECT aid, bid, abalance
                FROM public.pgbench_accounts
                WHERE ((aid >= 500000)) AND ((aid <= 500004))
```

PostgreSQL tries to send `WHERE` clauses to the remote server whenever possible. We can see from the `Remote SQL` lines that, aside from some inconsequential transformations, it sent the entire query to the remote server unaltered.

In the next query, we made a very minor change that should have caused the remote server to aggregate the `abalance` column as a `sum` and send it back to us. This will work with all PostgreSQL foreign data wrappers, but only versions 10 and later will properly forward aggregates for much-improved performance. Again, let's see the actual output on our test system:

```
Foreign Scan  (cost=100.01..628351.04 rows=1 width=8)
  Output: (sum(abalance))
  Relations: Aggregate on (public.pgbench_accounts)
  Remote SQL: SELECT sum(abalance)
                FROM public.pgbench_accounts
                WHERE ((aid >= 500000)) AND ((aid <= 500004))
```

The `Remote SQL` that PostgreSQL sent to the remote server includes the `sum` aggregate. Versions of PostgreSQL older than 10 were not capable of doing this, meaning they would need to fetch all records to the local system and aggregate them there. This is probably OK for such a small amount of data, but consider the overhead that would be involved if we requested a sum of one million rows. This alone is a great reason to upgrade!

What happens when we try to join two foreign tables? We only have the `pgbench_accounts` table, so we joined it with itself. The query still only asks for five rows, and both of its inputs are on the remote server, so we might expect the remote server to perform the join.

This expectation would be wrong. To illustrate, here's the EXPLAIN output for the last query on our test server:

```
Hash Join  (cost=628069.16..1630938.21 rows=5 width=12)
  Output: a2.aid, a2.bid, a2.abalance
  Hash Cond: (a2.aid = a1.aid)
  ->  Foreign Scan on public.pgbench_accounts a2
              (cost=100.00..927969.00 rows=20000000 width=12)
        Output: a2.aid, a2.bid, a2.abalance, a2.filler
        Remote SQL: SELECT aid, bid, abalance
                        FROM public.pgbench_accounts
  ->  Hash  (cost=627969.10..627969.10 rows=5 width=4)
        Output: a1.aid
        ->  Foreign Scan on public.pgbench_accounts a1
                    (cost=100.00..627969.10 rows=5 width=4)
              Output: a1.aid
              Remote SQL: SELECT aid
                              FROM public.pgbench_accounts
                              WHERE ((aid >= 500000)) AND ((aid <= 500004))
```

Don't worry too much about most of this output; just direct your attention to both of the Remote SQL sections. First, note that there are two of these sections. This means that our single query was transformed into two remote queries. Next, note that one of the queries has no WHERE clause and is fetching all 200 million of the rows in pgbench_accounts.

The foreign-data wrapper is literal in its interpretation of our WHERE clause. We supplied one WHERE clause for the first instance of pgbench_accounts, and in normal circumstances, this would be enough. Unfortunately, search conditions are not transitive where foreign tables are concerned. One of the queries returns five rows as we expected, while the other must process 200 million rows to find the matching aid values for those five rows.

Foreign tables are very powerful, but they must be used judiciously. Failing to observe the previous lessons will result in the same scenarios, or worse.

There's more...

While there are a number of notable caveats regarding foreign table usage, the situation is not entirely catastrophic. Foreign data wrappers continue to change as the developers work on them, and we can take advantage of those upgrades as they appear.

Explaining strange planner decisions

There's actually a very simple reason PostgreSQL fails to meet our expectations in the last query example. The answer lies in the structure of foreign tables themselves. When we defined the pgbench_accounts table, we specified four column names. PostgreSQL expects to see one or more of those column names within the SELECT clause in every interaction with the foreign table.

In versions of PostgreSQL older than 10, the second query example changes the SELECT clause to read sum(abalance). While the abalance column is part of our foreign table definition, sum is not. A functional transformation of any kind renders the column mappings moot, and PostgreSQL must apply them *after* data is retrieved from the remote server. Newer versions of the foreign-data wrapper optimize this, but only for recognized aggregate functions.

The third query example performs badly for a different reason. If we ignore the problem with the non-transitive WHERE clause, there's still another issue. We could add another WHERE clause for the second instance of pgbench_accounts in that query, but as the EXPLAIN output shows, we would still be executing two queries on the remote server instead of one.

This is due to how PostgreSQL currently handles foreign data. If we imagine the postgres_fdw wrapper as a worker carrying a large box, every box requires a new worker. In this scenario, every foreign table is a box, and every box is separate. Each time PostgreSQL encounters a foreign table, it dispatches a worker with their box and waits for the results. As JOIN is a distinctly separate action, we get two workers and two boxes.

There are, of course, exceptions to this behavior. With the introduction of PostgreSQL 9.6, certain combined operations become possible. Subsequent versions have improved query pushdown behavior even further.

Improvements in PostgreSQL 9.6

Two things that changed in PostgreSQL 9.6 are both associated with deferring certain actions to the remote server. In PostgreSQL 9.6, JOIN and ORDER BY operations are actually transmitted to the remote system, though there are some restrictions:

- Joined foreign tables exist on the same SERVER. In our case, this would be primary_db.

- The remotely joined tables must be distinct. Our third query example was a self-join, which is unfortunately not supported by the pushdown logic.
- We don't want to sort and join at the same time.

Basically, this means that we could create `pgbench_branches` as a foreign table and joining it with `pgbench_accounts` would be done by the remote system. We could also sort the results of a query from a single table, but not if we join them. In that case, PostgreSQL would sort the results from each table independently and again revert to performing the join locally.

In effect, PostgreSQL 9.6 could walk and chew gum, but not simultaneously. Still, this is a vast improvement over older versions that could accomplish neither task.

Improvements in PostgreSQL 10

PostgreSQL 10 improves things even further by adding the aforementioned ability to send aggregate functions to the remote server. This applies both to built-in aggregates and even user-supplied versions; however, the aggregate must exist on both servers to function properly.

Improvements in PostgreSQL 11

PostgreSQL 11 also improves foreign data wrappers by adding the ability to push aggregates down, even in the case of partitioned tables. The new declarative partitions in PostgreSQL 10 were missing several features, and one of them was proper handling by some elements of the foreign-data wrapper logic. That is no longer the case.

Optimizing foreign table access

If you read the end of the previous recipe, you might assume that we don't recommend that you use foreign tables at all. However, we would like to reassure you that foreign tables are not all doom and gloom. To prove it, we're going to use a disarmingly simple technique to optimize them: views.

It's true that PostgreSQL foreign-data wrappers cannot always combine queries for multiple tables on the same server. Provided we have access to the remote server, we can rectify this situation by creating a view to encapsulate the core of the query we want to perform. We can do this because PostgreSQL only knows the name of remote objects, not their composition. We can take advantage of this and use views to force remote joins.

In this recipe, we will describe how to use a remote view in place of a foreign table.

Getting ready

As we will be using the pgbench_accounts foreign table in this recipe, please complete all the previous recipes before proceeding.

How to do it...

For this recipe, we will continue to use the pg-primary and pg-report database servers. All queries should be performed by the postgres user in the pgbench database. Follow these steps to enforce better remote JOIN performance:

1. Create a view for the basis of the join on pg-primary:

```
CREATE OR REPLACE VIEW v_pgbench_accounts_self_join AS
SELECT a1.aid, a2.bid, a2.abalance
  FROM pgbench_accounts a1
  JOIN pgbench_accounts a2 USING (aid)
 ORDER BY a1.aid DESC;
```

2. Grant access to bench_user on the new view on pg-primary:

```
GRANT SELECT ON v_pgbench_accounts_self_join
    TO bench_user;
```

3. Create a foreign table that references the view on pg-report:

```
CREATE FOREIGN TABLE pgbench_accounts_self
(
    aid        INTEGER NOT NULL,
    bid        INTEGER,
    abalance  INTEGER
)
SERVER primary_db
OPTIONS (table_name 'v_pgbench_accounts_self_join');
```

4. Grant access to `bench_user` on the foreign table on `pg-report`:

    ```
    GRANT SELECT ON pgbench_accounts_self
        TO bench_user;
    ```

5. Examine the new query plan on `pg-report` with the following SQL statement:

    ```
    EXPLAIN VERBOSE
    SELECT aid, bid, abalance
      FROM pgbench_accounts_self
     WHERE aid BETWEEN 500000 AND 500004;
    ```

How it works...

For the first step, we create a view named `v_pgbench_accounts_self_join` on `pg-primary` that uses the same columns and the same self-join we attempted in the previous recipe. Then, we grant access to `bench_user` so that the view is usable on the `pg-report` server.

Next, we create a foreign table just as we did in the *Creating a foreign table* recipe, but this time, we name the local foreign table `pgbench_accounts_self` even though the view has a very different name. This should illustrate that names do not have to necessarily match and that PostgreSQL doesn't care whether the remote object is a table or a view. Once again, we grant access to the foreign table to the mapped `bench_user` user and our work is complete.

Before we finish this exercise, let's look at a verbose EXPLAIN that uses the foreign table. Here's the output from our test system:

```
Foreign Scan on public.pgbench_accounts_self
        (cost=100.00..144.35 rows=11 width=12)
  Output: aid, bid, abalance
  Remote SQL: SELECT aid, bid, abalance
              FROM public.v_pgbench_accounts_self_join
              WHERE ((aid >= 500000)) AND ((aid <= 500004))
```

This is much better! Now, we can see that the WHERE clause is being sent to restrict output from the `v_pgbench_accounts_self_join` view. As this view is evaluated on the `pg-primary` server, the join happens there as well. We have successfully combined two foreign tables into one. For users of PostgreSQL 9.6, which already provides this functionality, our view includes an ORDER BY clause that is also applied. We've successfully given PostgreSQL the ability to walk and chew bubblegum at the same time.

There's more...

As powerful as this technique might be, its utility is limited by the fact that we're using views to circumvent normal table access methods. This means that our foreign table now has the same limitations as views. Unless the view is very simple—which would defeat the purpose of using a view like this—we cannot perform any of the following actions:

- We cannot insert into a foreign table view
- We cannot update records in a foreign table view
- We cannot delete from a foreign table view

However, there is one thing that we can do with a foreign table view that we can't do with a local view. As foreign tables can be analyzed to gather statistics, we can analyze foreign table views as well. This produces local statistics that may include correlations that PostgreSQL would normally not find.

In the current state of the PostgreSQL foreign data architecture, this might not mean much. Yet as techniques and the underlying code improve, what is now merely an interesting fluke might become an advanced optimization approach. Only time will tell.

Transforming foreign tables into local tables

Remote tables provide an easy and convenient way to access remote data in a PostgreSQL database. This is good for highly available systems, as a properly compartmentalized system invites segmented maintenance. Yet, remote data comes with a rather drastic cost regarding data fetching and handling overhead.

PostgreSQL 9.3 introduced the internal support of **materialized views**. Traditionally, materialized views merely instantiate a view into a physical structure to avoid expensive or complicated query plans and result sets. They also make it possible to index or optimize a view in ways that are not normally possible. Now, imagine what we can do with such a structure when utilizing foreign tables.

In this recipe, we will explore how materialized views can drastically increase the local data-access capability within a PostgreSQL database.

Getting ready

As we will be using the pgbench_accounts foreign table in this recipe, please complete all recipes up to *Creating a foreign table* before proceeding.

How to do it...

For this recipe, we will focus on the pg-report database server. All queries should be performed by the postgres user in the pgbench database. Follow these steps to create and use a materialized view:

1. Rename the pgbench_accounts foreign table with the following SQL statement:

```
ALTER FOREIGN TABLE pgbench_accounts
      RENAME TO remote_accounts;
```

2. Use the following SQL statement to create a materialized view:

```
CREATE MATERIALIZED VIEW pgbench_accounts AS
SELECT *
  FROM remote_accounts
 WHERE bid = 5
  WITH DATA;
```

3. Add an index to pgbench_accounts to make it usable:

```
CREATE INDEX idx_pgbench_accounts_aid
       ON pgbench_accounts (aid);
```

4. Execute the following SQL statement to produce a simple query plan:

```
EXPLAIN ANALYZE
 SELECT *
   FROM pgbench_accounts
  WHERE aid BETWEEN 400001 AND 400050;
```

How it works...

In this recipe, we begin by moving the existing `pgbench_accounts` table out of the way. The intent, in this case, is to prove that we can treat a materialized view in a similar way to a local table. To do this, we want to create it with the same name that the foreign table currently uses. This means that `pgbench_accounts` becomes `remote_accounts` and better illustrates its relationship with the foreign server as a bonus.

Next, we create the actual materialized view. We could define all of the columns manually, but in this case, we want it to simply mirror the remote table. Think of this as object-oriented programming: we have a class named `pgbench_remote`, and we will instantiate it as `pgbench_accounts`.

Note, however, that we added a `WHERE` clause to restrict the results to rows where `bid` is 5. For our particular set of test data, this represents only 100,000 rows of the total 20 million. We did this to illustrate that we could have a central repository of data and maintain only a small subset on each local server for better scalability purposes. By finishing the statement with `WITH DATA`, PostgreSQL executes the query and stores the result in our new materialized view. If we had omitted this, the view would be empty and unusable.

At this point, we created an index on the `aid` column. This reflects the primary key that exists on the remote table, and it means that any local queries that expect it will perform normally. To prove this, our final step is to perform a basic query that retrieves 50 rows from the table and examines the path that PostgreSQL used to execute our request.

Our test system produced the following output:

```
Index Scan using idx_pgbench_accounts_aid on pgbench_accounts
      (cost=0.29..9.76 rows=50 width=97)
      (actual time=0.024..0.045 rows=50 loops=1)
   Index Cond: ((aid >= 400001) AND (aid <= 400050))
Planning Time: 0.276 ms
Execution Time: 0.087 ms
```

We can note a few important things from this `EXPLAIN` output. First, our results are being supplied by the `idx_pgbench_accounts_aid` index we created. The query runtime is reported as `0.276 ms`, which is roughly one-fortieth of a millisecond. This is the performance we would expect from an indexed retrieval with such a small amount of rows.

There's more...

There are a few unfortunate aspects of materialized views that we must consider:

- The contents are completely static
- They cannot be the target of `INSERT`, `UPDATE`, or `DELETE` statements
- Refreshing their contents may be slow

By static, we mean that the rows stored in the materialized view are the result of the `SELECT` statement that we used to define it. It would be a great way to bootstrap a reporting table of some kind, but then we encounter the next item in our list: no modifications. A natural consequence of this is that we can't build manual maintenance procedures designed to *top off* the contents. This means that we must refresh the contents of the materialized view all at once with the following statement:

```
REFRESH MATERIALIZED VIEW pgbench_accounts;
```

If the query that builds the output is slow and we have several materialized views like it, then maintenance times could increase dramatically. Some contributed materialized view architectures do not have this limitation, and it's entirely possible that future versions of PostgreSQL will also improve this aspect. For now, though, we'll want to limit our materialized view definitions to queries that are very well optimized.

Refreshing a materialized view requires an exclusive lock because its entire contents are replaced during the refresh. Be wary of queries or batch jobs that depend on these views, as they may be temporarily blocked until the refresh is complete. PostgreSQL versions 9.4 and beyond can prevent this blocking by using the following syntax:

```
REFRESH MATERIALIZED VIEW CONCURRENTLY
pgbench_accounts;
```

See also

The PostgreSQL documentation does a pretty good job of explaining materialized views. Please refer to the following resources to learn more:

- **CREATE MATERIALIZED VIEW**:
  https://www.postgresql.org/docs/current/sql-creatematerializedvie w.html
- **REFRESH MATERIALIZED VIEW**:
  https://www.postgresql.org/docs/current/sql-refreshmaterializedvi ew.html

You can also build your own materialized view library. Before PostgreSQL 9.3 incorporated the feature, users commonly applied the techniques described at https://tech.jonathangardner.net/wiki/PostgreSQL/Materialized_Views.

Creating a scalable nextval replacement

Now that we have all of the tools to communicate between disparate servers, we can start building a very rudimentary API to generate ID values that are distinct across a pool of database servers. By doing so, database-level function calls are available to the application and encourage data distribution, otherwise known as application-level sharding. This, in turn, increases our scalability and availability, as it will take far more than a single database outage to truly derail the application.

A company that did this early in the development cycle of its platform is **Instagram**. In fact, they're very open about the process they used, as described in their blog post at https://instagram-engineering.com/sharding-ids-at-instagram-1cf5a71e5a5c.

The idea they implemented may seem complicated but is actually deceptively simple. Here's a basic breakdown of what they were trying to create:

- The system should accommodate several thousand logical shards
- Generated SERIAL IDs should be unique across all logical shards
- The ID generator should remain viable for several decades at minimum
- The ID generator must handle extremely high insert traffic

For us to accomplish these goals in the same manner as Instagram, we can utilize a standard 64-bit BIGINT column type separated into three sections:

- Bits 1–42 represent the number of milliseconds since an arbitrary epoch. This is viable for roughly 140 years.
- Bits 43–53 represent the logical shard number for up to 2,048 shards.
- Bits 54–64 are used for the actual generated ID for up to 2,048 ID values.

This may not seem like much, but this means that we can generate 2,048 IDs per 2,048 shards per millisecond for almost 140 years. Taken to its extreme, this is over 4 billion IDs per second. It's possible that there are systems that have higher insert volumes than this, but we can't think of any.

In this recipe, we'll build such a function using PostgreSQL's plpgsql language and explain how each part works.

Getting ready

We will actually be starting from scratch in this recipe and will no longer use the pgbench tables. Instead, we want to start with new shell tables designed specifically for sharding. Execute the following SQL statements as the postgres user on an empty database to get ready:

```
CREATE SCHEMA myapp;
CREATE TABLE myapp.msg_log (
  id       SERIAL  PRIMARY KEY,
  message  TEXT    NOT NULL
);
```

We will be using this schema and table for the rest of this chapter.

How to do it...

Execute the following SQL statements as the `postgres` user to create a function that can generate IDs as we described:

1. Create the schema to hold shard-related functionality:

   ```
   CREATE SCHEMA shard;
   ```

2. Create a sequence to act as an ID generator:

   ```
   CREATE SEQUENCE shard.table_id_seq;
   ```

3. Create a function that will generate IDs:

   ```
   CREATE OR REPLACE FUNCTION shard.next_unique_id(
     shard_id INT
   )
   RETURNS BIGINT AS
   $BODY$
   DECLARE
     epoch    DATE := '2020-01-01';
     epoch_ms BIGINT;
     now_ms   BIGINT;
     next_id  BIGINT;
   BEGIN
     epoch_ms := floor(
       extract(EPOCH FROM epoch) * 1000
     );
     now_ms := floor(
       extract(EPOCH FROM clock_timestamp()) * 1000
     );
     next_id := (now_ms - epoch_ms) << 22
         | (shard_id << 11)
         | (nextval('shard.table_id_seq') % 2048);
     RETURN next_id;
   END;
   $BODY$ LANGUAGE plpgsql;
   ```

4. Execute the following query to generate an ID and view its contents:

   ```
   SELECT (newval & 2047) AS id_value,
          (newval >> 11) & 2047 AS shard_id,
          (newval >> 22) / 1000 / 3600 / 24 AS days
     FROM (SELECT shard.next_unique_id(15)
             AS newval) nv;
   ```

How it works...

Our first two steps aren't all that interesting; we merely create the shard schema and a sequence named table_id_seq for the IDs needed for value increments. Our design saves on implementation complexity by using the same sequence for every table within a shard, but this is not a requirement.

The bulk of the work is defined in the next_unique_id function we create. We start the function with the epoch variable, set to the beginning of 2020. This is an arbitrary starting date and could have been any date in the past. The important thing to remember is that this value is used as a baseline for how long the IDs will remain unique.

Next, we have the following section of code:

```
epoch_ms = floor(
    extract(EPOCH FROM epoch) * 1000
);
```

The extract PostgreSQL function will obtain the date in any format we want. By passing EPOCH, we get the date as the number of seconds since January 1, 1970, with a decimal representing the number of milliseconds as well. If we multiply this by 1000, then we're left with the number of milliseconds since the beginning of 1970 to our chosen epoch of 2020-01-01.

We repeat this process for now_ms, but this time, we use the clock_timestamp function instead of a static date. The clock_timestamp function always returns a timestamp obtained from the execution time of the function call. This is important because functions such as now will return the start time of the surrounding transaction. If we used now, then we could theoretically experience ID collisions after using more than 2,048 IDs.

In this block of code, we calculate the ID we return as a fully unique value:

```
next_id = (now_ms - epoch_ms) << 22
    | (shard_id << 11)
    | (nextval('shard.table_id_seq') % 2048);
```

Remember what we said about using the full size of a 64-bit integer. We begin with the time that has elapsed since our epoch and shift that value to the left by 22 bits. This left shift makes room for the shard ID and the generated ID, both of which should be between 0 and 2047.

Finally, we append an ID obtained from the sequence that we created at the beginning and modulo by 2,048 to ensure that we don't overflow the 11 bits we're using for this portion. In the end, we are left with an encoded ID with all of the attributes that we discussed at the beginning of this recipe.

If we call our new function once or twice, we should see it generate ID values; however, to prove it's doing what we claim, we need to reverse the encoding process to see what the ID actually contains. On our test system, one call of `next_unique_id` produces the following output:

```
myapp=# SELECT (newval & 2047) AS id_value,
          (newval >> 11) & 2047 AS shard_id,
          (newval >> 22) / 1000 / 3600 / 24 AS days
  FROM (SELECT shard.next_unique_id(15)

          AS newval) nv;
 id_value | shard_id | days
----------+----------+------
        9 |       15 |   11
```

We called the function and passed it `15` as the shard number to use, and after decoding the ID, we can see that it's unchanged. If we called this function several times in a row, we would see the `id_value` increment as well. We discarded a lot of information in our rush to decode the number of days since our `epoch` date, so we only see that `11` days have elapsed. In reality, that portion of the ID represents days, hours, minutes, seconds, and milliseconds since the beginning of 2020.

> If this looks similar to the timeshard global sequence type used by BDR as described in `Chapter 13`, *High Availability with Multi-Master*, then that's no coincidence. This is really an excellent way to guarantee no sequence collisions in clusters containing multiple writable nodes.

There's more...

If we wanted to use our new ID generator in a table, then we could do it very simply. Assuming that we already have our `myapp.msg_log` table, we could create a new table based on it with the following SQL statement:

```
CREATE SCHEMA myapp1;
CREATE TABLE myapp1.msg_log (
    LIKE myapp.msg_log INCLUDING INDEXES
);

ALTER TABLE myapp1.msg_log
```

```
ALTER id TYPE BIGINT,
ALTER id SET DEFAULT shard.next_unique_id(1);
```

This structure would correspond with shard number 1. All we need to do is modify the id column so that it can store our 64-bit integer and then set the default value to invoke our next_unique_id function. By doing so, we can create up to 2,048 schemas holding tables like this, and every generated ID will be unique across all of them.

Building a sharding API

When building a horizontally scalable system, we need a database library that facilitates its use. Without this, ad hoc tables can derail the whole process by producing a heterogeneous environment incompatible with a horizontal architecture. We need consistency if we also want reliability.

In the previous recipe, we discussed the necessary components of a function that can generate unique IDs across thousands of logical shards. This will form the core of our API, as it ensures that ID collisions are avoided within our application; however, what about the rest? How do we manage each shard? How do we add tables to the application? How can we automate as much management as possible to encourage adhering to the API?

This recipe will attempt to answer these questions and many more by having you create the necessary functions to manage a shard-driven system.

Getting ready

This recipe depends on the work we performed in the *Creating a scalable nextval replacement* recipe. Please review that part of this chapter before continuing.

How to do it...

Follow these steps to build a complete database-sharding API:

1. Learn one of the PostgreSQL procedural languages.
2. Create a table to track shard-configuration settings.
3. Write one or more functions to manage shard-configuration settings.
4. Create a table to track shard tables and source schemas.

5. Write a `next_unique_id` equivalent function.
6. Write one or more functions to control which tables are managed.
7. Write one or more functions to build or alter each shard's structure based on the tables it contains.
8. Create a table to track logical-to-physical shard mappings.
9. Write one or more functions to manage logical-to-physical shard mappings.
10. Define a role to grant sufficient permissions to users tasked with using all of the preceding functions.

How it works...

Before we discuss these steps, we readily admit that there is a lot of work involved here, and most of it is beyond the scope of this book. However, this is the minimum list of components necessary for a functional shard API. Fortunately, we only have to build this once!

The first step is to learn one of the procedural languages that PostgreSQL provides for database interaction. The core PostgreSQL server comes with PL/pgSQL, PL/Tcl, PL/Perl, and PL/Python as possible choices, though there are many more, such as Java, Ruby, or even PHP. Each of these has different performance characteristics and varying levels of difficulty, so choose whichever you are most comfortable with or whichever produces the best results. We used the pgSQL language for our `next_unique_id` function, but this doesn't mean you must follow our lead.

Next, we need a table and associated functions to manage shard-configuration settings; perhaps this means a table named `shard_config` and two functions named `get_shard_config` and `set_shard_config`. We use functions so that we can protect the boundaries of our 64-bit integer or to prevent changes to settings that would adversely affect the cluster of shards. Like any API, we should never trust user input.

After this, we need a table and associated functions to manage the architecture of our shards. For instance, the table of API-managed tables might be called `shard_table`. Then, we might create `register_base_table` to add tables to shard management and `unregister_base_table` to remove them.

Then we might add `create_next_shard` to increment the active shard counter and create an empty schema based on this new value. We might also want `create_id_function` to generate an optimized shard-specific ID generation function whenever a new shard is added. We'll probably need `init_shard_tables` to create table copies of all the base tables we've registered, which will also modify each copy to use our unique ID function.

Beyond managing the actual structure of the shards, we also need to control who can invoke all of these special functions, especially since there are so many of them. So it would be a good idea to create `shard_admin` role that we can grant to users or applications that need to invoke the API routines. Perhaps we may even want more granularity than this, and have a separate role for viewing shard metadata as well, among others.

Do we need more? Possibly. This core of functions provides the minimal structure necessary to create and maintain a working sharded database, but few systems exist with only minimal implementations.

There's more...

Due to the inherent complexity, there are a lot of sharding resources available that are beyond the scope of this book. Let's discuss some of them.

shard_manager extension

As we said earlier, building a fully functional API is beyond the scope of this book. However, we have written a reference implementation named Shard Manager, available on the **PostgreSQL Extension Network (PGXN)** at `https://pgxn.org/dist/shard_manager/`.

Shard Manager creates all of the configuration tables and functions that we discussed in this recipe, along with a couple of extras. Furthermore, it operates as a PostgreSQL extension—for example, to create a schema named `shard` to store the API and configuration tables, we would use the following SQL statements:

```
CREATE SCHEMA shard;
CREATE EXTENSION shard_manager WITH SCHEMA shard;
```

Documentation is currently somewhat sparse, but there is enough to install and use the provided functions, as well as some basic usage examples. Feel free to contribute to this documentation if you come up with fixes or enhancements!

Citus

While the `shard_manager` extension is more of a functional demonstration prototype, Citus is a fully functional data distribution extension. Though it does limit some PostgreSQL features by necessity, it transparently shards and distributes data among configured nodes. It is available from Citus Data at `https://www.citusdata.com/product/community`.

Each table can be configured to store data on multiple nodes as well for some overlap in case a node is lost. The proprietary enterprise version even has a feature for rebalancing shards in case new nodes are added or removed. It's a well-known solution for scenarios where it's neither appropriate to produce a homegrown shard management suite or otherwise too complicated.

Postgres-XL

While building a sharding API can be educational in some ways, if we're willing to embrace a bit of vendor lock-in, there's an alternative. Postgres-XL is a fork of core PostgreSQL that incorporates a lot of sharding concepts by distributing data to separately allocated data nodes. It is currently maintained primarily by 2ndQuadrant, and is available at `https://www.postgres-xl.org/`.

As with CitusDB, some features are restricted, but they are fewer in number. Generally, each node acts with nearly the full feature set of a standard PostgreSQL 10 installation. The main drawback to using this platform is that it requires a lot of manual setup: data nodes, coordinator nodes, and GTM nodes, along with GTM proxies, must all be installed and configured properly.

BDR AutoScale

Since we used BDR rather extensively in `Chapter 13`, *High Availability with Multi-Master Replication*, we figured we'd share this here as well. The BDR development roadmap currently includes a feature named AutoScale. The idea, in this case, is to leverage the multinode nature of a BDR cluster and also integrate sharding concepts, as we discussed in this chapter.

Early planning suggests that AutoScale will leverage the automated management of PostgreSQL 10-style declarative partitions by including multinode node affinity. This means that writing data to one multi-master node can distribute that information among a subset of the existing cluster within partition tables for better scaling and maintenance purposes.

See also

As we suggested that you learn one of the PostgreSQL procedural languages, here is a list of links to several popular choices:

- **PL/pgSQL**: https://www.postgresql.org/docs/current/plpgsql.html
- **PL/Perl**: https://www.postgresql.org/docs/current/plperl.html
- **PL/Python**: https://www.postgresql.org/docs/current/plpython.html
- **PL/Java**: https://tada.github.io/pljava/
- **PL/PHP**: https://public.commandprompt.com/projects/plphp
- **PL/R**: https://joeconway.com/plr
- **PL/V8**: https://github.com/plv8/plv8

Talking to the correct shard

In this section, we have chosen to represent database shards as PostgreSQL schema names. If our basic schema is named myapp, shard 1 would be myapp1, shard 15 would be myapp15, and so on. This is what we call the **logical shard** name.

Beyond this, shards should be independent of each other so that they can be relocated to another PostgreSQL server arbitrarily; however, if shards can be moved at will, how do we find them? In much the same way that LVM has a physical drive, logical shards have a corresponding **physical shard**. The physical shard is the server where the logical shard currently resides, as shown in the following diagram:

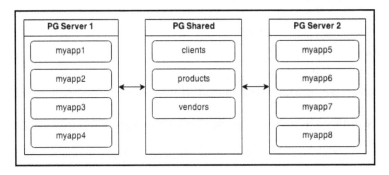

Elements such as **clients**, **products**, and **vendors** are shared resources that all PostgreSQL shard servers can use. This is where our foreign tables would be beneficial. The logical shards (schemas) **myapp1** through **myapp4** all reside on **PG Server 1**, and **myapp5** through to **myapp8** all live on **PG Server 2**. In this architecture, we have eight logical shards distributed to two physical servers.

In this recipe, we will explore various techniques to preserve and decode the logical-to-physical mapping necessary to interact with the correct data.

Getting ready

This recipe depends on the work we performed in the *Creating a scalable nextval replacement* recipe. Please review that part of this chapter before continuing.

How to do it...

All SQL statements in this recipe should be executed by the postgres database user. Follow these steps to build a table to map logical shards to their physical locations:

1. Execute the following SQL statement to create the shard-mapping table:

```
CREATE TABLE shard.shard_map
(
  map_id          SERIAL    PRIMARY KEY,
  shard_id        INT       NOT NULL,
  source_schema   VARCHAR   NOT NULL,
  shard_schema    VARCHAR   NOT NULL,
  server_name     VARCHAR   NOT NULL,
  UNIQUE (shard_id, source_schema)
);
```

2. Create a shard and register it with the shard map using the following SQL:

```
CREATE SCHEMA myapp1;
INSERT INTO shard.shard_map
  (shard_id, source_schema, shard_schema, server_name)
VALUES (1, 'myapp', 'myapp1', 'pg-primary');
```

3. Repeat the previous step to create a second shard:

```
CREATE SCHEMA myapp2;
INSERT INTO shard.shard_map
  (shard_id, source_schema, shard_schema, server_name)
VALUES (2, 'myapp', 'myapp2', 'pg-primary');
```

4. View the current status of our shard mappings:

```
SELECT * FROM shard.shard_map;
```

How it works...

If you wish, you can view this as another primer on preparing a shard-management API. Our first step towards this goal is to create a table to store the logical-to-physical location mappings necessary to locate a specific shard. At minimum, this table needs to track the shard ID (shard_id), the skeleton schema the shard is based on (source_schema), the shard name itself (shard_schema), and the server where the shard resides (server_name).

Some may wonder where the shard_map table should reside. There's a reason we introduced the shared PostgreSQL server in the introduction to this recipe: metadata should be stored on that central server. A combination of foreign tables and materialized views will ensure that all servers have immediate access to its contents if necessary.

Alternatively, a multi-master cluster could ensure that the shared resource tables exist on all shard servers directly.

Next, we create and save the location of two new shards for illustrative purposes. For our shard names, we chose to simply append the shard name to the source schema name. In addition, we created both shards on the pg-primary server that we used in various chapters of this book. This kind of naming scheme makes it simple to locate and interact with any particular shard in our cluster.

The final step is to visualize the data that we stored regarding our logical-to-physical mapping. On our test server, the mappings are as follows:

```
 map_id | shard_id | source_schema | shard_schema | server_name
--------+----------+---------------+--------------+------------
      1 |        1 | myapp         | myapp1       | pg-primary
      2 |        2 | myapp         | myapp2       | pg-primary
```

Note that the `shard_map` table is designed in such a way that we can create mappings for any number of schemas. Any schema can have all 2,048 shards, and we can find the physical location for any of them based on this table.

There's more...

While the mapping is an important step, we still need two things to really make use of the mapping. Let's see what they are.

Keeping things fast by creating a cache

In modern applications, it is becoming increasingly common to inject a secondary cache layer between the application and database. This layer stores commonly retrieved data in memory for immediate use. This layer might be composed of memcached or a NoSQL database, such as CouchDB, MongoDB, or Redis.

Once such a layer exists, it's important that the `shard_map` table is one of the first tables copied there. It has very few rows (a maximum of 2,048 is tiny in the database world), and storing it in memory removes the relatively expensive round-trip to the database. With this mapping in memory, the application will always and immediately know which physical server contains the data it seeks for a specific shard.

Choosing an application data to map logical shard

How does an application know which shard it should use in any particular situation? This answer requires one more modification to the table structure that our application uses. Our last decision involves adding a `shard_id` column to one table. This table can be anything, but should represent some defining aspect that can centralize related data.

A good choice for this is a `customer` table. In an order system, all interaction is eventually driven by customer activity. If we assign a customer a specific shard ID, all of their order data will be stored in that shard. As the application likely has the customer row information available at all times, it should also know the associated shard, and therefore where the data physically resides.

As a consequence, customer data should also be stored in the shared PostgreSQL instance that other shard servers can see. Customer data is relatively sparse compared to high volumes of order, image, or other types of activity that a customer can generate. If the customer table is too large to cache directly, we could create a `customer_shard` table in the shared database instead.

Moving a shard to another server

The final important aspect of database sharding that we are going to explore in this chapter is reorganization. The purpose of allocating a large number of logical shards is to prepare for future expansion. If we started with 2,048 shards, all of which are currently mapped to a single server, we will eventually want to move some of them elsewhere.

The easiest way to do this is to leverage PostgreSQL replication. Essentially, we will create a streaming replica for the server that we want to split and drop the schemas that we don't need on each server. Consider a database with two shards. Our end goal is to produce something like the following:

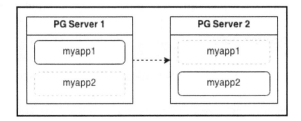

On each server, we simply drop the schema indicated by the dashed box. This way, we still have two shards, and only the location of **myapp2** has changed—its data remains unharmed.

This recipe will cover the process described here, making it easy to move shards to a new physical location.

Getting ready

This recipe depends on the work we performed in the *Creating a scalable nextval replacement* and *Talking to the right shard* recipes. Please go through these recipes before continuing.

How to do it...

In addition to our usual pg-primary PostgreSQL server, we will also be using pg-primary2 for this recipe. Database data will remain in the /db/pgdata directory. A server named pg-shared will play the role of our shared database as well. Follow these steps as the postgres system user and postgres database user where indicated:

1. Use pg_basebackup executed from the pg-primary2 server to clone the data from pg-primary:

   pg_basebackup -h pg-primary -D /db/pgdata

2. Create a file named recovery.conf in /db/pgdata on pg-primary2 with the following contents:

   ```
   standby_mode = 'on'
   primary_conninfo = 'host=pg-primary user=postgres'
   ```

3. Start PostgreSQL on pg-primary2:

   sudo systemctl start postgresql@12-main

4. When ready to split the shards, promote pg-primary2 to a writable state:

   pg_ctl -D /db/pgdata promote

5. Execute the following SQL statement on pg-shared to change the shard mapping:

   ```
   UPDATE shard.shard_map
      SET server_name = 'pg-primary2'
    WHERE shard_schema = 'myapp2';
   ```

6. Refresh any cached copies of the shard_map table.

7. Drop the `myapp2` schema on `pg-primary`:

```
DROP SCHEMA myapp2;
```

8. Drop the `myapp1` schema on `pg-primary2`:

```
DROP SCHEMA myapp1;
```

How it works...

We've already discussed the process of creating streaming replicas several times throughout this book, so we've elected to use a shortened version here. Our primary goal here is to create a full database clone of `pg-primary` on `pg-primary2`. This clone should continue to receive data from `pg-primary` until we are ready to split up our application data. When database activity is low or we can temporarily disable write activity to the `myapp2` schema, we can promote `pg-primary2` so that it acts as a writable server.

Once `pg-primary2` is writable, we execute an `UPDATE` statement on the `shard_map` table in `pg-shared`. Then we either refresh or invalidate cached copies of that table so that they are rebuilt. From this point on, all new requests to interact with data stored in the `myapp2` shard will be directed to the `pg-primary2` server.

With the `myapp2` shard's physical location changed and the caches updated, it should be safe to drop the unneeded schemas on each PostgreSQL server. The `pg-primary` server is only in charge of the `myapp1` shard now, so we can drop `myapp2`. Similarly, the `pg-primary2` server is only handling the `myapp2`, so we can drop `myapp1`.

If our data was evenly distributed, each PostgreSQL server would now be half the size of what `pg-primary` originally was. Furthermore, database load, IOPS and TPS requirements, and other metrics would also be scaled down. By doubling our server count, we've cut our per-server hardware requirements in half, and have thereby increased our query response times and availability.

There's more...

Though our example used only two schema shards, this process scales well to any number of preallocated segments. It's surprisingly easy to relocate schemas using the method described here, and there's no reason that we must limit ourselves to splitting one server into only two. The only real limitation is that we can't effectively recombine servers once they've been split this way.

There is, however, one important caveat that we must explain. This type of database sharding works best when the application is designed to accommodate it. In fact, it's even better to create all of the logical shards upfront, before data is inserted into *any* shard. Why is this?

Consider an existing schema with existing data. Foreign keys, customers, and customer activity have been accumulating for years. Redistributing this data into all of the necessary tables of our shard schemas will be extremely difficult and will likely be an entirely manual migration process.

This same problem exists if we only start our application with a small number of shards instead of allocating the maximum from the beginning. If we only have 4 out of 2,048 active shards and they're already on 4 physical servers, we will need to create new shards and manually distribute the data once again.

However, we can also start with all 2,048 shards at the beginning. From the very start, customers are assigned to shards, and data is inserted into the proper shard. Even if all shards start on one server, we can expand using the method described in this recipe. If we want to immediately grow to four servers, we merely create three clones and evenly distribute the shards to each system.

It's important to advocate and impose this architecture early in systems that are likely to require high transactional volume; otherwise, the path to horizontal scalability and the availability associated with it will be a long and hard one.

15
Zero-downtime Upgrades

A major version upgrade is the ultimate test of high availability for a database cluster service such as PostgreSQL. This process has advanced drastically since the early days. Consider the procedure required for some older versions:

- 6.5 – 8.2: dump and restore all databases
- 8.3 – 8.4: pg_migrator
- 9.0: pg_upgrade

Beginning with PostgreSQL 9.4 and the addition of logical replication, it became possible to leverage this process to upgrade to any future version without stopping the database service. However, the steps necessary to complete such an upgrade are non-trivial and utilize tools that are not officially provided by the standard community release.

That makes it important for us to explain how zero-downtime upgrades work. Perhaps more often than many will admit, upgrades are postponed to avoid costly downtime for extremely active database clusters with no clear maintenance window. Sometimes, this can last for years, and it can even risk running on a version of PostgreSQL that's no longer supported. At that point, the entire cluster is running on borrowed time. One unpatched bug could spell the end of everything, forcing a less-than-ideal rushed upgrade.

So how do we upgrade this way? The basic process is this:

1. Allocate a separate cluster architecture using the higher-version software.
2. Copy all data from the existing cluster.
3. Verify that the data matches as expected.
4. Switch connections to the new cluster.

Each of those steps appears simple, but includes a lot of preliminary work, allocation, configuration, waiting, and so on. The goal of this chapter is to break down each of those elements into one or more recipes to complete the entire upgrade successfully.

This is one of the final pieces for keeping a PostgreSQL cluster online through any possible action, and as we'll find out as the chapter progresses, it can even apply to more than upgrades. Taken as a whole, this chapter will free any **Database Administrator** (**DBA**) from worrying about their high-throughput database being offline, even for the dreaded major version upgrade!

In this chapter, we will learn how to upgrade a cluster while remaining fully online. We will cover the following recipes in this chapter:

- Preparing upgrade requirements
- Remembering PgBouncer and pglogical
- Creating a publication set
- Handling sequences
- Bootstrapping the target cluster
- Starting the subscription
- Monitoring progress
- Switching targets
- Cleaning everything up

Preparing upgrade requirements

Upgrading between major PostgreSQL versions without taking things offline is not a trivial exercise. There are many steps necessary to prepare, and we must integrate supplementary software to complete the process.

We've covered all the tools necessary to complete this maneuver through the course of the book, but that doesn't mean we know quite how to combine them, or what is involved. This recipe will make sure that we ask ourselves several questions about the PostgreSQL cluster, both to get ready for the upgrade and to ensure we have everything we'll need.

Let's get started.

Getting ready

Given the nature of this kind of process, it may be better to think of it as a data migration. As a result, we'll be asking several questions in the following instructions. Some of these may require acquiring hardware resources or expanding existing capacity. Please ensure these resources are available before continuing.

How to do it...

Ask and answer these questions about the cluster being upgraded:

1. How many nodes are in the existing cluster?
2. How much data is represented within each node of the cluster?
3. Do we have enough equivalent hardware to reproduce every node?
4. If not, can we subsist on a smaller server count for any duration?
5. If not, is there sufficient storage capacity on existing cluster nodes to host two copies of the data?
6. Do applications currently communicate through a proxy layer?
7. If not, would it be difficult to introduce a proxy layer?

How it works...

There should be an obvious theme to these questions. As we suggested in the beginning of this recipe, we will need a lot of resources to perform this task. Why? Consider this diagram for a company with a somewhat large PostgreSQL cluster:

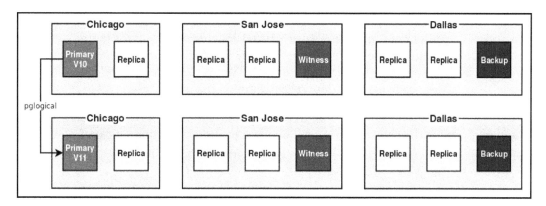

If every one of these nodes is in use while we are using the version 10 cluster, we must determine how many version 11 nodes we actually need.

The easiest way to proceed is to simply reproduce every node, as in the preceding diagram. In some cases, such as with an extremely busy **online transactional processing** (OLTP) cluster, it might be the only way. By migrating onto a cluster with the same node count, we know we have sufficient capacity to support the application stack. Backups of the second cluster will be up to date as soon as we activate it.

But what if we can't acquire so many extra servers? In that case, we could perhaps upgrade a cluster using a node configuration like that shown in the following diagram:

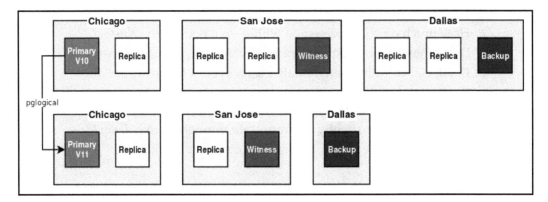

By using three fewer nodes, we could reduce the expense and required resources for the upgrade. Can we remove even more? If the platform can survive on diminished capacity, we could repurpose the deprecated version 10 nodes once the upgrade is complete. It would make the upgrade take longer and require more steps, but we would save resources.

 Many modern clusters use **Virtual Machines** (**VMs**) for their PostgreSQL clusters. If possible, try to allocate the same machine specification for the replacement VMs. We can then recycle the old VMs back into the pool once we finish the upgrade.

Perhaps we do not have an easy way to produce double the number of servers for a one-time upgrade. If that's the case, will our current hardware be sufficient? If we happen to have more than twice the required storage space to host our data, we can simply set up a second PostgreSQL instance on each server.

These extra instances will need to monitor a different TCP port and exist in a different directory, but they can reduce expenses significantly. If we know the size of our data on disk, we can decide to use the same hardware if we have more than twice as much available space. If there isn't enough space, can we add some? Often adding storage is much easier and cheaper than obtaining entire servers or VMs.

Beyond capacity, however, is the question of connection management. We learned about proxies in Chapter 4, *Proxy and Pooling Resources*. That chapter is very important to understanding just why we need a proxy in a PostgreSQL cluster. If connections directly contact our version 10 cluster, how do we transparently move them to the version 11 cluster? We absolutely need a proxy to complete this procedure.

The question is: do we have one already? If not, we must add one. Even a simple virtual IP address or CNAME makes it possible to move the application connection target to the new cluster once we're ready. But to do that, we would have needed to follow the recipes in this book, or have already built our architecture with the same concepts in mind.

If we don't have a proxy, what would be required to add one? How many applications will need to be reconfigured? Will we need to request an outage or maintenance window to restart the application stack to absorb that change? If so, can we then apply one or more recipes from this book to get the best proxy possible to take full advantage of the maintenance window?

Integrating a proxy layer may not be simple at this stage, but it is an utter necessity.

We will learn later that the preferred proxy layer for this chapter is PgBouncer. Don't worry if you're not currently using that! Simply having the proxy layer means it can be replaced with something else. The key is having some connection target separate from PostgreSQL itself, so we can masquerade the cluster that is actually active.

Remembering PgBouncer and pglogical

There are two essential pieces of software that drive the zero-downtime PostgreSQL upgrade procedure. Even though we covered both in previous chapters, we feel it is important to review why we chose these components. So, this recipe will explain just why PgBouncer and pglogical are critical to a seamless PostgreSQL upgrade.

Getting ready

There's really no preparation necessary for this recipe. Dive right in!

How to do it...

Follow these deceptively simple instructions:

1. Review all recipes related to PgBouncer in Chapter 4, *Proxy and Pooling Resources*.
2. Review all recipes related to pglogical in Chapter 7, *PostgreSQL Replication*.

How it works...

Why even have this recipe? We're glad you asked!

We introduced PgBouncer in Chapter 4, *Proxy and Pooling Resources*, and it gives us the ability to transparently redirect application connections from one server to another without interrupting transaction activity. This is the secret sauce that no other proxy approach can match.

A virtual IP address would interrupt active transactions unless we stopped the application. HAProxy would as well. The only proxy software that understands the PostgreSQL communication protocol is PgBouncer, and we want to take advantage of that.

The other essential capability PgBouncer provides is to PAUSE and RESUME session activity. Unlike RECONNECT, which only marks existing connections as needing replacement, and directs new sessions to the correct location, PAUSE waits for transactions to complete and then immediately closes the backend entirely. It also puts PgBouncer in a state that will not allocate a new backend until RESUME is called.

This PAUSE and RESUME cycle allows us to inject a short wait into application activity while we switch from the version 10 PostgreSQL cluster to the version 11 cluster. This wait is where replication lag is reduced to zero, and we reconfigure PgBouncer to connect to the PostgreSQL 11 replacement cluster. The application only perceives a short pause rather than rude disconnection messages, and resumes operating as if nothing has changed.

We explained how to use pglogical in Chapter 7, *PostgreSQL Replication*, as it allows us to copy data between two otherwise binary-incompatible PostgreSQL releases. The recipes in this chapter will rely on pglogical to transfer data from PostgreSQL 10 to PostgreSQL 11 while the platform is running.

We only scratched the surface of pglogical's full capabilities in `Chapter 7`, *PostgreSQL Replication*. Rather than copying only a small handful of tables, we can actually allocate entire schemas into publications. Unlike PostgreSQL 10 native logical replication, we can also replicate sequence values. This is extremely important, because it means sequences will resume at the correct values rather than being reset to 1 in the replacement cluster. It would be possible to set all sequences manually to fix this, but that requires extra steps that are otherwise not necessary.

With pglogical as our logical replication mechanism, we can build a replacement cluster, transfer all the data, and be immediately ready for the actual upgrade. And that upgrade is a mere PgBouncer `PAUSE`, reconfigure, and `RECONNECT` cycle.

The following recipes will explain how this is slightly different than how we used PgBouncer and pglogical in previous chapters, so pay attention!

There's more...

Consider this our last warning to ensure some kind of proxy is incorporated into your PostgreSQL cluster. In order to complete this upgrade, PgBouncer will be required. If there's already a proxy layer, we encourage either augmenting it with PgBouncer, or replacing it entirely. If there isn't, find a suitable maintenance window and begin working with application developers, management, infrastructure, and any other departments necessary to incorporate a layer of indirection.

It is a painful, one-time event that will prevent a far greater amount of problems in the future. From now on, this chapter will assume that PgBouncer is installed as part of the cluster and is available for certain upgrade steps. Trust us, it's worth the effort.

See also

It may be a good idea to refresh your memory on PgBouncer and pglogical functionality. We encourage at least skimming through these URLs:

- **pgbouncer command-line usage**: `https://www.pgbouncer.org/usage.html`
- **pglogical 2**: `https://github.com/2ndQuadrant/pglogical/tree/REL2_x_STABLE/docs`

Creating a publication set

The first component to successfully upgrading a PostgreSQL cluster while fully online is building a pglogical publication set. This publication set will represent all the data we want on the new cluster, and gives us an opportunity to *prune* anything that should be deprecated.

Unlike previous forays into logical replication, we will actually need to entertain some extra considerations. This recipe will explain how to build a publication set that ensures a smooth major version upgrade.

Getting ready

The *Remembering PgBouncer and pglogical* recipe already recommended reviewing the material on pglogical. We also suggest actually following the *Setting up pglogical* recipe in `Chapter 7`, *PostgreSQL Replication*, on the provider node so everything is fully operational before we begin.

How to do it...

Assuming we have a PostgreSQL 10 provider node that has pglogical installed, follow these steps:

1. Produce an unlogged table of all the schemas that should be transferred. Use a query like this to generate an initial list:

   ```
   CREATE UNLOGGED TABLE schema_list AS
   SELECT nspname
     FROM pg_namespace
    WHERE nspname NOT LIKE 'pg\_%'
      AND nspname NOT IN ('information_schema', 'pglogical');
   ```

2. Audit the resulting table of schemas and remove any subsequent schemas that should not be copied.

3. Produce a list of tables that do not have a primary key using the following query:

   ```
   CREATE UNLOGGED TABLE table_list AS
   SELECT n.nspname AS schema_name,
          t.relname as table_name,
          c.conname IS NOT NULL AS has_primary_key
     FROM pg_class t
   ```

```
        JOIN pg_namespace n ON (n.oid = t.relnamespace)
        JOIN schema_list s USING (nspname)
        LEFT JOIN pg_constraint c ON (c.conrelid = t.oid
             AND c.contype = 'p')
    WHERE t.relkind IN ('r', 'p')
      AND t.relpersistence = 'p';
```

4. Audit the resulting list of tables and remove any that should not be part of the migration.

5. Execute the following query to obtain a list of tables that have no primary key:

```
SELECT * FROM table_list
  WHERE NOT has_primary_key;
```

6. For any table that does not have a primary key, decide whether or not the table can be considered insert-only. If so, ignore it for now.

7. For tables that do not have a primary key and cannot operate as insert-only, either add a primary key based on existing columns or add a surrogate key, such as in this example with pgbench_history:

```
CREATE SEQUENCE pgbench_history_id_seq;

ALTER TABLE pgbench_history
  ADD _migrate_id BIGINT
     DEFAULT nextval('pgbench_history_id_seq') NULL;

ALTER SEQUENCE pgbench_history_id_seq
OWNED BY pgbench_history._migrate_id;

UPDATE pgbench_history
   SET _migrate_id = default
 WHERE _migrate_id IS NULL;

ALTER TABLE pgbench_history
ALTER _migrate_id SET NOT NULL;

ALTER TABLE pgbench_history
  ADD PRIMARY KEY (_migrate_id);

UPDATE table_list
   SET has_primary_key = True
 WHERE schema_name = 'public'
   AND table_name = 'pgbench_history';
```

8. Run the following query to add regular tables to the default replication set:

```
SELECT pglogical.replication_set_add_table(
        set_name := 'default',
        relation := schema_name || '.' || table_name
    )
  FROM table_list
 WHERE has_primary_key;
```

9. Run this query to add tables without primary keys:

```
SELECT pglogical.replication_set_add_table(
        set_name := 'default_insert_only',
        relation := schema_name || '.' || table_name
    )
  FROM table_list
 WHERE NOT has_primary_key;
```

How it works...

The job of this recipe is to either transfer everything, or some subset of the data we wish to retain. We start this process by listing all of the schemas in our database using a specially constructed query that omits any likely PostgreSQL catalog tables and the ever-present information_schema, as well as pglogical itself. From here we can decide to leave the list unadulterated, or remove rows for schemas we want to discard.

We then perform the same task for all tables in the database. It's important to know whether or not a table has a primary key. As a consequence, the query we use here is rather complicated, using PostgreSQL catalog tables such as pg_class, pg_namespace, and pg_constraint. The purpose of this query is to isolate, from the schemas we want to copy, any tables that are either regular tables or partition tables (relkind IN ('r', 'p')) and are not unlogged or temporary tables (relpersistence = 'p'). By including the pg_constraint table, we can identify which tables have a primary key and which do not, so we can use that information later.

Why do we need to know which tables have primary keys? For logical replication to operate efficiently, it must be possible to locate records on the subscriber system. Without a primary key, we would need to use the entire row as a key, which means a sequential scan for every update or delete. pglogical does not allow this kind of operation, so it enforces a rule that standard, logically replicated tables must have a primary key.

We can remove that stipulation if the table is insert-only, because any row inserted into the provider can simply be inserted into the subscriber as well. Our next step is to examine the tables that do not have a primary key. We can either add primary keys to each of these tables, or decide that would be too much unnecessary work. Some logging tables, for instance, may be purely for tracking activity, and as a result, could contain many millions or even billions of insert-only rows. Tables like this do not need special handling, and it would be extremely wasteful to retrofit a new key onto these for a one-time migration.

For other types of tables, perhaps through old design or by mistake, it may be that it's a historical accident that no primary key was assigned. In these cases, this is a good opportunity to fix that situation by adding one. If this itself is not possible, it may be necessary to add a primary key specifically for the purpose of the migration itself. In this case, the procedure is fairly complicated, and involves several steps:

1. Create a sequence.
2. Add a nullable default column to the table.
3. Alter the sequence so it's associated with the new column.
4. Update each record in the table, possibly in smaller batches in cases of extremely large tables.
5. Remove the nullable attribute from the new column.
6. Transform the new column to a primary key.
7. Lastly, update our table list to reflect that the table now has a primary key.

As in our example with the `pgbench_history` table, this can be a lot of extra work, especially if we have a vast array of tables that require this kind of procedure.

Whatever the case, our next step is to register these tables with pglogical so it knows to transmit them to the subscribing system. The easiest way to do this is to use our `table_list` as a source and call the `pglogical.replication_set_add_table` function for every applicable row. We need to call this function twice in two different contexts:

1. First for tables that do have a primary key, where we add it to the `default` replication set.
2. Second for tables that do not have a primary key, where we add them to the `default_insert_only` replication set.

This ensures every table we want to preserve through the migration is included, even those that don't work normally with logical replication.

There's more...

There is a much easier way to do this that may apply if all tables have primary keys. pglogical has a function specifically for this case that greatly simplifies the preceding procedure, especially if we want every table to be part of the migration. We could have obtained our list of schemas and then executed the following function:

```
SELECT pglogical.replication_set_add_all_tables(
        set_name := 'default',
        schema_names := array_agg(nspname)
      )
  FROM schema_list;
```

This would automatically register every table in each schema with pglogical for the `default` replication set. We hope your upgrade qualifies for using this function, but even if it doesn't, the procedure detailed in this recipe should work.

Handling sequences

Sequences are the primary reason we recommend using pglogical for major PostgreSQL version upgrades. Though they're often associated with tables, sequences are separate objects that only contain information about themselves. They're often overlooked because there are no events to capture regarding logical replication; there are no inserts, updates, or deletes to encode or decode.

Since pglogical is an extension and doesn't rely entirely upon logical decoding in order to operate, it also adds functionality to augment PostgreSQL. pglogical handles sequences by periodically refreshing the values on the subscriber system to ensure they're much higher than the last value on the provider. In the case of an upgrade, there should be no sequence conflict after switching to the new cluster.

This recipe will explain how to register sequences with pglogical, and other useful steps for managing sequences leading to an upgrade.

Getting ready

Please follow the *Creating a publication set* recipe before starting here.

How to do it...

Assuming we have a PostgreSQL 10 provider node that has pglogical installed, follow these steps:

1. Register all sequences with this query:

```
SELECT pglogical.replication_set_add_all_sequences(
        set_name := 'default',
        schema_names := array_agg(nspname)
    )
  FROM schema_list;
```

2. Verify registered sequences with this query:

```
SELECT s.set_id, ss.set_seqoid
  FROM pglogical.replication_set s
  JOIN pglogical.replication_set_seq ss USING (set_id);
```

How it works...

This is, thankfully, a short and easy-to-understand recipe. Unlike when we were registering tables and had to account for primary keys, sequences aren't tables at all, so when we register them with pglogical, we don't need to do anything special.

As a result, we can simply invoke `replication_set_add_all_sequences` to process all sequences for the schemas we want to copy, rather than using `replication_set_add_sequence` for each individual sequence. It's also a good idea to verify we added the sequences we expected, since we don't necessarily know how pglogical might interpret *all sequences in the listed schemas*.

As an example on our test system where we have a `sensor_log` table with a sequence, we saw these results:

```
 set_name |    set_seqoid
----------+-------------------
 default  | sensor_log_id_seq
```

It's only one sequence, but we didn't register it explicitly. Tables in a schema can have any number of sequences, which may not be properly associated. It's also not impossible for sequences to exist on their own, and not belong to any table or column at all. As a result, we recommend checking once sequences are added, to ensure all sequences are listed.

There's more...

When the time comes to synchronize these, we don't actually have to do anything. The subscriber sequences will be updated periodically to reflect updated values. However, should we want to follow a specific schedule, we can actually force a synchronization using a provided function.

Using the following query will manually update all sequences:

```
SELECT pglogical.synchronize_sequence(set_seqoid)
  FROM pglogical.replication_set_seq;
```

Keep in mind that this function, like many pglogical functions, is asynchronous. It merely injects the command into the pglogical process queue, and will not wait for the sequence to synchronize before returning.

Bootstrapping the target cluster

Another critical component of a major PostgreSQL upgrade using pglogical is that we need somewhere to send the data. Ideally, this is a cluster comprised of the same number of nodes, with identical hardware or better, and all the same supporting software, abstraction layers, and automation.

The goal of this recipe is to produce a target cluster using the newer PostgreSQL version so we can subscribe to the old one.

Getting ready

Though we'll technically be starting the new cluster *from scratch*, be sure to have completed the *Creating a publication set* recipe so we know pglogical is ready to transmit data to the new cluster we build.

Additionally, we will need to know the path to the `initdb` utility, as it is often obfuscated by software packaging. On Debian-based systems, it is usually found in `/usr/lib/postgresql/11/bin` for version 11, for example. Users of Red Hat derivatives can find it in the `/usr/pgsql-11/bin` path instead.

How to do it...

Assuming we have our old server (pg-old) and a new server (pg-new) to act as the subscriber, and our database to be copied is named myapp and stored in /db/pgdata, follow these instructions:

1. Bootstrap an empty PostgreSQL instance on pg-new using initdb as the postgres user:

   initdb -D /db/pgdata

2. Copy postgresql.conf and pg_hba.conf from pg-old to pg-new.
3. Copy the .pgpass file from pg-old to pg-new.
4. Dump all global objects on pg-old from pg-new as the postgres user:

   **pg_dumpall -g -h pg-old -U rep_user \
    -f global_objects.sql --database postgres**

5. Import all global objects in pg-new as the postgres user:

   psql -f global_objects.sql

6. Create the empty myapp database as the postgres user on pg-new:

   createdb myapp

7. Dump all **Data Definition Languages** (**DDLs**) from pg-old for structures and definitions:

   **pg_dump -s -h pg-old -U rep_user \
       -f myapp_schema_def.sql -d myapp**

8. Import the DDLs into pg-new so all tables, views, and so on exist:

   psql -f myapp_schema_def.sql myapp

9. Follow the instructions in the *Setting up pglogical* recipe of Chapter 7, *PostgreSQL Replication*, using pg-new as the subscriber.
10. Create any necessary replicas to reproduce the number of nodes decided on in the *Preparing upgrade requirements* recipe.
11. Install any supplementary software such as repmgr, Patroni, Barman, and so on to complete the cluster.

How it works...

The early portion of this recipe focuses on initializing a new cluster using initdb with the target version of PostgreSQL we want to upgrade to. For the purposes of demonstration in this recipe, we used version 11.

As usual when performing this kind of bootstrap, we copy all of the configuration files from the origin node. In this case, we want at least the postgresql.conf and pg_hba.conf files, as they define the majority of our configuration settings and connection access definitions. If your cluster uses the postgresql.conf include_dir directive, copy the full contents of any of those locations as well. It's important to capture as much of the original cluster structure as we can.

Don't forget to examine the postgresql.conf file for potential incompatibilities between versions. These are minimal between PostgreSQL 10 and 11, but are much more noticeable between 9.5 and 11, for example. It may be easiest to simply attempt to start the instance using the donated configuration file, and fixing things that PostgreSQL logs as errors that prevent it from running.

Part of this process is to use pg_dumpall to gather all roles defined within pg-old. These roles have been used by all portions of the application stack up to now, so we will need them in the new cluster as well. These will also be necessary for any object access GRANT or REVOKE statements within the database DDL. Once these are successfully exported, we can use psql and specify the file we dumped, and all users should then exist.

Now we want to start building database objects, including the database itself. We start by using createdb to create the myapp database in this case, as that is where our test application data resides. Do note that we'll need to perform this step for any databases we wish to copy from pg-old if we have multiple active databases per PostgreSQL service.

This time rather than dumping global data, we obtain object definitions with pg_dump by specifying the -s (schema-only) flag. We prefix the output file with the database name in case we need to do this for multiple databases. In our example, the file is named myapp_schema_def.sql, but just make sure it's unique and memorable. It may also be a good idea to timestamp the file so it can be used as a sort of record for what we did.

Once we import this schema definition into the correct database using the `psql` tool, everything is technically ready to start receiving data from the old system. This is why we recommend following the *Setting up pglogical* recipe of `Chapter 7`, *PostgreSQL Replication*, to finish setting up this server.

With the Primary node of the upgraded cluster ready, we can begin reproducing the remainder of the cluster, or at least the nodes we decided would be necessary in the *Preparing upgrade requirements* recipe. We need the Primary node at an absolute minimum, but it's a good idea to pre-provision any replica nodes at this time. This is because when we create the initial subscription, any replica nodes will begin accumulating the data as well.

Once we've begun to establish the data portions of our cluster, we can reproduce all of the helpful scaffolding. If we're using a failover system such as repmgr or Patroni, we would want to get these pieces installed at this point. Even if they're disabled to prevent a failover event until we've completed the upgrade, they will be ready to enable when we're ready. This applies to backup servers as well.

Why now? We want the replacement cluster to be as fully operational as possible, even while it's ingesting data from the old cluster via pglogical. This serves something of a dual purpose: first as a stress test, and second as proof that everything works prior to completing the upgrade. We will eventually have a parallel cluster containing all data from the old version, and it should reflect all the same capabilities.

There's more...

There may be some debate as to the efficiency of creating replicas now, rather than waiting for the subscription to complete. This is actually a valid and rather astute observation. In cases of extremely large clusters, it may actually be a much better idea to delay the creation of replica nodes, backup nodes, and other dependent servers until the initial synchronization step is complete.

The biggest justification for this is the fact that PostgreSQL physical replication uses **write-ahead logging** (**WAL**) traffic to maintain replicas. WAL is generally much larger than the originating data since it contains all page-level operations, including index creation. For a **very large databases** (**VLDB**) installation several terabytes in size, this may equate to several multiples of extra data transfer to each replica node during the initial bootstrapping phase.

In cases like these, we actually recommend skipping the last two steps of this recipe and waiting until after the *Monitoring progress* recipe indicates pg-old and pg-new are synchronized. With a less active upstream, it will be easier to create each replica, and any backup nodes will be interacting with a system similar to pg-old in volume.

Starting the subscription

The last ingredient in our high-availability PostgreSQL major version upgrade is to actually invoke the subscription. This is the point of no return, so we must ensure that everything is ready, and that nothing interrupts the synchronization process until it is complete.

This recipe will explain what is happening during the subscription process, and how to help make sure it completes without issue.

Getting ready

We will need two fully operational PostgreSQL clusters, so please follow all recipes up to the *Bootstrapping the target cluster* recipe before proceeding.

How to do it...

Assuming we have our old server (pg-old) and a new server (pg-new) to act as the subscriber, follow these instructions to start the subscription:

1. Execute the following query on pg-new to initiate the subscription:

```
SELECT pglogical.create_subscription(
    subscription_name := 'myapp_upgrade',
    provider_dsn := 'host=pg-old dbname=myapp user=rep_user'
);
```

2. Wait for the subscription to complete by executing this query on pg-new:

```
SELECT pglogical.wait_for_subscription_sync_complete(
    'myapp_upgrade'
);
```

3. Check for the following line in the `pg-new` PostgreSQL log:

```
LOG:  starting apply for subscription myapp_upgrade
```

4. Check for the following line in the `pg-old` PostgreSQL log:

```
LOG:  exported logical decoding snapshot
```

How it works...

Creating the subscription itself is the easy part; we simply call the `create_subscription` function as we did in the *Copying a few tables with pglogical* recipe of `Chapter 7`, *PostgreSQL Replication*. Of all possible parameters, we only need to supply the `subscription_name` parameter to label the subscription, and the `provider_dsn` parameter so pglogical knows how to contact the provider.

Observant readers may notice that we did not specify the `replication_sets` parameter. This is because, unlike in the chapter on replication, we did not create a subscription set. pglogical will subscribe to the `default` and `default_insert_only` sets unless told otherwise. Since that's where we placed all of the tables on the provider, `pg-new` should receive data without needing to list the sets.

We also did not set the `synchronize_data` attribute to `True`, as this is the default for any new subscription. The very act of creating the subscription should automatically start the synchronization process, which may take a very long time to complete.

In fact, that's the reason we also execute the `wait_for_subscription_sync_complete` function. Since most pglogical functions are asynchronous, this will explicitly wait until the subscription is fully established before returning the session prompt.

Once we've executed these two functions, we can actually check the PostgreSQL logs on both `pg-new` and `pg-old` to verify that it's doing as we asked. We should see something like this immediately in the `pg-new` logs once we invoke `create_subscription`:

```
2020-01-19 19:26:20.335 UTC [24850] [unknown]@myapp LOG:  starting apply for subscription myapp_upgrade
```

This lets us know that the subscriber has launched a pglogical apply worker that will begin making logical changes to the local `myapp` database; it even uses the subscription name so we know what is happening.

The story on `pg-old` is similar. pglogical will connect to the upstream provider as requested and request a subscription. This causes the creation of a replication slot as well as the creation of a background worker to start copying data to `pg-new`. In order for this data to remain consistent, pglogical also instructs PostgreSQL to export a transaction snapshot with the same transaction information as the replication slot.

This means all of the copied data will remain static until `pg-new` starts consuming from the replication slot and moves its transaction ID forward. We should see something like this in the PostgreSQL logs of `pg-old` when that process begins:

```
2020-01-19 19:40:41.945 UTC [46879] rep_user@pgbench LOG:  exported logical decoding snapshot: "00000007-00000576-1" with 0 transaction IDs
```

It may be a very long time before we receive any further messages from either PostgreSQL node. The exported snapshot must remain open and available for the duration of the initial subscription synchronization, and no further messages will appear until it completes. If either node is restarted, our progress is lost, and we must erase the contents of `pg-new` and start again.

There's more...

It probably seems dire when we say that the initial subscription requires success, or we must start from the beginning. This really is a natural consequence of how transaction snapshot exports work; if we lose the connection holding that snapshot, we don't have a consistent picture of the data.

In that case, and especially for larger databases, it may make more sense to avoid adding any tables or sequences to the subscription set we create on `pg-old`. It is quite possible to subscribe to an empty replication set, and this should succeed relatively quickly and establish a communication channel between both servers that is reliant only upon the replication slot.

Once we've done this, we can actually add tables to the replication set in small batches. Each of these batches will still require a separate synchronization, but depending on the size of the data they represent, it could be much less disruptive than attempting to copy all database contents in a single transaction.

All we have to do is skip the *Creating a publication set* recipe until we've established the subscription. Once the subscription exists, we can periodically add new tables like this:

```
SELECT pglogical.replication_set_add_table(
  set_name := 'default',
```

```
    relation := 'my_new_table',
    synchronize_data := True
);
```

The key here is the `synchronize_data` parameter, which we've set to `True`, though the default is `False`. Normally the `replication_set_add_table` function is only used to add new (and presumably empty) tables to a replication set. What we're saying here is that the table contains data, so any subscribed nodes will likely want those contents.

> In fact, we could modify the *Creating a publication set* recipe to account for this table batching. The recipe already creates a list of tables that should be synchronized, so imagine we added a numeric ID to the `table_list` as well. We could then copy 10 or 100 tables at a time, until everything was ready.

Monitoring progress

One important step for establishing an upgrade target is to watch and ensure all data from the old cluster successfully migrates to the new one. There are multiple methods for accomplishing this task, and we may choose to try all of them for safety, or just so we know how long we may need to wait until the new cluster is ready.

This recipe will explain a few easy ways to check the state of a subscription while it performs the initial data synchronization.

Getting ready

Please follow all previous recipes in this chapter before starting here.

How to do it...

Assuming we have our old server (pg-old) and a new server (pg-new) to act as the subscriber, follow these instructions to monitor the subscription progress of the myapp database:

1. Use this query on pg-new to check the state of the subscription itself:

    ```
    SELECT *
      FROM pglogical.show_subscription_status(
            'myapp_upgrade'
           );
    ```

2. Run this query on both systems to get an idea of the relative database size:

    ```
    SELECT pg_size_pretty(pg_database_size('myapp'));
    ```

3. Execute the following query on both servers to check the current table being synchronized:

    ```
    SELECT application_name, query, state_change
      FROM pg_stat_activity
     WHERE application_name LIKE 'myapp\_%';
    ```

4. Run this query on both systems to compare information for the table currently being copied, as is done for pgbench_accounts in this example:

    ```
    SELECT pg_size_pretty(pg_relation_size(
      'pgbench_accounts'
    ));
    ```

5. If possible, check to see the most recent ID is the same on both systems, as in this example on a table named sensor_log:

    ```
    SELECT max(id) FROM sensor_log;
    ```

How it works...

The first of our queries for checking status will provide a lot of information about the subscription, but is of somewhat limited utility. Here's an example from our test system:

```
-[ RECORD 1 ]-----+------------------------------------------------
subscription_name | myapp_upgrade
status            | initializing
provider_node     | origin
provider_dsn      | host=pg-old dbname=myapp user=rep_user
slot_name         | pgl_myapp_origin_myapp_upgrade
replication_sets  | {default,default_insert_only,ddl_sql}
forward_origins   | {all}
```

Note that the `status` field indicates the subscription is `initializing`. Everything else is basically a static field indicating some information about the subscription itself. When the subscription is complete, the `status` field will display `replicating` instead. It's not much in the way of diagnostics, but does at least confirm the subscription is still establishing itself.

The next check we can perform using the `pg_database_size` function is a very coarse comparison of overall database size. If, for example, we have a 1 TB database and the new cluster is still only 250 GB, we can generally predict how much time is remaining based on how long it took to reach that size.

Keep in mind that unlike the provider node, the subscriber system is a fresh installation receiving data that has yet to experience any modifications. As a result, the new cluster will not show any data bloat. If the provider system has more than 20% bloat, the final size of the new cluster may be much smaller than we might expect. Don't use this check as a final status, but it is safe to get a general idea of progress.

Next, we can actually inquire within the `pg_stat_activity` PostgreSQL catalog table to actually observe the initialization itself. The initial table synchronization step is not actually done through logical replication, but by pglogical itself. It connects to the remote server from the subscriber and initiates a `COPY` statement. This is one of the most efficient ways to load data into a table.

As a result, we can actually check to see when a `COPY` statement is running, and that tells us which table pglogical is currently synchronizing. Here is a sample from `pg-old` in our environment:

```
-[ RECORD 1 ]----+---------------------------------------------------------------------
application_name | myapp_upgrade_copy
query            | COPY "public"."pgbench_accounts" ("aid","bid","abalance","filler") TO stdout
state_change     | 2020-01-19 20:43:51.120447+00
-[ RECORD 2 ]----+---------------------------------------------------------------------
application_name | myapp_upgrade_snap
query            |
state_change     | 2020-01-19 20:43:51.06435+00
```

This output is actually slightly more informative than we'd implied. Consider the session labeled `myapp_upgrade_snap`. This is the session holding the transaction snapshot that ensures all `COPY` statements represent consistent data. As a result, we will only see this connection on `pg-old` rather than `pg-new`.

Meanwhile, a session performing the actual `COPY` should appear on both systems. The version on `pg-old` sends the data to `stdout`, while the session on `pg-new` consumes the data from `stdin`. We should see a pair of these on each server until the subscription has copied every table.

Unfortunately, the order of these tables is nondeterministic, so we can't use it as a progress indicator. However, we can see which table is currently being copied. If it is one of our larger tables, we can use the next indicator to estimate when it will complete.

The `pg_relation_size` function is very useful here, because it reports the amount of bytes consumed on disk by the object. If we ignore table bloat for now, the table should be about the same size on each system. If we execute the function on `pg-old`, we know the current size of the table, and `pg-new` will likely be some percentage of that amount.

If that value stops increasing, we know either that the table has completely transferred, or replication has been interrupted somehow. Assuming it's the former, we can confirm that by checking `pg_stat_activity` again. If the values still don't match, we also gain a new data point: the true size of the data on disk, barring any table bloat. This is another great benefit from upgrading in this manner!

Finally, we can examine each table more closely. This is something we can only do once the table has fully transferred, since the `COPY` statement is atomic. Regardless, we can use this on any table that has already synchronized, and it can confirm the most recent ID is represented on both systems.

There's more...

If the initial synchronization has been running for a protracted duration, the last check we supplied may report very different values. After all, `pg-old` is still receiving new rows for all tables, and the snapshot for the initial synchronization to `pg-new` may have been established hours, or even days ago.

Luckily, we can actually exploit the same trick pglogical used when creating the transaction snapshot. Since it needs the snapshot to ensure every `COPY` statement is consistent, we can actually use the transaction ID as well.

So long as we connect as a superuser, it's possible to specify the transaction snapshot ID and see the same thing as pglogical while it sends data to `pg-new`.

If we want to do this, we merely need to obtain the snapshot ID from the `pg-old` logs as we did in the *Starting the subscription* recipe. Then we can use a series of commands like this:

```
BEGIN TRANSACTION ISOLATION LEVEL REPEATABLE READ;
SET TRANSACTION SNAPSHOT '00000007-00000DB8-1';
SELECT max(id) FROM sensor_log;
```

Even if the transaction has been running for days, we have requested a `REPEATABLE READ` isolation level. This guarantees we see the same data as pglogical is exporting within its `COPY` statements.

This only works until the subscription is fully synchronized and switches to replicating status. Still, it's a great tool if we want to manually observe synchronization progress and validity.

See also

We used a few features of the PostgreSQL system catalog in this recipe. You can read more about them using these resources:

- **System Administration Functions**: https://www.postgresql.org/docs/current/functions-admin.html
- **The Statistics Collector**: https://www.postgresql.org/docs/current/monitoring-stats.html
- **SET TRANSACTION**: https://www.postgresql.org/docs/current/sql-set-transaction.html

Switching targets

We've now reached the point where the upgrade is possible. We have a brand new cluster running the newer version of PostgreSQL, all data has been copied, and we have tested the application on the new cluster to ensure compatibility. It is now time to switch the application stack to the new cluster and complete the upgrade transition.

PgBouncer will play a key role in this final step, and will ensure the application barely even notices the migration. This recipe will explain how the upgrade itself works, and the other steps we need to execute to ensure everything is fully synchronized.

Getting ready

Please follow all previous recipes before starting here.

How to do it...

These steps will assume we have our old primary (pg-old), a new primary (pg-new), and a proxy server running PgBouncer. Follow these instructions to complete the upgrade process:

1. Ensure there are no long-running transactions with this query on pg-old:

```
SELECT pid, state, client_addr, username,
       now() - xact_start AS duration, query
  FROM pg_stat_activity
 WHERE state != 'idle'
   AND now() - xact_start > INTERVAL '60s'
 ORDER BY duration DESC;
```

2. Terminate or resolve any transactions identified in the preceding execution.
3. Check the replication lag on pg-old with this query:

```
SELECT slot_name, database, active,
       pg_wal_lsn_diff(
         pg_current_wal_lsn(),
         confirmed_flush_lsn
       ) AS write_lag
  FROM pg_replication_slots;
```

4. If lag is relatively low, execute the following command as the `postgres` user on `pg-proxy` to pause the PgBouncer connections:

```
psql -U pgbouncer -h pg-proxy -c "PAUSE" pgbouncer
```

5. Run this query on `pg-old` to flush all pending replication traffic to `pg-new`:

```
SELECT pglogical.wait_slot_confirm_lsn(NULL, NULL);
```

6. Manually update sequences with this query on `pg-old`:

```
SELECT pglogical.synchronize_sequence(set_seqoid)
  FROM pglogical.replication_set_seq;
```

7. Modify the `pgbouncer.ini` configuration on `pg-proxy` to use `pg-new` as the connection target.

8. Reload the PgBouncer system service as a root-level user on `pg-proxy`:

```
sudo systemctl reload pgbouncer
```

9. Unsubscribe from `pg-old` with this SQL on `pg-new`:

```
SELECT pglogical.drop_subscription(
    subscription_name := 'myapp_upgrade'
);
```

10. Invoke the following command as the `postgres` user on `pg-proxy` to resume PgBouncer connections:

```
psql -U pgbouncer -h pg-proxy -c "RESUME" pgbouncer
```

How it works...

The first thing we want to do before upgrading is to examine any running transactions on the server. Anything that has been running for longer than one minute at the time we want to perform the upgrade is suspicious, and should be examined. It could be a batch job that may not complete for several hours, or a rogue connection that has languished after completing a desktop user's ad hoc query.

PostgreSQL can't tell the difference, and either of these connections will prevent PgBouncer from pausing the connections. PgBouncer must allow an executing transaction to complete before the PAUSE command will complete. Since we need this command to switch to the new cluster, we must remove these potential blockers before beginning.

The query we've chosen for that task will report the process ID (`pid`) of the session, along with the source of the connection (`client_addr`), the user, the duration of the full transaction, and the query that the connection last executed. This should be enough diagnostic information to figure out why the transaction is running or idle, and we can either contact the responsible party, or terminate it with the `pg_terminate_backend()` function.

Next, we should check for any replication lag. If the database infrastructure is very write-heavy or otherwise active, the upgrade cluster may be significantly behind. If there are tens or hundreds of GB of representative data lag, we do not want to initiate the upgrade. If we did, we might introduce a very long outage while we wait for the new cluster to catch up. Even if we need to reschedule the upgrade, that is better than such an outage.

Ideally, the query we included should provide results like this:

```
            slot_name                | database | active | write_lag
-------------------------------------+----------+--------+-----------
 pgl_myapp_origin_myapp_upgrade | myapp    | t      |         0
```

As we can see here, the slot assigned to our upgrade cluster shows zero lag. A few MB are nothing to worry about, but once we start seeing several GB, we may want to reconsider, reschedule, or find the source of the excess write traffic that is causing the lag.

Once we've established that nothing will prevent the upgrade itself, we can start the real procedure. We begin by using `psql` to issue a `PAUSE` command to the `pgbouncer` pseudo-database. This will cause PgBouncer to stop assigning PostgreSQL backends to clients after they complete their current transaction. All client connections will then be held in a wait state until we send a `RESUME` command to PgBouncer. At this point, we need to work fast to minimize the process.

Next, we should execute the `wait_slot_confirm_lsn` function. This function is provided by pglogical to perform several tasks, but for our purposes, it is a signal that the `pg-new` cluster has fully caught up to the last transaction at the time we ran the function. Basically, the function will not return until the lag is zero. Since PgBouncer is preventing any new write traffic, this should mean the `pg-new` cluster has all data on `pg-old`, up to the point we paused PgBouncer.

After we've eliminated logical replication lag, we should trigger one final synchronization of the sequences to ensure the values will be higher than those on the old cluster. As we did in the *Handling sequences* recipe, we can execute the `synchronize_sequence` function on all sequences tracked by pglogical. This is normally done periodically while pglogical is running, but since we don't know the time of the last synchronization, it's best to perform the process manually so we know all sequences are up to date.

If we haven't already, now is the time to alter the `pgbouncer.ini` configuration file so any database targets are directed to `pg-new`. This does not affect PgBouncer until we use `systemctl` to reload the service, causing it to re-read the configuration file. Make sure to `reload`, rather than `restart`, the service, or PgBouncer will automatically resume connections.

> To save time, consider preparing two configuration files before the upgrade. One configuration file will reflect the `pg-old` as the connection target, while the other will use `pg-new`. Then create a symbolic link from the appropriate file to `pgbouncer.ini`. This link is much faster and easier to change as part of an automated process.

Before we direct connections to `pg-new`, we really want to drop the subscription we created. If we don't, PgBouncer may still operate on the tables or sequences in ways we might not expect. For instance, since sequences are periodically refreshed and `pg-old` is no longer accepting writes, pglogical could reset the sequences on `pg-new` to some lower value even though we've been using them. Thus we use the `drop_subscription` function here to make sure that can't happen.

Finally, we can issue a `RESUME` command to the `pgbouncer` pseudo-database and resume traffic to our database cluster. Assuming everything worked properly, this traffic will interact with `pg-new`, and the old cluster no longer has any role.

Congratulations, you've upgraded a cluster without ever going offline!

There's more...

Some might claim the time between a PgBouncer `PAUSE` and `RESUME` counts as an outage. From the perspective of a user waiting for a response from the application, which is in turn waiting for a connection from PgBouncer, this is true.

This is why we strongly recommend automating *step 4* to *step 10*, from the second we PAUSE until we RESUME. Each of these steps requires no interaction, but should be completed so the upgrade is finished safely. Assuming there was no lag, this would mean the `wait_slot_confirm_lsn` function would immediately return. Sequences should update quickly with `synchronize_sequence`. The time required to swap a symbolic link for `pgbouncer.ini` is nearly zero. Calling the `drop_subscription` function is equally fast. A script can issue all of these commands back-to-back and even check for rare edge cases if there's time.

Cumulatively, no more than 2-5 seconds should elapse for the entire upgrade. As with any risky procedure, we always encourage testing everything in a development or QA environment until there are no mistakes and everything is fully documented and timed. We should know how long each step takes, so that when we perform the upgrade in our production environment, there are no surprises.

This may not be truly *zero* downtime, but we dare anyone to notice a single 2-5 second pause when moving from PostgreSQL 10 to 11.

Cleaning everything up

We've completed the upgrade, and everything is running smoothly. Now comes the time to dismantle or reuse any remaining hardware, nodes, and resources used by the old cluster. This may be a relaxing task, as all the hardest tasks have already been completed.

This recipe will discuss what steps are necessary to fully extract pglogical from the upgraded cluster, and what we can potentially consider regarding the old one.

Getting ready

Please follow all previous recipes before starting here.

How to do it...

These steps will assume we have our old primary (pg-old) and the new primary (pg-new). Follow these instructions to complete the upgrade process:

1. Optionally, execute this SQL on pg-new to remove the pglogical extension:

   ```
   DROP EXTENSION pglogical;
   ```

2. Optionally, remove pglogical from shared_preload_libraries in postgresql.conf, and restart PostgreSQL on pg-new.

3. If this has not already been done, enable any high-availability management software such as repmgr, Patroni, or Pacemaker for the pg-new cluster.

4. If this has not already been done, enable any backup software such as Barman or automated snapshots for the pg-new cluster.

5. Stop any high-availability management software on the pg-old cluster such as repmgr, Patroni, or Pacemaker.

6. Stop any backups or automated snapshots for the pg-old cluster.

7. Stop PostgreSQL on any nodes in the pg-old cluster.

8. Except for the Primary pg-old node, recycle or reuse any remaining nodes within the pg-new cluster.

9. If nodes are being reused in pg-new, modify settings in any configuration management software for these nodes. Otherwise, decommission the remaining pg-old node configurations.

10. If the upgrade was done on the same servers in extra storage space, erase pg-old data on all but the Primary node.

11. After a few days, remove the old Primary pg-old cluster data or node.

How it works...

This entire recipe is essentially optional, but makes a good checklist of elements we may wish to consider when cleaning up after such a major upgrade.

The first steps are optional because we may find that we need pglogical for transmitting table data to other parts of the cluster. So long as it's installed and listed in `postgresql.conf`, we could use it either for future upgrade needs, or managing any number of full or partial logical replicas. Some enterprises may dictate that any unused extensions should be uninstalled, and if that is the case, we may as well do that first.

Next, we need to enable any software that manages the cluster in ways that we may have temporarily disabled during the transition. We wouldn't want an automated failover being triggered for instance, so even if they're installed, we likely disabled repmgr, Patroni, or any other availability software.

This also applies to backups. Presumably, we're already backing up the `pg-new` cluster regularly to prove the process works as expected. But we may have also disabled any ongoing WAL consumption or snapshots for the period of the upgrade itself to avoid any disruptions. These should be enabled at this point as well. We might also consider invoking a post-upgrade backup so the process can complete while we watch.

Otherwise, the rest of the recipe involves decommissioning the remainder of the `pg-old` cluster. We tried to touch all of the major components here, but it's not really an exhaustive list. The first of these is high-availability software like repmgr, Patroni, and Pacemaker. Any resources these control might interfere with the `pg-new` cluster, or otherwise cause unnecessary failovers. We should disable all of that software now.

Once again, we want to perform the same operation on backups. Do not delete the backups themselves as we may need to refer to them later, but periodic scheduled backups or snapshots should be eliminated from the `pg-old` cluster. Even if we only prevent consumption of disk resources, we've accomplished something useful.

After disabling all of the automatic safeguards, we can safely shut down PostgreSQL on every node in the `pg-old` cluster. Any replicas we no longer need can either be permanently decommissioned, or perhaps reused in the `pg-new` cluster. We did, after all, potentially upgrade to a slightly under-provisioned cluster to preserve resources. Now is the time to start reestablishing the cluster as the original architecture intended.

The only exception here is the pg-old Primary node itself. There's still a very slim chance we need to revert the upgrade, and as unlikely as that may be, we should retain that node for at least a day or two until we know it's no longer necessary. Technically, this is optional, especially in container-based environments that are highly volatile in general, but we wanted to make sure it's considered.

One thing that may be overlooked is configuration management software such as salt, Ansible, Chef, Puppet, and so on. Any nodes we decide to reuse from pg-old to pg-new must have their profiles altered so they don't inadvertently revert to the old cluster settings. We don't want to manually integrate a node into the new cluster, only to have some automated framework undo our hard work sometime later, possibly even outside of work hours.

Any nodes that won't be reused should either be powered down or reabsorbed into the VM hypervisor at this point. Even if not for our pg-new PostgreSQL cluster, physical hardware can always be reused for something, or at least sold to recoup residual value. Hypervisors can always use more memory, CPU, and storage resources for reassignment to other VMs as well.

This still applies if we performed the upgrade inline on the same hardware as the pg-old cluster, but using a different PostgreSQL port. Rather than cleaning up nodes, we would be erasing data from directories associated with the pg-old cluster. This may or may not be a separate volume mount, but is still a resource to reclaim. And as we mentioned before, the pg-old Primary data should always be removed last. There's always the chance we need to refer to its contents, if only to verify older data in pg-new.

Eventually, however, even this stipulation will expire, and we should be able to safely recycle or decommission pg-old Primary resources as well. Once there are sufficient backups for the pg-new cluster, we can even remove any backup allocations for pg-old as well. These should be stored long-term in the cloud, a tape archive, or an offline server vault, but are not required to be online once the new cluster takes over.

Once we've accounted for all the various bits and pieces of the pg-old cluster, we can truly consider our upgrade complete. Congratulations on your online upgrade!

Other Books You May Enjoy

If you enjoyed this book, you may be interested in these other books by Packt:

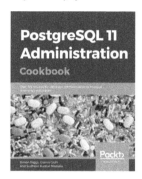

PostgreSQL 11 Administration Cookbook

Simon Riggs, Gianni Ciolli, Et al

ISBN: 978-1-78953-758-1

- Troubleshoot open source PostgreSQL version 11 on various platforms
- Deploy best practices for planning and designing live databases
- Select and implement robust backup and recovery techniques in PostgreSQL 11
- Use pgAdmin or OmniDB to perform database administrator (DBA) tasks
- Adopt efficient replication and high availability techniques in PostgreSQL
- Improve the performance of your PostgreSQL solution

Mastering PostgreSQL 12 - Third Edition
Hans-Jürgen Schönig

ISBN: 978-1-83898-882-1

- Understand the advanced SQL functions in PostgreSQL 12
- Use indexing features in PostgreSQL to fine-tune the performance of queries
- Work with stored procedures and manage backup and recovery
- Master replication and failover techniques to reduce data loss
- Replicate PostgreSQL database systems to create backups and to scale your database
- Manage and improve the security of your server to protect your data
- Troubleshoot your PostgreSQL instance for solutions to common and not-so-common problems

Leave a review - let other readers know what you think

Please share your thoughts on this book with others by leaving a review on the site that you bought it from. If you purchased the book from Amazon, please leave us an honest review on this book's Amazon page. This is vital so that other potential readers can see and use your unbiased opinion to make purchasing decisions, we can understand what our customers think about our products, and our authors can see your feedback on the title that they have worked with Packt to create. It will only take a few minutes of your time, but is valuable to other potential customers, our authors, and Packt. Thank you!

Index

Y

Z

www.ingramcontent.com/pod-product-compliance
Lightning Source LLC
Chambersburg PA
CBHW060633060326
40690CB00020B/4383